MAGILL'S
LITERARY ANNUAL
1979

*Essay-Reviews of 200 Outstanding Books
Published in the United States during 1978*

---

*With an Annotated Categories Index
and a Listing of 842 Review Sources*

Volume One
A-Mom

Edited by
FRANK N. MAGILL

SALEM PRESS
Englewood Cliffs

LIBRARY OF CONGRESS CATALOG CARD NO. 77-99209

ISBN 0-89356-279-3

First Printing

PRINTED IN THE UNITED STATES OF AMERICA

PREFACE

EACH YEAR provides a fresh challenge for our Annual Staff, charged with selecting and discussing critically a mere two hundred of the thousands of new books published during the year. The goal of this monumental task is to select a high percentage of works of an enduring nature, books that we believe will gain a permanent place in the body of American literature. The books of 1978 presented an especially interesting challenge, since there were so many good ones from which to choose. Represented here are 45 works of fiction, 27 volumes of poetry, 2 of drama, 20 collections of essays, 16 works covering autobiography, memoirs, diaries, letters, 7 volumes of literary criticism and literary history, 39 works dealing with historical subjects, 31 biographies, 3 books relating to science, 2 works concerning current affairs, and 8 excellent books that do not lend themselves readily to a specific category.

Among the leaders in the fiction category are Joyce Carol Oates's SON OF THE MORNING, one of her most artistically mature works; Richard Adams' THE PLAGUE DOGS, an imaginative tale rivaling in sensitivity the author's WATERSHIP DOWN; James A. Michener's CHESAPEAKE, a panoramic view of Maryland's Eastern Shore since Colonial times; Richard Schickel's ANOTHER I, ANOTHER YOU, a traditional "well-made novel" whose qualities reflect the author's experience as a film critic; FINAL PAYMENTS, a first novel of considerable promise by Mary Gordon; Émile Ajar's MOMO, winner of the coveted Prix Goncourt; Nobel Prize winner Heinrich Böll's AND NEVER SAID A WORD; David Madden's highly regarded THE SUICIDE'S WIFE; SHOSHA, a warm tale of the Warsaw ghetto by the winner of the Nobel Prize in 1978; THE UNDYING GRASS by the Turkish novelist Yashar Kemal, whose earlier works—especially MEMED, MY HAWK— have been well received in this country; and RUNNING DOG, a fine satire by Don DeLillo.

Other novels of note published during the year include those by John Updike, Peter Handke, Graham Greene, Ernest J. Gaines, Günter Grass, Jamake Highwater, Wilfrid Sheed, João Ubaldo Ribeiro, Françoise Sagan, and John Irving, whose THE WORLD ACCORDING TO GARP is a delightful excursion into the psyche of a free spirit.

A number of excellent short-story collections appeared during the year, led perhaps by THE STORIES OF JOHN CHEEVER, winner of the Pulitzer Prize in 1978. Barry Hannah's AIRSHIPS became the first winner of the Arnold Gingrich Short Fiction Award. Among other distinguished collections were INNOCENT ERÉNDIRA AND OTHER STORIES by Gabriel García Márquez and V. S. Pritchett's SELECTED STORIES, a superb collection.

As usual, poets contributed their share to the enjoyment of the literary year. One moving collection is CHIEKO'S SKY by Kotaro Takamura, a celebration of marital adoration animated by the lingering death of the poet's wife. Rudolph von Abele's A CAGE FOR LOULOU is a first collection by a middle-aged scholar, which is marked by its erudition and contemplative style. Diane Wakoski's THE MAN WHO SHOOK HANDS deals with the longing for acceptance and an end to loneliness. The title poem describes the *persona*'s depth of despair when her search for a personal commitment is rejected with a careless, unfeeling shrug (a handshake rather than an outpouring of love). BLOODFIRE is the second volume of Fred Chappell's four-book work in progress which he calls a "novel in verse." WHO SHALL BE THE SUN? is David Wagoner's fine collection of "Poems Based on the Lore, Legends, and Myths of Northwest Coast and Plateau Indians." Other volumes of poetry published during the year that deserve more than passing notice are those by Ann Darr, Karl Shapiro, Margaret Atwood, Robert Penn Warren, David R. Slavitt, Denise Levertov, Adrienne Rich, SELECTED POEMS by the former Poet Laureate of England, John Masefield (with a preface by John Betjeman), and a collection of poems and early writings by W. H. Auden edited by Edward Mendelson.

There were some excellent works of literary criticism and literary history published in 1978, among them Helen Gardner's THE COMPOSITION OF *FOUR QUARTETS*, in which Dame Helen provides an in-depth analysis of the background and development of perhaps the finest achievement of one of the major figures of English belles lettres. M. L. Rosenthal again examines the genius of T. S. Eliot, along with that of William Butler Yeats and Ezra Pound in his SAILING INTO THE UNKNOWN, in which study he seems to find that these three great artists infuse their poetry with an intangible energy that renews itself with each new reader. A VIEW OF VICTORIAN LITERATURE is an excellent study of nine Victorian writers by the eminent Victorian scholar Geoffrey Tillotson (completed by his wife Kathleen from notes after his untimely death). In WILLIAM FAULKNER: TOWARD YOKNAPATAWPHA AND BEYOND, Cleanth Brooks examines the non-Yoknapatawpha works of Faulkner, which in the main—but not entirely—comprise Faulkner's apprenticeship writings. This work complements Brooks's WILLIAM FAULKNER: THE YOKNAPATAWPHA COUNTRY (1963).

Letters and autobiographical writings account for considerable space in this year's Annual; their intimate revelations often delight the general reader, who usually has formed a distorted view of his favorite public or literary figure. Charles A. Lindbergh's AUTOBIOGRAPHY OF VALUES may serve to revise the superficial opinion that some readers may have had of this highly complex, philosophically oriented man. Volume II of Virginia Woolf's Diary (1920-1924) and Volume III of her Letters (1923-1928) appeared in 1978, and through them we reach the heart of her artistic development. Some six hundred letters of Count Lev Tolstoy were published in 1978, though this represents a mere seven percent of Tolstoy's prolific output. The value of this collection, however, lies not in its numbers but in the erudite approach of the editor and translator, Scottish Tolstoy scholar R. F. Christian. Selected Letters of John O'Hara and of Conrad Aiken also appeared during the year.

Numerous collections of essays were published in 1978, including volumes by Malcolm Cowley, Wright Morris, Eudora Welty, Howard Nemerov, Arthur Koestler, Hannah Arendt, Anthony Burgess, John Wain, Archibald MacLeish, Stephen Spender, and William H. Gass. All of these works bring messages that should not be overlooked by the serious reader.

History absorbs a substantial share of space in the current Annual and justly so. There was a plethora of historical literature in 1978, only a fraction of which could be dealt with in these two volumes. Though most readers are inclined to prefer studies of modern history, in A DISTANT MIRROR: THE CALAMITOUS 14TH CENTURY the art of Barbara W. Tuchman has provided a fascinating study of a time six hundred years ago when the basic problems facing humanity—wars, poverty, cultism, scorn for traditional institutions— were not unlike those present today. A more positive aspect is developed in Clive Bush's THE DREAM OF REASON, as he provides an overview of the re-markable development of the young American nation from 1776 to 1865. This same theme is present on a more limited geographical scale in Frederick Merk's HISTORY OF THE WESTWARD MOVEMENT, though the time span is greater: 1607-1975.

In IMPERIALISM AT BAY, Wm. Roger Louis shows the distinct American influence in the breaking up of the British Empire by substituting "trustee-ship" for "imperialism." The seed for this American viewpoint obviously springs from our Declaration of Independence, and in INVENTING AMERICA, Garry Wills treats the development of that political instrument admirably. Probably no year in modern world history has been more vital to civilization than the year 1945. John Lukacs argues this point well in 1945: YEAR ZERO.

Other historical works of unusual significance published during the year include Harrison E. Salisbury's RUSSIA IN REVOLUTION, 1900-1930, Saburō Ienaga's THE PACIFIC WAR, Maurice Baumont's THE ORIGINS OF THE SECOND WORLD WAR, and THE WHITE MAN'S INDIAN by Robert F. Berkhofer, Jr., a study long overdue.

Major literary biographies of 1978 include studies of Cervantes, Ernest Hemingway, Chateaubriand, Lermontov, E. M. Forster, Elizabeth Bowen, Milton, Samuel Beckett, and two highly capable editors: Maxwell Perkins and Saxe Commins. General biographies of note include those of Alexander Hamil-ton, Douglas MacArthur, Yeats's Maud Gonne (LUCKY EYES AND A HIGH HEART), Mary Tudor, Margaret Fuller, the Mellon family, Woodrow Wilson, William Wilberforce, and Daniel Webster.

The above mentioned works represent a small segment of the great outpour-ing of original thought and scholarly response inspired through the simple act of being alive and observant in the year 1978. We are fortunate that there are observers and writers who "see the light" and share with everyone their in-sights through published works. It has not always been so.

FRANK N. MAGILL

LIST OF TITLES

LIST OF TITLES

LIST OF TITLES

LIST OF TITLES

TITLES BY CATEGORY

ANNOTATED

FICTION

The story of the tragic consequences that result from the plan of a German officer to arrange the capture of his battalion by his American counterpart just prior to the Battle of the Bulge

The vibrant and violent world of T. S. Garp, full of comedy, pain, and great joy, a world that at first glance seems absurdly exaggerated but upon closer reading becomes a truthful reflection of the essence of contemporary America and contemporary humanity

A novel composed of forty-four vignettes which carry the hero from the childhood he remembers, through the middle age he endures now, to the future of old age he anticipates

POETRY
DRAMA

A volume of thoughtful, penetrating poetry by a man who composes in Polish, his native language, but who participates in the English translation

The second book of a four-volume "novel in verse" comprised of eleven narrative or meditative poems organized around images of fire

Erudite, contemplative poems which adopt a philosophic stance toward the human animal

The posthumous publication of a volume of poems expressing the deep and abiding love which the poet felt for his wife

The third collection by a poet of unusually intense vision and rare economy of style

Sixty-eight poems written over the past fifty years which demonstrate the austerity and erudition, as well as the poetic development, of one of this century's most conscious and modest literary craftsmen

Selections from ten volumes of poetry, along with new and uncollected verse, by the major contemporary American poet

LITERARY CRITICISM
LITERARY HISTORY

AUTOBIOGRAPHY
MEMOIRS
DIARIES
LETTERS

CURRENT AFFAIRS

THE SCIENCES

MISCELLANEOUS

CONTRIBUTING REVIEWERS FOR 1979 ANNUAL

Paul Ashin

Kenneth John Atchity

Peggy Bach

Terry Alan Baney

Carolyn Wilkerson Bell

Mae Woods Bell

Gary B. Blank

William Boswell

Kenneth T. Burles

Jack L. Calbert

John C. Carlisle

David B. Carroll

John R. Chávez

Ronald J. Cima

James W. Clark, Jr.

Gordon W. Clarke

Ronald D. Cohen

Phyllis DeLeo

Maurice E. Dixon

Leon V. Driskell

John W. Evans

Barry Faye

Kathryn Flaris

W. Bryan Fuermann

Faith Gabelnick

Betty Gawthrop

Roger A. Geimer

Robert F. Gish

Alan A. Gonzalez

William E. Grant

Joan S. Griffin

Michael Grimwood

Alan G. Gross

Manfred Grote

Max Halperen

Patricia King Hanson

Stephen L. Hanson

Antony H. Harrison

Robert L. Hoffman

Jeffry Michael Jensen

Willis Knapp Jones

Harold J. Joseph

Edward P. Keleher

Michael G. R. Kelley

Henderson Kincheloe

Anthony Lamb

Saul Lerner

Elizabeth Johnston Lipscomb

Mark McCloskey

Agnes McDonald

Willis E. McNelly

David Madden

Paul D. Mageli

Robert S. Metzger

Walter E. Meyers

Leslie B. Mittleman

Gordon R. Mork

Sheldon A. Mossberg

Joan Taylor Munger

James E. Newman

Robert E. Nichols, Jr.

Guy Owen

Mary Paschal

Susan Karnes Passler

Mary Reynolds Peacock

Doris F. Pierce

James W. Pringle

Anne C. Raymer

John D. Raymer

Bruce D. Reeves

Richard Rice

Larry S. Rudner

Richard H. Sander

Steven C. Schaber

Margaret S. Schoon

Hanna Scolnicov

Mary Jo Shea

Don W. Sieker

Sofus E. Simonsen

Gilbert Smith

Shirley F. Staton

Leon Stein

Linda Klieger Stillman

Nell Joslin Styron

James T. Sullivan

Henry Taylor

William B. Toole III

Stuart Van Dyke, Jr.

James R. Van Laan

Richard A. Van Orman

John N. Wall, Jr.

Thomas N. Walters

Susan I. Weaver

Bernard Welt

Mary C. Williams

Edward A. Zivich

ABOVE THE BATTLE
War-Making in America from Appomattox to Versailles

Author: Thomas C. Leonard (1944-   )
Publisher: Oxford University Press (New York). 260 pp. $12.95
Type of work: History
Time: 1861-1918
Locale: The United States and Europe

An attempt to show the variety of responses of American soldiers to their enemies and to the values and purposes of war from the Civil War through the end of World War I

> *Principal personages:*
> STEPHEN CRANE, author
> HARRY CROSBY, poet
> E. E. CUMMINGS, author
> JOHN DOS PASSOS, author
> JOHN J. PERSHING, soldier
> THEODORE ROOSEVELT, Rough Rider and President
> WILLIAM TECUMSEH SHERMAN, soldier
> PHILIP H. SHERIDAN, soldier
> WOODROW WILSON, President

Thomas C. Leonard sets several tasks in his volume devoted to what he terms the "culture of war." He presents the views of common line soldiers and of military professionals, of munitions manufacturers, and of the civilians who were not touched by the four military encounters faced by the American nation between 1861 and 1918—the Civil War, the Indian battles, the Spanish-American War, and World War I. The soldiers show us how they viewed themselves and their enemies and what they chose to remember and what to forget. The "preparedness" proponents such as the manufacturers of weapons discuss the values of always-newer machines of destruction, while the civilian media creates propaganda campaigns to portray the enemy as *worthy* of destruction.

It is this concept of "worthiness" which most surprises the casual or naïve reader, who might suppose that an enemy is an enemy, a person or a country whose purpose is to destroy him. Such is not always—or even frequently—the case in the wars the author chooses to discuss.

During the Civil War when brother often was pitted against brother, one perhaps strove to look "above the battle" to seek and find principles of freedom and politics which were worth defending and which made the enemy a worthy opponent even though he held opposite views. But as Leonard points out, the Civil War was "at times, orderly and chaotic, chivalrous and cruel." Above all else, it was not a glorious, flag-waving simplicity; it was a "scorched earth campaign."

Why then by the 1880's had most Americans, including the soldiers who had learned "more about diarrhea than saber charges" in the four years of civil war come to view the conflict as "comprehensible and humane," as a period of strife which had "unlocked America's energies and produced a glorious period of national growth"? Leonard gives no satisfactory answer to his own questions here.

He tells us that five hundred thousand soldiers deserted during this war which cost one military death for every six slaves freed. But he does not tell us whether those desertions were temporary such as Henry Fleming's in Crane's *The Red Badge of Courage*, caused by panic and fear, or whether they were permanent. Obviously, most deserters are not inclined to give detailed explanations or justifications of their actions, but the millions of men who did not leave the battles also must have had noncomplimentary comments about the destruction.

Unfortunately, those viewpoints either did not make it into print very often or were treated as typical complaints of the soldier in camp. What did reach print emphasized "the grand strategy of victory and defeat . . . not the human costs. Suffering was ignored or treated laconically—to illustrate some military virtue." At the same time war seemed to bring progress and prosperity; it brought "smoking factory chimneys, rails across the continent, free settlers in the West. . . ."

It is here that Leonard passes up the first chance to draw parallels to other times and to other wars. We must grant that this is a volume devoted to a specific time period and a particular theme; it is not a political tract, but it does seem it would not be totally inappropriate for the author to mention that many persons saw World War I as a great chance for pushing worldwide American economic hegemony, just as others secretly welcomed World War II twenty years later as a way to break the Depression of the 1930's. These and other parallels are obvious and important omissions in the book.

A second important point which is overlooked comes in regard to the battles with the Indians. With the end of the Civil War, the professional military staff turned its attention to bringing to the West a peace based upon unenforceable treaties which were broken more often by the government and the white settlers than by the Indians. Leonard presents an interesting picture of the officers "who had shed blood to keep their own society together" and who now were "ordered to dismember the culture of native Americans." According to Leonard's research, many officers did not enjoy the task given to them, especially as the job was complicated by the contradictions between public rhetoric and official orders to force the Indians farther and farther from their tribal lands.

Here was an enemy who certainly proved himself worthy on the battlefield and who seemed to have justifiable reasons for fighting. As General Sheridan admitted in 1878: "'We took away their country and their means of support, broke up their mode of living, their habits of life, introduced disease and decay among them, and it was for this and against this they made war. Could anyone expect less?'" Apparently only an obscure handful of officers felt strongly enough about the ambiguities to resign as a form of protest. The Indians might have a great deal of right on their side, but "the price of civilization" often was high. When the Indians proved to be resilient, the military responded by using more technology in an effort to end the problem quickly; "action seemed the thing to sweep away the complications of the Indian problem."

The obvious parallel to this nineteenth century military response to the "incomprehensibly wild" Indians is the twentieth century response to Vietnam. Billions of dollars in advanced technological equipment and hundreds of thousands of American troops were not enough to bring about the "light at the end of the tunnel" which the official press releases promised month after weary month. Whether draftees or professionals, many men in Vietnam must have felt the same frustrations which the Indian fighters felt. In fact, the generals in the Civil War and in Vietnam may have had similar thoughts: must one destroy one part of a nation to preserve another part, and must one destroy this part of the culture to save a different part?

Another unhappy parallel between the Indian battles and the Vietnam skirmishes—apart from the fact that neither affair was a declared war—comes in the responses of the soldiers. Social-psychologists perhaps will someday be able to tell the American nation whether the massacres in Vietnam could have been prevented or whether they were unavoidable aberrations caused by frustrations as the soldiers faced a losing test of the American myth of victory and right.

In the matter of advanced weaponry, readers of *Above the Battle* can see the similarities between the claims of the munitions manufacturers of that time and of this. Leonard quotes one preparedness proponent who is rather open in his sales pitch: "'As nations are bound to fight, it is far more merciful that they should be armed to the teeth.'" Today it must be granted that we have learned since then that machines still need men behind them and have lost the delusion that nations will be only "interested, ambitious spectators" of future battles between opposing groups of robots. There has even been an ironic twist in some rationalizations. Whereas, seventy-five or eighty years ago, weapons experts expected modern technology to bring about "less bloodshed even if destruction were increased at certain brief moments," the much-discussed neutron bomb proposed today will destroy human life but will preserve buildings and machinery. In any kind of objective view, such a development (it cannot be termed an "advancement" by any stretch of the imagination) becomes ludicrous; however, it is no more absurd than the "narcotic shells" proposed before World War I. What made them so appealing to popular and military journal and newspaper supplement writers was that the new bullets made "cleaner" wounds than did old-fashioned ones, and they deposited pain killing drugs in the wounds as they tore through the flesh.

As a journalist, Leonard justifiably could have pursued further the role of the media in our conflicts, especially beginning with the Spanish-American War. The metropolitan tabloid newspapers inflated the fight against a much-weaker Spain and ignored the philosophical and/or political bases for the clashes between American occupation troops and the natives in the Philippines. Twenty years later, it was the newspapers, magazines, and movies which created the Hellish "Hun," not the doughboys in the trenches. On the other hand, about fifty years after the media created an enemy in Spain, television destroyed the created enemy in Vietnam, for it was only when unsettling images of defeat and questionable priorities and "unAmerican" behavior began to enter our homes did the majority of Americans begin to call for an end to the war. This is not to say that television saw the fallacy of our involvement from the beginning, but it finally was able to shake the hold the military had on war-related news.

Thus, the nation, in fact, has changed in some ways; there are some positive aspects to the hundreds of thousands of lives and billions of dollars spent in the last one hundred years on wars. But we as Americans have stayed the same, have remained as blind as before in so many equally important ways. It is for both the positive and the negative sides of the story that Leonard should have drawn the parallels mentioned above and many others.

He does conclude his last chapter, a chapter devoted to silent, bitter veterans of World War I, with the comment: "Empty men have come home, unable to share their nightmare, and beyond anger." Perhaps if the concerned reader can extend Leonard's findings to a contemporary time, we will not need to say of our society what Leonard says of pre-World War I America: "Living with their hazy memories of the Civil War battlefields and their dreams of the benign weapons of tomorrow, Americans had neither a usable past nor a realistic future."

John C. Carlisle

Sources for Further Study

American Historical Review. LXXXIII, December, 1978, p. 1326.
Booklist. LXXIV, January 15, 1978, p. 792.
Choice. XV, April, 1978, p. 292.
Library Journal. CIII, February 15, 1978, p. 458.
Modern Age. XXII, Summer, 1978, p. 321.
Reviews in American History. VI, December, 1978, p. 445.

AIRSHIPS

Author: Barry Hannah
Publisher: Alfred A. Knopf (New York). 209 pp. $8.95
Type of work: Short stories
Time: Civil War to the present
Locale: The United States, mostly the South; Vietnam

A distinguished collection of twenty short stories, first winner of the Arnold Gingrich Short Fiction Award

Not literally tales about airplanes, the "airships" of Barry Hannah's collection of twenty dazzling stories are vehicles to transport our imagination. And what strange, fragile vehicles they are! Mostly grotesque, they hurtle into life a cargo of tormented souls, nearly all at their breaking points, yet defiantly passionate. Hannah's range is as remarkable as his penetration. From Vietnam to Mississippi, from the Civil War Confederacy to modern suburbia, his characters experience life at the narrow verge between disaster and redemption. A few of them attain a partial salvation; most are destined to fail, though they battle with stubborn pride.

Hannah's characters do not suffer from the pride of the Greeks, hubris — excessive confidence in their powers. On the contrary, they usually lack confidence. As the world judges them, most are failures: disappointed lovers, betrayed soldiers, futile dreamers. Yet they take full responsibility for their lives and never complain at the defeats they suffer. In their integrity they demonstrate their pride. "There's only tomorrow if you're lucky," says the old man in "Dragged Fighting from His Tomb"; many of Hannah's characters might repeat the same sentiment. Without delusions, usually without moral rationalizations, they face life squarely and accept reality with calm; and like the greatest tragic heroes of the Greeks, they are proud to be human.

In their tragic power, Hannah's stories remind the reader at times of the work of two other gifted Southern writers, William Faulkner and Flannery O'Connor. Like Faulkner, Hannah is interested in violence, not for the sake of sensation alone but for the psychological and artistic effects of terror. Many of Hannah's stories begin or end in fearsome violence. For example, in "Green Gets It," the psychotic narrator shoots a black man on a bicycle. "At least," he says, "I had the presence of mind not to kill him. I only shot him in the thigh." In "Quo Vadis, Smut?" a group of redneck hunters run down a cretinous farmer who had tied "his supposed sweetheart" to a bull, then strike a pitchfork in the animal's eye. In "Coming Close to Donna," the narrator, a self-styled "sissy," witnesses a battle to the death in a cemetery between two rival lovers of Donna, the nymphomanic; when she calls upon the horrified "fag" to have sex with her, he picks up a tombstone and crushes her head with it. These examples and many others that could be cited show how Hannah's treatment of violence seems almost comically grotesque. Yet it is never gratuitous, and the comedy, also reminiscent of Faulkner, is part of the Mississippi "tall tale." Like Faulkner's farcical yarns about the Snopeses, Hannah's broad comic sketches reveal characters who are both depraved and pitiable. We laugh at their madness, but the amusement is pained.

Further, in his treatment of the grotesque, Hannah resembles Flannery O'Connor. Like her, he creates a world of garrulous, compulsive, usually narrow-minded, and often dangerous types who barely glimpse a world of moral order that they cannot understand. For Hannah, the moral order is not precise — certainly not so precisely catholic; but it tantalizes his characters with its hint of reality. Without that hint, life could not be endured; yet the hint is only that, not a certainty. Good soldiers to the end for a cause that they only dimly perceive, Hannah's characters fight their lonely battles with courage or desperation and never whimper.

For Hannah, the image of the loyal soldier is General Jeb Stuart, peerless Confederate cavalry officer. In two major stories, "Dragged Fighting from His Tomb" (probably the finest piece of this collection) and "Knowing He Was Not My Kind Yet I Followed," Hannah re-creates the myth of Stuart's death. Again, in "Behold the Husband in His Perfect Agony," news of the death of Stuart has significance in the plot, although it is not central to the action. What does Stuart mean to Hannah? Certainly the figure represents the heroic age of the South: a Christian gentleman, charismatic leader in battle, masterful companion of men. But he appears to be more than a legacy of the old South — a memory part truth but a greater part myth. Hannah posits in Stuart the verities toward which other, weaker men and women merely aspire. Stuart knows who he is; he lives with conviction, dies with honor. Shot by his own trusted officer, Captain Howard, Stuart is the victim of the world's madness, although he is not mad. Rather it is Howard who is driven mad — maddened because he lacks conviction.

Most of Hannah's characters are poised delicately between madness and sanity. Desperate, they conceal their terror of chaos through fantasy, brutality, or lust. Rarely do they enjoy a completed romantic affair. Even when they love purely, with commitment — for example, Quadberry and Lilian in "Testimony of Pilot" — they are doomed. The chaos of accident, mere chance, destroys them. Or they surrender to their inner chaos. In "Our Secret Home," which treats a strange *menage à trois* involving deadlocked passion, the husband, Mickey, loves two women: his wife, Carolyn, and his sister, Patricia. He keeps them together in a house doomed by incest. Yet the three victims of accident struggle to love against all odds, against hope. Although the world breaks in upon them, they remain loyal to the mysteries of their hearts.

In general, Hannah's women are more sensitive to the promptings of the heart than his men. For his male protagonists, activity can serve to fill the inner void. So they may be soldiers ("Midnight and I'm Not Famous Yet"), athletes ("Return to Return"), or violent despoilers ("Green Gets It"). But women must come directly to grips with reality. In the two extraordinary stories that conclude the volume, "Deaf and Dumb" and "Mother Rooney Unscrolls the Hurt," Hannah examines with compassion the psychology of desperate women who endure the agony of truth. Resigned to their fate, they do not grumble at what cannot be altered. Minny dreams of the past, accepts the present, then drops off to sleep; but she is awakened violently by a hammer blow upon her mouth. Similarly, Mother Rooney — perhaps Hannah's most brilliant portrait — remembers her crumbling early life, the broach, symbol of her romantic dreams, and her betrayal. Old, unregenerate, and lewd, she is a modern version of Molly Bloom, now half in her grave but grasping for life. A triumph of Hannah's art, Mother Rooney demands comparison with the supreme female characters of Frank O'Connor or James Joyce.

To be sure, other stories lack the roundness of Hannah's best work. With a few exceptions, the short-short tales are inferior to the longer ones, not simply because they lack organic development, but because they seem to be experimental versions of stories yet to be written. The exceptions to this rule, however, are notable: "Water Liars," "Coming Close to Donna," and "Behold the Husband in His Perfect Agony." On the other hand, stories like "That's True," "All the Old Harkening Faces at the Rail," and "Pete Resists the Man of His Old Room" appear to be mere sketches, promising but unfinished. Among the longer pieces, only one is disappointing: "Return to Return." A sensitive account of the loyalties of three lifelong friends, the narrative never quite comes to life.

Rarely can the same criticism be applied to the range of Hannah's stories; they seize the imagination with abundant life. Indeed, because of their exuberant vitality, some may appear to be entertainments only, designed to amuse the reader by startling him; Hannah delights in all forms of sleight-of-hand that serve as fictional trickery. He often changes the direction of the story, so that a comic tale suddenly becomes serious, or a poignant plot develops an unexpected antic twist. For example, the opening sentence of "Water Liars" prepares the reader for a ribald plot: "When I am run down and flocked around by the world, I go down to Farte Cove off the Yazoo River and take my beer to the end of the pier where the old liars are still snapping and wheezing at one another." As the reader settles back in his chair, anticipating a fabliau about Sidney Farte, Jr., he is startled later in the story to discover a far more serious level of meaning. Exchanging fanciful yarns about ghosts, one of the characters, an old man, recalls how he stumbled upon his own daughter and her lover making love in the brush. And the narrator, in a hideous vision, imagines that he sees the former lovers of his wife. The story ends on the somber note: "We were both crucified by the truth."

Similarly, in "Green Gets It," the reader is tricked into supposing that the story is a droll yarn about Quarles Green, who "had never had a satisfactory carnal experience in his life." Midway through the story, the tone shifts markedly. We are conscious that the narrator is a fascist brute, a vigilante FBI agent. A black man speaks to him: "Pardon me. Is yo name Toid?" Before the reader has time to relax his mood for what appears to be a farcical scene, the incident grows nasty. Offended, the narrator stalks and shoots the black man, wounding but not killing him; then he resumes his amusing tale about Green.

To understand Hannah's art, one must be prepared for sudden, dramatic shifts in tone. For changes in tone, from ironic to farcical to tragic, signal changes in meaning. Often the change occurs in a single paragraph, sometimes in the middle of a sentence. For example, in "Return to Return," Celia and Levaster exchange philosophical ideas on nihilism and art. He says that "decoration is more important than art." She counters: "Is that what you learned in med school? That's dumb. . . . A boob is a boob is a boob." At this, "Dr. Levaster fainted."

In the Jeb Stuart stories, masterpieces of their kind, one can enjoy at best advantage Hannah's dramatic shifts of tone. The narrator of "Dragged Fighting from His Tomb" can be viewed, at different stages of the action signaled by shifts in tone, as a madman or philosopher, a murderer or a saint, Christ or Judas. Truly he is all these personalities. Captain Howard is a man crumbling before our eyes, one whose destiny is to destroy what he admires, then to destroy himself through remorse. Not since Ambrose Bierce has an American writer attempted to write so strange a story of terror and truth. For the story is terrible beyond the horrors of Faulkner or William Burroughs or Paul Bowles. Besides its strangeness, its quality is also visionary: an apparition of truth glimpsed though not fully perceived. With tones of rich ambiguity, Hannah mixes his loves and hates. And the truth of his best stories is a fearsome truth, part nightmare and part wild, derisive laughter. With *Airships*, the author establishes his claim to the front rank of contemporary American short fiction.

Leslie B. Mittleman

Sources for Further Study

Best Sellers. XXXVIII, September, 1978, p. 175.
Hudson Review. XXXI, Autumn, 1978, p. 521.
Sewanee Review. LXXXVI, July, 1978, p. 461.

ALLIES OF A KIND
The United States, Britain and the War Against Japan, 1941-1945

Author: Christopher Thorne (1934-   )
Publisher: Oxford University Press (New York). 800 pp. $29.50
Type of work: History
Time: 1939-1945
Locale: The China-Burma-India theater, the Pacific Ocean theater of war, Great Britain, and the United States

A history of Anglo-American political and strategic cooperation in the Asian theater during World War II which shows that there was friction as well as harmony between the two English-speaking allies

> *Principal personages:*
> SIR WINSTON CHURCHILL, Prime Minister of Great Britain, 1940–1945
> FRANKLIN DELANO ROOSEVELT, President of the United States, 1933–1945
> JOSEPH STALIN, Dictator of the Soviet Union, 1929–1953
> HARRY S TRUMAN, President of the United States, 1945–1953
> CHAING KAI-SHEK, President of China, 1927–1949; Head of "Free China" regime on Taiwan after 1949
> GENERAL JOSEPH ("VINEGAR JOE") STILWELL, United States adviser to the armies of Chiang Kai-shek, 1941–1944
> GENERAL ALBERT C. WEDEMEYER, United States military officer; Stilwell's successor in China
> LOUIS MOUNTBATTEN, Commander, British forces in Southeast Asia, 1941–1945

Christopher Thorne, a Reader in International Relations at Sussex University in Great Britain, is a leading authority on twentieth century diplomatic history. His earlier books in this field include *The Approach of War: 1938-1939* and *The Limits of Foreign Policy: The West, the League and the Far Eastern Crisis of 1931-1933.* Now, to these substantial works, Thorne has added the monumental *Allies of a Kind: The United States, Britain and the War Against Japan, 1941-1945.* With indefatigable energy, the author spent almost five years digging in the recently opened files of the British, Dutch, American, and Australian archives, and in the private papers of prominent Americans, Britons, and Australians. The fruit of all this labor is a new and searching look at the workings of the Anglo-American partnership during World War II.

Thorne's book is divided into six parts. Part One gives the reader the background of British-American relations in the Far East from 1939 to the Japanese bombing of Pearl Harbor to the Allied Conference of Casablanca, in January, 1943. Part Three treats the period from January, 1943, to the Cairo Conference of December, 1943. Part Four covers the period from the Cairo Conference to the second Quebec Conference of September, 1944, while Part Five carries the story to the time of the Japanese surrender to the Allies in September, 1945. Part Six is an epilogue in which the return of the European Powers to Southeast Asia after the war's end is briefly discussed. Throughout the book, the continuous Anglo-American debate over the future of postwar Asia is analyzed with regard to China, Southeast Asia, India, Australasia and the Pacific, and Japan herself. The structure of the book is thus rather complicated; and there is some inevitable repetition.

Unlike earlier historians of World War II, Thorne is not concerned with the reasons for either the early Japanese military successes or for the eventual defeat of the Japanese at the hands of the Allies. He does not, therefore, give a detailed history of military strategy and operations. Instead, Thorne is concerned with the reasons for the rapid crumbling of European power in East Asia after 1945. In the two decades following the war's end, France, Britain, and the Netherlands were all forced to give up their Asian Empires. Only Hong Kong remained under British control. According to Thorne, Japan's armed bid for supremacy in 1941-1945, although unsuccessful, considerably hastened this process of decolonization.

The stunning defeat of the British Army by the Japanese at Singapore in February, 1942, together with the Japanese conquest of Burma soon afterwards, laid bare the weakness of British defenses in Asia. To hold on to India, and to regain control of Burma, Malaya, Singapore, and Hong Kong, Britain required the financial and military help of her powerful Anglo-Saxon cousin, the United States. It was the United States Navy and Marines which, after June of 1942, were to carry the brunt of the fighting against Japanese forces in the Pacific Islands. Yet, as Thorne makes clear, both President Roosevelt and many of his military and diplomatic advisers were extremely skeptical about the moral rightness and the postwar political viability of Europe's Asian empires.

This basic difference of viewpoint, Thorne shows, often led to tension within the Anglo-American alliance. President Roosevelt championed the cause of a strong and independent China, which should take its place as one of the "Four Policemen" of world peace after the war. Churchill, on the other hand, tended to be somewhat more skeptical about the potential military and political power of Chiang Kai-shek's Republic. Roosevelt urged Churchill to cede Hong Kong to China and to make substantial conditions to the nationalist movement in India; Churchill firmly rejected these suggestions. Churchill wished to see a strong France, headed by Charles de Gaulle, with her colonial empire intact. Roosevelt, on the other hand, wished to see French Indochina (then under Japanese occupation) taken from France and put under some form of international trusteeship, to prepare the natives for eventual independence.

The most vivid passages of Thorne's book are the quotations illustrating the suspicion and antagonism to Britain found among many American officers and diplomats. Thus, we read about General Stilwell's hatred of the "Limies" and his biting characterization of a supercilious British general as a "monocled ass." We also learn of the belief, repeatedly expressed by General Wedemeyer and by such diplomats as Patrick Hurley and John Paton Davies, that a cunning, incorrigibly imperialistic Britain was scheming to keep China divided and weak. The author takes such examples of American Anglophobia from private diaries, personal letters, and memoranda written for internal circulation only. The superficial reader can all too easily get the impression that the wartime Allies did nothing but quarrel with each other.

By his frequent use of such evidence, Thorne inadvertently exaggerates the degree of hostility existing between Britain and the United States during the war years. Any alliance, unless it is a master-satellite relationship, is bound to involve some differences of opinion between the two partners. There was probably no more and no less such disagreement in the Anglo-American alliance than in any other alliance at any time in history. It is good for someone to remind us, as Thorne does, that Churchill and Roosevelt were human beings rather than plaster saints; but one should also remember that even imperfect human beings can work together for a common purpose.

If one reads Thorne's work closely, one realizes that Roosevelt and Churchill, despite their disagreements, were quite ready to compromise when the situation demanded it. Officials of Churchill's government did make attempts to reformulate the official philosophy of British imperialism to make it more palatable to American public opinion. President Roosevelt, while frequently expressing anticolonial opinions, never utilized the power of the United States in men and money in order to compel Churchill to change his colonial policies. When, in 1942, Churchill threatened to resign as Prime Minister if Roosevelt continued to pressure him over India, it was Roosevelt who backed down.

Furthermore, Thorne points out, Roosevelt's anticolonialism never became "embodied" within a "coherent and workable policy." Even within the State Department itself, there were those who preferred a more conservative approach to the colonial question than that of President Roosevelt. After Roosevelt's death, the United States government, fearing the danger of Communist expansion and hoping for a rapid economic revival of Western Europe, considerably softened its anticolonial stand. By the summer of 1945, Thorne points out, the new United States President, Harry Truman, had given his approval to the restoration of French authority in French Indochina.

The British and the Americans, Thorne states, had more in common than they sometimes realized. Thus, the British were not so firmly opposed to a strong China as some Americans thought, although they did not show the same blind faith in Chiang Kai-shek that some Americans did. The similarity between Briton and American existed not just on the level of policy, but also on the deeper level of ideas and sentiments.

Thorne argues that Americans, despite their professed anticolonialism, shared with their British ally, an instinctive belief in the superiority of the white, Anglo-Saxon race. While admitting that Churchill was a "racially arrogant reactionary" in his attitude towards colonial peoples, the author proves that Roosevelt himself, like many other Americans, expressed racist opinions at times. Similarly, the author points out that both Americans and Britons feared Japanese expansion at least partly because they viewed it as a threat to the role of the "white man" in Asia.

Thorne concludes, therefore, that there was an element of hypocrisy in the American "antiimperialism" of the 1940's. A firm belief in independence for colonies, the author notes, could easily coexist with an equally firm belief in the universal validity of "the American way of life." This latter belief, he implies, was really not that much different from the "White Man's Burden" ideology of traditional British imperialism.

Thorne shows that the shock of World War II helped loosen British ties not only with the nonwhite dependencies of East Asia, but also with the "white" Dominions of Australia and New Zealand. After the British defeats of early 1942, these two states decided, despite some misgivings, to look to the United States, rather than to the distant Mother Country, for their military shield. The result was the ANZUS Pact of 1951, from which Britain was completely excluded. Thorne's chapters on Australia and New Zealand, while interesting in themselves, do not fit well into the work as a whole.

Because of the professional historian's natural desire to be fair and judicious, Thorne sometimes writes sentences which are more cumbersome and convoluted than is really necessary. Aside from this minor flaw, his book is, on the whole, well organized and well written. The inclusion of maps, showing the Chinese, Southeast Asian, and Pacific theaters of war, is very helpful to the general reader.

By stressing the existence of friction as well as harmony within the Anglo-American alliance during World War II, Thorne makes an important contribution to our knowledge of those fateful years. The author's exploration of Allied attitudes towards racism and colonialism is also quite original. The work sheds light on some of today's most pressing foreign policy problems. Unfortunately, the sheer length of the book will discourage many people from reading it.

Paul D. Mageli

Sources for Further Study

Book World. June 25, 1978, p. G7.
Choice. XV, September, 1978, p. 927.
Library Journal. CIII, June 15, 1978, p. 1269.
Observer. March 5, 1978, p. 32.
Spectator. CCXL, March 4, 1978, p. 21.
Times Literary Supplement. June 2, 1978, p. 610.

AMERICA IN VIETNAM

Author: Guenter Lewy (1923-   )
Publisher: Oxford University Press (New York). 540 pp. $19.95
Type of work: History
Time: 1950-1975
Locale: Vietnam

An analysis of American involvement in Vietnam from its beginning to the collapse of South Vietnam, with special attention to the question of American guilt

> *Principal personages:*
> HARRY S TRUMAN, President of the United States, 1945-1953
> DWIGHT D. EISENHOWER, President of the United States, 1953-1961
> JOHN F. KENNEDY, President of the United States, 1961-1963
> LYNDON B. JOHNSON, President of the United States, 1963-1969
> RICHARD M. NIXON, President of the United States, 1969-1974
> GERALD FORD, President of the United States, 1974-1977
> WILLIAM C. WESTMORELAND, Commander of the United States Military Assistance Command in Vietnam, 1964-1968
> CREIGHTON ABRAMS, Commander of the United States Military Assistance Command in Vietnam, 1968-1975
> NGO DINH DIEM, Head of South Vietnam Government, 1954-1963
> NGUYEN VAN THIEU, Head of South Vietnam Government, 1967-1975

Perhaps one of the historian's most difficult tasks is to devote his attention to history which has recently ceased being current events. To address a very inflammatory issue still hotly debated makes an attempt at the definitive study almost impossible. Yet, Guenter Lewy boldly presents what his publisher calls "the first systematic analysis of the course of the war, American strategy and tactics, the travail of Vietnamization, and the causes of the final collapse of Vietnam." In justification of this claim, political scientist Guenter Lewy informs the reader in his preface that he is the first scholar to make use of classified defense information which had been unavailable until the passage of President Nixon's Executive Order 11652, of March 8, 1972, granting access to qualified researchers. Lewy's use of these documents as well as virtually every important book on the subject is attested by over fifty pages of footnotes to the eleven chapters, epilogue, and appendices which make up this book. The lack of a bibliography detracts only slightly from his scholarship.

The book is neatly divided into two major sections: the first six chapters detail the course of America's involvement in the conflict; chapters seven through eleven attempt to analyze the legality of this involvement. Lewy's analysis of the history of American involvement is certainly less controversial than those chapters which attempt to assuage the sense of guilt still lingering in the American conscience. In fact, the latter chapters tend to cast suspicion on Lewy's objectivity as a historian. The apologetic nature of the latter chapters casts doubt on Lewy's presentation of the factual account, upon which his analysis of guilt ultimately depends.

The first six chapters present a minutely detailed summary of the gradual escalation of United States involvement, from its inauspicious beginning during the Cold War when most of America's attention was directed to Korea, to its ultimate conclusion. Lewy convincingly puts the entire American mission into the context, often forgotten or overlooked, in which Vietnam and Korea were considered interdependent battlefields in the struggle against international Communism. While the United States was committing troops to Korea in 1950, no one seriously questioned the ten million dollars in aid sent to Saigon for what was essentially a French war burden. By the time of the fall of Dien Bien Phu in May of 1954, United States aid had passed the billion dollar mark. In retrospect, each escalation of money and manpower appears to be a logical step taken by the United States in an increasingly out of control situation in which the country did have a minor stake. Lewy recounts the frustrations precipitated by the ambiguous Geneva accords: South Vietnam's refusal to hold elections and North Vietnam's use of this failure as justification of its insurgency. Lewy uses recently declassified documents to argue that North Vietnam had planned its course of action from the very beginning.

Lewy's thesis that the armed struggle was planned in Hanoi in 1959 by the Central Committee of the Vietnamese Workers' Party is based, he says, on "captured documents and the testimony of defectors familiar with internal party directives." In this, as in most of his analyses, Lewy relies heavily on these "captures documents" and United States government files. He often cites "well informed" historians who reach similar conclusions, but is less convincing in discounting those he considers uninformed and/or biased.

In the crucial Gulf of Tonkin Resolution of 1964, Lewy finds no duplicity on the part of President Johnson's administration. He argues from the record that although congressional debate was short and perfunctory, Congress was aware of the full impact of the document. He quotes Senator Fulbright as saying that Congress "would authorize whatever the Commander in Chief feels is necessary." Lewy charges Senator Fulbright with inconsistency in later charging that the administration used deception. It is Lewy's conclusion that the subsequent escalation of the conflict was not originally intended, but that the threat of retaliation was thought to be a sufficient deterrent. As to America's entrance into the war in March of 1965 as a cobelligerent, Lewy maintains that the decision was not made until February, and he gives as justification that "the southern insurgency was never a spontaneous uprising but from the beginning was a deliberate campaign, directed and supported from Hanoi." To back this claim he cites the United States Department of State's "Working Paper on the North Vietnamese Role in the War in South Vietnam," and calls the "confirmed counts" of 28,000 North Vietnamese infiltrators into the south "a very conservative figure." One would have more faith in Lewy's sources if he would give some evidence of their reliability besides that they are "carefully researched and documented," and they are "based on captured documents." In most cases where he disagrees with other war analysts Lewy presents their case briefly and answers it with the assertion that subsequent information found in official United States documents disproves them. Although he admits frequent instances in which official policy differs from the actualities in Vietnam, he seems to have implicit faith in the official documentation.

From the time the United States was involved with ground combat units—the big unit war—Lewy feels that the United States military policy of trying to defeat a scattered, hidden enemy with traditional American war tactics of increased firepower was not only frustratingly ineffective, but also counterproductive; the South Vietnamese frequently sustained the greatest casualties, thus alienating the people from their supposed protectors. Added to this, as he points out, was the ineffectiveness and corruption of the South Vietnamese government. No one disputes these facts. It is their importance in the overall picture which is controversial.

Lewy is very critical of most American military policies except that of "Vietnamization," that is, gradually turning the combat over to native South Vietnamese soldiers. Unfortunately, Vietnamization did not begin on a major scale until after the Tet offensive of 1968, and its real results were not evident until much later. Then, although Lewy admits that the South Vietnamese army may have been too weak even with United States support, he blames the 1973 Paris Agreement and the Watergate affair for the ultimate collapse of the South. He calls the Paris Agreement a virtual abandonment of South Vietnam by the United States. But, he points out that President Nixon gave private assurances in two personal letters to President Thieu before the cease fire was signed. Because of his Watergate involvement, Nixon, according to Lewy, did not follow through on these commitments when Hanoi violated the peace accord.

The second part of the book, dealing with the justification of American intervention, is more suspect than the first. In this section Lewy states his purpose as an attempt "to analyze the legal status of certain controversial authorized battlefield practices in Vietnam."

His technique is consistent throughout. After presenting the charges, he presents the facts insofar as they are ascertainable; then he applies a strictly legal criterion, discounting unauthorized, isolated acts of individuals contrary to orders. He does admit that "some military men panicked and overreacted to provocation," and that officers should be held liable if they "could or should have known" of atrocities which were committed by their men. Yet, in most cases, he excuses instance after instance on the basis that the person acting in the height of battle was unable to assess the situation properly and was acting in good faith. Such a defense is acceptable in individual isolated cases, but it becomes suspect when used repeatedly as a blanket excuse.

Typical of Lewy's legal stance is his citing of the Rules of Engagement (ROE) published by the American command. These ROE incorporated the relevant rules of war and applied them to the situation in Vietnam. He calls these rules "impeccable," yet admits that "their implementation ran into numerous problems." Acquaintance with the ROE was spotty at best except among Air Force personnel. Officers usually relied on their "common sense" in most battlefield situations. Lewy does accuse General Westmoreland of "failure adequately to enforce ROE, a dereliction which in turn led to war crimes," but he finally begs off, stating that the determination of the degree of culpability is beyond his scope.

The various military tactics Lewy examines are: popular relocation of the civilian population and free-fire zones (areas which may be fired upon freely after due warning has been given to the populace); bombardment and destruction of populated areas; use of incendiary weapons, tear gas, defoliation and crop destruction; employment of cluster bomb units and the M-16 rifle. His conclusion is that,

the American record in Vietnam with regard to observance of the law of war is not a succession of war crimes and does not support the charges of a systematic and willful violation of existing agreements for standards of human decency in time of war . . . neither has it been a model of observance of the law of war.

The qualifications of terms in this conclusion are illustrative of the narrow legal distinctions being made. For example, on the effects of defoliation, on which solid scientific evidence is still lacking, he states, there is "no firm scientific evidence of any direct danger to human health caused by herbicides." Although this statement is technically true, there is a high degree of probability of such an effect which is still under study. The circumstantial evidence is very strong.

On the charges of terrorism, counterinsurgency and genocide, Lewy concludes that while not illegal, many things that occurred should not have happened. His main concern seems to be, however, that such tactics as counterinsurgency with high technology weapons do not achieve their intended purpose and are counterproductive, and in the end, self-defeating.

One chapter devoted to "Atrocities: Fact and Fiction," refers to what Lewy calls "the war crimes industry." He contends that war crimes occur in every war, but that the media publicized such incidents in Vietnam more than in any other war. He points out the one-sidedness of the International War Crimes Tribunal which opened in May of 1967 in Stockholm, Sweden. That the witnesses refused to name names made their stories impossible to verify and certainly would make their testimony inadmissible in most free courts of law. On the other hand, to state that it is unlikely that other incidents similar to the My Lai massacre occurred, as Lewy does, is contrary to evidence he himself presents. His study of court martial records shows that smaller scale atrocities did occur, and that punishment was often insufficient to serve as a deterrent for future actions. He states that strong commanders kept their troops under control, but admits that there were few strong commanders. He blames those atrocities which did happen on ineffective leadership, inadequate planning, lower enlistment standards, and inadequate training of the troops. He also points out that, by way of mitigation, treatment of American prisoners of war by the North Vietnamese was definitely inhumane.

In his epilogue, Lewy puts his entire study in perspective. He states that the main reason for United States failure was the conviction of the American public that the war was going badly and finally that it could not be won. He discounts the antiwar movement as a "small percentage of individuals," which did, nonetheless, comprise a large number of highly visible and vocal protesters. This sounds very much like Spiro Agnew's "silent majority" theory. Lewy considers the one-sided coverage of the war on television as the primary cause of American disillusionment. Finally, he cites subsequent history in Indochina as evidence that "the American attempt to prevent a communist domination of the area was not without moral justification."

Lewy's book is better at recounting the course of the war in Vietnam, but this account is hampered a little in that he supplies only two maps of South Vietnam, neither of which is very detailed. The reader unfamiliar with the terrain will have difficulty in locating many of the campaigns and skirmishes detailed. Also annoying is Lewy's habit of lacing his narrative with acronyms and abbreviations. Although he always gives the full title followed by the acronym in parentheses when he introduces these titles, it is cumbersome for the reader to wade through so many cryptic titles. The book does contain a helpful glossary at the end, but for the reader unfamiliar with military jargon Lewy would have been well advised to spell out some of the terms which appear infrequently (such as FWF [Free World Forces] which, incidentally, is omitted in the glossary).

It is also a bit surprising that in his recounting of the war, Lewy only once mentions the presence of television cameramen. In view of the importance of live television coverage and the attitudes of the American public, these instances should have been given a little more prominence in his narrative. Lewy's apologetic stance in his later chapters depicts him as much less the objective historian and more the advocate. His identification of some of his sources as "well-informed historian of that war" and "diehard Hanoi sympathizers" further lessens his credibility. Combined with his complete acceptance of official records, Lewy's evident partisanship makes it unlikely that his book will be acceptable as the definitive account of that painful chapter in American history. The passage of time and a less personally involved historian are required before such a book is to be written.

Roger A. Geimer

Sources for Further Study

Christian Century. XCVI, January 24, 1979, p. 83.
Commonweal. CVI, February 2, 1979, p. 54.
Kirkus Reviews. XLVI, September 1, 1978, p. 991.
Library Journal. CIII, September 1, 1978, p. 1642.
New York Review of Books. XXV, December 7, 1978, p. 19.

AMERICAN CAESAR: DOUGLAS MACARTHUR, 1880-1964

Author: William Manchester (1922-   )
Publisher: Little, Brown and Company (Boston). 793 pp. $15.00
Type of work: Biography
Locale: Primarily the Pacific Basin islands and archipelagoes
Time: 1880-1964

A definitive and exhaustive account of General Douglas MacArthur's extraordinary life, proceeding from the implicit thesis that this superb military leader's contributions to American, Philippine, Japanese, and Korean history are in danger of being underestimated by future generations

> Principal personages:
> MAJOR GENERAL ARTHUR MACARTHUR, Douglas' father
> GENERAL DOUGLAS MACARTHUR, five-star Supreme Commander in the Pacific during and after World War II
> ADMIRAL ISOROKU YAMAMOTO, a far-sighted Japanese naval officer whose wise use of air power almost defeated the American fleet in the Pacific
> HIDEKI TOJO, one of the Japanese "warlords," a ruling clique which led the Emperor Hirohito into a territory annexation which, in turn, led to the war in the Pacific
> EMPEROR HIROHITO, the shy and scholarly emperor who presided over Japan's entry into World War II
> MANUEL L. QUEZON, the Philippine leader who surrendered to the United States in the Spanish-American War

To many students of current history, the name William Manchester is inextricably linked with his two well-received studies of President John F. Kennedy: *The Portrait of a President: John F. Kennedy* (1962) and *The Death of a President: November 20-November 25, 1963* (1967). Though he has written three novels as well as a collection of essays, Manchester is primarily known for his histories and biographies dealing with such subjects as the Krupps of Germany, H. L. Mencken, and the Rockefeller family. This most recent work, *American Caesar: Douglas MacArthur, 1880-1964*, represents the author's finest biography to date, offering as it does a definitive and exhaustive account of five-star general Douglas MacArthur's extraordinary life proceeding from the implicit thesis that this superb military leader's contributions to American, Philippine, Japanese, and Korean history are in danger of being underestimated by future generations.

Following a standard biographical procedure, Manchester "begins before the beginning" by discussing the many accomplishments of Douglas' father, Arthur MacArthur, who began an exemplary soldier's career at the age of eighteen, joining the 24th Wisconsin regiment that stormed Missionary Ridge at the Civil War battle of Lookout Mountain. Later, after much service, Arthur was ordered to the West to fight marauding Indians; during this tour of duty, he married Pinky Hardy. Soon thereafter, in 1880, Douglas was born. Those years spent growing up in the wild West, riding horses, and scouting the range with Indian boys did much to form the adventure-hungry, free-from-fetters Douglas MacArthur the world would encounter in the next century. However, his Western experiences would be quickly put behind him, for in 1898 his father joined the fight against the Spanish; two years later, when Arthur was made military Governor of the Philippines, his son was to encounter islands and people that he would call home and family. In fact, the Pacific basin would be his "United States" from then on.

One could say with considerable justification that *American Caesar* is one lengthy refutation: a refutation of the allegation, perpetuated by World War II G.I.'s, that Douglas MacArthur was no more than "Dugout Doug," a pampered, spineless shirker who preferred the comforts of elaborate villas to the dangers of the front lines. Yet far from being a coward, Manchester's MacArthur knew no fear, directly confronting enemy sniper and shell fire without wincing or taking cover. Thinking himself somehow immune from a battlefield death, he frightened his subordinates with his reckless lack of concern for his personal safety. Indeed, MacArthur is absolutely magnificent as the nine-times-decorated commander of the famous Rainbow Division of Pershing's World War I army; he dashed over trenches with his men, defying the enemy to kill him. And he was magnificent in the Pacific as he boldly took on the forces of Emperor Hirohito's warlords: men such as Hideki Tojo, architect of the Pearl Harbor bombings, and Admiral Isoroku Yamamoto, dashing airman and naval strategist. With that absolute belief in "Honor, Duty, Country" learned in his youth at two military academies (the second of which was West Point) and in a world war, the General came into World War II well-equipped as a decision-maker. In fact, he only had contempt for those "nervous nellies" at the Pentagon and elsewhere who would deny him proper maneuvering room in "his" Pacific theater of operations. That his attitude would clash with the equally decisive attitudes of such people as Admiral Chester Nimitz (who was also to make decisions about the war in the Pacific) is hardly surprising.

As Manchester relates, it was MacArthur's genius for making the tough decisions that won the war with Japan and won it with so little loss of life (Allied losses during the entire army campaign in the Pacific totaled about the same as those sustained during the Battle of the Bulge in Europe). No one but the General—not even Nimitz—thought of "leapfrogging" around Japanese strongholds. During the operations, troops would be flown to islands far behind enemy lines in order for them to create bases of operation on which air strips could be built. The air strips, in turn, served as the starting points for new drives against the Japanese. This strategy allowed the Americans not only to avoid confronting the enemy island by painful island, but also to make giant leaps toward the ultimate objectives: the Philippines and Japan itself. As strategy, it was, without a doubt, one of history's cleverest tactical moves—something MacArthur was never hesitant about pointing out.

Politics had much to do with the General's ability to fight innovative campaigns like the one involving "leapfrogging." Because Franklin D. Roosevelt, President of the United States during most of World War II (dying in 1945 just before the cessation of hostilities), supported MacArthur's bold moves, the General could do almost anything he wanted without worrying about the opposition of his detested enemy: the so-called "Washington cabal." For a time after Roosevelt's death, MacArthur even got along with Harry Truman, President during the immediate postwar years. At the time Truman clearly did not wish to tamper with the revered Supreme Commander of Japan and the Philippines.

Certainly, MacArthur well applied the lessons he learned from history, a subject dear to him, especially the lessons gleaned from the North's treatment of the defeated South after the American Civil War and France's treatment of the prostrate Germany after World War I. In both cases, the victors behaved horribly toward the losers, creating bad feelings that would last for generations. MacArthur saw a chance to bring a defeated nation back to a normal state of civilization and, in taking a chance, won the love of the Japanese people. An eminently wise man, the General told his troops that he would abide no discourtesy toward their one-time foes and that they were to fraternize with them whenever possible. Under his benign rule, Japan, of course, did rise up again, becoming a formidable industrial power. And, in the Philippines, a new nation rose from the burned-out buildings the Japanese left behind after being driven from the Islands. There too, the people loved MacArthur, a man they treated like an emperor.

However, after North Korea invaded the South in 1950, things began changing for MacArthur. The support he enjoyed from President Roosevelt no longer existed; Harry Truman, a man not easily "talked down to" by anyone, was angered by the way the General countermanded his decisions—or simply ignored them. Increasingly worried about the Red Chinese pouring into South Korea, MacArthur decided to take drastic measures; he, as United Nations commander in Korea, would bomb and strafe Red China until she got out of the war. Truman would have none of this plan. When his command to call a truce was criticized by the recalcitrant MacArthur hellbent on expanding—not stopping—the war, Truman ordered him dismissed as commander, a decision which shocked and infuriated many Americans. MacArthur returned to the United States in 1951 not as a loser but as a great hero. His military career finished, he took up politics, presidential advising (when John F. Kennedy and Lyndon Johnson were in office) and memoir writing.

The Truman-MacArthur episode dramatically points to the essential character of the General: vain, he did not want a "Kansas City haberdasher" telling him what to do; proud, he wanted to be the man who reshaped Asian history; unbending, he could not admit that someone else could be right and himself wrong; resourceful, he believed he alone could overcome the "mediocre" thinking he found so prevalent in the Pentagon. And, as Manchester points out time and again there was a considerable measure of the actor in MacArthur, a man whose life was lived as if it were being acted upon a grand stage, the footlights following every gesture, the audience applauding his fabulous movements and crying at his fine speeches.

It is suggested by the author that all great leaders have the need to be actors and certainly MacArthur had more than an average need. The oversized corn-cob pipe, dark glasses, rakish and rumpled cap, and the stick he often carried were all theatrical props and with them he created possibly the most memorable *persona* of the entire war. But the occasional staginess of his speeches and proplike quality of his personal effects do not make MacArthur some sort of approval-hungry egomaniac—far from it. We are shown the man behind the gimmickry and that man is substantial: a fine and gentlemanly patrician who may have lacked the "common touch," but did not lack a heart.

Certainly, Manchester does a notable job of rescuing the reputation of General MacArthur, convincing the reader that the General's handling of the war in the Pacific and the subsequent occupation of Japan are among the brightest episodes in American history. And while he presents MacArthur, military genius and humanitarian *extraordinaire*, Manchester is not creating a one-sided, propagandistic biography, but rather an account which honestly portrays his subject, flaws and all.

John D. Raymer

Sources for Further Study

Christian Science Monitor. LXX, October 23, 1978, p. B14.

Harper's Magazine. CCLVII, October, 1978, p. 95.

Kirkus Reviews. XLVI, July 15, 1978, p. 792.

Los Angeles Times. October 1, 1978, "Books," p. 1.

National Review. XXXI, January 5, 1979, p. 36.

New Republic. CLXXIX, September 30, 1978, p. 27.

New York Review of Books. XXV, October 12, 1978, p. 14.

Village Voice. XXIII, June 19, 1978, p. 83.

— AND I WORKED AT THE WRITER'S TRADE
Chapters of Literary History, 1918-1978

Author: Malcolm Cowley (1898-   )
Publisher: The Viking Press (New York). 276 pp. $12.50
Type of work: Essays

Essays on American letters from World War I until the 1970's written during the last two decades

In a recent speech at a Modern Language Association meeting, Malcolm Cowley referred to himself as an unpaid national literary resource. No doubt he has become tired of reporters and writers of dissertations making demands on his time, but where else is there to turn? Simply by outliving all of his major contemporaries, he has become, like it or not, the dean of the Lost Generation—though he has come to deplore that term. He contends that the generation preceding Hemingway, Fitzgerald, and Faulkner was far more lost and tragic than the writers and artists who grew up during World War I. (Incidentally, Cowley now prefers the term "World War I generation" to "Lost Generation.")

Be that as it may, Cowley has become the leading authority on the literary situation of his times, and students of contemporary letters, especially fiction, should be properly grateful for the many essays, reviews, and books he has written during a long career at the writer's trade. His list of books includes such well-known titles as *Exile's Return*, his study of the postwar expatriates; *After the Genteel Tradition*; *The Faulkner-Cowley File*; and *A Second Flowering*, a study of the later careers of the Lost Generation. Cowley writes with grace, intelligence, and quiet humor (there does not seem to be a pedantic bone in his body), and his books are always enhanced by his intimate knowledge of his subjects, to say nothing of his compassion for the often messy lives of his writers. Not only did he know such figures as Fitzgerald, Hemingway, and Dos Passos well, but from the start he displayed an insatiable curiosity about their works and lives—as his use of his letters and journals later revealed. Since he was based in New York and Connecticut, however, his knowledge of, say, Southern or Western writers seems limited, and his "histories" of the contemporary literary situation are slightly unbalanced, tilting quite naturally to the writers he first knew at Harvard or met later when he was an editor of *The New Republic*. For example, the only Southern writers he knew well were Conrad Aiken, Allen Tate, his wife Caroline Gordan, and, later, of course, William Faulkner. This does not keep him from writing sympathetically of such novelists as Erskine Caldwell—but he is not as likely to write about writers here that he has not met and known in New York or Connecticut.

—*And I Worked at the Writer's Trade* is a difficult book to classify, but it is an easy one to read and enjoy. As are all his books, this one is informative and interesting, revealing on every page a consuming passion for the American letters of his time. Cowley's subtitle, "Chapters of a Literary History, 1918-1978," suggests more of a unity than the book has, for it is really partly memoir and partly literary criticism. (A number of the essays have appeared before as introductions to books he has edited or as magazine pieces that have appeared in the last two decades.) Certainly the author would not claim this as a definitive literary history of the period, though he touches on everything from the impact of World War I on the Lost Generation to the love children of the 1960's. Though he devotes a chapter to Faulkner and Hemingway, he has little to say of such giants as Eliot and Fitzgerald, devoting most of his space to minor writers he has known or admired. (There is even an informal history of the National Institute of Arts and Letters, of which he was president for a number of years.)

Perhaps a quote from the Foreword can best suggest the author's aim:

> These are chapters of literary history written at intervals over the last twenty years, though dealing with a longer period. I call them chapters, rather than essays, because they tell parts of a continued story and because each of them presents what I have learned about a particular situation or problem in the lives of American writers since the First World War. I was one of the writers, beset with the same problems as others, so the book tells part of my own story too.

Perhaps the autobiographical part of the book can be disposed of first—though the writer weaves his own life and experiences into all of the chapters. Malcolm Cowley is eighty years old now, and it is natural that much of his latest book concerns itself with more than a backward look at his career as a writer—primarily as a literary historian—though he began as a poet and reviewer. But even in the personal chapters, since he knew intimately and corresponded with so many important writers, he is constantly throwing fresh light on his contemporaries, as well as on himself.

Without attempting a full-fledged memoir, Cowley traces his development as a man of letters from his undergraduate years at Harvard, his first marriage, and his precarious life in New York supporting himself as a free-lance reviewer for the *Saturday Review* and the *New York Times*. Later came two years in Paris on a fellowship, where he met the expatriates of his *Exile's Return*. Back in New York and still struggling and poor, he eventually became an editor for *The New Republic*, where he had opportunity to meet (and often help) numerous young writers, to say nothing of participating in the literary feuds, fads, and tempests of the time. No one today knows more about the literary currents of the 1920's and 1930's.

As one might expect, the most important chapter here, entitled "The Sense of Guilt," is a reassessment of his left-wing activities before his break with the Communists in 1939. Here his tone is apologetic; he clearly regrets being taken in—especially as late as the late 1930's. One can experience with him the relief he felt when he quit *The New Republic*, resigned from his party affiliations, and retreated to his farm to write and work in his garden—where he remained for many years. Even so, admitting his errors, Cowley makes it clear that it was far better to be taken in by Stalin than by Hitler.

Other personal chapters deal with writers he first knew at Harvard, such as S. Foster Damon, poet and autobiographer of Amy Lowell, now all but forgotten; or such minor events as his and Kenneth Burke's reply to the Spectra Hoax, the subject of William Jay Smith's book in 1961. More important is his essay on Jules Laforgue, "Laforgue in America." In addition to the Frenchman's impact on his own book of poems, *Blue Juniata*, Cowley glances at his influence on his friend Hart Crane, as well as the early Prufrock period of T. S. Eliot, who introduced Laforgue to Ezra Pound. This is an edifying essay with enough quotes to make clear the appeal that Laforgue's harsh cityscapes and antipoetic images held for rebellious young poets in the 1920's—even those who had to struggle with the French as Cowley did.

A number of essays are intended to rescue Cowley's favorite writers from a new generation of unsympathetic critics. "Mr. Papa and the Parricides" is a defense of Hemingway, who has suffered at the hands of the academics since his death—and earlier, of course—many of whom are now ready to dismiss all of his fiction with the exception of *The Sun Also Rises* and a handful of stories. While defending Hemingway's artistry, Cowley attempts to refute the attacks of such critics as Dwight Macdonald and Leslie Fiedler (who feels that Hemingway is not a novelist but a short story writer), among others. While admitting Hemingway's shortcomings, Cowley points up again the freshness of Hemingway's famous prose and the importance of his experimental technique to the next generation. He asserts that Hemingway is being attacked because academics distrust writers whose books sell widely and because it is natural that the young generation "do in" their fathers (and betters), as they have others of Hemingway's generation, most notably Thomas Wolfe and John Dos Passos. But even if the critics could bury Hemingway, Cowley has no doubt that he would eventually make a comeback, as Melville did.

Similarly, in his essay on Faulkner, Cowley tries to rescue the novelist from his posthumous critics and interpreters, especially those who turn his characters into case studies. Here he narrows his concern to an examination of John T. Irwin's *Doubling and Incest—Repetition and Revenge* (1975), a "speculative reading" that Cowley calls Meta-Freudian criticism. Armed with his own groundbreaking work on Faulkner and the invaluable letters in his *The Faulkner-Cowley File*, it is not difficult for him to show the distortions and reductive nature of much recent Faulkner criticism.

Another impulse behind these so-called chapters is Cowley's plea for a reassessment of forgotten or neglected American writers. (Elsewhere he has called for a reevaluation of such diverse writers as Ramon Guthrie, Dawn

Powell, Harry Crosby, and Kay Boyle.) Here he includes an essay on Conrad
Aiken, whom he does not consider a Southern writer. Cowley knew Aiken
when he was at Harvard, and they corresponded and met infrequently until the
poet's death. In spite of what Cowley holds to be a major poetic talent, Aiken
never reached the audience he deserved (his *Collected Poems* sold less than
five hundred copies during its first year). No doubt part of the reason for this
was Aiken's refusal to appear in public and his inability to play the literary
game of lining up dust-jacket quotes and potential reviewers. In any case, after
many years of devotion to his craft and numerous books, both prose and poetry, Aiken was virtually unknown when he died.

Cowley makes a similar plea for his old neighbor and friend Robert Coates,
who wrote for *The New Yorker* for many years. His stories and novels are
impeccably crafted, but he is currently out of print.

Cowley seems on more certain ground with Erskine Caldwell than with
Coates or S. Foster Damon. Caldwell is an important writer, author of nearly
sixty books, and to date there is only one book on his work—and that a brief
study of racial themes in his fiction. Cowley did not know the Georgia novelist
well, though he met him before the success of *Tobacco Road* (1931) when he
was book review editor of *The New Republic*. He was drawn to Caldwell's
fresh stories in the little magazines in the late 1920's. In addition, he was
fascinated by the poetry in the autobiographical—and surrealistic—"The Sacri-
lege of Alan Kent," as well as the mixture of fact and fancy in Caldwell's later
autobiography *Call It Experience*. Cowley was among the first critics, along
with the editor Maxwell Perkins, to recognize the freshness of Caldwell's approach to his rural Georgia characters. He was correct in seeing the early influence of Sherwood Anderson and Hemingway on him—though he missed the
importance of D. H. Lawrence in his frank treatment of sex. Although he
admits the decline in Caldwell after the 1930's, when his vein of poetry
seemed to dry up, he continued to find readable such late novels as *Weather
Shelter* (1969) (Cowley is probably the only major critic to read the late Caldwell), as well as his nonfiction books on race and Southern religion, *In Search
of Bisco* and *Deep South*. Perhaps it is his interest in the underdog and his
left-wing sympathies that kept Cowley reading and defending Caldwell long
after others had written him off as a soft-core pornographer or commercial
hack. In any case, he and Kenneth Burke deserve credit for calling attention to
Caldwell's early stories and demonstrating that they contain mythic elements
and cannot be read simply as realistic fiction.

There is, perhaps inevitably, a nostalgic coloration in much of this book. As
Cowley confesses, he has "felt increasingly alone and beleaguered." He is
uncomfortable with the latest generation of writers (and he always groups them
by generations), finding them lacking in humanity. Although a rebel himself in
the 1920's, he cannot read the antistories of the 1970's, and he discovers nothing of literary value coming thus far from the so-called "love generation."

However, he is not a pessimist and he ends on a note of affirmation, for "fashions will change, as they always do."

In summary, one can say that Cowley's —*And I Worked at the Writer's Trade* continues to explore many of the themes and literary figures of his early works. Since much of it deals with minor writers, it is not his strongest book; nevertheless, it is worthy to stand beside his *Exile's Return* and *A Late Flowering*.

Guy Owen

Sources for Further Study

Booklist. LXXIV, March 1, 1978, p. 1075.

Choice. XV, September, 1978, p. 31.

Chronicle of Higher Education. XVI, April 24, 1978, p. 18.

Kirkus Reviews. XLVI, March 1, 1978, p. 278.

New York Times Book Review. April 30, 1978, p. 7.

Saturday Review. V, May 27, 1978, p. 62.

Time. CXI, May 1, 1978, p. 91.

AND NEVER SAID A WORD

Author: Heinrich Böll (1917-   )
Translated from the German by Leila Vennewitz
Publisher: McGraw-Hill Book Company (New York). 195 pp. $8.95
Type of work: Novel
Time: A two-day period sometime after World War II
Locale: Germany

A penetrating view of marriage and parenthood as examples of human relationships strained by war, poverty, and the inhumanity of a social system in which it is every man for himself

> *Principal characters:*
> FRED BOGNER, a man disillusioned with life
> KÄTE BOGNER, his wife
> CLEMENS, their son
> CARLA, their daughter
> FRANZ, the baby
> MRS. FRANKE, Bogner's neighbor
> MRS. RÖDER, Bogner's landlady
> YOUNG WOMAN IN THE SNACK BAR
> PRIEST WITH PALE PEASANT FACE
> SERGE, Fred Bogner's superior

When Heinrich Böll was awarded the Nobel Prize for Literature in 1972, the Swedish Academy cited his contribution to the revival of German literature after its demise during the Third Reich. The publicity surrounding the award of the Nobel Prize has led to a renewed interest in the U.S. in Böll's work. It is therefore not surprising to see this new edition of one of his early works, but it is a pleasant surprise that the publisher decided to release the novel in a new translation. This has proved a worthwhile effort. Leila Vennewitz possesses, after having translated so many of Böll's works, an exceptional feel for his language. The American phrases and the contemporary informality of the dialogue in this translation, which is approved by Heinrich Böll, bring the reader much closer to the intent of the German original than the former translation.

Up to this point in his career, Böll had experimented with the shorter and medium length literary forms and wavered in his choice between story, novel, long short story in the American manner, or collection of short stories around a single theme. *And Never Said a Word* is the second work Böll designated as a novel. In this early attempt at a new genre, the author chooses a narrow and finely delineated theme; namely, a marriage in danger of breaking apart. The structure is as simple as the theme. The novel has thirteen chapters, of which all odd numbered ones are narrated by the husband, Fred Bogner, and all even numbered ones by the wife, Käte Bogner. The time is limited to one weekend beginning as Fred is on his way from work on Saturday and ending very shortly after he returns to work on Monday morning.

Within this simple frame, Böll paints a broad picture of German society in the years after the war. In the center of this picture stands the Bogner family. Fred Bogner has left his wife and children because he, by nature peace-loving, opposed to any form of violence, now finds himself turning violent against his loved ones.

Fred Bogner is one of Böll's unheroic heroes who are victimized by forces beyond their control and comprehension. The hopelessness, inhumanity, and injustice around them pervert their natural emotions. Fred Bogner is incapable of keeping a job, he is doping himself with smoke and drink. When he is at home, he suddenly explodes and beats his defenseless children. Because of these uncontrollable fits of violence, he has left home and now roams the streets. He sleeps in bombed-out houses, stairways, and wherever he can find warmth without human obligations. An early interest in death, which started when he, as a seven-year-old-boy, secretly followed his mother's coffin to the cemetery is now perverted into a morbid fascination with death and dying. He attends funerals of strangers and is often invited home by the bereaved to listen to the life story of people of whom he knows nothing but their coffin.

Such perversion of human emotions leads Böll's characters either to superficial activity without any emotional involvement or to lethargy. On the one end of this spectrum is Mrs. Franke, who serves on all church and social committees. She is always on the move but only displays tenderness when she talks about money. At the other extreme are the people who are seen in some of the public places depicted in the novel. They merely sit there and let the world pass them by. They do not react to anything around them as they apparently have given up hope of ever influencing the course of events. Mrs. Röder, Bogner's landlady, is close to this stage of development. She is said to defeat any of Käte Bogner's complaints about the conditions of their room with her "overwhelming lethargy." Like Fred, Mrs. Röder takes schnapps as a cure-all; however, while she lacks incentive and energy to fight any longer, Fred still explodes. His anger may not be directed very rationally, but it shows some residue of life and hope, conscious or subconscious—he may still be able to change things. Mrs. Röder has lost this hope, as indicated by her admonition to Käte Bogner not ever to complain again for "there's no cure for poverty."

Fred Bogner's hope of improving the quality of his life has dwindled to the point where he is beginning to show signs of a suicidal fascination with defeat. This may be seen in his entire lifestyle, but is illustrated most clearly in his addiction to playing the slot machines. This addiction has gone so far that even money obtained at great sacrifice will end up in the machine. He will work extra hours or swallow his pride, asking acquaintances for loans to rent a room for a meeting with his wife. In most cases he will end up in front of a slot machine and not leave until all the money is gone. The initial fascination with winning has ceased, however. He has found a machine which almost never comes up with a winning combination, and even when it does, no money is paid out. Since finding this machine, he only plays this kind, the kind on which you lose even when you win. It is this stage of self-destruction which Fred has reached when Käte presents him with the ultimatum of either facing up to his responsibility as a husband and father or ending their relationship.

The author makes Fred's transformation plausible by developing circumstances around him and his wife which gradually lead them back towards each other and away from the influences which resulted in the breakdown of their relationship. This reorientation starts at the end of the first two chapters, after we have become acquainted with the two narrators and the situation in which they find themselves at the beginning of the weekend. At the end of chapter one, Fred goes to a church for the first time in years. At the end of the second chapter, we see Käte removing all the cheap prints of Renoir's women from the walls of her room and leaving only the crucifix and one picture of a maze of lines and sparse colors. She apparently is beginning to abandon the romantic escapist dreams represented by the Renoir prints and is beginning to face the cross of a complex, colorless reality. The Christian basis of their reformation as indicated in Fred's visit to the church and Käte's selection of the crucifix as the center of attention in her home is affirmed when Käte, on her way to meet her husband, enters the church where he had been only hours before.

This process of unwittingly following a track which will ultimately lead them together both physically and philosophically reaches beyond the church visits. During Fred's first visit to the bombed-out church, he had seen the priest with the pale peasant face and the woman from the snack bar. He followed the woman to the snack bar where the priest also showed up briefly. Similarly Käte happens into the snack bar on her way from the church where she had confessed but the priest had hesitated to grant her absolution. It is in the snack bar that the priest catches up with her and finally grants her absolution. Käte compliments the woman on her coffee, just as Fred had done that same morning. Once the couple has been reunited, they remain in the track which had led them back to each other. They both attend evening mass, and the next morning they go to the snack bar for breakfast.

More significant than the physical paths which lead the two together is the new philosophic orientation which they gain through the experiences of the weekend. The love and self-sacrifice of the woman in the snack bar counterbalances the selfishness and bigotry of Mrs. Franke. The priest from the bombed-out Church of the Seven Sorrows counterbalances the kind of Christianity which emphasizes the superficial as represented by the Bishop, the procession, or Mrs. Franke's association with the church.

The self-serving economic system in which man is viewed as no more than a prospective buyer and is appraised according to how much he appears to be able to pay, finds its opposite in the snack bar where human value takes precedence over money. It is this reorientation towards Christian and human values which will make a reunification of the Bogner family possible. There is no

deus ex machina at the end of the novel turning all evil into good. Reality for
the Bogner family remains the same: namely, bleak. The plaster will continue
to crumble from the walls in the overcrowded room, and Käte's battle against
the dirt and dust will remain as untriumphant as ever. The socioeconomic system is not changing, and the church is not becoming more sensitive to human
needs. But instead of expecting change from the outside, from everybody else,
the Bogners are now willing to change within themselves and are orienting
themselves on the simple, loving examples of the people connected with the
snack bar and the Church of the Seven Sorrows. They are going to place their
hope in prayer rather than in the slot machine, and from now on love and
charity will form the basis for their lives and actions rather than jealousy, hate,
dejection, and hopelessness.

Social criticism permeates the novel. While it is normally assumed that the
characters in Böll's early stories are people broken by the war, Fred does not
quite fit this mold. He himself finds that the influence of the war years on him
was minimal, that there is nothing to talk about from those years, that they
represent only boredom. What really broke him, or as he put it, made him
sick, was poverty, a poverty already experienced in his childhood before the
war. However, Käte's touching visual image of Fred gazing at the smoking
pile of rubble under which everything they had owned including their first and
only decent apartment lay ruined, as well as the references to the sickness and
death of their two babies, indicates that war had a more devastating effect on
their lives than their own words reveal. In the novel, however, Böll's major
criticism is directed towards the socioeconomic system; therefore, the root of
the problem with which the novel deals also lies within that system.

A somewhat naïve concept of the economic system, however, weakens the
effect of the criticism. Thus the tragedy of the two little children's death is
tainted when the reader is asked to believe that an effective medicine was
being withheld so that a useless remedy produced by the cousin of the Minister
of Health could be sold.

Böll's criticism of the church is more effective. The selfish and greedy Mrs.
Franke is a picture of hypocritical piety. This woman, who only shows tenderness when she speaks of money, is among the most prominent ladies of the
diocese, she receives Holy Communion every morning, and every month she
kisses the Bishop's ring. In return for these superficial actions, the church has
certified her urgent need for a fourth room, while the Bogners' application for
a two-room apartment receives an unfavorable reference.

The criticism of the church is sharpened when it is associated with the war.
Fred compares the communications from one cleric to another to those passing
among officers during the war. He also observes, while watching the procession, that the Bishop's stride is but a mild variation of the goose step. The
most effective criticism of a superficial church concerned only with itself and
its image is brought about by Böll's method of intermingling and paralleling

the images of the church procession and the advertising efforts of the druggists who are gathered in town for a convention. Flashing in the background of the broad picture painted in the novel are advertising signs which alternately promote the church and salvation and the druggists and their products.

The novel in its new translation is much more contemporary than one would expect. The theme and the structural simplicity bring it very close to the reader and should assure its popularity. But the dualistic moral philosophy which sees the world quite narrowly in terms of good and evil and the lack of differentiation in the portrayal of characters are weaknesses which are not uncommon in the early literature dealing with World War II.

Sofus E. Simonson

Sources for Further Study

Best Sellers. XXVIII, August, 1978, p. 139.
Christian Science Monitor. LXX, July 12, 1978, p. 18.
Kirkus Reviews. XLVI, March 15, 1978, p. 318.
Los Angeles Times. August 20, 1978, "Books," p. 4.
Library Journal. CIII, May 1, 1978, p. 993.
New Statesman. XCVI, September 29, 1978, p. 416.
New Yorker. LIV, August 7, 1978, p. 81.

ANOTHER I, ANOTHER YOU

Author: Richard Schickel (1933-   )
Publisher: Harper & Row Publishers (New York). 183 pp. $8.95
Type of work: Novel
Time: The 1970's
Locale: New York and London

An account of the emotional passages of two divorced people as they gradually learn to trust, laugh, and love again

> *Principal characters:*
> DAVID KOERNER, the recently divorced narrator
> ELIZABETH ADDERLEY, his lover, also recently divorced
> MORT CLINE, David's business partner
> SIR MILES POYNTER, a British television actor who befriends David and Elizabeth

Best known for his work as a writer, director, and producer of film documentaries about Hollywood movies, and as a film critic for *Life* and *Time* magazines, Richard Schickel has crafted a moving and memorable novel about marriage and love in *Another I, Another You*, a story required by our times. He accurately depicts the relationship between a mature man and woman thrown together by the breakup of their respective marriages, showing their search together, and their searches separately, for reevaluation and redefinition in their lives.

Our society has witnessed the increasing failure of marriage, the loss of love, and the bitterness of divorce. Schickel has confronted these traumas straightforwardly in this timely and engrossing novel. His portrayal of the psychic wounds inflicted by the contemporary marital state is mercilessly honest and, thereby, instructive. There is both wisdom and humor here. There is calculated truth in the book's jacketed subtitle: "A love story for the once married." Certainly the narrative will have more resonance, and provide more satisfaction, for those readers who have experienced divorce. Readers who "have been there" will spot immediately, and appreciatively, the discernment which Schickel brings to his task. He shows with knowing poignance the stages, plateaus, and fantasies privy to the divorced. He shows the needs and fears, the peculiar joys of shedding an old life and an old love, and the awesome possibilities of picking up the threads of the new life with the new love.

Schickel draws his book's title from lines by W. H. Auden: "For every news/means pairing off in twos and twos/Another I, another you." He captures the mood of contemporary society, in which one no longer asks an acquaintance about a spouse absent from the cocktail party. The ubiquitous answer has become Auden's "the news." Even though Schickel stoutly disclaims any autobiographical elements by writing in an authorial note: "I am not I; she is not she: they are not they," his novel rings true. The crises his characters experience are recognizable and painfully accurate—as if realized by one who indeed has had the new identity of "another I" thrust upon him.

The novel's major theme concerns the necessary, simultaneously rejuvenating and frightening redefinition of one's identity after a divorce. As much as a redefinition, the process is a rebirth, fraught with guilts and pangs of kaleidoscopic range. Schickel effectively captures the special tribulations his protagonist undergoes as he tastes the delight of sensual pleasure, only to bring himself up short with feelings of guilt for having allowed himself to feel good. This example is typical of the process: for years a person has been defined by being half of a partnership, part of a checks-and-balances relationship. With the dissolution of that arrangement, the partners become necessarily half-persons for awhile, stumbling along, no longer so clearly defined as before. The challenge of becoming, again, a person who can love and be loved is awesome. Schickel's novel brings this process into sharp focus by telling the story of a love affair between a man and a woman, both painfully divorced, who had convinced themselves that they were too weary, calloused, and hurt ever to be swept up into an old-fashioned romance again.

Thrown together by chance are David Koerner, the novel's forty-two-year-old narrator, and Elizabeth Adderley. Friends from the years of their former marriages, they begin seeing each other to assuage loneliness with someone "out of the past." They each are chagrined to learn that the past is unalterably lost, and that it is no basis for continuing a friendship. Astonished by an awakening awareness of each other's newly-perceived personalities and gifts, they drift into an affair which sharpens their senses of reality and ultimately broadens their concepts of life's possibilities. Theirs becomes an unashamedly sensual, romantic affair. They learn from each other how to give and accept love. They are not the foolishly eager youths who married early, struggled at jobs, had problems with in-laws, had children, had mortgages, suffered tragic, existence-denied differences and fights with spouses. Neither are they the uncertain, growing-gray, tired figures who watched their marriages die. Thrust into new existences, they are surprised to find advantages, though sometimes bittersweet, in their altered vision and tempered maturities. They no longer take anything for granted. They work very hard at being alive. They learn how to be benevolently selfish. What happens to them is both ancient and new. Together, they rediscover love and redefine it for themselves. In real ways, it is their first, best love. What preceded was a maturational dream become nightmare. Their growing appetites for each other, they discover in delight, extend beyond the physical. Moving together in love, they rediscover new-old concepts of kindness, grace, gentle affection, quietude, and humor. Together they begin, for the first time, to feel a commingled sense of decency and passion about themselves as individuals and as a couple. Fate, time, sociological circumstance—stimulating rather than depressing David and Elizabeth's particular sets of strengths and needs—combine to provide the new couple a life's moment of spiritual regeneration, human redemption, and unforgettable magic.

Such a novel requires firm control if it is to avoid two obvious extremes of stylistic form. Schickel tells his story in a crisply contemporary tone without ever becoming cynical or sensational. He also avoids becoming cheaply romantic. Obviously a man who tenaciously believes in—and celebrates with vigor—the possibilities of love and happiness between men and women, it would have been easier, perhaps, for Schickel to tell a more traditionally happy-ended story. He is too honest a craftsman for that. David and Elizabeth never marry each other. Rather, they learn, in time, that theirs has been a special, healing, learning-together interlude which they both wish could last, but which they know cannot. Their harsh, hurried century does not allow such magic to last. If at all, it must exist briefly; thereby its participants must themselves make it the more beautiful. Schickel knows no one lives "happily ever after." So, he tells no lies. He writes instead of our contemporary reality which is harsh and devastating, but which is rendered less cruel and destructive by the determined spirits of two characters who give of themselves to each other. He tells of their subsequent wisdom, acceptance, and growth—of their continuing strong affection and respect for each other even after, inevitably, they go different ways.

Schickel's story is a difficult one to tell. One of his most admirable traits is his capacity to make his story a deeply personal one with which readers, nevertheless, identify strongly. He causes us genuinely to care about his characters, to identify with them. Like us, they are not perfect. As in our world, there seems little of solidity or joy in theirs to which they may cling; they are trying to be the best people they know how; they want some modicum of happiness, and we identify with those needs and struggles. At the end of the book, the reader is hoping for fiction—for romance—for the beautiful lie to be told. Significantly, Schickel's novel teaches us, makes us feel more mature in the skillful way it denies us that every romance of ending. Without being bitter, he is simply realistic. We are encouraged by this honesty and come away from reading his novel strengthened. We tell ourselves that we too could survive this loss. He makes us feel strong and capable of continuing to grow in love and giving.

Schickel should be proud of having thus told his contemporaries an uncompromisingly real and, at the same time, an uncompromisingly encouraging story. In our age, divorces and affairs are not, it would seem, easy topics about which to maintain a sense of balance. *Another I, Another You* is an inspiring, instructive, cautionary tale.

Schickel has created a carefully restrained, tasteful yet powerfully evocative novel. In an age in which fiction seems intent upon killing off the mystique of heterosexual love, he has written a consciously virile, sensitive love story which will delight men and women alike. Rather than flying off into the provenly lucrative sanctuaries of fantasy or fuzzy-focused history as many other writers do today, Schickel has confronted his time and his people. He has penetrated to the center of some problems of contemporary life. He examines bravely the terrible damages which have been done to love, marriage, family, job, fulfillment, and friendship. Calmly, without relying on any but the recognizable events, he manages to impress his readers with capacities that they have not yet recognized in themselves. He believes in his characters and seems genuinely to like them. By liking his people, he makes us like them—thereby making it possible for us to begin liking ourselves through them. There are larger, more pretentious novels, by writers with more star-studded images, which accomplish much less. Perhaps we should not ask of a novel more than what Schickel has given us here. In addition to his interesting people and their real circumstances, he has offered us a grand lesson, very well told. And he gives us insights into our own inevitable versions of *Another I, Another You.*

Thomas N. Walters

Sources for Further Study

Booklist. LXXIV, April 1, 1978, p. 1241.

Kirkus Reviews. XLVI, February 15, 1978, p. 201.

Library Journal. CIII, April 15, 1978, p. 900.

New York Times Book Review. April 9, 1978, p. 14.

Publisher's Weekly. CCXIII, March 6, 1978, p. 88.

Time. CXI, May 1, 1978, p. 92.

THE ART OF WARFARE IN THE AGE OF NAPOLEON

Author: Gunther E. Rothenberg (1923-   )
Publisher: Indiana University Press (Bloomington). 272 pp. $12.50
Type of work: Military history
Time: 1790-1820
Locale: Western Europe

A historical survey of the tactics, weapons, and support services employed by the larger armies in extended campaigns which were characteristic of the Napoleonic age

> *Principal personages:*
> NAPOLEON BONAPARTE, Emperor of France and chief French military commander
> THE DUKE OF WELLINGTON, British military commander, Napoleon's chief adversary
> GEBHARD LEBERECHT VON BLÜCHER, Prussian field marshal
> ARCHDUKE CHARLES, Austrian military commander, brother of Austrian Emperor, Francis II
> MIKHAIL KUTUZOV, Russian field marshal

Readers who lose patience with the excessive technical detail of most military historians will find Gunther Rothenberg's approach refreshing. Instead of giving us every specific of each battle accompanied by obscure diagrams full of incomprehensible arrows, he gives us the essence of battle strategy and tactics, accompanied by diagrams of exceptional quality and clarity. Moreover, Rothenberg does not merely focus on the military details of military history; he also exhibits a serious interest in the social and political causes and consequences of that history. He seems as comfortable when he is describing the limitations of the late eighteenth century rifle and musket as he is in discussing the adverse impact of the ideas of the French Revolution on the treatment of prisoners of war.

Although from 1790 to 1820 Western Europe was shaken severely by the struggles of the French revolution, in fact, the art of warfare changed very little. This relative stagnation was partly the result of technical limitations which could not be overcome at the time. The results of such limitations can be easily seen by examining the deficiencies of the chief infantry weapon of the time: the musket. This weapon had a smooth bore and was loaded with improperly fitted balls, propelled by a charge initiated by a flint spark. The smooth bore and the irregularities in the shape of the balls were enough in themselves to interfere significantly with accuracy. In addition, the delayed charge caused the weapon to shake, and the absence of a rear sight made aiming difficult. In any case, the inaccurate front sight was often obscured by a fixed bayonet.

These deficiencies were evident when the musket was functioning well. However, this was seldom the case. The principle of interchangeable parts was well known, but the industrial revolution had not progressed far enough to translate theory into practice. Therefore malfunctions were common. In addition, the cumbersome firing mechanism was subject to fouling after a relatively small number of shots. The rifle, which existed at the time and was eventually to replace the musket, was certainly more accurate; but, as with many new inventions, was fraught with mechanical difficulties rendering it generally ineffectual as a battlefield weapon.

The inaccuracy and short range of the musket dictated battlefield tactics. Aiming of weapons made no sense and was forbidden. A slow advance in line, pointing and rapidly firing muskets, was the preferred tactic. This maneuver would create a hail of musket balls which would inflict wounds on the enemy in a manner analogous to the way buckshot effects a flock of wildfowl.

This tactic of pointing and rapid firing was necessarily engaged in at short distances. In fact a British ordinance officer estimated that "a soldier must be very unfortunate indeed who shall be wounded by a common musket at 150 yards, provided his antagonist aims at him, and as for firing at 200 yards you might well fire at the moon." Even at the short ranges of battle, it took a great many rounds to inflict a single casualty. At Vittoria it required 450; and since the average soldier fired sixty rounds at the battle, it took between seven and eight infantrymen, firing steadily, to wound or kill one of the enemy.

This wounded soldier—whether he was hurt by a musket round, a saber cut, or a cannon ball—could expect little in the way of medical attention. The wounded would lie out on the battlefield for hours, perhaps days, after battles were fought. They would die of shock, infection, or they would bleed to death. When they needed medical services, they were often not much better off. There existed no antiseptics (the germ theory of disease had not yet been formulated), anesthetics, or plasma. About all that army surgeons—there were never enough of them and many were ill-trained—could do was saw off a limb and apply a bandage. No wonder a cynical soldier stated that a wounded man's best medicine was a cannon ball.

Still, soldiers were more likely to die from disease than from battle wounds. In the Peninsula campaign the British army lost 33,819 troops, but only 8,889 were lost from combat-related injuries. In a dramatic instance, at Walcheren, there were only 106 battle casualties, but 4,175 died of malaria. "Disease, not bullets or bayonets of the enemy had destroyed an entire army." The filth and general inefficiency of military hospitals were notorious throughout all European armies and Florence Nightingale and the reform of military medicine lay in the future.

Not only common soldiers, but also commanders had problems. Intelligence and communications were two areas where difficulties were immense. The lack of adequate maps was especially vexing, for without such maps strategic and tactical maneuvering are twin nightmares: rivers not charted must be forded, mountains suddenly appear and forests turn to bare plains. Just as cartography was in its infancy, so were battlefield communication systems. It was standard for commanders to observe the progress of the battle from a rise of ground. Their exposed position was of no import, since they were not fired upon. To the military at the time, this practice made sense because without commanders no battle could be fought. From this rise, commanders could observe the dispositions of their troops at the beginning of a battle. After the start of action, however, the battlefield was so obscured by smoke that visibility was very much hampered. Furthermore, when commanders wanted to direct the course of action of their men, they had to resort to mounted messengers or runners. These methods were inevitably very slow and very much subject to the accidents of battle.

Difficulties in intelligence and communications were supplemented by difficulties in logistics—the means by which an army is clothed, fed, and equipped. Problems of supply plagued all European armies but especially those on the march, farther and farther from their base. Necessarily an army was no faster than the pace of its infantry; however, it could be much slower than that pace. It could be hampered by slow, lumbering supply vehicles maneuvering on bad roads. Moreover, the pace of individual soldiers could be slowed down by a heavy pack, full of extra food, extra clothing and tenting. The solution might be to lighten the pack and to eliminate the supply train. Soldiers could forage, could live off the land, and could sleep in the out of doors in all sorts of weather. But bivouac could lead to ill health and excess fatigue, and foraging could create ill will in the countryside and contribute to guerrilla warfare.

From what has been said thus far, it might be assumed that war in the late eighteenth and early nineteenth centuries consisted only of pitched battles. This is not entirely the case, since fortresses were still common and still besieged. These fortresses were built along elaborate lines on plans developed and perfected in the sixteenth and seventeenth centuries. Besieging a fortress was also done by plan when appropriate besieging equipment was available. However, whereas in earlier times the retention of a fortress was the key to victory, in the latter period this was not unalterably true. Napoleon's victory at Marengo was decisive, although the Austrians still held many of the Northern Italian fortresses.

In many respects—in armaments and logistics, for instance—the armies of the European powers were alike. They were also alike in that during this period, none lacked talented commanders. The British had the Duke of Wellington; the Russians had Kutuzov, the Austrians, the Archduke Charles; and Blücher led the Prussians. Nevertheless, towering above these leaders was the enemy commander, Napoleon Bonaparte:

Napoleon, absolute head of state and commander in chief, was able to achieve the realization of [his theories of rapid movement and efficient supply] and his short and relentless campaigns became a model for future generations of planners. Napoleon's army was to a large degree the product of its historical experience, transformed and made more powerful

by the charismatic genius of its leader. It served him well . . . and, even in extreme
adversity, the hard core of the army remained loyal to him.

Under Napoleon's inspired leadership, the French were able to triumph over
the rigid Prussians, the conventional Austrians, the brave, but amateurish British, and the brave, but disorganized Russians. Eventually, of course, Napoleon's "overweening ambition and his overcentralization, coupled with a
neglect of logistics and supply, proved his undoing and he was defeated by
attrition and greater numbers."

Mention of attrition and greater numbers leads to the inference that the size
of battle had increased, and so it had. The French Revolution was not a revolution in the way war was fought; however, it was a revolution in the personnel who fought—a transition from the professional armies of the eighteenth
century to the citizen armies of the nineteenth and twentieth centuries.
Whereas earlier commanders sought to avoid battle, later commanders sought
it eagerly. In the three hundred years between 1480 and 1790 only 713 battles
were fought; in the twenty years between 1790 and 1820 enemy forces engaged
each other on the battlefield 2,659 times. Moreover, armies were swollen by
the conscription of citizen soldiers—cheap and expendable manpower. In the
eighteenth century a whole military establishment might have consisted of
200,000 troops; at Leipzig Napoleon commanded 175,000 in one battle alone.

The large losses sustained by these citizen armies required the justification
of national hatreds which, in turn, had a deleterious effect on the treatment of
prisoners of war. More often than not, prisoners were massacred or allowed to
starve. While nationalism increased the brutality of war, it also led to the rise
of guerrilla warfare, especially in Spain, which "not only set the pattern for
future wars of national liberation," but "more immediately provided encouragement and inspiration for other national risings."

As *The Art of Warfare in the Age of Napoleon* makes clear, warfare in the
late eighteenth and early nineteenth centuries was both stable and changing. It
was stable in that weaponry, tactics, communications, logistics, siegecraft and
intelligence suffered from deficiencies in technical and scientific innovation
characteristic of the dawn of the Industrial Revolution. On the other hand, the
social nature of war indelibly changed. The Napoleonic period was the end of
small professional armies maneuvering to avoid battle. It was the beginning of
citizen armies, inflamed by nation hatreds, brutally directed to the complete
and ruthless destruction of the enemy.

Alan G. Gross

Sources for Further Study

Choice. XV, September, 1978, p. 937.
Contemporary Review. CCXXXII, March, 1978, p. 164.
Horn Book. VII, October, 1978, p. 4.
Library Journal. CIII, July, 1978, p. 1406.

AUTOBIOGRAPHY OF VALUES

Author: Charles Augustus Lindbergh (1902-1974)
Publisher: Harcourt Brace Jovanovich (New York). 423 pp. $12.95
Type of work: Autobiography
Time: The twentieth century
Locale: Predominantly the United States and Western Europe

Lindbergh offers a life study that is instructive as a philosophical commentary on the vicissitudes of this troubled century

> *Principle personages:*
> CHARLES AUGUSTUS LINDBERGH, pioneer aviator
> ANNE SPENCER MORROW, his wife, the daughter of the American Ambassador to Mexico, Dwight D. Morrow
> CHARLES AUGUSTUS LINDBERGH, JR., their fair-haired, blue-eyed son who was murdered after being kidnaped in 1932
> ROBERT GODDARD, a professor of physics at Clark University in Massachusetts who developed and tested the first liquid propelled rockets in 1929
> ALEXIS CARREL, Head of the Rockefeller Institute's Department of Experimental Surgery and winner of the 1912 Nobel Prize for Chemistry
> HERMANN GÖRING, *Reichsmarschall* of the German *Luftwaffe*

In the popular imagination, Charles Augustus Lindbergh is one of the greatest heroes of this century: that single-minded, serious farm boy from the American Middle West who flew nonstop across the treacherous vastness of the Atlantic Ocean by himself, a feat as astonishing today in an age of missiles and jets as it was in 1927; the gilded youth whose life was to be badly scarred by the kidnaping of his two-year-old son, Charles Augustus Lindbergh, Junior; the American hero who "stooped" to accept a medal from top Nazi, Hermann Göring, thus opening himself to charges of betraying his country. Those three images are what endure, but are they the images we should summon forth? In his *Autobiography of Values*, Lindbergh tells us "no." We come to know him as far more than the daring and naïve pilot of the *Spirit of St. Louis*, the grief-stricken father of a kidnaped, murdered son, or the man heralded by an evil State. We see him as a complex, opinionated, thoughtful, multifaceted man. He was statesman, cultural ambassador, businessman, scientist of amateur rank, writer, and philosopher.

That his autobiography, written in the twenty years preceeding his death in 1974, exists at all is due to the efforts of his friend, editor, and publisher, William Jovanovich of Harcourt Brace Jovanovich, who carefully went through enormous amounts of writing and sifted the essential from the irrelevant. The resulting manuscript is marred by a stylistic roughness and lack of flow which can be attributed to the fact that Lindbergh had not done the necessary rewriting before he died. As unpolished and dull as some of its chapters are, the *Autobiography of Values* is well worth reading, for the author is a latter-day Renaissance Man who did things most of us only dream about doing. Very often, he writes movingly:

> I cherish the illusion of being substance, yet I am as much the spatial nothingness of atoms. I am as empty and as potent as the space between stars. . . . I am a specter cleft by swords.

Yet, he can utter things specious and absurd as well. The book is a both irritating and tantalizing philosophical commentary which has as its subject not so much Charles Lindbergh, hero, but Charles Lindbergh, philosopher, trying to make sense out of his troubled century.

Much is to be learned from this autobiography that was heretofore unknown about Lindbergh: his reasons for marrying Anne Morrow, the extent of his belief in Social Darwinism, his reactions to war, his close escapes from death. We discover the complexity of a man too often simplified for the sake of "good press," for he was a practical visionary, a peace-loving fighter pilot, a privacy-loving celebrity, a patriot who believed that man must advance beyond nationalism. Yet, like any of the many books about Lindbergh, this one disappoints those readers searching for a definitive account of his life and times. He simply defies easy labels.

Perhaps one of the most apparent hallmarks of this autobiography is the author's studied "matter-of-factness," his straightforward way of discussing events. When those topics come up about which everyone wants to know as much as possible (the cross-Atlantic flight, his European reception after the flight, his married life, his feelings about the kidnaping, and his sojourn in Nazi Germany), Lindbergh passes them off as affairs of no real import. For example, his discussion of the landing of the *Spirit of St. Louis* is relegated to one sentence: "The sky was clear; the stars came bright; I circled Eiffel's tower and landed at the airdrome of Le Bourget thirty-three and a half hours after my take-off on Long Island." Yet, infuriating as this is, Lindbergh has his reasons for doing it. For one thing, all of the aforementioned events have been discussed many times by everyone from reporters to historians and for another, Lindbergh frees himself to discuss less well-known happenings.

Among the lesser known events Lindbergh describes are his pioneering work in the U.S. Mail Service where he flew "by the seat of his pants"; his piloting some of the first passenger planes (planes in which passengers had to wear parachutes); the early experiments with human organs done by Dr. Alexis Carrel of the Rockefeller Institute in New York; the war planning going on behind the scenes during the 1930's in Russia and Germany; and his daring flights in South America and the Caribbean where no real airports existed.

In all, Lindbergh speaks with considerable authority, being at once a visionary who dreams of a finer, more peaceful world as well as an eminently practical sort of problem solver never satisfied with quick or ill-thought-out answers. Although he is only expert in aviation, the author is an inspired dabbler in other areas. He is moved to know the secrets of life. As he confesses, "[To me] the important thing was the core. But what was it: how much of it was physical, how much mental, how much spiritual? How could one reach one's core?"

At times, Lindbergh's attempts at understanding himself, his place in that world, and the meaning of the universe are somewhat ludicrously conveyed. For instance, he belabors the dated notion that one who is endowed with phenomenal abilities of one sort or another must hunt for a mate genetically suitable; translating theory into practice, he hunts for a wife with the proper genes and finds her in the person of Anne Morrow. Yet naïve as he occasionally is, Lindbergh's overall understanding of the world is sound. For, having had the opportunity to travel around the world before flying from place to place became common, Lindbergh gained an appreciation of mankind's variety—and the sameness of men's lives for all the surface differences. Early on, the author discovered that differences between peoples were largely illusory and that wars, far from being necessary, were the by-products of ignorance. For all his understanding of his fellow man, Lindbergh did go to war against Japan in 1941 and did take an active interest in postwar nuclear technology; the depth of his commitment to peaceful pursuits is at times difficult to determine.

The most important question which Lindbergh tries to answer is this: "Is Civilization progress?" Having been to remote outposts where few Western people had ever been before, Lindbergh had the chance not only to observe, but also to participate in so-called "primitive" life and the freedom afforded to such people as Africa's Masai warriors, whom he found to be more congenial and beneficial than "civilized" men. Therefore, Lindbergh, though granting that civilization has its blessings, extolls the virtues of living unencumbered by technological society, feeling that such a society may have already overstepped the boundary separating man from nature. According to him, "Man is born with the God-given privilege of living on earth and water, under sun and sky. . . . Must we sacrifice the full appreciation of living for a narrowing culture of the mind?" The primitive, he feels, has reached a level of wisdom inaccessible to modern, technologically dependent man—a wisdom at once instinctual, intuitive, and subconscious rather than rational.

Lindbergh affirms what so many intellectuals are saying; namely, that civilization has its limits and that our environment can only be pushed so far before it collapses, unable to absorb the pollutants and disfigurement. To the author, such a breakdown can be avoided if we closely attend to the "survival values" of individuals. In other words, man must not worship his material creations, but rather look within to find meaning that endures. Without this peace that comes from within, he will destroy the world: a world he does not understand.

Surely, of course, such ideas are scarcely unique; one need only turn to any number of environmentally aware people—Norman O. Brown, Jacques Cousteau, John Kenneth Galbraith, Morris Udall—to find the same things being said (and often more eloquently). Yet, what makes these ideas worth reading in *Autobiography of Values* is the fact that Charles Lindbergh, symbol of the twentieth century man, has passed such judgment on his civilization. Somehow, one does not expect him to be as ardent an environmentalist and "one-worlder" as he is.

This book gives us a man different from the one whom we see in faded photos from the archives. Far from being a shallow technocrat or simple farm boy, Lindbergh reveals himself to be a deep thinker as well as a remarkable doer.

Thus, there is much worth reading in *Autobiography of Values*. We get to know the inner workings of the mind of the man who was the first to fly between continents, the first to see the world as a "global village," and among the first to recognize the Janus-faced nature of rockets and airplanes. We can learn much from him. For, "Once you lived with ghosts, you raged with storms, you cycled with the planets, and you knew a wisdom deeper than the mind, a reality beyond the touch of substance" and can write about such things, you are an author to be reckoned with.

John D. Raymer

Sources for Further Study

American Heritage. XXIX, April, 1978, p. 92.
Christian Century. XCV, May 17, 1978, p. 542.
Los Angeles Times. March 9, IV, p. 6.
Modern Age. XXII, Fall, 1978, p. 424.
Wall Street Journal. December 8, 1978, p. 18.

THE BAD LANDS

Author: Oakley Hall (1920-   )
Publisher: Atheneum Publishers (New York). 371 pp. $10.95
Type of work: Novel
Time: 1883-1911
Locale: The Badlands of the Dakota Territory

An examination of moral and ethical absolutes, this Western novel is concerned with the settlement of one of America's frontiers

> *Principal characters:*
> ANDREW LIVINGSTON, a New York banker-politician who comes to the Badlands on a hunting trip and stays
> LORD MACHRAY, a Scottish lord whose visions of glory and wealth bring him to the Badlands and to an empire
> YULE HARDY, a rancher with a fiercely individualistic point-of-view and one of Lord Machray's bitterest enemies
> MARY HARDY, Yule's daughter, a lovely young girl with a crippled hand and her own point-of-view
> BILL DRIGGS, a hunter, down-on-his-luck and one of the last of the old-timers in the Badlands
> CORA BENBOW, the madam of Pyramid Flats' only brothel

The latest novel of Oakley Hall, a writer of distinguished reputation and talent, is a Western. Having said this much with most Westerns is enough; with *The Bad Lands* it is no more than a beginning. This novel is everything that a Western should be: it is set in the Badlands of the 1880's; it has its cast of cowboys and cattle; it has its share of killings and violence. But to dismiss it as no more than a Western is unforgivable. It is also a novel of morality, of ecology, of ethics — in short, of life and its uncertainties. *The Bad Lands* is a novel of great importance.

Hall, who is the author of fifteen books, including *The Downhill Racers* and *Warlock*, presents in *The Bad Lands* a story whose debt to the life of Theodore Roosevelt is obvious at the beginning. The fact that Hall does not allow this influence to continue throughout the novel is the first hint of the restraint and the control that he exerts over every portion—indeed, over practically every word—of this novel. The story of Theodore Roosevelt's experiences in the Badlands with the Marquis de Mores is the starting point for the plot, but the real interest is Andrew Livingston's story. It is a compelling story, indeed, about men and their conflicts with other men, with progress, with life, with nature itself.

The themes of Hall's novel are universal, the conflicts ones that every reader can understand because they are still without solution. The universality of the themes is one of the major factors that lifts this story out of its context as a Western and gives it significance as a serious work of fiction regardless of genre.

The Badlands of the 1880's become a symbolic location for Hall as he addresses the problem of man's exploitation of the land. In the 1880's, the Badlands were a relatively unsettled and pristine wilderness, only recently taken from the Indians, a land that still remembered the blood that flowed from Indians and fur-trappers, that still heard in its memory the thundering hooves of herds of buffalo that had roamed its plains. But the Badlands were also the basis of the new dreams of cattlemen whose fortunes hinged on the upward swing of the cattle market and the unsettled prairies that this unspoiled land provided. It is significant that Hall should choose a setting in which the nearest sheriff was a hundred miles away, justice still operated with frontier swiftness, and blood seemed to flow regularly. The Badlands, so named because of their harsh environment and forbidding appearance, is the novel's principal metaphor.

The two main characters are almost as unique as the land itself. Lord Machray, a Scottish lord who had been decorated by the British Army time and again for bravery in campaigns in India, the Sudan, Egypt, and Abyssinia, came to the Badlands with dreams of growth and development. For Hall, Machray is a symbol of progress, of growth, of civilization, but to the local ranchers, he represents exploitation of the land, the aristocracy of wealth won by other men's labors and sweat. To the reader, he is a very real person with a dichotomy of traits: he is both strong and weak, coarse and gentle, a dreamer and a con-man.

Andrew Livingston, on the other hand, a New York banker and a member of the Liberal Republicans, is a man without dreams, hope, or purpose. His hunting expedition to the Badlands is designed to help him forget the drownings of his wife and daughter. Having cursed and condemned his God for such inexplicable cruelty, it is fitting that Livingston should come to such a Satan's garden as the Badlands to kill for sport; it is also fitting that here he should find meaning in death, purpose in living, and beauty in the ugliness of creation. Hall suggests that life is a balance of opposites: of beauty and ugliness, purpose and meaninglessness, creation and destruction. Livingston becomes an Everyman for Hall, as the characters and events he encounters on his journey allow him in the end to hold all things in a certain respect, to recognize a certain balance between opposites.

The plot is both simple and compelling. As a newcomer to the Badlands, Livingston is greeted with a certain reserve. As a hunter for sport, he is viewed with some disdain but without much enmity. When he decides to stay in this strange country, however, and purchases a herd of cattle, establishes a ranch, and puts down roots, the disdain is replaced with enmity and violence. It is interesting that Hall suggests here that the established residents of the Badlands see more evil in exploitation of the land than they do in the exploitation of the life of the land. Indeed, the price placed on life in the Badlands seems considerably less than the value placed on the land itself. In fact, Lord Machray is hated by his neighbors not because of any exploitation (although Yule Hardy uses this as rationalization for his hatred of Machray), but rather because he has fenced in the land he claims is his, land that before had been part of the open prairie, shared by all. In short, Machray attempts to own and control the land, not merely to live off it.

Livingston finds himself in the middle of a struggle that is both real (for the characters in the novel) and symbolic (for Hall and his readers). Livingston becomes, literally, the man in the middle, with his ranch between Lord Machray's to the north and Yule Hardy's to the south. Moreover, he is a newcomer, unwanted competition for grazing land already thought too scarce. Finally, he is a man caught between civilization and barbarism, between law and disorder. He must therefore live apart; he must maintain a balance between his neighbors, keeping the good will of both. In fact, it is when he loses the good will of one neighbor that the tension which had been simmering beneath the surface of the men's actions erupts into overt violence.

The Bad Lands is marked by strong, believable, and likable characters. They are neither saints nor devils; they are merely human, and as such are complex, with all the mixed emotions, confused motives, and misunderstood actions of real people. Here again, Hall's restraint strengthens the novel, as new facets of the characters' personalities are revealed gradually, in a real and credible manner. This restraint in Hall's characterizations is likely the novel's greatest strength.

Livingston is Hall's allegorical Everyman, a symbolic figure on the novel's thematic landscape, as well as a very human character, a strange blending of dichotomies and inconsistencies. It is through Livingston-the-artist's eyes that we view the other characters and events in the novel. In addition, we are shown Livingston's letters to his sister and son, which contain information essential for understanding forthcoming scenes and events. Since what background information is necessary is presented through letters, Hall avoids the risk of slowing down the narrative; in the letters all necessary information is crystallized, all nonessential information excised.

Hall's ability to capture a scene in a few words is a further indication of his talent and restraint. His description of a hanged man as "a limp question mark" is a fine example of his ability to convey the essence of a scene and its underlying question of morality. Hall does not allow his reader merely to observe the action and the violence; he must also participate through identification with Livingston. Only in this manner can Hall force his reader to consider the ramifications of violence and to identify each man's role and responsibility for it.

This constant questioning, whether it be of morality, justice, the past, or the future, is what *The Bad Lands* is really about. It is a novel of questioned values, of past and future, dreams and nightmares, life and death; it forces the reader to reassess his own values just as Andy Livingston must reassess his.

The Bad Lands is indeed a Western; but it is also a fine novel, marked by its author's restraint and talent.

James R. Van Laan

Sources for Further Study

Best Sellers. XXXVIII, September, 1978, p. 174.
Kirkus Reviews. XLVI, April 1, 1978, p. 387.
Library Journal. CIII, June 15, 1978, p. 1289.
New York Times Book Reviews. May 14, 1978, p. 12.
Newsweek. XCI, June 5, 1978, p. 98.
Publisher's Weekly. CCXIII, April 10, 1978, p. 66.

BELLS IN WINTER

Author: Czeslaw Milosz (1911-   )
Translated from the Polish by the author and Lillian Vallee
Publisher: The Ecco Press (New York). 72 pp. $8.95
Type of work: Poetry

A volume of thoughtful, penetrating poetry by a man who composes in Polish, his native language, but who participates in the English translation

While not widely known among American readers, Czeslaw Milosz is a poet of longstanding reputation in Europe; he has a well-deserved reputation, as well, for his work as an essayist, a novelist, and a literary scholar. Early in his life he began his work as a poet, becoming one of the leaders of "new poetry" in Poland during the 1930's. During the terrible years of World War II he was in the Resistance movement, editing an anthology of anti-Nazi writings entitled *Invincible Song.* A few years after the war ended, he left Poland for America, where he now teaches, in the Department of Slavic Languages and Literature, at the University of California, Berkeley. In addition to his writings in Polish, he has published a study of Polish poetry after World War II, a history of Polish literature, volumes of essays, a translation of the poetry of Zbigniew Herbert, and a volume of his own selected poems. In 1978 he was awarded the prestigious Neustadt International Prize for Literature.

At the center of Czeslaw Milosz's poetry is the realization that we humans are unable to grasp our experience, that as time passes what we have experienced becomes more and more difficult to comprehend. The poet relates this approach to life by writing poems in which he leads us to see the world as a manifestation of another, superior realm. Joseph Brodsky's written presentation of Milosz as a candidate for the Neustadt Prize explains: "Shortcutting or, rather, short-circuiting the analytical process, Milosz's poetry releases the reader from many psychological and purely linguistic traps, for it answers not the question 'how to live' but 'for the sake of what' to live." Not all the poems in *Bells in Winter*, it should be noted, are published for the first time in English, for some appeared earlier in magazines: *American Poetry Review, Antaeus*, and *New Poetry*.

One way to gain, or at least begin, understanding this excellent series of poems is to begin a second reading with "Bells in Winter," the title poem and final selection in the collection, as well as the sixth and last of a series of poems from "The Rising of the Sun." The poem starts with an imagined experience within an imagined experience. The "I" of the poem says that late one day, while on a journey, he stopped his horse and began to read in St. Paul's epistles. While reading he fell asleep and dreamed that a young man from Paul's Greece spoke to him. Then the "I" of the poem tells the reader that what has just been read is but an exercise in style, a prelude to something that is not invented. Apparently drawing from Milosz's own experience, the poem leads the reader to student days and a student's lodging in Literary Lane, to see an old woman named Lisabeth who brought firewood to the student's room. Why bring this back? asks the poem, replying that everything has a double existence, "both in time and when time shall be no more,"—the kind of belief held by St. Gregory of Nyssa, Johannes Scotus Erigena, and William Blake. Returning to the old woman and memories of her, the poem places her among the saints, among the souls of women abused in earthly existence by men and society. Returning to the "I" of the poem, the reader is led to contemplate a different world, the world of modern-day California, where firewood is cut with a chain saw and the towers of San Francisco can be seen in the distance. The poem ends by reminding us of the words of Old Testament prophets, and the promise of completion when every form will be "restored in glory."

One of the problems of being a poet is what appears to the poet's eyes when he has written a poem. In "Ars Poetica?" Czeslaw Milosz suggests that the poet produces something he himself did not know he had in him, that the written poem can make its creator blink his eyes as if suddenly confronted by a tiger lashing its tail. Still speaking of the poet, Milosz asks what responsible man wishes to be home to a collection of demons who, not satisfied with stealing the voice and hand of the poet, change his destiny to suit their convenience. He goes on to suggest that poems should be written "rarely and reluctantly," with the hope that good spirits, not evil ones, will choose the poet for their instrument. The purpose of poetry, he suggests further, is to remind the reader of the difficulty of remaining a single person, for we are, each of us, a house with unlocked doors, through which invisible guests go in and out at will.

In a different vein, as if to show the variety of poetry which Czeslaw Milosz can write, stand four poems from "The Chronicles of Pornic." Each of these poems takes a bit of local history and uses it not only for descriptive purpose, but also for an overt or implied irony. The first of the four, "Bluebeard's Castle," is about Gilles de Laval, Baron de Retz, educated in Latin and the liberal arts, staunch supporter of Joan of Arc in the fifteenth century. This is the same man who for his evil deeds was condemned by both lay and ecclesiastical courts to be put to death by strangulation. But, says the poem, there were those who said he was put to death because some members of his family, the prince, and the bishop all were greedy for his land. The second poem of this group, "The Owners," is about different owners of the same castle at different times, recounting how, during the French Revolution, the castle passed from the hands of its noble owners, after a period of emptiness, into the possession of a blacksmith, then a merchant, and finally into the hands of a cloth manufacturer. Third in the series of poems is "Vandeans," which accounts an episode of vengeance. The Vandeans, having taken Pornic, shoot a number of men purely for vengeance. Drunkenly celebrating their victory, they were themselves attacked and captured by men led by a priest-patriot. Two hundred fifteen of the Vandeans were killed in a brief encounter; another two hundred fifty, taken prisoner, were slaughtered on the beach near the castle. The fourth in this group of poems, "Our Lady of Recovery," is about miracles performed by St. Mary. Local people believed it was she who saved some of the local men who would otherwise have been lost at sea. The poem suggests that she also willed it that the survivors of a shipwreck should, in their celebration, become drunk and father children.

In "Encounter," an early poem written in 1936 and printed as the opening poem of the present volume, the poet shows the reader how some of the same questions have arisen for him throughout almost half a century; for this poem, like later ones, takes a piece of experience and asks what the poet, or the reader, should find as meaning in that experience and the memory of it. The poet relates how years before there was an occasion when he and a companion rode on a wagon across frozen fields at dawn one day. Suddenly a startled hare ran across the road before them, and the poet's companion pointed to it. Now, says the poem, both hare and companion are dead. But, it goes on to ask, where is "The flash of a hand, streak of movement, rustle of pebbles" going? And the poem adds that such a question is posed, not from sadness, but in wonder.

Czeslaw Milosz uses decades of experience in his poetry, frequently moving from his childhood before 1920 through time to the present, from his childhood's environment in eastern Europe to the West Coast of the United States, where he resettled. A portion of "Diary of a Naturalist," another of the poems from "The Rising of the Sun," illustrates this use of decades of experience. It recalls the poet's childhood with pictures of men, armed with scythes, cutting the summer's second mowing of hay while dressed in the unbleached linen shirts and dark-blue trousers which were the uniform of the farmworkers in the province. The same poem relates a recent experience when he visited Oregon's Rogue River, observing the banks of the boulder-strewn river and the wooded mountains above it. One of the details he noted was that the Alpine Shooting Star (*Dodecatheon alpinum*) grows in the mountain forests. Thinking of the flower, and the river, too, he comments on how language is deceptive, for language allows us, even forces us, to use different names for the same phenomenon at different times and places. He recalls that French-speaking trappers called the river La Riviére des Coquins, literally River of Scoundrels, now Rogue River. And he goes on to remind us that the name the Indians gave the flower and the river may well never be known. As he comments, "A word should be contained in every single thing/ But it is not."

Gordon W. Clarke

Sources for Further Study

Booklist. LXXV, October 15, 1978, p. 347.
Kirkus Reviews. XLVI, October 1, 1978, p. 1129.
Library Journal. CIII, October 1, 1978, p. 1987.
Nation. CCXXVII, December 30, 1978, p. 741.
Publisher's Weekly. CCXIV, September 4, 1978, p. 105.

BLACK ULYSSES

Author: Jef Geeraerts
Translated from the Dutch by Jon and Marianne Swan
Publisher: The Viking Press (New York). 268 pp. $12.95
Type of work: Novel
Time: The early 1960's
Locale: Belgian Congo, Spain

A grotesque portrait of an African medical assistant's retreat from and eventual complicity in the bloodshed that takes place after the Belgian Congo gains its independence from its European overlord, as well as a study of the larger implications of man's capacity for violence

> *Principal characters:*
> GRÉGOIRE-DÉSIRÉ MATSOMBO, a medical assistant and the "black Ulysses" of the novel
> MASUMBUKA, a witch doctor
> LIEUTENANT BOLEKO, rebel commander of the unit Matsombo joins
> DR. VAN DEN BERGHE, Belgian doctor and narrator of Part Two of the novel

Jef Geeraerts' first novel, *Gangrene*, won the prestigious Belgian State Prize for its literary and stylistic quality and for its wrenching portrait of a white colonial administrator governing an African village. This sudden praise also brought with it a storm of controversy. The novel was seized by the Minister of Justice and was put to trial for allegedly being bawdy and obscene. The added publicity sealed the success of *Gangrene* and it became a European bestseller, much to the chagrin of the Minister of Justice's office. The subject Geeraerts has brought to light, beginning with *Gangrene* and now in *Black Ulysses*, has been part of the author's actual experiences as an assistant administrator in the Belgian Congo; the violent emergence of the Belgian Congo as a nation is forcefully illuminated in *Black Ulysses*.

Many quite understandable but highly regrettable aberrations have occurred in modern history as a result of lack of planning when power changes hands. Such has been the case in the Belgian Congo, where there are constant reminders even today of colonial refusal to back out gracefully from Southern Africa. The early 1960's saw the final vestiges of Belgian control of the Congo crumble; the fight to fill the void began immediately, accompanied by an onslaught of atrocities across the land. *Black Ulysses*, written in stark and grotesque prose, relies on raw imagery which appeals to the reader through the nostrils, through the gut. The novel is repeatedly repugnant and apocalyptic. In vivid detail, African life as experienced by both the European colonialist and the native African is shown to be shockingly brutal. Geeraerts presents an uncompromising portrait both of European corruption and negligence in leeching off Africa, and of the black man's confused, fearful, hateful response to the circumstances in which he finds himself in his own territory.

The cultural clashes in the case of the Congo have left scars—some prominently visible, others hidden for years, carried around and left festering only to manifest themselves at a later date. Calm periods, therefore, enjoy a false security. It is difficult to measure adequately the damage done to a race of people who have been trampled, stripped of their traditions, and forced to conform to European bureaucratic and moral customs. As a European author who has lived and worked in Africa, Geeraerts has witnessed his share of broken lives and group behavior that passes into the realm of madness. His novel is designed to elicit disgust; and no heated room, comfortable chair, nor fluffy headrest can provide safe sanctuary from his searing images. A lesson is to be learned, and the reader turns each successive page only to be bombarded with raw evidence of what man is capable of doing to his fellow men when pushed to inhuman limits.

Comparisons can be made to other authors who have sought to describe incisively the evil in the environment and the evil within man, and the causes and the aftershocks of such evil: notably Jerzy Kosinski, V. S. Naipaul, and Joseph Conrad. Each in his own way has created a body of literature that is both brutal and instructive. The passages in Kosinski's *Blind Date* concerning the Manson murders make uncomfortable reading, but are essential to the lesson the author wishes to illustrate; Kosinski uses the scenes to make the point that there is a fragile balance between man and his environment which keeps the fabric of society intact, and which, when shaken, can easily lead to senseless brutality. *Black Ulysses* graphically dramatizes the flaw of inhumanity (and thus the ultimate culpability of the hero) that dwells within each man. The Caribbean setting in V. S. Naipaul's *Guerrillas* also dwells with corruption and revolution. Forces overwhelm the individual participants; and their natural response to them, if not death, is rage. Likewise, in *Black Ulysses* the desire for power has destroyed the rationality of both native and European alike. A powder keg has been lit, and people's lives are manipulated through fear and ignorance.

Probably the one work most comparable to *Black Ulysses* is Joseph Conrad's *Heart of Darkness*. Both works depict the Belgian Congo jungle, with its heat, disease, fever, and hidden death. Just as Marlow in *Heart of Darkness* describes colonial exploitation, so Grégoire-Désiré Matsombo, the "black Ulysses," gives the reader in frank detail the conditions under which he attempts to survive and to avert inevitable evil. Both Marlow and Matsombo search for an explanation of the inhumanity surrounding them.

Matsombo, having been educated by missionaries to be a medical assistant—an opportunity which sets him apart from his people—is forced to flee the security of the hospital in Bumba after he is involved in a tragic accident while operating upon an African. He sets off for his native village, taking with him all the penicillin and other medicines he can easily transport, and opens his own practice. Even though he is a little overbearing with the local villagers, Matsombo must acquiesce to their needs; he knows he is safe only as long as his "magic" medicines work their wonders. Mistakes, as he found at the Bumba hospital, are not tolerated, especially during these troubled times.

The balancing act has begun, and for him there is no turning back. He seeks personal escape in drink, drugs, and sex—appetites that seem to increase as the violence around him heightens.

Grégoire-Désiré Matsombo's voice dominates the novel; sometimes inciteful, sometimes pompous, his voice is that of a spokesman or a crusader. The chapters in Part One fluctuate between his personal recollections and a third-person narrative that describes Matsombo's native surroundings. In between these textual colorings are conversations Matsombo has with his patients, always having to dicker to get paid. His chief competitor in the village is the witch doctor Masumbuka. The magician, who formerly held together local society with his home remedies and philosophical edicts, can now only bemoan the coming of the white man and how the veneration of his powers has waned since the colonizers have set up camp in his country. Although the magician clearly is fighting a losing battle, Matsombo is not sure that his brand of medicine can be the salvation of his people either. Caught up in the realities of murder and mutilation, gonorrhea and gangrene, Matsombo knows he will be useful only as long as the penicillin holds out. Meanwhile, Matsombo sees that the tradition, myth, and sense of order that kept the individual African whole, at one with his people, at one with his land, and at one with himself, have been confused and frustrated by the implantation of European standards.

Geeraerts bases his novel in the Western literary tradition. Matsombo as a "black Ulysses" conjures up images of Homer's hero, who is shrewd and wily as well as generous and noble. Matsombo, however, because of his education and his practicing of the healing art of medicine, stands apart from the common man, and his character is closer to modern-day portraits of the Ulysses figure than to the Greek original. Matsombo shares with the Ulysses of *The Divine Comedy*, for example, a passion for knowledge that creates a distance between him and others; and, like the hero of Nikos Kazantzakis' epic poem *The Odyssey: A Modern Sequel*, Matsombo must attempt "to find deliverance by passing through all the stages of contemporary anxieties and by pursuing the most daring hopes." Physical deliverance for Matsombo does come in the form of his escape from the Congo to Spain where he settles—albeit still restless—in comfort after absconding with rebel funds.

Two themes recur throughout the various versions of the Ulysses myth: the quest for freedom, and the problem of exile and estrangement from society. For example, James Joyce explored the theme of exile in his masterpiece *Ulysses*, in which Leopold Bloom, a symbol of humanity, searches for fulfillment only to be rejected by his country, Ireland, because he is Jewish. Elements of myth, history, and religion are layered upon one another in both *Ulysses* and *Black Ulysses*. The Catholic Church has a hold on the conscience of Ireland, while in Africa, the Catholic missionaries have done their best to pound a love of Christ into the hearts of the natives. The pent-up hatred that Matsombo feels toward the Church, and his resentment over its imposition on his native culture, are illustrated in the story of his father's death.

When Matsombo's father was very sick and near death, a doctor was requested, but the nun in charge refused the request on the grounds that his father was an immoral man since he had two wives. Matsombo's father thus died an agonizing death, unable to comprehend why help did not come. Matsombo's hatred comes to a boil after he joins the rebel forces under the command of Lieutenant Boleko and participates in a number of killings. The rebel unit of which he is a member comes upon the convent in which the nun, now considerably older, who sealed the fate of Matsombo's father, is a boarder. This nun represents oppression to Matsombo; she is a symbol of all that has caused his exile from his land and family. He kills the nun, while his comrades rape and mutilate all the other nuns in the convent, under the orders of the bloodthirsty Lieutenant Boleko. Group behavior unleashes the primitive, uninhibited, violent passions of these individuals; the coward becomes a murderer, the educated man a barbarian.

As in James Joyce's *Ulysses*, in which Stephen Dedalus and Leopold Bloom cannot find the key to their frustration and loneliness, so Matsombo grabs at anything in hopes of finding something to hold on to, something to belong to, no matter how misguided and wretched. Because of the historical predicament in which he finds himself, no saving solution seems to be available, only disgusting moment-to-moment stopgap measures. Part One of *Black Ulysses* ends with Matsombo being beaten up by rebel forces while he attempts to practice medicine in his village.

Part Two takes place in Spain where Matsombo has sought refuge from the fighting. This half of the novel is narrated by a Dr. Van den Berghe, a Belgian doctor under whom Matsombo had studied and worked. The doctor is invited to stay with Matsombo at his villa, presumably so the two can catch up on news and renew their former friendship. Matsombo is at first hesitant and ashamed to relate his participation in the bloodshed; he concocts a story which rings false, and leaves both men feeling uneasy. Finally the silence is broken, and Matsombo peels away the layers of his pitiful life, confiding to the doctor his involvement with the rebel forces. He tells how his village had been ravaged and left in ruins, leaving him rootless and filled with hate. Dr. Van den Berghe's reaction is reserved, at first, as he tries to comprehend the situation and sympathize with the turmoil Matsombo had to suffer. But when Matsombo pulls out a piece of white linen stained with the blood of the nun he murdered, the doctor cannot feel sympathy, pity, or friendship; all that remains is repulsion and hatred for this man, this "black Ulysses." The reader is reminded of the last words uttered by Kurtz to Marlow in *Heart of Darkness*: "The horror! The horror!" *Black Ulysses* lays open for the reader the "heart of darkness" which beats within every man.

Jeffry Michael Jensen

Sources for Further Study

Booklist. LXXIV, May 15, 1978, p. 1475.

Kirkus Reviews. XLVI, March 15, 1978. p. 328.

Publisher's Weekly. CCXIII, August 24, 1978, p. 79.

BLOODFIRE

Author: Fred Chappell (1936-   )
Publisher: Louisiana State University Press (Baton Rouge). 40 pp. $9.95; paperback
$3.95
Type of work: Poetry

*The second book of a four-volume "novel in verse" comprised of eleven narrative
or meditative poems organized around images of fire*

Fred Chappell's *Bloodfire* is the second volume of a four-book sequence of
suite of poems which will eventually be published under the title *Midquest*, a
"novel in verse." The first book was *River* (1975) and a third, *Wind Mountain*, has already been announced. One gathers that as Chappell approaches
middle age (the work apparently began when the poet was thirty-five), he is
searching for meaning and pattern among his memories of growing up and
living in the South, specifically Western North Carolina. Interestingly enough,
each book has been organized around one of the four elements; the first water,
here fire; earth and air are yet to come—though many of the poems to be
included in the last volumes have appeared in a variety of literary journals.

One can only guess at the overall plan, of course, but thus far each slender
book has contained eleven poems and been organized around an overriding
image, as suggested. Moreover, each sequence of narrative and meditative
poems employs a wide variety of poetic forms, from free verse, couplets,
blank verse, and terza rima, to prose poems almost as relaxed as those written
by Peter Taylor a few years back. The variety of forms helps suggest the
diversity of the experiences being offered as samples from the poet's life. Thus
far each book begins with an image of dawn and returns to the same image at
the end.

No doubt Chappell intends for each volume to stand on its own, as the first
two obviously do. However, there are backward glances in *Bloodfire* to
"Cleaning the Well" of *River*—but there are also references to *The Inkling*,
one of Chappell's four novels, as well as to his Duke University Master's
thesis on Dr. Samuel Johnson. Further, the last line of the final poem in *River*
points toward the second sequence: "In the dew-fired earliest morning of the
world." Similarly, the last poem in *Bloodfire*, "Bloodfire Garden" suggests a
book organized around images of earth. In fact, it skillfully combines all four
elements in an affirmative conclusion that alludes to both the Bible and Eliot's
The Waste Land:

> Burnt-off, we are being prepared.
> The seeds of fresh rain advance,
> wind bearing from the south,
> out of the green isles
> of Eden.

Whether all four volumes will be similarly integrated, of course, remains to be seen—but one suspects they will be.

(Incidentally, Chappell staked out many of his themes in his first collection, *The World Between the Eyes* (1971): baseball, fantasy, movies, religion, and family relationships. The longer poems, such as "February," a haunting poem about a hogkilling, and "The Farm," seem to point toward his later autobiographical narratives.)

As one might suppose, Chappell interprets fire here as loosely as he did the water imagery in *River*. Sometimes it becomes love or desire, as in "Bloodfire Garden," where the garden is the marriage bed; once fire is equated with fever as the poet vividly recalls a childhood illness; elsewhere it is the sunlight burning the mists off the river and lighting up the world of "Fire Now Wakening on the River," which serves as a transitional piece between the two volumes. "Firewood" is a meditative poem, the poet's thoughts on his relation to matter, among other things, as he chops and wedges a log, the "red and yellow of honey of sun meat." This poem and others like it establish Chappell as a full-fledged Southern metaphysical.

On the other hand, nearly half of the poems in *Bloodfire* deal with actual fire, offering samples of the poet's experiences or memories of the destructive or cleansing element. For example, "My Grandfather's Church Goes Up" graphically describes the burning of a church seventeen years earlier on the spot where the poet and his wife Susan now picnic, a place reclaimed by nature and turned into "an enchanted chrisom/of leaf and flower. . . ." This particular poem employs an Anglo-Saxon line:

> Seventeen seasons   have since parted
> the killing by fire   of my grandfather's kirk.

(One assumes that this is the same grandfather of "My Grandfather Gets Doused" in *River*, thus providing another unifying device.) "My Father Allergic to Fire" is a seriocomic story of how the poet's father was forced to join the Ku Klux Klan when he was a youngster and was branded with a tiny cross. Another poem focused on the father is "My Father Burns Washington," written in a strictly rhymed six-line stanza, with subtle off-rhymes for variety. This is a serious memory of the Depression; in it his father protests the obsession with money by setting fire to a dollar bill. In the end, defeated, he stamps the fire out before the money is completely destroyed.

Perhaps Chappell's impressive range of styles can best be seen by looking at a pair of contrasting poems, "Firewater" and "Bloodfire," two of his most compelling poems. "Firewater" is a comic tale in loose blank verse in which Chappell's sense of humor and novelistic gifts are best evinced. Narrated by a backwoods character in the grocery store of a mountain community, it makes gentle fun of a centennial celebration in Clay County that involves a parade displaying the county's best-known products, among them moonshine. The entertaining narrative climaxes when things get totally out of hand: the smoke from the operating still, which is drawn on a wagon, makes a mule drunk to the point of passing out; and an officer tries to arrest the still operator, Big Mama, whereupon her three false-bearded sons erupt into a display of hill-country violence. The poetic line here is suitably relaxed and laced with appropriate folkspeech:

> Somebody hollered out, "That mule's drunk!"
> Sure enough he was. Drunk as an owl,
> Just from breathing the smoke that was pouring out
> From Big Mama's *model* still. . . .

"Firewater" is in the tradition of Robinson's and Frost's lighter blank verse narratives—and it stands up well under the comparison.

"Bloodfire," the title work, is a serious poem, in some ways an elegy for the fire-bombed and self-immolated victims of the Vietnam War. The poet, like Whitman, identifies with all of the victims: "I too suffered, I was there." But here the model is not Whitman's free verse, but the controlled lines of W. H. Auden's "Sept. 1, 1939" and, perhaps, beyond that, Yeats's famous poem on the Easter Uprising:

> Striving striving
> In the lightless void to know
> What best to make of guilty living
> In a decade without love or law.

The influence of Auden is patent, yet the poem is very much Chappell's own, and one of his most powerful.

As can be seen, the narrator shifts from poem to poem, though the focus is normally on the middle-aged poet. Chappell sometimes writes like a "good old Southern boy," fond of horror movies, baseball, and beer; but he is a sophisticated artist as well, an English professor who has translated Baudelaire and Rimbaud and alludes to René Char, Virgil, and Mary Shelley, as well as to the Bible and Protestant hymns. Also, there are mythic patterns concealed in his deceptively simple poems.

There is no question about the poet's technical competence. After three volumes of poetry and four novels, he seems able to bring off anything he sets his mind to. Here the subtle off-rhymes and internal rhymes are particularly effective, and for the first time he shows a mastery of Byronic comic rhymes: *au côté droit—raw*; *David Deas or—fertilizer*, etc. Perhaps the opening of "Feverscape: The Silver Planet" will suggest the subdued music of his terza rima stanza:

> Tensed lids or open eyes. Landscape the color of Jesus-words

in the testament, or color of sun on the gold-red edge.
Umber fire in my head the books and fevers drove me upon.

An autobiographical "novel in verse" is bound to involve risks, and Chappell cannot be accused of playing it safe. A wildly inventive and resourceful poet and storyteller, he nevertheless does not always sustain the reader's interest in his shifting memories, some of which cannot possibly interest the reader as much as the author. A few passages are so flat that they lack any semblance of poetic resonance. The strict stanzas sometimes lead to awkward inversions of stiffness, and a few of the Anglo-Saxon lines of "My Grandfather's Church Goes Up" seem awkward and occasionally read like a poetic exercise. Finally, although there is more humor in *Bloodfire* than *River*, with one or two exceptions the narratives here are not as compelling as "My Grandmother Washes Her Feet" or the superb "Cleaning the Well" in the first volume.

However, these are mere quibbles, for Chappell's *Midquest* is a unique undertaking in American poetry. The variety of its tones and language, its novelistic concern for character and narrative, and its dazzling diversity of forms make it a remarkable *tour de force*. When this "novel in verse" is complete, it will establish Fred Chappell in the forefront of the poets of his generation.

Guy Owen

Sources for Further Study

Library Journal. CIII, November 1, 1978, p. 2245.

BLOODY MARY

Author: Carolly Erickson (1943-   )
Publisher: Doubleday & Company (Garden City, New York). 533 pp. $12.95
Type of work: Biography
Time: 1511-1558
Locale: England

A life of Mary Tudor, eldest daughter of Henry VIII whose happy childhood as heiress presumptive to the English throne was shattered by the divorce and separation of her parents when she was fifteen

> Principal personages:
> ANNE BOLEYN, Queen of England
> CHARLES V, Holy Roman Emperor
> ELIZABETH I, Queen of England
> HENRY VIII, King of England
> KATHERINE OF ARAGON, Queen of England
> MARY I, Queen of England
> PHILIP I, King of Spain
> REGINALD POLE, Archbishop of Canterbury

Mary's birth in 1515 to Katherine of Aragon and Henry VIII was disappointing to her father, who had wanted and expected a son. At least the baby did not die immediately, however, as a boy-child had a few years earlier. Christening rites and celebration for the heiress presumptive to the English crown followed, according to the traditional formulas of the Roman Catholic Church and the English monarchy.

As a child, Mary was doted on by both her parents. Her father called her the "greatest pearl of the kingdom." Given a household of servants at age three, she was taught and groomed to prepare herself for marriage. It was expected that she would wed some foreign prince or prominent Englishman for political purposes as her mother had done. Her formal education was excellent, but she was constantly inculcated with current notions about the weakness and inferiority of females. She must, as a woman, conduct herself quietly, obediently, and modestly, and be prepared to serve in a wifely capacity any husband chosen for her.

Mary, as she grew up, did not develop into a beautiful girl, but she was sufficiently pleasing in appearance so that, with the crown she stood to inherit, her chances of making a favorable marriage were excellent. Numerous suitors and candidates came forth throughout her girlhood. One of the first was her cousin, Charles V, Holy Roman Emperor, to whom she was engaged when she was ten. Shortly after, however, her father canceled the engagement for political reasons. Mary, however, would continue to admire Charles and rely on him for advice throughout the rest of her life.

By 1525 it became evident that the aging Katherine would have no more children; Henry would have no legitimate sons by her. But Henry had an illegitimate son, known as Henry Fitzroy, to whom he now granted many titles and honors and prepared to legitimatize. At the same time, Mary was designated "Princess of Wales" and went to Ludlow Castle in Wales, where she set up court and had her first experience in ruling. The King, meanwhile, continued to try to arrange a marriage for his "pearl of the kingdom." There was some talk of Henry Fitzroy and Mary marrying. Instead Henry, in 1527, signed a marriage treaty with the French King, Francis I. It was arranged however, that because of the prospective bride's tender age, the marriage would be put off for at least three years.

At that point the first serious crisis in Mary's life emerged: her father decided to divorce her mother. Katherine, now old and ugly, was replaced in the king's affection by the twenty-year-old lady of the court, Anne Boleyn, who could presumably give Henry the son he so much wanted.

Four years of divorce proceedings followed; it was a time of shock, anguish, and disillusion for Mary. In the end, Anne was crowned Queen, Katherine's title was taken from her by the Convocation of the Church. She and Mary were sent into virtual exile from the court, forced to live in different residences, and forbidden to communicate.

An even greater humiliation for Mary followed. The Act of Succession (1534) designated Anne's offspring as the legitimate successors and Mary as a bastard. She formally and strenuously protested, but to no avail. Queen Anne, who hated both Katherine and Mary, prevailed upon the king to humiliate Mary even further. She was sent to Hatfield House as part of the household of the baby princess, Elizabeth. Her clothes, jewels, and other property were taken from her. She was to be treated as the unwanted child of her father, whom she was not allowed to see. Living at Hatfield became a constant torment for her. She began to suffer from a variety of illnesses which would plague her the rest of her life: stomach pains, headaches, amenorrhea, inability to keep food down, and melancholy, which surely must have been the psychosomatic source of her physical ailments. Rumors also circulated that she was being poisoned, and Mary herself feared that such might be the case.

Adding to her personal distress were the attacks that now began on her beloved Church. Her father had, in the matter of his divorce, defied and rejected papal authority and called himself the head of the Church in England. As the conflict between the Crown and the Papacy intensified Mary, along with many others, was caught between loyalty to the King and loyalty to the old faith. She tried to continue her obedience to both, but, as the schism widened, that became impossible. The persecution of the Roman clergy and the suppression of the monasteries touched her deeply, making her more devoted to her religion than ever.

Fearing for her own life when her mother died in 1535, Mary planned to escape England and find sanctuary with her cousin Charles. This plan proved impossible at the time; however, she repeatedly made escape plans in subsequent years. Her situation improved shortly after the removal and execution of Queen Anne, which was a blessing for Mary. It ended nine years of danger, constant tension and uncertainty. She was allowed to return to court, where she was better treated. At the same time, her father remarried, and his new wife, Jane Seymour presented him with the son he had so long wanted, Edward. Edward would displace Henry's daughters as successor to the throne, but Mary accepted that fact because she would be second in line of succession.

It would be eighteen years before she gained the crown, however. With the death of Henry VIII in 1547, Edward VI became King, and England turned more Protestant than before. Mary came to be regarded by the Protestants as an ever-present threat whereby the "rats of Rome might creep back" eventually. Pressure was put on her to stop her masses; her chaplains were arrested. Mary continued to swear loyalty to the King, her brother, while insisting that her soul and her faith belonged to God and the true Church. She showed her pride, courage, and strength of will more than ever in these years.

At last, Edward, the boy king, died in 1553. The Protestant faction tried to exclude Mary from the succession by elevating Lady Jane Grey as Queen. Mary, however, raised troops, overawed the Council, had Lady Jane and her associates arrested, and came to London in triumph to receive her rightful crown. On July 19, 1553, Mary was crowned Queen. She had survived. It was, she said in gratitude, a fulfillment of God's purposes.

Many people felt that "the idea of a woman as head of state was abhorrent on principle; kings were representative of God's image unto men as no woman could ever be." Still, Mary was in a strong position in the early part of her reign. She received widespread support and conducted herself prudently. As to the burning question of religion, she announced that she would force no man to go to mass, but she meant to see that those who wished to go should be able to do so freely. She herself was more fanatically religious than ever, celebrating six and seven masses a day. She did remove Protestants from the Council, and secured the release of Catholic bishops imprisoned during Edward's reign.

Then she turned to the matter of marriage and an heir. Charles V offered his son, Philip of Spain. She worried about the age difference—Philip was only twenty-six, while she was now thirty-seven—and about how far she should allow her husband to interfere in the governance of England.

After weeks of consideration, Mary put her doubts aside and in October, 1553, promised to marry Philip. A flood of outrage erupted in England. Her subjects feared that England would go to Philip as part of Mary's dowry and that Spaniards would come to rule over them. English Protestants said they would die rather than be ruled by Spain, and they tried to persuade the Queen to marry one of her English subjects instead. But Mary would have her own way; she would marry Philip. Marriage articles were agreed to and signed. Philip would have the title of king but no claim on the English throne. The oldest son of the marriage would inherit the Low Countries and England. It was quite a favorable arrangement for England, but the English Protestants were much opposed to it.

Meanwhile, at Mary's behest, Parliament repealed the Protestant legislation of the reign of Edward, and took the first steps toward restoring Catholicism. The divorce of Henry VIII from Katherine was revoked, making Mary the only legitimate child of her father once again. New rumors of plots to overthrow Mary in favor of her half-sister Elizabeth were rife in 1554. Said one Protestant, "the papists are having their turn, but Elizabeth will remedy all in time." A serious rebellion called Wyatt's Conspiracy did break out that year. Troops sent to stop Wyatt's advance from Kent to London joined the rebels instead, but Mary was able to gather enough London citizens to stop the rebels and save her throne. For months, executions of Wyatt and his rebels went on from gallows at every city gate in London.

Philip of Spain arrived in the summer of 1554, and he and Mary wed at Winchester to the accompaniment of much public pageantry. Shortly after, to her great joy, her doctors told her that she was pregnant; once again God had intervened.

Philip stayed in England and took over more and more of English affairs. He and Mary invited Cardinal Pole to England, Reginald Pole, a descendant of the Yorkist kings of England, had been exiled by Henry VIII for both religious and dynastic reasons. Pole was as ardent a Catholic as Mary or Philip. He now returned as papal legate to reunite England to the Church of Rome. When the Parliament formally requested that reunification, Pole absolved England of the sin of schism, and was named Archbishop of Canterbury. England was no longer outside the Roman communion. Parliament followed up with a revival of the medieval statutes regarding the treatment of heretics and other legislation to restore the old faith. But Parliament refused to restore the monastic lands to the Church, thus making a complete return of the old Church to power impossible.

It appears that the Protestants were still a minority at the time of Mary's reign, but they were a very vocal minority, committed as much to their various creeds as she was to her Church. The Protestants now showed their hatred of the official return to Rome by attacking Catholic priests, tearing down crucifixes, and speaking out against Romish practices. In retaliation, Mary forced numbers of Protestants to leave her realm; these exiles became famous as the Marian exiles who, from Switzerland and Germany, engaged in propaganda assaults against England's Catholic government.

Meanwhile, some of those who remained in England were now arrested as heretics. The first important arrest was that of Bishop John Hooper of Worcester. After undergoing imprisonment and torture, Hooper was burned at the stake for refusing to recant his heresies in February, 1555; this event marked the beginning of the persecutions. Erickson, in writing of this most remembered aspect of Mary's reign, says the records are oddly silent about

Mary's attitude and involvement in the persecution of the heretics. Mary found the heretics despicable for misleading others too ignorant to understand the truth and robbing them of their salvation, but she appears, in Erickson's estimation, to have been less determined to destroy them than were Philip, or Pole, or Bishop Gardiner, the Lord Chancellor.

During the last three years of Mary's reign, some three hundred persons were put to death—most of them in horrible ways—for their religious beliefs, including many clergymen and some women. Such slaughter for religion was unprecedented and without parallel in English history. Whether Mary sanctioned the killings directly or not, they earned her the odious title "Bloody Mary" forever after.

Mary's own griefs mounted. Her pregnancy proved false; she was barren, and there would be no Catholic heir as she had so devoutly hoped for. Indeed, it appeared there might not be a Catholic England. The burning of heretics reached a peak in 1555-1556, but their extirpation did not seem to return England to the true faith. Few of her subjects attended mass, few churches were rebuilt, and little enthusiasm was shown for Rome.

On the Continent, Philip had returned to war with France. He requested money from Mary to carry on the fighting. She responded with funds, which led to charges that she was going to ruin England to help the Spanish. She begged Philip to return to her side; he replied that the press of war and other matters made his return impossible. Now constantly ill, Mary conducted the business of ruling as well as she could, but her private life became reclusive, spent at her devotions.

Early in 1557, Philip returned to England, but only to raise money and troops, not to remain. At his request, Mary dutifully appeared before the Parliament to harangue them to declare war on France in alliance with Philip. The Parliament acceded, but Mary would find that the English people would not support Philip's war any more than they supported Mary's Church. In the fighting in early 1558, the French captured Calais, Guines, and Ham from the English. For Mary, the loss of those last English footholds on the Continent was grievous: "when I am dead and opened," she said, "you shall find Calais written on my heart."

The loss of Calais would not be the only sorrow in this last year of her life. Royal debts were high, the economy of the country was in bad condition, there were rumors that Philip intended to dissolve their marriage, and her health was failing. Her culminating sorrow came when she received the news that Cardinal Pole, upon whom she had relied for so long, had died. Upon this news, Mary fell into deep malancholy; she lost her will to live and peacefully expired. The day of her death—November 17, 1558—would be celebrated by Englishmen for generations as a time of rejoicing because it brought Mary's half-sister Elizabeth to the throne. Few mourned the passing of Mary Tudor.

Most historians and biographers have, in the four centuries since Mary's death, shared the dislike for Mary that so many of her contemporaries expressed when she died. Almost without exception, books about Mary have condemned her "poor, short, despised reign" and her failures as a ruler. Carolly Erickson is somewhat more sympathetic; she does not completely redraw the traditional portrait, but she does offer insights into Mary's personality and actions. Despite her book's unfortunate title, Erickson offers a thoughtful, vivid biography of an often misunderstood woman. Erickson has used the sources well; her descriptions of the pageants, jousts, festivals, and celebrations are particularly striking. Such occasions were of great importance in Renaissance England: they fortified the prestige of the rulers, preserved religious and secular traditions, and gave pleasure to the participants and observers. One might wish, however, that Erickson had devoted somewhat less space to these celebrations, and more to such matters as the operation of government and the condition of the economy in Mary's time to give a more balanced picture of the times.

James W. Pringle

Sources for Further Study

Booklist. LXXIV, February 15, 1978, p. 973.

Christian Century. XCV, April 26, 1978, p. 452.

Choice. XV, May, 1978, p. 456.

Guardian Weekly. CXVIII, March 5, 1978, p. 18.

New York Times Book Review. January 15, 1978, p. 10.

Observer. June 25, 1978, p. 26.

A CAGE FOR LOULOU

Author: Rudolph von Abele (1922-   )
Publisher: Louisiana State University Press (Baton Rouge). 51 pp. $8.95
Type of work: Poetry

Erudite, contemplative poems which adopt a philosophic stance toward the human animal

At the age of fifty-six, with a distinguished record in teaching and literary scholarship as well as two published novels (*The Vigil of Emmeline Gore* and *The Party*) behind him, Rudolph von Abele seems rather an unlikely figure to be publishing a first collection of poems. He was, after all, already a graduate student at Columbia University when Allen Ginsberg entered there as an undergraduate more than thirty years ago. The intervening years have been a particularly active and exciting period in American poetry; hosts of groups and individuals have brought forth manifestos, both political and aesthetic, linking the course of our literary tradition with the Beats and the "Counterculture," with the antiwar movement and the sexual revolution. With these changes in what, somewhere along the way, began to be known as the "national consciousness" have come corresponding changes in our notions about poetry. Through all of this instructive turmoil, von Abele's talent as a poet appears to have lain dormant, and now that his first book of poems has appeared, he presents something of a puzzle. While his work seems to reveal no direct influence by his contemporaries, von Abele still writes a kind of poetry that is very much of our time.

One reason why von Abele's poetry seems so appropriate for the late 1970's is that it focuses so consistently upon its author. The poems in *A Cage for Loulou* do not, for the most part, dwell upon autobiographical detail—quite the opposite. Yet no matter what their subjects, the typical situation in these poems is that of the author explaining himself—in a very literal sense—to the reader. In the era that Tom Wolfe, and everybody else by now, has called the "Me Decade," this emphasis on the self might be considered so universal as to make it hard to determine whether it is actually a feature of a text or an inevitable interpretive strategy. Yet it is precisely because of the indirection of their method—throwing widely disparate types of data at the reader, and introducing the author as a figure in this flux—that we can see von Abele's poems stressing the self as relentlessly as those of the Confessional poets of the 1960's: Robert Lowell, Anne Sexton, John Berryman, and Sylvia Plath. At his best von Abele continues along the path trod by these poets and speaks more eloquently than most others who have done so.

Many of von Abele's poems ground themselves in the details of a breadth of knowledge few American writers could match. Besides its frequent references to works by Flaubert, Joyce, Beckett, Stendhal, and the like, von Abele's poetry often draws upon twentieth century developments in mathematics, physics, philosophy of language, aesthetics, and music theory. *A Cage for Loulou* is, in fact, a virtual compendium of contemporary esoterica. And this is another way in which von Abele's poetry is right for its time: Few enough of our poets actually inhabit Einstein's universe, trilling lines of verse in curved space among the black holes and red shifts. Yet the erudition of these poems, especially the presence in them of fairly complex ideas from philosophy and the sciences, is rather like the spirits that spoke to Yeats through his wife: it is there not to draw attention to its own existence, but to provide metaphors for poetry. Ideas are not used to intimidate the reader, but to serve as a common object of contemplation for him and the past.

This shared contemplation is not easy for either of the parties in the process. The self the poems present is perplexing and perplexed. But the puzzles in which it engages itself and the reader, though framed in intellectual terms, are moral and emotional rather than intellectual. The poems do not serve to expand and comment on scientific ideas, but to chart emotional life, as in "Astronomer's Complaint." In this poem, the phenomenon of the red shift in the light emanating from receding stars, with its corollary idea that the universe continues to expand, is used economically and intelligently to describe the relationship between two people—almost after the manner of the scientific metaphors of the Metaphysical Poets. Similarly, in the poem "Une Semaine de Bonté" (the title is taken from Max Ernst's famous collage, a surrealist story without words), a meeting between two lovers is expressed by the formula, "Let A conduct himself toward Z in the modality p,/ Let Z conduct herself toward A in the modality q."

In these two poems, the first drawing upon physics and the second upon symbolic logic, metaphors from science and philosophy seem to be used for two main reasons. First, in each case the author is talking about communication, and he wants, quite seriously, to adopt a stance that will allow him to observe human phenomena objectively; hence, at the end of "Astronomer's Complaint," the lines "When I was younger I/ never knew how cold/ observatories have to be." Second, the use of material from the sciences operates, in a contemporary poem, like the introduction of God or the Imagination in a nineteenth century work. It provides something unchanging, above and beyond the sphere of human relationships, something to serve as a matrix or background of meaning to set those relationships against, as in the last stanza of "Une Semaine de Bonté":

> A febrile hand or two contracted all those eyes to zeroes,
> after which, feathers gave way to scabrous fingernails,
> and these, in turn, to blood, and bone, and marrow,
> as each fought the other down into the dizzy absolutes,
> of which neither dreamed they might be merely in the mind.

There is fairly subtle play here with the notion of the transcendent or sublime, an implication that the poet will concede the possibility of the real existence of the "dizzy absolutes" beyond the particulars of human life, without relying upon such extrahuman entities to redeem the human world from its frequent disappointments and occasional brutishness. Von Abele's intellectual openness here, as well as his frequent use of questions rather than declarative sentences throughout the book remind one of Keats's remark on "Negative Capability": "The only means of strengthening one's intellect is to make up one's mind about nothing—to let the mind be a thoroughfare for all thoughts." After the manner of Ludwig Wittgenstein (1889-1951), then, whose influence appears in such poems as "Die Welt Ist Alles, Was der Fall Ist" and "About That of Which One Cannot Speak, One Must Be Silent," von Abele presents to the reader more questions than axioms, more puzzles than solutions.

Yet, just as it was Wittgenstein's contention that he embarked on his complicated path through language theory in order to arrive, eventually, at a system of ethics, so von Abele's play with ideas is not free, undirected play—his games with language and with the processes of reasoning are rarely light-hearted. Here again von Abele is a twentieth century man, one who has absorbed the idea that game theory is a serious matter. We might say that whereas a poet such as Frank O'Hara—whose work also abounds in references to figures in the arts, and who also indulges in frequent games with the reader—strives usually for the exuberance of a boy playing kickball with words, von Abele achieves the tone of a determined and sometimes grim chess master. Occasionally, as in "Am I Not Your Son?" and "Will the Black Watch Hesitate to Shoot?," von Abele, like the Knight in Ingmar Bergman's *Seventh Seal*, plays a game with Death. But always, no matter who his partner is, his stakes are peace of mind, intellectual growth, and, above all, moral integrity.

Like Gertrude Stein's Melanctha, von Abele seems to be forever asking, "What is the right way for me to do?" The first poem in *A Cage for Loulou* sets the tone for the book: "Poet Counterpoet" describes the Chinese philosopher-poet Li-Po "lying back/ drunk in a boat, without oars, among reeds," contemplating the image of himself engaged in relatively aimless contemplation. In the course of the poem the poet gets so involved in reflections that he seems to become entirely passive, and this is a kind of serenity, a goal some poets might work towards. But for von Abele it seems to be also a moral abdication, and this cannot be allowed; he transfers Li-Po from his *bateau ivre* to a "down-screaming fiery plane,/ studying the Jersey meadows." It is as though he says here that serenity belongs to the realm of language and signs, or mathematical symbols; to the process of analysis and description; but never to the things analyzed and described. Out of our wish for serenity we may construct, in Yeat's phrase, "beautiful lofty things," yet life as it is lived more often recalls the lines from the Irish poet's "Crazy Jane Talks with the Bishop": "Love has pitched his mansion in / The place of excrement."

The poem "Moons and Caves," besides providing the memorably wry comment, "The real estate of man is such that any sensitive/ proprietor ought to find the form and file for bankruptcy," stresses once again the distinction between the world of words and symbols and the world we must live in. Within its context in the poem, the phrase "find for form" is like "real estate," a pun: the idea of poetic, perhaps even of Platonic, form is being toyed with here; and the suggestion is that the moons and caves of poets, existing in individual imaginations, may be of less use than a few cold, hard, palpable, and unpoetical facts, the physical presences in the world we live in.

Still, poems are made of words, not things. Though in "Variations on a Paradox"—which appropriately enough provides the title for the first section of the book—von Abele says, "That we must make poems is a perplexity," it seems to be the kind of perplexity he can find both engaging and morally instructive. So, as "Moons and Caves" suggests, he continues to look for appropriate forms; a dedication to life becomes a dedication to speaking about life. Like Samuel Beckett at the end of *The Unnamable*, von Abele's poems seem to say, "I can't go on, I'll go on." The search for appropriate symbols, subject matter, and objects of contemplation often leads to other literary works; Beckett and his characters, for example, appear more than once in *A Cage for Loulou*, and with good reason; Beckett constitutes probably the most important contemporary influence to be found in von Abele's poems.

James Joyce, too, appears in the background of von Abele's book, not merely in the author's fondness for wordplay, but in the consciousness running through all the poems that human beings are made of flesh and blood—and several other, grimier substances often bypassed in our thought and literature. Von Abele's is a profoundly *physical* world, but one which through language attempts to make myth of the poor human body, as Joyce begins to do in *Ulysses* and does on such a grand scale in *Finnegans Wake*. In the cycle of "Dublin Poems," von Abele builds on Joyce's use of the personification of Dublin's river to make one of the loveliest, most balanced poems in this book: "Four Movements of Anna Liffey" uses a kind of symphonic form—note the pun in the title—to express compassion for a female river about to merge with a male sea. The conceit is convincing because the compassion is genuine. Yet here the reliance on Joyce is not particularly marked; it is as if von Abele inhabited Joyce's world but viewed it from another perspective.

In a similar fashion, von Abele builds upon Gustave Flaubert's short story "A Simple Heart" in the long title poem of *A Cage for Loulou*. Flaubert's Loulou is a gaudy-colored parrot belonging to the housekeeper Felicité, who has the bird stuffed and mounted upon its death, making of it a kind of shrine that soon becomes tattered and infested with worms. On her own death, Felicité sees the stuffed bird in a kind of vision as the Holy Ghost, conventionally portrayed as a dove. It is important for both Flaubert's story and von

Abele's poem that the bird be a parrot, mimicking human speech, but without the force of consciousness and intention behind its locutions. But von Abele takes this figure a step farther; the subject of his poem is not really the parrot in the story, but the stuffed parrot Flaubert kept on his desk to serve as a model while writing the story.

In "A Cage for Loulou," then, von Abele brings together all of the major themes and attitudes we have seen controlling the rest of the poems in the book. The poem is compassionate, but frequently ironic; playful and grim at once. It employs metaphors derived from both literature and science, setting up a series of reflections of reflections that may well become too complex for many readers; yet the poem sincerely attempts to guide the reader through a genuinely labyrinthine reality. Finally, "A Cage for Loulou" is authentically humble: It does not provide manifestos, but modestly asks whether there is, or can be, a way of bringing words and human life together for the elucidation and enrichment of both. Though the focus is, as we have said, on the self above all, the emphasis on moral integrity in this poem, as in the other poems in *A Cage for Loulou*, makes Rudolph von Abele a welcome new voice in our poetry—especially at the end of the "Me Decade."

Bernard Welt

CAPTAIN PANTOJA AND THE SPECIAL SERVICE

Author: Mario Vargas Llosa (1936-   )
Translated from the Spanish by Gregory Kolovakos and Ronald Christ
Publisher: Harper & Row Publishers (New York). 244 pp. $10.95
Type of work: Novel
Time: 1956-1959
Locale: Peru

A serio-comic novel about the Peruvian army's official agency of prostitutes, directed by Captain Pantoja, whose personal involvement in his job leads to the destruction of the agency and his own career

> *Principal characters:*
> CAPTAIN PANTALEÓN PANTOJA, the director of the Special Service, a corps of prostitutes serving the Peruvian army
> POCHITA, his wife
> MOTHER LEONOR, his mother
> GENERAL FELIPE COLLAZOS ("TIGER"), Chief of Administration, Supply, and Logistics for the army
> GENERAL ROGER SCAVINO, Army Commander of the Amazon region
> SINCHI, a popular radio announcer
> BROTHER FRANCISCO, leader of the Brotherhood of the Ark, a cult of religious fanatics
> OLGA ARELLANO ROSAURA ("THE BRAZILIAN"), the most desirable of the prostitutes

This excellent translation of the 1973 novel *Pantoja y las visitadoras* is a significant contribution to the substantial body of Hispanic fiction that has been made available in English in recent years. Mario Vargas Llosa is not as well known in this country as some other contemporary Latin American prose writers, such as Gabriel García Márquez, Carlos Fuentes, and Julio Cortázar. The publication of this translation should enhance his reputation among English-speaking audiences.

Captain Pantoja and the Special Service presents clear evidence that Vargas Llosa is very much a part of the Latin American group, for there are many similarities between his approach to the creation of a fictional world and theirs. His experimentation with narrative techniques is reminiscent of Carlos Fuentes' in *The Death of Artemio Cruz* and of Manuel Puig's in *Heartbreak Tango*. Much of the storytelling is developed through a montage of letters, official communiques, and news reports reproduced verbatim with annotations by the correspondents of those documents. When the narrator does speak, his voice is objective and his role is limited to presenting the dialogue without commentary. He always speaks in the present tense, and constructs a broad view of concurrent happenings by moving freely within a passage from one set of characters to another.

This combination of official documentation and objective present-tense narration gives the novel a sense of immediacy and authenticity. Because the narrator is so unobtrusive, almost all the information comes from the characters themselves. There is no authoritative voice to tell the "truth" about the world of Captain Pantoja, nor is there a subjective narrative opinion to distort the reality. The reader witnesses the events as they occur or as they are reported by the characters who participate in the action.

The reader of serious contemporary fiction is surely acquainted with this type of narrative and will recognize these techniques as typical of the work of the Latin American novelists. Because Vargas Llosa is participating in a trend and developing his fictional reality in a familiar way, his challenge to be innovative is much greater. The originality that he achieves is due to the story that he tells. His novel is ingenious primarily because the plot material is directly related to the familiar techniques of contemporary fiction that he uses to tell the story. There is a clear relationship between form and content.

The novel presents the story of Pantaleón Pantoja, an army lieutenant who is promoted to captain and charged with creating the Special Service—an official corps of prostitutes to serve the army men stationed in the remote areas of Peru. Pantoja moves his wife and mother to Iquitos, where he does an extraordinary job, always working undercover in civilian dress. After the local radio announcer broadcasts a sensationalist exposé of the Special Service, Pantoja's wife leaves him; he subsequently falls in love with Olga the Brazilian, the most beautiful of the prostitutes. When Olga is killed in the line of duty, Pantoja delivers a eulogy at her funeral in military uniform. The army command immediately demotes him and refuses to acknowledge its complicity in the creation and maintenance of the Special Service. Pantoja, convinced that he has acted honorably and served his country well, returns to Lima to a reunion with his family.

The novel is primarily a story spotlighting the bureaucratic process at work. The narrative techniques enhance the plot material, for the devices used to tell much of the story are the forms of the typical government agency. The development of the Special Service is told in great detail through official reports written in superb bureaucratic jargon. The prostitutes are "specialists." The soldiers are "candidate-users" who engage in "utilization activities" with the specialists. This is a "pilot project" the success of which will be evaluated once it has reached its "maximum operational volume." Obviously, this is all rather ludicrous, since the Special Service is in fact just a group of whores dedicated to satisfying the sexual desires of the soldiers. The humor of the novel is derived from the fact that Vargas Llosa begins with a ridiculous premise and then proceeds to deal with it as if it were not ridiculous. There is no narrator to comment on all this, and the characters are so involved in the events that they cannot maintain the distance necessary to see the absurdity of the situation.

The novel also presents a delightful portrayal of the fervent bureaucrat.

Captain Pantoja is a simple, childish man who always wanted to be a "soldier-administrator." When he gets this job, which he must execute as a sort of undercover agent, he throws himself into his task with an amazing enthusiasm. He sends out formal questionnaires to the soldiers to determine exactly how many "services" will be needed in a given week. He strives for efficiency by placing the prostitutes in the right place at the right time and then checking the results to find out if the right number of minutes were allotted for each service. In other words, he tries to anticipate the demand and adjust the supply in a very orderly manner, as if he were charged with distributing shoes and socks instead of sex.

When Pantoja discovers that the demand for sex is greater than the supply, he works for greater efficiency. He distributes pornographic literature to the candidate-users waiting in line for their utilization activity, so that they will be more aroused and require less time with the specialist. This is a clever presentation of what happens when things become official. The Special Service was established to satisfy the men so that they would not be dominated by their unfulfilled sexual urges, yet the result is quite different. Their sexuality becomes their most important concern, and the system tries to find ways to increase their sexual urge rather than to decrease it. In effect, the product and the way it is marketed become more important than the consumer for whose sake the agency was created.

In exploring and satirizing the bureaucratic process, Vargas Llosa is doing what many other novelists have done. However, he goes beyond his predecessors, primarily because he selects as his "case study" an example which is both absurd and socially controversial. The paternalistic army command sets out to satisfy through official channels this particular need of the men in its charge—the need for frequent sexual relations. The inanity of the impersonal administrative procedures becomes more apparent and more humorous than usual, because of the incongruity of applying the bureaucratic mentality to the most intimate of human activities. At the same time, the sanctimonious reactions from certain sectors of the community reveal the hypocritical notions about sexuality that pervade Western society. The religious interests of the region are shocked by the rumors of an official brothel sanctioned by the army, and also by the spreading hysteria of a religious cult led by Brother Francisco—a fanatic who instructs his followers to crucify insects, animals, and people. Even a large number of the soldiers and some of the prostitutes are secretly converted to his Brotherhood of the Ark.

The novel is particularly interesting for this analogy between the activities of the Special Service and the attitudes toward sexuality of the religious institutions of this society. In establishing the official agency to take care of the men's sexual needs, the army is attempting to compartmentalize the biological urge. Give the men a regular diet of sexual activity, at an appointed time, and even stimulate them as much as possible as they wait in line, and then there will be no problem with sexuality at other times. This is precisely what the religious zealots would try to do—separate the sexual urge from the rest of life, isolate it, and hide it so that it will not offend polite society. In either case, it is an attempt to control people by regulating their private lives.

Vargas Llosa's novel is a very humorous version of the theme of man's nature in conflict with the civilizing forces of Western society. The army creates an agency to harness the destructive flaw of man, his biological need for regular sexual release. This "weakness," with its potential for destroying the mechanized efficiency the army hopes to attain in its soldiers, is reduced to a programmed activity that constantly must be refined to create greater productivity and efficacy.

The problem is that this bureaucratic mechanization of man's nature does not work. Despite all the official reports and documented studies, the project exudes the very sensuality that it attempts to control. Everyone, soldiers and civilians alike, becomes so obsessed with the agency and the regulations that the system dissolves into chaos. Captain Pantoja contributes to the disintegration of this bureaucratic invention because he cannot maintain an impersonal stance. He cannot let a day pass without trying out one of his "recruits," and he finally destroys his career because he falls in love with Olga.

Even in this mechanized, depersonalized bureaucracy, man and woman play their roles of the tempted and the temptress, the hunter and the hunted. Brother Francisco attracts followers like flies because he offers what the Special Service threatens to take away, the earthy experience of unbridled nature. In spite of all attempts to turn him into a programmed machine, man inevitably returns to his original sin of animalistic sensuality.

In the last chapter of the novel, Vargas Llosa develops an extraordinary satire of society's hypocrisy. Pantoja is censured not because of his role in maintaining an official whorehouse for the army, but for having publicly acknowledged the existence of the Special Service. The narrator shifts the scene from each army officer scolding Pantoja to that officer commenting on the scandal as he instructs his own favorite prostitute just what to do to increase his own sexual pleasure.

The novel is a very effective treatment of sexual mores and of the ways in which people in power attempt to control what other people do. The Special Service is a failure because of what Captain Pantoja is. He is too naïve and emotionally involved in his work to be a good bureaucrat. In effect, Pantoja is not the impersonal, disinterested, lethargic director that every good agency needs to function inefficiently and perpetuate itself indefinitely.

Vargas Llosa succeeds in revealing some truths about human nature and the inevitable forces of society. This is a novel about the individual and the system, but it is particularly interesting because the novelist has chosen a system that cannot work because it attempts to control a part of human nature that will always defy all such efforts. This premise allows Vargas Llosa to portray, somewhat pessimistically but with a great deal of humor, the essential flaws of man and of the society he has invented for himself.

Gilbert Smith

Sources for Further Study

Booklist. LXXIV, January 1, 1978, p. 732.
Library Journal. CIII, February 1, 1978, p. 387.
Nation. CCXXVI, April 1, 1978, p. 377.
New Republic. CLXXVII, May 20, 1978, p. 36.
New York Times Book Review. April 9, 1978, p. 11.
Saturday Review. V, February 4, 1978, p. 32.

CATHERINE, EMPRESS OF ALL THE RUSSIAS

Author: Vincent Cronin (1924-   )
Publisher: William Morrow and Company (New York). Illustrated. 335 pp. $12.95
Type of work: Biography
Time: The eighteenth century
Locale: Russia

The story of the day-to-day life of Catherine the Great that reveals personal details of her private life as well as describing her public achievements

Principal personages:
EMPRESS CATHERINE I, an eighteenth century despot of German birth who revolutionized Russian life
EMPRESS ELIZABETH I, daughter of Peter the Great who arranged the marriage between Catherine and her heir designate
TSAR PETER III, Catherine's husband who ignored her through most of their marriage
FIELD MARSHALL GREGORY POTEMKIN, Catherine's great love and secret second husband
GRAND DUKE PAUL, Catherine's older son and heir

Drawing on primary sources such as love letters, diplomatic dispatches, diaries, and Catherine's personal memoirs, Vincent Cronin presents an intimate, detailed biography of the only woman ruler in history designated as "Great." His compassionate and refined tone to her story line reflects Cronin's respect for the woman and her achievements. Catherine's private life, which was filled with a series of love affairs sensationalized by French revolutionary writers and other critics, is described in the context of a long, distinguished reign and from this perspective, Catherine emerges as an enlightened despot.

Cronin commits himself on key historical problems eclipsing Catherine's successes: the disputed paternity of her children, the number of her children, the intensity of her interests in sex, her rumored secret second marriage, and her role in murdering her consort, Tsar Peter III. Catherine's reputation repeatedly has been vilified by biographers; Cronin reevaluates evidence which exonerates her from committing regicide and proves that she was not a nymphomaniac, but rather an overworked ruler who regarded sex as a non-exploitative and needed physical outlet.

Catherine is introduced as Sophie of Anhalt-Zerbst, a minor German princess with no claims to greatness. Her hard-won battle with scoliosis, her strict early education, and her warm relationship with her French governess, Babet, are intimately detailed and serve to establish the character traits of endurance, resilience and loyalty, which Sophie later manifested as Grand Duchess and Empress of Russia. From the beginning, the reader perceives Catherine as a real person rather than a remote, though important historical figure.

Her rise from a General's daughter to Empress was a feat attributable more to her determination than to outside political pressure. To bind an alliance,

Prussian Kaiser Frederick II helped arrange the marriage between Sophie and Grand Duke Peter Ulrich, the heir to the Russian throne. However, it was Sophie who brought it about by undergoing a process of russianization that necessitated her name change to Catherine and her conversion to the Orthodox religion. That same determination enabled her to withstand eighteen years of persecution by Peter and the Empress Elizabeth and to connive ways to placate their anger. She survived Tsar Peter's growing unpopularity by publicly defying his policies, such as his alienation of Austria and war with Denmark, and by staging a *coup* that deposed him and empowered her. Her victories over such dynamic and dramatic vicissitudes made her mistress of her own destiny in a country rife with assassination. She looms as a person who could act well on her own despite setbacks.

As Cronin shows, Catherine's reign of thirty-three years was often challenged by pretenders claiming to be Peter III or a close relative. For example, Emilyan Pugachev, one of the most threatening, led successful peasant uprisings in South Russia in 1773-1774. Astute action by the Empress and powerful military figures saved her throne, but the public imagination was stirred by these potential usurpers, who, unlike the foreign-born Catherine, were Russian.

In addition, her rulership was not accepted without criticism by some major supporters, such as her son, Grand Duke Paul, who was haunted by the image of his slain father and his mother's possible part in the murder. Catherine's silence in the matter created a rift between them that made Paul constantly question her right to the throne, though he never acted against her. Cronin convincingly argues that the Empress was silent in order to conceal her adultery with her first lover and Paul's real father, Serge Saltuikov, and also to conceal her plot to depose Peter. She also feared that any revelation about Paul's paternity would weaken her authority since she claimed to be preparing the throne for Peter the Great's descendant. Historians disagree on whether Peter III fathered Paul, but Cronin's stand is well supported. The comparison of physical features of the three men demonstrates remarkable similarities between Paul and Saltuikov.

Catherine was less inhibited in other relationships with her lovers though as firmly in control. Generous and forgiving in nature, she retained the loyalty, if not the love, of the eleven men in her life. Cronin theorizes that she lost the love of six suitors because they were dynamic men who rebelled against subservience to a woman. Catherine was predominant in decision-making even with her idol, Field Marshall Gregory Potemkin, who was influential in government affairs. (Together they planned the Greek Project—a partitioning of Turkey's European holdings among Russia and allies.) Her love letters betray a dependant, devoted side to her nature which Potemkin could easily arouse, but never conquer. Cronin demonstrates that Catherine was devoted to her career above all else.

Cronin manages to portray Catherine, the private person, and Catherine, the public person, cohesively by showing how she was always politically aware. She survived persecution and humiliation as Grand Duchess by befriending former enemies such as Empress Elizabeth's physician and close adviser, Dr. Armand Lestocq, and her husband's mistresses. She broke through Peter's indifference by taking such an interest in the affairs of his native Holstein that she became its key administrator, for which she was dubbed Madam La Ressource. Her friendship with British Ambassador Charles Hanbury-Williams became the basis for her covert promotion of British interests in Empress Elizabeth's court where she was a political nonentity. While she lost the love of Gregory Orlov, who along with his brother, Alexis, provided the muscle for her *coup*, she bestowed lavish honors on both soldiers to prevent an estrangement that could dethrone her. She strengthened Russian control over Poland by arranging for Stanislaus Poniatowski, an ex-lover and father of her daughter, Anna, to be elected king. In public life, Catherine did not allow personal unhappiness and emotional needs to interfere with political ends.

Catherine's Russia was a backward, ignorant land that she civilized through radical administrative and social reform. Because she was a neglected wife, she filled idle hours as Grand Duchess studying modern European thought and familiarizing herself with Russian life. Appalled by widespread illiteracy, disease, and superstition, and influenced by reformist writings of Voltaire, Montesquieu, and other *philosophes*, she created towns, schools, hospitals, orphanages; administrated provinces (her crowning achievement); and sparked a flowering of the arts and native industry. She corresponded with progressive thinkers and invited talented craftsmen and artists to work in Russia and instruct her people. Cronin praises Catherine's reforms, particularly her encouragement of social criticism and religious toleration and disputes legends characterizing her as insincere and tyrannical. He portrays her as a ruler who loved her adopted country and indefatigably worked to improve it culturally, socially, and politically. There is no mention of the cruel excesses charged against the latter part of her reign by other historians. In Cronin's biography, Catherine never commits atrocity, but advocates compassion in government.

With the same underscoring, he vindicates her attitude toward serfdom explaining the Empress' abhorrence of the institution, but her inability to end it during her lifetime. She reasoned that in educating public opinion against serfdom, emancipation would be possible under a future ruler. To ease oppression, she promoted her *Instruction*, a guideline for making just laws for all classes and urged the gentry to refer to it in dealing with their serfs. The reader is given the impression that Catherine's efforts improved the everyday life of the serfs and reduced their number. In an otherwise trustworthy presentation, this impression is an aberration since Catherine allowed serfdom to expand to parts of the Ukraine by transferring large tracts of land to favored noblemen.

In outlining her major foreign policy triumphs, the author reveals Catherine's natural administrative skills. Under her rule Russia established a protectorate over Poland; became the dominant power in the Middle East; annexed the Crimea; partially broke up the Ottoman Empire; cemented Russia's hold on the northern Black Sea Coast; extended Russia's western boundary into the heart of Central Europe; and gave Russia a strong voice in European affairs. Whether she extended Russian influence by conquest or skillful diplomacy, she increased the power and prestige of her adopted country in an unprecedented way, unequaled except in modern times. Cronin is justified in presenting these achievements as a measure of her greatness.

Despite all achievements, Catherine refused to consider herself a great ruler. Always practical in outlook, she viewed herself as a hard worker with many projects in the future. Cronin refers to the writings of her secretary, Khrapovitsky, and other court staff in detailing her disciplined work schedule and her broad range of interests. She never wearied of the minutiae of day-to-day politics and even found time to write stories and plays. While she may not have Europeanized Russia for posterity through rigorous reform, her toil certainly aroused a dormant force and gave Russia a strong voice in world politics.

Illustrations, appendices, and a "Source and Notes" section expand upon the narrative and Cronin's favorable presentation of Catherine. Of special emphasis are letters from English and Danish ambassadors, and passages from Catherine's early love letters that are published here in book format for the first time. High scholarship is reflected in this wealth of research making Cronin's biography authoritative as well as factually entertaining.

Anne C. Raymer

Sources for Further Study

Books and Bookmen. XXIII, June 18, 1978, p. E1.
Guardian Weekly. CXVIII, April 30, 1978, p. 22.
Kirkus Reviews. XLVI, February 15, 1978, p. 213.
Library Journal. CIII, June 1, 1978, p. 1164.
Spectator. CCXL, January 21, 1978, p. 20.
Times Literary Supplement. April 28, 1978, p. 471.

CERVANTES: A BIOGRAPHY

Author: William Byron
Publisher: Doubleday & Company (Garden City, New York). 583 pp. $14.50
Type of work: Biography
Time: 1547-1626
Locale: Spain and other Mediterranean countries

A biography of Miguel de Cervantes Saavedra, sixteenth century Spanish novelist, poet, and playwright, author of Don Quixote de la Mancha

Cervantes has had many biographers, but only a few have directed their work toward a general readership. In English, the most recent are R. L. Predmore and Manuel Durán. This new book is an exhaustive biography in which William Byron organizes all the facts that are known about Cervantes into a manageable adventure story. As he states clearly, it contains no new facts, for all extant documentary evidence about the life of Spain's greatest novelist has already been published in some form. Rather, this is a work of revision which puts everything in the perspective of the historical circumstance in which Cervantes lived. Predmore and Durán write for an educated general audience, and they assume a certain amount of sophistication in the area of literature and literary criticism. Byron does not. He addresses the average reader who knows little and cares even less about what literature is, or what the proper approach to literature should be. Predmore's biography (1973) and Durán's (1974) are clearly the work of scholars of Hispanic culture with specialized training in literary criticism. Byron's book indicates that his interest lies more in the field of history and that he does not have experience in literary analysis. His biography of Cervantes tries to be all things at once: biography, cultural history, literary history, and literary criticism. As it synthesizes all the previous work on Cervantes' life and works, it is sometimes successful, sometimes disappointing, and occasionally irresponsible.

For the first 150 years after the publication of *Don Quixote*, there was no interest in the life of its author. Then, in 1737, Gregorio Mayans y Siscar published his *Life of Cervantes*, which in 1738 received wider exposure as a preface to an edition of *Don Quixote*. From that point on, Cervantes' life received a great deal of attention as various scholars unearthed new documents related to the facts of the author's life. The culmination of this trend was the massive seven-volume work by Luis Astrana Marín, published from 1947 to 1958, the *Vida ejemplar y heroica de Miguel de Cervantes Saavedra, con mil documentos hasta ahora inéditos y numerosas ilustraciones y grabados de época* (*Exemplary and Heroic Life of Miguel de Cervantes Saavedra, With One Thousand Previously Unpublished Documents and Numerous Illustrations and Engravings of the Period*). After Astrana Marín's research, it is almost inconceivable that anything new could be added, but his title—*Exemplary and Heroic Life*—betrays his lack of objectivity in the evaluation of all these facts.

Byron's task has been to transform all this material into a narrative accessible to the general reader in English, and provide a new evaluation of the documented facts.

The biographer is always faced with difficult decisions in writing about a person who lived centuries ago, particularly if he does not have access to contemporary accounts. There are no contemporary biographies of Cervantes, only numerous documents that provide rather scanty knowledge of his involvement in the events of his time. In such a case, the biographer may write a kind of historical novel, in which he presents his central character doing things which he probably did, given the evidence. Or he may limit himself to telling only what the person definitely did, according to the specific documents or reliable eyewitness accounts of his contemporaries. In either case, the biographer has an obligation to present that person's life in the context of his times. This is usually the least difficult of the tasks, for the historical *milieu* can be reconstructed from a wide variety of sources. Byron does a very capable job of creating that historical ambience. He does not do so well in choosing an approach to Cervantes' actual participation in the events of his time. In fact, he never quite decides what his approach will be. The result is a strange combination of fact and speculation. Byron is entirely honest about his blending of truth and fiction, but his constant vascillation between what Cervantes did and what Cervantes must have done turns out to be very irritating. The problem lies mainly in the style of Byron's writing.

This passage from his examination of some fragmentary evidence of a duel between Cervantes and one Antonio de Sigura is a good example of the flaws in this book.

> A fight could nevertheless have started in the arcaded palace courtyard. . . . Cervantes might have encountered Sigura there. But why cross swords with him? . . . Did a Cervantes too impressed with his new friendships tease Sigura for his illiteracy? . . . Or was there a crude gibe at the young man's virility, pointed enough to release the mechanism of sexual disorientation in Cervantes' heart? . . . Cervantes was never to refer directly to the incident in his writing; it was nothing to be proud of. The theme of dueling does recur in his stories, however, and such patterns sometimes point to personal experience.

Byron's point of view has value, given the lack of complete, reliable accounts of Cervantes' life. Throughout the biography he tries to find commonsense explanations for the things that the documents prove that Cervantes did. However, as this passage illustrates, he regularly tells the story in terms of what Cervantes must have done, or what he could have done, or what we can imagine him doing. Thus, we have extensive passages describing the social circumstances in which Cervantes found himself, followed by a tentative placing of the novelist in that circumstance, probably doing what most people did at the time in such a situation. Such a method becomes somewhat distracting, since this is ostensibly a biography—a narrative of what Cervantes *did*. The problem is most evident when Byron becomes too specific. He approaches the techniques used in developing content in a historical novel, but he does not allow himself to adopt the narrative form of the historical novel. It is to Byron's credit that he does not invent history by saying that Cervantes did such and such a thing if the evidence for that does not exist. Yet, it simply does not work to say repeatedly that one can imagine Cervantes doing and saying all the things that he might have done and said. Byron puts himself in a difficult situation by not making a clear decision about whether he is writing history or historical fiction.

The most serious problem of this biography, however, is a result of Byron's concept of the relationship between life and literature, and particularly the relationship between the artist and the art that he creates. In the passage quoted above, Byron says that patterns such as the recurring theme of dueling "sometimes point to personal experience." He may be right, but he also may be wrong, and a very large part of his biography is based on what Cervantes' *characters* say and do. This is Byron's way of dealing with the uncomfortable fact that Cervantes wrote almost nothing in his own voice. The only writings that can be regarded as direct, truthful statements from the author himself are the prologues and dedications that he wrote for his own works. Even these are highly suspect, since they show many signs of being as "fictional" as his novels and stories. Byron frequently uses the statements from the novels, stories, plays, and poetry as if they were the words of Cervantes himself, rather than the words of his narrators, characters, and poetic voices.

This failure to separate the fictional, created voices of literature from the "real" voice of the artist speaking for himself indicates that Byron does not adhere to the principles of literary criticism that have been accepted as valid for the last hundred years. It is true that many authors use their own personal experience as they create their works. To suggest otherwise would be to ignore the many instances in which we have proof that an artist's work does bear some relationship to the events of the artist's life. However, to use an author's work to build a case for the way the author feels about things, or what he believes, or what he did in his own life, is to ignore completely the questions of narrative irony and artistic creativity. For example, it is possible to find in *Don Quixote* all kinds of characters saying all kinds of contradictory things about almost anything. How does one decide which of those coincide with Cervantes' opinions or experience? To try to do that is folly when one is writing biography, or history, or literary criticism.

One example of the distortions resulting from this confusion of life and literature is evident in the above quotation, where Byron speaks of Cervantes' "sexual disorientation." Throughout the biography, he creates a portrait of a man very limited in his sexual experience, suffering at times from guilt about his sexuality, and generally very indecisive in his relationships with women. Yet there is no evidence for this in the reliable documents. Byron gleans all this from the fact that there is very little information about Cervantes' involvement with women. To fill this gap in the sources, he draws from the artistic creations of the author quotations that indicate a sexual disorientation. He shows no awareness of the importance of separating life and art. These quotations are the words of Cervantes' fictional personages. As such, they indicate absolutely nothing about what Cervantes felt about his own sexuality, or about the kind of sexual experience that he actually had.

Time and again, Byron reveals this concept of the works of Cervantes as a possible proof of what the author did and felt. This is a serious flaw, particularly because this book is directed to a general audience that probably does not have a clear understanding of what literature is. This biography perpetuates some common misconceptions about the relationship between real life and fictional life, between the artist and his artistic product. This is the same error cultivated by the successful Broadway musical based on Cervantes' novel, *Man of la Mancha*. According to that version, the story of the sublimely ridiculous knight-errant is the story of Cervantes' own experiences, transformed into an ideal form through his fanciful imagination. This works beautifully on the stage and results in one of the better products of the American musical theater. However, it is an irresponsible perversion of the masterpiece on which it is based. It represents a perpetuation of the erroneous concepts that the majority of people have about literature and its relationship to its creator.

In spite of these very serious flaws, Byron's biography of Cervantes has considerable merit. The author creates a fascinating account of the quality of life in the sixteenth century in Spain and provides an abundance of detail about the historical events affecting this extraordinary novelist. The reader who is not sensitive to the problems of artistic creation will find in the book a great deal of accurate factual information, with some interesting analyses of the Spanish cultural experience in Cervantes' time. It is unfortunate that Byron does not accept the challenge of educating his readers in the question of the relationship between reality—which is one thing—and art—which very clearly is something else entirely. To promote the notion that an artist's work is primarily an expression of the artist's own experience is to ignore a century of very important work in aesthetic theory.

Gilbert Smith

Sources for Further Study

Booklist. LXXV, November 1, 1978, p. 448.
Kirkus Reviews. XLVI, August 15, 1978, p. 914.
Library Journal. CIII, September, 15, 1978, p. 1748.
Publisher's Weekly. CCXIV, August 14, 1978, p. 56.

CHANCE AND CIRCUMSTANCE
The Draft, the War and the Vietnam Generation

Author: Lawrence M. Baskir and William A. Strauss
Publisher: Random House (New York). 312 pp. $10.00
Type of work: History
Time: 1964-1973
Locale: The United States

A comprehensive study of the operation of the Selective Service laws during the Vietnam War, with a thorough analysis of their effect upon young Americans

Lawrence M. Baskir served as general counsel and chief executive officer of President Gerald R. Ford's clemency board for draft evaders and deserters, and William A. Strauss was director of planning and management for the board and director of the staff that prepared its final report. From these pivotal positions in the controversy surrounding the administration of the nation's selective service laws during the Vietnam era these two men have written an exhaustive study of the operation of the selective service laws throughout the course of the war and have concluded that these laws were blatantly unfair on their face and hopelessly complicated from an administrative point of view, finally collapsing, for all practical purposes, in the depth of the conflict. If that is true, one is left with the inevitable conclusion that the United States was not only bound to lose the war in Indochina but indeed deserved to lose it.

The Vietnam conflict was America's most painful war by any standard. It was the nation's longest war, and one that eventually ended in defeat. It was a war where the only heroes were prisoners, who in earlier conflicts were largely forgotten or even the objects of shame. The war saw a majority of those eligible for service evade that service either legally or illegally, while many within the military deserted their posts and fled to foreign countries willing to receive them. Finally, as it became clear that America was not going to win, supporters of the war within the United States turned the greater part of their frustrations upon those Americans opposing the war, much more than upon the enemy in Indochina, and particularly upon those who openly defied the draft or deserted the military. A climate of disorder and hatred within the United States itself followed.

The thesis of this study is that the majority of young men subject to the draft during the war legally evaded service through a multitude of loopholes in the selective service laws. Those loopholes were there because the American people as represented by Congress wanted them there, and the Selective Service concurred. The system had been built up piecemeal since the resumption of the draft in 1948 and was supposedly designed to ensure that the military drafted only those men fit to serve and those not needed in the civilian economy. The problem was that such categorization was very loosely and politically defined, so that by the time the unpopular Vietnam War rolled around, clever youth, mostly from privileged and educated backgrounds, simply took advantage of the abundant legal opportunities available to them for evading military service. They did not go, and they received no public censure for not going. Even if no loophole were available to a youth, once drafted into service there were yet other ways for the clever and the manipulative to avoid combat.

The complexity of the draft laws, with all their loopholes, together with all of the bureaucratic procedures and "safeguards" in the administration of the laws, meant that the system would collapse if enough people wanted to "gum it up." This apparently was what happened by 1971, when the system began to fall of its own weight. A body of complex law and procedure, administered by local boards composed of citizens who were often totally ignorant of the law, assisted by low-level civil service clerks, was a perfect target for draft resisters with clever lawyers. There were plenty of courts presided over by sympathetic judges willing to listen to cases where incompetent draft boards made errors in administering a hopelessly complex set of laws. These courts increasingly found that local boards were in violation of Supreme Court rulings on the operation of the law, and draft offenders generally went free. The fact is that the law was so complicated that no board could really avoid making a fatal error in a controversial case, unless it had the best and most expensive of legal counsel. That of course was not the case; usually the boards had no counsel at all. Consequently, most boards after 1971 just gave up on controversial cases. Had they not done so, and had they been successful in prosecuting their cases, federal prison space would have had to be doubled to accommodate all those found guilty.

Who, then, was drafted to serve in the war? Assuming that millions of the poor never even bothered to register for service, and that other millions of the affluent got off legally, a large hole was left in the potential pool of applicants for service in Vietnam. Certainly many youths did support the war and felt morally obliged to serve, but the study indicates that most Vietnam draftees were of the lower socioeconomic classes, and thus either legal loopholes were lacking or they did not have the imagination, initiative, or money to take advantage of what technicalities might have been available to exploit. Others were simply unwilling from a moral standpoint to cooperate with such a system and refused the "outs" that were available to them; they preferred to attack the system and the war in the courts as being immoral. The latter were invariably identified by the public as disloyal and generally lost their cases, since judges were unwilling to venture into constitutional quagmires and felt they had to administer the law as it stood. This group probably would never have seen service or been sentenced to jail had they taken their "loops" and kept quiet about it.

The result of such a draft law was that the military was filled with people from the lower socioeconomic classes, bringing with them all the problems that their background entailed. Secretary of Defense Robert M. McNamara had instituted "Project 100,000" which aimed to rehabilitate and train 100,000 recruits from the lowest intelligence levels; but Congress never adequately funded the program, with the result that the military was burdened with tens of thousands of men whom it simply could make no use of. These men never adjusted to military life and discipline, and consequently the services mired down in the racial and drug problems that still afflict them.

Much has been made of the problem of military desertion during the Vietnam years. But here again the authors argue that what might appear to have been desertion by politically active soldiers opposed to the war was usually not that at all. It was true that some recruits did experience a belated political awakening and deserted rather than serve in the war, usually seeking refuge in some sympathetic foreign country. Others were plainly criminal types, unfit for service. But the great majority had more basic reasons, as have most deserters throughout the history of warfare. Men from the lowest socioeconomic order have frequently felt that family problems at home provide sufficient grounds for desertion. Poor families are often in trouble, even hungry, and beg a soldier to return home to help with this or that problem. Such men are historically not cowards, or not politically conscious, but merely simple men overwhelmed by personal and family crises. These men during the Vietnam War were poorly paid soldiers usually ignorant of their legal right to aid for their families; or at least they were incapable of coping with the military bureaucracy in charge of administering such help. Consequently they deserted.

The military itself made the further error of issuing an elaborate series of numerically coded discharges, resulting in untold numbers of men receiving numbers on their discharges that, if decoded, stigmatized them for life on the basis of nothing more than a clerical error. For example, such an error could brand a man as a homosexual. The system of military discharges had long been entirely too complicated to be understood by the public, as well as by potential employers, and the codes only served to compound a problem long in the making. Many discharged veterans were so unsophisticated that they did not know the effect of their discharge category on their future employment possibilities.

President Ford, bowing to public opinion, announced an amnesty program for draft evaders and deserters of the Vietnam era which was administered by the authors of this study. They maintain that in fact Ford's program was far less lenient than the policies pursued for some years previously by the courts, the Department of Defense, and the Justice Department, and that the President soon lost all interest in the program. It became just one more bureaucratic boondoggle, tossed around by Defense, Justice, and Selective Service, and providing bureaucrats the opportunity to spend time and money on something of little value to men in trouble with the law. Consequently the latter showed little interest in it.

Jimmy Carter, in fulfillment of a campaign promise, did give a full amnesty and pardon to all draft evaders of the Vietnam era, but declined to extend this clemency to deserters. The authors maintain that this was most unjust since the latter usually deserted for reasons other than political opposition to the war, and theirs was in fact the most pitiful of all the cases arising from the conflict. However, it seems that they have little hope of rehabilitation; large sections of the public continue to vent the wrath of defeat upon a group of men whose only crime was that they were ignorant and poor, while the great majority evaded military service legally, suffered no criticism whatsoever, and have in many cases gone on to lucrative and secure careers. The draft laws apparently have terminated in the same injustice in which they were originally conceived.

Jack L. Calbert

Sources for Further Study

Book World. June 11, 1978, p. E4.
Kirkus Reviews. XLVI, March 1, 1978, p. 272.
Library Journal. CIII, April 1, 1978, p. 735.
New York Times Book Review. June 11, 1978, p. 9.
Newsweek. XCI, June 5, 1978, p. 100.
Publisher's Weekly. CCXIII, February 6, 1978, p. 98.

CHANCE MEETINGS

Author: William Saroyan (1908-   )
Publisher: W. W. Norton and Company (New York). 135 pp. $8.95
Type of work: Memoir

The eighth memoir by the Armenian-American novelist, short story writer, and playwright, in which he attempts to define his theory of friendship

This is William Saroyan's forty-sixth book. Like most of his latter-day works, it is anecdotal, sentimental, and professionally Armenian. There are small glimmers of the Saroyan of the mid-1930's, the man who wrote so movingly in the short story collection *The Daring Young Man on the Flying Trapeze*, but not many. On the law of averages there would not be, since the memoir is only 135 pages long, and those pages are about one-third margin; and what the book lacks in length it makes up in incoherent paragraph-long sentences. Consider the following:

What these geniuses put forward is very little, compared with the potential, or with the original itself, all things already and for billions of years real and in place, but it is the only thing we have that is our own, that we have made, and after ourselves, after our continuous putting forward of ourselves, through the procedure invented or given as a gift by nature to all continuing things, after our most astonishing falling in with the procedure, our successful recreation of ourselves over billions of years, in all of our various forms, these things, this art, made by our madmen, our disgruntled boys, our violent girls, our geniuses, our refusers, our frequently sick boys and girls, these homemade things are all that we have, all that we call culture, civilization, and mortal glory.

If Saroyan has a valid place in American letters, it is as a short story writer. Memoirs such as the current work do nothing to enhance his reputation; this, his eighth work in the genre, is plotless, pointless, and prolix. He manifests none of the keenness of septuagenarian V. S. Pritchett, nor the wit of the late P. G. Wodehouse, despite the fact that he is barely three score years and ten and makes much of it. *Chance Meetings* offers no surprises to those who have followed Saroyan's career.

Saroyan's effort in this work is to define ideal friendships as brief chance meetings, complete in themselves, with no past and no future. The chance meetings in this memoir, however, are spotty and lack any central theme other than that suggested by the title. There are a few bright spots, but by and large this thin book is not rewarding. As Saroyan meanders down memory lane, however, he does introduce us to a few interesting characters.

In some of the sketches the reader will recognize the germ of a tale, as in the chapter concerning a Mormon beauty and a would-be writer, and the lie that the writer lived. Yet even in these, Saroyan does not take the reader into his confidence, thus leaving him frustrated. There is humor in the story of an undertaker who has been in the business for forty years and has worked his way up in the company to the vice-presidency of Cypress Lawn Cemetery. He continually writes advertisements subsequently ruled out by the head of the company, such ads as "Inter here," or "Cypress Lawn Cemetery. We give you a lot for your money." Yet Saroyan does not go beyond superficial telling of the tale; we really do not know the undertaker.

In another chapter, the reader meets Black Jack, small both in stature and in the seriousness of his crimes of robbery. When an influential editor pleads his case, Black Jack is let out of jail. Released, he must play the game of reformed criminal and be on display with his talks to civic clubs and the deserving poor. It should be clear that he is free only in the physical sense. Under these circumstances, the reader is not surprised when Black Jack commits suicide.

The ever present "I" in his works has led to charges by critics that Saroyan is narcissistic and pompous. It should be noted that his "I" is not always the "I" of the writer; sometimes he uses it as a symbol of the human condition. In the instances where both the reader and the author recognize this, Saroyan's strengths are to be found. Sometimes his characters do work and the reader does care, yet even under these circumstances it is difficult to decide whether one is reading too much into his words. His recollection of wanting to touch a nesting bird and of observing, but being unable to catch, a ditched catfish, could be the story of man's attempt to reach the stars. It could be; but when Saroyan questions why memory chose to preserve these events, he steps on his lines and the philosophical impact is lost.

These stories offer no evidence that they were written by the same man who also became, for a while, an important force in the American theater—unless that in them he continues to opt for freedom in style: a nonstyle self-described as "easy going, natural and American." It is easygoing to the point of sloppiness in these memoirs. To its credit, however, *Chance Meetings* does have a measure of the Saroyan buoyancy that is evident in some of his works such as *The Human Comedy*, which Saroyan wrote originally in drama form as a screenplay. The most that can be said for this current work is that it is mildly amusing in spots.

William Saroyan's place in literature has slipped in the past three decades; he has not progressed with the times. In the beginning, although his stories were often written about sad and desperate men, he captured a willing audience. The stories radiated an uncritical optimism and faith in a Grand Dream. The Depression-weary reader escaped into the optimism generated by Saroyan's naïve faith in a better life to come. As time passed and times grew better, Saroyan's work did not change; but with the return of a shaky economy, Saroyan may be bidding for a new following. If such is his motive, the publication of this lightweight memoir is excusable, or at least understandable, since there is a clumsy transcendentalism about his work that has a certain positive appeal today.

During the 1930's Saroyan was a better writer than he is now credited with being. If he would only return to writing short stories and sparing the readers the memoirs, there would be room for a regenerated Saroyan on our bookshelves.

Mae Woods Bell

Sources for Further Study

Christian Science Monitor. April 5, 1978, p. 19.
Critic. XXXVI, Summer, 1978, p. 93.
Library Journal. CIII, February 1, 1978, p. 366.
National Review. XXX, May 12, 1978, p. 599.
New York Times Book Review. March 12, 1978, p. 11.

CHATEAUBRIAND: A BIOGRAPHY
Volume I (1768-93): The Longed-for Tempests

Author: George D. Painter (1914-   )
Publisher: Alfred A. Knopf (New York). 327 pp. $15.00
Type of work: Biography
Time: 1768-1793
Locale: France

The first volume of a biography of a leading French romantic writer

> *Principal personages:*
> FRANÇOIS-RENÉ DE CHATEAUBRIAND, novelist and politician in early nineteenth century France
> RENÉ-AUGUST DE CHATEAUBRIAND, his cold, unloving father
> JOSEPH GESRIL, a childhood friend who strongly influenced Chateaubriand
> CHRÉTIEN DE MALESHERBES, *philosophe* and statesman who became Chateaubriand's mentor

Chateaubriand: The Longed-for Tempests is the first volume of George D. Painter's monumental three-part study of the French romantic writer and politician of the early nineteenth century. A retired incunabulist at the British Museum, Painter has long been known to the literary world for his biographies of André Gide, William Caxton, and Marcel Proust. In this new work, Painter presents Chateaubriand as a bright, impetuous young aristocrat in search of himself during the decline and fall of the old regime in France.

The early life of François-René de Chateaubriand is known to us largely through his memoirs. It is a basically gloomy story. Born at St. Malo, Brittany, on September 4, 1768, Chateaubriand was the youngest of five children of a relatively poor noble family. His mother, more concerned with society and religion than with rearing an infant son, sent François-René to live with his grandmother until he was three. "On leaving my mother's womb I underwent my first exile," Chateaubriand later recalled. He received no more love from his father, René-August, who dedicated himself to the task of restoring his family's ancient lands and titles through a career at sea.

René-August's career as a privateer and slave trader paid handsome dividends and by the time he was nine, François-René found himself ensconced at Combourg Castle. Long walks through the woods and heaths of the family's ancestral homeland on holidays and school vacations developed in Chateaubriand an enduring love of nature. But he remained a troubled youth who on several occasions expressed a desire for self-destruction. During adolescence he developed a morbid fascination for his youngest sister, Lucille, who perhaps served to compensate for parental affection denied inside the cold and damp walls of Combourg Castle. Painter carefully weighs the evidence for incest between Chateaubriand and Lucille and concludes tentatively against it.

Painter considers that three persons had a crucial formative impact on Chateaubriand's emotional and intellectual development: his father René-August, a schoolmate, Joseph Gesril, and the *philosophe* and statesman Malesherbes. Chateaubriand's relationship with his father is viewed by Painter as a basically negative experience. René-August's cold, authoritarian attitude produced in Chateaubriand's character a deeply rooted strain of "melancholy" and "isolation."

As a student in clerical schools at Dol, Rennes, and Dinan, Chateaubriand was a restless, undisciplined achiever. He excelled in Latin, Greek, and mathematics and was encouraged to pursue an interest in writing. Upon the urging of Joseph Gesril, who showed him the "bright eyes of danger," Chateaubriand often found himself in trouble for defying school rules and regulations. His propensity for dangerous living is well documented by Painter. Chateaubriand's near miss with death at Niagara Falls is only the most harrowing of a number of rash, possibly suicidal incidents in his life recounted by Painter.

Chateaubriand's introduction to Parisian literary society in the late 1780's was facilitated by his entrance into the military. As a younger son of noble birth in the Province of Brittany, François-René had little hope of inheriting family lands and titles under the prevailing rule of primogeniture. His restless soul yearned to travel and led him to follow his father's example by seeking a career in the Royal Navy. Failing to obtain the much-desired commission, Chateaubriand was promptly enrolled in the Navarre Regiment of the Army. The event was fortuitous for François-René. The liberal leave policy of the Royal Army allowed him to take advantage of his close proximity to Paris and Chateaubriand was soon exposed to the main currents of enlightenment thought.

At the home of his sister Julie, now married and living in Paris, Chateaubriand made the acquaintance of a number of second-rate writers such as Delisle de Sales, Carbon de Flins des Oliviers and Jacques Ginguené, from whom he gained beliefs in "universal brotherhood, the perfectibility of man and the noble savage." But the most important influence on Chateaubriand's literary and political life was undoubtedly the eminent *philosophe* and statesman Chrétien de Malesherbes. The links between Chateaubriand and Malesherbes were both organic and spiritual. François-René's brother Jean Baptiste had recently married Malesherbes' granddaughter Aline de Rosanbo. The old Malesherbes, impressed with the potential of the aspiring young author, assumed the role of mentor. In Painter's opinion, Malesherbes became a "new father" to Chateaubriand, though the relationship may actually have been more that of a benevolent, eccentric grandfather.

Under the tutelage of Malesherbes, Chateaubriand explored the philosophical underpinnings of the eighteenth century concept of natural rights, personal freedom, and constitutional monarchy. His support for political reform did not extend beyond his own social horizons, however. When the counter revolutionary armies under Prince Condé marched against the Convention in 1793, Chateaubriand returned from America to enlist in the effort. One seeks in vain in Painter for any sign of opposition to his father's trade in slaves expressed by Chateaubriand. As for the peasants of Combourg facing the "misery" and "death" of winter in 1785, Chateaubriand was apparently unconcerned as he and Lucille "trod in bliss over the dazzling snow."

Painter finds parallels in the lives of Malesherbes and Chateaubriand and the reader should probably expect to find more in subsequent volumes of the biography dealing with Chateaubriand's career as adviser to Napoleon and Ambassador to Berlin. During the course of the Revolution, both men committed themselves to the cause of King and class against the violently emerging nation. As Chateaubriand makes clear, his hastily arranged voyage to America owed as much to the sight of "heads on pikes" as to his desire to meet an Indian.

Chateaubriand's voyage to America in 1792 forms the longest section of the biography. The trip is explored in great detail by Painter beginning with the "Hyperborean Strands" which provided its rationale. Voltaire's depiction of a Breton orphan nurtured by savages in *L'Ingénu* was inspiration for Chateaubriand's novel *Les Natchez*, the story of an Indian captured and brought to France. The ubiquitous Malesherbes, hopelessly misinformed about the geography of North America, urged the novice explorer to include in his voyage an attempt to discover the elusive Northwest Passage. Faced with the realities of life on the American frontier, Chateaubriand quickly shelved the idea.

Painter is least effective when trying to dispute earlier commentators' suggestions that Chateaubriand may have fictionalized parts of his travelogue. Rejecting their assertions that topographical descriptions in Chateaubriand's *Memoirs* sharply diverge from reality, Painter reconstructs an itinerary for Chateaubriand from his own "poetic" narrative, the "circumstances of the time," and accounts of contemporary travelers. The result is tedious as well as unconvincing and the reader may wonder about the extent to which the memoirs and novels of at least one romantic writer were cast from the same mold.

Painter's *Chateaubriand* is a well-organized and meticulously detailed account of Chateaubriand to the age of twenty-five. Its lethargic pace will not endear it to the nonacademic reading public, and its cursory attempt at psychoanalysis will perhaps annoy scholars familiar with the works of Erickson, Mazlish, and others in psychohistorical studies. Painter's *Chateaubriand* will nevertheless become an indispensable guide to the life and thought of this leader of French Romanticism of the early nineteenth century.

Sheldon A. Mossberg

Sources for Further Study

Booklist. LXXIV, February 15, 1978, p. 971.

Library Journal. CIII, March 1, 1978, p. 566.

New Republic. CLXXVIII, April 22, 1978, p. 25.

New York Times Book Review. May 7, 1978, p. 10.

Newsweek. XCI, May 1, 1978, p. 82.

Publisher's Weekly. CCXIII, March 13, 1978, p. 99.

Time. CXI, May 1, 1978, p. 92.

CHESAPEAKE

Author: James A. Michener (1907-   )
Publisher: Random House (New York). 865 pp. $12.95
Type of work: Novel
Time: 1583-1978
Locale: Maryland's Eastern Shore

The examination of a tidewater community's history from pre-Colonial life of the native Indians through the Watergate years

Principal characters:
PENTAQUOD, a Susquehannock brave
THE STEEDS, descendants of an English Catholic gentleman
THE PAXMORES, a Quaker family of boatbuilders
THE TURLOCKS, a clan of hunters and fishermen

The historical novel seems to be enjoying a rebirth in our literary tradition. Particularly in the recent television broadcasts of James A. Michener's *Centennial* and Alex Hailey's *Roots*, we see the phenomenal success of watereddown history on the video screen. An accompanying surge in book sales suggests we may be in for more of the same rediscovery of our origins. Whether such a movement should be welcomed is debatable, but, in any case, writers are sure to come forth with all kinds of derivations on the already successful theme.

Some writers, of course, are old hands at employing the credibility of history as a basis for fiction. In doing so, they have sought to provoke realizations about where we are now based on where we were at some past time. The lessons of history, ignored or not, usually provide compelling reading matter, as wise novelists have long known.

Chesapeake, James Michener's latest novel, in its examination of nearly four hundred years of American history, follows a pattern already familiar to his readers. Through strong characterization and an episodic organization, Michener weaves a compelling tale of a community on Maryland's Eastern Shore. Centered on a fictional town called Patamoke located on the very real Choptank River, the novel traces events from the period prior to English colonization through the Watergate years. It concentrates on the lives of several early families and their descendants, the generations that, along with later immigrants, populate the region. But perhaps most important, *Chesapeake* creates a scenic paradise through Michener's masterful description. It is this powerful sense of place that unifies the book. At every turn, human interaction with the natural environment is an underlying theme of the narrative.

Michener's love for the Chesapeake Bay and its environs is evident. His painstaking detail superbly captures the spirit of the place, surrounding readers with the sense of comfort which bay area inhabitants have long enjoyed. Moreover, Michener seems to adhere to E. M. Forster's principle that a "spirit of place" informs the actions of those men and women who are sensitive to the spirit. Like Forster, Michener sees an inextricable bond between men and their surroundings, so that the generally tranquil setting encourages serenity in the affairs of men. Certainly there are tensions that arise, but they are subsumed to the overall tendency toward tranquillity. Very often the most tension-filled moments in the novel result from natural catastrophes, when men are pressed by elemental forces to overcome the power beyond their control. In general, however, *Chesapeake* emphasizes that this region is a land of pleasant living, a place conducive to human life and inviting habitation.

As a body of water, the Chesapeake Bay is unique in the world. Fed primarily by the Susquehanna River at the north, the bay maintains a variable mixture of salt and fresh water which changes concentrations with the seasons. For the most part, the waters are shallow except for a deep central channel and notches where various side rivers join the main current. In these broad expanses of shallow brackish water vast numbers of shellfish and finned fish make their homes. Along the extensive shoreline, wading birds and migratory waterfowl inhabit saltmarshes teeming with small fish and other wildlife. Situated midway along America's east coast, the bay moderates both the winter's cold and the summer's heat by virtue of its constant sea-land breezes. Without doubt, life on the bay is comfortable, providing for man's needs with everything from spectacular scenery to abundant food supplies.

Into this scene Michener first introduces a lone Susquehannock brave on his way south in search of a haven. Driven from his own warlike tribe because of his pacifist nature, Pentaquod comes to the Choptank in search of peace and finds a paradise. He soon learns that shellfish in the estuary waters are available for easy taking. He sees that waterfowl are everywhere. In time, he connects with the peace-loving Choptank Indians and is selected as their chief. What he recognizes at his first encounter with this region is how easy life here can be. Later, after he has encountered the first white men to explore the Chesapeake, he realizes that these new men will soon recognize what he has come to know, and their recognition means the doom of his people.

In part this doom is a threat to the ecology of the region, for with English colonization a change must occur. The early settlers carve plantations out of the wilderness, clearcutting virgin forests to make way for agriculture. Immense tobacco fields replace what were endless miles of timber. By nature tobacco production requires extensive land use because the plants quickly exhaust minerals from the soil, making mandatory further clearing operations. Combined with continual settling on the part of new immigrants and the proliferation of descendants, these land requirements make certain the destruction of valuable tracts of timber. In most cases the wood is merely burned, there being no ready use for the tremendous amounts of wood cut. To the modern mind such waste is appalling, a fact Michener emphasizes while establishing the necessity of the early practices.

Continually through the novel Michener underscores the characters' reaction to the abundant resources at their disposal. As with the land, the wildlife is used rather recklessly, eventually hunted in wholesale slaughters to provide income for the hunters and supply restaurants in Baltimore and Annapolis, on the other side of the bay. A lengthy description of duck hunting and a special type of gun used to kill hundreds of ducks at a time vividly enforces the idea that environmental exploitation becomes a way of life in the region. In the midst of bountiful game, the gamest men make their fortunes.

Later, as game and territory are diminished, pressure to conserve creates tensions between the conservation-minded and those committed to exploiting the land. Enforcing legal restrictions in an area where individual freedom has long governed men's actions provokes confrontation, in some cases leading to violence. Michener is adept at presenting all sides of the argument and examining its eventual resolution. As a matter of course, he centers his examination in the lives of individual characters, probing motivation in terms of past experience and individual perceptions of need and greed.

Michener's characterizations are realistic, and he probes the diverse types which make up the Patamoke community. Pentaquod and his brethren are early eliminated from the scene, though through a marriage into one of the lower class families, the Turlocks, the Indian strain is minimally preserved. Central to the novel are the Steeds, founders of the original tobacco plantation and the dominant agricultural operation in the area. The Steeds are gentlemen descended from Edmund Steed, an English Catholic fleeing persecution in his homeland. Eventual slave owners, the Steeds represent a conservative element tied closely to tradition and maintenance of the *status quo*. It is in their interest to foster stability and economic growth based in an agrarian social structure.

Counterbalancing the Steeds are the Paxmores. Edward Paxmore is himself the victim of persecution at the hands of New England Puritans. Whipped and tortured out of Massachusetts, the Quaker comes to the peaceful Choptank and finds a home where he can employ his considerable skills as a woodworker. His wife, Ruth Brinton Paxmore, also the victim of Puritan persecution of the Quakers, joins him in establishing a family that becomes the conscience of the community. From the outset, the Paxmores oppose slavery, with later members of the family playing a significant part in the Underground Railroad.

By profession Edward Paxmore and his sons are boatbuilders, which establishes them as central figures in the development of the region, since their ships carry the trade so essential to the community. Later Paxmore ships also become famous in battle because of their swift, sleek designs and sturdy construction. Finally, smaller Paxmore boats are fitted superbly to do the work of the bay's watermen, who depend on easily maneuvered boats for their livelihood. Oystering, clamming, and crabbing—done in the shallow estuary waters—require boats of shallow draft, but boats capable of withstanding the sometimes tempestuous vagaries of Chesapeake weather.

Both the Steed and Paxmore families are made up of men and women of principle. They establish the standards upon which the community florishes. Equally stubborn in defense of their sometimes contradictory views, they nevertheless hold to an overall toleration of differences, thus representing a keynote in the history of the Maryland colony. For them human dignity and concern for the less fortunate are ways of life. Though slave owners, the Steeds manage their slaves with an enlightened attitude, one which cultivates respect and fairness in the essentially unfair situation.

Contrasting these two prominent families are the Turlocks, descendants of Timothy Turlock, scandalous runaway from Virginia who makes his home in the marshes along the river. Timothy and his heirs make their living by hunting and fishing, living close to the land and water, and coming to know and understand both. In a sense, the Turlock clan embodies the tenacity with which early settlers conquered the wilderness in which they chose to exist. For the Turlocks, living in the vast marshes means discomfort and hardship, but it also brings knowledge of a complex environment and the basic skills of survival. The wedding of marine and terrestrial elements supplies these careful observers with unique opportunities, so that the Turlocks become excellent hunters and fishermen, seemingly endowed with animalistic awareness of their surroundings. Michener implies that their way of life, in a sense, is the vital core of what remains most unique about life on the Chesapeake.

With time, various other elements are added to this three-family society. Immigration introduces a wide variety of cultural strains to the area, and with each new group new niches are established in the societal framework. Freed blacks and indentured servants, having worked out their commitments, become integral parts of the community and assume prominent places in the events of the region. Tensions result at times, and the resolution of these tensions is one of Michener's vital concerns. Racial issues especially present themselves as painful experiences for the community, eventually erupting in riots and hostility. Again it is important to emphasize that Michener presents these conflicts as being generated by individuals; conflicts are the results of individuals' actions and beliefs.

In general, however, the lives of Michener's characters are commonplace, without extraordinary circumstances. Even the few exceptions to this rule are, at bottom, lives of average men and women caught up in situations or problems much larger than themselves. Michener's focus remains of the interactions of men as they exist relative to place and time. *Chesapeake*, then, almost assumes the character of a *paean* devoted to place.

As a result, readers will most certainly be struck by the massive research which has produced this novel. Throughout, *Chesapeake* seems a labor of love, and Michener is quite candid in his opening acknowledgments, pointing out that his first encounter with the bay came in 1927 and that from his earliest days he considered writing about it. He provides an extensively detailed list of sources of information, and in one sense the book might be considered a compendium of bay lore. Without doubt *Chesapeake* is an informative experience for any reader. Even natives of the Chesapeake region will find themselves constantly intrigued with details about the bay's history, wildlife, and occupations.

Concentrating on its small section of Maryland's Eastern Shore, *Chesapeake* provides a microcosmic look at the development of the region; but, in a broad sense, the novel also provides interpretations of United States history. The weaving of stories here is representative of the type of development in any part of our nation, and the concerns examined are similar to problems encountered, to some extent, by Americans of all backgrounds.

Such breadth of scope, however, creates what might be considered a few distractions. In a few places, particularly where Michener deals with nature, the narrative may seem overly detailed. The reading may even be a bit tedious for some readers. In other places Michener intrudes to point out obvious lessons to be learned from the history or from man's foolish actions toward the environment; such didacticism becomes heavy-handed. When Michener is given to hyperbole, the result can be a bit syrupy. But perhaps the most unsettling problem is the novel's pace, which is somewhat slow to moderate at the beginning, but very fast toward the end. Some readers may feel rushed in the later stages because of the significant jumps in time. The problem is understandable in a book of this size and ambition. Moreover, the faster pace at the novel's end might suggest the quickening pace of life with the coming of the twentieth century and the inroads of the external world on this relatively isolated region; Michener suggests as much when he talks about the construction of the Chesapeake Bay Bridge and how that span brings the cities of Baltimore and Washington within commuting distance of the Choptank.

Certainly changes have been wrought in the way of life on the Eastern Shore. Once isolated areas are now accessible. Marshes are being drained to create land for houses and businesses to accommodate a new wave of settlers seeking retreat from the complicated life on the western side of the bay.

A local Baltimore brewery has long advertised that its beer comes "from the land of pleasant living," the shores of the Chesapeake Bay. More and more, that title in its original sense seems only applicable to Maryland's Eastern Shore. The western shore, filled with the hectic Baltimore-Washington urban sprawl, while not yet totally unpleasant, requires too fast a pace of its inhabitants. But the Eastern Shore, long a politically and geographically isolated area, preserves much that is traditionally encompassed in the brewer's phrase.

Indeed, the sensitive intruder will still feel the slower pace. His mental pulse will quiet, as through generations other men's have quieted. He will absorb the place as it absorbs him. He will enter the timelessness of life beside water, life determined by estuary rhythms, life long obedient to natural systems for survival. Possibly he will, like the youthful James Michener, think a book should be written to address the uniqueness of this place, explaining the binding of human history to the fabric of the natural environment. But such a writer has quite a job ahead of him if he hopes to match the depth of feeling and the penetrating understanding evident in Michener's *Chesapeake*.

Gary B. Blank

Sources for Further Study

America. CXXXIX, September 23, 1978, p. 182.

Best Sellers. XXXVIII, September, 1978, p. 171.

Book World. July 9, 1978, p. 171.

Booklist. LXXIV, July 15, 1978, p. 1719.

Library Journal. CIII, July, 1978, p. 1436.

New York Review of Books. XXV, August 17, 1978, p. 31.

Newsweek. XCII, July 24, 1978, p. 82.

CHIEKO'S SKY

Author: Kotaro Takamura (1883-1956)
Translated from the Japanese by Soichi Furuta
Publisher: Kodansha International Ltd. (Tokyo). 68 pp. $12.95
Type of work: Poetry

The posthumous publication of a volume of poems expressing the deep and abiding love which the poet felt for his wife

During his lifetime Kotaro Takamura was a widely popular and highly respected poet in Japan. He published a number of volumes of verse which were highly acclaimed, and one, *Tenkei,* won the Yomiuri Literary Prize in 1951. He was also noted for his translations of poetry and prose, and wrote a biography of Auguste Rodin. He pursued these diverse literary activities while simultaneously devoting himself to a lifelong career as a sculptor. Despite his long established position as a leading modern poet in Japan, his work is scarcely known outside his own country. This posthumous volume, which is a revised version of a book of verse first published in 1938, then updated in 1974, is one of the few publications of Takamura's which has received any real international attention. It is an attention long overdue.

Takamura was an extraordinarily creative artist, equally adept at shaping language or stone, carving wood or arranging words. Whether his verbal talent in any way affected his sculpture would be difficult if not impossible to say, but his sculptor's vision—the compelling impulse to embody the abstract idea in the concrete representation—lends to his poetry a singular impact, a unique effectiveness. His poetry is very translatable because words for concrete images have so much more nearly identical counterparts in other languages than do abstractions or intangible ideas. This is not to suggest that the ideas are not there, for Takamura's poems are much more than interesting images conjured up through words. The images, metaphors, and similes he uses are special vehicles, yoked to his ideas, infused with his vision, and expressed through his poetic control of words.

The poetry in this volume is not only intensely visual, but often sensually tactile as well. He refers to Chieko's body as agatelike, maintains that she is "phosphorescing in my cells," and describes how in the hour of her death her "clean teeth bit fresh into the lemon," and the juice restored lucidity for an instant.

Chieko's Sky has a single unifying subject, Chieko, and an unrelieved seriousness and directness of approach. The poet speaks in his poems of playing, laughing, and romping with his beloved wife, but he does not play, or laugh, or romp with words. There is no comedy, no satire, no merriment in his verse. It is lyric verse, expressing a vast range of human emotions from anguish and despair through exhilarating joy; but the verse itself is straightforward, solemnly intent on conveying the message of the moment.

The poems span the years from the time Kotaro met Chieko in 1912 until 1951, just five years before his death and thirteen years after she had died of tuberculosis. These verses are a lyric panorama of the long love affair which illuminated the poet's life. The intimacy and the explicitness of the moments captured in these lyrics—some of them revealing his reflections while alone, and others describing hours shared with Chieko—provide the reader with an almost unparalleled entrée into the personal world of the poet. He is generous in his candor and the effect is an awesome impression of the magnitude and sustained force of his love.

One expecially moving group of lyrics is that containing poems written between 1948 and 1951. In these poems there is a renewed sense of life and a tone of placid joy after his despair during Chieko's madness and the years following her death. Here the poet asserts in various ways that she is really always with him—infused into his very being and into all of nature. These final poems are especially exemplary of the sculpture-mindset of the poet; for Chieko dead, the disembodied spirit is affirmed by the poet to have entered into and become a living element within his own flesh where she maintains a genuine identity. He asserts that Chieko exists in absolute reality, and that to the extent that we can have contact with that reality, so much the better people we are. Kotaro plainly idolizes Chieko, and his obvious sincerity makes the reader realize that he really does not know any other way to think or talk about her.

It is impossible fully to appreciate the melody and cadences, or the sounds of the words in Japanese when one is reading translations in English. But it is surely only just to mention that the translator, Soichi Furuta, has performed his job well; for the English translation is characterized by a pleasing rhythm, melody, and grace of phrasing. The verses celebrate simplicity, wholeness, and totality. They sing of simple meals, quiet moments, and of the total commitment of love. Above all, they celebrate, whether joyously or sadly, the intense bond of devotion between these lovers.

In addition to the poems contained in the volume, there is a section devoted to prints of Chieko's paper cuttings. Most of these are representations of flowers, and they have a harmony of line and color which make them delightful to view. Another section of the book is a brief prose essay narrating the circumstances of the meeting, marriage, and life together of Kotaro and Chieko. It also tells of her lapse into insanity, and the subsequent years of anguish. It is an account which in its simple dignity achieves the grace of the poems themselves.

The poems have the quality of combining intense passion with high seriousness and mature dignity. They evoke images of Chieko's beloved sky, the mountains, grasses, scents, and sounds of the beautiful countryside of Japan. The delight the pair experienced in romping playfully over the hills and fields is as carefully and passionately etched in verse as is the tragic suffering that came later. The poems are infused with the splendor of an abiding love, and this love is expressed with warmth, candor, and dignity, in language that is touching, and in images that are beautiful and haunting. This moving book of lyrics is an excellent way to become acquainted with Japanese poetry.

Betty Gawthrop

Sources for Further Study

Booklist. LXXV, September 15, 1978, p. 148.
Sewanee Review. LXXXVI, July, 1978, p. R108.

CHINESE FOREIGN POLICY AFTER THE CULTURAL REVOLUTION, 1966-1977

Author: Robert G. Sutter
Publisher: Westview Press (Boulder, Colorado). 176 pp. $14.50
Type of work: Diplomatic history
Time: 1966-1977
Locale: Peking, China

A succinct chronicle and summary of Chinese foreign policy from 1966 to 1977

> *Principal personages:*
> MAO TSE-TUNG, chairman of the Chinese Communist Party and its preeminent theoretician until his death in 1976
> CHOU EN-LAI, Chinese Communist Party leader and the premier of the People's Republic of China (PRC) until his death in 1976
> LIN PIAO, Chinese Communist Party leader and the minister of defense of the PRC until his death in 1971
> HUA KUO-FENG, chairman of the Chinese Communist Party
> TENG HSIAO-PING, deputy chairman of the Chinese Communist Party and senior vice premier of the PRC
> CHIAO KUAN-HUA, minister of foreign affairs of the PRC

This timely review of the significant developments in Chinese foreign relations since the so-called Great Proletarian Cultural Revolution appears as one of the Westview Special Studies on China and East Asia. Robert G. Sutter, now with the Congressional Research Service of the Library of Congress, was for nine years an analyst on Chinese foreign affairs in the Central Intelligence Agency. He endeavors to present materials of interest to both the general reader and the specialist. For this purpose he has divided his slim volume into two equal parts. The first part provides a general overview and summary of the major turning points of the period; the second part concentrates on the policy of the People's Republic of China (PRC) toward specific countries and regions, as well as major policy issues. Throughout the volume the author makes use of a textual analysis of recently declassified reports of the New China News Agency (NCNA), as translated and published by the government of the United States.

The astounding internal upheavals of the Cultural Revolution had a tremendous impact on Chinese foreign policy. During this time China was reduced to relative inactivity in its external relations. Its propaganda posture was rigidly dogmatic. Only when the turmoil within China subsided was the strong ideological emphasis on furthering the world revolution gradually abandoned. Instead, a more rational and pragmatic pursuit of the national interest was adopted. It may be said that after the Cultural Revolution the PRC returned to "normal" diplomacy.

The Cultural Revolution began in May, 1966, when classes were stopped before the school term ended. Mao Tse-tung had encouraged the students to forego their studies and to exert themselves on behalf of the proper political "line." Chairman Mao exhorted China's youth to fight against elitism and privilege. This meant, in effect, to turn against the established Communist Party organization. Irregular so-called Red Guard organizations sprang up everywhere and spread the revolutionary fever. Allowed to roam freely, the Red Guards effected total disruption of the educational system. Faculty members, in particular, fell victim to humiliations and purges. Under the slogan "seizure of power from below" the Cultural Revolution gained momentum and led to the purging of many prominent leaders who had been identified as opponents of Mao's proper line.

Ostensibly, the network of Maoist forces battled the regular party organization to eradicate revisionism. Mao continued to place the same high value on egalitarianism and mass participation that he had insisted upon during the original revolutionary struggle. Perhaps he was sincere in wanting to fight an apparent historical pattern, wherein revolutions, once institutionalized, promptly allow for the emergence of a new privileged class. However, it is more plausible to view this period as an elemental power struggle. By throwing China into chaos, the Maoists sought to regain absolute control over the shaping of China's destiny. In the end, the moderate elements, looking to Chou En-lai for guidance, seemed to prevail. They were able to call a halt to the Cultural Revolution in the latter part of 1968.

The Ministry of Foreign Affairs was severely affected by the disruptions and the disorganization. Thus, the new Chinese foreign policy emerged only gradually. Some conflict within the leadership group over the general orientation of foreign policy remained. The major issue was the nature of relations with the two superpowers. Lin Piao, earlier considered Mao's heir, apparently opted for a renewed association with the Soviet Union. In this he was strongly opposed by those working strenuously to free China from any Soviet influences whatever. Ultimately, Lin's violent death in 1971 appears to have settled the matter. In any event, it helped clear the way for the eventual normalization of relations with the United States.

As an indication of the limited resumption of diplomacy in 1968, Sutter notes a succession of official visitors to Peking from Third World states. Clearly, Peking sought to gain a position of leadership respecting the nonaligned developing countries of the world. To further this objective, a posture of fervent opposition to both superpowers was assumed. However, the thrust of Chinese diplomatic activities was obviously designed to achieve more leverage against the Soviet Union. Cases in point were the stepped-up efforts to solidify relations with Albania and Romania. Regarding Romania, the Chinese were able to take advantage of that country's strong desire to free itself from Soviet domination by refusing to go along with certain Soviet-sponsored measures affecting Eastern Europe. The efforts to improve relations with such Asian neighbors as North Vietnam and North Korea, although of mixed success, may also be noted in this context. In general, Peking sought to exploit every opportunity in relations with countries in the Soviet sphere which could lead to a reduction of Soviet influence over them.

By 1970 China was following a clearly discernible pragmatic foreign policy. The guiding theme was the improvement of its position vis-à-vis the Soviet Union. When the United States signaled readiness to adjust its China policy, discussions between the two countries commenced in Warsaw. These first exploratory talks were suspended for a while by China, in protest over the American incursion into Cambodia. Yet, even at this stage China's propaganda was projecting the United States as being far less a threat to world peace than the Soviet Union. With the ending of the American involvement in Southeast Asia, the stage was set for the normalization of affairs. President Richard Nixon's trip to China in February, 1972, signaled the advent of a new era in Sino-American relations. It was an event of enormous symbolic importance, and it set in motion the process which culminated in the assumption of full diplomatic relations in January, 1979.

At the Tenth Congress of the Chinese Communist Party in August, 1973, ranking officials exuded a new confidence respecting China's international position. In part this may have been a necessary maneuver to justify the new pragmatic approach. The moderate group was being challenged by leftist elements led by a group later condemned as "the gang of four." A so-called anti-Confucius campaign was launched to discredit the moderates. This challenge was successfully deflected and did not significantly disrupt the foreign policy process.

The perceived security threat posed by the Soviet Union has been the overriding concern of the foreign policy makers. Countless warnings of the designs of the Soviet Union have been issued. Invariably, that country has been branded as "the most dangerous source of war." During the last several years of the period under review, China has tried strenuously to undermine Soviet-American détente. The European Security Conference in Helsinki was condemned as the "new Munich," and the Western powers were warned about the dire consequences of appeasement.

The causes of the Sino-Soviet conflict were complex and varied. In good measure they were, of course, of an ideological nature. Following the death of Stalin, the Soviet Union was seen as pursuing a revisionist course, leading to a resumption of capitalism and resort to imperialism. To some extent personality clashes were also a factor. Specifically noted in this connection has been the dislike Khrushchev and Mao had for each other. The historical conflicts of claims over territory added yet another dimension to the problem. China's relations with the Soviet Union began to deteriorate noticeably in the late 1950's. In retrospect, the expanding Sino-Soviet split must be seen as having had the most powerful influence on the course of Chinese foreign policy. There were some mutual gestures to improve relations in 1970. However, they obviously were not very fruitful, for the tone of China's anti-Soviet propaganda became more strident than ever.

1976 brought major leadership changes to China. Three of the foremost leaders died in short succession. These were the chairman of the Chinese Communist Party Mao Tse-tung, the chairman of the National People's Congress (China's chief of state) Chu Te, and the premier Chou En-lai. Hua Kuo-feng emerged as Mao's successor. Chou's protégé Teng Hsiao-ping was removed from his posts a second time in the ensuing power struggle, only to make a third comeback. Eventually Teng would become the effective head of government, indicating the clear ascendancy of the moderate, pragmatically oriented faction.

These leaders have realized that a foreign policy essentially free of ideological encumbrances can most effectively serve China's vital national interests. According to Sutter, the desirable goals include reestablishment of control over regions traditionally subject to China; gaining a stronger position in world affairs and as a result, being more secure in the face of the Soviet threat; and the creation of favorable conditions for the rapid development and modernization of China. China has made impressive strides in the past. However, particularly in regard to internal development, it has a long way to go before satisfactory levels are reached. For this reason the normalization of relations with the United States and Japan assumed a very high priority. The Chinese leaders had come to realize that the isolation of their country brought heavy liabilities and dangers, with very little security. Thus, as soon as conditions permitted, Peking looked outward again. Its more flexible foreign policy led to a broadening of relationships with the non-Communist world.

The result of these developments was the emergence of a multipolar pattern, assigning nearly equal positions to four powers: the United States, the Soviet Union, Japan, and China. This pattern entailed at least the potential for greater stability and the lessening of the likelihood of big-power military confrontations in regional conflicts. More recent developments have reaffirmed, however, that the greatest danger lies in an open conflict between the Soviet Union and China. Teng Hsiao-ping continues to promote a united front in opposition to "hegemony," the Chinese codeword for Soviet expansionism. China has been countering Soviet moves to fill the power vacuum in Southeast Asia created by the American withdrawal. Teng noted pointedly to the countries in the area how foolish it would be to let the wolf come in through the back door after they had rid themselves of the tiger in the parlor. Meanwhile, Vietnam had moved into the Soviet orbit and received the necessary assistance for its own expansionist designs in Laos and Cambodia. More recently, and outside Sutter's coverage, Vietnam confidently dared to invade and occupy Cambodia. The Cambodian regime, however despicable, was under the protective mantle of China. To the Chinese, therefore, the Vietnamese action was an unacceptable provocation, requiring a strong response. As will be recalled, shortly after

Teng's visit to the United States in January, 1979, a punitive military action against Vietnam was launched. By teaching the Vietnamese a lesson, China hoped to erase the blemish on its prestige in the region. At this point, of course, it is still an open question as to who, the Soviet Union or China, has overplayed its hand in Vietnam.

More importantly, however, the Chinese actions in Vietnam fit into Peking's general scheme of attempting to upset the détente policies of the superpowers. Thus, strong countermeasures on the part of the Soviet Union would play directly into the hands of Peking in this regard. At the same time, a weak response, or none at all, would discredit the Soviet Union as a superpower. In either case China would appear to benefit. The general situation in Asia is very fluid, containing many unanswered questions. These considerations go beyond the scope of Sutter's volume. Sutter does not indulge in speculations regarding the future. He presents a straightforward review of Chinese foreign policy. As such, it is not particularly helpful for reflection and evaluation, but it is certainly very useful as a reference and information source.

Manfred Grote

Sources for Further Study

American Academy of Political and Social Science. Annals. CDXLI, January, 1979, p. 207.

Choice. XV, July, 1978, p. 754.

CLEARED FOR LANDING

Author: Ann Darr (1920-   )
Publisher: Dryad Press (Washington and San Francisco). 76 pp. $8.95; paperback $3.95
Type of work: Poetry

The third collection by a poet of unusually intense vision and rare economy of style

In her earlier collections, *St. Ann's Gut* and *The Myth of a Woman's Fist*, Ann Darr established herself as a poet of enviable gifts. Her range is wide, from short poems which seem to arise from fleeting impressions, to long poems which grow from long meditation on hard matters, some of them too painful to be handled by any but the most strongminded of poets.

Like many other poets in recent years, Darr has gone from a commercial publisher to a small press. Her first two books were published by William Morrow; *Cleared for Landing* is published by Dryad Press, an energetic small publisher. The particular reasons for this do not much matter. Whether Morrow had a chance at this book and missed it, or whether Darr simply began to see the disadvantages of placing poetry with large companies whose policy is that poems do not sell, she has found in Dryad Press a publisher willing to present her poems in a handsome format, and to stand by the book until it is sold out. Increasingly, established poets as well as relative beginners find in the small presses a hospitality to their work which the commercial publishers could not have mustered even in the best of times.

This collection takes its title from "Cleared for Approach, Cleared for Landing," a long and harrowing poem which makes up the book's fifth and final section. But the title resonates as well throughout the first four sections; the phrase comes to be a metaphor for all sorts of clearings and landings. The ten poems in the first section, "What Shall We Say to Our Sister?," are various in tone, but most of them hover successfully between some private event—their source—and full disclosure. "Dear James Wright," for example, in the form of a note to that poet, touches upon a private matter, and goes on to something even more private, yet more interesting and haunting. Halfway through the poem, the speaker says "I am glad/you are on the wagon. Lengthening/your life is a good idea." Then there is a recollection of having hidden a wagon beside a river before going out in a canoe; the wagon disappears, because thievery turns up in the countryside as well as the city. Then the poem turns back, but more deeply, on the old cliché for giving up drink:

> but you know about rivers—
> the goddamned ever-flowing
> junk-clogged rivers flowing
> inside and out. If I can ever
> find another wagon I ought to

> climb on. All my braincells
> are washing downstream.

The mystery in this small poem is a result of the skill, not only with which
the phrase "on the wagon" is worked until its power is renewed, but also the
skill which keeps the reader from knowing for certain whether the wagon was
stolen by a person or by rising water. Things wash downstream in either case,
and we are left at last with those few essentials which we might seem to take
with us when we die.

This view is hauntingly presented in "It Is the Breathing," a beautiful short
poem about the death of an old woman. Here again, the private aspects of the
experience are withheld: we do not know anything about the old woman's
relationship to the poet or to the speaker of the poem; it is clear only that the
relationship matters. In the first stanza, the speaker and the old woman are
placed far apart:

> Nine hundred miles away I hear the breathing.
> Under the oxygen, the little flippety door
> moves open and shut, open and shut.
> It is the breathing that keeps her alive
> and somewhere under the lonely tick of the clock
> the air comes on like muffling comforters.

The economy and power of this stanza are worth trying to explain. There is
intrinsic force in the apparent subject matter, as it is presented in the first and
fourth lines, flat and expository in tone. But the language is equal to the subject: "the little flippety door" is a frightening image, everything coming
down, at last, to a trivial mechanism; and the oxymoronic "muffling com-
forters" suggest that, if the breathing "keeps her alive," the air will finally
smother her.

The woman's age is mentioned in the second stanza:

> She is standing at the window
> gasping for air she breathed in
> 90 years ago. She hears the wind
> in her ears but the leaves hang limp.
> *They* are calling her to come over, come over.

The echo of a childhood game leads into another recollection, which swims
up, dreamlike, with such particularity that a manufacturer's name is included;
in a poem of such vagueness about certain facts, this specificity is brilliantly
placed:

> She steps out the window onto the keyboard
> of the old Knabe grand. Its leaves, its grapes,
> its lion feet uphold her. Now the river
> is running through Grand Street
> and on her piano raft, she floats away.

This stanza turns back to echo the "limp" leaves of the second stanza as they become part of the upholding piano, the "grand" in Grand Street, and as she floats away, the old woman has all that she wished for as she stood at the window. There is much that one might like to ask about her, but most of the questions are gossip, and to have answered them might have filled the poem with the cold humorlessness of confessionalism. All that this poem needs is here.

The second section of *Cleared for Landing*, "Relative Matter," begins with a poem of the same title. It is addressed to someone who had been invited for a visit, but who is no longer welcome, because hatred has washed through the household like a volcano, leaving nothing unscarred. The end of the poem, in a flat malediction that has some of the force of ancient curses, makes it clear that the person addressed is somehow responsible for all that has happened:

> We have only the slightest clue
> as to the beginnings. Someone
> mentioned your name. the way you dam-
> age things.

Here, as in a few other passages in the collection, Darr deviates from normal typography in small ways, catching the exact tone of a voice by letting an uncapitalized sentence follow a period, and by breaking the next-to-last word. (Here, incidentally, is another advantage of working with a small press that cares about its work: one does not automatically assume that there are typographical errors in the above stanza.) Out of context, these lines might make the broken *damage* appear to be a metrical necessity, since the other three lines are octosyllabics. But in the rest of the poem, though the fourth lines are all disyllabic, there is enough variety in other lines, which range from five to ten syllables, to draw attention away from the meter toward the word itself.

"Relative Matter," as a section title, might suggest a too-cute grouping of poems about relatives. The first poem dispels this notion immediately; there is nothing cute here. There are poems about births, daughters, anniversaries, and gifts for loved ones, but they all carry beneath their surfaces the heavy knowledge that things run toward their slow conclusions. When this fact is faced with some humor, the result is like "The Pot-Bellied Anachronism," in which the speaker explains why she has "this bulging belly." The stanzas make up a list of reasons, some of them wistful, but most of them direct and almost hard-nosed, as in the last stanza:

> I am making a statement. That I can be any
> shape I want, even pudding-shaped and
> nobody can stop me.

And yet, at the end of the poem, one notices the force of that *nobody*, there at the head of the last line, and realizes that it includes the speaker: *nobody, not even I*, it says—and that is one of the central themes of this book.

The third section of the book is a long poem—one hundred and eleven lines in four parts—called "What Are You Most Afraid Of?" On the surface, it is an account of a reading trip involving Darr and the poet Samual Allen, and much of the description recounts a mad drive over the Maryland countryside, Darr and Allen trying to keep up with a fresh-faced young lunatic who has offered to lead them to some social engagement connected with the reading. There are passages of genuine humor here, especially if one has any familiarity with the awkwardnesses that come up regularly during reading trips. But the poem finally fails to hold together, because too many things are attempted, too many tones and deep questions introduced which need more leisure to develop, even in a poem whose fragmentary, transitionless progression is earned by the high-speed setting. Too much is left to the imagination, given the fact that one must have some experience of poetry-reading trips to enter fully into what is happening here.

The fourth section of *Cleared for Landing* is called "Filling in the Blanks." It contains eleven poems, one of them bearing that title; all the same, it is tempting to think of the section title as a way of saying that these poems are more miscellaneous than unified. This is not to say that they are inferior to the other poems; several of them are quite fine, notably "For Great Grandmother and Her Settlement House," "'Things Are Still Coming Ashore,'" "And the Temperature Dropping," and two strange poems spoken by imaginary characters, "Mad Hannah" and "Gussie Wears Her Red Suspenders."

These last two are interesting as examples of a poetic method which increases in currency these days. Many poets, feeling perhaps that their established voices have cut them off from subjects or tones which continue to engage them emotionally and imaginatively, have adopted *personae* in order to gain a certain freedom. In the modern period, of course, several poets, Eliot among them, took cues from Browning's monologues; but the current phenomenon is not quite the same thing. Darr's use of Hannah and Gussie, who have turned up in her earlier books, is more like Yeats's use of Crazy Jane, or Berryman's use of Henry. These poets returned to their characters from time to time, so that their poems might say things the poet felt unwilling to say without a mask; but through the mask, the poet speaks for himself in a way that Eliot did not in "The Love Song of J. Alfred Prufrock." So it is easy to imagine Darr, confronting an idea for a poem, wondering how it might go, and deciding that this is a time when Hannah should speak.

In this case, the anecdote involves an exchange between Hannah and "Old Uncle Solemn," who warns Hannah that his brother will not respect her womanhood "now/our mother's gone." She appears to understand him, he is relieved, and the poem ends,

> Who would tell him that his message came

years and years too late?
Nobody. Nobody nobody.

The anecdote alone has not quite the power that the voice gives it, the care-fully placed period in the last line being one instance of the distinctive inten-sity toward which the poem rises.

The title poem, "Cleared for Approach, Cleared for Landing," is based on the crash, about five years ago, of TWA Flight 514 into the western side of Mount Weather, on its approach to Dulles International Airport. The subject's intractability is awesome; Darr has a handle on it, first, because she was within earshot of the crash, and is familiar with the terrain; and, second, because she understands aviation, having flown with the Woman's Airforce Service Pilots in the Army Air Force during World War II. Her physical proximity to the event makes possible an emotional involvement which often must seem willed in poems about public disasters. By facing her foreknowledge of the crash, Darr places herself in the midst of the event:

> At eleven 09 on Sunday morning
> the plane droned low over our house.
> 20 seconds later it flew into Weather Mountain.
>
> I am not responsible. I have accurately
> figured that I could not have reached
> the telephone, called the field . . .
>
> Now you know who I think I am. And
> guilty of everything.

Darr's knowledge of flying enables her to work with some of the docu-mentary residue of the crash; the fifth and sixth sections of this long poem consist largely of transcripts, first of the communication between the plane and the tower, and then of the interrogation of the controller during the F.A.A. investigation. This latter section is particularly strong; Darr has the nerve to give the controller an unspoken interior monologue, set in italics, amidst the questions and answers from the transcript. The effect, however, is not to at-tribute thoughts to a real person, and thus risk presumption; rather, the *per-sona* of the whole poem enters the controller, as Tiresias in *The Waste Land* has "foresuffered all."

"Cleared for Approach, Cleared for Landing" is a large, ambitious, and successful poem. It is one of the triumphs of the collection that the shorter poems are not obliterated by it.

Henry Taylor

Sources for Further Study

Book World. December 3, 1978, p. E6.
Library Journal. CIII, October 15, 1978, p. 2116.

COLLECTED POEMS

Author: Basil Bunting
Publisher: Oxford University Press (New York). 152 pp. $10.95
Type of work: Poetry

Sixty-eight poems written over the past fifty years which demonstrate the austerity and erudition, as well as the poetic development, of one of this century's most conscious and modest literary craftsmen

In 1949, Basil Bunting wrote a short poem which he called "On the Fly-Leaf of Pound's Cantos." It opens with the comment, "There are the Alps. What is there to say about them?" The implications are clear, and to most students of English literature of the twentieth century, inescapably true: the accomplishment in verse of the late Ezra Pound is as baffling as it is massive.

Bunting ends that poem with the words, "There are the Alps,/ fools! Sit down and wait for them to crumble." Though Bunting's poem pays homage to Pound, it provides good advice, which the Northumbrian poet took a few years later. Bunting's publication in 1966 of his long work "Briggflatts," an auto-biographical work as he calls it, marked his final declaration of independence from the method and manner of Pound. Rather than to deny the prosodic and technical lessons to be learned from Pound, Bunting absorbed the lessons so wholly that he could, at last, return wholeheartedly to the language of his region and the concerns of his homeland.

Reading the collected poems of Basil Bunting seems, in some ways, like embarking on a highly selective survey of twentieth century English poetry. Unlike most surveys, it lacks inferior work, for Bunting excises and revises ruthlessly. As early as 1929, he addressed a poem "To a Poet who advised me to preserve my fragments and false starts." The upshot of the poem is that Bunting's "numerous cancellations" prefer the garbage can to "printed ignominy."

The preface to the 1968 Fulcrum Press edition of Bunting's *Collected Poems* says that "heaped together," the poems he had written "here and there now and then over forty years and four continents . . . make a book." Now, ten years later, Bunting has added a three-line preface to the new edition of his poems. The new edition, this diffident poet writes, gives him a chance "to put right a few words and stops the compositor got wrong, and to add four short new poems." His admirers in England and the United States will regret that by the writer's stern standards, a fifth new poem "seemed better lost."

Sixty-eight poems may seem a slender stock on which to base a literary reputation, but that reputation by now is established. The future may raise or lower Bunting's stock in accord with literary vogue, but he is unlikely to drop from sight. He has never claimed a place among the major writers, but the nature of his originality wins admiration from more readers—particularly other poets—every year.

A friend of Ezra Pound (with whom he worked to edit the *Active Anthology*, 1931) and of Louis Zukofsky, Bunting acknowledges their influence upon his work—along with that of "poets long dead whose names are obvious." Bunting's 1968 preface names those influences: Wordsworth and Dante, Horace, Wyatt and Malherbe, Manuchehri and Ferdosi, Villon, Whitman, Edmund Spenser. The list underlines Bunting's eclecticism and erudition. For a biographical dictionary, he wrote of himself: "educated at Ackworth, Leighton Park, Wormwood Scrubs Prison and the London School of Economics. Successively music critic, idler, soldier, diplomat and journalist. Travelled much. Read much in several tongues."

The final section of Bunting's *Collected Poems* is devoted to what he calls "Overdrafts," or translations. A note cryptically warns the reader—"It would be gratuitous to assume that a mistranslation is unintentional." He does not hesitate to intrude the expression "fit wine for a pope" into a translation of Horace, and, after several verse paragraphs in another poem, he breaks into his own work with the comment, "—and why Catullus bothered to write pages and pages of this drivel mystifies me." In a neat turn-about, he provides ("Verse and Version") a poem in English by Louis Zukofsky followed by his Latin Version.

These are not the poems for which Bunting is best known, though his proficiency in the classical languages and modern languages doubtless aided him in honing his diction to its present fine edge. Bunting writes (in his preface) that he has set down words "as a musician pricks his score, not to be read in silence, but to trace in the air a pattern of sound that may sometimes . . . be pleasing." The reader who takes this statement at face value may safely forget the poet's considerable learning and his allusions. As Bunting writes, "unabashed boys and girls" may enjoy his poems.

Unfortunately, such "unabashed boys and girls" are hard to find. Poems so self-consciously hewn, even when they achieve perfectly natural rhythms, repel readers accustomed to plentiful "filler" in language. The taut muscles of Bunting's verse shame the sloppy speaker and reader—who retaliate by finding Bunting "hard to understand."

Perhaps it will help some readers to know that Bunting's concern is not to be understood; he writes in the firm belief that, like music, poetry is to be heard. The "living voice" of the poem *is* the poetry; extracting a bundle of maxims or philosphic ideas is not the point. Too often, however, Bunting assumes knowledge, both linguistic and factual, which few of his readers today will have—or care to secure.

Early and late, Bunting's poems reflect the breadth of his reading and experience. He has lived in Italy and France as well as in Iran. He has visited the United States, and, for a time, he was captain of a private yacht sailing the Mediterranean and crossing the Atlantic. His long poem "The Spoils" (1951) is sensuously redolent of the Middle East, where he served as a Royal Air

Force officer and later as a civil servant and journalist. An earlier long poem, "Villon," written in Rapallo while he was with Pound in 1925, derives in part from his experiences in prison as a conscientious objector during the final years of World War I. The Nazi threat to civilization in the 1930's led him to abandon his pacifism.

Among the earliest poems Bunting has preserved, "Villon" demonstrates the depth of Pound's and T. S. Eliot's influence on the young writer. Bunting objectifies a very personal experience, that of his imprisonment, and through a shifting time-focus allows the events and details of the poem to grow larger and more generally significant. To dismiss "Villion" as either "Poundian" or "Imagistic" misses the mark. Bunting *was* an imagist; *Poetry Magazine*'s editors, he writes, "have been kind to me one after another." At the magazine, with Pound as its foreign correspondent, writing which deviated from the rhythms of the metronome and which dealt directly and concretely with its subject was likely to win editorial approval. *Poetry Magazine* nurtured modern poetry.

"Villon" moves toward the hardness and precision of much of the best recent poetry. The poem's reliance on the historical, as well as its diction, makes one think more of a poet like Browning than of Wordsworth. Rhyme works frequently, but freely, in the poem. As early as "Villon," Bunting apparently recognized the importance of quantity, or duration, in English verse. In 1966, his "Briggflatts" would exploit that awareness more fully.

Bunting opens the notes of the new edition of his *Collected Poems* with the statement that notes "are a confession of failure, not a palliation of it, still less a reproach to the reader, but may allay some small irritations." Most readers will find the notes to "Briggflatts" more useful than any of the other notes: the poet fills better than a page with simple definitions of Northumbrian words. One note, for instance, says "we have *burns* in the east, *becks* in the west, but no brooks or creeks." Bunting's notes emphasize the importance of the Northumbrian tongue. "Southrons," he writes, "would maul the music of many lines in 'Briggflatts.' " One writer has said one should read "Briggflatts" with broad, soft vowel sounds and sharply enunciated consonants. Another critic says Bunting marries "dour, arresting imagery with suggestive abstractions" to produce a poetry "of barren magnificence and no ease."

Bunting labels "Briggflatts" as an autobiography, "but not a record of fact." He adds, "The truth of the poem is of another kind." "Briggflatts" marks the poet's return to his region and his rediscovery of his native dialect. Like much twentieth century literature, the poem is as much "about" poetry and the making of poetry as it is about anything else. The poem's first section sets in opposition (or perhaps complementary relations) a "slowworm" and a stonemason. Both will recur, and sometimes the slowworm recurs at climatic points in sections of the poem; Section Three, for instance, concludes: "So he rose and led home silently through clean woodland/where every bough repeated the slowworm's song." Both the slowworm and the mason relate to themes of persistence and dissolution. "A mason times his mallet/ to a lark's twitter." The mason works until the "stone spells a name/ naming none,/ a man abolished." The poet then names the "shining slowworm part of the marvel." The mason stirs: "Words!/ Pens are too light./ Take a chisel to write." A page later, the first section ends with these lines:

> It is easier to die than to remember.
> Name and date
> split in soft slate
> a few months obliterate.

Bunting's poem opens, then, with variations of the *carpe diem* theme and with an echo of Theophile Gautier's injunction to the artist to work in durable materials. With true Anglo-Saxon fatalism, Bunting allows the "sweet tenor bull" of the poem's first line to become *beef*—and he gives concrete form to passing time with the statement that "amputated years ache."

Section Two of "Briggflatts" touches upon the relationship of the poet to the rest of society. The "Poet appointed," writes Bunting, "dare not decline/ to walk among the bogus. . . ." The poet, "sick, self-maimed, self-hating obstinate," mates "beauty with squalor to beget lines still-born." The section ends with an extended allusion to the Queen of Crete, Pasiphae, whose desire for a bull led to her giving birth to the minotaur. Neither flesh nor spirit flinched, Bunting writes, "till it had gloried in unlike creation."

The entire poem achieves unity through reiteration of specific images and variations of those images. The poet manages through sharp precision of language and juxtaposition of images to make the familiar strange and the strange familiar. The poem's coda opens, "A strong song tows/ us, long earsick," thus suggesting again the power of native speech and native rhythms to *move* people—both literally and figuratively.

"Briggflatts" is Bunting's most important achievement, but he could not have earned that poem, with all its austere richness, without what came before. Such poems as "Chomei at Toyama," written in 1932, reveal much about the strategies of Bunting's mind and his ability to make poetry of foreign sources; still, that poem stands more nearly as a literary artifact than as a poem with its own life. Interest in the Orient inevitably accompanied the imagist and *avant-garde* literary activities of the 1930's, but Bunting's erudition is rarely as satisfying as his purely poetic efforts.

The ordering of poems in Bunting's *Collected Poems* sometimes disturbs, as, for instance, when one goes abruptly from "Briggflatts" to "Chomei at Toyama." The book's third section, "First Book of Odes," ends with strong poems of the 1940's, followed by the "Second Book of Odes," with poems dating from 1964 to 1975. The final three poems in this section are among the four short new poems Bunting added to the new edition. The fourth new poem is a translation of Horace (1971). Going from Bunting's work of the 1970's to a translation of 1927 provides a jolt, particularly since the final poem in the "Second Book of Odes" is the truly extraordinary "At Briggflatts meetinghouse."

In twelve lines, this particular ode recapitulates the themes of "Briggflatts." Bunting proves here what he has gained in some fifty years of writing. As much as any poem in the collection, this short one makes the reader think of the naturalness of art. "True ease in writing comes from art, not chance," wrote Alexander Pope. The lines here are as natural as they are memorable. They make one think also of the contemporary American poet James Dickey, who has said that he revises his poems to take the "worked-on quality" out of them.

Useful though it is to have all of Basil Bunting's poems in a single volume, many readers will prefer to linger over the major accomplishments since 1951, "The Spoils," "Briggflatts," and the odes of "The Second Book of Odes." Other poems in the collection deserve study, but the later poems give sheer pleasure. Hugh Kenner was right when he said there is no poet better than Bunting.

Leon V. Driskell

Sources for Further Study

Book World. July 9, 1978, p. E6.
Books and Bookmen. XXIII, May, 1978, p. 43.
Christian Science Monitor. LXX, September 18, 1978, p. B10.
Harper's Magazine. CCLVII, November, 1978, p. 81.
New York Times Book Review. July 2, 1978, p. 7.

COLLECTED POEMS 1940-1978

Author: Karl Shapiro (1913-   )
Publisher: Random House (New York). 341 pp. $15.00
Type of work: Poetry

Selections from ten volumes of poetry, along with new and uncollected verse, by the major contemporary American poet

With the publication of *Collected Poems 1940-1978*, Karl Shapiro's high standing among a select group of major mid-twentieth century American poets may be more firmly established. The collection includes poems from ten volumes: *Person, Place and Thing* (1942), *The Place of Love* (also 1942 but printed in a limited edition), *V-Letter and Other Poems* (1944), *Trial of a Poet* (1947), *Poems 1940-1953* (1953), *Poems of a Jew* (1958), *The Bourgeois Poet* (1964), *Selected Poems* (1968), *White-Haired Lover* (1968), and *Adult Bookstore* (1976). In addition, Shapiro includes fifteen new, uncollected poems. With very few exceptions, the poet's choices are judicious. Here are all his famous (that is to say, widely anthologized) poems. Also included, of course, are poems that have been slower to find their audience. For example, Shapiro selects sixty-nine pieces — the greatest number of poems from any single volume — from *The Bourgeois Poet*, a collection that originally was received with mixed reviews by the critics, some of whom were disappointed by the author's stylistic experimentation. In retrospect that volume, together with several other later books that have extended the technical range of Shapiro's craft beyond the already familiar work of the 1940's, seems part of the poet's organic achievement.

To appreciate the magnitude of that achievement, one must examine the full range of Shapiro's work, from the early sharply detailed, often grimly realistic poems of his first two major volumes, to the more leisurely style of his later books of verse. In *Person, Place and Thing*, Shapiro adopts for common, often banal modern subjects a witty metaphysical mode, involving the ironies, paradoxes, and arresting metaphors typical of seventeenth century verse. "The Fly," for example, is a contemporary conceit that may well be compared to Donne's "The Flea." In vigorous, unsentimental poems such as "Auto Wreck," "Waitress," "Mongolian Idiot," and "Elegy Written on a Frontporch," Shapiro anatomizes the modern mechanical world like a deft surgeon cutting away at gristle and bone. Skeptical of romantic idealism, Shapiro in his early poems writes: "I see too many who romanced/Defeat, unmasculine, debased;/The striptease puritans who danced/The long lewd ritual of waste." If these lines remind one of Ezra Pound, Shapiro also sounds much like T. S. Eliot in such poems as "The Glutton" or "Guineapig," showing his revulsion toward vulgarity. Perhaps the most characteristic poem of this volume, "Scyros," is a masterful expression of anger and disgust at the corruption of the modern world.

But Shapiro's sensibility is not the same as Eliot's or Pound's. Poems of his first volume (an earlier slim collection, *Poems*, appeared in 1935 but has not been reprinted), though brilliant in execution, now seem emotionally forced, strident. The tensions of authentic seventeenth century verse spring from metaphysical oppositions in the thinking of poets like Donne or Herbert. But in Shapiro, the metaphysical technique is intellectually simulated, although the poet's energy in creating conceits is certainly real enough. Often Shapiro creates tensions from the arresting metaphors of his opening lines: "The doctor punched my vein/The captain called me Cain" ("Scyros"), or "O hideous little bat, the size of snot" ("The Fly"), or "To hurt the Negro and avoid the Jew/Is the curriculum" ("University"). In working out these metaphors, however, the poet rarely expresses an emotional equivalent of his intellectually structured conceit.

With his second significant volume, *V-Letter and Other Poems*, for which he received the Pulitzer Prize at the age of thirty-one, Shapiro more closely welded the sensibility of wit to that of emotion. Most of the poems in this book reveal the technical virtuosity of *Person, Place and Thing*; the same unsentimental, shrewd observation of sharp details; the same mixture of anger and disgust. But the truculence of that collection gives way to the poet's more characteristic voice of reasonableness, of generosity and compassion. In celebrated poems like "V-Letter," "Elegy for a Dead Soldier," "Christmas Eve: Australia," "Troop Train," and "The Intellectual," he speaks as the conscience of the war-embattled generation—a generation neither "lost" nor muddled, but grimly fighting an unglamorous, necessary struggle for survival. Shapiro reduces his ironies to ambiguities ("Piano," "The Second-Best Bed"); and in "Satire: Anxiety" and "Lord, I Have Seen Too Much," he writes with tenderness about his own and mankind's limitations. To these poems that deal more personally with waste and disaster he adds pieces that reflect a lifelong examination of his Jewishness (his father was a Jew, his mother a Roman Catholic). In "The Synagogue," "Jew," and "Shylock," he attempts to comprehend the dominant side of his mixed heritage.

Shapiro's third major volume, *Trial of a Poet* (1947), continues the process of introspection. "Recapitulations," the most ambitious work from that volume, is a brief (perhaps partly ironic) intellectual autobiography. Included in this book are other notable poems, chiefly "Homecoming," "The Progress of Faust," and "In the Waxworks." Also included are prose poems such as "The New Ring" and "The Dirty Word," which show the poet's attempts to loosen his style to a more conversational manner.

In the retrospective volume *Poems 1940-1953*, Shapiro continues to experiment with different subjects in a more relaxed structure. The major achievement of this volume is his seven-part *Adam and Eve*, in which Shapiro's fine lyrical voice, evident even in his most abrasive pieces, sings with seductive harmonies. In *Poems of a Jew* (1958), the poet advances his lyrical range in

introspective verse of great intensity, such as "The Jew at Christmas Eve,"
"The First Time," and "The Crucifix in the Filing Cabinet."

   With *The Bourgeois Poet* (1964), Shapiro marks his most significant departure from his tightly constructed early verse. In this volume he treats details of
the commonplace as well as of the great world, not as a detached, ironical
observer, but as a participant. A middle-class intellectual, "professor with
tenure," he laments his loss of hair ("one by one my troops desert"), saunters
by the window of a publishing company ("And I know, like a secret, they are
printing my book of poems"), and gossips casually about a dermatologist, a
poor relation, about "editing *Poetry*" (for he was indeed editor of *Poetry, A
Magazine of Verse* from 1950 to 1956)— mixing trivial and serious subjects.
Some reviewers, mistaking the *persona* of the poems for the living poet,
criticized Shapiro as a poet in maundering decline, concerned mostly with
banalities. They neglected to perceive, however, that the poet had always been
a keen observer of small details; now, without affectation, he was placing
himself in the landscape of the verse. A representative poem from this volume,
"I Am an Atheist Who Says His Prayers," describes the writer less as the seer
of his generation than as an ordinary man who stumbles along with his fellows:
"I am of the race of the prematurely desperate."

   Similarly, *White-Haired Lover* (1968) reveals the poet vulnerable, ironies
turned upon himself. At times playful ("Words for a Wall-Painting"), passionate ("How Do You Walk?"), joyful ("I Am the Clown"), the poems of
this volume are understated, classical. Like Yeats, in his later verse Shapiro
becomes more receptive to joy. In "You Call These Poems?" (from *Selected
Poems*, 1968), he summarizes his poetical career:

> For years I used to write poems myself
> That pleased the Moslems and Hindus of culture,
> Telling poems in iambic pentameter,
> With a masculine inversion in the second foot,
> Frozen poems with an ice-pick at the core,
> And lots of allusions from other people's books.

   Shapiro's most recent poetry, influenced as he says by William Carlos Williams, continues to experiment with both open and tightly constructed forms.
They reveal Shapiro's authentic concerns, neither "frozen" from artifical
strategies nor allusive of "other people's books." For his accomplishments he
shared the 1969 Bollinger Award for poetry with John Berryman. Like Berryman and a number of other major American poets of his generation — Theodore Roethke, Robert Lowell, James Merrill, Delmore Schwartz, Howard
Nemerov, to mention some conspicuous names—he has been both poet and
professor, both artist and critic, both private and public man. As a public man,
a voice of conscience, he has written poetry in the liberal tradition of skeptical
humanism. Serious, honest, realistic, decent: he has never sentimentalized his

vision to appeal to a mass audience, never betrayed his trust as an artist. Similarly, as a private man, he has written with candor and sensitivity about what it is like to be a human being in this troubled century: a Jew, a lover, a bourgeois poet. Though many writers of his generation in despair took to excessive drink, to drugs, or died by their own hands, he has chosen to live with dignity: conscientious, intelligent, resourceful. In "The Old Poet," he speaks with affection about "that radiance of old poets (those who surrendered power with a smile)." Shapiro has such a radiance. Let us hope that he has many more poems to write.

Leslie B. Mittleman

Sources for Further Study

Best Sellers. XXXVIII, September, 1978, p. 199.

Choice. XV, September, 1978, p. 874.

Commonweal. CV, November 10, 1978, p. 725.

Hudson Review. XXXI, Autumn, 1978, p. 543.

Nation. CCXXVII, November 11, 1978, p. 518.

THE COMPOSITION OF *FOUR QUARTETS*

Author: Helen Gardner
Publisher: Oxford University Press (New York). 239 pp. $32.50
Type of work: Literary history

A well presented, valuable study revealing the sources and experiences which lie behind T. S. Eliot's major work

In *The Composition of* Four Quartets, Dame Helen Gardner examines the process by which Eliot arrived at the final text of his major work, identifying the sources and experiences that lie behind Eliot's poem and presenting all of the changes Eliot made in the text. It is an admirable work of scholarship and an immensely rewarding one, not only for the richness of material Dame Helen has tenaciously gathered from her many years of researching what Eliot called the "litter" of composition, but for the economy, tact, and restraint of her presentation. This volume is, and is likely to remain, the finest study of *Four Quartets* that we have.

In Part One Gardner focuses on the origins and sources of the poem. She informs us that *Four Quartets* was not planned but grew into a unified whole over a period of eight years, from 1935 ("Burnt Norton") to 1943 ("Little Gidding"). Each poem is steeped in the experiences, both actual and remembered, of a man in his middle years:

> So here I am, in the middle way, having had twenty years—
> Twenty years largely wasted, the years of *l'entre deux guerres*-

Each poem arises from or is associated with a specific place, season, and element which helped Eliot in locating his thoughts and unifying his poetry. Although Gardner had remarked in *The Art of T. S. Eliot* (1950) that the sources of the poem are completely unimportant, that "no knowledge of the original context is required to give force to the new context," she now argues that a familiarity with the background of the poem is necessary in understanding the deeply personal, confessional nature of Eliot's work.

Many of the biographical sources Gardner cites are familiar. We already know, for example, that Eliot visited Burnt Norton, East Coker, and Little Gidding before writing each poem, and that the Dry Salvages refers to an area off the coast of Cape Ann, Massachusetts, which Eliot visited every summer in his childhood. But Gardner fleshes in these bare, known facts with qualifications (she tells us, for example, that Eliot knew nothing about the sinister history of Burnt Norton) and with additional details that enrich the possibilities of Eliot's intentions and reveal his dependence on deeply felt experiences as catalysts for the creative process.

For instance, Gardner remarks that Eliot visited Burnt Norton in the autumn of 1933 with Emily Hale, a close friend from his graduate years at Harvard, whom, she suspects, he had seen the year before while on a lecture tour of the

United States. It was after his reunion with Hale and his return from America that Eliot began to survey his life, questioning how he might have acted differently in his past. "It was a time of painful reflection," Gardner writes, "on what had been and what might have been, of memories intertwined with the scenes of childhood and young manhood."

In this reflective mood Eliot composed "Burnt Norton," with its theme of the actualities and potentialities of the past, as well as a series of landscape poems under the title "Words for Music," one of which, "New Hampshire," shows Eliot looking back to his Harvard days: "Children's voices in the orchard. . . . Twenty years and the spring is over." The similarity of the two poems is evident in their feeling, imagery, and musical patterning. But a further connection may also be made: that in both, Eliot had Emily Hale in mind. This connection between Hale and "Burnt Norton" is strengthened further by the fact that the garden referred to in the opening lines of "Burnt Norton" carries with it associations with another garden, that of Hale's aunt, Mrs. Perkins, which Eliot visited in the mid-1930's and to which he alludes directly in an unpublished poem, "A Valedictory/Forbidding Mourning: to the Lady of House" (1935) and indirectly in "Burnt Norton" in the lines: "Will the sunflower turn to us, will the clematis/Stray down, bend to us; tendril and spray."

Although "Burnt Norton" revolves generally around thoughts of what might have been, these biographical details offer a more specific interpretation: that in the poem Eliot is addressing Emily Hale on their former ties together. The evidence lends itself to this reading, but Gardner does not draw any conclusions about it nor does she gossip about its implications, as some critics have done. Rather, she steadfastly refrains from speculating on what might lie behind the background of "Burnt Norton" or of any of the other quartets. What matters, she implies in her cautious presentation, is that Eliot's four poems are meditations on the meaning of experience itself, and those experiences which inspired each poem, whether immediate, ancestral, or national in character, should be treated as impersonally as her remarks on the inclusion of the kingfisher in "Burnt Norton": "Just as, when asked for the significance of 'autumn,' Eliot replied simply that 'it *was* autumn' so here he might answer those who look for mystical meanings in the sunflower, clematis, and kingfisher: 'There *was* a clematis; there *was* a kingfisher.' " Gardner's approach is not only tactful but critically sound, for it pays attention where it is due—to the poem itself and not to matters that lay outside it.

Throughout Part One, Gardner emphasizes the biographical over the literary sources because so much of the poem comes from Eliot's life, and the literary sources, which are central to *The Waste Land*, are ancillary in *Four Quartets*. "The poems are poems of experience," she writes, "and are not built upon literary sources."

Those literary sources that are important to Eliot's intentions, however,

Gardner does examine, discriminating the allusions that warrant consideration of the context of the source from those which are merely occasional references or reminiscences of a lifetime's reading and thinking. (In her commentary in Part Two Gardner cites these latter sources.) She informs us, for example, that in "Burnt Norton" Eliot unconsciously combined Kipling's "They" with Elizabeth Barrett Browning's "The Lost Bower" in rendering his responses to time's losses and gains. In "The Dry Salvages" his indebtedness to Indian philosophy and literature is evident in a general way in such terms of expression as "you know and do not know" or "world not world, but that which is not world," and more specifically in Krishna's advice to Arjuna in the third movement of the poem. And, in what is her finest account of Eliot's literary sources, Gardner discusses how he attempted in "Little Gidding" to reproduce in English Dante's *terza rima* style with its simple alteration of masculine and feminine endings. On all of these matters and a great many more Gardner is germanely informative.

Occasionally, however, Dame Helen does fall into the trap of allusion-hunting. Her detailed discussion of the connection between Eliot's, "ruined millionaire" in "East Coker" and the character of Zeus in Gide's *Le Prométhée mal enchaîne*, for instance, is unpersuasive and not in keeping with her established guidelines. So, too, are her remarks on the influence of J. H. Shorthouse's *John Inglesant* on "Little Gidding." On the whole, however, Gardner's treatment of the literary background of *Four Quartets* is balanced and restrained in her interpretations.

In Park One Gardner places *Four Quartets* in its contextual setting. In Part Two she gives us the text itself, including all of the changes in wording, phrasing, rhyming, and organization which Eliot made in the writing of the poem as well as his published comments on it. In the text of "Little Gidding," for example, Gardner presents all five drafts of the poem, ten letters from Eliot commenting on it, the first corrected proof, and the final text. The record of these revisions on which Gardner has judiciously chosen to be complete rather than selective offers us a unique opportunity to examine how Eliot's mind worked and how he wrestled with words and their meaning to find the truth of his feelings, and the truth feelings point to. As he writes in one of the most eloquent, confessional passages of the poem, this "toil with language" was almost always an effusive yet exciting venture for him:

> Trying to learn to use words, and every attempt
> Is a wholly new start, and a different kind of failure
> Because one has only learnt to get the better of words
> For the thing one no longer has to say, or the way in which
> One is no longer disposed to say it. And so each venture
> Is a new beginning, a raid on the inarticulate

Also included in Part Two are the comments, queries, and changes in the text which Eliot's friends and advisers made during the composition of the poem. The fact that these suggestions were committed to paper is, Gardner remarks, rare, providing us with a certainty of attribution which contrasts sharply with the confusions surrounding the manuscript of *The Waste Land* and Ezra Pound's editorship of it. The reason for this abundance of available material is the circumstances in which *Four Quartets* came to completion. Because the last three quartets were written in wartime and his friends were scattered ("Burnt Norton" was written in 1935, which helps to explain the small amount of available material on the poem), Eliot had to rely on correspondence for their advice and suggestions about the poem. Thanks to John Hayward, Eliot's loving collaborator, the record of these exchanges as well as the manuscripts have been preserved and are now in the library of King's College, Cambridge.

Thus it is to Hayward that the world owes Eliot's decision to reshape "Little Gidding" in the light of "some acute, personal reminiscence," and to him that it owes the lines: "And that to be restored, our *sickness* must grow worse," rather than the less forceful *malady* or *ailment* which Eliot had originally written; or "And as I fixed upon the down-turned face/That pointed scrutiny with which we challenge/The first-met stranger *in the waning dusk,*" rather than "the first-met stranger *at dawn*" which Eliot had first written or "in the first faint light" or "after lantern-end . . . lantern-out . . . lantern-down . . . lantern-time," none of which adequately conveyed the "shades before mourning" with a "precise degree of light at that present time of day" which Eliot was striving for. To Hayward's final suggestion Eliot replied: "I cannot find words to express a proper manifestation of my gratitude for your invaluable assistance."

Similarly, to Geoffrey Faber, Eliot's publisher, we are indebted for two of the finest descriptive lines in "The Dry Salvages": "Often together heard: the whine in the rigging/The menace and caress of wave that breaks on water," rather than *soothing menace* which would have upset the euphony of the line; and "under the oppression of the silent fog/The tolling bell/Measures time not our time" instead of "under the silent stillness" which struck Faber as too weak. The publication of these exchanges confirms that *Four Quartets*, like *The Waste Land*, would not be the masterpiece it is without the collaboration of friends whom Eliot trusted and upon whom he depended for encouragement and advice.

The organization of textual material is never an easy matter for editors, particularly so when as much exists as there does with *Four Quartets*. Dame Helen and Oxford University Press, therefore, are to be congratulated for the clarity of their format. As notes to the final text Gardner has included all of the revisions and comments which Eliot and others made. She thus keeps the final text before the reader while sparing him the annoyance of flipping back and forth in uncovering Eliot's work in progress. For years to come readers and scholars of Eliot's poem will find in Part Two an immensely rich source of material on which to reflect on the whole process by which Eliot created *Four Quartets*.

There is little to complain about in Gardner's book, but two oversights should be mentioned. Eliot had originally chosen as the title of his poem *Kensington Quartets*, a reference to the area in London in which he lived during the writing of much of *Four Quartets*. But, although Gardner gives us Eliot's objections to the title, she does not tell us why or when he rejected it or how the eventual title was selected. This is a minor point. More disturbing is the fact that Gardner does not include in her textual study the American edition which preceded the English edition by a year. Since this edition contains changes which Eliot later discarded in his final edition, it should have been included as part of the record of the composition of the poem.

One final note. Gardner hopes that her book will be read not only by Eliot scholars but by a larger public interested in Eliot's work. At $32.50 it seems highly unlikely that many of the public will be able to afford this admirably written, beautifully presented, and enriching study of Eliot's major work.

W. Bryan Fuermann

Sources for Further Study

Encounter. LI, July, 1978, p. 69.
Library Journal. CIII, July, 1978, p. 1410.
Listener. XCIX, June, 1978, p. 713.
New York Review of Books. XXV, December 7, 1978, p. 16.
Times Literary Supplement. September 15, 1978, p. 1006.

THE COUP

Author: John Updike (1932-   )
Publisher: Alfred A. Knopf (New York). 299 pp. $8.95
Type of work: Novel
Time: 1973, with frequent flashbacks to the years 1954-1957
Locale: The fictional sub-Saharan country of Kush, and the fictional town of Franchise, Wisconsin

A witty and ironic novel that is a unique mixture of realism and fable, dealing with opposing political and cultural ideas struggling for control of a fictional, sub-Saharan, Third World country

> *Principal characters:*
> COLONEL HAKIM FELIX ELLELLOÛ, President and Chairman of the military government of Kush
> MICHAELIS EZANA, Minister of the Interior of Kush, and a political rival of Ellelloû
> KADONGOLIMI, Ellelloû's first wife
> CANDACE, his second wife, an American
> SITTINA, his third wife
> SHEBA, his fourth wife
> KUTUNDA, his mistress
> EDUMU IV, deposed King of Kush
> OPUKU, Ellelloû's bodyguard
> MTESA, Ellelloû's chauffeur
> DONALD GIBBS, USAID official
> ANGELICA GIBBS, his wife
> KLIPSPRINGER, an American State Department official

What, in the name of the muse, is John Updike, that elegant chronicler of blue-collar Pennsylvania and Northeast suburbia, doing in Africa? He is searching for a novel, and, on reflection, the territory of his search should not be as surprising as it at first seems. In the "Convoy to West Africa" section of his *In Search of a Character*, Graham Greene hints at the enticement that "the black unexplored continent the shape of the human heart" has long held for writers. Major English language novelists from Evelyn Waugh to Greene, from Hemingway to Saul Bellow to Paul Theroux, have found within the physical, moral, and human landscape of this vast territory a liberating force for the literary imagination. Bellow has said that the African setting of *Henderson the Rain King* served, at that point in his career, as an inhibition-breaking, imagination-provoking stimulus, and a reading of that exuberant novel will underline his point.

Did Updike also succeed in his search? The answer has to be a resounding yes. *The Coup* is a dark comedy about the Dark Continent, a witty, ironic, ingeniously plotted novel that combines an acute knowledge of its West African setting and a sarcastic but accurate portrayal of current international political tensions with a fablelike story that becomes thoroughly convincing in the telling. Add the vivid writing that is Updike's personal trademark, and this book has to be ranked as one of Updike's better novels. The story concerns the short but eventful career of a would-be Marxist-Muslim dictator, Colonel Hakim Félix Ellelloû, who is never quite successful in his attempts to wield power. Ellelloû, who may be the most completely realized character that Updike has created since Rabbit Angstrom, is an engagingly honest fellow who admits that he suffers from "ambivalences," and his ambivalent nature and career set the tone for the novel.

The Coup is a novel of opposing ideas battling for control of a fictional, sub-Saharan, Third World country that Updike has given the Biblical name of Kush. The opposing ideologies are of two types: one political and the other cultural or moral.

The political battle leads to a showdown between Ellelloû and his Minister of the Interior, Michaelis Ezana, but its catalyst, of course, is the obligatory struggle between the Soviet Union and the United States, the two "superparanoids," for influence over the development of Kush. Ellelloû, a devout Muslim given to quoting the Koran on almost any occasion, sees the Russian-American conflict as one between "freedom from disorder" and "freedom from inhibition." Hating such trashy aspects of American culture as junk food, rock music, and drug permissiveness, all of which he sees as an affront to Allah and his own Islamic orthodoxy, Ellelloû becomes a halfhearted Marxist, allowing the Russians to build missile bases. The more sophisticated and cynical Ezana is the opposing halfhearted capitalist, gravitating to the Americans because he is more interested in the development of his country's meager resources than he is in its spiritual potential.

Though the political battle is mainly a contest between the philosophies of Ellelloû and Ezana, the cultural conflict pits Ellelloû, to his sorrow and disgust, against all of his people. The influence of "America, that fountainhead of obscenity and glut" has a strong pull upon the people of Kush, threatening to ruin the Colonel's dream of a pure Islamic state. Ellelloû likes to wander among his fellow citizens in disguise—as a gum vendor, a messenger boy, and an orange seller, among others—to discover what is really going on in the streets and on the nomadic trails. He is often disconcerted by what he sees and hears. A brief blast of rock music from an unknown source can cause him to send his soldiers on a systematic search for transistor radios, cassette players, and hi-fi systems. Ellelloû's odd method of intelligence-gathering often gets him in trouble because very few of his people have ever seen a photo of their leader. Several of the novel's best comic scenes are developed from the basic situation in which a disguised Ellelloû suddenly finds it necessary to try to prove his identity.

The two major creations of the novel are Ellelloû and his country. Both, like the novel itself, are combinations of reality and fable. Ellelloû is, in various ways, both larger-than-life, as befits a legendary dictator, and very ordinary, leading to his aforementioned "ambivalences." Kush, though a fictional creation with its own boundaries and special features, is a thoroughly researched composite of several of the Sahel countries of West Africa. The physical aspects of its arid, empty landscape, as described by Updike in some of his most beautiful writing, are obviously accurate, but the geography has been manipulated somewhat to aid Updike's careful, circular plot. Both Kush and its dictator seem perfect instruments to serve Updike's unique blend of reality and fantasy.

The history of Updike's Kush, like the career of his Colonel Ellelloû, is troubled not only by ambivalent ideas and situations, but also by that force of irony which seems to be a major factor in so much of the history of this troubled century. The time of the novel is 1973, and Kush is in the midst of a terrible drought. (This part is historically accurate, for the Sahel countries did suffer through a prolonged drought from 1968 to 1973.) Kush became an independent nation in 1968, throwing off the shackles of its French colonialists in a military-led revolution, but the never-easy plight of its people has been getting worse ever since. Their peanut crops, the country's main source of revenue, have been devastated.

As a child born as the result of the rape of a Salu tribeswoman, Colonel Ellelloû has come a long way from his beginnings to his shaky throne. Joining the colonial regiment of the French army at seventeen, he rose quickly in the ranks until he deserted in order to avoid fighting in the Algerian War. Making his way to America, he enrolled at (Joseph) McCarthy College in Franchise, Wisconsin, where he earned a degree during the years from 1954 to 1957. The novel contains several extensive flashbacks to Ellelloû's college years as an alien student and a deserter. They are mainly used for characterization: they show how Ellelloû developed his hatred for some aspects of American culture; how he became rededicated to the religion of Islam at Elijah Muhammad's Temple Two in Chicago; and how he acquired the second of his four wives, Candace, a blonde American. Ellelloû, who is puritanical in most ways, is no puritan in matters of sex. Returning to his country in time to become a minor leader of the revolt of 1968, he found himself elevated to his leadership role by the assassination of the General who had led the revolution.

Without spoiling its suspense or any of its delicious surprises, it should be noted that the plot of *The Coup* is one of the best in Updike's prolific career. It is a convoluted maze of small ironies which leads to the large irony of its climax in Kush's Balak Mountains, the Bad Quarter, "Where not even the *National Geographic* has been." Everything comes full circle here. Nothing is wasted. There are no throw-away characters or incidents. The reader may be sure that when Ellelloû first sees Candace trying on sunglasses in a Franchise drugstore, the setting and the situation were chosen with a purpose; the reader should realize that. And when Ellelloû, driving across the desert in his Mercedes, spies a truckload of flattened American automobiles and a strange pair of golden arches, the reader knows that something ominous is waiting in the wings. Every detail is important, from the descriptions of the blind old king down to the picture of his attendant reading the Koran to him; old Edumu IV will be heard from again. Updike's story is continually surprising, yet always consistent. Everything is in its proper place.

Ellelloû, as we have noted, has a way with women, although he has about as much luck in maintaining their loyalty as he does in trying to stop the permeation of American influence among his people. This condition is due to his tendency to neglect them, both because of his wandering ways and the fact that he must keep his four wives domiciled at four different locations. The ladies, understandably, do not have much appreciation for one another. Because four wives is apparently the limit under his Muslim law, and since his eye (which also wanders) has been attracted by still another female, a beautiful nomad picked up on one of his trips, he must settle for taking her as his mistress. These women are not included just to give us a picture of Ellelloû's love life—they are an intrinsic part of Updike's evolving plot, and of the tone and theme of the novel. A short examination of each of them may help demonstrate how everyone, as well as every incident, has a special place in Updike's plan.

Kadongolimi, Ellelloû's first wife, a person of basic "earth-strength," is the traditional African. Long-neglected by her husband, she has grown fat in her middle-age, and sits in her house surrounded and served by a bevy of children, none of whom are Ellelloû's. She implores the Colonel to abandon Allah and go back to the old African gods of *juju* because she believes that only by so doing can he persuade the rains to fall again.

His second wife, Candace, is a white American, a former fellow student at McCarthy College. As an undergraduate, she thought it would be daring and romantic to be married to a black African; now she is bored and bitter, desperately wanting a divorce which Ellelloû will not grant for political reasons. She is the quintessential American liberal, deeply involved in a situation she does not understand.

Sittina, the daughter of a Tutsi chief, is wife number three. She also went to school in America, gaining some fame as a track star at a small, all-black Alabama college. She is now drawn to "artistic" pursuits such as music and painting, but remains a novice because she is "too variously talented to push anything through to mastery." Instead, she haunts the shops, and wants Ellellou to be more receptive to the Americans so that there might be nicer things to buy. Sittina seems to represent the midpoint in Kush's progression (or regression) toward Western values. In her pursuits of ideas, she is virtually indistinguishable from millions of American housewives.

Sheba, Ellelloû's fourth wife, is young, beautiful, mindless, blatantly sexual, and addicted to popular music and the African versions of hallucinogenic drugs; most of the time she is stoned from kola nuts and other natural drug-bearing plants of her native land. Ellelloû does not notice that Sheba is an African version of many of the facets of American culture that he despises, because he is fond of her, and because he indulges his women in ways he would never tolerate among the populace.

Kutunda, the concubine, turns from a sexual into a political being, and becomes, in essence, the modern, self-made, successful career woman, as well as a thorn in Elleloû's personal and political side.

One can see that these women are employed by Updike to illustrate the progression of Western ways in Kush, but this does not mean that they are stereotyped characters. They are, especially considering the limited space available for each in the novel, expertly fleshed-out, and they stand out as individual human beings, rather than the types which they represent.

If there is any element missing from this brilliant novel, it is emotion. Judging by Conrad's three criteria for great fiction, Updike makes us see and hear, but fails to make us feel deeply for any of the characters. They are meticulously created, but with an omniscient, ironic detachment rather than with human warmth. *The Coup* is, after all, a novel of ideas, not of emotion, and, as such, it will hold a high position in literary circles for a long time to come.

William Boswell

Sources for Further Study

Atlantic. CCXLII, December, 1978, p. 94.

Booklist. LXXV, November 1, 1978, p. 461.

Kirkus Reviews. XLVI, October 1, 1978, p. 1090.

New York Review of Books. XXV, December 21, 1978, p. 3.

Publisher's Weekly. CCXIV, October 23, 1978, p. 52.

CRISIS ON THE LEFT
The Cold War and American Liberals, 1947-1954

Author: Mary Sperling McAuliffe
Publisher: University of Massachusetts Press (Amherst). 204 pp. $12.50
Type of work: History
Time: 1947-1954
Locale: The United States

A discussion of changing ideas and political forces in the United States during the decade after World War II

Power attracts attention. This is nowhere so evident as in our modern media, which mobilize and focus vast amounts of attention on those who are powerful, without regard to how temporary or illusory that power may be. Of course, it is understandable that journalists and the general public should be fascinated with the glamour and excitement surrounding those obviously capable of influencing events. No one expects the everyday observer to seek an understanding of more subtle social forces—even if these are, in the long run, more powerful in their effects. The detection of these quieter trends we leave to historians and social scientists. But scholars too are very often mesmerized by the appearance of power. The most telling argument of those who debunk history as mere storytelling is the tendency of many historians to focus on the most trivial details concerning national leaders while entirely neglecting the nation itself. There are dozens of books about Adolf Hitler for every study of the roots of Nazism. Many famous historians have based their careers on Presidential "portraits" and biographies; but who can name an authority on the American Congress? Probably more has been written about the personal peculiarities of Franklin Roosevelt's advisers than about the complete transformation of American labor during the New Deal. This bias towards the charismatic or spectacular may not only disguise the past but also distort it.

Joseph McCarthy provides a perfect example. So much has been said and recorded of the man that we tend to forget the movement. The very name "McCarthyism" reveals how the general fear and hatred of Communism in the decade after World War II has been absorbed and identified, in our minds today, with the personality of the Senator from Wisconsin. McCarthy was actually only influential for a few years during the height of the Cold War, from 1950 to 1954. His influence was due to the fact that he voiced the deepest fears of the average American conservative—suggesting that the entire American government was riddled with Communists. Many influential anti-Communists recognized that McCarthy's charges had no substance and that the man was a walking time-bomb: impressive but ultimately self-destructive. After McCarthy was censured by the Senate in 1954, and the fear of domestic Communism began to recede, both liberals and conservatives tended to blame the Red Scare on his excesses; they either forgot or excused their own.

Crisis on the Left is a book about McCarthyism that barely mentions McCarthy; in avoiding the temptation of the glamorous, author Mary McAuliffe has produced a perceptive and innovative book. Rather than looking to the seats of power on the conservative right, she seeks an explanation of anti-Communism from the liberal and radical left—groups for whom the postwar decade was one of frustration and impotence. Her investigation is based on the belief that the Red Scare was "a far more pervasive and subtle mood than the McCarthy image allowed for." Through a careful examination of ideas and movements on the opposite end of the ideological balance, she has argued convincingly that leftist conflict powerfully shaped postwar anti-Communism.

Liberal politics in the United States has almost always been unusual in two respects. First, it has drawn much of its inspiration from radical parties or governments in Europe—thus going against the grain of an America suspicious of foreigners. From the end of the eighteenth century, when Jefferson's party was attacked for supporting the French Revolution, radical groups of all kinds carried with them a vaguely treasonous, foreign air about them. Also, leftists in the United States have often been united into a sort of "popular front." Instead of breaking into a number of splinter parties, as has generally occurred in Europe, American leftists have often united behind candidates: Andrew Jackson in the 1830's, William Jennings Bryan in the 1890's, Robert LaFollette in the 1920's, and Franklin Roosevelt in the 1930's.

These two factors contributed to the nature of New Deal liberalism. The Depression created a need for innovative thought, and the Roosevelt Administration was openly experimental. New activity on the political left quickly blossomed in response. Traditional progressives, liberals, socialists, and Communists appeared, offered ideas, and worked in the government. Those on the extreme left, though never in the seats of power, were entirely acceptable as political participants. This new tolerance of Communism extended overseas, and Roosevelt extended American recognition to the Soviet Union. The mood on the left was cooperative and optimistic.

This "popular front" alliance was somewhat shaken in 1939, when Nazi Germany and Stalin's Russia joined in pillaging Poland. The Soviet Union seemed ruthlessly opportunistic, and domestic Communism lost favor. But when Hitler invaded Russia in 1941, and the Japanese attacked Pearl Harbor, the United States suddenly found itself in alliance with Communism. To be sure, the American public did not come to think of Stalin as another Churchill; still, the Soviet Union and the United States shared an ideological fervor in the war against Fascism, and Communism appeared as a positive force. The popular front in America was stronger than ever, since everyone was against Hitler; and the American Communist Party soared in membership. Moreover, the nature of the war suggested a clear postwar agenda, which almost all leftists supported: international organizations to prevent future wars, renewed activism by the government to prevent a postwar depression, and zealous protection of the civil liberties that German Fascism attacked.

In the wake of victory, however, this concensus began to fall apart. With the death of Roosevelt, the central unifying voice on the left was lost. His successor, Harry Truman, was seen as a political moderate at best; hope for another "New Deal" quickly faded. The economy provided another shock. Instead of faltering, business experienced a powerful postwar boom, arousing fears of excessive inflation and calls for restrained government spending. Unlike Great Britain, which elected its first Socialist government in 1945, the United States seemed to be shifting in a conservative direction. This trend was heightened by a rash of postwar strikes, which alienated much support for labor and further divided the liberals. These events did not in themselves ensure conservative victory at the next elections, nor did they effect the disintegration of the " popular front." Similar events occurred in Europe, where Labor, Socialist, and Communist parties were enjoying unexpected success. In the United States, however, the postwar situation disturbed an established equilibrium among leftists: as new solutions were offered, old differences resurfaced.

Into this environment came the spectre of anti-Communism. Months before the war ended, Soviet-American cooperation began to erode. Sharp exchanges over the question of Poland's future led to the swift realization, by both countries, that their interests and values would conflict sharply in the years ahead. The divergence of interests was underlined by an even greater divergence of values. To American leaders, Stalin's Russia represented everything the United States had fought against. This animosity was rapidly communicated to the general public. Within a year of the war's end, American foreign policy largely reversed itself, and confronted the Soviets at every step.

As McAuliffe points out, this chain of events produced a threefold division in the left. At one extreme were the Communists, with a small (50,000) but articulate membership, who tacitly (sometimes explicitly) supported the aims of Russian foreign policy and denounced American policy as imperialistic. At the other extreme was a much larger group of liberals who distrusted the Soviet Union and gave Truman's foreign policy increasingly strong support. In between were leftists of various shades who disliked Stalin but questioned whether the Soviets aimed for world domination and definitely rejected the American policy of confrontation. These last two groups, indistinguishable in their political beliefs during the war, took on increasingly clear identities and by 1947 had formed two separate organizations: the Americans for Democratic Action (ADA) and the Progressive Citizens of America (PCA).

By small increments, these two groups developed polarized positions on two parallel issues: American foreign policy, and the control of domestic Communism. The ADA, sympathetic to Truman, found itself supporting a wide range of measures to combat the Soviet Union, from the Marshall Plan to the Korean War. Its members tended to believe that liberalism must staunchly oppose all forms of Communism if it was to survive. This feeling was strengthened as conservatives gained power in Congress and the states. Consequently, they supported efforts to ensure that Communists did not hold high government office. The PCA, in contrast, fervently believed that liberals must unite against the emerging Cold War. Soviet-American conflict appeared to be a prelude to militarism and reaction within the United States; and attacks on American Communists seemed to be the first sign of repression. Consequently, the PCA found itself playing devil's advocate—defending Soviet intentions, pointing out excesses of American actions, and justifying the rights of American Communists. The positions of both groups, the ADA and PCA, had considerable merit; both sought similar ends—a progressive, free United States; but the open bitterness of their conflict fed the spreading fire of anti-Communism. The ADA, in defending a basically conservative spectrum of policies, weakened the influence of liberals and gave extreme conservatives a freer hand. The PCA, in defending Communism, made the Communist "threat" appear much larger than it was, and enabled anti-Communists to point at millions of "fellow-travelers" instead of a few thousand genuine Communists. Despite their best efforts, both groups contributed to the powerful mood which allowed Joe McCarthy to prosper.

This apparent paradox is the starting point for McAuliffe's subtle and careful argument. She proceeds to follow the interaction of leftist conflict with the broader trends of American politics in the late 1940's, ending with an analysis of the new liberalism which emerged in the early 1950's. This liberalism represented the triumph of the ADA over the PCA, and found expression both in the campaigns of Adlai Stevenson and in such influential books as Arthur M. Schlesinger, Jr.'s *The Vital Center*. Such men saw themselves as bulwarks of embattled moderation, defending democracy both from the Communist threat on the left and the anti-Communist extremists on the right.

The subject matter of *Crisis on the Left* is difficult to grasp, because the left was composed of so many different and competing groups: labor unions, intellectuals, political parties, and millions of concerned citizens. McAuliffe, however, has succeeded in encompassing these centers of activity without reducing her analysis to vague generalizations. This is partly accomplished by the organization of the book. The chapters revolve around a series of crises and decisions, chronologically arranged; each successive event focuses on the internal workings of some particular group. Thus the reader turns from the annual CIO convention of 1946, to the formation of the ADA in 1947, to the presidential bid of Henry Wallace in 1948. Clarity is also introduced by following certain key individuals through the pattern of events. In watching Phillip Murray, President of the CIO, become steadily more hostile to Communism, while Henry Wallace, former Vice-President, becomes steadily more radical, the complexity of the period is cogently brought home to the reader.

The basic reasons for the success of this book have nothing to do with its composition, however. It works because it ignores the demagoguery of the period and focuses on the interaction of politics and ideas. McAuliffe shows how the events of the postwar period exploded some basic liberal tenets— faith in the goodness of man, the possibilities of world peace, and the need to restructure American institutions—and divided the left over Communism, leading to a new and very different sort of liberalism, stressing the need for moderation at home, "toughness" abroad, and greater trust in national institutions. By writing about these unnoticed aspects of the McCarthy era, Mary McAuliffe has broken intriguing new ground. The book tells us much not only about the 1950's, when liberals were out of power, but also about the policies of Kennedy and Johnson.

Richard Sander

Sources for Further Study

Choice. XV, June, 1978, p. 606.
Chronicle of Higher Education. XVII, October 2, 1978, p. R13.
Commonweal. CV, August 4, 1978, p. 503.
Political Science Quarterly. XCIII, Fall, 1978, p. 532.
Progressive. XLII, August, 1978, p. 41.

DANIEL WEBSTER

Author: Irving H. Bartlett
Publisher: W. W. Norton and Company (New York). Illustrated. 333 pp. $12.95
Type of work: Biography
Time: 1782-1852, with a concentration on the period 1815-1852
Locale: The northeastern United States, primarily Washington, D. C.

A biography of Daniel Webster, the nineteenth century orator, lawyer, politician, and statesman

> *Principal personages:*
> DANIEL WEBSTER
> ANDREW JACKSON, President of the United States, 1829-1837
> WILLIAM HENRY HARRISON, President of the United States, 1841
> JOHN TYLER, President of the United States, 1841-1845
> MILLARD FILLMORE, President of the United States, 1850-1853
> JOHN C. CALHOUN, statesman from South Carolina who argued in favor of slavery
> LORD ASHBURTON, representative of British in establishing present Maine-Canadian boundary

Most Americans know Daniel Webster from grade and high school history texts which praise him, along with Henry Clay, as one of the "giants" of nineteenth century political life and a major defender of the Constitution of 1787 and the American Union. Serious historians would add that his life and achievements were important not only in opposing internal threats to the Union but also in securing the American nation from the greatest external threat of the nineteenth century: the presence of Great Britain in North America. Webster did indeed labor long and hard to convince domestic disunionists that theirs was a course that could only end in disaster, above all for themselves, and to convince both Americans and the British that the United States and Canada could peacefully share the North American continent. It may be difficult for a late twentieth century American to appreciate fully Webster's work and accomplishments, since Appomattox and an unfortified, "open," 3,000-mile United States-Canadian border (across which people and trade flow unhampered) are now taken for granted; but Webster's achievements on behalf of the internal and external security of the Union must be acknowledged as among the most meritorious in American history.

Unfortunately for Webster, but fortunately for historians whose work thrives on complexities, conspiracies, and general corruption, these achievements were not easily or even honestly reached, and his reputation has tarnished considerably during this century. Even before his death in 1852 he had lost the support of the moral and intellectual leadership of New England, a section that he faithfully represented in Washington for a lifetime and from which he undertook three unsuccessful presidential campaigns. Because of his refusal to condemn slavery as an outright evil to be eradicated at any cost, and for his acquiescence in the provisions of the Compromise of 1850, which gave slavery new legitimacy within the union, Webster was condemned as the evilest of men and as one who had failed to live up to his promise. Then, after his death it was discovered that most of his career had been spent living off of other people's money; and this from an acknowledged expert on fiscal policy. Generally, historians have been forced to conclude that his personal finances and public obligations were a tangle of political favoritism and nepotism, and Bartlett devotes much of his biography to putting this side of Webster's existence into perspective, emphasizing Webster's undoubted accomplishments, and explaining his inability to take up the cause of reform as the great war over slavery neared. Still, one is left with the feeling that Webster's life was lived on the borders of corruption, that he was expedient and self-serving, and that perhaps he really was "Black Dan" after all.

Webster was reared in New Hampshire by a father of strong personality, a veteran of the French and Indian wars and of the Revolution and a strong supporter of George Washington and the Federalist party; his religious training was of the conventional, Calvinistic, New England variety. Thus anchored as a youth in federalist politics and Calvinistic religion, Webster developed a certain conservatism which remained with him throughout his life. As a child he displayed great talents of speech and intellect, on which his later successful political career was built; and his father saw to it that he received a good education. After graduating from Dartmouth College, Webster became a law clerk and reader of the law under one of Boston's most prominent practitioners, and thus he was launched on what was to be a most lucrative career.

All his professional life Webster was a lawyer for the monied class and a great believer in a society based on private property. He believed that the American experience both ensured and depended upon the maintenance of private property rights; that such rights were the basis of social equality; and that the government should do all it could to enhance the general prosperity through the private property system. Webster eloquently represented New England and the propertied interests in Congress from the War of 1812 until the paralyzing arguments over slavery in the 1850's, encompassing the time of General Jackson and his successors in the White House, and consequently a period of *laissez-faire* governmental policy. He usually found himself at odds with Presidents Jackson, Van Buren, Tyler, Polk, and Taylor, who generally opposed governmental intrusion into the economy in such matters as internal improvement projects. Webster labored long and hard to overcome the strict constructionist policies of the Jacksonian era, generally without success. He opposed, as well, the increasing threats of disunion originating with Southern slavery interests headed by John C. Calhoun of South Carolina. His life was spent in an effort to achieve a stronger and more comprehensive federal union; and while he achieved only limited success during his lifetime, he did lay the bedrock on which Lincoln would later build a firmer foundation for the country.

Politics has always been a costly affair, and Webster needed plenty of money to stay in public life and to live in the ostentatious style which he maintained throughout his career. He managed to be not only a prominent and successful politician but at the same time a very highly paid lawyer; in fact, he was perhaps the most highly paid lawyer of his time. As a member of Congress he represented the claims of New England merchants and bankers before the government and argued cases before the Supreme Court; he helped steer various indemnities to private citizens and merchants through the Congress while acting as counsel for those same persons before the government. Needless to say, his friends were to be found all up and down State Street in Boston and throughout the New York business community. They raised numerous "loans" and "funds" over the years to keep him in office—debts which Webster apparently never intended to repay. He took it for granted that somebody had to pay his gigantic personal expenses and that his benefactors needed political access to him and to the government. Webster also intervened on numerous occasions to get government appointments and contracts for his son, whose private law practice never really flourished. He clearly lived and worked in a way that one hopes might not be followed by a member of Congress today.

As Secretary of State for President Tyler, Webster concluded negotiations with his British counterpart, Lord Ashburton, establishing the present Maine-Canadian boundary, and then proceeded to expend a great deal of government money buying newspaper support for the agreement. Some historians have even charged that Webster took money under the table from Ashburton in exchange for the agreement, though Bartlett spares his readers this most damaging charge. Webster, nevertheless, even when at his best, seems never to have been far removed from corruption.

Why was Webster always so hungry for money and so careless about favoritism? Probably because he was careless about his own personal finances and could not conceive that money, either his or somebody else's, was of any real importance. Webster had not only one of the biggest heads in Washington (supposedly filled with brains) but also possessed one of the city's biggest bellies, which he kept filled with expensive food and drink; he boasted frequently that if there were a fine bottle of wine lodged under any roof he would surely find it. He maintained comfortable residences in both Boston and Washington throughout most of his career and lavished tens of thousands of dollars on his country estate, Marshfield, on the Massachusetts seacoast; at the same time he continued to maintain his parents' farm in New Hampshire, as well as other properties in Illinois which he purchased for speculative purposes. Webster apparently ran through money like water and was given to both conspicuous personal consumption and speculation, to which he was particularly susceptible. At one point he was saved from bankruptcy by the fact that his chief creditor, the Bank of the United States, itself went bankrupt before it could foreclose on the man who had been for years its chief political sponsor in Congress.

Bartlett emphasizes that Webster was generous with his friends, his family, and supporters who needed help; but it should be noted that Webster lived for years off of these persons, as well as anyone else foolish enough to pause long enough at his doorstep to be talked into a "loan." Whatever Webster's accomplishments—and they were monumental—one shudders to think what would have resulted had any of his presidential campaigns actually been successful. Webster achieved greatness through eloquence and diplomatic tact brought to bear on some of the major questions of his time, but he would have made a miserable and divisive President because he totally lacked basic integrity, to say nothing of administrative skill. Brilliance in his case rested on a shaky foundation.

Jack L. Calbert

Sources for Further Study

Best Sellers. XXXVIII, September, 1978, p. 181.

Booklist. LXXV, November 1, 1978, p. 452.

National Review. XXX, November 10, 1978, p. 1426.

New York Times Book Review. July 23, 1978, p. 12.

New Yorker. LIV, September, 25, 1978, p. 170.

THE DIARY OF VIRGINIA WOOLF
Volume II: 1920-1924

Author: Virginia Woolf (1882-1941)
Edited, with a Preface and notes, by Anne Olivier Bell and Andrew McNeillie
Publisher: Harcourt Brace Jovanovich (New York). 371 pp. $12.95
Type of work: Diary

The second volume of a complete edition of Virginia Woolf's diaries covering the years in which she began to emerge as a major literary voice

If the first volume of *The Diary of Virginia Woolf* had a somewhat insulated, claustrophobic quality, the second volume leaps immediately and triumphantly into the midst of that busy British *cénacle* known as Bloomsbury. Early in 1920 Woolf can complain of the many interruptions she has had to contend with, but it is clear that the life of clubs, conversation, gossip, teas, and dinners was absolutely necessary to her existence as a person and as a writer: "For some time now life has been considerably ruffled by people. Age or fame or the return of peace—I don't know which—but anyhow I grow wearied of 'going out to tea'; and yet can't resist it. To leave a door shut that might be open is in my eyes some form of blasphemy." And at the very close of the volume, in the entry for December 21, 1924, she notes, rather complacently, "All our Bloomsbury relationships flourish, grow in lustiness. Suppose our set to survive another 20 years, I tremble to think how thickly knit & grown together it will be. At Christmas I must write & ask Lytton [Strachey] if I may dedicate the common reader to him."

Time after time the diary reads like a social calendar. In fact it becomes one: "Tuesday the Squires & Wilkinson & Edgar to dinner; Wednesday tea with Elena; Thursday lunch with Nessa, tea Gordon Square; Friday Clive and Mary here. . . ." She may write of being spread thin, but she clearly rejoiced in her world. While the diary overlaps only in part the recently published third volume of *The Letters*, the two publications indicate clearly enough the difference between what she told her diary and what she poured out in her hundreds of letters. The letters provide a series of masks carefully adjusted to the recipients; emotionally, at least, it is difficult to trust any single one of them. The diaries not only outline her days but attach to each moment the feeling associated with it.

In 1920 Virginia Woolf was just beginning to acquire a literary reputation in her own right and was also finding that she enjoyed the feeling: "At a party now I feel a little famous—the chances are people . . . whose names I know, also know my name." She was quite clear and self-conscious on the personal value of such recognition. Visiting Roger Fry, who, despite his standing as an art critic had failed as a painter, she describes him as filled with "an obscure irritation" and too willing to adopt an aggrieved tone. In such a mood Fry was scarcely capable of praising the work of another—Woolf's, for example. "I sometimes fancy," she points out to her diary, "that the only healthy condition is that of doing successful work. It's the prime function of the soul." In the five years covered by this volume of the diary, Woolf attained her literary majority—publishing her first genuinely experimental novel, *Jacob's Room*, completing *Mrs. Dalloway*, and assembling the collection of critical essays entitled *The Common Reader*. There were shorter works of fiction as well, over a hundred articles and reviews, and, of course, those scores of letters. And there was that most important, increasingly time-consuming but increasingly gratifying venture, the Hogarth Press, which in 1923 published Eliot's *The Waste Land*. It also, of course, enabled Woolf to feel relatively free of the pressures of the literary marketplace since she could, and did, publish her own work.

As one would expect, it was to her diary that she also confessed her doubts, dilemmas, and hunger for praise when it was not forthcoming. After a conversation with Eliot, she feels that her husband, Leonard, shone more than she did, and asserts, determinedly, "but I didn't much mind." Very shortly, however, her diary notes, "But I think I minded more than I let on," and the writing of *Jacob's Room* comes to a halt; she feels listless, doubts the value of what she is doing, and admits to some jealousy of Leonard: "Perhaps at the bottom of my mind I feel that I'm distanced by L. in every respect." She conducted a love-hate relationship with Katherine Mansfield, and part of it, at least, was the result of professional jealousy. Admitting that she was delighted to hear Mansfield abused after the publication of *Bliss*, she tells her diary that she feels Mansfield deserved the abuse because of her penchant for self-advertising, but then herself has a fit of honesty and confesses that in her heart "I must think her good, since I'm glad to hear her abused. When news of Mansfield's death reaches her, she attempts, carefully and honestly, to assess her real feelings. At first, she notes, "one feels—what? A shock of relief?—a rival the less?" She goes on to a moving disquisition of her reactions, noting, without self-abasement, her jealousies, her pettiness, and her sense of loss. Mansfield was, apparently, one of the few people she could talk to about her work and feelings, and assume that she would be understood. Earlier in the diary, Woolf registers a period of estrangement and then a meeting with Mansfield; after the usual careful conversational skirmishing, the two writers fall into conversational lockstep with each other: "To no one else can I talk in the same disembodied way about writing; without altering my thought any more than I alter it in writing here."

Readers will no doubt mine the work for its comments on such celebrated contemporaries as Joyce and Eliot. Her strictures on Joyce were, of course, famous before the publication of this edition, having appeared in Leonard Woolf's one-volume collection of extracts, *A Writer's Diary*. Some, at least, are the result of Woolf's uncertainties and jealousy at a time when her own reputation was scarcely assured: "I reflected how what I'm doing is probably better done by Mr. Joyce. Then I began to wonder what it is that I am doing"—this is 1920, when she was at work on *Jacob's Room*, and when *Ulysses* was available only in the splintered publication of *The Little Review*. Later, with the whole of *Ulysses* in front of her and with *Mrs. Dalloway* in progress, she is far more certain of her dislike; it is also clear that part of her reaction is the result of T. S. Eliot's fulsome praise of Joyce. Having read to the conclusion of the Hades episode, she tells her diary that she was interested at first, then "puzzled, bored, irritated and disillusioned as by a queasy undergraduate scratching his pimples. And Tom, great Tom, thinks this on a par with War & Peace! An illiterate, underbred book it seems to me: the book of a self-taught working man." An odd mixture this, of criticism, jealousy, *ad hominum* attack, and the rather unfortunate air of snobbery that reveals itself more than once in the book. Disliking *Ulysses* more and more, she finally concludes it at the point where the galley proofs of *Jacob's Room* arrive, and she determines firmly that *Ulysses* is a "mis-fire," "diffuse," "pretentious," and, of course, "underbred." But when Leonard has her read an intelligent review analyzing the novel in some detail, she admits that another look might be in order.

T. S. Eliot figures as something of an enigma in these pages, since, at least at times, Woolf found him so. Early on, she scarcely knew what to make of him since his type, she admitted, was so different from hers. Nevertheless, both here and in the letters, Eliot appears often as a figure of fun. While Woolf feels that there is in him a "great driving power some where," she describes him personally and socially in, to say the least, rather unflattering terms: "Pale, marmoreal Eliot was there last week, like a chapped office boy on a high stool, with a cold in his head, until he warms a little, which he did." Since her diaries were the places where she not only caught her feelings but examined them as she did, she can wonder whether Eliot will ever become "Tom" to her; later she decides that she might well become intimate with the poet and still later is rather "disappointed" to discover that she is no longer afraid of him. Once, to her vast delight, "Tom" gets drunk, then sick, and then, the next day, nervously and effusively apologetic.

Her snobbery could extend even to Henry James, whose *Wings of the Dove* she found merely ingenious, the sentences taut but the book as a whole nevertheless "much emasculated by this timidity or consciousness or whatever it is. Very highly American, I conjecture, in the determination to be highly bred, & the slight obtuseness as to what high breeding is."

But there was method in the Bloomsbury madness. Sometimes the members' efforts to help and support one another went wildly, comically astray. The effort to raise money enough to enable Eliot to leave his bank job created nothing but problems, for Eliot and everyone else. The plans designed to force a book out of Desmond MacCarthy were bound to fail, despite a number of meetings of the Novel Club and then the Memoir Club, at which members were to read their work aloud, including, hopefully, MacCarthy. At one meeting of the Memoir Club, Woolf made the rather irritating discovery, through a memoir read by Clive Bell, that Bell had been having an affair with a woman at a time that "coincided with his attachment to me." Nevertheless, there was the case of E. M. Forster, discovered in a very despondent state after his return from India: "depressed to the verge of inanition. To come back . . . to an ugly house . . . an old fussy, exacting mother . . . without a novel, and with no power to write one—this is dismal, I expect, at the age of 43." But the Woolfs, particularly Leonard, encouraged him, and it was to them that he sent a jubilant letter saying he had just written the last words of *A Passage to India*.

Max Halperen

Sources for Further Study

Booklist. LXXV, October 15, 1978, p. 346.

Economist. CCLVIII, August 26, 1978, p. 94.

Listener. C, August 24, 1978, p. 251.

New Statesman. XCVI, August 25, 1978, p. 245.

New York Review of Books. XXV, December 21, 1978, p. 31.

A DISTANT MIRROR
The Calamitous 14th Century

Author: Barbara W. Tuchman (1912-   )
Publisher: Alfred A. Knopf (New York). 677 pp. $15.95
Type of work: History
Time: 1300-1400
Locale: Primarily France

A reappraisal of the history of events of the fourteenth century in France by means of a narrative biography of Enguerrand de Coucy VII

Principal personages:
ENGUERRAND DE COUCY VII
JEAN II, King of France, 1350-1364
EDWARD III, King of England, 1327-1377
CHARLES V, King of France, 1364-1380
RICHARD II, King of England, 1377-1399
CHARLES VI, King of France, 1380-1422

Barbara W. Tuchman is one of our most distinguished historians, being the author of such previously acclaimed works as *The Zimmermann Telegram*, *The Guns of August*, *The Proud Tower*, and *Stilwell and the American Experience in China*. She has twice been awarded the Pulitzer Prize.

The extent of the seven years of research for *A Distant Mirror* is partially indicated by a seventeen-page selective bibliography of sources and by the thirty-four pages of reference notes, both gathered at the end of the volume. The book is divided nearly in half by sixteen chapters in Part One which predominantly relate the conditions of life in the first three quarters of the fourteenth century in France, and the twelve chapters of Part Two which follow the military exploits of Sire Enguerrand de Coucy VII. The author has found it best to concentrate on the details of one person's life and so provide multiple perspectives. The device is a good one because as we read of armies, battles, wars, crusades, and uprisings, we also appreciate how events shaped one life during those times; we can the better judge and empathize with conditions of a time which the intervening six hundred years may have made relatively inaccessible to us.

Europe in the fourteenth century seems remote, owing primarily, as the author explains in the foreword, to a scarcity of reliable facts, figures, and dates with which to reconstruct the times. For the Middle Ages, the data we do have are inexact, partial, biased, exaggerated, and contradictory. Any objective observer needs to weigh the descriptions and accounts carefully in order judiciously to assess probabilities. Such is the eminently fair attitude Barbara Tuchman has employed in producing a very reasoned and readable re-creation of the 1300's.

This work's subtitle is "The Calamitous 14th Century" and the adjective is easily justified by noting such major calamities as: the Hundred Years War between England and France, begun in 1337, which, besides its destruction and strife, continued the political upheaval of the century; the removal of the Papacy to Avignon in 1309, and then the eventual schism in 1378 which divided loyalties of the ruling class as well as of the religious leaders; and the Black Death in 1348 which killed one third of the population of Europe and recurred approximately every twelve years thereafter for the rest of the century. In sum, all authority must have seemed to be defective and the curse of the plague to condemn all human effort.

These three major disturbances are very well described in the first part of the work. In the political arena, we are given interesting facts about the important nobles, as well as being instructed in the governing principles of the time. For example, it was a salient operating fact of politics that intermarriage among the nobles of any area of Europe was exclusively for purposes of political aggrandizement. Thus, specifically, the central figure of this book, Enguerrand de Coucy VII of France, was married to the daughter of Edward III of England because Coucy was a very important nobleman with extensive properties and income. The most important political theory of those days had to do with the concept of chivalry. Soldiering was made fitting for nobles by a creed which exalted their mission. They became knights with the high ideals of bringing aid to the oppressed, safeguarding the virtue of women, overcoming terrible foes, and doing all for a high religious cause. As with all war propaganda, however, time after time we are shown that in the battles neither side was more moral, neither was more courageous, neither gave more genuine service to the chivalric codes than the other. Furthermore, the winning of battles was more a result of chance than anything else; and the outcome of most of the fighting was largely inconclusive. Nevertheless, we receive a strong general impression: warring, pillaging, and ruthlessness were never more rampant than in the fourteenth century. It was almost a necessary condition of human life.

In the disturbances within the Catholic Church during the fourteenth century, not only was there no clear leadership or order among the prelates, but the spiritual meaning of religion was either abandoned or neglected in favor of material and political benefits for the clergy. Like the nobility, the clergy lived by oppressing the common people. Both ruling classes taxed the people excessively and constantly, to the point of causing minor revolts. Furthermore, the church became so thoroughly materialistic that it sold everything from small bones supposed to be the relics of some saint to special dispensations for the forgiveness of almost any sin. Religion was a business as well as a "government." So it was that the nobles attempted to give high moral purpose to what was essentially a base human instinct for aggression, while the clergy was busy turning high moral purpose into oppressive avarice of its own. The results were the same in both cases: the lower classes suffered greatly.

With the physical destruction accompanying the plagues, the chaos of the century must have seemed complete, and indeed Barbara Tuchman says that common people were sure that the wrath of God was upon them and that they were doomed. Details of the first epidemic, called the Black Death, which lasted two years, 1348-1350, include the facts that the disease was bubonic plague and, as we now know, was carried by rats from the ships and then to human beings by way of fleas that infested the rats. The symptoms were horrible, including the black sores that gave the plague its name. Death could be lingering, or it could come within a day after contracting the illness. The dead were carted away in charnel wagons and burned; no one was safe.

Against such a general background of major disturbances, Barbara Tuchman has provided us with many specific insights into the daily lives of the general population during those years in France. These details of the varied fabric of life are most numerous in Part One of the volume. The castles of the nobles are described, especially that of the family of Enguerrand de Coucy VII in Picardy, northeast of Paris; we learn of the plan of the rooms, the defensive battlements in case of attack, and the manner in which life went on. Other descriptions inform us of the entertainments of the noble classes — their falconry, feasts, and balls. A realistic picture of Paris is painted, including the city's layout, shop signs, public baths, market places, and customs. We are shown the traffic jams, the hordes of students, the noise and the smells. Descriptions of the life of the highest clergy include the sumptuous courtlike elegance of the Papacy at Avignon, with its huge crowds of seekers. The lack of proper sewage for a small city experiencing such a massive population growth caused many to complain of the vile smells. Finally, the peasants' daily lives and lack of comforts are detailed, even to the clothes worn, the food eaten, how the days were ordered. People stayed indoors after dark; work after sundown was prohibited; beggars were everywhere. Potatoes, coffee, tea, and tobacco were unknown, as was, happily, syphilis; but leprosy was not uncommon. People living in town often kept monkeys as pets. Upper-class women plucked their eyebrows, and were censured, as were the men who wore those peculiar medieval pointed shoes.

Many other interesting things emerge from this volume, including evidences of some bizarre behavior. People were generally superstitious and believed in sorcery. Flagellants appeared from time to time: groups of people beating themselves in religious fervor to express remorse for their sins and to induce God to forgive mankind. Alchemy, the search for a way to transform base metals into gold, was the popular science of the day; and astrology, next to God, was thought to be the greatest determinant of affairs. Even demonology was practiced by some.

More important than the deviant behavior, however, were other social attitudes which were more prevalent and much more inimical to well-being: prejudices. First was the egregious prejudice of the two ruling classes, the nobles and the clergy, toward the peasants and shopkeepers; this tyrannical attitude was the cause of much grief and formed the basis of a consistent complaint of the lower classes; namely, that in addition to being ruthlessly victimized, taxed, and enslaved, they were also despised. Another traditional object of class hatred was the Jew, who, as Tuchman very aptly demonstrates, has been ostracized from the Christian world since its early days and was more actively assaulted during the times of the Crusades in medieval Europe. In the mid-fourteenth century, Jews were blamed for the plagues, were said to have "poisoned the wells" of Christians. The fact that Jews died in equal proportions to the gentiles did not prevent them from being attacked and even burned at the stake. A third prejudice was that against women. They were often roundly condemned as playthings of the devil. As a rival force to that of the Church and the State, a woman was to be despised as a "hindrance to devotion," a "confusion to man." The only tolerated state for woman was as a wife, and there she must be totally obedient to the man. Original sin was traced to the female, the temptress. A mother's care was necessary but the father was to be the real source of the child's internal and external welfare. The Salic law forbade females from inheriting the throne, one of the serious objections being that a woman could not bestow judgment on a man, since man is intrinsically nobler than woman. Much writing about women in medieval literature portrays them as cuckolding, gossiping, and shrewish. It is perhaps particularly annoying by our standards to notice that while women were held in low esteem, nevertheless the cult of courtly love fostered the fantasy of damsels as lofty, chaste, pure, and unattainable. Never were the ideal and the real more at odds.

In Part Two, the military exploits of Enguerrand de Coucy VII are chronicled, including his campaigns in Switzerland, Italy, North Africa, and Bulgaria (Nicopolis). Through the accounts of these battles we appreciate the futility of what was then a defeated sense of chivalry; the end of the era of crusades had come. Simultaneously, we witness a rising sense of nationality among the people of France as they resist English control of their provinces. This sense of nation is fulfilled during the next century by French military victories.

One may ask whether in this book the case has indeed been made which the title suggests; namely, that the fourteenth century is a distant mirror of the twentieth. Certainly Tuchman has intended that we draw many parallels. When she does not openly state the parallel, as "For belligerent purposes, the 14th century, like the 20th, commanded a technology more sophisticated than the mental and moral capacity that guided its use," she allows us to form our own. The nearly continual state of war then is hardly different from this century's two World Wars, the Korean and Vietnamese conflicts, and the civil wars in China, Russia, Spain, South America, Africa, the Middle East, and India. Belief in traditional institutions such as church, government, even marriage and traditional life styles, have all been challenged or upset in this century. Perhaps certain aspects of bizarre behavior then, such as flagellation, sorcery, and other superstitions, correspond to the extreme cultist activities of our day. Assuredly, however, parallelism is more a device than an actuality. The plague, for instance, is not mirrored in this century. In any case, corresponding human activities in any two eras of history can easily be compared; the so-called "lessons of history" have been called to our attention before. So the point of this re-creation of a remote and calamitous century is not whether all of its aspects are directly reflected today. The point is that by adopting such an attitude of comparison we approach this distant time without the usual condescension, ready to condemn the medieval period as barbaric. Nor do we automatically consider our times to be intrinsically better in all respects. Tuchman, attesting to certain deficiencies of those days, of sanitary conditions or medical knowledge, say, is quick to point out that there were other aspects worthy of praise. For example, the usual treatment of the plague, by letting blood and putting on plasters, was either useless or perhaps even harmful, yet the doctors of those times did know how to set bones, pull teeth, take out bladder stones, even remove cataracts. We appreciate balance in such a presentation of history and we gain from it a feeling of kinship with the people of those times.

A Distant Mirror is not without flaws. Some may find the events hard to follow because of chronological and spatial interruptions and dislocations. The life of Enguerrand de Coucy VII does not inspire much sympathy and he does not ever "come alive," since we learn only the events of his public career. There are some lapses of style; for instance, "Frenchmen did not lack who were ready to accept union. . . ." is more French than English. And, finally, historical facts nearly always belie proclamations about the grand order of things, so that when one reads, concerning the next (fifteenth) century's Joan of Arc, that "The moment required her and she rose," one objects to any historian explaining the "Exigencies of History" as some celestial predestination.

A Distant Mirror should be required reading for all students in high school and college. As a history text it is vivid, resourceful, altogether interesting. As an example of re-creation of the past, it is an absorbing narrative full of all kinds of pertinent information to help us better understand those times, our own times, and ourselves.

Anthony Lamb

Sources for Further Study

America. CXXXIX, November 11, 1978, p. 334.
Library Journal. CIII, September, 1, 1978, p. 1635.
New Leader. LXI, October 9, 1978, p. 18.
New Yorker. LIV, November 13, 1978, p. 246.
Saturday Review. V, October 28, 1978, p. 40.

THE DIVIDED LEFT
American Radicalism 1900-1975

Author: Milton Cantor
Publisher: Hill and Wang (New York). 248 pp. $11.95
Type of work: History
Time: 1900-1975
Locale: The United States

A succinct and scholarly history of American leftist groups and their difficulties through the first three-quarters of the twentieth century

Principal personages:
DANIEL DELEON, Curaçao-born founder of the Socialist Labor Party
EUGENE V. DEBS, the most famous leader of the Socialist Party during its early years
WILLIAM ("BIG BILL") HAYWOOD, miner and leader of the Industrial Workers of the World
NORMAN THOMAS, respected leader of the Socialist Party during the Great Depression
EARL BROWDER, Communist Party leader during the Great Depression and World War II
MIKE KLONSKY, theoretician for the Students for a Democratic Society

Milton Cantor obtained his Ph.D. from Columbia University. He is currently Professor of History at the University of Massachusetts at Amherst. Prior to the publication of *The Divided Left*, Cantor edited six books and authored two others. His articles have appeared in a variety of liberal publications. Cantor's research interests span labor, radical, and intellectual history.

Cantor begins his study of the left with an examination of Daniel DeLeon and his Socialist Labor Party (SLP)—the first major Marxist organization in United States history. Curaçao-born, DeLeon was "a professor without a professorship" and a man intensely concerned with maintaining the "revolutionary purity" of his Marxism, regardless of the consequences. As a result, though DeLeon was one of the tiny handful of first-rate leftist theoreticians to emerge in the United States, his "monopoly" on *the* correct strategies led to the first appearance of factionalism—something that would decimate DeLeon's SLP and *all* subsequent left-wing groups in the country. DeLeon was, as a result, the ultimate leader of a small sect, made up predominantly of non-English-speaking immigrants, with no substantial roots in the labor movement. The scenario of the early SLP set the tone for what was to come. Leftist movements would come and go, but all would suffer from the same liabilities. First, the left would remain isolated from the very working class so essential in any Marxian plan for revolution. Under varying circumstances, no left-wing group in American history sank deep roots in the labor movement. And, second, as each group failed to secure a mass base for its outlook, members would turn inward, closing ranks around whatever was deemed the true and proper path to revolution—and expelling any and all members with doubts or disagreements.

Witness the rise and fall of the Socialist Party (SP), founded in 1901. Its early charismatic leader, Indiana-born Eugene V. Debs, was a product of various railroad workers unions, and had led the massive Pullman Strike of 1894. Debs made several runs for the U.S. presidency, with his greatest success coming in 1912, when he polled 900,000 votes. Socialists were elected to many state and local offices in the years before World War I. Socialists also controlled several of the trade unions in the American Federation of Labor. Then came World War I.

Socialist Party voting strength, where it existed, was based on reform rather than revolution. The crucial point is this—the SP gained a substantial degree of public acceptance, perhaps greater than any other leftist party in United States history, but it did so by abandoning revolutionary principles. Much of its voting strength was based among middle-class reformers and populist farmers, *not* the working class. Finally, with the coming of the war, the SP proved vulnerable to factionalism and it split over the issue of support of the war. It was further torn over the issue of the Bolshevik Revolution. Militants pulled out to form two Communist parties in 1919. The SP was left as an isolated sect, recovering only slightly under Norman Thomas' leadership during the Great Depression.

During the 1930's and 1940's, the Communist Party (CP) underwent a similar rise and fall. It emerged from isolation to gain its greatest credibility during the Congress of Industrial Organizations (CIO) drive to organize industrial workers, and later through its fervent support for the war effort during World War II. But, to gain acceptance, the CP became overtly revisionist under the leadership of Earl Browder. Communism was proclaimed to be "twentieth century Americanism." The CP was doomed by the postwar Cold War period. The "red scare" ended CP influence in the CIO and in society in general. The year 1956, with the Krushchev revelations of Stalin's crimes and with the Soviet intervention in Hungary, left the CP with a tiny core of aging true believers.

The last major movement chronicled by Cantor is the New Left of the 1960's. This movement suffered from several major difficulties. It embraced a diverse following of young people. At the same time, New Leftists tended to shun theory, giving much of their activities a "naysaying" quality. Members were largely confined to the nation's campuses, and engendered the overt hatred of the working class through their "counter-cultural" life style. Additionally, there was only one major issue that provided this movement with unity —the Vietnam War. As Cantor notes, once Nixon began concrete steps to end the war, the New Left's clientele disintegrated into special interest groups such as the current Women's Liberation movement. The biggest issue was gone. In addition, the long hair and other elements of the "counter-culture" were absorbed into the general American culture, ending the movement's distinctiveness.

Thus does Cantor present the major radical movements that have appeared in our century. Why did these organizations fail? Cantor's title gives a large part of the answer. All leftist groups have been marked by fierce internal hairsplitting over ideology. More time and energy has been spent fighting among themselves than fighting the capitalist "enemy." But, as Cantor notes, the results would have been no different even if the American left *had* been unified. To secure a larger public following, as did the SP and CP, revolution had to take a back seat to reform. In the process, the SP and CP failed to acquaint members and followers with a truly revolutionary perspective. On occasion, with government repression like the Palmer Raids or McCarthyism, firm revolutionaries were few in number, and organizations were subsequently crushed. Finally, where radicals did gain entry into the labor movement, their labor activities, by necessity, had to come first. The very union security provided in part by radical organizers in the 1910's and 1930's had the highly ironic result of defusing worker support for radicalism. The more concessions exacted from employers by unions in the SP or CP orb, the more secure workers felt *within* a capitalist framework. As Cantor observes, American capitalism has proven most durable as a result, impervious to the periodic onslaughts of devoted radicals going nowhere.

Cantor's book is a valuable contribution to intellectual and labor history. Beyond the major groups he describes, however, Cantor may lose the general reader, for the number of sects and individuals is extensive indeed. Some prior knowledge of radical history is helpful in approaching this scholarly account, and Cantor's excellent bibliography provides readers with the leads they may need for further reading. Cantor's book remains a succinct, highly readable account, a true work of synthesis by an important historian, on a topic of great interest if not impact.

Edward A. Zivich

Sources for Further Study

Library Journal. CIII, July, 1978, p. 1404.
Washington Monthly. X, July, 1978, p. 59.

THE DREAM OF A COMMON LANGUAGE
Poems 1974-1977

Author: Adrienne Rich (1929-   )
Publisher: W. W. Norton and Company (New York). 76 pp. $9.95; paperback $2.95
Type of work: Poetry

Poetry which investigates women's relationships with one another in the context of historical, political, and family experiences

This is the tenth volume of poetry which Adrienne Rich has published. It includes her ninth volume, *Twenty-One Love Poems*, which was first published in a hand-printed, limited edition at Effie's Press, Emeryville, California. *The Dream of a Common Language* is a continuation of *Poems, Selected and New, 1950-1974*, which documented the poet's social and psychological upheavals as she tried to work in a heterosexual world. The primary imagistic pattern was the circle, the symbol of unending search and pain which women and men encounter: "For us the work undoes itself over and over:/The grass grows back, the dust collects, the scar breaks open" ("Ghazals: Homage to Ghalib 7/14/68:ii"). Beyond the repetition of old patterns and injuries, however, the poems charted the emergence of a feminist sensibility as they attempted to create a new language which would convey women's social experiences. They moved from tight, rhymed analyses of dead-ended relationships in the 1950's and 1960's to fuller, more prosaic, daring statements about female/female relationships in the 1970's.

The Dream of a Common Language is clearly the product of twenty-five years of personal and poetic turmoil and continues themes begun in her last single book of poetry, *Diving into the Wreck, Poems 1971-1972*. With this new collection, Rich explores women's love, women's history, women's living in the present. Importantly, *Of Woman Born: Motherhood as Experience and Institution* (1976), which is Rich's only book-length prose work to date, is written concurrently with the poems in *The Dream of a Common Language*. The title suggests Rich's familiar concern with woman's life as manifested in micro- and macrospheres and examines intellectually the nature of motherhood. *The Dream of a Common Language* is concerned less overtly with motherhood but openly explores women's relationships with one another, not only as mothers and daughters but as sisters and lovers. Much of the imagery is familiar to readers of Rich, but here we see the patterns used in a new way. There is a daring freshness about the poems, an unabashed candor about her own love life, and an admirable availability of her consciousness to women's search for commonality and self-understanding.

The volume consists of seventy-six pages divided into three sections: I. *Power*, II. *Twenty-One Love Poems* and III. *Not Somewhere Else, But Here*. The poems in Section I were composed during 1972-1975, in Section II during 1974-1976, and in Section III, during 1974-1977. The lack of a strict chronology supports the cyclic, ruminating style of this collection. The poems are grouped ostensibly by theme, but the themes of women loving women, of women struggling to discover their own metaphors for experience, of women dying in the process of being reborn, pervade each section. The divisions thus seem arbitrary, the poems in each section appearing to be contemporaneous with the ones in another section and pointing to the culminating poem, "Transcendental Etude":

> There come times—perhaps this is one of them—
> when we have to take ourselves more seriously or die;
> when we have to pull back from the incantations,
> rhythms we've moved to thoughtlessly
> and disinthrall ourselves, bestow
> ourselves to silence or a severer listening. . . .

These poems convey that tone of thoughtful, quiet seriousness to which "Transcendental Etude" speaks. Several of them ("Power," "Phantasia for Elvira Shatayev," "Paula Becker to Clara Westhoff," "A Woman Dead in Her Forties") ponder the deaths of women explorers, poets, scientists. Many repeat, in variation, lines written in "Ghazals":

> A decade of cutting away
> dead flesh, cauterizing
> old scars ripped open over and over
> and still it is not enough ("Toward the Solstice")

Section I, *Power*, contains seven poems which concern silences and survival. "What does it mean 'to survive?'" writes Elvira Shatayev, leader of a women's climbing team who was killed as she climbed Lenin Peak. "Is not a heroic death a kind of survival?" muses the poet: is not Madame Curie's continued work despite obstructive cataracts and "cracked and suppurating skin" a statement of her heroism? Is not "scraping eggcrust from the child's/dried dish/ skimming the skin/from cooled milk" ("To a Poet") an extraordinary tribute to survival and to silence? Writes Rich:

> Silence can be a plan
> rigorously executed
>
> the blueprint to a life
>
> It is a presence
> it has a history a form
>
> Do not confuse it
> with any kind of absence ("Cartographies of Silence")

Women who have lived lives of silences are here reclaimed; they have been present in history; they have influenced the course of our civilization; they have been "living in the earth-deposits of our history." In order to liberate these histories, women need to blend, almost symbiotically, into their sisters' visions and to speak out the closed memories, the caged will.

> I come towards her in the starlight.
> I look into her eyes
> as one who loves can look,
> entering the space behind her eyeballs,
> leaving myself outside.
> So, at last, through her pupils,
> I see what she is seeing. . . .
> Lashed bars.
> The cage.
> The penance. ("The Lioness")

Twenty-One Love Poems conveys the experience of a poet in love with a middle-aged woman like herself. The poems, which move sequentially and mosaically, present an ironic, unlikely romance between two who have shed their morning youth and are creating a fresh, exciting life together ("No one has imagined us"). The poems move back and forth among the histories, personal and cultural, as the poet compulsively recreates her lover, her self, in order to dive deeper into her past, her inner consciousness. The cultural, historical silences, tentatively explored in Section I, here confront the poet as aspects of her lover and as historical imperatives needing to be excavated:

> whatever's lost there is needed by both of us—
> a watch of old gold, a water-blurred fever chart,
> a key . . . . Even the silt and pebbles of the bottom
> deserve their glint of recognition. I fear this silence,
> this inarticulate life. (IX)

What she discovers as she explores new/old history, familiar/strange bodies are differences within oneness:

> We have different voices, even in sleep,
> and our bodies, so alike, are yet so different
> and the past echoing through our bloodstreams
> is freighted with different language, different meanings. (XII)

This exploration, unlike the love relationships charted in her earlier poetry, is hopeful because it is self-exploration. The differences are undeniable, but the possibilities seem richer. The poet, loving another woman, must inevitably confront her own individuality; her own mind projecting love and stories onto another. She remains, as a survivor in history, alone yet sharing her solitude. Like the moon Diana, she is "half-blotted by darkness"; yet she is choosing "to walk here," to live within the present, to face the pain of a partially understood love. Clearly, we have returned to the poems in Section I, to the search for an adequate articulation of silence, of commonality, of individual existence:

> How do I exist?
>
> This was the silence I wanted to break in you
> I had questions but you would not answer.
>
> I had answers but you could not use them
> This is useless to you and perhaps to others. . . .
>
> Language cannot do everything. ("Cartographies of Silence")

Section III is the longest of the book and reconfirms the poet's commitment to immersion in the present while investigating the past. There is a ferocity about these poems which contrasts sharply with the restrained passion in Section II. Rich speaks of courage and of needing to be separate:

> I have written so many words
> wanting to live inside you
> to be of use to you
> Now I must write for myself. ("Upper Broadway")

It is not surprising that these poems of separation and individuation concern mothers and sisters as well as lovers. The poet returns not only to historical mothers dying in childbirth ("Paula Becker to Clara Westhoff"), but to her sister who shares her history which must be recaptured, reexamined, reintegrated into a dynamic present. In "Sibling Mysteries," the poet asks her sister to remind her of their childhood, early adolescence, marriage, and motherhood, and of how they are united inevitably by their primary attachment to their mother: "Tell me again because I need to hear/how we bore our mother-secrets/straight to the end. . . ." As the poem moves, Rich again confronts the reality of her separateness and her commonality with her sister. The paradox of difference within sameness obsesses the poet and seems resolved only in the womb of the mother. The sister speaks differently, lives a different life; "yet our eyes drink from each other/our lives were driven down the same dark canal." The daughters, united through the mother as woman, are united with each other through the facts of their own lives.

Still, the act of reclaimed separation haunts the poet in the final poems of the book.

> If some rite of separation
> is still unaccomplished
> between myself and the long-gone
> tenants of this house,
> between myself and my childhood,
> and the childhood of my children,

it is I who have neglected
to perform the needed acts. . . . ("Toward the Solstice")

Relentlessly, like scars breaking open, Rich moves back over history, women's lives, the violence of men's politics "requiring women's blood for life/a woman's breast to lay its nightmare on" ("Natural Resources"), to expose and reexpose atrocities which, though named, escape expurgation. "My heart is moved by all I cannot save." ("Toward the Summer Solstice")

The final two poems of the collection simply restate in a more cerebral tone the paradoxes the poet finds. If one examines history, writes Rich, one is confronted repeatedly with half-truths, uncompleted lives, silences without reference. If one examines one's own history, one meets the mirror or a partially obscured reflection. Finally, if one confronts one's inner self, one finds the fragments, the half-remembered homesickness for the mother, the woman who is/was ourselves, fused, separate, permanent. In language highly reminiscent of very early poems such as "Aunt Jennifer's Tigers," "Afterward," and "Mathilde in Normandy," Rich returns to the mundane, to women's work, to sewing, tapestries, making new garments. There is a quiet vision in such activity, "a whole new poetry beginning here." Rich, using her intellect and her discovered self-love, begins to recover her present and to cherish her past.

> Such a composition has nothing to do with eternity,
> the striving for greatness, brilliance—only with the musing
>   of a mind
> one with her body, experienced fingers quietly pushing
> dark against bright. . . with no mere will to mastery,
> only care for the many-lived, unending
> forms in which she finds herself. . . . ("Transcendental Etude")

Faith Gabelnick

Sources for Further Study

Best Sellers. XXXVIII, August, 1978, p. 166.
Booklist. LXXIV, July 1, 1978, p. 1659.
Harper's Magazine. CCLVII, November, 1978, p. 81.
Yale Review. LXVIII, Autumn, 1978, p. 83.

THE DREAM OF REASON
American Consciousness and Cultural Achievement from Independence to the Civil War

Author: Clive Bush
Publisher: St. Martin's Press (New York). 397 pp. $28.00
Type of work: History
Time: 1776-1865
Locale: The United States

An interdisciplinary study of the developing American nation during its early stages of growth and sophistication in terms of its literature, science, painting and sculpture, and politics

In the course of a year's production of scholarly volumes, there are so few which even come close to the scope and perspective of Bush's compilation of American intellectual, artistic, and material artifacts that we must applaud both the author's vision and the publisher's bravery for *The Dream of Reason*.

Students and critics of American Culture (or American Studies or American Civilization, depending upon one's institutional perspective and affiliation) are, of course, familiar with the "pioneering" works: Perry Miller's *Errand into the Wilderness*, R. W. B. Lewis's *The American Adam*, Vernon L. Parrington's three-volume series on *Main Currents in American Thought*, Barbara Novak's *American Painting of the Nineteenth Century*, and Alan Gowan's *The Unchanging Arts*. Each of these authors deals with one or more of the concerns of Bush, but only Bush attempts to put fine and popular arts, elite and popular literature, mechanical and technological progress, and political events into one compelling overview of the new, awkward, and uncertain nation from 1776 to 1865—all in approximately four hundred pages.

Obviously, Bush is almost forced to make some too-sweeping generalizations if he is to cover that much time in that number of pages; yet some of the generalizations leave the reader with an uneasiness about what has been said. But, by the same token, Bush pulls into one place many seemingly unconnected aspects of the culture and makes the reader, in fact, see that political change did not exist in a vacuum apart from literary and painting-style changes or mechanical changes which gave the workers of that era the steam engine and the wheat thresher. And Bush does it all with the additional advantages (and disadvantages) of the foreign observer, for he is a lecturer in English and American literature at the University of Warwick, in England.

Because he views Americans and the American culture from a psychological and environmental distance, Bush is able to laugh at some of the foibles which we find too sacred for humor, and to avoid laughing at some pomposities which to the twentieth century viewer seem almost beyond belief.

For example, Americans traveling in China today are often disturbed by the number of pictures of Lenin and Mao and Marx on display. Such deification seems inappropriate, even ridiculous, especially in our post-Watergate age. Yet George Washington's pictures hung in every classroom and village hall in the United States well into the twentieth century, and no one took offense. As Bush points out, such portraits "became visual incitements to public virtue and private honour." For the popular canonizers, Washington's death actually made their job easier; a dead hero is a much safer commodity than a live one. Many persons have always felt that sculpture is more fitting for a hero than a simple portrait. The portrait can be duplicated and distributed more quickly and inexpensively than a statue, but the stone or bronze form with its three-dimensionality gives the viewer a more realistic feeling for the depicted subject. Washington did not escape such depiction, and Bush is to be credited for resisting the opportunity to laugh at Horatio Greenough's 1836 *George Washington*—a larger-than-life sculpture which has the former President seated on a monumental chair, scepter in his left hand, right hand raised toward the skies, with drapery around only the lower half of his body. Although intended for the rotunda of the Capitol Building, this more-or-less copy of a statue of Zeus in the temple at Olympia with its superimposed head of Washington, finally wound up in a dusty corner of the Smithsonian.

With the popular arts, Bush places the monthly magazine stories of Kit Carson and Mike Fink, the lithographs of Currier and Ives, and candid photography into the meaningful perspective of the growing middle-class American society. Unfortunately, his views of the popular arts and of the popular content—visual and narrative—are some of Bush's weakest comments, in that he sometimes finds himself forced into a corner by his own reason. For example, he devotes a chapter to "The Hero as Representative" and attempts to discuss the role of the hero in American culture. However, he begins the chapter with the statement that "the need for heroes reflects a clamour for social identity and is deeply allied to thwarted social needs." Whether such yearning for heroes is a function of frustrations, or whether it is a function of a desire to emulate someone closer at hand than a mystical God-figure is not the problem here. What is of concern is that Bush would almost have us believe that Americans are the only persons who have or want or need heroes. Further, when he says "the intense and hysterical involvement of many Americans in the deposition of a recent president shows the continuance in American life of the politicopsychological phenomenon of hero-worship," such admiration somehow becomes a mental aberration. But on the other hand, he lauds the movement in popular taste from the refined gentleman, Natty Bumppo, to the raucous frontiersman, Kit Carson, and from "battle piece" paintings to the William S. Mount genre studies and the Currier and Ives prints, which brought art into every living room. Finally, he can herald the arrival of the camera as the instrument which destroyed the hold of the elitists on pictorial realism.

He also would have us accept that painting and poetry "were at first felt to be too aristocratic ever to admit of their practice in a republic. . . . The scientist became more important than the artist as an expounder of the nation's consciousness." This, then, is one of those sweeping generalizations which at first reading seems to be full of valuable meanings, but which on second perusal cannot be accepted, even in a survey such as this one.

In the first place, although the actual power of the New England churches was much less by the time of the revolution than it had been, the views of the church still pervaded much of the thinking of the general public in regard to art. The Puritans mistrusted poetry, painting, drama, and almost any other form of decorative or self-expressive creative arts. Although such art was decried by the Puritans when it was part of the Church of England such as in the "aristocratic" high-church format, the unhappiness felt by the Puritans was with the fact that such art was too "Popish" and too inclined to distract the weak soul in its pursuit of salvation. That is, it is not the aristocratic aspect which made the arts unacceptable to the Puritans, but the antireligious aspect; however, as the religious viewpoint lost much of its power, the anti-artistic attitude—now attached to kings and courts and nondemocratic agencies—remained. In addition, for the new republic, which constantly was sending some of its best and strongest and brightest persons into the ever-expanding Western frontier, there was not enough time or money to be trained as a painter. As everyone "knew" back then (and continued to believe well into the present century), the only way to be trained as an artist was to study in England or Germany or France. Such training required independent wealth or the support of a wealthy patron. Such patrons were found on the East Coast almost exclusively until the second half of the nineteenth century; it was there, too, that a growing wealthy, upper class (America's "aristocracy") was forming.

Finally, the "scientist" to which Bush frequently refers, during the eighteenth and nineteenth centuries, was a mechanic, a technological tinkerer. Such a statement is not meant to denigrate the valid advances in American science during this time, but Bush and others who would decry the support given to these practical men must remember that it was easier to be a "scientist" and to be trained as such than it was to be an artist. One good, practical machine or mechanical improvement could support a lot of scientific "discoveries" which were of no value or of no practical use. The scientist was not condemned when he produced a nonfunctioning machine or a functioning but impractical tool. (Such impractical machines, of course, were thought of as not contributing much to progress, but then neither did the impractical artist contribute much to progress.) In addition, the scientist to a greater extent could train himself at his own pace in his own home by reading the growing number of scientific journals or by establishing a correspondence with others interested in the same subjects. As indicated above, with rare exceptions the artist must be trained if he is to reach a level of ability which will bring him renown. That concept—renown and the concomitant potential for exploitation—perhaps explains better than anything else why scientists and not artists are viewed by

some as more important "expounders" of a culture's "consciousness."
(Perhaps if Benjamin Franklin had spent as much time and had achieved as
much success as a poet or an artist as he achieved as a scientist, the entire
course of the Republic would have been different.)

Exploitation was the prime factor in the expeditions by Lewis and Clark
through the newly acquired Louisiana Purchase territories. That fact, that most
of the important expeditions which followed were conducted by military or
ex-military men, is not lost on Bush. The role of the military as he portrays it
in this time period is not as harsh as some have shown it to have been, but he
does not play down the growing influence of the professional soldier on
government. Again though, Bush perhaps goes too far when he says it is the
surveyor "who is the true folk hero of the developing West, the man who
created boundary, not the man like Daniel Boone . . . who operates in the
undifferentiated space of a psychically pure wilderness." Folk heroes are people who are larger than life, persons who roam freer and farther and faster
than the average person, than the settler who comes along behind to convert
"nature into a nation." The person who prescribes limits, who encloses the
open land, whether those enclosures are lines on a paper map or the barbed
wire fences which came later, hardly seems to fit any description of a hero.
Someone must draw the lines, someone must close up the open land or chaos
will reign, but the settler who accepts and desires the boundary lines perhaps
can do so because he can roam free with the Kit Carsons of his dreams in a
landscape which is free of limits, except those set by nature.

If there is an overriding image of the United States both in the eyes of the
citizens and of the Europeans who became the immigrant flood of later decades, it is that of the free and open landscape, whether it is the gently rolling
hills of the Hudson River Valley or the broad, sweeping plains of the midwest,
or the rugged Rocky Mountains. The land, whether a wilderness or a garden,
whether benevolent or threatening, becomes the dream of the American. From
Jefferson's calls for a nation of small farmers to Daniel Boone's feeling
cramped when his neighbor is less than a day away, Americans have discussed, dreamed about, painted, and stolen the land. Thus it is appropriate that
the first major painting "school" in the new land is that of the Hudson River
Valley painters who depicted a landscape both rugged and sophisticated. "Rip
Van Winkle" contains eloquent passages devoted to descriptions of the "fairy
Mountains" of the Catskills. Even George Caleb Bingham's paintings of river-
boatmen become a landscape. The rugged mountains and the smooth-flowing
Mississippi River presented a problem also to some persons in the early part of
the nineteenth century as the nation began to feel a growing sophistication and
cultural awareness. This great, open, fertile land had no ruins of temples, no
crumbling monuments to forgotten heroes and gods of ancient lore. How then
could we expect to develop a civilized, artistic nation if we had no ruins? In
some cases, the landscape artists painted in ruins of their own creation, but the

popular Currier and Ives prints often populated the landscape with buffaloes, trains, Indians, and covered wagons.

Books such as *The Dream of Reason* are so rare they must be supported in as many ways as possible. At the same time, because there are few such books for students of the American scene, the problems in style and in approach in Bush's work become glaring. He has two rhetorical techniques which are especially irritating. On the one hand, his style is almost turgid. Obviously no one expects or wants pulp magazine simplicity, but when one must stop to reread a sentence just to try to determine what is being said because of its convoluted condition, erudition is inappropriate. It hampers the reading, and it hampers the comprehension of what is being read. A second irritating characteristic is his continual use of compound adjectives such as "sociogeographic," "religiopolitical," "metaphysicoliterary," "religioscientific," "psychopolitical," and "politicosexual." Perhaps the most disturbing flaw comes when Bush becomes a twentieth century Freudian critic to interpret nineteenth century art. For instance, in reference to a painting of an Indian family, a visual grouping which he admits comes straight from Christian "flight into Egypt iconography," Bush says the painter "unconsciously expresses the wish that they would abandon their hectic sexual lives and become a model . . . happy family." How the author can determine the state of the couple's physical relationship—unless one child equals a "hectic" sexual life—is beyond understanding. Later, when discussing a story by Cooper, Bush comments that the protagonist's efforts to better himself draw on the "psychic energy of pre-orgasmic foreplay."

Despite these nettling flaws, Bush's book is still a valuable contribution to our study of our past. *The Dream of Reason* perhaps could serve as a first contact to American Culture for a beginning student, as long as the individual studies cited above follow it.

John C. Carlisle

Sources for Further Study

Choice. XV, December, 1978, p. 1430.

DULLES
A Biography of Eleanor, Allen,
and John Foster Dulles
and Their Family Network

Author: Leonard Mosley (1913-   )
Publisher: The Dial Press (New York). 530 pp. $12.95
Type of work: Biography
Time: The twentieth century to 1976
Locale: The United States and Europe

The story of the famous Dulles trio who dominated the American political scene in the 1950's

> *Principal personages:*
> JOHN FOSTER DULLES, United States Secretary of State from 1953-1959
> ALLEN WELSH DULLES, C.I.A. Director under President Dwight D. Eisenhower
> ELEANOR LANSING DULLES, famous economist and author

British journalist-biographer Leonard Mosley has produced a triple biography of John Foster, Eleanor, and Allen Dulles that meets a definite need. The lengthy text is anecdotal and occasionally humorous, but lacking in analytical insight. Some sections are trite and boring while historical inaccuracies—for example, that Stalingrad fell during World War II—are annoying. On the whole, the biography is worth reading because it presents an engaging group portrait of the three siblings and reveals the character flaws that led to the Dulles brothers' foreign policy miscalculations during the early part of the Cold War period.

Mosley clearly dislikes John Foster, a self-righteous, self-serving father figure for the triad. He describes how Foster (as Mosley calls him) sacrificed family, friends, and colleagues to protect his career. To avert charges of nepotism when he was first made Secretary of State, he even tried to force Eleanor out of her Berlin desk job. Foster also helped Allen and Eleanor, but always from a position of dominance. Since Allen owed Foster his job at the prestigious Sullivan and Cromwell law firm, he was forced to endorse Thomas E. Dewey for President in the 1940's against his will. Seldom were Foster's views defied.

The brothers had long careers in diplomatic service before their pinnacle appointments in President Dwight D. Eisenhower's Administration where Foster formulated U.S. foreign policy and where Allen made the Central Intelligence Agency (CIA) his personal domain. Eleanor, though the most human and possibly the most brilliant member of the group, never attained more than a middle level desk officer's job in the State Department. Mosley states that she was thwarted in her ambitions because of her sex, a fact that she rebelled against all her life. It is too bad that Mosley devotes the least attention to her life and achievements, since of the three she exhibited the most depth of character and the greatest involvement with different social groups.

The early life of the trio has been popularly re-created with a heavy reliance on Eleanor's reminiscences, since she is the only surviving member who could be interviewed. The picture that emerges is that of a disciplined, austere home life where children were taught to suppress emotions and mask physical weaknesses. With their sisters, Margaret and Nataline, the three were reared to be strict Presbyterians by their minister father and proud mother, daughter of a former Secretary of State. Foster, the eldest, was the most stoic and cruel. However, behind composed veneers, they all were subject to physical problems. Allen suffered terribly from gout which was linked to a birth defect: he was born with a club foot (a family secret). Mosley is successful in presenting Foster, Allen, and Eleanor as basically very volatile people. The other two Dulles sisters receive little attention, so the reader is limited in judging the emotional interplay within the entire family network. Mosley's scope is not as wide as his title indicates.

The narrative opens dramatically on a party scene at the Allen Dulles home on Christmas Eve, 1968, where the ill and retired head of the CIA is merely "the man upstairs" whose presence is not missed by the partygoers or his wife. This sets the tone for what is essentially a depressing biography, despite its inherent historical interest.

Bound by a belief that they could help shape American history, the trio held many reunions in spite of frequent squabbles stemming from deep personality differences. Mosley finds the greatest contrast between the two brothers. Foster was the cool, detached statesman who alienated colleagues, while Allen was the sophisticated and popular *bon vivant*. Whereas Foster was faithful to his wife, Allen was notoriously unfaithful to his. In addition, religion played a key role in Foster's decisions, while Allen was motivated by adventure. Foster despised the British and Allen admired them. Moreover, Foster was the more opportunistic and self-centered. When Senator Joseph McCarthy subpoened members of the State Department to testify concerning charges of Communism, Foster did nothing to protect his subordinates. Allen, to the contrary, refused to throw his to McCarthy's wolves, a stance that not only increased his popularity with subordinates but also furthered the autonomy of the CIA. Foster leaked secrets to the press, while Allen was more trustworthy. However, Allen was as despicable in his support of illegal covert CIA operations as Foster was in interpersonal relations. Both men lacked self-criticism, without which they exaggerated their political importance.

Mosley draws heavily upon the Allen Dulles papers in detailing his World War II adventures in Berne, Switzerland, where as an OSS (Office of Strategic Services) operator, Allen became a master spy. Other sources, some of which Mosley mentions, such as the recollections of the British defector, Kim Philby, challenge Allen's claims. Yet, the author lauds his accomplishments to the point of hyperbole. These wartime successes contrast sharply with Allen's later failures as CIA chief, the ill-conceived Bay of Pigs invasion of Cuba being among the most disastrous. Mosley does not satisfactorily reconcile this dichotomy. A revealing letter written in Moscow by Kim Philby indicates that Allen was lazy, but there is no further elucidation.

On the whole, Allen's cloak and dagger escapades and womanizing provide a touch of enjoyment to the narrative and offset the almost insufferable behavior of Foster—particularly his hardline diplomacy as Secretary of State. Dour and overbearing, Mosley's Foster has few redeeming qualities and few political successes. He is given high marks for negotiating the Japanese peace treaty in 1951 and is favorably portrayed in his role as Bernard Baruch's young assistant on the "Reparations Committee" at the Versailles Peace Conference after World War I. Otherwise, his life unfolds as a series of misjudgments, from his refusing a job to William O. Douglas at the law firm in which he was a senior partner, to his virulent anti-Communist policy of the 1950's which positioned America on the brink of nuclear war. Mosley makes clear that Foster's praise of his brinkmanship resulted in lost opportunities, especially, the chance for better relations with the Soviet Union and friendship with Communist China. His snubbing of friendly overtures by Chou En-lai at the 1954 Geneva Peace Conference is a classic example of poor statesmanship. Yet, Foster was steel-willed and conceited in his convictions. Repeatedly criticized for leaking news favorable to himself at every major conference he attended (and consequently jeopardized), Foster remained self-righteous. Mosley, unfortunately, does not question Foster's ideology; so the reader is denied a probing psychological study. Townsend Hoopes's *The Devil and John Foster Dulles* is a more revelatory biography.

Mosley's chronology effectively demonstrates how by the 1950's Foster became the Republican party's chief spokesman on foreign policy and how much he influenced President Eisenhower's foreign policy decisions. In response to Foster's advice, Eisenhower even rebuffed old personal friends such as Anthony Eden during the Suez Canal crisis. However, the reader is not given enough information about Foster's special relationship with Eisenhower to form firm judgments.

Mosley holds Foster responsible, at least in part, for major international crises such as the Hungarian Revolution and the Suez Canal British and French invasion. Though encouraging both enterprises, Foster reneged in support. Anthony Eden's descriptions furnish the backdrop scenario for the Suez invasion, a version that shows Foster endorsing the intervention, then withholding his support. Mosley's explanation is that Foster wanted to destroy the last vestiges of British hegemony and succeeded. His motivation was personal and probably stemmed from his abhorrence of British reparations demands at the Versailles Peace Conference. Ironically, as Secretary of State, Foster exemplified the *Realpolitik* he deplored at Versailles.

An illuminating assessment is made of Foster's protective influence over Allen when the latter was CIA director. Allen was free to plan assassinations, fund lethal chemical experiments, and expand espionage activity without supervision. Their moral values, while widely divergent, never conflicted, and Foster as Secretary of State never censured Allen for lavish expenditures on covert gadgetry. Allen's downfall came after Foster's death, when the older brother was not around to smooth over his failures.

Eleanor's career reflects greater professional competence. As a welfare worker in Paris during World War I she was the only member of the trio under fire and the only one deeply concerned with the underprivileged. Married against family wishes to a Talmudic scholar, David Blondheim, Eleanor wrote several scholarly works on her own and in collaboration with her husband. After his death by his own hand she gave birth to their only child, a boy, and resumed her political career in Europe after World War II. She is especially remembered for her procurement of Marshall Plan aid for a devastated Austria. In Mosley's portrayal, Eleanor constantly served humanity and rose above personal tragedy, although she always deeply felt the loss of David Blondheim. Her life with her husband is intimately recounted—unfortunately, at times, to the point of tedium. Nevertheless, the details are noteworthy because there is a dearth of published biographical material concerning both Eleanor and Allen.

Minimal attention is given to the trio's children, although the conversion of Foster's son Avery to Catholicism, and his vocation as a priest, is spotlighted. Father Avery Dulles, S.J., was one of Mosley's prime sources of information about how his Catholicism was used to benefit his father politically. For the most part, however, the children's lives fade into the background, while our attention is directed to the silly behavior of Foster's and Allen's wives, topics more for gossip than for a critical biography. But Mosley tells his gossip well. The narrative ends as it began, with a party; this time at Eleanor's where the eighty-two-year-old matriarch entertains her descendants, none of whom is involved in politics. A final ironic note: despite the clamor of the triad for political recognition, the Dulles family as a political dynasty ended with Foster, Allen, and Eleanor.

In writing this biography Mosley relied heavily on personal conversations with family members and former associates, as well as the brothers' personal papers at Princeton University. As a result, he adequately covers American Cold War politics during the Eisenhower era. But one may wonder if many international confrontations of the 1950's can be explained in terms of Russian aggressiveness and American thoughts of nuclear retaliation. Mosley's overview may be too simplistic.

Anne C. Raymer

Sources for Further Study

Choice. XV, July, 1978, p. 748.
Critic. XXXVII, July 15, 1978, p. 6.
Economist. CCLXVIII, July 8, 1978, p. 99.
Spectator. CCXLI, July 8, 1978, p. 140.
Virginia Quarterly Review. LIV, Autumn, 1978, p. 140.

EARTHLY DELIGHTS, UNEARTHLY ADORNMENTS
American Writers as Image-Makers

Author: Wright Morris (1910-   )
Publisher: Harper & Row Publishers (New York). 193 pp. $10.95
Type of work: Essays

A collection of brief essays exploring the works of representative major American fiction writers and analyzing the effect of image-making on their individual literary styles

That Wright Morris is a writers' writer has seemed the case for nearly forty years. He has many admirers; he should have more. Americans should appreciate him; he understands us. He is a protean storyteller. He has remarkable energy, having produced some thirty volumes, including eighteen novels, a collection of short stories, four photo-texts, an anthology, and four collections of essays, of which *Earthly Delights, Unearthly Adornments* is the most recent. He has written adventurously, always daring to push to new limits his craft, always changing and growing. Despite the size of his canon and his tenure on the scene, he has never quite caught the fancy of the general public—and he has never tried to. That is as it should be, but it is also a shame, because he succeeds cogently in showing Americans to themselves. Although he did win, twenty-three years ago, the National Book Award for his novel *The Field of Vision*, his is clearly not the purpose of the bestseller author. Instead, he is that rare artist who is equally interested in substance and technique: a stylist and craftsman.

Morris loves his stories, and he loves the process of deciding among the immense variety of possible forms for their telling. Art for him is heightened reality. His dual regard for reality and its rendering makes him special among American fiction writers and makes him a challenge to read. He is tough, eccentric, and clear-sighted. He does not comfort or delight readers with cheap easiness. He possesses an unapologetically hard-edged and angularly analytical intelligence; his truths are not always pleasant, and to appreciate his prose, one must love honesty. His combination of story and style makes his work of fascinating interest both to other writers and to readers willing to confront nonformula fiction, willing to live with zany, memorable, real characters, and willing to be startled and changed by what they read. Such adventurous writers and readers appreciate the crispness of Morris' style, his aptness of scene and setting, his precision of phrase and picture, his ear for American idioms, his deep affection for the human condition, and his stories. They respect his restless search for new structures, for fresh nuances of diction, tone, and texture to add to a scene or a character. He is never lazy. Rather, he celebrates complexity and flux. It is unfortunate that Morris has not reached that wider audience which other, less gifted writers do achieve; the respect his fellow writers accord him must suffice for now. They know how hard he works to make the process of writing fiction look so much simpler than it is; they know he is America's living master of *le mot juste*.

This collection of essays celebrates American writers and writing. It is obviously a labor of love and gratitude. Morris deeply admires those American writers who so fused themselves with their beginnings, their landscapes, and their language that they developed into artistic representatives of a nation. As a writer, he has aimed for this fusion himself. He sees American writing as a singular stream flowing up to him, around him, beyond him, and he is unabashedly proud to be part of it all. It is apparent that he has read American writing prodigiously, remembered much, and thought unceasingly and perceptively about his readings. He loves his craft and is grateful to those strong writers who stimulated and guided him in learning his craft. This book is his testimonial to those writers and an elucidation of how they accomplish their art.

Morris' pleasure at being part of a tradition is obvious throughout this collection. For him, the greatness of the American literary tradition stems from the language itself, which is rich and various. It is a strong and sinewy language, capable nevertheless of astonishing grace, subtlety, and imagery, and superbly resistant to stultification. Morris believes that, in the hands of a perceptive author, the language has the power to shape our very lives.

Earthly Delights, Unearthly Adornments is a successful attempt to define, clarify, and illustrate Morris' basic premise that images provide the hallmark to any writer's style, "the signature by which we recognize them." He shows how various representative American writers filter memory through their emotions and intellects, producing great works of art through singularly effective images.

The first essay in the collection is personal and places Morris consciously in the American tradition. In "Of Memory, Emotion and Imagination," he explores his own growing consciousness of and delight in the combination of work, craft, and ineffable mystery which forms a literary product. He analyzes his need as an artist to create, delineates the decisions he makes, and gives credit to the elusive factor of creativity. Out of all this he attempts to understand the origin of his own unique style.

In the volume's middle portion, Morris analyzes in separate, pithy, and memorable essays on each artist, these same concerns and concepts as they apply to the lives, personalities, and works of such American writers as Melville, Whitman, Twain, Henry James, Willa Cather, Gertrude Stein, Katherine Anne Porter, Fitzgerald, Dos Passos, Faulkner, Hemingway, Richard Wright, James Agee, and Carson McCullers. As a unifying transitional device, he ends each essay with an intriguing comparison or contrast to the work of the writer to be treated in the next essay.

In the last two essays, "Origins: The Self-Imaged Image Maker" and "Unearthly Adornments," Morris comes full-circle back to himself. He reiterates that those writers he has explored in the book are uniquely American, uniquely bound in the resilience of the language. It is our search, he suggests, for ". . . telling imagery . . . rooted in memory and emotion" which makes our literature singular. He maintains, "the whiteness of the whale, the lineaments of death, the speech of groping hands, water purling over rocks, the recurrent voices of impotence and rage provide us with clues to the writers' obsessions, the chimed notes of their emotion. . . . Which is either positive and life-enhancing or negative and life-negating." After this generalization, Morris homes honestly in on his own purpose as a writer, his own needs to make certain kinds of images: "Much of my own plains-based fiction grew out of my need for an experience I came too late for." The compelling force, he concludes, is our hunger, our necessity to search for something profoundly elusive, to seek an image more life-enhancing than the one we have exhausted. Thus, his book's title: writers create "unearthly adornments" for "earthly delights." Morris, as Marianne Moore expressed it earlier, engages in speaking of imaginary gardens with live toads in them.

This volume is an important study for students of American literature; Morris' assessments of a score of American writers are valuable for their freshness and exactness. A helpful index is provided which includes interesting citations of minor figures. Morris' lively, inquisitive, and inventive intellect never fails to delight, even when one disagrees with a specific point. The collection is also of value to writers of fiction; it will aid them in relinquishing false burdens and in better shouldering worthwhile ones. When Morris writes of writing, he is to be trusted as the scout who knows the territory from firsthand experience. Finally, the volume should be of value to the general reader, since it is charmingly instructive, remarkably free of critical or scholarly jargon, easily accessible, pungent in its perceptions. One is constantly underlining passages as being truly outstanding. Of Twain, for instance, Morris muses, he was a man grown bitter, "exiled from what he held most dear—the image he had made of his boyhood." Morris writes of Hemingway that he did not understand how much he had to love before he could write at full power, uninhibited by his reputation. In an eccentric and thought-provoking re-evaluation of Hemingway's much-maligned posthumous novel, Morris maintains ". . . he must find new objects of affection, of attachment. *Islands in the Stream* . . . finds him at ease with sentiment, indulgent with humor and admitting of binding ties with a cat named Boise." Of Leo and Gertrude Stein he observes, "Compared with his sister, Leo's egotism was self-absorbing and superficial. Slowly and in a way astonishing she was knowing she was a genius." Each of these essays is packed with such keen perceptions. Each one, in a way, points toward Morris' conclusion to his essay on McCullers: "We do not see the hard facts of life . . . until they are transfigured by the image-maker. The world itself is unfinished until he goes around and finishes things up." Throughout these essays shines Morris' admiration for the energy, tenacity, bravery, and hard-won brilliance of these writers—even when he does not find them altogether successful in certain works. What excites him consistently is their skill in transforming into higher truths their own memories and realities through their images.

Overall in these essays, Wright Morris has fashioned a marvelously warm and human book, rich in detail and reason. He sheds much light on literary reputations all too often accepted unquestioningly. His ideas are provocative and instructive, and because of its crystalline quality, the collection seems lighter than it is. The author's infectious curiosity about the whys and the whats of writing will stimulate readers to come back to the volume again and again. Morris cares about us, our language, and our perceptions. He loves to read and to write; he does both uncommonly well and makes it possible for us to join him in enhancing those delights.

Thomas N. Walters

Sources for Further Study

Booklist. LXXV, November 1, 1978, p. 449.

Kirkus Reviews. XLVI, August 15, 1978, p. 934.

Library Journal. CIII, September 15, 1978, p. 1750.

Publisher's Weekly. CCXIV, August 28, 1978, p. 382.

ELIZABETH BOWEN

Author: Victoria Glendinning
Publisher: Alfred A. Knopf (New York). Illustrated. 331 pp. $12.50
Type of work: Biography
Time: 1899-1973
Locale: Principally Ireland and England

A richly detailed life of the last of the great Anglo-Irish novelists, the brilliant and fascinating Elizabeth Bowen

In this biography of Elizabeth Bowen one learns about the woman herself and why she wrote as she did. Author, Victoria Glendinning has documented her work thoroughly with quotations from living people, letters, radio addresses, acquaintances' reminiscences, diaries, publishers' comments, and reviews. There are more than a hundred people who have helped with this perceptive treatment of Elizabeth Bowen's life and work, which is illustrated with sixteen pages of photographs of Elizabeth, her parents, her husband, her homes, and her friends. Elizabeth Bowen had a rich assortment of notable friends, among whom were T. S. Eliot, Virginia Woolf, Iris Murdoch, Rose Macaulay, Cyril Connoly, John Buchan (Lord Tweedsmuir), Lord David Cecil, A. E. Coppard, E. M. Forster, Graham Greene, L. P. Hartley, Rosamond Lehmann, Cecil Day Lewis, William Maxwell, Carson McCullers, William Plomer, May Sarton, Muriel Spark, Stephen Spender, Evelyn Waugh, Eudora Welty, Alfred and Blanche Knopf, Sean O'Faolain, and Lady Ottiline Morrell.

Elizabeth Bowen was Anglo-Irish. She was born in Dublin on June 7, 1899, and died in London on February 22, 1973. She was buried in the family graveyard in Ireland, near Bowen's Court.

Her father, Henry Charles Cole Bowen, was the eldest of nine children, and her mother came from a family of ten; but Elizabeth was their only child. Her father inherited Bowen's Court, given to his family by Oliver Cromwell, and here, during the summers, Bitha, as Elizabeth was called, lived her first seven years. Then her father suffered a nervous breakdown and went voluntarily to a mental hospital outside Dublin when she was seven. So began Bowen's life in England, where she and her mother were taken over by a "network of Anglo-Irish relatives."

Her vague and ethereal mother, Florence, was apprehensive of Bitha's health and insisted that she drink plenty of milk, never become overtired, wear gloves in order not to get freckles on her hands, and not be allowed to read until she was seven. She felt that the Bowens were mentally overworked, and even after Bitha was in elementary school, her mother withdrew her from time to time so as not to "tire her brain." Bitha started her "campaign of not noticing" when they left Bowen's Court and continued this protective device after her mother died of cancer when Bitha was thirteen. She never allowed herself to overgrieve outwardly. Her cousin Audrey, who shared a room with her, heard her sobbing in the night; but she could never talk about her mother or her own sorrow. Audrey believed that she never got over losing her mother. Bowen was well aware of the stammer that afflicted her throughout her life, and which may have been brought on by the trauma she felt over her mother's death. (The stammer was described as a pronounced hesitation—and a complete stalling on certain words, one of which was "mother." Forty years later, after several successful lecture tours, an agent replied to inquiries: "Not at all disturbing, but if I may say so, 'endearing' rather than distracting. She is a most successful lecturer," he said, "with a most successful stammer.") As a woman of forty, she wrote that her mother, when away from her, had "thought of me constantly and planned ways in which we could meet and be alone."

Upon the death of her mother, her upbringing was taken over by a committee of aunts. She was sent to Harpenden Hall and then to Downe School in 1914. Downe School had as head mistress Olive Willis, who did not say "Don't" but "Need You?" She told the girls that it did not matter if they were happy, so long as they were good. She also put much stress on conversation and chattiness, tact and resource. Elizabeth said that as a result "many of us have turned out to be good hostesses." Another graduate of Downe wrote: "To this day, the briefest lull at a luncheon or a dinner party is instantly filled by me with remarks of an inanity which startles even my children."

All this time her father had been gradually recovering from his mental illness, and when she left Downe House in the summer of 1917, at eighteen, she went to Bowen's Court to live with him. She and her cousin Audrey Fiennes had a delightful social time, going to balls and even giving one at Bowen's Court. But she was never the typical debutante, not being pretty enough, silly enough, or confident enough. She showed her unconventional side in the way she dressed, always with large earrings, necklaces of false pearls or great glass baubles, and other flashy fake jewelry that she wore with great *éclat*.

A year later, in 1918, her father remarried. The new wife was agreeable to Elizabeth's high spirits and they got along very well. Then Elizabeth had her first real love affair. The man was five years older than she, a soldier, Lieutenant John Anderson. The relationship broke off before marriage, Elizabeth sending back his ring from Italy where she was visiting an aunt. She got over her disappointment in time, but traces of John Anderson show in the character of Major Brutt in her novel *The Death of the Heart* (1938).

Elizabeth began writing stories when she was twenty. At first she had no luck getting them published. Then she met Rose Macaulay, an established novelist, through her old head mistress Olive Willis. In 1923 her first book, *Encounters*, a selection of short stories, was published. In the same year she was married to Alan Cameron; she was twenty-four and he was thirty.

Alan Cameron was intelligent, well-read, and sensitive, though not an "intellectual." He was extremely conscientious, and "hearty in manner." He was the safe harbor for Bowen's dislocated life. Their marriage, which, as the years passed, sometimes seemed incomprehensible to the outside world, nevertheless lasted. There were, however, aspects of Elizabeth's nature that were never satisfied by Alan. She had several affairs, always with men younger than she. Alan was always protected from knowing about the affairs, since Bowen considered that they had no bearing on her marriage. "Guilt is squalid," she believed, and her attitude may be regarded as masculine rather than feminine. Her last affair, with Charles Ritchie, lasted until her death; he was with her when she died.

In 1925 Alan was appointed Secretary for Education for the city of Oxford. This was most propitious for Elizabeth, who came into her own professionally, socially, and emotionally during the ten years that they lived in Oxford. She formed many friendships. Lord David Cecil and Maurice Bowra, professors at Wadham College, were among her intimates. Bowra wrote of her:

> She was tall and well built and had the manner of someone who has lived in the country and knows its habits. She was handsome in an unusual way, with a face that indicated both mind and character. . . . She had a masculine intelligence which was fully at home in large subjects and general ideas. . . .

The stimulus of Oxford was responsible for two books in 1929, *The Last September* and the short story collection *Joining Charles*. After that she produced a book every year except one until she and Alan left Oxford in 1935. Meanwhile, Elizabeth's father had become ill again, and Elizabeth went to Bowen's Court to be with him; he died in May 1930, leaving Bowen's Court to her.

Bowen's Court was much as it was when the third Henry Bowen moved there in 1776. There was no bathroom at all. Maids brought up tin baths to the bedrooms and hot water in wickerwork containers. There were two ancient but adequate lavatories. The rooms were hard to heat and one visitor tested the sheets by placing her hand mirror in the bed; finding it fogged over, she slept in a raincoat. Elizabeth nevertheless entertained at Bowen's Court constantly, having house guests for weeks at a time. Her American publisher, Blanche Knopf, an exquisite woman addicted to cleanliness, warmth, and comfort, wrote to Elizabeth in August, 1938, after a stay there: "I cannot even begin to tell you what staying at Bowen's Court has meant to me. I have never seen anything quite like it of course, but I never realized how living that way could possibly be." Though the accommodations were spartan in the early days, Elizabeth always provided the best of food and drink and took care of all the expenses connected with entertaining, even though there was never really enough money. She felt that Bowen's Court, her inheritance, was home. In 1949 Elizabeth's book *The Heat of the Day* made some money for her, and she spent part of it putting bathrooms in Bowen's Court. A little later, planning to live permanently there instead of in England, she redecorated the big drawing room with curtains made, surprisingly, of pink corset-satin.

Elizabeth and Alan had spent their summers at Bowen's Court for years, but when Alan had to retire in 1951 for reasons of health, their plans to live there the year round were interrupted by his death in August, 1952. She wrote to a friend who had been a recent guest:

> It was a great thing that, as a crown to our life of nearly thirty years together, we should have had these months here in this house—as you know, the life we had just begun here was what we'd been looking forward to for so many years. We had such a lovely spring and summer and everything.

And to William Plomer she said in 1955, "Alan never seems dead, in the sense that he never seems gone; I suppose that if one has lived the greater part of one's life with a person he continues to accompany one through every moment." They never had any children.

As a widow Elizabeth continued to entertain, but she also threw herself into lectures, travel, and teaching. In 1956 she was awarded a fellowship at Bryn Mawr for the autumn term. She was writer in residence at the American Academy in Rome in 1959. None of these activities brought the kind of money that she needed to keep up Bowen's Court, so in 1959 she sold it to Cornelius O'Keefe, hoping that he and his family would live there. However, it was torn down. She lived briefly in Oxford and then bought a little house in Hythe on the Kent coast where she had lived with her mother fifty years before. She continued to travel. From 1950 until her last illness there was no year in which she did not spend some time in the United States. Lecturing and being a writer in residence at American universities was a source of income and pleasure. Also, she could see something of Charles Ritchie, who was the permanent representative of Canada at the United Nations 1958 to 1962.

Many studies have been written about Elizabeth Bowen; so she decided to write her own: an unconventional autobiography with "the relationship between art and life" as its theme. It was never completed, but on her deathbed she instructed her literary executor, Spencer Curtis Brown, to publish it. It was included in *Pictures and Conversations* (1975). Bowen suffered from a chronic smoker's cough and had bouts of recurring bronchitis from 1970 until she died on February 22, 1973.

Nell Joslin Styron

Sources for Further Study

Choice. XV, June, 1978, p. 544.
Critic. XXXVII, July 15, 1978, p. 6.
Sewanee Review. LXXXVI, July, 1978, p. R88.
Yale Review. LXVII, June, 1978, p. 615.

E. M. FORSTER: A LIFE

Author: P. N. Furbank
Publisher: Harcourt Brace Jovanovich (New York). 619 pp. $19.95
Type of work: Biography
Time: 1879-1970
Locale: England and the East

A biography divided into two parts, the first covering Forster's first thirty-five years and development as a novelist, the second covering his remaining fifty-six years and maturity as a man of letters. Furbank captures the spirit of the age and intellectual climate so instrumental in Forster's growth, and reveals in a sensitive and sensible manner those parts of Forster's life so long undisclosed

Among American readers, the name of E. M. Forster does not loom large. Because *A Passage to India* has sometimes been taught in high school and college curricula as a representative of the modern British novel, some readers will remember Forster's name; but the majority will have forgotten him. An unassuming character himself, Forster wrote unassuming novels. He dealt with central human concerns in his books, but he was never the flashy kind of writer who starts trends. His characters were types he was familiar with in Edwardian England, holdovers from the Victorian period. In a sense his life was also a kind of holdover, with a cognizant refrain from sexual liberation and inherent frustrations but with a deep-felt affection for associates.

Forster was a fine man and a fine writer, and P. N. Furbank has written a fine biography to present his life. *E. M. Forster: A Life* follows a prescription Forster himself uttered forty-five years ago. In a letter to Joe Ackerley in which he commented on the necessity of omissions from Lowes Dickinson's biography, Forster asserted that he should want "every thing told, everything" when his own biography was to be written. As a result of following such a direction, Furbank has written not only a sensitive biography but also a sensible one that answers those questions we are likely to ask about Forster's life, with its richly diverse mixture of experiences, acquaintances, and frustrations.

A certain attitude prevails throughout Forster's works, and in the present biography, passages from the author's letters and other writings continually affirm that attitude. Forster asserted the necessity for connections between human beings, sensible relationships that showed warmth and compassion. In his own life, he was studiously attentive to relationships, working at them, analyzing them, fretting about them. Upon the base of friendship he anchored most of his beliefs. Forster's friendships were myriad. Homosexual or non-sexual, they filled his attention. Attachments to all types of people, so long as they were sensitive to others, kept him young and intellectually energetic. He spread his good fortunes with others and himself required very little, except in the form of attention from those he held dear.

At bottom, Forster's most formative friendship was his enduring love relationship with his widowed mother. He barely knew his father and grew up in a household dominated by Lily Forster and the women with whom she socialized. The family was middle-class, adequately provided for, and able to pamper the boy. Lily devoted herself to her dear Morgan. He attended a series of day schools and boarding prep schools but was seldom happy in these situations because of his frail constitution and old-maidish ways. Recollections by schoolmates in later years emphasized the latter trait above all others, save for his clumsiness.

Not until Forster entered Cambridge did he feel at ease with his peers. At Kings College his intellectual and social life blossomed, whereas he had suffered in the public schools. At Kings he encountered kindred spirits and began to fashion the network of close personal relationships that would fill his lifetime. Furbank, in presenting these early details, provides clear images of Forster's developing sensibilities, and we clearly anticipate later characteristics of the writer. Especially important are the details of the Cambridge years because of their later effect on his novels and the shaping of his vision.

Through these details we gain valuable insight concerning what relationship Forster's childhood and development had to later attitudes and behaviors he was to espouse through a long public career. Furthermore, we see how these early years shaped his private life and attitudes.

To a degree, we must examine his private life to understand Forster's literary contribution. Because Forster enjoyed associations with such a widespread circle of prominent figures (notably, members of the Bloomsbury group), his observations are valuable to our assessment of his era. Because in his novels he deftly probed the social milieu of middle-class England, we are richer for his letters to friends, which often show the basis for his fiction. Forster was a copious letter writer, and his dispatches during travels provide sometimes hilarious, always illuminating commentary. We can see developing images and attitudes that later emerge in his wonderfully entertaining novels and in his penetrating essays.

Perhaps more important literarily, however, Furbank enlightens us concerning key questions about Forster's difficulties with writing. Obvious reasons for suppression of certain homosexual short stories and the homosexual novel *Maurice* are made more understandable in the context of Forster's life. His misgivings about the stories, their effect upon and reception by friends, are clearly revealed. Through the biography we see that Forster's firm sense of propriety and discretion was a direct product of his upbringing. Moreover, we clearly see that he was conscious of protecting his reputation in the public eye, no matter how he conducted his private affairs, no matter how fine the questionable works were artistically.

Why Forster never wrote another novel after *A Passage to India*, however, has been the most debated question concerning his literary career. Here Furbank provides valuable insight that should help resolve the question; three chief reasons are given. First, Furbank calls to mind that Forster was superstitious despite his rationalist frame of mind. In a sense, success created sterility in him, an almost irrational fear that things were going too well to continue.

Second, Furbank cites Forster's central problem as an early twentieth century novelist. Being a homosexual, he was bored at having to deal with the relationships of men and women, the problems of marriage, and matters of bisexual love. This, Furbank indicates, was Forster's practical explanation. Furbank also cites Forster's frustration at having written *Maurice* and recognizing the impossibility of its publication; his feeling that *Maurice* would have been a better novel if written for publication was frustrating. But ultimately the most damaging thought was that writing *Maurice* had been a substitute for having a homosexual affair.

Furbank's third explanation perhaps has the most merit. He suggests that Forster's novels all follow similar lines of development and include the same character types and plot materials. Furbank does not mean that Forster repeated himself, but rather that one central vision informed all Forster's novels, and that "the social types and manners which ruled his imagination were those of his Edwardian youth." Therefore, Forster, as a realistic novelist, was in a difficult position in the modern age, fashioning contemporary themes from somewhat outdated materials.

To whatever degree these reasons were mixed, the fact is that *A Passage to India*, published in 1924, was the last novel Forster wrote. While he started to sketch out several more novels at later points in his career, none ever developed. He did write a number of fine stories, but the bulk of his work took the essay form, where without a doubt he also excelled.

In his long life Forster covered diverse subjects in his essays. He spent considerable effort on book reviews and felt them to be rather important. He championed other writers and was ever on the lookout for ways to help the less favored. Moreover, he was not afraid to step boldly into areas of controversy, as in cases involving civil liberties and obscenity rulings. One such case, involving Radclyffe Hall's novel *The Well of Loneliness*, prompted Forster to organize a host of writers to testify on behalf of the book. Later, as a member of the International P. E. N. Club and the National Council for Civil Liberties, he lent his voice to various writers' causes. After his sojourns in India and Alexandria, he gained something of a reputation for speaking lucidly and forcefully on Indian politics and British colonial policy, of which he was usually critical. He spoke out fervently against war and attended numerous conferences throughout Europe for the purpose of advancing peace among nations.

Altogether, Forster's life was full with travel, friendship, literary fame, and sexual frustration, the latter being an undeniable part of Forster's existence. He was relatively mature before he had any significant sexual encounters, and these were not wholly satisfactory. Several of the men he most loved in his young manhood either were not in love with him or expressed their love in ways different from Forster.

Throughout Forster's adult life, sexual questions continued to dominate his relationships. Relationships that turned into affairs and the affairs of fellow homosexuals are reported faithfully by Furbank. Yet Forster's desire to leave behind an accurate record has created the one significant drawback of the biography: Furbank tells us so much about the fears, foibles, and frustrations of Forster's circle of homosexual friends that at times the biography becomes tedious with detail, the pace slows, and the reader tires of the account.

On the whole, however, the generous inclusion of details through most of the book supplies interesting footnotes to our knowledge of modern literary history. Forster's encounter with D. H. Lawrence, for example, juxtaposed two of the early twentieth century's major British authors. Their relationship, touchy from the outset, never developed, but it had important repercussions, such as convincing Forster to show *Maurice* to his friends—major steps in his development. Forster recognized a homosexual side to Lawrence, particularly through his reading of *The White Peacock*, and thought him to be purposely self-blinding. Lawrence, however, trusted Forster as a critic, at one point saying "I can trust you to take me seriously, and really to read. Because whatever I may be, you *do* listen."

Another relationship of Forster's, with C. P. Cavafy, brought to light the realm of modern Greek poetry. Forster felt Cavafy was the greatest discovery among the modern Greeks and championed his work. For Forster, Cavafy epitomized Alexandria, and Furbank cites a passage from *Pharos and Pharillon* in which Forster speaks of the "Greek gentleman in a straw hat, standing absolutely motionless at a slight angle to the universe." The details of their encounters, as with so many other encounters in Forster's life, reveal a sensitive man seeking meaningful, thoroughly human connections with other people.

Forster was an intellectual in the most positive sense of that label. He was naïve about some subjects and approached politics with certain blind spots. He could be indolent, and he often lacked specific direction in his writing. For the most part, however, he maintained a tolerant and humanistic objectivity toward the world, and he took an active part in the shaping of it. His long association with the East, his deep love for India and high regard for her people, his love of the Mediterranean—all blended in a moderating influence upon his English middle-class stance.

Explaining that stance is Furbank's central concern. Forster wanted such a book because he knew there were things in his life that would interest us and things that were necessary for us to understand more than the public roles of his long career could ever reveal. The Forster who emerges from these pages presents the ideal humanistic model, a man deeply in touch with his culture and the humanity that creates that culture. Furbank's image of Forster's personal side reinforces the public image we have so long had of Forster and does nothing to change our perception except to enrich it.

Furbank is an engaging writer who has captured the flavor of Forster's literary style in the biography; readers will find themselves remarking time and again, "how like Forster this sounds." The careful excerpting from Forster's writings does much to create this effect, but Furbank's skill goes beyond the excerpts, and he is always sensitive to his effect. Thus, he fashions a cohesive document that is thoroughly illuminating. This is not a critical biography, but the wealth of information it provides makes possible a greater degree of understanding of Forster's works. It is not a sentimental biography, but its revelations expose the sentiments fundamental in Forster's canon. It is a highly readable literary biography, important for its subject but also important because of the lucid style and comprehensive treatment. Forster devotees will find here a book to cherish for its sensitive and sensible handling of E. M. Forster's life.

Gary B. Blank

Sources for Further Study

Books and Bookmen. XXIII, May, 1978, p. 25.
Library Journal. CIII, September 15, 1978, p. 1748.
Newsweek. XCII, October 30, 1978, p. 96.
Publisher's Weekly. CCXIV, July 31, 1978, p. 87.
Time. CXII, November 6, 1978, p. 113.

THE END OF THE OLD ORDER IN RURAL EUROPE

Author: Jerome Blum (1913-   )
Publisher: Princeton University Press (Princeton, New Jersey). 505 pp. $12.50
Type of work: History
Time: The eighteenth and nineteenth centuries
Locale: Europe

A study of the social changes that transformed much of Europe from a society of hierarchical orders to one of economic classes

Principal personages:
ALEXANDER II, Czar of Russia, 1855-1881
NICHOLAS I, Czar of Russia, 1894-1918
FREDERICK II, King of Prussia, 1740-1786
CHARLES EMMANUEL, Duke of Savoy
MARIA THERESA, Archduchess of Austria and Queen of Hungary and Bohemia, 1740-1780
ARTHUR YOUNG, English traveler and author

Studies of the lives, labor and status of European peasants in the Old Regime did not attract the attention of historians to any extent until the later nineteenth century. Since then, there has been a spate of works on the subject by historians of many countries. In this book, Jerome Blum, a distinguished American historian, has performed a useful service by bringing together and synthesizing a good share of the published materials concerning the life and liberation of the peasants of the eighteenth and nineteenth centuries. His "List of Works Cited" covers forty-five pages and ranges from John Quincy Adams, *Letters on Silesia* (1804), through the classic studies of peasant emancipation in Prussia by G. B. Knapp, to the masterly work of Fernand Braudel in the 1960's and 1970's.

The End of the Old Order in Rural Europe is divided into three sections. The first, called "The Traditional Order," explains the internal structure of the feudal hierarchy of the Old Regime and the activities of the two orders: seigniors and peasants. The second section, "Transition," deals with the forces and elements that emerged, particularly in the eighteenth century, to undermine the traditional structure of European rural society. The last section, "Emancipation," tells where, how, and when the peasants were given their personal liberty.

Blum uses the phrase "servile Europe" to mean those lands from France in the west to the Russian Empire in the east in which a process of rural change and of emancipation formed a common experience that lasted for more than a century. He does not include Spain, Britain, most of the Italian states, or the Ottoman Empire as part of servile Europe because the transition from servility to liberation of the peasants in those countries did not follow the same pattern, or come at the same time, as in the servile Europe.

Servile Europe in the eighteenth century contained more than one hundred million people, of which seventy to ninety percent—depending on the country—were rural peasants working the land of their seigniors and burdened with a host of obligations and services that had to be furnished to support the ruling orders. The peasantry of servile Europe was the "broad patient back who bore the weight of the entire social pyramid." Above the peasants in the social structure of the Old Regime were the clergy and the nobility or seigniors. Each order or estate had its defined rights, functions, and obligations which had been formulated in the Middle Ages and which persisted through laws, customs, and habits. Some movement of individuals between orders was possible, as when a peasant became a clergyman, but that was relatively rare. In all, it was a hierarchical, fixed society resting on a "gradation of powers, authorities, eminences and distinctions" with each man born to his place.

Blum takes issue with some historians who hold that by the eighteenth century most peasants of servile Western Europe were no longer serfs because they had been freed from personal servility, and their dependence now adhered only to the land. This is technically true, but the distinction is specious in terms of practical consequences. Virtually all peasants, he points out, still owed servile obligations to a seignior and stood in servile relationship to the seigniorial order as a whole. Only remnants of serfdom may have remained to confine and oppress the peasants of Western Europe by the eighteenth century, but those remnants were sufficient to cause the peasantry to feel their servile status and wish to end it. In the "cahiers of grievances" sent to Paris on the eve of the French Revolution, peasants from all parts of that country complained of the multitude of servile obligations and seigniorial privileges that still existed.

At the same time, Blum acknowledges that, relatively speaking, the peasants of Central and Eastern Europe were much more servile and degraded than those of Western Europe. In Russia and elsewhere in Eastern Europe the peasants were serfs to be sold, mortgaged, exchanged, or gambled away by their seigniors as if they were chattel property. "Hybrids between animal and human," said one Russian lord of his serfs, while another called the peasants "lazy, drunken, irresponsible louts . . . who were kept at work only by fear of the whip."

Throughout servile Europe, almost all peasants were required to furnish a variety of dues and services to the seigniors. Blum cites many examples. In the province of Moravia, for instance, the peasants were susceptible to 246 different money payments for various dues. Not all the peasants of Moravia owed all those money payments, but most of them owed a large proportion of them. He also mentions a certain Livonian peasant household of eight members, male and female, which was obligated to provide 356 days of unpaid labor service annually to the local lord or to the local church. Labor services of all kinds were the most universal of the peasant obligation in Eastern Europe. The payment of the tithe was the major obligation of Western European peasants. Originally the tithe had the pious purpose of supporting the churches and helping the needy. By the eighteenth century it was no more than a tax collected by the government, the nobles, townsmen, and even by some peasants from other peasants. The tithe is probably the best example of the perpetuation, and perversion, of the old medieval social order and its burdens on the peasantry.

Also onerous and widely hated by the peasantry were the numerous surviving seigniorial privileges. These included the so-called monopolies, such as local seignior's control of grain milling or of the manufacture of alcoholic beverages. Seigniors throughout Europe also retained the privilege of hunting wild animals; indeed seigniorial hunting privileges increased during the eighteenth century. Lords of the manor, particularly in Eastern Europe, still had the privilege of granting or refusing permission for their peasants to marry. The administration of justice by the seigniors over their peasants was another privilege which continued from medieval times: seigniors in parts of Eastern Europe often kept a gallows on their estates to facilitate the swift carrying out of the judicial decisions.

Looking at the conditions of life of the peasantry of servile Europe generally, Blum finds that, although there were some prosperous members of the order by the eighteenth century, the great majority were forced to endure a hard existence. Obligatory dues and services took away most of what they produced, forcing them to live in "animal-like squalor and filth." Many of them survived only by turning to beggary or vagabondage. The society of the Old Regime, Blum asserts, failed to provide even a minimally satisfactory standard of living for most of the population.

Entering upon the scene in the eighteenth century were those rulers who came to be known as the enlightened despots. It was they who prepared the way for the liberation of servile Europe and the ending of the traditional order of society. The enlightened despots were primarily interested in enlarging their own absolute authority but, in so doing, they undercut the authority and privileges of the seigniors and aided in the freeing of the peasants. On the other side, the seigniors of the eighteenth century began to insist that the traditional obligations of the peasantry and the ancient privileges of the nobility be reaffirmed and fulfilled. That resurgence of noble demands was basically an effort to halt the growth of absolutism by the monarchs. An intense struggle between the monarchs and the seigniors emerged. The ultimate winners of that conflict would be neither the despots nor the nobility, but the peasants, who gained their freedom as a consequence.

As part of the attempt to restore the status of their order, many eighteenth century seigniors expropriated lands that had fallen into the hands of peasants, especially in Eastern Europe. The monarchs countered by expropriating ("engrossing") peasant lands also, and adding those holdings to the crown lands. But the enlightened despots were persuaded to introduce reforms in the status and tenure of the crown land peasants, whereas the nobility never made any reforms in the lives of their peasants. Maria Theresa of Austria and Catherine II of Russia in the later eighteenth century both reduced peasant obligations on manors belonging to the crown. An even more sweeping reform was made by the absolutist Nicholas I of Russia, who, by royal fiat, made the obligations of all state peasants lower and more equitable. Nicholas even talked of the eventual emancipation of all Russian peasants.

Another ingredient in the growing movement for reform and emancipation was the trend toward agricultural improvement in the later eighteenth century. Throughout Europe large stretches of land were being reoccupied, and newer methods of farming were being tried: root crop planting, green fallowing, ending of the three-field system, and enclosure of the common lands. The trouble was that, more often than not, the peasants could not be persuaded to plant the new crops or adopt the new techniques. The peasants took little interest in agricultural improvements and would work only in the same ways as their fathers had. It was apparent to many agricultural reformers, such as Arthur Young, the English traveler, that no real improvement of European agriculture could come about until the burdens were lifted from the peasants and they were liberated.

Thus Blum sees a combination of conditions coming together all over servile Europe to form the matrix from which the emancipation of the peasants emerged: "reforming princes, improving landlords, new crops and new techniques, new economic opportunities, discontent with the economic inefficiencies of the servile order, and new and disturbing ideas about the equality of man and the injustice of privilege. . . ."

The first emancipation decree by an absolute ruler was that of Charles Emmanuel of Savoy in 1762. It was followed in 1789 when the peasants of France and Switzerland were freed from their servile status; but then there was a halt in the movement because of the French Revolution. Such reforms as peasant emancipation became associated in the minds of other European rulers with the "poison of Jacobinism," which they feared and hated.

Momentum toward the liberation of all peasants of servile Europe had been only delayed, however, not stopped. In 1804, the peasants of Schleswig-Holstein were given their freedom, and those of Prussia in 1807. Emancipation of the peasants of Eastern Europe did not come until the middle years of the nineteenth century; the Austrian peasants were liberated in 1848, the Hungarian peasants in 1853, and the Russian peasantry—the largest group of all—was emancipated by a decree of Alexander II in 1861.

Personal emancipation did not mean complete freedom for most peasants, however; elements of seigniorial privilege and authority still persisted in many places. The Russian peasants, for example, would be required to give two additional years of obedience and service to their former lords. Many of the old seigniorial monopolies continued to be recognized and preserved: the hunting and fishing privileges, among others. In several of the German states, the lords retained police and judicial authority over the peasants until well into the nineteenth century.

Nevertheless, although some vestiges of the old seigniorial authority persisted, the fundamental fact was that by the last quarter of the nineteenth century, servile Europe was no more. All men were now equally citizens of the state, and society was seen as an "aggregate of individuals." Economic and social classes replaced the hierarchical order of the Old Regime.

The End of the Old Order in Rural Europe is a fine piece of scholarly research and graceful writing. To have organized a great amount of material in a coherent fashion and make it understandable and interesting, as Blum has done, is commendable. Any student of European social history will find the book a rewarding study.

James W. Pringle

Sources for Further Study

Journal of Economic History. XXXVIII, December, 1978, p. 975.

THE ENGLISH AUDEN
Poems, Essays and Dramatic Writings, 1927-1939

Author: W. H. Auden (1907-1973)
Edited by Edward Mendelson
Publisher: Random House (New York). 469 pp. $17.95
Type of work: Poetry, essays, and dramatic writings
Time: 1927-1939

A collection of the writings that earned Auden his reputation as the major poet and author of the 1930's in England, this volume makes possible a reassessment of the first major phase of Auden's career

The career of W. H. Auden reflects the paradoxical nature of literary relations between the United States and England. Sharing a common language, a common cultural and artistic background, the two countries seem at once close and remote, sharing in the modern artistic revolution against inherited forms, and yet, in the final analysis, refusing to merge into a single literary tradition. T. S. Eliot, born in St. Louis, became an English citizen and a major force in the English literary scene; Edward Mendelson, Auden's literary executor, notes in his introduction to this volume that Auden's literary career really began with a rejection by Eliot of his first volume of poetry. Yet Eliot remains, for most literary historians, an American poet, distinctively American in his poetic voice, no matter how much he seemed to take on the appearance and demeanor of the English literary classes. Auden's career parallels Eliot's, except in reverse. Taking up residence in New York in 1939, Auden became an American citizen in 1946. If Eliot needed a retreat from America into England, and Englishness, to become a major American poet, Auden needed a retreat from England to become the poet *he* wished to be. He wrote a friend in 1939: "I adore New York as it is the only city in which I find I can work and live quietly. For the first time I am leading a life which remotely approximates to the way I think I ought to live." Yet, in spite of Auden's long sojourn in America, no one doubts that he was an English poet. This volume goes a long way toward showing why.

Auden, of course, unlike Eliot, was established as a major contemporary poet before he made his transatlantic pilgrimage. He published the first collection of his verse (entitled simply *Poems*) in 1930; together with Christopher Isherwood, Stephen Spender, and others, Auden quickly made clear that a new generation of English poets was to be heard in the land. Building on the revolutionary modernism of Eliot and Pound, Auden and his contemporaries forged a new era in poetry—clearly modern in its style and voice, but possessing a wider awareness of the social, economic, and political realities confronting Europe in the years leading up to World War II. Auden was later, as we will see, to be profoundly uncomfortable with at least some of the ideas he voiced in his early poetry and prose. Nevertheless, as this volume attests, Auden's early reputation was well founded. The three volumes of poetry anthologized here, along with the essays and reviews, show us a poet of vigor, of clarity and force, as well as a man who has thought deeply about the state of English language and letters. What Mendelson has done in this volume is to make possible a clearer view of Auden's poetic origins, his early verse, and his preliminary reflections on art and society: in sum, the English roots of his poetic career.

The bulk of this volume is given over to Auden's poetry, a substantial quantity of verse for any poet's lifetime, and a truly remarkable amount for the first twelve years of a poet's career. Reprinted here are all the poems from Auden's first three volumes, *Poems* (1930, reprinted with seven substitutions in 1933), *Look, Stranger* (1936), and *Another Time* (1940), with the exception of some poems from *Another Time* written after Auden emigrated to America. Also included are the early verse drama *Paid on Both Sides*, poems previously uncollected, and a few poems previously unpublished. Rounding out this overview of Auden's early verse are poetic sections from a number of Auden's published and unpublished plays. Readers familiar with Auden's work from more recent collections will be happy to have in this volume a number of poems suppressed by Auden, perhaps in reaction to his later unease with the political positions taken in them. Notable among these is the poem "Spain 1937," originally written after Auden's experiences during the Spanish Civil War. Stephen Spender, in his recent memoir of this period (*The Thirties and After: Poetry, Politics, People, 1933-1970*), describes this poem as "a serious application of the Marxist view of history to the Spanish Civil War"; he suggests that Auden came to dislike it because it expressed an attitude he felt intellectually forced into but never truly felt. Spender recounts Auden's striking the last two lines of the poem in Cyril Connolly's copy, and writing in the margin, "This is a lie." The lines read, "History to the defeated/May say Alas but cannot help or pardon."

One of the delights of a volume like this one is that it makes possible reading through Auden's poetry in chronological succession. Clearly displayed are the early experiments with form, tone, and voice, and the movement toward a more mature style and a richer vision of the poet's world. Frequently-anthologized pieces, such as "Musée des Beaux Arts," take on new life and fresh vigor when they are returned, as here, to their original poetic context. And, while time has taken Auden from us, it also allows his editor to restore to his texts manuscript readings changed in printed versions to avoid charges of libel, obscenity, or discourtesy. As a result, we are closer, in this volume, to the true process of Auden's development than we have ever been before.

Mendelson rounds out this volume with a generous selection of Auden's early prose. Offered here are Auden's essays and reviews that concern his development as a poet and his changing ideas of poetry's social role. His essay on writing (placed third in this volume) will, for example, interest those who want to know how Auden viewed the purposes of his craft; other essays suggest his views on social issues, while still others help us piece together Auden's biography.

Auden has, it seems, been well served by his literary executor. Mendelson introduces this volume with a brief but insightful sketch of Auden's early poetic career, locating his writings in an outline of the poet's biography. Working with both manuscripts and the various editions of Auden's works, Mendelson has been careful to give us the text of Auden's works that represents the poet's final intentions. This means that on occasion he has incorporated into the text changes made by Auden in copies of his poems. However, all emendations, as well as early versions of poems, or whole poems, revised or dropped from later editions, are noted in the appendices, where early or deleted verses or poems are reprinted in full. Mendelson is clear as to his editorial method; the extent to which he followed through on it will have to be determined by those who share with his access to all the relevant documents.

In sum, *The English Auden* provides us with a unique opportunity to observe one stage in the career of a major modern poet. As Mendelson repeatedly makes clear, Auden was not to repeat himself after 1939; if we can take the poet himself seriously, his work after his move to New York was to be his major poetic statement, that for which he will chiefly be remembered. Nevertheless, if Auden *did* live as he wanted to live, and write the poetry he wanted to write, after he came to America, his post-English work is inevitably based on what went before. What Mendelson has made possible is for us to have in one convenient volume the material we need to assess the process of Auden's poetic development. With this volume in hand, we can gain a sense of Auden's Englishness, as well as the foundations on which Auden built his later career. Students of Auden must be ever in Mendelson's debt for a thorough and handsome volume, while they hope for a series of equally careful volumes tracing the career of the American Auden.

John N. Wall, Jr.

Sources for Further Study

Yale Review. LXII, June, 1978, p. 609.

ERNEST HEMINGWAY AND HIS WORLD

Author: Anthony Burgess (1917-   )
Publisher: Charles Scribner's Sons (New York). Illustrated. 128 pp. $10.95
Type of work: Literary biography

Burgess attempts to reveal the life of Hemingway the man as a parallel to his fiction

Is there anything left to say about Ernest Hemingway? There is possibly no other American writer in the twentieth century about whom every critic or student has spoken with so absolute a sense of assurance. Many of the older generation of critics have, in fact, abandoned the author for newer horizons, leaving behind a heritage of scholarly disdain. Their traditional critical view portrays Hemingway's world as one of natural and human violence in which characters struggle to survive and to assert the integrity of self. According to these critics, war, sports, and sometimes love are the games played by the Hemingway hero, but in the conventional sense these games are always lost and the hero ends as victim.

Some past scholarship has discovered, however, more than material for scorn. A few critics have admired the saturation of Hemingway's works with the memory of physical pleasure and its costs. Others have cited the author's lean, hard-hitting sentence structure which dramatizes the action of his narrative.

Now a new breed of critic is starting to drift back to Hemingway, determined to venture into the inner turbulence of the author's mind and craft. Sadly, many of these scholars seem to rely on archetypal myths or Freudian approaches to explain the secrets of Hemingway's art in relation to his psyche. Hemingway remains, however, a slippery quarry, and we often learn more about the critic than about his subject.

In truth, the relationship between Ernest Hemingway's life and his art has never been wholly explained, despite the appearance of several major biographies in recent years. One simple but compelling explanation is that the author's life style, which drew more attention to himself as a man and attracted more nonliterary copy than any other American writer in our century, was as dramatic as was his prose but much more flamboyant. It is significant that at times his life-style became outrageously disproportionate to his work.

There is, however, a deeper level inherent in the relationship between the man and his work. Anthony Burgess, the English literary critic and novelist, explores this area in *Ernest Hemingway and His World* in order to clarify the events of the author's life as sources of inspiration for his writing. To his friends, Hemingway was, as one noted when he died, "a man who lived it up to write it down"; but to his enemies, what he wrote shrouded rather than revealed the truth about his inner self. Both groups of observers are shortsighted in that they fail to perceive arbitrary and necessary distinctions between the life and the work.

In his balanced portrait, Anthony Burgess evokes both sides of Hemingway —the compulsive arrogance and the frustrated literary artistry. He is aided in this endeavor by the many rare photographs that adorn the text. These unique and relatively fresh glimpses serve to highlight and further clarify some skillful critical analysis. His essay effectively traces the events of Hemingway's life in an attempt to be selective without oversimplifying. As is the case with other contemporary critics, Burgess finds much that repels him in the author's personality, but his feelings concerning aspects of Hemingway's behavior do not decrease his regard for the artistry embodied in many of the novels and short stories.

Hemingway the man, states Burgess, was as much a creation as his books, but a far inferior one. The author was not content with mere excellence as a hunter, fisherman, boxer, and guerrilla leader. He desired to turn himself into a Homeric myth, which meant posing, lying, and treating life as fiction. While some of his lies are transparent, according to Burgess, it is difficult to sort out the self-made legend from a reality which was less glamorous, though still colorful enough. Unfortunately, we know Hemingway the man not from letters and diaries, but primarily from tales told by himself in bars, on shipboard, on safari, from tales retold by others, and finally, from reminiscences which conform to the legend and which grow continually less reliable.

Hemingway the legend is treated skeptically by Burgess, but Hemingway the writer is dealt with more realistically. The young author had an austere ambition: to write what he called "a true simple declarative sentence." In accomplishing this ambition, he instigated a revolution in feeling. He made narrative prose into a physical medium shorn of the cerebral and fanciful, apt for the Hemingway hero, tough, stoical, suffering, and exhibiting the kind of Hemingway courage that we have been taught to call "grace under pressure."

Yet to speak of the young Hemingway as possessing a literary ambition would probably be false, emphasizes Burgess. He was possessed of an instinctive aim, both simpler and more complex, to draw the aesthetic disposition of language away from its traditional locations in the head and the heart and to attach it to the nerves and muscles. Burgess rightly signifies this as Hemingway's greatest achievement.

The English critic treats the middle-aged Ernest Hemingway as a man who had been and could still be a marvelous writer. He had a sustained, though not always coherent or visible, inner life. It was during this period that the legend of Hemingway overshadowed the work, as if an abundance of adventure compensated for a scarcity of art. The man behind the legend often presented a disagreeable picture, and it is to Burgess' credit that he neither avoids nor makes too much of this fact.

The Hemingway of the middle years watched the fat collect upon his soul and upon his style, and most of the time he knew what was happening. In his stories he transformed these personal troubles into the materials of aesthetic detachment. A significant example of this trait is seen in his story "The Snows of Kilimanjaro" in the description of a writer slowly dying of gangrene in Africa. He has followed the wrong gods and wasted his talent, and now he is dying on a hot African plain, looking up at the snowcap of Kilimanjaro— where, Hemingway had learned, the frozen corpse of a leopard had been found. The scene is ostensibly an allegorical diagnosis of the mythical "crack-ups" of F. Scott Fitzgerald in which the beast signifies the artist who dies nobly seeking the summit, while the dying writer's gangrene represents the corruption and mortification of talent misused. Burgess sees it as an insight into the concerns of the aging Hemingway. The writer can, on the surface, be taken as a kind of Fitzgerald who has been endowed with the stoic insights of a Hemingway, concedes Burgess. Yet he can also be perceived as "a kind of Hemingway corrupted by the attractions of the role of man of action, neglecting his true vocation while the vultures and hyenas of devouring time close in."

Simply to identify this character with Hemingway would, of course, be foolish, as Burgess well knows, but it would be still more foolish to suppose there is no connection. Not many modern writers have charted their spiritual conditions as accurately as Hemingway did in his fiction.

The Hemingway of the final years is pictured by Burgess as a battered but unbowed veteran. Following World War II, he indicated, by statement and by action, a commitment to a fresh start in life and art. After a somewhat disappointing 1950 novel, *Across the River and into the Trees*, the author returned to his sources of inspiration of the 1930's: big game hunting and fishing. He nearly died in two successive African plane crashes in 1953, but his luck, although running out, was still running good. He survived and wrote a long account of his African experiences.

It was fishing, though, that provided Hemingway with the source material which was totally to recoup literary losses in his later years. Drawing upon a sketch of a Cuban fisherman that he had written fifteen years earlier for *Esquire*, Hemingway produced *The Old Man and the Sea*, which won the 1952 Pulitzer Prize and was undoubtedly a major factor in winning for the author the 1954 Nobel Prize for Literature.

The mature author of the middle and late 1950's pressed harder to recapture the past. He turned to Paris of the 1920's for *A Moveable Feast*, which emerged as a sort of autobiography of the author's years of literary apprenticeship. Burgess notes the aptness of the religious connotation of the title. The young Hemingway and his friends, according to the critic, were hungry and poor enough to regard any meal as a sacrament, a feast of faith and hope. The "vie de Bohème" of the 1920's, says Burgess, "happened in fact and, held in memory, can happen again and again like a potent liturgy revivifying a present that, paradoxically, is well fed but empty of nourishment."

In 1961, however, the liturgy ended. The ardor of writing had become excruciating. In the spring the author had received twenty-five electric shock treatments to alleviate growing depression. Burgess speculates as to the causes of this depression and reasons that it was possibly caused by a deepening gloom at the author's failure to actualize his own myths. "He could not cope with the stress that most men endure gracefully; he was too godlike to be expected to have to cope." On the morning of July 2, 1961, Ernest Hemingway placed the muzzle of a silver shotgun in his mouth and pulled both triggers.

"All stories, if continued far enough, end in death," Hemingway writes in *Death in the Afternoon*, "and he is no true story teller who would keep that from you." Anthony Burgess does not keep that fact from readers of *Ernest Hemingway and His World*. His strength as a critic and, indeed, the strength of the book is the conveyance of a sense of balance and of perspective. The Hemingway style was a new and original contribution to world literature, he concludes, emphasizing that the Hemingway code of courage, the Hemingway hero and his stoical holding on against odds, have exerted an influence beyond literature. Ultimately the insufficiencies of the man, as delineated by Burgess, maimed the creative work.

In summation, however, Hemingway at his best is regarded by the British critic as a seminal force as patent as Joyce or Faulkner; and even at his worst, he is a constant reminder that to engage literature one has first to engage life.

Stephen L. Hanson

Sources for Further Study

America. CXXXIX, December 2, 1978, p. 414.

Atlantic. CCXLII, October, 1978, p. 116.

Critic. XXXVII, November 15, 1978, p. 7.

New Republic. CLXXIX, October 7, 1978, p. 37.

Spectator. CCXLI, November 25, 1978, p. 23.

THE EYE OF THE STORY
Selected Essays and Reviews

Author: Eudora Welty (1909-   )
Publisher: Random House (New York). 355 pp. $10.00
Type of work: Essays and reviews

One of America's finest writers of stories and novels presents a selection of her essays, reviews, and occasional pieces published over a period of more than thirty years in numerous periodicals

For nearly forty years Eudora Welty has been recognized as one of our finest writers of fiction, particularly of short stories; but her infrequent nonfiction writings have been comparatively little known. In her latest book she has gathered together her critical writings on a number of her contemporaries and several nineteenth century fiction writers, and has added eight brief pieces about her native South. *The Eye of the Story* is a selection of thirty-five essays, reviews, and personal and occasional pieces, most of which originally appeared in the *New York Times Book Review*, *Atlantic Monthly*, *New Republic*, *Harper's Bazaar*, and other periodicals. The volume contains most of Miss Welty's nonfiction writing which has been published in the past thirty-six years.

In the first group of essays, "On Writers"—Jane Austen, Henry Green, Katherine Anne Porter, Willa Cather, and Anton Chekhov—Welty writes sometimes objectively, sometimes subjectively with frequent use of "I think," "I feel," "it seems to me," so that the essay becomes a personal appreciation of the writer she is analyzing and discussing. The appreciation is both intellectual and emotional. Of Jane Austen's novels she remarks in "The Radiance of Jane Austen": "Their high spirits, their wit, their celerity and harmony of motion, their symmetry of design appear unrivaled in the English novel. [Her] work at its best seems as nearly flawless as any fiction could be."

Commenting on the work of a contemporary English novelist whose nine novels have often portrayed an exterior life very different from that in Jane Austen's, Welty says: "Henry Green seems to me to be a romantic novelist who has chosen to write from inside the labyrinth of everyday life, whose senses and whose temperament are and have remained romantic and whose reason and experience are lying in wait for the romantic at every turn." She sees Green as a novelist of the imagination who is "inside his characters' *world*, totally and literally" even though the reader may sometimes wonder whether the novelist is, at a particular moment, writing of the exterior or the interior world.

Like Henry Green, Katherine Anne Porter often writes from within her characters' minds; and, says Welty, "As her work has done in many respects, it has shown me a thing or two about the eye of fiction, about fiction's visibility and invisibility, about its clarity, its radiance." Readers of one of Welty's best-known and most beautifully written stories, "A Worn Path," may see how she has developed her own "eye of fiction." In the story she easily, almost unnoticeably, shifts from the exterior description of Phoenix Jackson's trip to town, into the busy mind of the old woman as she moves, half-led by memory which aids her age-dimmed eyes, along the familiar path.

Welty, as she makes clear in "The House of Willa Cather," has been stirred by the way in which Miss Cather makes the landscape seem a living presence to her characters and to the reader in her novels. She is impressed by Cather's artistry in juxtaposing the present against vivid reminders of a distant past, when prehistoric monsters bathed or swam in waters that washed where cattle now graze in sweeping fields, or later, when long-vanished people lived in the cave dwellings of the Southwest where one may still flake off the carbon left by the smoke of ancient cooking fires. "Another of the touchstones of Willa Cather's work," says Welty, "is her feeling for the young." One thinks of Welty's own love for the young and her understanding of them, as in her early story, "A Piece of News." In this story young Ruby Fisher, finding her name in a murder account in a scrap of newspaper, luxuriates in the fantasy of imagining herself shot to death by her gruff husband. When he returns from tending his moonshine still, he brings her back to everyday reality by explaining that it was another Ruby Fisher who died, and then good-naturedly spanks her.

A critic in 1962 noted a resemblance of Welty to the Russian Anton Chekhov: ". . . a basic spiritual kinship marked by a lack of an 'attitude,' the view of the world as an enigma, a pervasive tolerance and compassion, an eye for the ludicrous and the pathetic, and a tragicomic vision." Welty's critical essay, "Reality in Chekhov's Stories," did not appear until 1977, after Welty had published nearly all of her fiction. Reading it, one feels that her appreciation of the form, the themes, the content, the tone, the people, the kinds of reality in Chekhov must surely have influenced to some degree the writing of many of her own stories. It is either that or the fact that she could have been struck by what a Russian author had done several generations before her as she recognized her spiritual or artistic kinship to him. She comments, "In Chekhov's stories, reality always had its origin: it comes to us through the living human being—and not anonymously. It lives, was born, in the particular—not in the general humanity but in this man, that woman, their child." Concluding the essay she says, "Chekhov showed the implacable facts of existence—the illusions, the deceptions, the mystery, the identity—that reality variously stood for among many characters." Edna Earle Ponder's reality in Welty's *The Ponder Heart* is not the reality her eccentric Uncle Daniel Ponder perceives, but her awareness of his peculiarities does not lessen her love for him. Old Mr. Marblehall, in the story which bears his name, escapes from the dullness of one reality into a more exciting one as Mr. Bird. The creator of Uncle Daniel and Mr. Marblehall does not mock either of them; to her they are more comic than pathetic, and her amusement is kindly, not cruel.

In her second group of essays, "On Writing," Welty discusses the reading, writing, and analyzing of stories; place in fiction; the vocabulary of fiction; the limitations of fiction writers as crusaders; the misreading of one of her own stories, "A Worn Path"; and the manipulation of time in fiction.

Through brief analysis, comparison, and contrast, Welty uses stories by Hemingway, Chekhov, Lawrence, and Faulkner, among others, to show, in "Looking at Short Stories," that the best modern stories have much more to offer readers than mere plot or action: they offer theme, style, characterization, symbolism, even a bit of instruction sometimes about ourselves, about others, and about the world we live in.

In "Place in Fiction," Welty states that in fiction, place may seem less important than other elements such as character, plot, symbolism, or feeling. Yet place, ". . . one of the lesser angels that watch over the racing hand of fiction . . . can be seen, in her own way, to have a great deal to do with [the] goodness" of a good novel:

> . . . with the goodness . . . in the raw material of writing . . . with the goodness in the writing . . . with the goodness—the worth—in the writer himself: place is where he has his roots, place is where he stands; in his experience out of which he writes, it provides the base of reference; in his work, the point of view.

The reviews which make up the third section of *The Eye of the Story* show a wide diversity of authors and works: Washington Irving's *Western Journals*, George R. Stewart's *Names on the Land*, two books by Virginia Woolf, a children's story by E. B. White, a Faulkner novel and a volume of his letters, two books by E. M. Forster, two by S. J. Perelman, a literary biography, a suspense novel, Isak Dinesen's *Last Tales*, a book of stories by Patrick White, and Elizabeth Bowen's posthumously published autobiography. Fitting the tone of her writing to the nature of the author or the work being reviewed, Welty is naturally serious in most of the reviews. She is critically negative in judging only one book, Arthur Mizener's biography of Ford Madox Ford which, Welty admits, shows intelligence and much earnest labor but which sadly lacks the imagination needed to do justice to such a man as Ford. In contrast, the amused and amusing review of E. B. White's *Charlotte's Web* must have greatly pleased Mr. White when he read it, and the double review of two of S. J. Perelman's books not only contains a potpourri of samples of his ingenious wordplay but also a confession that the reviewer fell in love with Mr. Perelman at fifteen while surreptitiously reading him in a Latin class in Jackson, Mississippi.

The personal and occasional pieces which complete *The Eye of the Story* include "A Sweet Devouring" in childhood of books from the local library and from the Welty home shelves; some notes on Mississippi River country; an excellent analysis of Welty's first novel, *The Robber Bridegroom*, a marvelous blending of history, myth, and fairy tale; an evocative description of a pageant in a Mississippi Negro church in which both children and adults, dressed as birds, imitate by flapping wings the birds they represent, and dance to syncopated piano music; a nostalgic picture of Welty's home town remembered from childhood; a similar recollection of the little store to which young Eudora Welty was sent most willingly to buy things for her mother; a remarkable portrait of Ida M'Toy, a black woman who was a secondhand-clothes dealer for twenty-six years after having been a midwife for thirty-five, and whose best remembered gesture was her outflung hand accompanied by the exclamation, "Born in this hand!"; and finally the brief introduction to Welty's *One Time, One Place*, a snapshot album of pictures taken in Mississippi during the Depression.

As readers, we can be truly grateful that Eudora Welty chose to gather in one place and in durable form these varied writings that might otherwise have lain neglected or forgotten in the many scattered pages where they first appeared. Gathered together now, they may continue in future years to inform, to instruct, and to please.

Henderson Kincheloe

Sources for Further Study

America. CXXXIX, October 7, 1978, p. 232.

Best Sellers. XXXVIII, October, 1978, p. 225.

Commonweal. CV, September 29, 1978, p. 632.

Harper's Magazine. CCLVII, October, 1978, p. 89.

Virginia Quarterly Review. LIV, Autumn, 1978, p. 127.

A FAMILY ALBUM

Author: David Darryl Galloway (1937-   )
Publisher: Harcourt Brace Jovanovich (New York). 225 pp. $8.95
Type of work: Novel
Time: 1880-1975
Locale: The American South

A series of six loosely related "images" in which six cameras are described and six photographs are analyzed for the purpose of creating a character, life, and destiny for each of the six photographers and their twelve subjects

> *Principal characters:*
> ELIHU ZACHARIAH MORTON,
> JOHN PRESLEY JARVIS,
> MARTHA MARY TUPELO PEARL INDEPENDENCE DAY MCBRYDE,
> CYRUS LAWRENCE MACDONALD,
> JUANITA ROSE LOWNDES, and
> DAVID BONNER DYER, the photographers
> BOY WITH HIS DOG,
> DOROTHY KATHLYN JARVIS,
> MARGARET ELAINE JARVIS AND DOROTHY KATHLYN JARVIS IN A
> GOATCART DRAWN BY A GOAT NAMED "GENERAL LEE,"
> JAMES AND DOROTHY HENRY,
> JAMES AND HIS SON, DAVID HENRY, and
> HUGH BOYCE JARVIS, EILEEN JARVIS BRILLEAUX, DAVID FRANKLIN
> JARVIS, AND DOROTHY KATHLYN JARVIS DYER, the subjects

David Darryl Galloway, distinguished essayist, teacher, lecturer, literary critic, and connoiseur of art, is also a first-rate novelist. *A Family Album*, unconventional in format and meticulously executed, could well serve as a model for ambitious new writers. With skill and artistry the writer combines in his short book much about the social history of the South since 1880 and the history of photography—an ingenious combination and one which would pose difficulty for anyone less knowledgeable about both.

Leafing through family photographs leads to capricious imaginings about those who operated the cameras and the subjects who posed for the pictures. Not content with authentic identifications, the viewer prefers to analyze completely each detail in the picture before assigning to characters the names they might have had, the lives they might have lived. In interpreting these representations, past, present, and future are considered; emotions and moral attitudes are analyzed; physical characteristics are described.

The mood of the novel is established by a prefatory letter purportedly written in 1832 by Joseph Nicéphore Niépce (1765-1833) to his son Isidore Niépce. An artful blend of fiction and fact, the letter is introduced by a quotation from an actual letter of October 23, 1829, in which Joseph Nicéphore Niépce agreed to cooperate with Louis Jacques Mande Daguerre (1787-1851) in perfecting Niépce's heliographic method of producing images. Galloway obligingly fills in gaps which exist in documented accounts of the Niépce-

Daguerre partnership. Such wariness between the two men as the novelist describes, however, is entirely credible and makes for good reading.

Several passages in the Niépce letter announce the themes that will be developed in the body of the book. Images, says Nicéphore, may seem "fixed" when they catch one moment forever, but in fact true images can only be fixed after death. Then an accurate assessment can be made. He deplores Niépce's failure to "fix" an image; but, he ponders, "Are the images of the mind more stable, or do they not undergo similar commutations?" Unlike a photograph, the mind cannot be fixed. What the eye of the mind perceives *is* the image. The world, he thinks, is not a good judge of people or of true merit: "M. Daguerre's enthusiasm often overrides his modest sense of propriety and convention, though his perhaps is the tone of the new world. . . ."

In closing the letter, Nicéphore suggests that each generation is subject to the whims of fortune. He cannot correct the mistakes of Claude, or complete what he had hoped to do about fixing images; symbolically, in passing on the ivory miniature of his own mother and the opportunity to continue his own research, Nicéphore passes on the future to Isidore. An editorial note at the close of the preface states that Isidore Niépce lived out his life in poverty despite a pension granted him by the French government in 1839 when the daguerreotype process was recognized by the Academy of Science. The struggles, futility, and near successes of the Niépces announce the prevailing theme in the novel.

A precise format is maintained in constructing the book. With undeviating precision, like the hands of a clock or the dimensions of old photographs, each chapter, or image, conforms to a pattern. There are six images. Each begins with a significant quotation which reflects the philosophy of photography.

The second part of the image, called "The Camera," includes a detailed physical description and a concise history of each instrument used in producing the picture. Through the cameras is traced the evolution of modern photography. Simple enough to be understood even by the amateur, these descriptions are accurate and complete enough to interest the professional. Inanimate though they are, the cameras might well have been listed with the cast of characters: A Lancaster Instantograph; a Bulls-Eye; a collapsible bellows-type camera by J. Valette; an Argus "Model A"; a 3A Autographic Kodak Special; the Minox.

"The Camera" section of each image is followed by a sketch of the photographer. Some of the best writing in the book occurs in these six sketches. Bare genealogical statistics—birth date, death date, marital status, birth and death sites—are a cold, factual listing not unlike the items on a tombstone. Yet it is remarkable how quickly, in a few deft lines, life and vitality are given to the bare bones of the four cameramen and the two camerawomen. Absence of visual image minimizes the importance of physical appearances, so there is more emphasis on storytelling and less on critique.

The picturetakers vary greatly in social class and situation. Two generations of a middlebrow family are represented in the characters of John Presley Jarvis and David Barnes Dyer, second and sixth photographers respectively. Jarvis, "Uncle John," one of the most admirable persons in the novel, is stable, entirely respectable, moderately successful. Much as cameras become outmoded and must be replaced by newer models, Uncle John's generation is superseded by the next. This feeling of succession is achieved by using young David Barnes Dyer as the sixth photographer. Family names found in earlier portions are repeated in the sixth image. "David," "James Henry," "Dorothy Kathlyn"—all common Southern names—serve to give an illusion of continuity, although there is no central plot at all. There are only fragments and small plot outlines employing characters with the same names.

Four of the photographers might have been chosen at random, but close analysis indicates that they are representatives of particular types peculiar to various periods in Southern history. Elihu Zachariah Morton, aimless and shallow, simply exists and lets "life take care of itself." Predictably, he becomes a photographer by chance but manages to derive both pleasure and profit by picturing "young ladies in swimming suits or underwear" and selling his mass-produced copies to traveling salesmen. The salesman who would have bought Morton's "art" is the fourth photographer, Cyrus Lawrence Mac-Donald, coarse, rough, uncouth, purveyor of "everything from heavy-duty serviceables to naughty Parisian novelties," and a frequenter of whore houses. Nonetheless, MacDonald loves his mother (as much as he can love anyone) and has one almost real romance. In the sketch of MacDonald is reflected the rural, frontier huckster of the South in the early 1900's.

Two of the most appealing persons in the novel are the camerawomen. It is an amusing surprise to discover a black female photographer in business in the South during the post-Civil War years. In the dilineation of Martha Mary Tupelo Pearl Independence Day McBryde Jackson, antebellum days are recalled. A free black, Pearl lives for forty-two years on a plantation operated much as it has been before the war. Only when the "mistress" dies and the "master" sells the plantation is Pearl truly emancipated. From this point on, Pearl's adventures with her goat named "General Lee," a goat cart, and his mistress' camera bought at auction provide comic relief from the grim realism of most of the sketches. Pearl is never ecstatically happy or cruelly sad; she harbors no hostility toward anyone, is self-sufficient, dependable, and lets life have its way, able somehow to keep her own lens in focus.

Black Pearl and white Juanita Rose Lowndes have many similar characteristics. Juanita, child of a glamorous circus queen and an improvident, indulgent father, was, like Pearl, an accepting child, dependent on others. Both can cope with changing fortune; both are supportive of the men on whom they had depended—Pearl of her master, and Juanita of her father. Juanita finally marries a man who really loves her, and the reader hopes that at least one story may have a happy-ever-after ending, but such hopes are short-lived. The ex-prize fighter husband dies, Juanita continues to serve others, and finally succumbs to kidney failure. (Galloway never permits a romantic death.)

Each of the six photographs is dissected in astonishing detail. Such absorption with minutiae tends at times to become tedious, but the tedium is outweighed by the brilliant, kaleidoscopic moments of insight caught by the camera's lens. The storyteller deftly explores the intellect, character, and sex life of every person pictured. Even the dog portrayed with the newsboy has personality and a physical life of his own.

Each individual comes to life replete with a past, present, and future, but the inevitable transience and brevity of existence is suggested in every vignette. "Their moments of joy are so few and so brief that we are right to pause over this rare document." Humanity's frailty is implied in the description of Dorothy Kathlyn Jarvis, aged four, as "ruthlessly diminished by parched earth, sky, fields, and woods." It is particularly frustrating to the reader not to have a good reproduction of this photograph in the book because there is at all times the uncontrollable urge to compare viewer impressions. However, reproduction of the photographs on the jacket is appropriate and appealing.

Enough fragmentary narrative is interspersed with the photographs to tease. A story line is dropped and picked up as quickly as a cameraman can change his lens. At times this changing of direction is disconcerting. For a second the focus is on possible romance and beauty; with a slight shift in angle, there is only crudity, ugliness, disease, and death.

Careful attention has been lavished on style and technique. With each shift in image, there is a shift in time and a successful evocation of mood and memories. The poverty and despair in the South after the Civil War (and still, in some areas) are painfully present in the picture of little Kay. "Jimmy and David" is particularly effective in its nostalgic references to the 1940's, with all the deprivations of World War II. Galloway's clever use of letters—T, V, C, U, and S—in this sketch is superb; he even manages to use "Tennessee Valley Authority." Wartime slogans ("V for Victory") and organizations ("NRA," "WPA,") come to mind. There are occasional indications of Galloway's appreciation of the works of Henry James and Edgar Allan Poe.

In its freshness of concept and sensitive treatment of subject matter, *A Family Album* is an extraordinarily successful experiment.

Mary Reynolds Peacock

Sources for Further Study

Best Sellers. XXXVIII, July, 1978, p. 103.

Christian Science Monitor. April 21, 1978, p. 26.

New Republic. CLXXVIII, May 13, 1978, p. 37.

New York Times Book Review. April 16, 1978, p. 15.

New Yorker. LIV, May 15, 1978, p. 157.

FIGURES OF THOUGHT
Speculations on the Meaning of Poetry & Other Essays

Author: Howard Nemerov (1920-   )
Publisher: David R. Godine (Boston). 198 pp. $15.00
Type of work: Essays

A collection of essays, chiefly on modern poetry, in which the author seeks to understand the essential nature of the craft and its relationship to modern concepts of thought

Howard Nemerov has long been concerned with the nature of poetry, its status as a form of human discourse and the distinctive ways it uses language. This interest he shares with many poets before him; unlike most poets, however, Nemerov is given to ordering his thoughts into essays and publishing them in books. When he does so, as in this volume, he enters a world of discourse in which the requirements for success are often quite different from those desirable in a poet. The poet must be a good writer of poems; Nemerov is clearly that, as his distinguished career and numerous awards attest. The critic, on the other hand, must be above all else a good reader of other people's poems, one who can enrich and illuminate and enliven for us the poetic achievement of someone else. Nemerov is certainly a capable reader, at least of some others' poems; particularly, his discussions of Yeats in this volume are moving and insightful. However, Nemerov clearly feels a tension between his role as poet-critic and the place in literary culture of critics who are not poets. That tension informs the tone of many of the essays in this book.

Such tension underlies the testy attack Nemerov makes on Harold Bloom's *The Anxiety of Influence* in the essay which gives its title to this volume. In the midst of a radically simplified summary of Bloom's complex argument, Nemerov lets slip the problem; he just does not understand Bloom's theories. Our choice of one interpretation over another, he says, is chiefly a matter of whether we like it or not; it suffices to say that Nemerov does not like Bloom's. Nemerov's stance in this essay is one which basically says, "I do not understand all this, and you, dear reader, needn't either, because I am a certified poet, and who is Bloom, not a poet, to tell us what poetry is all about, anyway?" While one may or may not agree with Bloom's admittedly complex and controversial theories about the development of poetry since the Romantic Age, Nemerov's basis for objecting to it is hardly adequate.

Nemerov's attack on the academic criticism of literature in this essay and in others scattered throughout the volume points to a serious division which exists in our literary culture at this time between the professional scholar and critic and the amateur or dilettante. Nemerov, *as a critic*, belongs to the latter camp; he faces the company of professional scholars who devote their lives to furthering our understanding of the major works of our literary heritage, equipped with high standards of learning and documentation. While it is understandable why an active poet whose reputation is to some degree in their hands would feel threatened by such people, it is not clear why he feels it necessary to attack directly or by condescension those whose careers are devoted to the study and dissemination of our literary heritage. One can understand why writers on literature in the popular press who are busy with their careers as poets, or whatever, cannot, or do not want to, reach the standards for publishing professional literary criticism. This does not prevent them from making an occasional insightful observation, as Nemerov does in a few places in this volume. The cost of not holding to such standards is, however, also clear. At one point, for example, in this book, in an essay in which he makes a number of fine points about Yeats, Nemerov belabors the commonplace that World War I had a decisive influence on the course of modern poetry. Clearly he believes this; clearly, also, it is true. But to offer it as an original observation is to ignore all those who have made the point before, and made it more cogently.

The major usefulness of this volume must be seen not in terms of how true a picture of modern poetry it presents but in terms of its presentation of the view of modern poetry held by one practicing modern poet. For that, those interested in Nemerov's poetry will find its lengthy discussions of how poems *mean*, how thought is expressed in words, how modern poetry is to be read, to be helpful for what they tell us about Nemerov's poetry. The best essays in this book are those casual ones in which the author ruminates about his experience of time, the complexities of poetic language, and the low estate of poetry in our day. Students of Nemerov's artistic works should find such pieces extremely helpful in understanding his own aims and techniques in his verse.

The most interesting is probably the first essay in the volume, entitled "Thirteen Ways of Looking at a Skylark," in which Nemerov offers some reflections on the nature of poetry and poetic uses of language. His basic point is that poetry works with those experiences which seem wonderfully unique but which, under examination, turn out to be of universal applicability. From this beginning, he moves on to suggest that poetry resists precise definition, but invites a variety of definitions; it is both that form of discourse which inspires human purpose and the chief means by which human beings confront the hopelessness of their lives. Poetry is thus paradoxically both didactic and an end in itself; it calls attention to itself as much as it directs our attention to its subject.

A similar point is made in another essay, "Poetry and Meaning," which really focuses Nemerov's two concerns in this book. Here, Nemerov states that poetry is "getting something right in Language"; he wonders whether we have not lost the ability to feel the "rightness" which is basic to poetry. Much of the blame for our loss of this ability he lays at the door of academic treatments of literature, which share, he argues, the cultural tendency to seek results at the expense of mystery. As a result, Nemerov wonders whether we are not approaching the end of poetry in English. The vigor with which poetry is being written and published in our day would seem to give the lie to his concern. But this misses the point: it may well be that poetry as Nemerov understands it and likes it is coming to an end. That idea is something different altogether.

In sum, the admirer of Nemerov's poetry will find this book fascinating as a view of the world from Nemerov's perspective and as a gloss on his work. Those interested in a truer and more just picture of literature and literary criticism must look elsewhere.

John N. Wall, Jr.

Sources for Further Study

Library Journal. CIII, March 15, 1978, p. 665.
New Republic. CLXXVIII, April 8, 1978, p. 29.
New York Times Book Review. April 16, 1978, p. 11.

FINAL ENTRIES, 1945
The Diaries of Joseph Goebbels

Author: Joseph Goebbels (1897-1945)
Translated from the German by Richard Barry
Edited, with an Introduction and Annotations, by Hugh Trevor-Roper
Publisher: G.P. Putnam's Sons (New York). 368 pp. $14.95
Type of work: Diary
Time: February-April, 1945
Locale: Germany

A first-hand look at the leaders of Nazi Germany when it became clear that defeat was imminent as revealed through the diaries of the Minister of Propaganda

Principal personages:
JOSEPH GOEBBELS, Minister of Propaganda and Public Enlightenment in the Third Reich, 1933-1945
ADOLF HITLER, the *Führer*, 1933-1945
HERMANN GÖRING, Commander-in-Chief of the Luftwaffe, 1933-1945
JOACHIM VON RIBBENTROP, German Foreign Minister, 1938-1945
WINSTON CHURCHILL, Prime Minister of Great Britain, 1940-1945
JOSEPH STALIN, political and military leader of the U.S.S.R., 1924-1953

It has been thirty-four years since Russian tanks rolled into Berlin, and American, British, and French troops crossed the Rhine and conquered central Germany. It has been that many years since Adolf Hitler and his Propaganda Minister, Joseph Goebbels, and their families swallowed poison in the bunker under the rubble of the Reich Chancellery in Berlin and finally abandoned their dream of controlling the world. Yet the memory of the vast destruction they caused is still vivid, and it remains the most important touchstone for the West. The fact that people who share our culture could produce evil of this magnitude brings into question our entire way of life, for with the weapons of death now available, a repetition of the Nazi experience threatens to end that life altogether. Knowledge of the past has never been sufficient to change the future; nevertheless, an awareness of what human beings have done is one of the few fragile tools we have with which to try to learn enough to preserve the civilization which has made human existence something more than a mere struggle for survival. This is what is now at stake.

It is fortunate, therefore, that a microfilm copy of the daily diary kept by Joseph Goebbels has passed to the West from East Germany, where it was recovered, and can now be published. The first segment, issued in 1978 under the title *Final Entries, 1945*, will not by itself explain how Nazism could have occurred; but it does add a piece to the jigsaw puzzle by providing a revealing first-hand look at one of its leading practitioners at the moment of truth, when it was clear that his movement was being defeated and he himself was going to die.

The roots of Nazism were buried deep in Germany's past. At its origins lay the political institutions of feudalism and absolutism. Although extant throughout Europe, they were particularly pronounced in Prussia, where the Junker landlords maintained serfdom into the nineteenth century, and the monarchy required unflinching duty to the state. Thus, the social and political values which prevailed were far different from those of France or England, where more liberal relationships were established generations earlier. Furthermore, the fact that the German lands were divided into obsolete political entities made them vulnerable to foreign intervention and meant that the German people remained untrained in the management of their affairs on an international level.

The most extensive foreign intervention came during the Napoleonic wars when the French overran Germany. This traumatic experience, combined with the growing awareness of the commonality of all Germans helped produce the chauvinistic nationalism which maintained that the Germans were superior to all other peoples. Unification did not come until Prussia, under the guidance of the Junker nobleman Otto von Bismarck, defeated Austria in 1866 and France in 1870. Thus, the old Prussian autocratic order remained the dominant social structure in the new Germany. At the same time, however, industrialization was revolutionizing the living conditions of large numbers of peasants who moved into the cities and entered factories, breaking the ties which had been the base of this traditional order. The discrepancy between the new economic system and the Prussian values created unresolved tensions which were one of the contributing causes of World War I.

Germany's loss of this bitterly fought contest and the resultant collapse of the monarchy produced both a power vacuum and a generalized disorientation. The constitutional government set up at Weimar won the support of large numbers of Germans, but important and highly visible groups were disloyal. On the left, Communists, spurred on by the revolution in Russia, were active in street demonstrations and vocal in their calls for an overthrow of the government. On the right were grouped conservatives who hoped for a return to the monarchy, patriots of all classes who were humiliated by the defeat and the Treaty of Versailles, and citizens who were disturbed by the Communist demonstrations and the manuevers of opportunistic politicians in a multiparty system.

The agitation on the right might not have gotten out of hand had it not been for the economic disasters which fell one on top of the other. First came the inflation of 1923 which destroyed the currency and thus monetary savings; and then in 1929 the depression hit, leaving six million men unemployed and further shaking the belief that the established institutions of society were capable of assuring a tolerable life. For twenty years, from 1914 to 1933, a Germany fissured by deep economic and social cleavages was exposed to a succession of extremely demoralizing crises, radicalizing millions of citizens.

These were the circumstances which enabled the racist and simple-minded ideology of National Socialism to flourish. By blaming the economic troubles on the Jews, calling for a revision of the peace treaty and a return to a *völkish* way of life and elevating the *Führer* cult to a dogma, the Nazi world view provided shelter for those distraught by the turmoil of the 1920's and eager for a belief system which absolved them of responsibility and offered hope for a quick return to stability.

For its leaders, however, Nazism was more than a convenient ideology; it was the means by which they could take over absolute control of the state and eventually the world. Yet one of the most unsettling aspects about this fanatic leadership is that it emerged from the most ordinary backgrounds imaginable. In coming to terms with Nazi megalomania, therefore, one must recognize that the destructive impulse which drove it on is not the preserve of any one class, profession, or region.

Goebbels is a good example. The son of a hard-working clerk who was a devout Catholic, he was born in 1897 in the Rhineland, the most western-oriented region of Germany. Through sheer industry, the Goebbels family had painfully climbed into the middle class, and in his secure foyer, young Joseph was lovingly taught the precepts of Christianity. Although handicapped by a deformed foot, he had a quick mind and did well in the rigid German *Gymnasium*. Even at this time, though, he had a reputation as an opportunist, ready to "tell on" his friends if it would improve his standing with his teachers. Naturally, he was rejected by the army during the war, a blow which deeply affected him and helps explain his need to prove his manliness during the violent struggle of the Nazis.

After high school, he was able to go to the University, with financial help from the Catholic Church, and he earned the coveted degree of doctor. His college years were ones of tremendous tumult in Germany, with the loss of the war, the collapse of the government, revolution and counter-revolution, the Allied blockade, the invasion of the Ruhr by the French, German passive resistance, and inflation. For Goebbels, who thought very highly of himself and who wanted to prove his heroic qualities, it must have seemed clear that he was living in an age in which Germany was fighting for her existence and great political decisions would be made. Like many others, he did not know at first which side he wanted to be on, and before joining the Nazis he flirted with left-wing ideas. Above all at this time, though, he wanted to be a writer, and for two years after graduation he tried unsuccessfully to get his articles and fiction published. Unwilling to believe that his work was simply trite and uninteresting, he placed the blame on Jewish control of the press and publishing houses, and when this unemployed intellectual was offered a job writing for a Nazi newspaper in 1925, he accepted.

Almost immediately, he proved himself to be an excellent propagandist, with a marked talent for invective. He turned out to be a first-rate public speaker as well. As a result, he soon became one of the growing Nazi Party's most important assets in the Rhineland and came to the attention of Hitler in Bavaria. Goebbels was known for his radicalism, favoring an appeal to the working class, a position which conflicted with Hitler's strategy of cooperating with wealthy supporters in order to gain respectability and funds. At a showdown between the radicals and Hitler, Goebbels was impressed by the affluence and power of the Bavarian organization and switched sides without a qualm. It was not so much that Goebbels abandoned his radicalism, but rather that his ambition to reach the top convinced him that joining Hitler was the right way.

He was rewarded for his decision by being named *Gauleiter* of Berlin, a heady promotion for a young man. It was here that he made his name, founding a newspaper, *Der Angriff (The Attack)*, where he continued to demonstrate his ability to taunt his opponents mercilessly. As Party leader he built up a mass following among the increasing numbers of unemployed, and he successfully challenged the Communist control of the street through violent confrontations. Elected to the Parliament, he was named Minister of Propaganda and Public Enlightenment when Hitler became Chancellor on January 30, 1933.

In this post, his boundless energy and inventiveness enabled Goebbels to take over almost every facet of public information in Germany. By means of this control, and with a good deal of skill, he perfected the propaganda techniques which presented a uniform and idyllic picture of Nazi principles and the *Führer* cult. In so doing, Goebbels was extremely important in consolidating the Nazi regime and interjecting it into every aspect of German life, making him one of the crucial architects of the Third Reich. As war approached, Goebbels actually disapproved of Hitler's military ambitions, but he was unwilling to oppose them. Once the war turned against the Germans, Goebbels' mastery of propaganda became important once again in order to maintain morale. With the Allies closing in on the Reich, Goebbels exhorted his countrymen to remain firm and pushed the Nazi high command to adopt all possible measures for total war. *Final Entries, 1945* begins in February, with the English, Americans, and Russians already on German soil.

Goebbels displays a number of very revealing attitudes in the diary. The most striking characteristic is his unrelenting determination to continue the war at all costs. Given the unbroken string of German defeats since Stalingrad, and the overwhelming superiority of the Allies, this determination is surprising. Although generally optimistic about the prospects of victory, Goebbels did at times recognize that the end was at hand. His determination, therefore, was not so much the strategy of a military commander who genuinely felt his lines could hold, but rather the inflexible egotism of a man who could not admit defeat. It is commonly held that revolutionary leaders, such as Napoleon and Hitler, become so psychologically committed to the belief that they are superior to ordinary mortals, that, once proven fallible, they cannot accept a more prosaic self-image and must go on trying to prove that they are super-men. Goebbels obviously suffered from this defect as well; it is the fatal flaw of movements which are based on the notion they can do no wrong, for it means that they deny reality. It may be that members of the middle class, such as Hitler and Goebbels, are the most likely to exhibit this trait, since their superior gifts combined with their commonplace background give them the idea that they are well above everyone else in sheer ability. Whatever the origin of Goebbels' fierce will, it made him a formidable enemy, who in the end could be broken only by being destroyed.

The fact that Goebbels had an extraordinary ego is amply demonstrated in this volume. Considering that his world was collapsing around him, that German cities were being reduced to rubble, and that millions of fellow citizens were being evacuated from their homes, it is almost unbelievable that there is not one iota of self-criticism in these pages. Aside from two references to the fact that the Nazis overplayed their hand, Goebbels does not admit to making a single mistake or misjudgment; nor is there the slightest hint of guilt over the 6,000,000 deaths brought about by his colleagues and himself. Instead, Goebbels is incredibly self-assured, maintaining that he was right at every turn and that if he had only had his way, things would be much different. The fault is always someone else's. Göring and Ribbentrop were idiots, the German generals cowards, Franco pompous. Mussolini had no backbone, Stalin only wanted to loot, Churchill was the gravedigger of Europe, and England was responsible for all of Europe's misery. Goebbels had created a world of his own, and if he had not been so terribly dangerous, all of this would be some-what pathetic. Apparently he hoped that his diary would be a testimony to the courage and vision of Nazi Germany, but actually it leaves the reader wonder-ing how anyone could have wanted to preserve a document which frequently makes its author appear simply stupid. Yet, had the Germans won, Goebbels' distorted version would have rolled out of his propaganda machine, and the ability to see the obvious contradictions might have disappeared with our free-dom.

It was not the truth which motivated Goebbels, but the power which enabled him to force the world to accept the perverted views he spewed forth. The constant use of lies and their justification in this book will not come as a surprise to those familiar with Nazi techniques. Despite his untruthfulness, his boundless ego, and his nihilistic determination, Goebbels does engage in a certain amount of the hard-headed political realism, for which he was also known. His acumen is most apparent during the entries for the first few days in March, when he analyzes with some sophistication the deteriorating relation-ship between the Soviet Union and the Anglo-Americans, concluding nonethe-less that the alliance cannot be broken up. Once the line of the Rhine was crossed on March 7, though, military prospects disappear, and Goebbels, un-able to assess his own role in the catastrophe, is left without much to say.

In addition to its great value in unveiling Goebbels in defeat, the diary offers useful information on other Nazi leaders. Goebbels sees Hitler rather often, and although he records his disintegration (for instance, the appearance of a twitch), the reader can still watch the *Führer* manipulating his Propaganda Minister and retaining his power over him to the end. The viciousness, competition, and terror which existed among Hitler's chief lieutenants is also set forth by Goebbels, who makes it clear that the lust for domination which characterized them was not curbed by the sense of solidarity which had once been one of the proudest boasts of the Nazis.

Final Entries, 1945 is important for showing us the bankruptcy of one of the most prominent Nazis. Goebbels was immoral, untruthful, shamelessly self-centered, and ruthless—until the day the combined might of Russia, Britain, the United States, and France, finally crushed him.

Stuart Van Dyke, Jr.

Sources for Further Study

Atlantic. CCXLII, July, 1978, p. 88.

Book World. May 21, 1978, p. E1.

Kirkus Reviews. XLVI, April 15, 1978, p. 473.

New York Times Book Review. May 14, 1978, p. 9.

Newsweek. XCI, June 5, 1978, p. 100.

Saturday Review. V, May 27, 1978, p. 48.

Village Voice. XXIII, May 1, 1978, p. 78.

FINAL PAYMENTS

Author: Mary Gordon (1949?-   )
Publisher: Random House (New York). 256 pp. $8.95
Type of work: Novel
Time: The present
Locale: New York City and New York State

*The story of a woman who must make a new life for herself after eleven years of
caring for her invalid father*

> *Principal characters:*
> ISABEL MOORE, a thirty-year-old woman
> ELEANOR LAVERY, and
> LIZ O'BRIEN RYAN, her oldest friends
> HUGH SLADE, a married man with whom Isabel falls in love

Isabel Moore, the central character is Mary Gordon's first novel, *Final
Payments*, is the sort of woman one would like for a friend. For eleven years
before the novel begins, she has been caring for her father, who has suffered a
series of strokes. She has established a ritual of feeding him and bathing him,
of reading to him, of sleeping when he sleeps, that has not only dulled her but
has consumed the years when most women are establishing themselves in careers and in important adult relationships.

The novel opens with the father's funeral. Isabel is thirty. The shape of her
previous existence has suddenly dissolved, and she must, quite literally, make
a life for herself. Into this staggering task she moves by fits and starts, making
rapid, almost dizzying progress once she is launched, only to become para-
lyzed by memory and grief toward the end of the novel. Her problems, intensified by her circumstances, are those every woman must face: how to come to
terms with one's parents; how to discover satisfying, useful work; how to carry
on friendships; how to deal with sex. Because these questions are so familiar,
and because Mary Gordon allows Isabel to narrate her story in the first person,
the reader immediately adopts Isabel's view of the world and easily shares in
her triumphs and failures.

As the novel unfolds, Isabel must deal not only with her father's death, but
also with the meaning of her relation to him during his life. Father and daughter have been alone together since Isabel was two, and her intelligence and
self-scrutiny will not allow her to avoid acknowledging the jealous possessiveness of their attachment. The possessiveness has been sanctioned by her
conservative Irish-Catholic upbringing and by what she perceives to be the
Church's teaching about filial duty. She has a clear memory of how, at thirteen, she contrived the firing of a housekeeper, a whining, damp-handed
woman with designs on her father. At nineteen she slept with one of Moore's
young associates out of frustration at what she viewed as her father's readiness
to give her up. Three weeks later he suffered his first stroke, and Isabel, out of

guilt, accepted with no hesitation the responsibility of caring for him.

As she reflects on all these events, she gradually comes to understand how she and her father have punished each other, albeit out of a deep and sometimes admirable devotion. Her growing clarity about her feelings toward her father reveals the sensitive hand of a novelist who refuses either to romanticize Isabel's devotion or to psychoanalyze it away. Gordon also carefully develops the role of the Church in encouraging what is in some ways an unhealthy relation. Although she cannot hide from her father the loss of her virginity, Isabel does manage to hide from him that she has lost her faith. Despite this lapse from daughterly perfection, she respects her father's orthodoxy, and she solicitously entertains the priests who come to visit him and who praise her for being so dutiful. She may not be going to Mass on Sundays, but she is still, in the eyes of the Church, a good girl.

Not only is the author clear-sighted in treating the complicated relation between daughter and father; she is equally convincing in her account of Isabel's friendships with Eleanor and Liz, long her neighbors and schoolmates, and still her best friends. She has seen less of Liz than of Eleanor, whose beauty and taste Isabel alternately admires and finds cloying. Her friend takes intense delight in fruit and clothing, in their colors and textures, in the pleasures of a warm bath or a cool glass of wine. It is Eleanor who helps Isabel select a new wardrobe for her new life, who encourages her to undertake contraception, who shares her own growing sense that relations with men may be so difficult that celibacy offers an attractive alternative. In the weeks following Moore's death, Isabel and Eleanor manage to acknowledge and endure their first serious disagreement; they also discover the dangers of indulging themselves in the comforts of staying at home together, of sitting around in their housecoats, of undertaking prolonged and intimate conversations.

Isabel leaves Eleanor to visit Liz and her husband and children. Liz's wit is astringent, her view of the world as no-nonsense as Eleanor's is dreamy, her skin as brown and tough as Eleanor's is pink and fragile. Isabel learns that Liz has energetically accepted both the conveniences and the unhappiness of her marriage to John Ryan, a politician who claims sexual possession of anything that wears a skirt, including, eventually, Isabel herself. Fortunately, Ryan's attentions to Isabel are not limited to sexual ones; he also gives her a job in a county welfare office: she is to visit county residents who are being paid to care for elderly people in their homes. Isabel's job offers Mary Gordon an opportunity to create a poignantly witty series of vignettes. There is the senile woman who believes herself to be a rock-and-roll band; the kind, sensible man who gives Isabel helpful advice about men and asks to look at her breasts; the folks who are dying in a crowded home which is physically inadequate but filled with affection and activity, the primary activity being illegal off-track betting in which the elders vigorously participate. Gordon handles these vignettes with great economy, humor, and tenderness; they, like Liz and Eleanor, also serve as vehicles for Isabel's growing understanding of herself, her past, and her future.

Gordon's portrayal of Isabel's job and of her friendships with Liz and Eleanor are the most successful and satisfying achievements of *Final Payments*. Because the three women have been friends since childhood, they connect themselves to their common Catholic past, and they measure their growth away from it. Yet much as Liz and Eleanor both love Isabel, they can hardly bear each other. The women are not a threesome, not a "group" in the Mary McCarthy sense. Gordon makes Isabel deal with her friends' antagonism, as well as with the separate conflicts that arise between herself and each of the other two. The three manage to tolerate, to absorb, to work within these conflicts simply because, underneath it all, they share a great deal of affection. At the end of the novel it is Liz and Eleanor who help Isabel make a bridge to the future. These women speak to one another frankly, intimately, Their talk is warm and supportive, the sort of conversation which women recognize immediately as taking place in real life, but which seldom seems to take place in novels. Perhaps Virginia Woolf's prediction—that one of the major contributions of women writers would be to explore positive friendships between women—has at last been realized.

Partly because Gordon's handling of Eleanor and Liz is so sure, her characterization of Hugh Slade, the man with whom Isabel falls in love, seems less successful. Isabel responds to the same masculine authority in Hugh that she respected in her father, and she is drawn to the strength of his wrists and back, even though she is aware that she is inviting pain by becoming involved with a married man. We can see that Isabel loves Hugh and that her sexual feelings toward him are intense, but it is not easy to understand what it is about him that so attracts this complicated, intelligent woman. Not only does Hugh suffer as a character by comparison with Liz and Eleanor, but the novelist has also encumbered him with Cynthia, a wife so unappealing that we cannot imagine what the basis of their marriage might ever have been, not what competition she poses for Isabel. Because his marriage offers him so little, Hugh's distress as he vacillates between Isabel and Cynthia seems unjustified.

Cynthia Slade does, however, serve the important narrative purpose of confronting Isabel with guilt. She forces Isabel to see that she is no longer the devoted daughter giving up her own life to care for her father; instead, she is a free woman who is having an affair with another woman's husband and enjoying it. Isabel's confrontation with Cynthia precipitates the novel's emotional crisis: all Isabel's repressed grief finally erupts, overwhelming her in a severe depression. She refuses to see Hugh, Liz, or Eleanor; her job ends, and she decides that the only course open to her is to live with the housekeeper she fired seventeen years before—the odious woman she hates more than anyone else—so as to end her days in complete self-abnegation. Such sacrifice, she believes, is what the Church requires; and besides, it will make her good. It is not until she has moved in with the housekeeper, fattened herself out of all her newly purchased clothes, and started sleeping more hours than she stays awake, that Isabel reaches the bottom of her grief. The bottom is firm, and she can build on it. Eventually she sees that Jesus Himself does not require constant self-sacrifice, even if the Church seems to; He sanctifies affirmation as well.

Mary Gordon delicately and suspensefully times the novel's resolution, and its optimism succeeds because it has been so hard won. There is even a hint of parody in the final pages: we begin to wonder whether Isabel's sleepiness and weight gain might be symptoms of a pregnancy that will force her to go back to Hugh. But this is no conventional soapy novel. Isabel triumphs over circumstances, upbringing, and, more significantly, herself. Mary Gordon has triumphed too. In prose filled with delightful surprises, she has matter-of-factly presented a female protagonist who likes sex without being a slave to it, who is capable of genuine love for women as well as for men, who can deal with her past and move beyond it to a life that is full, complicated, and thoroughly contemporary.

Carolyn Wilkerson Bell

Sources for Further Study

Atlantic. CCXLI, May, 1978, p. 94.

Christian Science Monitor. May 25, 1978, p. 23.

Harper's Magazine. CCLVI, April, 1978, p. 84.

New York Times Book Review. April 16, 1978, p. 1.

Newsweek. XCI, April 10, 1978, p. 91.

Saturday Review. V, March 4, 1978, p. 32.

Time. CXI, April 24, 1978, p. 92.

THE FIVE STAGES OF GRIEF

Author: Linda Pastan
Publisher: W. W. Norton and Company (New York). 62 pp. $8.95
Type of work: Poetry

A collection of poems classified according to the five phases involved as a person learns to cope with the idea of his/her own mortality

In her book *The Five Stages of Grief*, Linda Pastan combines concrete and ethereal imagery as she records her feelings about the steps in the gradual acceptance of death. Each stage is represented by its own group of poems; each group has its unique tone and dimension of feeling. Although the images peculiar to the different stages do overlap, they are utilized in different contexts and so evoke varying emotions. The book jacket depicts a winding staircase whose upper steps cannot be seen, though the balcony is in partial view and the lower steps are in full view. The reader is invited to ascend in understanding as he learns about the poet's comprehension of mortality and moves with her through "Denial," "Anger," "Bargaining," "Depression," and "Acceptance."

The poems in "Denial," the first stage of grief, vary in their handling of experience but are united by the thematic concept of the nonacceptance of death. The cumulative effect of the deaths of friends and relatives upon the poet, the recapitulation of her failures, and knowledge of her own mortality are recorded in a highly personalized manner. Intertwined with these concrete images are ambiguous words, phrases, and stanzas which clarify the reader's understanding of denial. One is drawn into the *poet's* experience, but the ambiguity and universality of the experience enables him to relate in principle, as well, to the denial of death.

Many facets of denial are dealt with in this section. In the poem "Funerary Tower," the poet, visiting her father's grave with her mother, defies her forty years by the recollection of childhood. She carries these remembrances, not the grave site, home in her arms. Furthermore, she denies change and growth, which connote the passage of time and, therefore, death, after she returns home from a trip to Europe. This experience is masterfully delineated in the poem "After." Then there is the homelier image of an egg; like the figures on Keats's Grecian urn, it too is frozen in perfection, until it "succumbs" briefly to life and then death. Still another poem questions the reality of life after death; this leads to an escape into the imagination in order to reaffirm evanescence or perhaps to freeze one's thoughts in still perfection before "we go down in darkness."

Presenting the reader with the difficulties and fears of being a poet, Pastan, in "Voices," describes how she is preoccupied with writing; she composes, for instance, in a car and drives through a stop sign. Her fears are focused on the denial of the end of her writing career and, in a juxtaposition of images, she considers burying her poems to preserve her talent. Another form of denial occurs in "Adultery" and "Argument" as the poet refuses, by declining to listen to unpleasant words or to recognize dark shadows, to acknowledge the estrangement of her friend and lover. Like a cat living its ninth life, on her ninth journey, in the poem "Waking in Norway," she studies nature with a calculating eye and denies life. She only sees death and separation—even grass grows like the hair of the dead after they are buried. Finally, in the last poem, "Self Portrait at 44," she copes with the imperfections in her life by inviting her failures to sit down beside her; then she escapes by falling asleep.

The absolutes of life and death do not exist in parallel structure within the first stage of "Denial." Rather, it is death, not life, that is the absolute. Through varied images of a father's grave, a lover's absence, an egg, journeys to Europe, adultery, argument, and self-evaluation, the poet attempts to quell the force of change in each. Such concrete objects, as they are used as subjects of denial, only reaffirm death as an inevitability.

In the second stage of grief, anger, there is a feeling of disgust with human relationships, including those of the family. She also views the poet within her as a stranger. Death is a reality that cannot be denied, and recollections of conflict, disease, and personal mistakes incense and irritate her. Emotions and time wasted in senseless argument, prejudice, and illogical thinking appall her; however, these thoughts, as poems, are kept from becoming too maudlin through the use of unusual, topical metaphors. For instance, in "Death Is the Final Consumer," Pastan looks at her life as a thing that has a registered handgun. When she tries to flee from it into death, which is the only product that is one hundred percent pure, she sees television antennae gleaming like crucifixes. The poet becomes one of Nader's Raiders fighting angrily against mortality.

Another poem in "Anger" that typifies the poet's irritation with people is "In the Old Guerrilla War." The conflict between her husband and her son is analogous to a war in which she tries unsuccessfully to bring about peace. She irons handkerchiefs of truce and rolls socks "instead of bandages." When she intervenes, the combatants become irritable and are united only by the "family tree," breaking bread, not their wrath with each other. Through this experience she can merely survive, not live, as she is angered by the realization that in this wasteful period she is an ineffective mediator who will be a field soon "where all the flowers/On my housedress/Bloom at once." Since she cannot affect any action, it is not surprising that in the final poem in this section, she wants to be left alone—off stage with the scenery—and orders everything to go away.

Moving to another stage, "Bargaining," Pastan observes the processes of life and death in terms of the flow of all living things that have gone before. The macrocosmic and microcosmic views of human existence are placed in perspectives of the historical past that help her to come to terms with her life.

As she explores the past, whose visions of history vary from Judaic religious beliefs to the American bicentennial year, she learns from the evolution of thoughts. Thus, the histories of experience are related to her understanding of life cycles.

The two poems that best exemplify Pastan's personalized view of mortality as a part of the universal cycles of life are "Physics for Poets" and "Terminal." In the former, the motion of electrons around a nucleus is compared to the moth that circles around a light or earth that revolves around the sun. Both movements mean eventual death or destruction; and this idea is internalized by the further extension of the analogy when the poet defines and bargains with the thought of dying herself. "Dreams revolve around our heads—/dark planets,/dark questions;/is God so stingy with form?/Is each of us no more than metaphor/for something else?" The poet, who finds no immortality in herself, but sees a glimpse of life in her form, clutches tightly onto another in the final lines of this poem. The other poem, "Terminal," a treatise about life and death, is somewhat reminiscent of *Ecclesiastes*. The themes of arrival and departure are primary; it is the law of the seasons or nature, and thus leaves, flowers, and snow all fall. The ". . . light from a star/that started towards us/ a million years ago/arrives at last." She is learning to bargain with her own mortality, and through a universal view, she can understand.

However, the poet has not yet learned how to cope with this knowledge and so enters the fourth stage, "Depression." The primary movement in this series is one of falling, although once again the images are concrete. Paperweights, mirrors, the radio, animals, hotel stationery, a television late show, final examinations, and a high school reunion serve as metaphors for her feelings. This depression has affected her memories and they are fragmented. When these bits and pieces are placed together, a whole pattern is created for the reader who can, then, understand the poet's depression. Though the tone and quality of the poetry remain consistent, there is a nervousness and anxiety that underlies each poem. Individually, they lack, like depression, the *panache* of those that have preceded.

In the final section, "Acceptance," the vitality of movement returns to the poems. Pastan's acceptance is not passive; rather, she is in accord with the knowledge of her mortality. For example, in "Old Woman," when her griefs sing to her, she sings back; in "Caroline," death is compared to a coat that can be buttoned by the wearer who then will be ready to depart. Several of the other poems in this section help the poet to review her relationships with her family and come to terms with the past decisions in her life.

Especially delightful is "Arithmetic Lesson: Infinity." Preceding the poem is an excerpt from Shakespeare's *Antony and Cleopatra*: "In nature's infinite book of secrecy/a little I can read. . . ." These lines are fitting since the cadence of this work suggests a light Shakespearean piece. Numbers are assigned characteristics, and images that have been utilized previously in other poems depict the special nature of the numbers "one," "two," and "three." Generally, even and odd numbers are classified, as are the ways in which the poet counts impressions. She writes: "The negative numbers squabble/among themselves; imaginary numbers/count the number of kisses/that dance on the head of a pin./And the parade goes on."

The book concludes with a poem that delineates the five stages of grief and gives its title to the book. Like it, the poem is masterfully written. Although Pastan's work is not as sensual as Jong's, nor as feminist-oriented as Plath's, her poetry has the common touch. The reader, upon finishing the book, wishes to ascend the winding staircase of imagery once again.

Kathryn Flaris

Sources for Further Study

Best Sellers. XXXVIII, May, 1978, p. 59.

Booklist. LXXIV, May 1, 1978, p. 1407.

Kirkus Reviews. XLVI, February 1, 1978, p. 168.

Library Journal. CIII, February 15, 1978, p. 465.

New Republic. CLXXVIII, February 4, 1978, p. 39.

Saturday Review. V, March 4, 1978, p. 33.

THE FLOUNDER

Author: Günter Grass (1927-   )
Translated from the German by Ralph Manheim
Publisher: Harcourt Brace Jovanovich (New York). 547 pp. $12.00
Type of work: Novel
Time: The Neolithic age to the present
Locale: Primarily Danzig

A many-faceted work which may be read as an exposé on the rise and fall of male domination, as a history of Danzig, or as a treatise on culinary art

> *Principal characters:*
> Incarnations of ILSEBILL beginning with the Neolithic matriarch:
> AWA
> WIGGA
> DOROTHEA OF MONTAU
> MARGARETE RUSCH (FAT GRET)
> AGNES KURBIELLA
> AMANDA WOYKE
> SOPHIE ROTZOLL
> LENA STUBBE
> SYBILLE MIEHLAU (BILLY)
> MARIA KUCZORRA
> Earlier incarnations of the FLOUNDER (narrator) include:
> BISHOP ADALBERT
> ALBRECHT, the Swordmaker
> MÖLLER, the town painter
> MARTIN OPITZ
> AUGUST ROMEIKE, Inspector for King Frederick II
> FRIEDRICH BARTHOLDY, a young revolutionary
> PASTOR BLECH
> JEAN RAPP, Napoleonic Governor of the Republic of Danzig

Before Günter Grass's latest novel appeared in Germany in 1977, it had raised great expectation among critics and readers. The author had been at work on it for five years and had promised it for the celebration of his own fiftieth birthday in November of that year. Enough information about the book had been released to whet the appetite of the reading public. When it did appear, it without a doubt disappointed some, but also fascinated many others; and soon it was a best seller and a favorite topic of conversation among German readers.

In this novel Grass—if possible—outdoes himself in his natural propensity for shocking the bourgeoisie. All taboos are lifted. The novel is definitely bawdy, scurrilous, gross; and yet it is fascinating, captivating, and challenging. Unfortunately the novel loses some of its immediate appeal in the English translation. Grass's language is earthy, sensual, and very rich. By his choice of words, the author plays on all the reader's senses; he creates associations which are revealing and contribute to the understanding of the novel but which also may be strikingly funny. In this respect Grass's imagination knows no limit, and there is little doubt that some of these delightful expressions are of Grass's coinage. The visual image and the intimacy of embrace are heightened by substituting, for the common German word for "to embrace" *umarmen* (to put arms around), his own *umbeinen* (to put legs around). When the flounder is originally caught, he informs the fisherman-narrator in his early know-it-all manner that he has prepared himself for this event by learning the dialect of the Baltic coast. This, the flounder explains, was not too difficult since what is spoken there seems at best a wretched *Gemaule* (a low animalistic form of language; *Maul* is the mouth of an animal). In the English edition this word is translated as "stammering," thus suggesting nothing but the most basic meaning. What has happened to the reader's delight in seeing something expressed as it has never been expressed before? What has happened to the pun, the humorous twist, of hearing from the mouth of the high and mighty flounder, an animal, a term intended to show his disdain for the people of the region, but which at the same time makes them his equal?

All too often this richness of Grass's language is lost, either as described above, or through a circumlocution which lacks all the newness and the pointed ready wit of the German original. A beautiful coinage like *Fürundfürsorge* (*für und für* is of course "for ever and ever"; *Fürsorge* is "provision," "care," but also suggests social welfare) becomes "perpetuation of loving care," and loses in English its stunning newness as well as its cynical implications. This also happens when very earthy expressions are translated by overly scientific terms, as, for example, "incarnation" for *Fleischwerdung* (becoming flesh). Here the associations with food, gluttony, and cooks and their dealings with flesh are lost. But even with these weaknesses of translation, *The Flounder* is a fascinating book which will intrigue the American reader as it does the German.

The novel gets its name from the legendary talking flounder which in the Grimm brothers' tale is caught and released by a simple fisherman after it informs him that it can and will grant his wishes. When the fisherman's wife, Ilsebill, hears of the catch, she sends her feeble husband back to the water to relay her ever-increasing demands: first for a cottage, then a castle, then a kingdom, and even elevation to the papacy. When she finally demands control of the sun and the moon, the flounder draws the line and returns the couple to the hovel they had lived in to begin with.

In the novel this misogynistic fairy tale is retold with variations and ostensible corrections. The flounder is caught again by three women and tried in a feminist court for having enticed the male to break away from matriarchy and advised him through the ages in his quest for superiority over women.

Parallel to and closely interwoven with the court action runs the narrator's story told to his wife, Ilsebill, during the time of her pregnancy. The historic span of this narration reaches from the Neolithic age to our time—or, more specifically, to a 1970 dockworkers' strike in the author's native city of Danzig (now Gdansk, Poland). Within this time frame the narrator moves with ease since he is equally well at home in all ages, having lived through them all in some male incarnation or other.

The incidents related always center around a woman, beginning with the arch-archetype of the matriarch, Awa, who has three breasts and who satisfies man's every physical need, thus keeping him in the mental state of suckling infant. This prevents him from dreaming and yearning and robs him of the initiative to bring about change. It takes the flounder centuries of prodding before the man makes even as much as a quickly aborted attempt to free himself. He decides to follow the Goths as they move south from the Baltic coast, but quickly has enough of the unknown and returns to the matriarch's breast. But slowly the age of myth is left behind, the age in which nothing beyond the number three, the number of Awa's breasts, is quantified, and in which the individual is of no significance and no single deed is deserving of recognition. The heroic age begins, the age of the male principle, of change, of progress, and of wars.

Now the narrator is often incarnate in some historic person, a fact which adds an additional dimension to the novel. The reader gains the feeling of being made privy to personal information about historic figures. Memorable are the descriptions of a fictional meeting between Martin Opitz and Andreas Gryphius, as well as the story of how the miserly and pedantic Martin Opitz attracts the plague by giving a beggar a silver coin and demanding change.

It is significant that almost all male persons in the novel have some historic authenticity, starting with Bishop Adalbert and continuing on to Willy Brandt. This is not the case with most of the women characters. Nevertheless, it is the woman who stands out in the novel as the pillar of society. She is, with exception of some of the "new women" on the "Womenal," the feminist court, of almost mythical dimensions, overshadowing everything and everybody else during the age in which she reigns as cook. The contemporary Ilsebill is described as landscape and in terms normally associated with descriptions of nature. This endows her with dimensions which are otherwise not as obvious in her as in her predecessors. The women have permanency and it is not unusual that one cook outlives two or more incarnations of the male narrator. While the narrator may be split up into several personalities simultaneously, as, for example, Friedrich Batholdy, Pastor Bleck, and Jean Rapp, the women are unique. Although they do not make history that is recorded in books, each age within the novel is determined by and gets its special characteristics from the heroines.

The portrayal of women is not all positive—nothing is in this novel. The early matriarchs were reactionary, forbidding things new, and thus retarding artistic production and technical progress. Initially man is prevented from quantifying anything beyond the number three, the number of Awa's breasts.

Later that is extended to 111, the number of dimples on Awa's body. Men originally are refused permission to traffic in metal objects, but before having all such objects destroyed, the matriarch herself hides away a kitchen knife for use in her cooking.

The imagination and creativity of women become apparent primarily in what they do to satisfy man's physical needs. When it comes to cooking or supplying food, their imagination and resourcefulness are limitless. The recipes and descriptions of food preparations show never-ending innovation. Awa teaches man to fish and invents the cooking spit; Wigga plants and hybridizes beets; it is Amanda Woyke who introduces the potato into Prussia. Amanda not only develops the innumerable recipes for utilization of the potato but supervises the growth of potatoes throughout northern Europe. Naturally her singular efforts at providing food during a time of need are not recorded in the history books. This honor goes to Count Rumford, with whom Amanda corresponded.

When women leave cooking pots and beds and reject their traditional roles, they become unlikable, as evidenced to a degree by Dorothea of Montau and then by the feminists Maxie, Frankie, and Siggie, the lesbians who catch the flounder in modern times and bring it before the "Womenal." These three, who think of themselves as the "new sex," encompass all the negative elements of the male psyche. But when their male mania is driven to its extreme at the Father's Day festivities and they successively rape the Awa-type woman, Billy, men immediately demonstrate that they can behave in an even more dastardly fashion. The technology that has supplied Maxie, Frankie, and Siggie with plastic penises has also provided man with artificial extensions of his sexual organ, in this case motorcycles. With their cycles the Black Angel gang repeatedly ram and kill Billy, who has just escaped her earlier tormentors. Thus even the most dismal portrayal of women is topped by an even more derogatory statement about men.

Günter Grass has been accused of jumping on the bandwagon of the feminist movement with this novel. He has also been accused of male chauvinism, and the German feminist publication, *Emma*, designated him as "Pasha of the Month" when the novel first appeared in Germany. Such criticism is superficial and leads nowhere since it is as easy to prove that the author favors one side as the other; indeed, it is obvious that neither the male nor the female principle, as the flounder expounds them, would lead to the salvation of the world. The final scene of the novel is not very promising. The woman, Maria, confers at length with the flounder, which again has been released into the Baltic Sea. When she emerges from the water, it is not Maria but all women or womankind which takes on mythical proportions and overlooks and oversteps the male, who is lying spent on the beach. As she walks off in her new majesty, he humbly follows. We know what the flounder's one-sided counsel of the male has led to. In the novel we are given no indication that his jumping the fence to throw his support to the other side is going to be any better. Therefore, this last scene seems to indicate a repetition of history instead of a new beginning.

What, then, is the thrust of the novel? While *From the Diary of a Snail* and *Local Anesthetic* show definite tendencies, *The Flounder* seems to avoid that, and this may be its strength. The growing didacticism and moral and political fervor in Grass's works from *The Tin Drum* to *From the Diary of a Snail* are paralleled by a loss of vigor and dynamics in the narration. Whatever has been said in praise of Grass's prose style in *The Tin Drum*—it has been called vitalistic, sensual, visual, and effervescent—is true for *The Flounder* as well; and that is very important. It is the vitality in the smallest structural components of the novel—the word, the sentence, the image—which counterbalances the lack of dynamics in the overall structure of the novel. There is no simple narrative development, beginning with the Neolithic age and continuing up through history to the present. A linear concept is missing both with respect to time and space. Everybody and everything are interrelated and interdependent. This is structurally illustrated by having the first and the last incarnation of Ilsebill appear contemporaneously with all other incarnations, and by the breakdown of the traditional distinction between past and present, before and after. The spacial interrelationship is, among other things, shown by some seemingly superfluous passages, such as the Calcutta chapter. The repetitiveness and "static" caused by this method would become tedious were it not for the vitality of the language and for the insertion of some fifty passages of poetry. These poetic summaries or comments at the end of most of the chapters are pointed and witty and provide relief for the reader in breaking the voluminous flow of the sixty-some episodes of the book.

Sofus E. Simonsen

Sources for Further Study

Atlantic. CCXLII, December, 1978, p. 98.

Booklist. LXXV, September 15, 1978, p. 155.

Harper's Magazine. CCLVII, December, 1978, p. 80.

Library Journal. CIII, September 1, 1978, p. 1660.

Newsweek. XCII, November 6, 1978, p. 22.

Time. CXII, October 23, 1978, p. 104.

Times Literary Supplement. October 13, 1978, p. 1441.

FOREVER YOUNG

Author: Jonathan Cott
Publisher: Random House (New York). 219 pp. $10.00; paperback $5.95
Type of work: Essays and interviews

Conversations between a noted poet-essayist and eight significant artists and intellectuals whose creative imaginations make them seem "forever young"

To be "forever young"—ah, that is impossible. But in every generation some few lucky people have managed to defy the stereotypical image of old age; their hopes are young. Creative people, in general, keep alive their faculty for wonder. To them, each day seems fresh with the glory of a child's vision, no matter how many years they number. In *Forever Young*, Jonathan Cott records, either through formal interviews or informal conversations with distinguished artists and intellectuals, their rich and vivid life experiences.

An associate editor of *Rolling Stone*, Cott first published between 1974 and 1977 most of the pieces in that magazine, although he has slightly altered the form of several interviews for this volume. Among the notables interviewed are Oriana Fallaci, herself a famous (to some a notorious) interviewer; Glenn Gould, the virtuoso Canadian pianist; Stéphane Grappelli, master jazz violinist; Werner Herzog, German experimental film producer-director; Walter Lowenfels, poet and unrepentant Communist; Henry Miller, influential novelist and essayist; Harry Partch, *avant-garde* composer; and Maurice Sendak, author of adult fantasies disguised as children's books. Diverse though these creative figures are, they share certain traits: childlike imagination, humanistic vision, exuberant enthusiasm for the greatest of all the arts—that of living. From the standpoint of freshness and creativity, these people have learned how to be "forever young."

Nevertheless, one must cavil with the author's choice of title. To a reader unfamiliar with Cott's high critical standards, the words might suggest a self-help book on cosmetic or gymnastic approaches to youthful vitality. In fact, this collection has nothing at all in common with popular manuals on health fads and the like. It is a serious work devoted to the creative experience. Less pretentious than the *Paris Review* interviews ("Writers at Work"), Cott's pieces are amiable, relaxed, but thoroughly professional. Whereas the *Paris Review* staff of interviewers tended to cross-examine most of their subjects as though they were in a courtroom, and, for the sake of posterity, had the obligation to discover from the artists their concealed motives, Cott converses with his subjects like a friend instead of a prosecutor.

Compared with the *Playboy* interviews, moreover, Cott's conversations are far less theatrical, though more incisive. The author has a genuine interest in his subjects, he has a scholar's knowledge of their work, and he shares most of their creative interests. A musician, poet, author of children's books, and anthologizer of children's literature, Cott is attracted precisely to the people whom he interviews because of his own artistic curiosity. And his curiosity is contagious; his interviews become collaborative sessions, mutually stimulating to subject and author. They are remarkably fluent, spontaneous, and lively, as though the participants had, in the excitement of their conversations, forgotten the presence of the tape recorder and exchanged ideas without stress.

What qualities make a good interview? Most interviewers hope that their subject will reveal a startling confidence—perhaps a confession never before exposed in public. To catch the subject in an unguarded moment, the interviewer generally structures his session like a lawyer's examination, purposefully directing the course of the discussion. *Playboy* interviews, for example, generally try to elicit from the subject some sensational revelation concerning sexual attitudes or practices. Oriana Fallaci's interviews are usually stormy emotional confrontations, during which she is often able to shatter the subject's defenses. Sometimes the result of this strategy is a significant disclosure of the subject's psychology. For example, in famous interviews with Henry Kissinger and former President Thieu of South Vietnam, she drove these usually self-controlled politicians to passionate outbursts that offered strange insights into their character. But the lawyer's method has certain limitations: the interview reveals only an aberrant moment of the subject's consciousness. Through guile we may penetrate into the speaker's inner soul for that brief time, but we cannot truly say that we understand the subject. In ordinary social intercourse, just as we would hesitate to judge a person solely on the basis of overhearing his sudden outburst of rage or passion, so we should be suspicious of any interview that goads a subject into erratic behavior, no matter how sensational or psychologically revealing.

Cott's interviews, in contrast, attempt to capture the true nature of the subject, just as a photograph reveals one's true form. His special talent is to show the representative individual, not to catch the subject unaware for public exposure. In some respects, Cott's methods are more difficult to appreciate than those aimed at sensational disclosure. He must not only show sympathy for his subjects, but in truth *be* sympathetic toward them, if he is to gain their confidence. Relaxed, they talk freely, not defensively. What they reveal is their general nature, not a momentary lapse of behavior. And if they are indeed interesting people, they will—to use the metaphor of verisimilitude—photograph themselves, without the pressure of the interviewer. The result of such an approach may perhaps be less dramatic, but it is a human document nevertheless.

Cott's subjects are, without exception, interesting people. Many of them are old (as we would expect from the title): Harry Partch (1901-1974) and Walter Lowenfels (1897-1976) have since died, and their interviews may more properly be called memoirs; Stéphane Grappelli and Henry Miller are, respectively, in their seventies and eighties. But Oriana Fallaci, Glenn Gould, Maurice Sendak, and Werner Herzog certainly are on the green side of middle age—indeed, Herzog is the *Wunderkind* of modern German cinematography. So it is not a question of advanced age that unifies the subjects of Cott's book; rather, it is their shared enthusiasm for life, their "childlike aliveness to the feelings of the world and to the world of their feelings."

To discover their enthusiasms, the author participates with them in dialogues that probe their own—not necessarily the interviewer's—concerns. He compares his method of "quasi-interviews" to that of Boswell's *Life of Johnson*, Eckermann's *Conversations with Goethe*, or to the works of Oscar Lewis and Studs Terkel. On the level of art, the first two books are masterpieces of empathetic conversation; the second two are superb examples of sensitive sociological reportage. But to understand Cott's method best, one should keep in mind the judgments of Martin Buber, whom the author quotes: "Dialogue between mere individuals is only a sketch; only in dialogue between persons is the sketch filled in." In Cott's dialogues with his subjects, his role is neither that of lawyer nor flatterer, critic nor patronizer. He holds his own: an intelligent, sensitive, informed partner of the dialogue, no less interesting than his famous subjects.

Because those interviewed represent such diverse talents in the creative arts, a reader necessarily will have to choose his favorite sessions on the basis of personal taste. Cott's interview with Fallaci is perhaps the most provocative from the standpoint of observing a volatile personality in action. Fallaci is a passionate, opinionated, often abrasive woman whose rudeness, excitable temper, and theatricality make her an interviewer worthy to be feared by any pretentious or shallow subject. But for Cott she shows another, more attractive side of her nature. "Only Nixon," she once said, "knows more about tape recorders than I do." Contemptuous of most of her subjects, she yearns to interview people of substance. In her imagination, she would have wished to record conversations with Jesus, Julius Caesar, and the Emperor Augustus ("because he was such a damn fascist Nazi"). Instead of such people of substance, she records—much to her fury—insignificant rascals, whom she excoriates for their pettiness. But if she had a chance to interview the first being from outer space, she "would do it like a child. That's the secret. . . ."

From his two-part interview with Glenn Gould, Cott captures a picture of a pianist entirely absorbed in music. His anxiety dream is that somehow he might be forced to perform on stage in a different art form—as a singer perhaps. Stéphane Grappelli tells Cott that his jazz violin music springs from exuberance: "When I'm playing I'm blissful, I'm happy, I improvise." Werner Herzog describes how he is obsessed by terrible images of chickens, by symbols of deformity in ordinary things, by acute silences. In a touching interview, Walter Lowenfels talks about his battle with cancer and his greater battles in life with ignorance, cruelty, and hatred. An old-fashioned idealistic Communist, he is the ecstatic poet of futile causes. Henry Miller, the "cosmic tourist," is caught in a quiet, genial mood; much of his anger has long since drained away (although he hates the movie *Bonnie and Clyde* for its violence, and he speaks with disgust about Los Angeles). On the other hand, he discusses fondly the mysticism of Chuang-Tze and of the Chasidic Rabbi Nachman; reviles the memory of his cold, selfish mother, but speaks with generosity about his love for women; and he even offers the olive branch to Germaine Greer, one of his detractors among militant feminists. "I don't just like," he says, "I love. I go overboard." With Harry Partch, Cott discusses the composer's innovative techniques, his friends, his memories. On Maurice Sendak he offers six brief conversation-essays concerning the child's vision of reality, the artist's recollection of the child within himself.

Cott's pieces on Sendak, whimsically titled "Overture: Little Brother, Little Sister," "Brooklyn Kids," "The Hunger Artist," "Mozart and the Man in the Moon," "The Shape of Music," and "Inside and Outside: The Meadow," combine elements of the conversation-interview and the familiar essay. From them we can best assess Cott's special qualities as an artist whose dialogue transcends "its simple pragmatic function of eliciting information" and becomes "a dramatic interchange resulting in a realized embodiment of the meaning of personality." Cott's dialogues reveal the workings of the creative personality. Although the artists are different and understandably have some conflicting viewpoints (for example, Gould detests Mozart's mature music, whereas Sendak adores Mozart), they are alike in their ability to retain a sense of childlike wonder.

To be forever young, one must keep bright the vision of youth. All of the creative personalities whom Cott interviews treat life as play—the imaginative play of the child full of wonder. For his epigraph to *Forever Young*, Cott quotes a line that epitomizes his advice to his reader of whatever age: "Those who wonder shall reign, and those who reign shall wonder."

Leslie B. Mittleman

Sources for Further Study

Booklist. LXXIV, March 15, 1978, p. 1153.
Harper's Magazine. CCLVI, February, 1978, p. 91.
Kirkus Reviews. XLV, December 1, 1977, p. 1300.
Library Journal. CIII, February 1, 1978, p. 360.
New York Times Book Review. January 15, 1978, p. 6.

FREAKS
Myths and Images of the Secret Self

Author: Leslie Fiedler (1917-   )
Publisher: Simon and Schuster (New York). 367 pp. $14.95
Type of work: Social commentary
Time: 2800 B.C. to the present

Physiologically deviant human beings from the myths of Ancient Greece to the present era of film and pop culture are examined to determine what elements govern the shifting popular attitudes toward these anomalies

Leslie Fiedler has been a critic of international reputation for several decades. Many of his viewpoints have stirred controversy in the literary world, and his latest work, *Freaks*, is sure to arouse commentary both favorable and unfavorable. This history of those he terms "freaks" discusses human beings unfortunate enough to be doomed, from causes science has yet to explain, to a life of "otherness." It is largely a history of exploitation, and Fiedler's fascination with the subject is apparent in chapter after chapter on what P. T. Barnum called "curiosities."

The oldest surviving record of freaks is a Babylonian clay tablet dated about 2800 B.C. The abnormalities described thereon were considered auguries of the future, and were classified as those with something extra, those with something less, and those with something doubled. The "something extra" might include children born with six fingers on each hand, considered by diviners as omens of ill portent. Those children born without one or more essential body parts were ambiguous signs, sometimes presaging good furtune, sometimes ill. "Something doubled," *monstres doubles*, were likewise ambiguous: the birth of a hermaphroditic baby boded ill, while a janicepts infant (one with a head upon his head) was good fortune. Fiedler notes, however, that the more prosaic Romans thought of all classes of monsters as ill-omened.

The Romans, like many other cultures ancient and modern, disposed of malformed children at birth by culturally determined methods, including exposure or ritual sacrifice. In modern times the method may be the withholding of life-support systems or, in the case of therapeutic abortions, direct action to destroy the life of what may only be suspected to be a monster. Chang and Eng, the most celebrated of modern Siamese twins, who gave the popular name to what is more scientifically described as conjoined twins, may have narrowly escaped infanticide in nineteenth century Siam. Likewise, the Egyptians, who numbered animal-headed creatures among their deities, mummified the bodies of dwarfs and other anomalies, perhaps after ritual sacrifice.

But as Fiedler notes, genocide has never been directed against freaks in general until modern times, first when Hitler included dwarfs in the ranks of those to be removed from the Aryan race.

Fiedler explains that, despite the expressed wish of these unusual people not to have the term "freak" applied to them, he prefers the word to the more doubtful "monster." He thinks that since the 1930 appearance of C. J. S. Thompson's *The Mystery and Lore of Monsters*, which studied physically deviant humans, the term "monster" has been preempted (due no doubt to movies and television) for creatures of artistic fancy like Dracula, Frankenstein's monster, the Wolfman, and King Kong. He feels justified, moreover, by the acceptance of the terms "freak" and "freaking out" by young people who use them to describe their antipathy to contemporary society and its values. Youth, of course, do not confuse monsters (make-believe horrors) with anomalies of nature such as dwarfs, giants, hermaphrodites, Siamese twins, and multi-limbed individuals whom Fiedler covers with the term "freaks."

The acceptance by society of some types of unusual people seems to be a matter of some interest to Fiedler. As he notes, the dwarf or midget has been a well-documented, and in most cases well-loved, addition to royal families since the Renaissance. We know what dwarfs are long before we leave babyhood, and indeed even young children know the twenty-one or more words in modern English for little people. The oldest name, "pygmy," derives from a Greek word meaning the distance from the elbow to the knuckles of a normal-sized man. Thus, when nineteenth century European explorers discovered tribes of dwarfs in Africa, the most obvious name for them was "pygmy." They are, however, not noticeably different from any of their neighboring tribes except in size.

Dwarfs have a long and varied history, dating in modern times from the dwarfs of Bartholomew Fair in Elizabethan England, through the dwarfs of the court of Catherine de Medici to the last dwarf kept as a pet, by novelist William Beckford in England of the nineteenth century. Contemporary dwarfs have fared well, serving in almost every capacity that normal-sized people fill. During World War II, for example, the insides of bomber wings were worked on by crews of dwarfs; and in contemporary entertainment dwarfs have played many roles. Members of the Earles family were cast as munchkins in *The Wizard of Oz*, and the serious actors Michael Dunne and Bill Barty have distinguished themselves in *Ship of Fools* and *The Day of the Locust*, respectively. And *Star Wars* could not have been filmed without dwarfs who played the diminutive Jawas, and especially the robot hero Artoo Detoo.

The wide acceptance of dwarfs by taller people has come about, Fiedler thinks, because all normal-sized adults were once little people themselves. We have all had to sit in large chairs with feet swinging, to jump to put something on a high shelf, and to find ourselves in crowded elevators staring at the backs of knees. We can therefore sympathize with the hardships of these people as they try to live normal lives in a world of giants.

Just as the modern acceptance of dwarfs is almost universal, big people, "giants," have fared nearly as well. Modern basketball and football teams are benefited by those whom nature has made very tall and relatively agile. It is ironic to think that the "Irish Giant," Patrick Cotter, would have now been well paid for his 7' 7" as a basketball player, while in his own time his only function was to serve as a source of fun and wonder. Fiedler distinguishes between the dull and sluggish people who are made giants by being victims of pituitary or gonadal defects and true or genetic giants. These latter can compete physically and mentally with any normal-sized person. The book includes many photographs of giants, including Robert Wadlow, who at 8' 11½" and 491 pounds was the tallest man, probably, who ever lived. Wadlow died at age twenty-two on July 15, 1940, of cellulitis of the feet, aggravated by his immense weight and the braces he had to wear in order to walk.

Other supermen and superwomen have not done badly in the normal world. Fiedler notes that almost without exception, the fat ladies of circus fame have had no trouble finding husbands (sometimes more than one). This Fiedler attributes to our earliest memories as babies of being held and nourished in what to our seven-pound bodies must have seemed giant breasts and arms. He notes that many cultures prefer opulence in female flesh. The living skeleton, however, does not share the possible happiness of the fat, for to Western man, the skeleton symbolizes famine, hunger, and death. The living skeleton is a reminder not of abundant life and eros without guilt, but of love lost or denied.

Acknowledging the temptation for the normal to desire sexual union with the "ultimate other," Fiedler sees all freaks as somehow erotic. Thus, although the modern perceives immense ugliness as in some way lower on the evolutionary scale, this consequent beastliness is also associated with greater sexual potency, and therefore felt to be menacing. Among the grotesquely ugly Fiedler classes the bearded ladies. That they often seem titillating he supports by advancing the evidence of Pepys' seventeenth century diary, in which the author recorded his reaction to a Dutch bearded lady: Pepys found her strange, but also mighty pleasing. Bearded women include among their number witches (being hirsute was considered *prima facie* evidence in witch-hunts) as well as saints: St. Galla, St. Paula, and St. Wilgeforte. Like fat ladies, bearded women have apparently no trouble finding a spouse. Julia Pastrana, once billed as "The Ugliest Woman in the World," was married to her manager.

Wild men and feral children are dismissed along with legends of wolf children as fabrications from the start, in Fiedler's opinion. He joins skeptics such as Daniel Defoe, Claude Levi-Strauss, and Bergen Evans in this debunking.

The chapters dealing with hermaphrodites and conjoined twins are long and detailed, containing information such as the correction of the misconception that Siamese twins would be different sexes. Since the twins are products of incomplete cell division at an early embryonic state, the twins, produced from one fertilized egg cell, must be of the same sex. Despite the richness of mythology about freaks, Siamese twins have no prehistoric archetypes. They do not figure in cave drawings or paintings, nor do they appear in folk legends or tales. As Fiedler notes, there have been two-headed gods like the Roman

Janus, or the three-headed Cerberus, or the many-armed Shiva, but these are not freaks; rather, they are iconic representations of divine or Satanic super-strength or superability.

Investigations into the causes of genetic mutation are outlined, along with detailed descriptions of modern accidental maiming, such as that resulting from the use of thalidomide by pregnant women in 1961-1962. Fiedler questions the ethics of experimenting on unborn human beings, whether benefits for the future fetus occur or not. He applauds those who called for the withdrawal of thalidomide, and he discusses what he terms "value problems" involved in a decision to "interrupt" a pregnancy likely to result in an abnormal birth. Fiedler points out that many termed freaks have proved able to cope with life as well as any "normal" person. In the final analysis, he questions whether anyone has the right to deny life to a child merely because it will be expensive to nurture, either by its family or by the state.

In an excellent overview of the media handling of the myth of the freak, Fiedler points to attempts as early as Shakespeare's Caliban to portray the freak as a touching human being. His list includes movies such as Carson McCullers' *The Member of the Wedding* and her later *Reflections in a Golden Eye* as good examples of Hollywood's attempt to present a true portrait of the freak, not as a sideshow attraction but as a valuable member of society. However, Fiedler feels that the greatest of the films on this sort is the 1932 version of *Freaks*, a creation of Todd Browning. Even critics who find its situations and ending contrived have been driven to reflect on the implications, both moral and philosophical, of this film. Although it was Browning's intention to portray freaks living as normal people live, the effect of the film on the viewer is likely to be just the reverse, leaving the impression that there is something magical and evil about them. Nevertheless, the film at least attempts to present freaks as people, not as oddities or curiosities but as flesh-and-blood humans who desire the same fulfillment as their more genetically and glandularly fortunate brothers.

Fiedler ends his portrayal of the world of freaks with a look at the subculture whose musical heroes—Alice Cooper, Mick Jagger, and the like—are self-made freaks—we note the popularity of songs urging the young to "freak out." Perhaps there is something hopeful here: if therapeutic abortion shows a fear of freaks better suited to the cave than to the hospital, perhaps the young can do what the old have failed to do, and reverse the trend to barbarism by seeing nature's infinite variety where the old see only freaks.

Walter E. Meyers

Sources for Further Study

Atlantic. CCXLI, February, 1978, p. 93.

Harper's Magazine. CCLVI, February, 1978, p. 90.

Library Journal. CIII, March 15, 1978, p. 664.

New York Times Book Review. March 5, 1978, p. 9.

Newsweek. XCI, February 20, 1978, p. 82.

Time. CXI, February 20, 1978, p. 95.

THE FUTURE OF CHINA AFTER MAO

Author: Ross Terrill
Publisher: Dell Publishing Company (New York). 331 pp. $9.95; paperback $4.95
Type of work: Current affairs
Time: 1976-1977
Locale: China

An analysis of the internal affairs of China during the critical years of 1976 and 1977 which examines the implications the events of those years have on the future of China and the world view of China

Principle personages:
MAO TSE-TUNG, leader of China since 1949 and responsible for unifying the country around his interpretation of Marxism
CHIANG CH'ING, Mao's widow and part of the Gang of Four, a leftist group which struggled for power after Mao's death
CHOU EN-LAI, Premier of China for twenty-seven years and one of the founders of the Chinese Communist Party (CCP)
TENG HSIAO-P'ING, Vice-Chairman of the CCP, purged in 1967 and 1976, but restored to his former position in 1977
HUA KUO-FENG, Chairman of the CCP and leader of China since 1976

Ross Terrill may well be one of the most readable authors of Chinese current events, and in *The Future of China After Mao*, he maintains this reputation, even though this is probably his most intellectual analysis of the country. The book is based on the events which shook China during 1976 and 1977, including the death of Prime Minister Chou En-lai, the earthquake of Tangshan, the death of People's Liberation Army (PLA) leader Chu Teh, the death of Party Chairman Mao Tse-tung, the struggle between leftist Chiang Ch'ing (Mao's widow) and her Gang of Four against present Chairman Hua Kuo-feng, and China's economic and strategic position in the world.

Unlike his other books, in which he weaves the contents around his travels in the People's Republic of China and uses different incidents to emphasize points he wishes to make about life in China, much of the information in this book consists of Terrill's interpretation of articles which appeared in the *People's Daily* and other publications. The author retains his colorful use of the English language. For example, he describes Hua as having "The charisma of an insurance clerk," and mentions "The Year of the Snake—1977—slithering in." Given a few facts, he vividly reconstructs major events, such as Hua's *coup* over the Gang of Four.

A chronological list of the major events of 1976 and 1977 prefaces the book and allows the reader to keep time sequences straight during some of the extensive descriptions. Also included is a glossary of important persons and events which is very helpful to the reader who may still be easily confused by Chinese names and terminology. Terrill's introduction, consisting of an overview of America's changing attitudes toward China, is a refreshing change from the usual descriptions of Imperial China and the Dynastic Cycle which generally comprise the introduction of most books about China. After establishing China's place in the world today, Terrill describes the events in China at the time of Mao's death by giving brief biographies of major persons such as Mao, Chou, Teng Hsiao-p'ing, Hua and Chiang Ch'ing and the Gang of Four, and the part they played in Chinese political affairs in 1976-1977. Finally, Terrill offers an analysis of Chinese relations with Russia, Taiwan, and the United States.

Many of the chapters overlap, and Terrill's major points, such as the establishment of diplomatic relations between the United States and China, are discussed in the light of the main topic of various chapters. A chapter on Chou En-lai, for example, reveals the effect this man had on opening talks between the United States and China. Another chapter, on the Gang of Four, mentions the leftist reaction to United States-Chinese relations and speculates as to what might have occurred had the Gang won the struggle for power following Mao's death. Finally, Terrill uses his chapter on Sino-United States relations to reiterate and thereby emphasize his major premises and objectives.

Terrill makes no attempt to conceal his feelings toward many of the people he mentions. In the chapter on Chou En-lai, it is clear that Terrill feels a tremendous respect for Chou and considered him a better statesman and politician than Mao. His animosity toward Chiang Ch'ing and the Gang of Four is apparent, although it is difficult to determine whether this reaction springs from the groups' leftist ideology, or from Terrill's belief that ideology would hinder China in establishing diplomatic relations, and certainly cultural exchange, with other countries. One of the major points Terrill uses to discredit the Gang of Four is the conflict over ideology which has been brewing in China during the past two decades and which was demonstrated in the Cultural Revolution in the 1960's.

According to Mao, the purpose of the Cultural Revolution was to let young people experience revolution by purging the bourgeoisie and "capitalist roaders" who were gaining control in China, and at the same time to set up the controlled contradictions which would move China toward its goal of "pure" Communism. However, Terrill considers the Cultural Revolution a power ploy directed by Mao against the growing bureaucracy of the Chinese Communist Party. He states that China at the time was "classless" and that the villains against whom Mao rallied the country, economically speaking, did not exist, which created a credibility gap in the ideology of the party.

Terrill accuses Chiang Ch'ing of prolonging the Cultural Revolution in terms òf the credibility gap, but does not show how it relates to the "red-expert" conflict, which was one of the major movements of the insurrection and which, in reality, formed the basis of the conflict between the Gang and the Hua-Teng regime. In the Cultural Revolution, the "red-expert" conflict was illustrated in the "Hsia fang" movement, assigning "experts" consisting mainly of students to common laboring jobs in the country. Chiang Ch'ing stressed redness (political purity) and used this philosophy to control educational and cultural programs throughout China. Hua, and especially Teng Hsiao-p'ing, favored the goal of making China technologically equal to the West before the end of the century—a goal which could not be achieved by sending the "experts" to the countryside.

Terrill mentions that the Chinese call the Gang of Four "rightist extremists" (creating another credibility gap since the Gang's theories are "obviously leftist") without really explaining why the Chinese persist in referring to them as rightists. But Terrill does not mention whether the label "revisionists," used by Hua and Teng to rally the people against the Gang, is another misnomer, even though the label was given to intellectuals, who constituted the growth of bureaucracy, by Mao during the Cultural Revolution.

Terrill prefers to compare the growth of bureaucracy in China today to ancient China rather than to the Soviet Union (perhaps to avoid offending Chinese officials reading the book). However, in view of China's long history, it is difficult for modern historians to escape the Dynastic Cycle theory and view the present regime as more than another stage in the cycle. Terrill labels the growth of bureaucracy as neo-Legalism—after the theory of state established by the Ch'in Dynasty which first united China in 221 B.C.; the growing apathy of the people as neo-Taoism—after the philosophy which endorses withdrawal from worldly concerns; and the leftist slant of Chiang Ch'ing toward political ideology over technology as neo-Confucianism—after the sage whose philosophy of morality governed China throughout the Imperial Age.

Terrill speaks of this neo-Legalist growth of bureaucracy as winning out over neo-Confucianism through the fall of the Gang of Four. However, in Imperial China all three philosophies coexisted and were, in fact, essential for the perpetuation of the Dynastic Cycle. Legalism provided the structure for the state; Confucianism, the method of rule by the relationships outlined by Confucious; and Taoism, an outlet for the people from the rigidness of Confucianism.

Confucianism also stressed the "Amateur Ideal," the theory that statesmen must be philosophically sound rather than skilled in a particular field to achieve a bureaucratic post. This might prove to be an analogy to the red side of the red-expert conflict. In view of China's recent exploitation by major powers, it seems logical for the Chinese to stress the expert side of the conflict to increase military technology, preventing further chance of invasion, and to criticize the redness represented by the Gang—even though, particularly in his later years, Mao stressed redness, perhaps from fear of a growing bureaucracy and a separation of the experts from the masses. However, should this separation occur, it would follow Marx's theory of contradictions and provide a natural contradiction instead of the structured one Mao tried to set up in the Cultural Revolution.

At times the reader gets the impression that Terrill is directing the book toward American and Chinese statesmen, because one of his focal points is the establishment of diplomatic relations between the two countries. Terrill's recent appearance before the House International Relations Committee may have led him to decide that Americans needed some sort of education on current events in China. Knowing that one of the major arguments against United States-China diplomatic relations was the fear of damaging shaky relations with the Soviet Union, Terrill goes to great lengths to demonstrate how the establishments of such relations would ease tensions between China and the U.S.S.R. and, in effect, create a more balanced power triangle.

In his discussion of a possible thaw in Sino-Soviet relations, Terrill notes overtures Teng had already made with the Soviets and warns against their establishing ties before the United States has a chance to finalize relations. In his discussion of the slight thaw with the U.S.S.R. following Mao's death and the rise of Teng, Terrill mentions China resumed anti-Soviet propaganda because the "Russians were not prepared to match words with deeds," perhaps implying that the United States ought to start following up on some of the agreements made in the Shanghai Communiqué of 1972. So far, the establishment of United States diplomatic relations with China has not produced any thaw toward the Soviet Union—in fact, anti-Soviet slogans are raging stronger than ever, and the Soviets are clearly uneasy about this new turn of events, which to them is throwing the triangle out of balance.

Terrill rather glosses over Taiwan's role in deterring the establishment of diplomatic relations between the United States and China by stating that China's concern was directed toward United States military involvement on the island province, rather than worry about Chiang Kai-shek's Republic of China. Terrill makes no attempt to dispute the two governments' claim that there is only one "true" government of China, and that Taiwan and the mainland should be reunited, even though this statement discounts the nationality of the Taiwanese, who comprise one of China's minorities.

Terrill also mentions Yeh Chien-ying, the former defense minister and technically the second most powerful man in the country (Yeh gave up his position in 1978). Terrill notes that Yeh was one of the key figures in helping Hua establish control of the country through the People's Liberation Army. Indeed, the PLA gained prominence and power through the role it played in restoring order after the Tangshan earthquake and by providing credibility to Hua by arresting the Gang of Four and openly publicizing their support of Hua through the media. This growth in the PLA's power, which had decreased after Lin Piao's attempted *coup* in 1971, is most obviously seen in China's recent invasion of Vietnam. It will be interesting to see if Hua and Teng can justify the invasion's lack of success, and what effect it may have on their leadership.

Terrill is not so bold as to make an absolute prediction for the future of China, being well aware of the major ideological swings which can change

Chinese internal and foreign policies even overnight. Diplomatic relations between the United States and China had not been finalized when Terrill wrote this book, and though he advocates the establishment of those ties, he also suggests the possibility of Sino-Soviet ties and other solutions.

Terrill correctly predicts that before 1980 the future of United States-China relations would be resolved: either the countries would have reached an agreement or broken off ties completely. However, he seems to have had some foresight in the positive resolution of diplomatic relations. For example, he makes a reference in favor of United States ties with China by saying the growth of the Chinese middle class will necessitate the growth of a better standard of living, including ". . . soft drink machines in factories . . ."—a very curious statement in view of China's recent trade negotiations with Coca Cola.

Terrill notes that the future of China after Mao depends largely on the ability of Hua and Teng to resolve the ideological crises resulting from the growth of a middle class in China. They must allow for the development of technology and provide a better standard of living for the people without the experts becoming too widely separated from the masses. And, in their race to become technologically equal to other major powers by the end of this century, the Chinese must rely on a major power to facilitate their growth. Although Terrill does not say it, he might well agree that the growth of United States-China relations has developed from "Ping Pong Diplomacy" (competition) to Coca Cola Diplomacy (trade oriented).

Susan I. Weaver

Sources for Further Study

Choice. XV, December, 1978, p. 1439.
Kirkus Reviews. XLVI, April 1, 1978, p. 427.
Library Journal. CIII, May 15, 1978, p. 1060.
New Republic. CLXXIX, August 19, 1978, p. 37.
New York Times Book Review. July 2, 1978, p. 4.

THE GERMAN ARMY, 1933-1945
Its Political and Military Failure

Author: Matthew Cooper
Publisher: Macdonald and Jane's (London). 556 pp. $17.95
Type of work: Military history
Time: 1933-1945
Locale: Europe

The history of the German army emphasizes that its military and political failure consisted of its subjugation to Hitler, who was a military incompetent

Principal personages:
ADOLF HITLER, Chancellor and *Führer* of Germany, 1933-1945
FIELD MARSHAL WALTHER VON BRAUCHITSCH, Army Commander until Hitler took over completely in 1941
GENERAL HEINZ GUDERIAN, famed panzer commander
GENERAL FRANZ HALDER, Chief of General Staff
FIELD MARSHAL ERICH VON MANSTEIN, key German commander
FIELD MARSHAL ERWIN ROMMEL, well-known tank commander

The dilemma of personal conscience in an immoral state is perennially fascinating, and no more vivid historical example of this dilemma exists than the history of the German people under Nazism. To what extent were the Germans responsible for the evils of the Nazi state? To what extent was the German leadership responsible? The latter question, especially, seems pertinent and arresting, since neither the mass exterminations at home nor the brutal wars abroad would have been possible without the help of thousands of the elite at the heads of large industries, enormous bureaucracies, powerful armies. In *The Germany Army, 1933-1945: Its Political and Military Failure*, Matthew Cooper grapples with the reaction of the German army leadership to the advent of Hitler and their dilemma in following his increasingly insane commands.

At the beginning, Hitler's leadership gave no cause for alarm. The army and Hitler enjoyed a period of mutual admiration that lasted from 1933 to 1938 when Hitler, distrustful of his generals' judgment, made himself Supreme Commander. In 1941, when Field Marshall von Brauchitsch ceased to be Commander-in-Chief, Hitler became Commander-in-Chief as well. From this time on, Hitler took over more and more of the operational command of his armies—until his generals were little more than puppets responding to the tugs of his mind. It was the *Führer* who decided to attack the Soviet Union, to stand at rather than withdraw from Stalingrad. It was Hitler who made the numerous military decisions which led to disaster in both the East and the West. The generals' opinions constantly poured forth and were persistently ignored. Hitler, in fact, insisted on directing his armies in detail. For instance, in 1941, during the invasion of Russia, Hitler ordered:

In the northern sector of the Eastern front the main attacks will continue between Lake Ilmen and Narva towards Leningrad, with the aim of encircling Leningrad and making contact with the Finnish Army. . . . the intended thrust by Panzer Group 3 against the high ground around Valdi will be postponed until armoured formations are fully ready for action. . . . Estonia must first of all be mopped up by all the forces of the 18th Army. Only then may divisions advance toward Leningrad.

By 1945 this interference with army operations had progressed further. Hitler ordered:

1. Commanders-in-Chief, Commanding Generals, and Divisional Commanders are personally responsible to me for reporting in good time:
   a. Every decision to carry out an operational movement.
   b. Every attack planned in divisional strength and upwards which does not conform with the general directives laid down by the High Command.
   c. Every offensive action in quiet sectors of the front, over and above normal shock-troop activities, which is calculated to draw the enemy's attention to the sector. Every plan for disengaging or withdrawing forces.
   d. Every plan for surrendering a position, a local strong point, or a fortress.

Such progressive interference on the part of Hitler is usually justified on the grounds that he was a military genius who in the face of the opposition of his pusillanimous generals forged his new weapon, *Blitzkrieg*, or lightning war, utilizing the highly trained, well-equipped, motorized German army to win quick victories in the West. Matthew Cooper is concerned with destroying that myth, with showing that Hitler was not a military genius, did not have a new method of war, or a well-equipped army.

Standard German military practice emphasized *Vernichtungsgedanke*:

the total destruction of the enemy's forces, not by means of relatively slow, costly frontal attacks, but of swift decisive blows from the flanks and the rear. Victory was seen to be in strategic surprise, in the concentration of forces at the decisive point, and in fact, far-reaching concentric encircling movements, all of which aimed at creating the decisive *Kessel schlachten* (cauldron battles) to surround, kill, and capture the opposing army in as short a time as possible.

Against this older idea was opposed the newer—that of armored infiltration. Following the British theorists Fuller and Liddel Hart, the German generals Guderian and Rommel promoted the idea that the way to victory consisted of an armored thrust deep and swiftly into enemy territory, well ahead of infantry. The goal was not the annihilation of the enemy forces but the disruption of his communications, the disintegration of his morale. This was victory just as sure, but conceived of in a new way. Combined with the activities of para-troops and dive bombers, this was *Blitzkrieg*.

Cooper's point is that, strictly speaking, there was no *Blitzkrieg*. In the first place, in 1939 the army table of organization was such that only one division in twenty was panzer; moreover, one quarter of the existing tanks were not

incorporated in panzer divisions, but were used for infantry support. Furthermore, ninety percent of German tanks were obsolete. Thus Germany went to
war with less than five hundred tanks of modern design. Moreover, of over
two thousand motor vehicles in a panzer division, not one was wholly tracked.
This deficiency meant that support vehicles could not adequately follow tanks
in their lightning, off-road thrusts. Finally, panzer troops were never given
equal status with infantry, cavalry, and artillery. These conditions did not
markedly improve throughout the six years of the war.

With few exceptions the German army was used to procure victories—often
brilliant and decisive victories—not by the armored thrusts, but by the traditional means of a battle of encirclement and annihilation. Guderian's thrust
through France was an example of the major use of armor, but it was constantly thwarted by interference from above—a concern about the swiftness of
Guderian's pace and the nakedness of his flanks. Rommel's strategy and tactics in the North African desert was another example. Rommel was substan-
tially not interferred with, but was constantly starved for equipment and fuel
and by Hitler's lack of appreciation for the importance of the war in the desert.
Other than these two campaigns, there was no significant use made of the idea.

The emphasis on *Vernichtungsgedanke* is as much a function of the conservatism of the general staff as it is of Hitler's lack of military insight. But the
conduct of the war—in large strokes and in detail—also suffered markedly
from Hitler's incompetence as a military commander. According to Cooper, on
the issues of larger strategy Hitler failed badly. His attack on the West succeeded more because of the incompetence of his enemies than because of his
brilliance. The attacks on the East failed because of Hitler's stupidity in beginning a two-front war, his foolishness in fighting an enemy that could lose—and
did lose—ten men for every one of his, his incompetence in ignoring the only
strategy that might have led to victory. To Cooper, Hitler's military leadership
consisted of "his unrivalled capacity for self-delusion, his suspicion of the
professional military caste, his oft-expressed belief in the power of a fanatical
will, his fear of taking risks, his disinclination for long-term plans, his propensity to place political before military considerations, his inability to distinguish
between the important and the trivial," and, with defeat, his "frequent outbursts of rage." This opinion finds ample support in the opinions of the generals. To Halder, "A man, with dynamic intellect, energy, and bold daring may
go beyond what the average military mind sees as the limits of possible
achievement, but he will never fail to recognize and heed the fact that ultimately such limits do exist. He will not, as did Hitler, base all his actions on
wishful thinking rather than on what can be achieved." Von Manstein felt that
"the basic issue was between two incompatible conceptions of strategy and
grand tactics: *Hitler's*, which arose from [his] personal characteristics and
opinions [and those] based on the traditional principles of the German General
staff." To the author, therefore, the failure of the German Army was the fail-

ure of its leadership to draw the line when Hitler began to assert his control of operational matters.

This is to take a narrow view of responsibility and to place too much reliance on the self-serving opinions of the General Staff trying to excuse themselves after a war which they had lost and in the conduct of which they had distinguished themselves only by moral cowardice and political ineptitude. In fact, the truth seems simpler. At first, Hitler was right and the generals were wrong. The West was vulnerable and stunning victories were won. Drunk with success, the German General Staff, along with the German people, ignored their ultimate weakness in the face of the overwhelming manpower of the Soviet Union and the overwhelming industrial might of the United States. They were able to brush aside the fact that Hitler was criminally insane, a man whose plan included making the murder of millions a national industry. With a presumably clear conscience, the generals were able to issue orders which stated that "the soldier in the east is not merely a fighter according to the rules of war, but also a protagonist of a merciless racial idea, who must fully understand the necessity for hard, but just, punishment of Jewish sub-humanity." The point is not, as Cooper asserts, that Hitler was an incompetent military commander; the point is that he was mad, and that, by and large, the generals followed his orders unswervingly. The point is not that the generals experienced a conflict between honor and duty, but that they ignored the welfare of the German people and led millions under their commands to disablement and death. Without the generals' connivance, Hitler could not have pursued his mad ambitions. The generals gave him their help unstintingly, and are therefore culpable. Evil does not exist because there is a devil but because men follow him.

Alan G. Gross

Sources for Further Study

Library Journal. CIII, September 1, 1978, p. 1633.
Times Literary Supplement. October 20, 1978, p. 1206.

GERMANY 1866-1945

Author: Gordon A. Craig (1913-   )
Publisher: Oxford University Press (New York). 825 pp. $19.95
Type of work: History
Time: 1866-1945
Locale: Germany

A balanced survey of German history in its brief period of unity that emphasizes the tragic consequences of the failure of German liberalism and social reform

Principal personages:
THEOBALD VON BETHMANN-HOLLWEG, Prime Minister of Prussia and Chancellor of Germany, 1909-1917
OTTO VON BISMARCK, Prime Minister of Prussia and Chancellor of Germany, 1871-1890
HEINRICH BRUENING, Chancellor of Germany, 1930-1932
PAUL VON HINDENBURG, President of Germany, 1925-1934
ADOLF HITLER, *Führer* and Chancellor of Germany, 1933-1945
WILLIAM II, Emperor of Germany, 1890-1918

Many important works on the social, cultural, political, and economic history of modern Germany have appeared in the past ten years. Gordon Craig, a military and diplomatic historian, has produced an important synthesis of this recent scholarship. While the new social and economic emphases applied to modern history have made the discipline more analytical than before, Gordon Craig has reaffirmed the status of history as an art. The stylistic qualities and the suppleness of Craig's narrative line combines a tragic story with trenchant analysis.

Craig effectively prefaces each chapter with selections from German poetry that capture the theme of the period. The author sets the tone of his story by characterizing Germany not as the usual Faust, but rather as Hamlet who symbolizes the fatally indecisive character of German liberalism. The character of this political and social liberalism proved to be manipulated by the rulers, fearful of the masses, timid and divided. In 1866 Hamlet gives way to Fortinbras, who symbolizes the arrogance and rigidity of Bismarckian and Wilhelmian Germany. The weaknesses of the Weimar Republic led to a longing for a new Fortinbras who leads Germany to disaster. The *Kulturvolk* (people devoted to culture) of the nineteenth century is transformed into a *Machtvolk* (people devoted to power) of the twentieth century. The emphasis of this book on political, personal, and cultural themes against a backdrop of social and economic forces puts Craig in the great tradition of liberal German historiography exemplified by Hajo Holborn and Fritz Stern.

At the outset of his excitingly written story Craig feels rightfully obliged to rehabilitate the "old fashioned" emphasis on the role of personalities from its near oblivion at the hands of social and economic historians. His story begins with the Prussian victory over Austria in 1866. This made possible Otto von

Bismarck's unique accomplishment of preserving the authoritarian structure of Prussia-Germany in a modern world that was evolving toward more libertarian structures. It is from the inadequacy of Bismarck's solutions that many subsequent problems of German history derived. Craig's assertion that had it not been for Bismarck, Germany would have been united but not in the same way, is an astute and balanced observation on the relationship of personality to larger historical forces. The fearful prediction of Friedrich Nietzsche that a nation's misconstrued victory can sometimes be more dangerous than a defeat, is one of the many illuminating literary citations employed by Craig. These references cast light both on the great writers of the time and on the problems of the time they observe.

From 1871 on Bismarck became a "culture hero" and authoritarian attitudes and institutions became enshrined in the structure of the Second Empire. The author's analysis of the formation of an authoritarian alliance of industry and agriculture in 1879 illustrates not only an economic and social event, but also Bismarck's opportunity to consolidate the hold of his political system on the nation. Bismarck's persecution of the socialists was also a partial success of the authoritarian regime, for it pressed into service such institutions as the bureaucracy and the police.

As in his *Studies in German Statesmanship*, Craig clearly analyzes the complexities of Bismarckian diplomacy. Germany's alliance with Austria and Russia was designed to isolate France, but failed because Austria and Russia had opposing interests. The diplomats chosen by Bismarck tended to be mediocre yes-men who could later not agree on whether to favor Russia or Austria. By 1890 Germany chose Austria and a policy of overseas expansion.

The campaign of the ruling classes against the socialists failed to discourage the growth of the Social Democratic Party. However, Bismarck's astute introduction of social insurance laws in 1883 helped to split the socialists, while the purge of the bureaucracy, the expansion of the reserve officers corps, and the support of the reactionary educational system all served to bolster the authoritarian regime. By 1890 the desperate Bismarck was contemplating a coup to abolish the pseudoliberal constitution. It is important to note here that at least one future German Chancellor, Franz von Papen, contemplated a coup in 1932, as did the conspirators against Adolf Hitler in 1944. German authoritarianism lent itself to such solutions.

Craig's treatment of German cultural developments is superb. Not only does he display a great understanding of German poetry and drama, but he constantly puts his wide knowledge of the German social novel to good use. This helps to cast light on the relationships between German social and cultural developments. Craig's study of the divergence of politics and culture in Wilhelmian Germany stresses both the alienation of literary figures from the regime and the increasing drift of scholars and professors in the universities toward nonpolitical irresponsibility and hypernationalism. A short but trenchant discussion of the struggle for women's rights in the Second Empire does a valuable service of synthesizing current scholarship.

Craig provides a penetrating characterization of Kaiser Wilhelm II as an insecure and unintelligent amateur politician who was devoid of common sense and given to vacillation. Wilhelm's need to give Germany a "place in the sun" was shared by the nation at large. This German craving for recognition was an important force in Germany's drive for world power. Perhaps Craig should have more fully related the awesome facts of German industrialization to politics, society, and diplomacy.

The author's portrait of Chancellor Theobald von Bethmann-Hollweg as "the quintessential *Geheimrat*," possessing "all the best and worse qualities of the Prussian bureaucracy," is one of the most devastating judgments in the entire book. It is also a bitter commentary on the brittleness of the unimaginative elite who ruled Germany from 1890 to 1914. The socialists continued to grow in numbers while the authoritarian pillars of the regime sought to avoid reform by appealing to the industrialists, the anti-Semites, the expansionists, and the nationalist academics.

Unlike other historians of the period, Craig does not argue that a crisis of the Second Empire was inevitable in 1914. Though the Reichstag passed a vote of no confidence in the government in 1913, the socialists did not want to take power. Craig implies here that had World War I not destroyed the system, reformist socialist attitudes might have worked to reform the system peacefully. Though this is a corrective to the strictly determinist view that an explosion was inevitable, the argument remains hypothetical.

Emphasis on the relationship between foreign and domestic policy helps to explain the coming of World War I. East Elbian aristocrats supported tariffs that antagonized Russia; the industrialists supported a Navy that alienated Great Britain; and the military developed great influence over the government. The result was an increasing German arrogance of wealth and power that produced overconfidence and recklessness on the world scene.

Craig's detailed narrative of Germany in World War I is worthy of the quality of military history he has written in the past. His theme is the victory of the reactionary annexationists and the army over the forces of peace and reform. We learn the little-known fact that the annexationist movement was supported by the German princes who craved territories to enlarge their states. For example, the Prince of Bavaria coveted the area of Burgundy. Craig might have pointed out that Burgundy was the area promised to the SS in World War II.

If the imperial regime of Germany had been hampered by the arrogance and lack of perspective of those in power, the Weimar Republic was plagued by vacillation and self-doubt. The similarity between the reactionary Empire and the democratic Republic was the poor quality and rigidity of the leadership and the party structure. The failure of the Weimar Republic effectively to liberalize

and socialize Germany; the German hatred of the Versailles Treaty; the alienation of the intellectuals; and the persistence of the older elite doomed the republic. The socialists and middle classes remained divided. The civil service,
the judicial branch, the army, and the educational system remained in the
hands of the old order. Craig puts the problem of the Weimar Republic in a
nutshell in an ironic statement that is characteristic of his fine prose style:
"Germany, in short, had been defeated by the very people who were now
running it." Finally, the disastrous inflation of 1923 destroyed the morale and
the economic well-being of millions of Germans and left great wounds in the
body politic.

The divisions in politics and society were also characteristic of Weimar
culture. Craig's description of that culture is vivid and succinct. The experimentation of these topsy-turvy years renders the period one of the great
creative eras of cultural history. Yet the fragmentation of intellectual life into
antigovernment factions of left and right, the proliferation of fads and schools
of thought, the withdrawal of intellectuals into an inner nonpolitical world,
were all signs of trouble. The cultural landscape of Weimar revealed a lack of
assurance and an absence of unifying norms and common goals. Craig argues
that Weimar produced a culture of extremes. Even libertarians such as Kurt
Tucholsky attacked the German republic as a sham. Given the nature of the
republic, this was understandable. Meanwhile, such right-wing intellectuals as
Moeller van den Bruck were searching for a new Fortinbras who would revive
the character of the true nationalistic Germany. Despite the poverty of right-
wing ideas, they were to triumph with a vengeance in 1933.

The major revisions offered by Craig in the area of late Weimar politics lie
mainly in the role of personality. Craig sees Article Forty-eight of the Weimar
Constitution, with its provision for presidential emergency rule, as a republican substitute for the personality of the monarch. President Paul von Hindenburg emerges as an "effective and moderate" supporter of the republic until
the crisis of 1930. Foreign Minister Gustav Stresemann becomes a brilliant
practitioner of German self-interest, not the "good European" he has sometimes been called. Craig effectively argues that Heinrich Bruening was not the
last defender of the Weimar Republic but rather its first gravedigger. Bruening
lacked the "psychological gifts" of leadership and inaugurated rule by decree.

Craig's handling of the Nazi phenomenon looks upon the movement and its
leader as "*sui generis*, a force without a real historical past . . . ." Yet such
historians as George Mosse have made a convincing case that many Nazi attitudes had roots in the period since 1870. Mosse's argument by no means
minimizes Craig's correct assessment of Hitler's uniqueness and brilliant but
contemptible qualities of leadership. Craig clearly traces the political machinations that led to Hitler's appointment as Chancellor. As in some of his previous
writings, the author views the army as a crucial force in Hitler's coming to
power. Unfortunately, he devotes too little attention to the economic, social,

cultural, and psychological forces that combined with the political success story of the Nazi takeover.

The book aptly assesses the uniqueness of the Nazi experience as a combination of the "traditional and revolutionary." The themes of Nazi history emphasized by Craig reveal that he is fully abreast of recent trends of research and interpretation. Nazi government was a conglomeration of rival agencies and satrapies where all roads led to the *Führer*. The SS emerged as the most effective dominating force of the regime. The Nazis craved popular support, and provided a halfway revolution where a vaunted equality of status and opportunity became a novel feature of German social life. However, the Third Reich was ultimately conservative, for it sought to solve its social and economic problems through total war and genocide.

Craig's chapter on Nazi culture is perhaps his best analysis of German cultural history, for it is here that he effectively analyzes the relationship between politics, society, and culture. Most German intellectuals hailed the Nazi regime out of a mixture of nationalism, naïveté, and fear. The Nazis destroyed the older creative intellectual elite of Germany. We learn that the Nazis burned not only books but hundreds of paintings. Craig is right to show that new methods and techniques of propaganda were perhaps the most innovative features of the regime.

The churches, universities, and army lacked the will to resist Hitler. German resistance movements rested on a social base narrower than that in France. What resistance there was coalesced, not around the intellectuals who took the road of "inner emigration," but around the army. All the army could offer was the old solution of the coup, a basically illiberal, backward-looking, and authoritarian solution.

An analysis of Nazi diplomacy leaves little doubt in the mind of the reader that the Nazis prepared for war. They sought to wage total war by means of modern military technology, extermination, and propaganda. But they were brought down by the opposition of much of the civilized world. By 1945 Germany was in a shambles and had no choice but to start over again.

Gordon Craig's conclusions reflect the arguments of some recent social historians who maintain that Hitler's work of destruction took the old Germany with him. Thus, the obstacles that had stood in the way of political reform and social modernization had been removed. The options open to the Germans in 1848 were possible in 1945 with the memories of disaster to help them choose the path of reform. For such a fine work of history, Craig's conclusions are somewhat ahistorical, for they seem to overemphasize the break between the period of German unification and the era since 1945. Germany is still a divided nation. The Eastern half of the country remains within an authoritarian, albeit modernized, framework. Though a democracy, the Western portion of Germany contains a neo-Nazi movement and a radical sectarian left that threaten to polarize the nation in a future time of testing.

Germany 1866-1945 is the most lucid synthesis of the complexities of modern German history that has yet appeared. It is characterized by a superb style, a careful balance between political, cultural, and socioeconomic perspectives, and an eye for illuminating quotations from the Germans themselves. Its major theme of the consequences of illiberalism and the failure of social reform also encompasses the tragic story of those who tried in vain to create a free Germany. Craig's mastery of the vast body of the recent historiography of modern Germany brings new evidence and meaning to an old theme; his fine prose style gives life to it. The result is a notable achievement.

Leon Stein

Sources for Further Study

Economist. CCLXVIII, September 16, 1978, p. 122.

New Statesman. XCVI, September 15, 1978, p. 336.

New Yorker. LIV, September 11, 1978, p. 162.

Spectator. CCXLI, November 4, 1978, p. 18.

Times Literary Supplement. October 6, 1978, p. 1113.

THE GREAT FEAR
The Anti-Communist Purge Under Truman and Eisenhower

Author: David Caute
Publisher: Simon and Schuster (New York). 542 pp. $14.95
Type of work: History
Time: The 1940's and 1950's
Locale: The United States

A history of the persecution of "subversives" during the McCarthy era

Principal personages:
JOSEPH McCARTHY, Senator from Wisconsin who accused many individuals of subversive activity
ROY COHEN, his special assistant
JOHN HENRY FAULK, a blacklisted radio commentator

Americans worried about many things in the 1950's: the high unemployment rate, increasing racial tension, and the invincibility of the Yankees. They even worried about a ridiculously low level in inflation. But the main concern of the United States during this period was Communism. The anxiety of the arms race, the secrecy of the Soviet state, and the strange responsibility of being the world's dominant power—all of these led to a remarkable preoccupation with the Communist issue. Government and public reaction to this issue was suffused with that vague fear which led to security programs, persecution of domestic radicals, and a remarkable concentration of power in the hands of a demagogic Senator named Joseph McCarthy. In the late 1970's, the American view of Communism is far more sophisticated. We concede that China, Yugoslavia, and Russia are not part of a monolithic whole, but are very different societies; that the Russian military can be as bungling as the Pentagon; and that many Russians are not only good people, but fairly content with their lives and even with their government. The older, one-dimensional division of the world into good and evil, free and Communist, seems hopelessly simplistic by comparison. Why the older view held such a powerful grip on America is a fascinating and complex question, and one which few historians have tried to answer.

The Great Fear does try, but fails to add much to our understanding of McCarthyism. It is a disappointing book chiefly because it could have been so good. In recent years, a wealth of new information has become available as government documents have been declassified and old radicals have concluded that the national mood is safe enough for the revelation of their secrets. This material is largely unworked, touched only by journalists and a few specialist students. David Caute, brings to his book an established reputation for research and an understanding of the political left. A long and well researched book, *The Great Fear* is nonetheless inconclusive and riddled with defects.

The basic problem with the book is Caute's utter lack of objectivity. Rather than conforming to the standards of fairness historians expect in the 1970's, Caute falls instead into the shrill tone of J. Edgar Hoover in the 1950's—the only difference being that he is denouncing not the Communists, but the anti-Communists. Each chapter is a compilation of case studies exposing the slim pretexts and weak reasoning which led to the firing, silencing, or imprisonment of hundreds of people during and after the Red Scare. Many of these people were entirely innocent of any Communist connection; virtually everyone was innocent of "treason" as we now conceive of it. This is interesting material. The problem is that Caute cannot help imbuing the persecuted leftists with all the attributes of Christian martyrs—determination, virtue, idealism, intelligence—while their persecutors are cast either as Gestapo-like inquisitors or hopeless buffoons. As a result, the book sounds like the work of a muckraker writing in 1953, trying to awaken the world to the dangers of McCarthyism. Unfortunately, Caute is writing more than two decades after McCarthy was censured for the very practices condemned in the book. There are few things more tedious than an exposé of what has already been exposed.

Caute's biases seep into the book through an uneasy mixture of sarcasm and self-righteousness. On the one hand, he views Communism with mock indignation, pretends to take seriously the most outlandish conspiracy theories, and parodies the statements and intentions of any and all investigators. On the other, he seems to be sometimes overcome with anger at his subject, and venom spills onto the pages. He calls Roy Cohn, McCarthy's special assistant, a "spoiled child"; says that Congressional committee members "hounded" innocents; and so on. At times the anger in the writing almost obscures the meaning of the phrases: "The victim whose stubborn and courageous fight against those who had vindictively destroyed his career called down the curtain on the blacklisters was an utterly non-Red Texan called John Henry Faulk. . . ." Most discouraging of all are the wild exaggerations that sprinkle the chapters. The author suggests, for example, that Los Angeles teachers were all in a "state of constant anxiety" for six years from fear that their teachings would be construed as "subversive."

The organization adopted in *The Great Fear* does not lend itself to an understanding of the period. The book is arranged according to the various groups in which persecution occurred (Army, science, Civil Service, unions, and so on), not according to phases of the Red Scare. Consequently, the reader gets little sense of the building momentum of the period of the late 1940's and early 1950's. Each chapter is subdivided into even narrower topics, which appear to have been written at different times, often repeat one another or fail to explain obscure references, and generally fail to produce coherent reading (one joke made by Arthur Miller at the expense of a Congressional committee is retold by Caute in three separate sections). Moreover, the book focuses so heavily on the individuals who suffered at the hands of an intolerant America that one loses sight of the country itself; we learn of the fear that followed fellow-travelers, and not of the larger, more important fear that gripped the nation.

The heart of the problem in *The Great Fear* is that, while Caute seeks to explain McCarthyism, he in fact pays only cursory attention to its causes. His research and the cases he cites are all centered around the effects—the impact upon radicals or suspected radicals. But this, of course, is not the truly interesting aspect of the Red Scare. Repression can be found in almost any society during almost any period, including the American past. The herding of Oriental Americans into California internment camps during World War II, the treatment of Southern blacks, and the repressive measures taken against thousands during the first Red Scare (1919-1920), all make the effects of McCarthyism seem comparatively mild. The sources of intense anti-Communism are, by contrast, unique and intriguing.

Although it is difficult to pinpoint exactly what the Red Scare was, one can clarify with some confidence what it was not. It was not, first of all, an elitist, fabricated movement. Regardless of the influential role of a few demagogues, it is clear that they were responding to, not manipulating, a powerful current of popular feeling. If anything, the exaggerated charges and unjustified inquisitions of some anti-Communists tended to discredit the movement in the long run. Nor was it a partisan phenomenon. Though the leading anti-Communists were Republicans, and their targets were often Democrats, much of the scare was initially fueled by the policies and statements of Democratic President Harry Truman. As Mary Sperling McAuliffe makes clear in *Crisis on the Left*, a great many liberal intellectuals became strong voices against domestic and foreign Communism by the early 1950's. Finally, it is clear that McCarthyism lasted far longer than most movements of its kind. The Red Scare that followed World War I, for example, reached its climax a few months after the war's end and declined within a year. After World War II, on the other hand, the scare remained strong for well over a decade and dominated issues in Congressional elections from 1946 to 1954. Despite all this attention, and despite such occasional "revelations" as the Alger Hiss and Robert Oppenheimer cases, no one has ever turned up strong evidence that significant espionage occurred during the Cold War, that the American Communist Party ever planned any sort of insurrection, or that any sort of "indoctrination" took place in the nation's schools.

What forces, then, could have fueled such powerful fears? Caute mentions a few possibilities. One is nativism—the fear of foreign influence that is particularly strong in a nation at once "isolationist" in its traditions and a land of immigrants. Recent immigrants were often prominent in radical movements and hence confirmed the suspicions of nativistic groups. Another is class hostility, felt by farmers and the middle class for workers who were in a rebellious mood after the war, which could be easily transformed into an ideology like anti-Communism. Although unwilling to commit himself to a systematic Marxist analysis, Caute seems to favor the notion that class antagonism—perhaps even a middle-class attempt to prevent working-class unity—was at the heart of McCarthy's support. The evidence marshaled for this position, however, is minimal.

One possible explanation for part of the Cold War hysteria lies in the nature of the Cold War itself. From 1946 on, the United States felt itself confronting a clear enemy. Russia was hostile to American ideals, economic interests, Western power, and the entire American plan for the postwar world. Rarely, if ever, had the United States been so united on foreign policy as when it opposed Soviet expansion. But for all this hostility, the United States was peculiarly impotent in the conflict (as was, indeed, the U.S.S.R.). The possibility of total war was unthinkable—particularly after the Soviet Union developed its own atomic weapons. The Cold War had to be conducted carefully and with restraint. In other words, aggression was repressed and, to extend the metaphor, pent-up within the country. The search for an outlet led inevitably to a domestic version of the Soviets: the Communist Party.

American Communists played their part in fanning the fire of persecution—once the FBI and the Congressional committees had ignited it. One of the most interesting chapters in *The Great Fear* follows the Party into the 1950's. As hostility towards Communism grew, and leading Communists were put on trial chiefly for just belonging to the Party, members became frenetic. Many went "underground," assuming new names, new lives, often new facial features. Elaborate subterfuges were arranged as a prelude to secret meetings. Important messages were chewed and swallowed. The stories informants could tell of Communist behavior were enough to make even the staunchest civil libertarian question the motives and purposes of the Party. To less tolerant observers, such evidence confirmed all their worst suspicions. Anti-Communism was thus a self-renewing force, providing an increasing array of beliefs and actions that might be viewed as subversive. The credulous could easily find more suspects who fell outside the narrowing band of conformity, further fueling suspicion and fear.

Caute has thoroughly and effectively documented the consequences of that fear. His work will be useful to future researchers in understanding the extent of repression. But he mistakes this terrible part for the whole of American society. Neglected are the foes of McCarthyism, the absence of red-baiting in presidential politics, the moderation of many judges, politicians, and citizens. Neglected too are those aspects of the period which had nothing to do with Communism and foreign policy—unemployment, segregation, and the other issues which gradually supplanted anti-Communism in ideological and political importance. In trying to portray the America of this period as an utterly repressive state, Caute both distorts and overstates his case. His detailed facts suggest a more complex picture than his analysis allows for; on close examination, the "machinery of repression" he presents appears to be, instead, simply nuts and bolts.

Richard Sander

Sources for Further Study

Best Sellers. XXXVIII, July, 1978, p. 128.
Chronicle of Higher Education. XVII, October 2, 1978, p. R13.
Listener. C, September 28, 1978, p. 401.
New Statesman. XCVI, September 15, 1978, p. 334.
Times Literary Supplement. November 17, 1978, p. 1331.

THE GUGGENHEIMS: AN AMERICAN EPIC

Author: John H. Davis
Publisher: William Morrow and Company (New York). 608 pp. $14.95
Type of work: Biography
Time: 1775 to the present
Locale: Lengnau, Switzerland; Philadelphia; New York

An engrossing rags-to-riches history of America's richest and most philanthropically active Jewish family

> Principal personages:
> MEYER GUGGENHEIM, the Swiss-born patriarch of the American Guggenheims
> DANIEL GUGGENHEIM, the mining czar of the Guggenheim second generation
> HARRY FRANK GUGGENHEIM, called "Harry the Magnificent," the most able businessman and most noted philanthropist of the Guggenheim third generation

In *The Guggenheims: An American Epic*, John H. Davis, an honors Princeton graduate, Fulbright scholar, and author of *Venice* and *The Bouviers*, tells much that is engrossing about the Guggenheims of Philadelphia, New York, and California—the richest Jewish family in America. A study of this length (608 pages) is needed, if only to remind Americans that the Guggenheims, while not as famous as the Astors, DuPonts, and Mellons, contributed vastly to their country.

An "all-American" story in the Horatio Alger vein, *The Guggenheims* portrays Jews who, though fearfully downtrodden in Switzerland, come to Philadelphia in 1848 and, in record time, put together a colossal fortune. Although luck entered into their success, it was the ability of the father and five of seven sons to work together that made the Guggenheims so rich so quickly. No other American success story revolves around so many cooperating family members, most of whom add their own brand of expertise to the running of Guggenheim Brothers. In fact, almost any other great American fortune of the nineteenth century was largely the result of one individual, whether that person be a Frick, an Astor, a Vanderbilt, or a Morgan.

Davis offers a good account of the Swiss Guggenheims, who lived under appalling restrictions (virtually the same as those established in the Middle Ages) placed upon them by their Christian neighbors. Jews of the village of Lengnau, in the valley of the river Surd, were not allowed to enter most occupations (the usual exceptions were usury and peddling), to enter a Christian threshold, to speak to Christians, or to have tiled roofs like Christians. Routinely swindled, burned out of their homes and beaten, the Jews of Lengnau were also forever being taxed by the local Landvogt, a type of robber baron having life and death powers over "his" Jews. It is small wonder, then, that Simon Guggenheim, son of the ghetto leader Isaac (the "Icicle") Guggenheim, left Lengnau for America.

Of the Jews' frustration at not having sufficient outlets for their talents in Switzerland, Davis notes: "So tightly did the centuries of restriction, repression, and persecution . . . wind the spring of Guggenheim ambition that it would take many a generation before the spring would wind down, the momentum give out." And Davis gives readers a fine sense of exactly how tightly wound that spring was in his portrait of Meyer Guggenheim, the son of Simon, who wasted little time before marrying and using his Philadelphia home base to painstakingly build an empire based upon stove polish, then lace, and, most importantly, mining. Barbara Guggenheim assisted in this empire building, giving Meyer eight sons, five of whom (Daniel, Murry, Solomon, Simon, and Isaac) would fashion the mining and smelting network of Guggenheim Brothers and American Mining and Smelting.

To Davis, Meyer remains the most astonishing member of an astonishing family—a man "never to be surpassed in . . . imagination, daring, cleverness, perseverance, industry, courage, energy, [and] faith." Unfortunately, he also emerges as that stereotypical Jew of racist tracts: tightfisted, at times mean-spirited, cunning, avaricious, unsociable, and money-hungry. (Whether such a Shylock-like portrait does justice to Meyer is difficult to say, but one does want to know more than Davis provides about this fascinating man.)

Meyer blazed the financial trail for his sons, first investing wisely in skyrocketing ventures (the Hannibal and St. Joseph Railroad, for one), then buying the right real estate: the "A. Y." and "Minnie" silver mines of Leadville, Colorado. The latter paid off so fabulously that the Guggenheims were well on their way to being millionaires. Later, Daniel Guggenheim would use some of the proceeds from the two mines to start the first of many family smelting enterprises in Monterrey, Mexico.

After making the move from Philadelphia, a city known for its closed society, to the more open New York of 1888, Meyer let his sons know that they should all become millionaires or, even better, multimillionaires. At his death in 1904, most of them had done as he had wished. In the latter decades of the nineteenth century, the "five brothers against the world" piled up victory after financial victory, founding tin, copper, gold, and diamond mines and smelters over the globe: in Utah, Nevada, New Mexico, the Yukon Territory of Canada, the Alaska Territory, Mexico, Chile, Bolivia, Angola, and the Congo. Their financial triumphs were paralleled by social conquests, for the Guggenheims moved in the best society, Jewish and Gentile. Moreover, they were even able to form a partnership with WASP tycoon J. Pierpont Morgan, resulting in the formation of the gigantic Alaska Syndicate in 1907, an enterprise requiring the construction of a multimillion-dollar railroad through the wilderness, an entire harbor complex, a manmoth breakwater for the harbor, and the purchase of steamships to transport copper ore from Alaska to the smelter at Tacoma, Washington.

The Guggenheim Brothers' Alaskan exploits were so full of chicanery and so obviously inspired by greed, that average Americans, no longer so cowed by big businessmen as they had been in the nineteenth century, denounced the hated "Morganheim" or "Guggenmorgan" connection as monopolistic and predatory. While praising the Guggenheims rather extravagantly for their ingenuity and business acumen, Davis sides with those who saw in them a monstrous force: he finds the first and second generation Guggenheims guilty of exploiting the earth, gouging out holes in once glorious mountains and destroying the natural beauty of streams and forests.

Always on the lookout for new ventures, the Guggenheims showed a singular lack of concern over whom they did business with: for example, Belgium's notorious King Leopold II (nicknamed "the Butcher" by those who knew of his Congo massacres) or the German munitions manufacturers preparing for the outbreak of World War I (no doubt "Old Icicle" Isaac Guggenheim would have approved of such machinations).

Though the American public decried such commerce with the "forces of darkness and destruction," the Brothers Guggenheim found that such dealings worked wonders, especially during the war, when the hard-pressed Allied Powers, in desperate need of metals, paid them their high asking price. By controlling seventy-five to eighty percent of the earth's silver, copper, and lead, the Guggenheims were in a perfect position to dictate prices; in so doing, they accumulated the second largest Jewish fortune in the world (only the Rothschilds had more money), estimated to have been between $250,000,000 and $300,000,000.

After the war's end, the Guggenheims still having business interests are portrayed as having weakened family ties: "From now on the Guggenheims would devote themselves more to spending than to making." Pioneers in business, the Guggenheims went on to be pioneers in philanthropy, devoting money to individuals and groups that would reshape the world.

Finding that they really had not done much to help alleviate suffering and assist creative people discover new artistic horizons, several of the Guggenheims gave away huge amounts of their money. Previously, relatively small amounts of money had been given to organizations such as Mount Sinai Hospital in New York and the home for Jewish refugees in Lengnau, Switzerland.

To help mankind rather than exploit it, each brother involved in Guggenheim Brothers contributed to laboratories, medical institutes, universities, foundations, museums, and studies of the arts and sciences. Their gifts are still very much in evidence: the Daniel and Florence Guggenheim Foundation, the Daniel Guggenheim Fund for the promotion of Aeronautics, the Jet Propulsion Laboratory in Pasadena, California, the Solomon R. Guggenheim Foundation, and the Solomon R. Guggenheim Memorial Museum, to name but a few.

Of the following generations of Guggenheims, the most able was Harry

Frank Guggenheim, an outstanding businessman, administrator, diplomat, and man of the arts. His story, while told at some length, is not really as interesting as that of the family's third generation ne'er-do-wells and rebellious types like Colonel Bob, Peggy, or Harold Loeb, all of whom led fascinating (if often disoriented) lives.

Since the fourth generation harbored so few persons with even the slightest amount of interest in the family's mining business, Harry, unable to rely upon anyone in the family to manage business affairs after his death, turned to an outsider, Peter O. Lawson-Johnston. Ironically, the last male to bear the name Guggenheim had condemned the things of this world and turned to transcendentalism in his search for meaning.

So ends Davis' tale of a great family. The spring that Simon and Meyer Guggenheim had so tightly wound had completely unwound. Davis' contributions to Guggenheim family history are many, for he engagingly portrays the majority of Guggenheims exactly as they must have been: hardbitten business tycoons able to sacrifice the homely pleasures of lesser mortals for the pleasures of money-making. With care, Davis sets the foibles and failures of the minority of the Guggenheims against the fabulous success of the majority. Yet, however fascinated he is by the family's wealth, Davis is almost always able to step back from the abyss of Guggenheim worship and offer a basically objective view of his subjects. His book offers much in the way of human interest, while at the same time giving the reader a feeling of what it was like to be one of the lordly Guggenheims—America's Medici.

John D. Raymer

Sources for Further Study

Business Horizons. XXI, October, 1978, p. 81.
Commentary. LXVI, July, 1978, p. 72.

HELLO, DARKNESS
The Collected Poems of L. E. Sissman

Author: L. E. Sissman (1928-1976)
Publisher: Little, Brown and Company (Boston). 294 pp. $9.95
Type of work: Poetry

A collection which contains the texts of the poet's three earlier books and a "Post-humous Collection" of thirty-nine poems selected by Peter Davison, whose Preface to the book provides an account of the poet's life

The 134 poems in *Hello, Darkness* pain as often as they delight, and some-times the delight arises directly from the pain. Unfortunately, many readers of contemporary poetry will never discover the pain or the delight in L. E. Siss-man's work, for they will be unwilling, or unable, to penetrate his dense tex-tures or to hear the subtleties of his rhythms. Sissman's erudition and his pas-sionate commitment to craft combined to enable him to produce perhaps fifty poems important enough to stand with the best of his time.

Sissman wrote nearly all the poems in *Hello, Darkness* in a single, intensely lived decade. The book contains the texts of Sissman's three earlier books, and concludes with a "Posthumous Collection" of thirty-nine poems. The poet's friend and editor Peter Davison, aided by the poet's widow Anne Sissman, and writer friend John Updike, selected the poems for the posthumous collection. Davison has written a Preface for *Hello, Darkness* in which he provides the main lines of Sissman's short life and evaluates his friend's poetic achievement.

As early as 1963, Sissman was compiling a book of poems to be called *Homage to Cambridge*; that book never appeared, for the poet discovered a far grander, far more immediate theme than celebration of his adoptive city and his days at Harvard. That theme was his own death. After learning in the autumn of 1965 that he had Hodgkin's disease, the poet (in Peter Davison's words) "for the rest of his life wrote like one possessed of a knowledge remote from most of us, the knowledge of real time." The bulk of Sissman's collected poetry—all but ten poems—came between that time and 1974. Other work not collected here is on deposit at Harvard.

Born in Chicago in 1928, Sissman at the age of seventeen went to Harvard, where he initially failed to prove himself academically, but later, after a time out of school, was graduated *cum laude*. Discovering his talent in advertising, Sissman made a lucrative career for himself in Boston. After diagnosis of his terminal illness, he retained his advertising post and, in addition to his poetry, began contributing a regular column to *Atlantic Monthly*, later collected in book form under the title *Innocent Bystander* (1975).

Before his death in 1976, Sissman collected significant honors in recogni-tion of his poetry. Perhaps the most important to him was the invitation to be Phi Beta Kappa Poet at Harvard in 1971. For the most part, however, Sissman's work falls outside the supposed mainstream of his most active years; his work strikes many poets and critics as bookish and mannered. Certainly, Sissman's work makes no concession to the demands for open forms and spontaneity of statement fashionable in the 1960's and early 1970's. His work makes its own terms, and though Peter Davison is right when he says that the poet's writing after 1965 "only apparently resembled the thickly textured formalities of his undergraduate writing," the words "thickly textured" and "formal" characterize Sissman—at his best and worst.

Sissman writes, in part, from the experience of "Dislocation," which Davison says affected an entire generation. Dislocation is important in Sissman's best poems, but historical forces are not always responsible for the dislocation. Sissman's sensitive powers of observation permit him to capture a generation's—perhaps an age's—dislocation, yet one feels that the world would never have cohered for him, no matter when he had lived. The artist's need to discover meaning in form has never made for conformity, or adjustment.

The best poems in Sissman's "Posthumous Collection" extend the mortal concerns he announced in his first book, *Dying: An Introduction*. Like the earlier books, the posthumous collection combines the trivial with the significant in disturbingly jarring ways. One wishes that Peter Davison had decided to violate the usual conventions of "collecting" a poet's work and had put together instead a thematically ordered collection called *Hello, Darkness: The Best of L. E. Sissman.*

No one reading for the first time the poems with which *Dying: An Introduction* opens is likely to suspect the power of which Sissman will prove capable in his title poem and the one which follows it at the end of the book. Those poems had to come last, for their impact would have blunted anything which followed. Strangely enough, the poems evoking Cambridge, college days, parents, and early loves betray far more self-indulgence that do the poems about the poet's impending death. The echoes of Eliot—when they are only echoes—do little for the poems, and annoy the reader who recognizes them. A poem with a title like "Sweeney to Mrs. Porter in the Spring" announces itself as a period piece.

But from such unpromising beginnings, *Dying: An Introduction* takes the reader to the richly textured, honestly motivated poem called "The Marschallin, Joy Street, July 3, 1949," the evocative power of which goes beyond the literarily allusive or topical concerns of some other poems. Sometimes gently, sometimes whimsically, this poem allows the reader to discern the pathos of passing time, and, quietly dramatic, it suggests the emptiness of apparently full lives. The poem's dramatic center emerges as both general and particular, and the skill of the verse amplifies the portrait of the woman who haunts the lines. At the end, the act of going "belowstairs . . . /To put her windows down against the rain" sums up the lifetime of coping everyone must face.

Dying: An Introduction is composed of five sections, each laconically titled and progressing from the poet's initial medical examination, through medical testing and pathology reports, to knowledge. Two lines from Philip Larkin, serve as epigraph: "Always too eager for future, we/Pick up bad habits of expectancy." The lines are quietly prophetic, and serve a function quite different from the kind of epigraph which provides the information on which the poet has built his work. The first section is called "Ring and Walk In"—a marvelously low-key beginning for what will be a drama of life and death. Section II echoes in all our ears; "Probably Nothing," it is called: the usual medical encouragement to the probably dying patient. Section III, "O.P.O.R.," dramatizes the taking of bone marrow for testing, and Section IV, "Path. Report," brings intimations of X-ray treatment and the death to come.

The poem's final section is called "Outbound," and Sissman here allows his concern for form to give way, in its technical sense, to a larger sense of form. The lines taper down to knife points, and the poet brings together his past, his present, and his future. In what looks for Sissman shockingly like free verse, he writes: "Through my/Invisible new veil/Of finity, I see/November's world—/Low scud, slick street, three giggling girls." The poet finds this, "oddly, not as sombre/As December,/But as green/As anything:/As spring."

"Canzone: Aubade" closes *Dying: An Introduction* with a restatement of what has been learned: "All of our love must go the same old way." And, later, "memory at noon/Springs on us all the secrets that we know/About ourselves, to try if we can know/The agony of aloneness." The poem's envoy is both bleak and promising, for it tells us that "though our pain persists in sleeping still,/It will arise and flourish at high noon." Furious and constant, the poet tells us, our pain will "seek to find a way/Out of our time, the only one we know."

Sissman's second book, *Scattered Returns* (1969), is less uneven than his first, but the trivia of poems such as "Small Space" annoys as exquisitely as a chipped tooth. A poet as conscious of his tools as Sissman has no business trading on the inanities of such doggerel. What *might* be amusing in another context annoys when dropped into a book which opens with a poem like the devastating "A Deathplace." This is not to deny the validity of juxtaposing light verse with statements of a larger sort: still, the parody which sneers on one level and, at another level, panders to elitist taste has no business in a serious book. "Make these three/Mistakes in speech?" Sissman asks in all-capital letters. "Hear them mermaids/On the beach," he asks, "Singing real low/Each to each?" Then, by way of *coup de grace*, "Had I ought to/eat a peach?" The vulgar may be with us always, but summoning them up ought not to require textbook allusiveness.

Scattered Returns opens with an epigraph and with a dedication to Howard Moss, poetry editor of the *New Yorker*. The "highest artist," says the epigraph, "grapples up his art one-handed," while the other hand "reaches out-/To those below him" in a "grasp of love." Some of the poems which follow measure up to the high-minded ideal. Others do not, and one wonders why the poet set such a high standard only to violate it.

Perhaps the problem is that Sissman as poet rarely seems one-handed; hence, he seems to expend his effort in behalf of the "art," not the fellow human in danger of falling into the abyss. In the long run, Sissman's two-handed poetic technique, promiscuously applied, levels the peaks of human experience to a humdrum effect. Had Sissman sometimes failed, or had he discriminated among the possible ranges of feeling, the poems in *Scattered Returns* and in the collected works might have spoken more loudly to the needs of human life. As things stand, Sissman dignifies the trivial and the consequential with such equal craft that the reader despairs of determining what really matters to the poet. Eventually, instinct dictates that the "dying" poems matter most, and the reader necessarily grieves that Sissman's poems must live so precariously with one another.

"A Deathplace" opens with the observation, "Very few people know where they will die,/But I do. . . ." Closely observed details of the hospital in which Sissman will die, rendered humorously and ironically, provide the setting for his imagined death. By avoiding the somberly predictable details and seeing others, Sissman gets by with what lesser poets would have botched. What could have been an exercise in self-indulgence becomes instead an unblinking look into the terror of annihilation. Sissman follows the surprise of corridors said to be "jaundiced and distempered" with an amusing rhyme of *cringe* and *syringe*. Here, restrained and ordered verses prove their effectiveness:

> I will cringe
> Before the pinpoint of the least syringe;
> Before the buttered catheter goes in;
> Before the I.V.'s lisp and drip begins
> Inside my skin; before the rubber hand
> Upon the lancet takes aim and descends
> To lay me open. . . .

The diction surprises with its precision and insists upon the homely, not the technical, term—"the buttered catheter" and the "I.V.'s lisp and drip." The unexpected words confer newfound horror upon the trappings of hospital pain. Later, at the imagined final hour, the poet again surprises the reader by distancing himself from the solemnity of death. He writes that he'll feel his blood "go thin, go white, the red,/The rose all leached away, and I'll go dead." The precision is admirable, but the poet turns away and lapses into the childlike "go dead" to express the final extinction. If not childlike, this pattern nevertheless lets the poet suggest death as a state like limpness or rigidity hence knowable.

Such strategies of ironic discourse brought to bear on our shared extremities help the reader face up to them; one imagines also that they helped Sissman face up to what faced *him*. In such poems as "A Deathplace," the enormity of Sissman's subject, his awareness of the dangers of sentimentalizing conspired to make him every bit the poet. In other poems—an unfortunately large number of them—Sissman brings to mind Howard Nemerov's technique robbed of Nemerov's nerve.

Sissman seems, as Davison writes in the Preface, to be a "divided, complex man." In his family and in college, Sissman was called Lou; in business, he was Ed. Sometimes, Davison notes, in writing about Lou Sissman, Ed Sissman refers to himself as "Mr. Edwards." The split in Sissman's person suggests a fundamental dichotomy, the tension of which aggravates the two extremes of his poetry. Lou Sissman—the perennial undergraduate and son—persists side by side with Ed Sissman—the businessman and poet, the man facing death, and drawing on his total experience to cope with a knowledge Lou Sissman wishes fervently to avoid. The split nature helps explain both the power and the unevenness of the body of work in *Hello, Darkness*.

That split nature is nowhere more apparent than in Sissman's apparent inability to recognize and excise glib and often *jejune* allusions. One winces when Sissman writes of his "marching feet,/Which now tread out the vintage where the grapes/Of drought are stored." The poem, "A Common Prophecy," gains nothing from the cuteness; in fact, the allusion obscures the point. Just a page later, in "Bethlehem State," Sissman yields to the urge again, and gives us the anticipated Yeats allusion, but with a twist: "Rough beasts who slouched to Bethlehem to die." The worst of it is that gratuitous allusions sometimes mar fatally the short poem which lacks sufficient bulk to absorb the foolishness. One of the most promising short poems arises from Sissman's finding *Dying: An Introduction* remaindered. The final lines are marvelously terse: "Well, if you/Preach about dying, you must practice it too." Inexcusably, the poem opens "I wandered lonely as a cloud. . . ."

Scattered Returns (1969) concludes with what may be Sissman's single best poem. Though "A War Requiem" does not specifically treat the poet's illness, its sections provide recurrently "A sense of last times." Written in five parts, it moves from "New York, 1929" through time and space to a final section "In the New Year." The single poem in that section is "Twelfth Night, 1969." The Vietnam War continued in 1969, and the poet writes "I hide/Out in my hideout from the memory/Of our unlovely recent history,/And of those fresh divisions just gone west." The poet hears a crack, which may be a tree "cleft by the cold," but is "likelier . . . a gun down at (Fort) Devens."

The poet is ready for his epiphany and ends the poem with snow lancing the window, and his seeing a "murderous shadow"—

A snowy owl,

Cinerous, nearly invisible,
Planes down its glide path to surprise a vole.

The lines achieve Sissman's purpose through indirection, all the more powerful for understatement. Having named the "snowy owl," synonymous with the
"murderous shadow," Sissman allows it here merely to "surprise a vole." The
poet's perception brings together the private and the political person. From
what he has earlier named his "warm isolation," Sissman expressed meanings
far more lasting than either the "hawk" or the "dove" rhetoric in the divided
America of the late 1960's. The rhetoricians of both peace and war generally
stopped short of such universal observations.

Like all of Sissman's books, *Pursuit of Honor* (1971) contains several
poems of real magnitude, but the title poem seems merely long. For all the
poet's attention to his business, the poem does not rise above its content.
Honor is a girl in the beginning, a successful career woman at the end. The
protagonist, partly at his friends' urging and partly for lack of anything better
to do, makes her the object of his adolescent yearnings, both physical and
vaguely romantic. Honor has an emotionally retarded father, for whom she is
also a romantic object. The poem intends to suggest that both Honor and her
"lover" are victims of the smothering love of a father who uses his daughter
for selfish ends. That reading, however, suffers from the protagonist's failure
to raise *his* love above the trophy-seeking, sexual-exploitation level. Perhaps
the reader is supposed to observe that the physician father's mounted fish is for
him what a bedded virgin would be for the Harvard boys in the poem, but
when the sveltely successful Honor meets the middle-aging protagonist in the
final section, the implication is that both have missed something major in their
lives.

The opening poem in *Pursuit of Honor* is another matter; "The Big Rock-
Candy Mountain" tells, poignantly, of a person's life and death. The person is
Sissman's half-brother, an itinerant farm worker, and Sissman makes common
cause for his half-brother and for all other itinerant farm workers of the nation.
The poem's epigraph comes from Basil Bunting's great autobiographical poem
Briggflatts:

A mason times his mallet
To a lark's twitter . . .
till the stone spells a name
naming none.
a man abolished.

Even in a poem so personally grasped, Sissman cannot resist the urge to
absorb other poets into his work. The opening line of "The Big Rock-Candy
Mountain" takes off on Robert Frost's famous poem read at the Kennedy inau-
guration: "The land was theirs after we were the land's," writes Sissman. The

echo is like an itch, but ends up signifying little or nothing. Similarly, one wonders why Sissman's funeral home had to be named Goebel's; that name's association with Nazi Germany renders it worse than useless in a poem like this.

"Among School Children" begins allusively, and then gets on with important things. The poem has nothing, or scarcely anything, to do with Yeats's poem of the same name. Part I shows us senior citizens being served lunch at a public school; Part II provides the sad spectacle of a school reunion. The sadness arises partly from the wives' degeneration and partly from the fact that the "shining husbands" are "most like firstborn sons." The point may tell a great deal about Sissman's wavering between schoolboy and adult. The third part gives us Sissman, in a role somewhat like Yeats's, being questioned by students and cheerfully regarding the confrontation of generations as "without result." The poem gives us Sissman between youth and age. While Yeats accepted being regarded as a "smiling public man," Sissman—childless in both his marriages—observed the "nonce senses" of the students' language. Condescension does not here serve the purpose.

"Dying: A Resurrection, 1969" amounts to a high point in *Pursuit of Honor*. At the end of the poem, which dramatizes Sissman's rematch with death (his second bout with cancer), the poet awakes, ashamed of his dramatics, and creeps back "into life as into much/Too large a pair of trousers." The poem concludes in obviously triumphant acceptance and in what John Updike has called Sissman's middle way:

> Evident-
> Ly even desperation leads a charmed
> Life, valetudenarians go unharmed
> At times, self-sorrow often sobs in vain,
> And morrows rob us of our mortal pain.

Poems of this sort, without posturing and without self-consciously affected wit, represent the best of Sissman. Such poems occur among those in the "Posthumous Collection," as Sissman masters metaphors which extend into conceits. "Getting On: Grave Expectations" provides evidence of a new daring as the poet imagines himself drinking "glass after glass of days" and then going on to "squat seven-packs of weeks" and "flat fifties of full years." All this time, he thinks "of how tomorrow, mastered at a swallow,/Would taste. . . ." Here, the metaphor of consuming and being consumed provides the poem's form and the language remains at once direct and concrete.

"Getting On: Grave Expectations" climaxes with awareness of "the warning bells of closing time" and the need for courage to "dissolve our marriage/To our dear self,"

> the lost boy in the burning
> Building of bone—the fat being in the fire—

The poem indicates that Sissman continued able to *detach himself from himself*, to recognize that his adolescent self "sired a haggard Double," but the division in such poems provides the distance needed to speak of the death Sissman knew to be imminent. "Spring Song," one of Sissman's most clear-eyed but lyric celebrations of life and knowledge of death, presents the poet as "agent for my slowly failing/Senses, my withering sinews, drying juices."

Sissman's "Posthumous Collection" has four parts—poems Descriptive and Satirical, poems Nostalgic and Narrative, poems Light and Dreamy, and finally five poems under the heading "Hello, Darkness." Several in the first section, including the two poems just cited, take their places among Sissman's enduring achievements. Most of what appears in sections II and III tends to blur the dramatic impact of the final section.

Not a false sound, certainly not a false line, mars the brilliance of the concluding five poems. The opening poem plays the X-ray negative against the portrait shot. In awesome "glossy X-rays," Sissman is laid bare: "my skull glows like a moon/Hewn, like a button, out of vivid bone." In a poem called "December 27, 1966," the poet's illness merges with a loving description of sky and moon in an invocation of death. "Homage to Clotho: A Hospital Suite" and "Cancer: A Dream" bring us closer to the dread moment, and the final long poem, "Tras Os Montes," comes as close to realization of the individual's place in time's progression as the reader can bear.

With "Tras os Montes," the poet properly elects the Portuguese expression, which avoids the dramatics or vulgarity of "over the mountain." Again, Sissman places himself in a progression: his parents, himself, first in company, then with another, and finally alone. The sections devoted to his parents' deaths provide their birth and death dates. The third section repeats the title and, parenthetically, announces (197-). Precise death date unknown, the poet accepts his movement toward the final truth of "the final climb/Across the mountains to the farther shore,"

> Of sundown on the watersheds, where self,
> Propelled by its last rays, sways in the sway
> Of the last grasses and falls headlong in
> The darkness of the dust it is part of
> Upon the passes where we are no more.

It was a glorious passage which gave such verse. The poet moved toward wholeness, and the faults of *Hello, Darkness* are not his. He wrote, as we all must, in anticipation of discovering the outcome. That discovery made, the poems stand and demand an ordering to let their dark lesson be learned.

Leon V. Driskell

Sources for Further Study

Booklist. LXXV, September, 1, 1978, p. 20.

Nation. CCXXVII, November 11, 1978, p. 517.

Poetry. CXXXIII, November, 1978, p. 100.

Times Literary Supplement. July 28, 1978, p. 847.

HIMSELF!
The Life and Times of Mayor Richard J. Daley

Author: Eugene Kennedy
Publisher: The Viking Press (New York). 288 pp. $10.95
Type of work: Biography
Time: The recent past
Locale: Chicago, Illinois

The story of Chicago's most illustrious and controversial mayor and how he stayed in power for two decades

Principal personages:
RICHARD J. DALEY, Mayor of Chicago, power behind the mighty Chicago Democratic political machine
JOHN F. KENNEDY, President of the United States, 1961-1963
LYNDON BAINES JOHNSON, President of the United States, 1963-1968

Himself! The Life and Times of Mayor Richard J. Daley is neither recommended for hard-core Daley haters nor for those who would ask for a completely balanced account of "the life and times" of this most controversial of American mayors. While purporting to be "even-handed," author Eugene Kennedy, professor of psychology at Loyola University in Chicago, actually is a Daley enthusiast; his vision of the man about whom he writes says as much.

To Kennedy, Mayor Daley was best seen as an Irish chieftain along the lines of mythical Cuchulainn, surrounded by fanatically devoted warriors and retainers who would do virtually anything for their strong-willed lord. As chieftain, Daley loved his tribe (Chicagoans), his native soil (Chicago), made all the big decisions for that tribe and "native land," yet never forgot from whence he had come (the humble Bridgeport area in central Chicago) or those humble folk who helped him become chief. Although perhaps overused throughout the book, Kennedy's image of Daley-as-Chieftain does hold water: after all, Daley was all of those things that made up the image. Born to parents having real ties with Ireland and living in the midst of Irish-Americans on the South Side, Daley learned to trust members of his "tribe," later looking to them for both emotional and political support and giving them high offices in City Hall as mayor. Moreover, Chieftain Daley gave his total allegiance to the city's Irish Catholic groups and promoted their interests.

To be sure, Daley was almost born to the office of mayor, having been involved in the political infighting of a city known since he was a young man for ferocious political struggles. His inspired leadership established real emotional links with white ethnic Chicagoans, and created a sense of community among peoples of many backgrounds. While he often labored mightily with the English language (to the delight of the "North Shore liberals"), what he said was manna to most Chicagoans—a fact attested by the present-day way many conversations about the city begin: "I remember what late Mayor Daley used to say about that. . . ."

The Mayor knew all there was to know about stirring up his constituents at party rallies; after the parades, food, musical salutes, and the rest of the introductory hoopla, he would let the people know he was with them, rather than the bank presidents downtown, by talking about their neighborhoods, their children, and their values: homelife, religion, and patriotism. (And yet he would not find it difficult to address the bank presidents the following day, letting them know he supported their enterprises.) As Kennedy observed, Daley really did believe in what he told the people of his city, and his belief in traditional values made him Chicago's most-loved father figure. If Chicago is what poet Carl Sandburg termed the "City of the Big Shoulders," then Daley could be called the "Mayor of the Big Shoulders."

A thoroughgoing pragmatist who could easily lapse into sentimentality, a big city boss who ruled absolutely yet fairly, a backroom dealer who was deeply religious, Daley was, as Kennedy points out, one of those complicated and wholly unique politicians who wielded real power yet had the nearly unanimous consent of the governed. In short, he was something of an Irish chieftain and something of a twentieth century American political dynamo.

Unfortunately, Kennedy pushes the Daley-as-Chieftain notion too hard and too long, making one wish he would concentrate more on Daley-the-Chicagoan or Daley-the-Midwesterner rather than cloaking his man in outworn trappings of ancient heroes. And if one wanted another image of Daley taken from mythology, he might look to Achilles-of-the-unprotected-heel.

Daley's Achilles' heel was his inability to assess accurately the meaning of events transpiring during the Democratic Convention in Chicago during August, 1968, a year of violent antiwar protests. A rag-tag army of genuine radicals, would-be radicals, and mainstream college students from across the United States assembled in Chicago's parks during that month. Their presence there created a series of events culminating in the now-famous "police riot," a riot which badly hurt the Mayor's national reputation. With his policemen's actions having given Chicago the title of "fascist city," Daley was completely baffled by the bizarre events of August and tried as best he could to live down the infamy of it all; he was, however, a man transformed by these events.

Kennedy finds it highly ironic that Daley, feeling that Vietnam was wrong and even telling President Lyndon Johnson that it should be terminated, was finally left with the label of party loyalist and war supporter. His popular image as demogogue and hawk, therefore, conflicts with his real self. He was, Kennedy argues, an outwardly rough, though inwardly gentle, man who found himself surrounded by youths who could wreck his Chicago, and acted to save that city from destruction. In so doing, he made the greatest mistake of his life.

It is no secret that Daley became agitated every time his city was abused by the media. Kennedy's account emphasizes the love Daley felt for his city: he could never say enough about her skyline or hear "Chicago" played often enough. Moreover, whenever visiting VIP's were in Chicago, the Mayor would act as tour guide, pointing out this building or that park. Thus, when demonstrators threw rocks at Chicago store windows and damaged park property, it was no wonder he reacted so vigorously.

The year 1968 was the beginning of a gradual decline for Chicago's leader. Though his authority would never once be in serious question, the spirit of politics seemed to go out of the Mayor. In 1972, Daley's national reputation suffered further as the leading contender's supporters at the National Democratic Convention actually spurned Daley and his Cook County political machine, choosing to oust a Daley-picked group of delegates, and replace it with a "more representative" one. Angry and bitter, Daley was "like a swaying sea animal that lives out of ordinary time and space." His own party seemingly had deserted him. Even though Daley's national image had been tarnished by the events of 1968 and 1972, he retained his tight control over the Chicago political machine until his death in 1976.

Perhaps one of the most commendable aspects of *Himself!* is the attention the author gives to the day-to-day functioning of this infamous political organization—the last of the big city machines. Readers, for example, note how the influential aldermen of the city's wards did their part to support Daley, behind-the-scenes, during City Council meetings, and during election time when they had to deliver the vote. The aldermen acting as Daley's footsoldiers kept close tabs on their constituents, listened to their complaints, comforted them after a loss, and noted their suggestions about how the city could be better run. If garbage was not collected regularly in the Eleventh Ward, the alderman of the district found out about it and informed someone "downtown" of the problem. However, if nothing was done and the Mayor heard about this, the alderman had to answer to him. Again, such concern for the "little person" by the Mayor of Chicago was real. A neighborhood resident himself (he lived in the Bridgeport section of the city), Daley sympathized with the ordinary white Chicagoan and his problems.

However, there was another side to Daley—the side that failed to take much interest in the well-being of black and Latino Chicagoans. And of this side, Kennedy tells us little except that Daley's myopia contributed to the racial explosions of the late 1960's. A more complete portrait of the Mayor would, by necessity, deal with his inability to understand Chicago's people of the South and West sides.

Despite his shortcomings, the Daley depicted by Eugene Kennedy is a man who possessed courage and a capacity to care for other people. Though completely in charge of Chicago's political affairs, Daley was careful not to offend those upon whom he relied for support, nor to ignore those who would disagree with him. Pledging to his followers early in his career that he would

". . . embrace charity, love mercy, and walk humbly" with his God, Daley was, at least in Kennedy's estimation, a fundamentally decent, upright person who kept his power-and-influence hungry aldermen away from the public till.

In *Himself!* we are given only a glimpse of Daley—husband and father. The real focus of the book is on how the Mayor made it to the top of Chicago politics, how he became the man who promoted John F. Kennedy in the 1960 presidential campaign and helped him to win the election, and how he encountered diminishing returns toward his later years in politics. It is not a particularly valuable study of Daley's "times," but it is a satisfactory and sometimes exciting introduction to this most popular and interesting American mayor.

John D. Raymer

Sources for Further Study

Best Sellers. XXXVIII, July, 1978, p. 118.
Critic. XXXVII, August, 1978, p. 2.
Saturday Evening Post. CCL, September, 1978, p. 90.

HISTORY OF THE WESTWARD MOVEMENT

Author: Frederick Merk (1887-1977)
Publisher: Alfred A. Knopf (New York). 660 pp. $20.00
Type of work: History
Time: 1607-1975
Locale: The American West

A history of the American West from Jamestown to the present

> *Principal personages:*
> DANIEL BOONE, one of the first explorers of the trans-Appalachian West
> JOHN QUINCY ADAMS, American President concerned about extending American institutions to the Pacific
> JAMES K. POLK, American President who, through the Mexican War and diplomacy, acquired the Mexican Cession and Oregon

Frederick Merk was one of America's great Western historians. Born in Wisconsin in 1887, he received his B.A. degree in 1911 from the University of Wisconsin where he worked under the dean of Western historians, Frederick Jackson Turner. In 1916 he followed Turner to Harvard where he received his Ph.D. In 1921 he became a member of Harvard's History Department.

His early fame came primarily through the teaching of the course the "Westward Movement," which his students called "Wagon Wheels." It became one of the most popular courses offered at Harvard, constantly undergoing changes in content, and covering the grand sweep of the Westward movement from the first Atlantic settlements to the Pacific, emphasizing the economic and political developments. Spending much of his time on the refinement of this course, Merk's record of publication was necessarily limited. But with his retirement in 1957, he published a number of significant works—*Manifest Destiny and Mission* (1963); *The Monroe Doctrine and American Expansion, 1843-1849* (1966); *Essays in Anglo-American Diplomacy and Politics* (1967); and his last volume, *History of the Westward Movement*, published a year after his death.

This book is a compilation of Merk's lectures to his graduate students in Western history. Because of that lecture format, there are sixty-four chapters, some of them consisting of only five or six pages. This creates a certain sloppiness in the work.

The hand of Merk's teacher, Frederick Jackson Turner, is seen throughout the book. Merk stresses the interrelationships of political, economic, and social history. He spotlights the powerful influence of the availability of land on the growth of American society, as pioneers went through the changes brought about by social evolution. Merk emphasizes geographical rather than chronological continuity in the settlement process. He views American expansion as a series of conquests in which one physiographic province after another was overrun by pioneers. Each new conquest differed from the previous one as the special environment of the new land put its stamp on the Americans. An exponent of the theory of multiple causation, Merk shows that there were numerous forces behind the development of the various regions that make up America. It was the creation of the different "civilizations" resulting from these interactions of men and nature which accounted for the sectional conflicts that almost destroyed the nation in the 1860's. Like Turner, Merk saw that the important controversies essential to the interpretation of early American history could be understood only by emphasizing the close interaction between the pioneers and the environment in which they lived; in other words, the stage was as important as the players.

The first chapter is a short one on the American Indians that accepts many of the usual myths. For example, Merk states that the Iroquois "were a ferocious people" who took sadistic delight in torturing people. Yet nowhere in the book does he mention the Camp Grant or Sand Creek massacres where whites perpetrated massacres on Indians. Otherwise, the Indian is given little attention. And when he *is* presented, it is usually only to serve as a backdrop for the more important white advance. But this oversight has its compensation: the name of George Armstrong Custer does not appear once.

Merk discusses the early settlements of Virginia and Massachusetts Bay and the later expansion of New England, as well as the pioneer advance into the Great Valley of Virginia. Then he continues with the story of the first conflicts between the colonists and the Indians and the collision of the British and French interests, ending with the victory of the British in the French and Indian War.

Emphasis is given to the period after 1763; and the author, unlike Turner, gives sufficient attention to the land speculators and the role they played in the settling of the Allegheny Plateau. Attention is also paid to the important role that the West played in the War for American Independence.

The next six chapters deal with the period between 1783 and 1800. Among the topics discussed are the land cessions of the states, postwar land speculation, and American diplomacy in the Southwest with the Spanish, and in the Northwest with the British. Entering the nineteenth century, Merk relates how sectional differences began to develop in the early part of the period over primarily economic issues, such as tariffs, internal improvements, and banks. He shows his special interest in the mid-nineteenth century. Some of the best chapters in the work are those dealing with the annexation of Texas, the Oregon Question, and Manifest Destiny.

Next, the author turns his attention to the critical issue of slavery. Four chapters are devoted to slavery and the new territories, the Kansas-Nebraska Act, the Dred Scott Decision, and the West and Slavery.

The opening up of the West meant the obtaining of vast national resources: verdant farms, national transportation routes, forests, grasslands, and mineral deposits. America became a continental nation. The author describes how in the twentieth century the semiarid regions were opened up through dry farming: the utilization of drought resistant, hybridized grains, and new methods of cultivation that retained the moisture in the soil.

As with most textbooks, there are problems of emphasis. The major question is how much attention some subjects should receive. Here, there is certainly an overemphasis on agriculture. For example, of the last fourteen chapters, eleven could be considered as dealing largely with farming. There are also certain gaps. There is no comparative analysis of different frontier movements, such as occurred in Russia, Australia, and South Africa. These happened at about the same time as the opening of the American West; there were similar encounters between native peoples and the pioneers, with the same tragic results for the natives. If this comparative aspect of the frontier had been considered, it would have given the reader both an enlightening and a challenging view.

Merk pays no attention to the explorers. The men who in the early nineteenth century opened the West and advertised its potential are somehow neglected. The Lewis and Clark Expedition of 1804-1806 is given two pages, while Stephen Long and Zebulon Pike do not even appear in the index. By way of contrast, Henry Wise, whose influence on the West was negligible, has four entries, while Louis Philippe, the King of France, has two.

No mention is made of urbanization. Much research in the last two decades has been devoted to the Western city; yet the author has no place in his work for this important subject, even though the West was one of America's most urbanized sections. This hiatus may be traced to the Turner influence, which takes little notice of cities. Also, there is no mention of the important events that took place in the West during the Civil War. If one looks for Quantrill's Raiders, Sibley's New Mexico Campaign, or the Battle of Apache Pass, he will not find them.

But if there are weaknesses in the work, there are also strengths. Unlike most Western history texts, Merk's extends to the twentieth century. It would be difficult to find better surveys of modern soil conservation, irrigation projects, and Western agriculture than those given here. The chapter on the "Columbia Basin and Central Valley Projects" traces the history of those efforts from the 1930's to the present. Concisely presented, it offers well-selected photographs and tells of the difficulties that the federal government faced during these years.

This work may well be the last grand summation of the Turnerian thesis in textbook form. But while the Turnerians have opened up the study of Western history and presented many interesting ideas, they have often refused to undertake new approaches to the subject. And this is one of the important weaknesses of Merk's text. For example, if one compares the chapter titles of this book with those of Ray Billington's earlier *Westward Expansion*, which was dedicated to Merk, there is a great similarity—"The West and Slavery" and "Settlement of the Gulf Plains"—and, with few exceptions, in their treatment of the eighteenth and nineteenth centuries they deal with the same topics.

In comparing these two books that owe so much to Turner, there are some positive statements to make about the Merk work. First, he includes the period of the twentieth century, while Billington ends his book with 1890. Merk's chapters on the Oregon Question and the period of the sordid nineteenth century are more interesting than Billington's. And Merk's ability to handle the subject of agriculture is greater than Billington's. In many ways, of course, the works are similar. Both are large volumes: Merk's has over 600 pages while Billington's has nearly 800. Both were written with evident affection for the subject. Both authors use maps effectively and possess a thorough knowledge of American geography. But Billington's is the superior work. It is better written than Merk's. One gets the impression that Merk simply lifted his book from his lecture notes, with few changes. Another significant difference is in the two authors' bibliographies. Merk's is simply a listing of a few significant works, while Billington's is in the form of a bibliographical essay and is one of the great compilations of the works of Western history, as worthwhile as the text itself.

As the culmination of the career of one of the foremost authorities on the West, Merk's is an important one-volume history. In telling this comprehensive story, the author brings to the dramatic events a pleasing blend of his own lively style, narrative talent, and thorough familiarity with the basic sources for these grand events. The narrative is a lively synthesis. Interpretations and judgments made by the author are based on intensive study. Merk knows how to use his sources—primary and secondary—to good advantage. His maturity as a scholar and his ability to use the English language well produce a solid work.

Richard A. Van Orman

Sources for Further Study

Booklist. LXXIV, July 1, 1978, p. 1661.

Chronicle of Higher Education. XVII, October 16, 1978, p. R13.

Library Journal. CIII, July, 1978, p. 1405.

New Republic. CLXXIX, May, 1978, p. 827.

HITLER'S SPIES
German Military Intelligence in World War II

Author: David Kahn (1930-   )
Publisher: Macmillan Publishing Company (New York). Illustrated. 671 pp. $16.95
Type of work: History
Time: 1803-1945, with a concentration on the period 1939-1945
Locale: Germany, Nazi-occupied Europe, and centers of German espionage activity throughout the world

In this comprehensive study, David Kahn reveals the complicated and cumbersome organization of German intelligence during World War II

> *Principal personages:*
> ADOLF HITLER, Chancellor and *Führer* of Germany, 1933-1945
> ADMIRAL WILHELM FRANZ CANARIS, head of the *Abwehr*, German military intelligence
> REINHARD HEYDRICH, head of the *Sicherheitsdienst* (*SD*: Security Service), the intelligence organ of the National Socialist German Workers Party; and the *Reichssicherheitshauptamt* (*RSHA*: Reich Security Administration) until his assassination in 1942
> WALTER SCHELLENBERG, head of *SD* foreign intelligence and after June 1, 1944, most branches of the defunct *Abwehr*
> GENERAL REINHARD GEHLEN, head of Foreign Armies East
> COLONEL ULRICH LISS, head of Foreign Armies West
> JOACHIM VON RIBBENTROP, Foreign Minister of Germany

David Kahn, a distinguished journalist and historian, is the author of the widely celebrated book, *The Codebreakers*. His latest study, the outgrowth of a doctoral dissertation completed under the direction of H. R. Trevor-Roper at Oxford University, represents the most comprehensive work to date on the intelligence operations of Nazi Germany during World War II. The title of Kahn's book, *Hitler's Spies: German Military Intelligence in World War II*, is, however, doubly misleading. In the first place, as the author notes in the preface, the term "spies" is used metaphorically to include all forms of intelligence gathering, not just espionage. Thus, for example, Kahn covers in great detail the structure of Nazi Germany's communications intelligence, which, in part, involved codebreaking, the interception of radio messages, and the censorship of mail and telegrams. In addition, he devotes considerable space to the analysis of all the intelligence gathered, by whatever means. The second misleading term in the book's title is the word "military." The book does not deal solely with intelligence gathered by the German armed forces; it also encompasses the intelligence gathering activities in political and economic areas by various government ministries, the National Socialist Party, and private individuals. Collectively, of course, the goal of those people working within these four areas was to insure the military victory of Nazi Germany.

Chances for the realization of ultimate victory would have been immeasurably improved if the intelligence gathering activities within these four areas of Nazi society had been unified from the outset of the war. Contrary to Nazi Germany's monolithic façade, Kahn notes, no single high-level body controlled intelligence. The disorganized nature of German intelligence, with several competing agencies performing the same functions, was but a microcosm of Adolf Hitler's dictatorship. Hitler purposely created overlapping spheres of authority in order to perpetuate endless squabbling among his subordinates, thereby safeguarding his own position.

Among the German intelligence gathering agencies which Kahn describes at length are the *Abwehr*, Foreign Armies East, the Foreign Office, the *Forschugsamt* (Research Department), and the *Sicherheitsdienst* (SD: Security Service). Within the command structure of the armed forces, the *Abwehr* (meaning "defense") and Foreign Armies East were especially important. Kahn devotes an entire chapter to the *Abwehr*'s military espionage and counterespionage activities and to the career of its legendary leader, Admiral Wilhelm Franz Canaris. Early in 1944, Hitler, angered by the ineffectiveness of the *Abwehr* (which was a major center of the anti-Nazi resistance), removed Canaris as its head and subordinated the agency to the *Reichssicherheitshauptamt* (RSHA), the Nazi Party Reich Security Administration. More effective than the *Abwehr* was Foreign Armies East, administered after April 1, 1942, by Reinhard Gehlen. Through his efforts, the Germans always knew what units of the Red Army stood opposite them on the Russian front. Kahn, however, contends that Gehlen frequently failed in his important task of predicting major Soviet offensives, notably the one launched by the Red Army at Stalingrad in November, 1942.

Two important agencies of intelligence in German government circles were the Foreign Office and the *Forschungsamt*. Under the leadership after 1938 of Joachim von Ribbentrop, the Foreign Office expanded its intelligence gathering activities. Now, in addition to the traditional methods used by its diplomats in gathering information, Ribbentrop created a spy service based on German missions abroad. The success of this operation in gathering information paled, however, in comparison with the *Forschungsamt*, one of the most successful of Germany's intelligence agencies, set up in 1933. This agency, according to the author, tapped wires, intercepted radio messages, and broke codes in the entire gamut of political and economic intelligence. Kahn sheds much light on the *Forschungsamt* and eight other related agencies which together comprised Nazi Germany's highly effective communications intelligence network.

The Nazi Party had an intelligence organ of its own, the *Sicherheitsdienst*, or SD, organized in the early 1930's under the leadership of the brutal Reinhard Heydrich. The SD had a domestic and a foreign arm which in 1939 were incorporated with government police agencies, into a party-state organization known as the *Reichssicherheitshauptamt*, also under the leadership of Heydrich until his assassination by Czech resistance fighters in the spring of 1942.

A year before his death, Heydrich had named Walter Schellenberg as head of the foreign intelligence branch of the SD. Hereafter, as Kahn relates, Schellenberg's power and influence in intelligence matters grew steadily. On June 1, 1944, some months after the dismissal of Canaris as head of the *Abwehr*, the decision was made to dissolve the *Abwehr*. Most of its branch agencies were transferred to Schellenberg, who, for the remainder of the war, headed the nearest thing Nazi Germany ever had to a unified intelligence agency.

Kahn's analysis of the nature of German intelligence includes an engrossing chapter on espionage. It was in this area that the Germans experienced their greatest intelligence failures of World War II. Their worst setback was in Great Britain where, according to the author, every single German spy was in fact a double agent. In one of the greatest double deceptions in the history of intelligence gathering, the spies in Great Britain on which Germany relied passed on only the information—real or faked—that the British fed to them. This deception, amazingly enough, had begun in 1936 and lasted throughout the war. Kahn attributes much of the overwhelming failure of German espionage to the lack of sufficient long term peacetime preparation.

As a means of illustrating the shortcomings of German intelligence, Kahn provides absorbing case studies on major turning points in the war, including Hitler's decision to invade Russia, and the Allied landings in North Africa and Normandy. In planning the invasion of Russia, Hitler made no use of his intelligence apparatus to consider the ultimate question of strategy: could Germany mount a successful campaign of conquest against the largest country on earth? Instead, German intelligence was limited to such secondary and technical matters as establishing enemy troop locations. Hitler's attitude toward intelligence was the result, by 1940, of his arrogant conviction, shared by many of his associates, that Germany could conquer any country in the world. In the case of Russia, Kahn observes, this arrogance was compounded by the Nazis' contempt for Communism and their racial hatred of the Slavs. The Nazis, moreover, were so convinced of the weakness of the Red Army, whose officer corps was so recently decimated by purges, that they considered elaborate planning and information gathering to be a pointless exercise. Thus, they never learned until it was too late the true size of the Red Army or how the Russian forces were equipped. Surprisingly, as Kahn points out, the Germans underestimated by more than half the total number of Soviet tanks; and, worse, they had no inkling of the most successful tank of World War II, the T-34. Faulty intelligence thus contributed significantly to the ultimate disaster which befell Nazi Germany on the Eastern Front.

Nor did German intelligence fare much better in the West. In March, 1942, Colonel Ulrich Liss, head of Foreign Armies West (the counterpart of Foreign Armies East) issued a top secret document in which he assessed the possibility of a major Anglo-American thrust against Axis-dominated Europe and North

Africa. Liss concluded that "the great demands placed on tonnage by Japan's entry into the war make major British-American undertakings against the defended coasts of Europe improbable in the year 1942." Furthermore, he did not think that the Western Allies could mount any attack against French North Africa. Kahn explains how German intelligence failed completely to improve upon this assessment during the months that followed. As a consequence, the Germans were taken completely by surprise when the Anglo-American landings took place in French North Africa on November 8, 1942. The success of this Allied venture convinced everyone, including Hitler, that a cross-Channel assault against his European fortress would take place some time in 1943 or 1944. The passing of 1943 without the invasion only served to intensify the feeling that it would come in 1944.

In order for the invasion to succeed, Allied counter-intelligence had to deceive the Germans into thinking that the main landing would come in the Pas de Calais area—just twenty-one miles across the Channel from England—rather than in Normandy, where in fact the greatest amphibious invasion in history would take place. Kahn, in a lengthy chapter, shows how perfectly this deception worked; once again, at a critical juncture of the war, German intelligence failed to provide anything like an accurate assessment of Allied plans. Remarkably, for several months after the invasion began on June 6, 1944, Hitler and many of his advisers continued to believe that another attack would be launched, against the Pas de Calais area.

Kahn concludes his study with an analysis of the reasons for the overall failure of German intelligence during World War II. German intelligence experienced only limited success in operational and tactical situations, and complete failure at every one of the strategic turning points of the war. Germany, as Kahn puts it crisply, "underestimated Russia, blacked out before the North African invasion, awaited the Sicily landing in the Balkans, and fell for thinking the Normandy landing a feint." Five basic factors, according to the author, were responsible for this failure: (1) Germany's unbridled arrogance, which caused her to lose touch with reality; (2) aggression, which led to a neglect of intelligence; (3) the tendency of the German General Staff and the officer corps as a whole to regard intelligence specialists as rivals threatening their position; (4) the tangled authority structure of the Nazi state, which seriously impaired intelligence operations; and (5) anti-Semitism, which deprived German intelligence of many outstanding minds, who then lent their cryptographic talents to the Allied cause.

In discussing these factors in some depth, Kahn tries to show that each of them had origins in Germany's past. He attributes German arrogance and the feeling of superiority to a tradition of authoritarianism going back to the teachings of Martin Luther, whose ideas on the necessity of absolute obedience to the ruler took root in such predominantly Lutheran states as Prussia. This rather simplistic interpretation of authoritarianism in German history ignores the fact that the National Socialist party was founded and experienced its early growth in predominantly Catholic Bavaria. Kahn is correct in stating that Germany's arrogance, which broke her contact with reality, also prevented intelligence from seeking to resume that contact. This and the other factors, combined with Hitler's obstinate refusal to listen to any opinions contrary to his own, doomed the intelligence operation from the start.

David Kahn's *Hitler's Spies: German Military Intelligence in World War II* has broken important ground, but it is by no means the definitive work on the subject. Kahn, in appealing to a mass audience, writes in a brisk, journalistic style which is both a major strength and a weakness of his study. Thus, although his numerous stories and anecdotes make for lively and colorful reading, their excessive employment frequently obscures the comprehensive picture of German intelligence which he seeks to convey. Kahn organizes his material primarily for the dramatic impact it will have; consequently, he often treats the same subject at several different points in the book, thus making his narrative sometimes difficult to follow.

If in the style of *Hitler's Spies*, David Kahn the journalist is paramount, in the research for the book, David Kahn the historian clearly emerges. His massive thirty-four page bibliography contains references to numerous unpublished documents and to interviews with a host of Germans involved in the intelligence operations of the Third Reich. A casual glance at the bibliography explains why the book took almost ten years to complete. Overall, then, Kahn's study is a major contribution to the burgeoning literature on intelligence operations during World War II.

Edward P. Keleher

Sources for Further Study

Book World. August 13, 1978, p. E1.
Booklist. LXXIV, July 15, 1978, p. 1714.
Guardian Weekly. CXIX, September 24, 1978, p. 21.
New Statesman. XCVI, October 27, 1978, p. 552.
Time. CXII, July 10, 1978, p. 82.

THE HUMAN FACTOR

Author: Graham Greene (1904-   )
Publisher: Simon and Schuster (New York). 347 pp. $9.95
Type of work: Novel
Time: The present
Locale: London and suburbs

The conventional elements of the spy thriller become metaphors of the secret games of life in which each of us is a double agent

> *Principal characters:*
> MAURICE CASTLE, a double agent
> SARAH, his black wife
> ARTHUR DAVIS, Castle's young assistant
> COLONEL DAINTRY, a security officer within the British Secret Service
> DOCTOR PERCIVAL, a medical officer in the Secret Service
> SIR JOHN HARGREAVES, a high-ranking official in the Secret Service
> CORNELIUS MULLER, a South African agent

Graham Greene's twentieth novel, *The Human Factor*, not only reminds us quite forcibly that at seventy-five the master is still doing what no other writer can do, but assures us that we probably need not fear that the novels he produces in his declining years will reveal a diminishing of creative energy, imaginative power, or moral force. *The Human Factor* shows little trace of the weaknesses of his last novel, *The Honorary Consul*: an apparent arbitrary use of point of view, a looseness of structure, an aura of contrivance, and predilection for theme-mongering.

If Maurice Castle is less memorable and Greene's style less brilliant than the protagonists and style of his finest novels, one still feels the control of the supremely professional novelist who knows how to use an entertainment genre, the espionage thriller, as a metaphor of man's basic condition: interdependence among people in love and hate, euphoria and fear, loyalty and betrayal, comradeship and loneliness, confession and silence, youth and old age, habit and chaos.

Greene uses alternating points of view to structure his vision of relationships that corrupt, and to generate the suspense that lures one to espionage novels. Maurice Castle, a double agent of sixty-two with thirty years in the British Secret Service, is the character through whose point of view Greene most often filters the action and his meditations on it. When we view events through the eyes of Colonel Daintry, a security officer within the Service whose assignment is to uncover Doctor Percival (the double agent who devises ingenious ways of disposing of double agents), and through the eyes of Sir John Hargreaves (the new commander who supervises the investigation and disposition of the double agent), we observe parallels among all four men; and our feelings for Castle, who is unable to perceive many of the parallels, are enhanced. For instance, each of them faces the specter of old age (as does Greene himself) and retirement. Their differing attitudes and strategies for coping give us more complex perspectives on the man who most interests us, Castle. Because his wife is young, he realizes that they cannot share old age. Past retirement age, Castle would like only to change his job, not to retire. Percival's cynical dismissal of his error in killing the innocent Davis makes Daintry, who is most like Castle, want to resign, rather than conspire in a coverup. Knowing "he would exchange one loneliness for another," he does resign, and feels free, but somehow strangely alone.

In this as in most of Greene's best novels, espionage suspense also derives from his adroit point of view strategy. By rendering no events from the point of view of Arthur Davis, Castle's assistant, whom Percival and Hargreaves wrongly suspect of being the double agent, Greene keeps the reader in suspense as to who that double agent really is. Once Davis is dead, Greene allows Castle to act and think more directly in his role as double agent; thus, not until halfway through the novel do we discover that Castle is the man they seek. Another kind of suspense sustains the reader's interest thereafter: when and how will the other three old men, Daintry, Percival, and Hargreaves, discover Castle and deal with him? At midpoint, we are more interested in Castle as a complex character and in following Greene's delineation of his varied relationships than in conventional espionage intrigue; and the suspense becomes more an acceptable device for heightening our responses to the pathos of Castle's psychological traumas than a major element in a spy story.

As undeserved exiles within the Secret Service, Castle and young Davis are the only agents in the small Eastern and Southern Africa division. Nothing in Africa, says Hargreaves, the commander, is ever urgent. When Daintry discovers a leak in security, it is the public revelation that a leak is possible that poses the problem; scandal and the exposure of a court case would do much more harm than the information a double agent might reveal. It is imperative that the double agent die quietly, "naturally." Arthur Davis, a romantic who joined the service expecting a James Bond excitement and who retains an incredible innocence, finally tells Castle, "We aren't the stuff of double agents, you and me." When Percival tells Hargreaves of his plan for having Davis die a natural death, Hargreaves tells the doctor that he sometimes gives him the creeps. The commander's liaison officer with the bacteriological warfare division, Percival is amoral; to him, the word "traitor" is old-fashioned. He is "a little stout rosy man in tweeds" and silver-rimmed spectacles whose love of trout Greene belabors a little too mechanically as a character tag. In strict confidence, Percival tells the suspect, Davis, a bogus story about weapon researches; then, with insufficient proof, he impatiently takes it upon himself to proceed with the elimination of Davis.

Greene generates the pathos of Davis' predicament through the points of view of Castle and Daintry. When his daughter tells him she is getting married, Daintry happens to catch sight of Davis in the restaurant. At the wedding, he and Castle learn that Davis is dead; when Daintry accidentally breaks his ex-wife's owl figurine, she tells him it is irreplaceable; he replies that Davis is too. Cynthia, the daughter of an official who works in the office and whom Davis loved, says, "All I ever did for him was—was make his bed," when the fatal illness set in. Castle imagines that "perhaps somewhere far away a microphone and a recorder were being detached from the line. Davis would no longer be under surveillance. He had escaped." It is an effective chapter ending that anticipates the end of the novel.

To some extent, Greene uses the British Secret Service structure as a metaphor for life as a game. The game becomes more complicated when Cornelius Muller, a South African agent, arrives to share with the British an American project with the code name of "Uncle Remus," the goal of which is to prevent a race war that threatens to close the gold mines and cut off the uranium supply. Castle passes this information on to the Soviets, but the notes he steals from Muller are the wrong set. Muller, whose notes are headed "A Final Solution" and who declares that there is no such thing as ancient history, is part of a historical context that Greene creates. And in Castle's own part in history, certain relationships recur. Muller is a "racialist" who once tried to blackmail Castle under South Africa's race laws; Ivan, who was once his Soviet control in London, had also tried to blackmail Castle. An exile in Moscow, Castle must again deal with Ivan.

Castle, who lives a very private life is conscious that he has no friends. He is estranged from his mother, and his father is dead. He does not even have the satisfaction of close contact with his wife's son, Sam, by her Bantu husband (who may or may not have died in prison). Although he does not wish Sam were his own child, the thought of Sam living among the Bantus, dying of starvation or radiation if the Uncle Remus plan should ever be put into effect, makes Castle feel justified in betraying the plan.

In all his novels, Greene's characters discover that the ties that bind sometimes strangle, that our interdependence forces us in some ways to become double agents who must in time end in old age, loneliness, silence, and exile. A comparison of Greene's works with Joseph Conrad's would reveal many illuminating parallels. The epigraph of *The Human Factor* is from Conrad: "I only know that he who forms a tie is lost. The germ of corruption has entered into his soul." Love and gratitude form the major ties in Castle's life, beginning with his relationship with a Bantu black woman and her child. During World War II, while Castle was away in the Secret Service, his first wife was killed in the London blitz; his guilt for not being there to protect her partially explains his exaggerated sense of gratitude to Carson, a Soviet agent, for helping him get Sarah out of South Africa years ago when he broke the apartheid laws with her. She did not learn until later that he had used her to contact his African agents. She tells him she sometimes wishes she were still his agent.

"You tell me so much less than you did then." He is now a double agent out of gratitude to Carson, who died in prison; thus, he puts himself and Sarah in even greater danger.

Castle's mother once told him that when he was a child he "always gave away too much in a swap." Because he fears, hates, and loves, he is convinced he should quit the Service; human emotions have no place in it, and are actually a detriment to the job. In Moscow, Castle is forced, like other defectors, to live on Russia's gratitude; and Sarah's efforts to join Castle in Moscow are a reversal of Castle's efforts to join Sarah at the Hotel Palana in Lourenco Marques (which, ironically, is where Davis wanted to be transferred to).

The compassion that is part of his character also causes Castle to form ties with Davis and Daintry. When he leaves a note in a tree for Boris, he remembers leaving a love note for a girl when he was ten years old. She was a girl nobody liked, and "he was there to right the balance. That was all." When Daintry plaintively asks Castle to attend his daughter's wedding with him because he will not know a soul there, Castle realizes that he cannot resist any call for help. Castle does not see, as the reader does, that his loneliness and inability to communicate with others parallels Daintry's predicament. When Boris is not there to talk to, and other attempts to communicate (including trying to confide in a priest, who rudely tells him he needs a doctor) fail, loneliness compels Castle to expose himself to Daintry, who feels the same aching loneliness and need to speak. Both men suffer from the rule of silence imposed by their profession; out of frustration, Daintry, also, talks too much, telling strangers about his mother and father. He has bored his wife into "that chilling world of long silences." Lonely, he calls his daughter, but when he mispronounces her new last name, his son-in-law tells him he has the wrong number, and hangs up. Likewise, in the end, the line to Moscow will go dead, cutting Castle off from Sarah. Greene contrasts Percival and Hargreaves with Castle and Daintry; each is the other's only friend.

In every story of double agents, a doublecross must surface; in Greene's symbolic use of the spy genre, the doublecross contributes to the novel's meaning. To pass messages to Boris, Castle buys classics such as *War and Peace* and Trollope's *The Way We Live Now* (the titles are a little too pat) at a used book store; he tricks the proprietor into passing on to his son, who runs a pornographic book shop across the street, passages taken from the books. But when Castle must go into exile in Moscow, Halliday, the father, reveals himself to be the real contact, a loyal Communist; another lonely old man, he tells Castle he felt less lonely when Castle visited the shop. "It came as a shock to Castle to realize how little he had been trusted even by those who had the most reason to trust." In Moscow, Castle learns that the messages he sent to Moscow were passed back to the British to give the impression they had an agent in place in Moscow. Castle has risked everything only to lend a few panes to a hall of mirrors.

Castle's exile in Moscow is but a literal culmination of a series of existential exiles every human being must experience. Greene conveys a sense of that exile in his imagery. Early in the novel, a light rain gives "a black glitter to the pavement like a policeman's raincoat." That rain becomes in Moscow "a snow in which one could expect the world to end." In Moscow, he is "safe at the center of the cyclone." He feels like Robinson Crusoe in his little room, another image that seems a little too mechanical.

To emphasize our sense of Castle's exile in Moscow, the physical and psychological atmosphere of which suggests the universal limbo of old age and retirement, to which the dangers of double agentry lend poignance, Greene shifts at the end for the first time to the point of view of Castle's black wife, Sarah, herself an exile from South Africa. She and her son are the only "country" to which Castle feels any loyalty. During a long distance call from Moscow, Castle tells Sarah that perhaps she and Sam will join him in the spring, but the only certainty his tone expresses is that of old age. "She said, 'Maurice, Maurice, please go on hoping,' but in the long unbroken silence which followed she realized that the line to Moscow was dead." On that note, echoing all the themes and techniques Greene has developed, the novel ends. One hopes the line to Greene remains open.

David Madden

Sources for Further Study

America. CXXXIX, November 11, 1978, p. 338.
Hudson Review. XXXI, Summer, 1978, p. 352.
Observer. July 23, 1978, p. 21.
Saturday Evening Post. CCL, December, 1978, p. 86.
School Library Journal. XXV, October, 1978, p. 162.

THE HUNDRED YEARS WAR
The English in France, 1337-1453

Author: Desmond Seward
Publisher: Atheneum Publishers (New York). Illustrated. 296 pp. $11.95
Type of work: History
Time: 1328-1453
Locale: England and France

A short narrative account of the Hundred Years War

> *Principal personages:*
> EDWARD III, King of England, 1327-1377
> JOHN II, King of France, 1350-1364
> CHARLES V, King of France, 1364-1380
> RICHARD II, King of England, 1377-1399
> CHARLES VI, King of France, 1380-1422
> HENRY V, King of England, 1413-1422

The decade of the 1970's has seen a generous outpouring of historical writing by Desmond Seward—*The First Bourbon: Henry IV of France and Navarre* (1971), *The Monks of War: The Military Religious Orders* (1972), *Prince of the Renaissance: The Golden Life of François I* (1973), *The Bourbon Kings of France* (1976), and *Eleanor of Aquitaine* (1978). To this considerable list the Paris-born, Cambridge-educated Seward now adds *The Hundred Years War: The English in France, 1337-1453*, another popular, which is to say for the general reader, medieval history.

For that general reader who enjoys feasting on rich diction, Seward's prose offers the sumptuousness of a medieval banquet, giving substance to the world of peers and prelates and paladins; of magnates, dukes and barons; of vassals, seneschals and sorcerers. To enhance the feeling of noblesse, knight-errantry, feudal loyalty, and the Blood-Royal, Seward often introduces an anglicized French word (retroussé, melée) and sprinkles virtually every page with discriminating dashes of French itself, each term carefully explained (*bastide, chevauchée, gabelle, seigneurs*). Seward's language alone engenders the aura of the age.

Because the general reader is the target, Seward's writing is, happily, quite readable. Sentences flow well, without convolution, and paragraphs are reasonable in length. The liberal use of short quotations from contemporary chroniclers, a number of whom actually knew the people being discussed, and the careful integration of those short quotations into the movement of the paragraph not only aids readability but invests the explication with a firsthand feeling. Thus, "The French knighthood—'good chivalry, strong of limb, and stout of heart, in great abundance'—was Philip's most daunting asset."

Not that Seward is without some peculiarities of style. His use of "in the event," for instance, may prove to be a bothersome idiom to Americans more familiar with the phrase, "in any event." His practice of omitting the comma following a long introductory adverbial clause has the tendency of requiring some second readings. ("When the fortress of Marke in the Calais march fell to the French he retook it the same day.") And his mannerism of omitting a controlling topical sentence from some paragraphs can leave a reader floundering and uncertain: *One* paragraph begins on the matter of the armor of the archers, shifts to the origin of the longbow, moves on to the fire power of the weapon, and concludes with a discussion of other sidearms.

Seward obviously revels in ironies, some mined from the chroniclers and some of his own invention, as in his observation that many of the bow-staves stored in the Tower of London had been imported from Guyenne. He also finds a sardonic humor in many of the incidents of war, as when he explains that firearms were seldom lethal, "except to those firing them," or when he describes Clarence returning to winter quarters, laying waste the land "in the good old style." It is a grimness of humor not unlike that of early medieval literature.

The author's sense of irony even infiltrates what one might call personality miniatures, as in his reference to "the Holy (though excommunicated) Roman Emperor Ludwig IV." Indeed, one of Seward's strengths as a retriever of the past is his superb ability to propound a thought-provoking characterization with admirable succinctness, combining taut analysis of data and contemporary opinion. He describes John the Fearless, for instance, as "a taciturn little man, hard, energetic and charmless and, to judge from a famous contemporary portrait, singularly ugly. . . . "

The fuller portraits occur at paced intervals throughout the book. The name and exploits of Sir John Fastolf, for example, appear with regularity, but Seward reserves the more ample portrait for almost the end. Such pacing is technically understandable, though one can never be sure whether Seward will settle for physical description, as in the case of Philippa of Hainaut, or will add matters of motivation, as in his pondering of the inner tensions that may have caused Henry V's "brutal single-mindedness." By and large, such intimations remain minimal in number and degree.

Seward has many personages to treat, of course, so his inclusion of four genealogy charts proves to be a useful device. The charts are scattered, however, in three separate locations; a single section would have spared some inconvenience. And, although the pedigree charts obviously had to be limited, the omission of some prominent figures of the York line might be considered another flaw.

Battle charts and maps represent another enriching component. The charts sketch out not only the deployment of opposing forces in several key encounters, including the composition of those forces, but also the terrain and prominent natural and man-made features in the vicinity. The three page-size maps, unlike the genealogy charts, *are* printed in a single section, facilitating ready reference. Inevitably, the maps fail to show some of the sites dealt with in the text. In the waxing and waning of English and French fortunes, cordoning off varying portions of the French countryside, perhaps three maps have been too few to portray the passage of more than a century. Furthermore, the maps depict France to the virtual exclusion of England, thus demanding a knowledge of English geography sufficient to comprehend a healthy list of English place names, a list emphasizing ports and the manor towns of noteworthies.

Photographs and drawings reveal a concern on the part of the author and his editors for visual enrichment: The book contains a four-color frontispiece, thirteen black-and-white plates, and ten other illustrations. The plan may have been to enliven the text by emphasizing people over things, for two-thirds of the illustrations are pictures of persons. But they tend to be static, lacking in drama—unlike the dizzying success of various modern efforts to capture the reach of the age. Particularly pronounced is the sameness among the seven photo-reproductions of English knights made from brass rubbings; with thoughtful captions, these could have traced major trends in English armor during the period. And where illustrations could greatly abet prose description, as in Seward's extensive delineation of the importance of the English warship known as a *cog*, there is no illustration. In fact, though line drawings of the longbow and crossbow supplement descriptions of those weapons, the text lacks comparable pictures of the French cannon (other than the frontispiece, which has no gloss), even though the role of the cannon in the ultimate defeat of the English is integral to Seward's thesis.

If the main illustrations fail to provide the most thoughtful support for the text, there is, nevertheless, a happy use of artwork in the visually appealing chapter headings designed for each chapter. At the head of each, beside the chapter title and two brief quotations, rests the drawing of a knight's helmet. In the first five chapters, the helmet is an early visored type; in the next three chapters it is a later type, and in the final chapters yet another type. Can it be editorial symbolism that places the helmet left to right in the chapters covering 1337-1398, only to have it reversed, along with England's fortunes, in the chapters thereafter?

Though scarcely original, the quotations accompanying the chapter headings continue to be an appealing idea. Thus, at the head of the first chapter, "Valois or Plantagenet, 1328-1340," Sir Geoffrey Scrope is quoted, asking, "Sir, does it not seem to you that the silken thread encompassing France is broken?" Yet there is, after a time, a fair degree of repetition, even as in the illustrations to the text. Given the variety of sources, why, for example, should *The Raigne of King Edward III* be quoted in each of the first four chapters? When authorship is known, should not that be cited for the benefit of the general reader? And, in a book where non-English words are carefully explained in the text, should not a similar scruple guide the choice of the quotation?

In the final measure, the unevenness in handling the efforts at visual enrichment is symptomatic of a certain unevenness of detail throughout the book. For example, Seward amplifies his notion of Edward III's approach to propaganda. But he gives the most minimal treatment to such significant events as the breakdown of the manorial system following the Black Death, or the linguistic shift from Anglo-Norman to Middle English. In the closing chapters numerous allusions to the crown's money problems seem to be the hollow echo of an issue which cannot be developed because of its complexity. Did the editors simply say, "Three hundred pages and no more"? At one point Seward reveals a certain pressure when he writes, "Due to lack of space there is not much about chivalry in these pages, but its ideals were real enough. . . ."

The unevenness extends to interpretation, as well. It takes Seward but a sentence or two to postulate Edward III's military ambitions, Charles VI's phobias (including the possibility of porphyria), the implications of warfare on noncombatants, the harnessing of national resources, and the growth of Parliamentary power. Yet, even that sentence or two is lacking in the reference to Edward III's promised reforms in government, Henry V's reaction to the price-gouging and hostility which greeted his victorious army at "friendly" Calais, or Bedford's purposes in temporarily resigning the Regency because of alarm at Joan of Arc's offensive.

The unevenness extends to Seward's own sense of drama. He is, unquestionably, at his very finest in the battle scenes. Crécy, Agincourt, Verneuil, Formigny, Castillon: These, despite their compression, capture something of the tension and spirit of medieval battle poetry. He draws on the chroniclers most astutely in depicting the misery of the besieged and the plight of the noncombatant; and he uses their words with poignancy in such a summing up as the burial of Bedford, the Regent. But often Seward hides the dramatic key, or gives it away too soon. Overall, he has transmitted a sense of the dilemmas and a taste of the agony. Yet distance and dispassion keep his portrayal outside the circle of the most powerful narratives.

Robert E. Nichols, Jr.

Sources for Further Study

Booklist. LXXV, September 1, 1978, p. 23.
Kirkus Reviews. XLVI, September 1, 1978, p. 1003.
Library Journal. CIII, October 1, 1978, p. 1981.
New Statesman. XCVI, July 21, 1978, p. 89.
Times Educational Supplement. August 11, 1978, p. 18.

ILLNESS AS METAPHOR

Author: Susan Sontag (1933-   )
Publisher: Farrar, Straus and Giroux (New York). 88 pp. $5.95
Type of work: Essay

A cogent essay on the modern metaphors correctly or incorrectly applied to illnesses, particularly to tuberculosis and cancer

An incisive extended essay, *Illness as Metaphor* exposes mythologies connected with two of the most fearful of maladies, tuberculosis and cancer. During the greater part of the nineteenth century, tuberculosis was either romanticized and sentimentalized, or made the object of terrified speculation. Until 1882, when the tuberculosis bacillus was isolated and established as the cause of infection, the nature of the disease was believed to be mysterious. Around this mystery, which could be emotionally but not intellectually apprehended, an elaborate pattern of metaphors developed. Lacking medical facts to explain the true pathology of the illness, people invented a fanciful tuberculosis, using language that communicated their ambiguous, often contradictory feelings. Sontag points out that this fantasized tuberculosis scarcely resembles the real, scientifically described disease. As the inaccurate judgments of nineteenth century science gave way to factual investigation in our own time, so the metaphors of the past were seen to be inadequate. In the same manner, Sontag argues, contemporary metaphors applied to cancer will give way in the future to more exact language describing that malady. In time, cancer will be demythicized as tuberculosis has been. Sontag's thesis is that we must understand the tyranny of false metaphors in order to liberate ourselves from the language of fears and superstitions that have no basis in reality.

To develop this thesis, Sontag carefully examines the older metaphorical concepts of tuberculosis as a pattern against which the reader can compare the modern metaphors of cancer. She has little interest in the medical or pseudo-scientific notions of the disease prior to this century. Instead, she chooses as examples a wealth of material from literature. Because the metaphors concerning pathology either originate among writers, or because literary masters express in definitive form the most nearly representative metaphors derived from popular speech, writers serve as her primary source. With extraordinary erudition, Sontag assembles information from such diverse writers as Stendhal, Kafka, John of Trevisa, Muger, Hugo, Dickens, Henry James, Turgenev, Stevenson, Joyce, Goldsmith, Shelley, Mann, Gautier, and so on. Citing examples from fiction, drama, biography, letters, and diaries, she synthesizes enough material for a convincing essay on a topic such as "Literary Uses of Tuberculosis Prior to the Twentieth Century." But she is less concerned with the impact of tuberculosis—either as metaphor or fact—upon literary figures than with the mythology that these writers perceived to be associated with the disease.

For most of them, tuberculosis was romanticized as an illness that spiritual-ized its victims. Even as the so-called consumptives seemed physically to waste away, they were believed to have gained spiritual resources. Considered sufferers from a disease of passion, tuberculars were supposed to be either individuals who were recklessly sensual, or, in contrast, people who denied themselves sexual energy. Either way, their disease was linked to excesses or repressions of love. Furthermore, victims were romantically associated with a malady that was to terminate following a prolonged but not agonizing illness. The fact that the progress of the disease seemed to be uncomfortable rather than painful, that its signs were pallor (or ruddy complexion) and emaciation rather than any horrible outward physical disfigurement, and finally that it seemed to heighten rather than diminish perception—all these observed condi-tions contributed to make tuberculosis seem "interesting." Indeed, even those who were its victims appeared to accept the mythology of the disease with some satisfaction.

Yet, as Sontag demonstrates, the mythology failed accurately to describe tuberculosis as a pathology known to science. Although in its early stages the malady might seem to the victims to be only uncomfortable, in its final stages its ravages could be terrible. And the supposed spiritualization of the consump-tive was actually a process of bronchial disintegration. Finally, the supposed etiology of the disease was entirely false. Passion had nothing to do with the causes of tuberculosis: a bacterial infection was responsible. As soon as Koch and others explained the nature of the disease, it lost its glamorous mythology. Contemporary writers speak of tuberculosis in accurate, rather than metaphori-cal language; and when a great writer, Thomas Mann, uses the older meta-phors for the disease (for example, in *The Magic Mountain*), he can be under-stood on a symbolic level of meaning but not on a scientific level. Because contemporary writers are less likely to use the unscientific metaphors, they are less likely to become attracted to the mysterious aspects of tuberculosis. In fact it is cancer, not tuberculosis, that modern writers invest with metaphors.

These metaphors, Sontag believes, are remarkably similar in many ways to those formerly applied to tuberculosis. Cancer is also seen as a disease of passion—although usually repressed passion. A modern myth is that certain personality types are especially susceptible to cancer. Like victims of tuber-culosis in the old metaphors, cancer-prone individuals are supposed to have an inner disposition that brings the malady upon them. Thus, the cancer-type is somehow seen as responsible for his disease. But there is this difference: the old metaphors concerning tuberculosis types romanticized the person as (in some sense) fortunate, whereas the current metaphors for cancer show him to be miserable and doomed. Like tuberculosis, cancer is understood to be nearly always fatal; the very word conjures up a sentence of death. To explain the pathology of the malady, writers use metaphors of aggression. The body is "attacked" by cancer; the body's "defenses" are broached by a spreading malignancy that resembles an advancing army. So to fight cancer, we are urged to join a "crusade," to battle its forces until we are victorious.

These metaphors, as Sontag points out, are only partly accurate in describing the real ravages of cancer. From what we know so far, the malignancy appears to be of several types with varied kinds of effects upon the body. Some cancers are very rapid, while others are slow to develop. Not all, certainly, are—or need be—fatal. Sontag makes the point that some victims of cancer might expect to outlive those struck by heart trouble, yet the heart patient is probably more sanguine about his condition. According to the metaphors of his malady, his bodily organ is wearing down, like a machine, so he attributes his disability to the mechanism itself, rather than to a mysterious foreign source leading to internal disintegration, such as cancer is supposed to be, and he is less apprehensive. The cancer-personality, on the other hand, accepts as true the frightening mythology that his body has been invaded—defiled—by a corrupt force that invaribly will kill him. Worse, the death is always supposed to be painful, even though in fact some victims die quickly, with little suffering.

Because the cancer metaphor threatens one's sense of completeness, it drives its victims to irrational conduct. To Sontag, that result is particularly unfortunate, inasmuch as the cancer patient must thus contend with a poor mental attitude in addition to his obvious medical problem. As an example of irrational conduct, the author shows how cancer patients react to the metaphors by trying to drive the malady from their systems by will power or by some form of mental manipulation. Yet if cancer may be shown to have a purely physical cause, like tuberculosis, it would seem as irrational to hope to drive it from the body through concentration, yoga exercises, or will power, as it would be ineffectual to attempt to treat tuberculosis by these same mental disciplines.

Of course, Sontag's argument hinges at least partly upon the similarity between the metaphors of cancer and tuberculosis. We already understand the scientific causes and effects of the latter, but our knowledge about cancer is far less complete. Consequently, it is easy to discover fallacies in the old metaphorical language associated with consumption. At the present state of our investigation of cancer, however, we cannot be certain whether the metaphors that have accumulated around it are mostly true or false. Sontag's analogy is, after all, a metaphor also; and she argues on the basis of language, not of scientific evidence. Most of her evidence is drawn from the limited but highly significant literature written by people distinguished in the arts or letters. For the most part she ignores the popular use of metaphors describing illness. Are the popular stereotypes of cancer disseminated in the mass media identical to those that appear in literary sources? Probably they are very similar; but Sontag neglects to establish a case for their connection. In addition to the metaphors derived from important writers, we would hope to examine metaphors on cancer, let us say, that derive from the press, from television, or from the theater.

Similarly, the author neglects to investigate fully the medical/scientific metaphors concerning cancer. Are many doctors ill-prepared to discuss with their patients the nature of serious maladies because they rely upon faulty scientific metaphors from their specialized fields? For example, when they describe the effects of cancer as "invasive," are they influenced by metaphor or by scientific fact? Or should doctors avoid metaphorical language altogether, until the precise etiology and treatment of cancer may be understood? Certainly, the author is correct in showing that many stereotypical descriptions of cancer may be called "punitive"—threatening and punishing—and she is also correct in warning us that such punitive language can dishearten the patient suffering from cancer. But if the medical effects of cancer are indeed understood to be dreadful, then punitive metaphors would appear to be the most nearly accurate in describing the malady. For if the nature of cancer is punishing, it stands to reason that any euphemisms intended to conceal the punitive metaphors would serve neither the physician nor the patient.

Despite these few limitations in the scope of Sontag's essay, *Illness as Metaphor* is an extremely valuable contribution to our understanding of the ways in which language as metaphor contributes to the mythology of the disease. Lucid, erudite, serious but never solemn, the book is a model of its type: a lively analysis of metaphor as a key to the structure of ideas. Sontag shows how language can either communicate accurately or distort our concepts of illness. More, she shows how language can influence our reaction to illness, to make that illness seem less or more grave. So it is a pity that readers who could profit the most from her discussion are not likely to read the book; the mass audience of readers, including those who suffer from cancer and other illnesses, will probably not be attracted to an essay so finely composed, so rich in allusion, so pithy and unsentimental.

Instead, a small number of readers who are concerned with the uses of language will learn to become more keenly critical of their own metaphors on sensitive issues. "Modern disease metaphors," Sontag insists, "are all cheap shots." And she admits that, on at least one occasion, she has been guilty of misusing metaphor. "I once wrote, in the heat of despair over America's war on Vietnam, that 'the white race is the cancer of human history.' " Somehow it is comforting to reflect that even Susan Sontag may—though very rarely, to be sure—use the "cheap shot." Unlike most of us, however, she has the intellectual probity to assess her errors and, through the learning experience, to perfect her metaphors.

Leslie B. Mittleman

Sources for Further Study

America. CXXXIX, October 7, 1978, p. 230.
Atlantic. CCXLII, November, 1978, p. 98.
New Republic. CLXXIX, July 8, 1978, p. 37.
New York Review of Books. XXV, July 20, 1978, p. 18.
Virginia Quarterly Review. LIV, Autumn, 1978, p. 127.

THE ILLUSION OF PEACE
Foreign Policy in the Nixon Years

Author: Tad Szulc (1926-   )
Publisher: The Viking Press (New York). 882 pp. $20.00
Type of work: History
Time: 1969-1974
Locale: Washington, D.C.

A comprehensive account of the foreign policy of the United States during the Presidency of Richard M. Nixon

Principal personages:
RICHARD MILHOUS NIXON, thirty-seventh President of the United States
HENRY ALFRED KISSINGER, special assistant to the President on national security affairs, and the Secretary of State
WILLIAM P. ROGERS, Secretary of State
ALEXANDER MEIGS HAIG, General and chief assistant to the President
MELVIN R. LAIRD, Secretary of Defense
RICHARD HELMS, Director of the Central Intelligence Agency
ELLIOT L. RICHARDSON, Undersecretary of State
JOSEPH J. SISCO, Assistant Secretary of State for Near Eastern and South Asian Affairs

Tad Szulc was for many years a highly respected diplomatic and foreign correspondent for *The New York Times* and has several notable publications to his credit. His account of President Nixon's foreign policy, therefore, might well be expected to arouse interest, despite the fact that it involves a largely familiar story. Many publications covering this fascinating period in American foreign relations have appeared in recent years. It is the story of the relaxation of tensions with the Soviet Union, known as détente; the Strategic Arms Limitation Talks (SALT); Henry Kissinger's hectic shuttle diplomacy in the Middle East; the stunning diplomatic overture to Mainland China; and the Paris negotiations over the war in Vietnam, to mention some of the highlights of the period. It is, also, the story of the bizarre world of the Nixon White House, a setting in which key officials distrusted and spied on one another, and in which a climate of hostile suspicion deeply affected the policy-making process.

Szulc strives to shed some additional light on the available record. He incorporates into his account information from unpublished official papers and a large number of interviews with high government officials, public figures, and diplomats. This plan does allow for occasional revealing "inside" perspectives, spotlighting the contrast between the public and the private attitudes of the Nixon administration. Szulc's expressed objective is the exposition of Nixon's preoccupation with images: specifically, the creation of images which had little or no relationship to reality and obscured the truth. In the final analysis, according to Szulc, President Nixon's proclaimed achievement of a "struc-

ture of peace" was no more than the *illusion* of peace. Incidentally, the
phenomenon of illusion has been noted in other assessments of the Nixon administration. Nevertheless, Szulc's basic theme indicates his intent to provide
a fresh and more searching coverage of the Nixon years.

The two dominant figures, the President and Henry Kissinger, special assistant on national security affairs and later the Secretary of State as well, formulated major new policies and made consequential decisions. Some of these
turn out to have been flawed, but most still await proper historical assessment.
Nixon and Kissinger complemented each other remarkably well. The President
had a deep interest in international relations and considerable practical experience, while Kissinger was known for his brilliance of mind and impressive
scholarship on foreign and security affairs. Both shared a strong distrust of the
bureaucracies and were in full agreement on by-passing the State Department
and establishing direct communication links with foreign governments in vital
policy areas. Kissinger had a free hand in reorganizing the National Security
Council. He made it the instrument through which he would assume complete
control of foreign policy. It enabled him to neutralize or to diminish the influence of the two most important traditional actors, the Secretaries of State and
Defense.

Szulc recounts the Nixon-Kissinger foreign policy in strictly chronological
order, dividing his material into six books, one for each year of the Nixon
administration. Such a diarylike treatment seems inappropriate for the subject
matter and the considerable amount of material involved. The reader has much
difficulty grasping from the thicket of detail the grand policy designs and the
linkage between such important policy areas as détente, the opening of relations with China, and the Vietnam peace settlement. Thus the lack of an effective organizational framework must be noted as an unfortunate shortcoming.

When Nixon began his term in office, the Vietnam war assumed the highest
priority in United States foreign policy. The "Vietnamization" of the war was
the formula designed to deal with the most critical public irritant over the
conflict, the loss of American manpower. The administration was able to
withdraw sizable American troop contingents. However, this policy was accompanied by an escalation of the use of air power over Vietnam, Cambodia,
and Laos. Previously imposed constraints were removed, and the enemy was
subjected to unprecedented levels of punishment. These moves were designed
to entice the enemy into serious negotiations and, at the same time, to give the
South Vietnamese the opportunity to become more self-reliant. While much of
the public resentment abated in apparent proportion to the decline in American
casualties, many college campuses exploded into hostile demonstrations pro-
testing the escalation of the air war. These student protests, compounded by
the Kent State University shootings, posed serious political problems for the
Nixon Administration. They undoubtedly contributed to the perception in the
Nixon White House of being under a state of siege.

During Nixon's first year in office, the possibility of inducing the Soviet Union and China to apply pressure on North Vietnam came more clearly into focus. Indeed, the Sino-Soviet conflict offered opportunities which it was high time to attempt to exploit. The President's trip to China in February, 1972, was a spectacular diplomatic and personal triumph. Its chief accomplishment was the initiation of a process of normalization of relations between Peking and Washington. Both governments agreed to the principle of the existence of only one China. However, the status of the Republic of China on Taiwan was left unresolved, and each side maintained its own previous position. This led to the establishment of "liaison offices" in the respective capitals, instead of full-fledged embassies. Prepared in utmost secrecy by Henry Kissinger, the announcement of the Peking summit was truly sensational news. Its impact was especially strong in Japan, where it came to be known as the first of two "Nixon shocks," the second one resulting from the drastic promulgation of policies designed to ameliorate the United States balance of payments problems.

The Moscow summit was held in May, 1972. Just prior to this event the North Vietnamese had launched a massive assault on South Vietnam and scored significant gains. The President responded by ordering the mining of all major North Vietnamese ports and the resumption of massive air and naval attacks. This severe American military action was to force Hanoi to return to the negotiating table in Paris. In ordering the strong action, Nixon took the calculated risk that the Soviets might call off the summit as an expression of solidarity with their client North Vietnam. Such a reaction on the part of Moscow would have upset Nixon's electoral strategy, which counted heavily on an improved relationship with the Soviet Union. Evidently the Soviets, too, were desirous of continuing the cautious move toward limited cooperation. The Moscow summit meeting was held on schedule and brought forth the first set of agreements on strategic arms limitation (SALT I).

Such brilliant diplomatic achievements, in addition to the fact that the Hanoi delegation had returned to the Paris peace talks, holding out the prospect that the Vietnam conflict could at last be settled, allowed the President to look with confidence to the 1972 elections. Alas, an ominous cloud began to appear on his otherwise clear political sky; it was the burgeoning Watergate scandal. When the Vietnam cease-fire agreement was signed in January, 1973, it should have freed Nixon to move vigorously and innovatively in other foreign policy areas and to devote more attention to those areas suffering from neglect because of the concentration on the Vietnam conflict. Tragically, it was at this particular juncture that the Watergate scandal began to absorb more and more of the President's time and energy. Gradually, but inexorably, the scandal ruined his political reputation and impeded the conduct of foreign policy.

As the problems of Watergate became more acute for the President and his status deteriorated, that of Henry Kissinger grew more formidable. Kissinger became the dominant figure in United States foreign policy. In 1973 he assumed the position of Secretary of State, while continuing his position in the White House as the President's special assistant on national security affairs and continuing in charge of the National Security Council apparatus. 1973 was to have been the "year of Europe." However, the Yom Kippur war and the subsequent oil embargo changed that. The Atlantic powers were slow to cooperate in establishing a united posture to cope with the oil shortage and to deal with the Organization of Petroleum Exporting Countries (OPEC).

The attack by Egypt and Syria during the observance of Yom Kippur caught Israel by surprise. Szulc suggests that the surprise element was due largely to a failure to act on available intelligence pertaining to Arab preparations for the attack. Both Egypt and Syria made important initial gains, but were stopped and thrown back by the recovering Israeli forces. Israel was left utterly dependent on the United States for quick resupply and, therefore, susceptible to American pressure. Both sides were persuaded to accept a cease-fire in a place, at a time, when the Egyptian forces were threatened by complete defeat. Szulc states that the war was a "cruel sideshow" for Kissinger, who wanted a stalemate in order to engage in his long-range peace diplomacy. Subsequently, of course, Kissinger was able to bring about the disengagement agreements through his exhausting Middle East shuttle diplomacy.

In general, the 1973 war in the Middle East significantly reduced the Soviet presence in the area. However, it also elevated oil into a tremendously powerful tool of Arab diplomacy. The oil embargo, followed by the sudden quadrupling of oil prices to consumer nations, caused a sharp economic setback to the industrialized nations of Western Europe, Japan, and the United States. The dependence on Arab oil made it imperative to assume a more even-handed position regarding the Arab-Israeli conflict, as well as to effect the formation of a united posture toward the oil cartel.

A review of the Nixon-Kissinger foreign policy would have to conclude that it gained more flexibility for the United States in its relations with its allies, the Third World countries, and its two major adversaries, the Soviet Union and China. The altered American posture, referred to as the Nixon Doctrine, called for more regional self-reliance. The new assessment of China envisioned that country as posing far less of a threat to smaller Asian powers than had previously been thought. The reassessment enabled the United States to reduce its physical presence in Asia considerably.

The overall conception of the Nixon-Kissinger foreign policy, having as its objective the change from the "era of confrontation" to the "era of negotiation," is accepted by Szulc as entirely sound and desirable. However, the actual achievement of a "structure of peace" eluded the Nixon administration. What was obtained in this regard was, indeed, a mere illusion. There is much about this period which should be subjected to critical scrutiny. Yet, Szulc's treatment of it is essentially a descriptive account. Szulc fails to present an incisive analytical study. His assertions are often unconvincing and insufficiently supported. His heavy reliance on confidential oral statements of individuals is questionable. The total absence of any reference to source material is certainly an irritant from a scholarly point of view. Understandably, a reporter may have to protect the confidentiality of sources in the form of unpublished papers and personal interviews. However, most of the book is obviously based on published documents, often quoted extensively, as well as other secondary literature on the subject. These sources should have been identified and cited by Szulc.

In its total impact, *The Illusion of Peace* falls considerably short of expectations. It is not the kind of illuminating and critical assessment of the Nixon-Kissinger foreign policy that should have been possible at this stage. The lack of organization, the repetitive nature of much of the coverage, the inclusion of a vast amount of tangential and extraneous detail, and the complete absence of source citations have greatly reduced the book's usefulness.

Manfred Grote

Sources for Further Study

Christian Science Monitor. LXX, June 26, 1978, p. 23.
Choice. XV, October, 1978, p. 1124.

IMPERIALISM AT BAY
The United States and the Decolonization of the British Empire
1941-1945

Author: Wm. Roger Louis
Publisher: Oxford University Press (New York). 612 pp. $19.95
Type of work: History
Time: 1941-1945
Locale: Great Britain and the United States

A tracing of the development of the idea of trusteeship during World War II, and its incorporation in the Charter of the United Nations in 1945

> *Principal personages:*
> SIR WINSTON CHURCHILL, British Prime Minister, 1940-1945
> FRANKLIN DELANO ROOSEVELT, President of the United States, 1933-1945
> CLEMENT ATTLEE, Labour Party member of the Churchill coalition cabinet, 1940-1945; Prime Minister, 1945-1951
> HERBERT VERE EVATT, Foreign Minister of Australia during World War II
> LORD CRANBORNE, British Colonial Secretary, 1942; Dominions secretary, 1943-1945
> HAROLD STASSEN, United States delegate to the San Francisco Conference, April-June, 1945
> OLIVER STANLEY, British Colonial Secretary, 1942-1945
> SIR ANTHONY EDEN, British Foreign Secretary, 1940-1945
> HENRY STIMSON, United States Secretary of the Navy during World War II
> ARTHUR CREECH-JONES, leading British Labour Party expert on the colonial question during the World War II period
> CORDELL HULL, United States Secretary of State, 1933-1944
> EDWARD STETTINIUS, United States Secretary of State, 1944-1945
> SUMNER WELLES, Undersecretary of State, 1933-1944
> BENJAMIN GERIG, United States State Department expert on the colonial question

Wm. Roger Louis, Professor of History at the University of Texas, is an authority on the history of European colonialism. Among his earlier books are: *British Strategy in the Far East, 1919-1939*; *Ruanda-Urundi, 1884-1919*; and *Great Britain and Germany's Lost Colonies, 1914-1919*, the latter being a study of the origins of the League of Nations Mandate system. Louis has now written a detailed, scholarly study of the Anglo-American debate over colonialism during World War II: *Imperialism at Bay*. This work is based on the recently opened files of the British and American archives, and on the private papers and personal diaries of British, American, and Australian statesmen and other high officials.

The title, "Imperialism at Bay," might conjure up the image of a cornered lion about to be shot by a band of hunters. The story the book tells is, how-

ever, much less dramatic. The subtitle, "The United States and the Decolonization of the British Empire," is also somewhat misleading, since Britain
did not give up any of her colonies during the period covered in this book.
What Louis narrates is not the clash of battle between rival armies, but the
struggle between two ideas: "imperialism" *versus* "trusteeship."

In 1919, colonial territories taken from the Central Powers had been handed
over to various Allied Powers, to be administered by them, subject to the
supervision of the Permanent Mandates Council of the League of Nations.
After 1945, former colonies of the Axis Powers, together with some former
"Mandates," were administered by various Allied Powers under the supervision of the Trusteeship Council of the United Nations. United Nations supervision of the Trusteeships would prove to be far more vigorous than League of
Nations supervision of the Mandates had been. The natives' right of petition to
the United Nations, and the right of that world organization to send inspection
teams to the trust territories, helped considerably to accelerate the process of
decolonization in the years after World War II. It is to a study of the origins of
this Trusteeship system that Louis devotes his new book.

The book consists of four parts. The first is a rather lengthy introduction, in
which the author first presents the main themes before dealing with them at
length. In part two Louis traces the trusteeship controversy from the time of
the Atlantic Charter (August, 1941), when common Anglo-American peace
goals were first stated, to the Cairo Declaration of December 1, 1943, in
which the abolition of the Japanese colonial empire was proclaimed as an Allied war aim. In part three, the author takes the narrative up to the Yalta
Conference of February, 1945, where the "Big Three," Russia, Britain, and
the United States, approved the application of the Trusteeship principle to certain types of dependent territories. In part four, the author shows how, at the
San Francisco Conference of April-June, 1945, the Trusteeship principle was
formally incorporated in the United Nations Charter. The story the author has
to tell is a rather long and complicated one.

As a result of the Japanese bombing of Pearl Harbor, on December 7, 1941,
the United States formally entered World War II on the side of Britain. Even
before that date, however, President Franklin D. Roosevelt and British Prime
Minister Winston Churchill had been *de facto* allies. In August, 1941, the two
leaders, meeting on a ship off the coast of Newfoundland, had proclaimed the
so-called "Atlantic Charter." In this press release, the self-determination of
nations had been declared a key Anglo-American goal for the postwar world.

Louis shows that after the stunning defeat of the British Army by the Japanese at Singapore, in February, 1942, there was a wave of criticism of the
British Empire by American politicians and journalists. How, it was asked,
could Americans fight for the national self-determination mentioned in the Atlantic Charter, while simultaneously defending the colonial Empire of their
closest ally? It was in this atmosphere that President Franklin D. Roosevelt

began to speak, on numerous occassions, of the need for reform of the British and other European colonial empires. "Imperialism," he believed, must be abolished.

To Roosevelt, Louis explains, "imperialism" meant the exploitation of colonies by the European Powers for their own benefit, without regard for the welfare of the indigenous peoples. "Trusteeship," on the other hand, meant the international supervision of the European powers' administration of their colonies. Under such supervision, Roosevelt believed, the European powers would be forced to improve the standard of living of their colonial charges, and to prepare them for eventual independence.

The author contends, in a somewhat sarcastic fashion, that Roosevelt viewed trusteeship as a "panacea," to be applied to all sorts of dependent territories and politically unstable areas. Thus Roosevelt, at one time or another, proposed trusteeship regimes for British Gambia, French Morocco, the Japanese-ruled country of Korea, and the then Japanese-occupied French colony of Indochina. In addition, Roosevelt wanted Hong Kong, which he hoped Britain would cede to China, made into a free port under international supervision.

Between 1942 and 1944, while Roosevelt was airing his ideas, State Department officials, in committee meeting after committee meeting, tried to formulate American plans for the future of colonial territories after the war. Many such officials, such as Undersecretary of State Sumner Welles, were just as enthusiastic about international supervison of colonies as was the President himself.

Both Roosevelt's plans for trusteeship, and those proposed by State Department officials, met with opposition from British Prime Minister Churchill, who was extremely reluctant to see British colonies subjected to any form of supervision by an international organization. The tension between the American advocacy of trusteeship, and the British desire to keep outsiders from meddling in the affairs of their colonies, is a major theme of Louis' book.

In dealing with this subject, the author scrupulously refrains from oversimplifying complex issues. He does not present the history of the trusteeship question merely as a battle between British imperialism and American anti-imperialism. Instead, he shows that differences of opinion concerning the future of colonialism existed not only between the British and American governments but also within each of the two governments.

Although British Prime Minister Churchill's government was a Coalition Cabinet, comprising both Labourites and Conservatives, there was no bitter debate within the Cabinet over the colonial issue. Instead, Louis states, such Labour Party Cabinet members as Clement Attlee tended to "rally round the flag" when faced with what they regarded as unjust American criticism of the British colonial record.

Yet, if there were no sharp disagreements over trusteeship in Churchill's Cabinet, there were certainly differences of emphasis. Colonial Secretary Sir Oliver Stanley, for example, wished to see foreign interference with the Empire warded off even if it offended American public opinion. Stanley also wanted Britain to turn her Mandates into colonies pure and simple. Foreign Secretary Sir Anthony Eden, however, insisted that the alliance with the United States was all-important, and that maintaining this friendship required at least verbal concessions to American criticism of the Imperial System.

To fight the war, and to maintain her position in the postwar world, Britain had to keep the friendship not only of the United States, but also of the "White" Dominions of the British Commonwealth. Yet, it was a statesman from one of these Dominions, Australian Foreign Minister Herbert Vere Evatt, who again and again demanded that British colonial rule be subjected to international supervision. While faulting the Australian statesman for being "abrasive," Louis praises him for having contributed, by his continual championship of trusteeship, to the enshrinement of that concept in the United Nations Charter.

Within the United States government, Louis makes clear, the most enthusiastic partisans of trusteeship, aside from Roosevelt himself, were to be found in the State Department. The most determined foes of trusteeship, on the other hand, were the Secretaries of War and the Navy, and the heads of the Joint Chiefs of Staff.

By the autumn of 1944, therefore, a bitter quarrel between friends and foes of trusteeship had broken out in the United States government. Each side hoped to win over Roosevelt, but he refused to take sides. Navy Secretary Henry Stimson argues that American national security imperatively demanded the American annexation of the Japanese-ruled Mariana islands. United States sovereignty over these islands, Stimson believed, had to be absolute: foreign interference could not be permitted. The military officers of the Joint Chiefs of Staff, some of whom wished the annexation of French and British Pacific islands as well as Japanese ones, accused the State Department experts of being fuzzy-minded idealists, whose indiscriminate espousal of international supervision of colonies would weaken the justifiable American claim to sovereignty over strategic bases. The position taken by the United States Navy, Louis notes ironically, was very close to that espoused by the British Colonial Office.

After Roosevelt's death, a compromise was reached. To mollify the military, the State Department agreed to demand, at the upcoming International Conference at San Francisco, that the Pacific islands be given a special status as "strategic trust territories," which could be fortified in the interests of world peace by the United States. The new President, Harry S Truman, approved this solution.

In the meantime, Anglo-American differences over trusteeship had gradually been resolved. At the Yalta Conference, of February, 1945, Churchill had, at the urging of Foreign Secretary Eden, conceded that trusteeship should be applied to former Axis colonies and to former Mandates (including British Mandates), though not to all British colonies. Louis shows how, at the San Francisco Conference of April-June, 1945, Harold Stassen, a leading figure in the American delegation, was able to work out a common position on the trusteeship question with British delegate Lord Cranborne. After hurried talks with delegate after delegate, Stassen succeeded in keeping Russia, China, and the smaller powers from inserting even stronger anticolonial wording in the United Nations Charter.

For by now, Louis points out, many United States State Department officials were not so sure as they had once been that their country should be in the forefront of the fight against colonialism. Some of them now believed that the United States would soon be involved in a struggle with Russia, and would need the support of those European states which possessed colonial empires. President Truman, by approving the return of French authority to Indochina in the Autumn of 1945, showed that he shared the State Department's sober second thoughts about antiimperialism.

Louis is careful not to exaggerate the anticolonial sentiments of either President Roosevelt or the officials of the State Department. No American at this time, Louis contends, "foresaw the speed or the fragmentation of decolonization." Louis argues that Roosevelt himself did not believe in immediate freedom for all colonies, but only in their gradual preparation for such freedom. Thus, Roosevelt "aimed at stabilizing, not undermining, the colonial world." To Louis, the "antiimperialism" of World War II America was more high-sounding rhetoric than a practical call for action. Louis also implies that the United States Navy's plan to annex islands in the Pacific was itself a form of imperialism.

Louis' scholarship is exhaustive and meticulous. The author breaks new ground in his study of Anglo-American attitudes towards colonialism. The wave of decolonization after World War II was made possible, not only by the rise of indigenous nationalist movements, but also by the kind of collective bad conscience about imperialism which Louis' work so thoroughly describes. By investigating in depth the process of bureaucratic decision-making, rather than merely studying the interaction between Churchill and Roosevelt, Louis also sheds new light on the history of inter-Allied relations during the war.

Imperialism at Bay is a book for scholars, not for the general reader. It is far too detailed for the beginning student. Without some background knowledge of both late nineteenth century imperialism and the post 1945 process of decolonization, it is very difficult for the reader to understand the thesis of Louis' book. The complete absence of any maps or illustrations makes it difficult for the nonspecialist to visualize just who the faceless bureaucrats were, and precisely which colonial territories they were talking about.

Paul D. Mageli

Sources for Further Study

Choice. XV, October, 1978, p. 1108.
Reviews in American History. VI, December, 1978, p. 537.

IN MY FATHER'S HOUSE

Author: Ernest J. Gaines (1933-   )
Publisher: Alfred A. Knopf (New York). 214 pp. $8.95
Type of work: Novel
Time: 1970's
Locale: Louisiana

A haunting portrayal of a man's search for himself and the meaning of his life

Principal characters:
PHILIP MARTIN, a minister and civil rights leader
ALMA, his wife
ROBERT X (ETIENNE), his illegitimate son
CHIPPO SIMON, his old friend

Best known for his highly successful novel *The Autobiography of Miss Jane Pittman*, Ernest Gaines's new book *In My Father's House* is at least as notable in its unflinching presentation of the modern black man's dilemma as the earlier work is in its poignant portrait of the black man's past. In *The Autobiography of Miss Jane Pittman*, Gaines celebrates the indomitable spirit of blacks as they struggle out of the degradation of slavery and do battle with racial hatred and ignorance to claim their due as full human beings. In *My Father's House*, through its lean plot and echoing rhythm, exposes another kind of slavery in the making in modern America: it is slavery dressed in the guise of material success. *In My Father's House* is a cautionary novel that reveals the terrible danger that lies beneath the beauty and allure of the American dream. Blacks who now have the opportunity to make a place for themselves in middle-class society, to live the "good life" in America, can be so blinded in their quest that they can fall victim to an influence which would more effectively and insidiously strip them of their humanity than could any slave master in the past.

Gaines's restrained style and serious tone effectively reveal the genuine depth of his feeling and the concern with which he views this very real problem. Although the author is sympathetic to the central figure in the novel, Philip Martin, he makes effective use of irony to strip away those trappings of affluence and power which hide the real Philip.

Philip is the pastor of a large black church in St. Adrienne, Louisiana, and is a leader in the local civil rights struggle. Thus he has attained position, prestige, and authority. He has all the external symbols of middle-class success: an elegant, ranch-style brick home, a luxury sedan, a station wagon for his wife, and an "ideal" family consisting of a wife and two children (one boy and one girl). Gaines's use of irony is quite apparent here. Philip is described as tall, large, and very handsome. He is so satisfied with his apparent success that he finds no need to question or examine his life. Then a mysterious figure from his past comes to town, and Philip's world collapses. The focus of the novel rests on Philip's attempts to face himself and his life for the first time in order to know who he is and what his life means.

The action begins when a wraithlike Robert X appears out of the rain and winter cold, a ghost from Philip's past. He is a hollow man, a shell, the remnants of a son Philip had abandoned more than twenty years before. The X in Robert's name reflects his lack of substance and identity; it also underscores the fact that Philip no longer remembers his son's real name (Etienne). When Robert X appears in his father's living room during a party, Philip starts to move forward to greet him, stumbles and suddenly falls to the floor. Symbolically, Robert X is the spiritual and emotional commitment that Philip had long ago rejected, as he had rejected Robert X and his mother, Johanna. Philip is pathetically estranged from true spiritual and emotional understanding. When he attempts to move closer to it, he falls; he lacks the necessary strength of conviction even to approach it much less to embrace it. The fact that Philip is a minister and yet suffers such spiritual deprivation is another example of Gaines's use of irony.

Robert X also represents the future of men like Philip Martin, and, in particular, their sons. As Gaines presents it that future is bleak indeed. For if it is the fathers who make a place for their sons, who provide the models and guidance and strength, what kind of place is it going to be when fathers do not even know their sons, when fathers abandon their sons, or when, even though they are physically present, they essentially ignore their sons? What would such a world be like?

Gaines provides a glimpse of the awful answer through the agonized figure of Robert X as he ponders the empty colored bottles strewn in the alley beneath his window: ". . . used to be something good in them. . . . Somebody went through a lot of pain making them. . . . Look at them now. Busted. Nothing but trash. Nothing but trash now."

The heart of the novel lies in Philip's torturous struggle to face his past and thereby avert this disastrous future. *In My Father's House* is a moving tale of a man's attempt to face, first of all, the fact that even in 1970 he is still operating under the influence of the slave mentality—that, in fact, he has inadvertently accepted the damning myth that he is a stud, a buck, an animal. What else but an animal would sire children and then leave them as he, Philip, had done? Second, in order to compensate for the underlying doubts about his own self-worth, he has wholeheartedly adopted the desire for power, individual gain, and material possessions—in other words, the white value system that underlies the whole structure of American life. In so doing, he has lost sight of the values of human dignity, community, and compassion for which black people have fought so long. In relinquishing these largely spiritual and emotional values, Philip has created an unbridgeable gap between himself and his wife and children.

Philip symbolizes many upwardly mobile blacks who play the game of getting ahead, but who, somewhere along the way, lose sight of where the game begins and where it ends. In the process, they often also lose sight of who they themselves are. Repeatedly, Philip asks himself: " 'Who really was Philip Martin, and what, if anything, had he really done?' "

In his uncomplicated and straightforward style, Gaines deals with themes of tremendous significance to every reader who is concerned about the direction that life in this country has taken. The novel is not all darkness and pain, however. For in the midst of the winter, the season in which the action of the novel takes place to emphasize the theme of psychic death, Philip's cry of "I am lost" can be recognized as his most honest statement. Within it are contained the seeds of hope.

Joan S. Griffin

Sources for Further Study

Book World. June 18, 1978, p. E5.

Horn Book. LV, October, 1978, p. 546.

New York Times. CXXVII, July 20, 1978, p. C19.

School Library Journal. XXV, November, 1978, p. 81.

IN SEARCH OF HISTORY
A Personal Adventure

Author: Theodore H. White (1915-   )
Publisher: Harper & Row Publishers (New York). 561 pp. $12.95
Type of work: Autobiography
Time: 1915-1963
Locale: The world, particularly China and Western Europe

Personal reminiscences of major historical events from the late 1930's through the early 1960's that the writer covered in his capacity as a professional journalist

The major events of this century have been chronicled by professional journalists, both print and nonprint, who have been in the midst of the action, recording for us every detail of each event of major or minor significance. Theodore White is a journalist whose good fortune and sense of history have enabled him to be present at and active in many pivotal events of this century. His sense of the historically important has been the underlying force in the decisions that shaped his professional career. Over several decades, White has kept carefully written, detailed notes of the events he has witnessed and the conversations he has had in his capacity as a writer for various news media. He has a passion for detail, especially political detail, and a keen insight into the meaning of an event in human terms. Since his notes are made with an eye toward publication, they are greatly inclusive. His talent for colorful writing is evident not only in the present volume, but in the details which he chose to record so many years ago.

In Search of History is an autobiographical account of the historical events White witnessed from the 1930's through the 1960's. The book is organized chronologically into several major segments: his childhood, the years that he spent in China as a war correspondent, his European experiences, and his coverage of American presidential politics. Each of these major sections is written in the first person, but each is also prefaced with a third-person narration set in a different style of type to emphasize the shift. This device of stepping aside from the story line, though somewhat awkward, is effective in adding perspective through which the reader can adjust to the upcoming events.

White's fascination with history came about as part of his extraordinary educational background. His home life included discussion of current events and an emphasis on reading. He attended the Boston Public Latin School, a rigorously academic institution, instead of a neighborhood high school. In order to pay his transportation costs to and from the Latin School and to help with home expenses during the Depression, he sold newspapers on the streetcars. It was in this very practical arena that he first became aware that history as it was happening could sell newspapers, and that the more colorful the story being told, the more newspapers he could sell.

White attended Harvard on a scholarship, aided by a grant from the Burroughs Newsboys Foundation; after graduating *summa cum laude*, he was awarded a fellowship which gave him the opportunity to increase his knowledge through travel. He went to China to see at first hand the culture whose language and literature had been his university major.

The fellowship which provided him the money to get to China was not sufficient to allow him to remain there indefinitely without a job. Henry Luce of *Time* magazine needed a writer who could mail colorful background stories covering major events, which would be just as pertinent six weeks after mailing as when written. This assignment gave White the opportunity to use his knowledge of Chinese language and culture and to interview many important people in Asia during the years 1938-1945.

Some of these interviews, punctuated by deft, incisive descriptions of leaders both in their official capacities and at a more personal level, are printed in White's book. His description of Henry Luce, for example, includes such phrases as "Conversation with Luce . . . was like conversation with a vacuum cleaner." Such phrases capture the sense of urgency and the probing mind of the subject. Whether writing of Chou En-lai's "silken courtesy" or Dwight D. Eisenhower's "clean, hard prose," White describes personalities as much as persons.

One concept with which White grapples throughout the book is the image of America as the embodiment of goodness and virtue, a theme which he addresses frequently in his explanation of the American presence in Asia before World War II and in Europe during the postwar years. In each case, Americans felt that their expertise and money was needed if the civilization in question was to survive and if its valued elements were to flourish. In particular, White discusses American support of Chiang Kai-shek's Nationalist government. Since Chiang and most of his advisers were American-educated, and many were Christian, they received American support. However, because of Chiang's mismanagement and the resulting chaos as exemplified by the dreadful Honan famine, it was Mao Tse-tung's Communist party that held the trust of the Chinese people. Through his explication of these events, White clarifies for the modern reader the reason for Mao Tse-tung's success and the historic inevitability of the recognition of Communist China by the United States. In Europe during the years of the Marshall Plan, American Aid was administered, according to White, coextensively with the interests of the people and consequently was perceived as positive.

White had the opportunity during World War II in China, and after the war in Europe, to watch the activities of the local Communists in each area during active periods of development, and he draws particularly interesting conclusions from his observations. He contrasts the Europeans, who engaged in general terrorism as a way to convert the people forcibly to the desired point of view, with the Chinese Communists, whose terrorizing was more planned and directed less against the common people. The Communists in China were

offering the peasants an orderly government in the midst of the chaos left by
the Nationalists, while those in Europe were creating chaos in the midst of the
old order. As a free-lance writer, White covered the Marshall Plan in Europe
because he felt that the next important thrust of history would develop out of
the reconstruction of Europe and the economic, social, and military ground-
work that was being laid for the development of a European community.

During his stay in Paris, White met Dwight D. Eisenhower, who was in
Paris at this time because of his involvement in defense plans, and who was
also becoming a long-distance candidate for the Presidency of the United
States. Through this acquaintance, White became interested in Presidential
politics, and both Eisenhower and White came to realize that the future thrust
of world power would come from the office of the President. For that reason,
both returned home—one to run for office and one to write about it.

Although he does not dwell on it, White makes it plain that his early interest in socialism, in connection with his sympathetic understanding of the Chinese Communists, had combined in the early Cold War era to blacklist him as a
writer in the United States. His free-lance writing in Europe about something
as dry as the Marshall Plan was a way of wiping his journalistic slate clean. It
did not work completely, and his account of the difficulties he encountered
with the State Department during the McCarthy era is revealing.

The last section of the book deals with American politics, but it is far from
a rehashing of White's *The Making of the President* series. The account in this
volume concentrates more on the meaning of the events—partly, no doubt, a
function of time and distance promoting better perspective. It is this quest for
the overall meaning of his experiences over many decades and in so many
contexts that seems to have spurred White to write this book. He decides in his
conclusion that the Kennedy election and assassination mark the departure
from the old America to a new one, less in tune with the old American myths
of goodness and virtue and more attuned to the task of creating new ones to
take their places. He feels that the great Opportunity that had been the hallmark of the American dream and that delivered White himself from the Boston
ghetto to the seats of power had been enlarged by Kennedy and had redefined
America. The sudden removal of the guiding force for all of this change,
White claims, allowed various opportunists to scramble ahead in a frenzy that
covered the next ten years. One wonders, however, if White's sense of change
in American purpose ("his old ideas no longer stretched over the real world as
he saw and sensed it to be") might stem at least partially from his own growing older.

These are public reminiscences, and in the simplicity of hindsight they are
rather pat in the dovetailing of the early influences in the author's life and his
future interests in history and writing. What does come through, though, is
White's belief in himself, his confidence in his ability to achieve whatever he
strove for. Although White's personal journey from socialist ideals to Repub-

lican values is left unexplicated, he seems to find himself at the end of the volume liberal of mouth but conservative of heart. Hurt by the sight of his old neighborhood as an urban ruin, he seems angry and puzzled, suddenly aware that it takes more than high hopes to change people, that wishing will not make it so. He seems, as he ends the book, to grasp at the hope that through a further analysis of power, especially the political power wielded by our leaders, he can discover the patterns for solutions to our current problems and point the way for the future. There seems with this hope to be the promise of at least one more volume of memoirs, the next to concentrate on these patterns of American power.

Margaret S. Schoon

Sources for Further Study

Business Week. August 21, 1978, p. 8.

Commentary. LXVI, November, 1978, p. 74.

New Leader. LXI, October 23, 1978, p. 16.

New York Review of Books. XXV, November 9, 1978, p. 6.

Newsweek. XCII, August 14, 1978, p. 66.

INNOCENT ERÉNDIRA AND OTHER STORIES

Author: Gabriel García Márquez (1928-   )
Translated from the Spanish by Gregory Rabassa
Publisher: Harper & Row Publishers (New York). 183 pp. $8.95
Type of work: Short stories
Time: The present
Locale: Colombia and other unnamed places in Latin America

A collection of twelve short stories, written between 1948 and 1972, which trace the development of García Márquez as a writer of fiction

Colombian author Gabriel García Márquez is best known for his major novel, *One Hundred Years of Solitude*, first published in Spanish in 1967 and in Gregory Rabassa's English translation in 1970. Acclaimed as a work of extraordinary originality, the novel had an astounding impact on the world of fiction both in the Hispanic countries and in the United States. The title story of this collection and two other selections date from about the same period (1961-1972) and are quite reminiscent of *One Hundred Years of Solitude*. The other stories are interesting as evidence of the other styles and themes with which García Márquez experimented before 1960. Some of the stories are lovely, others are merely adequate, and at least one is disappointing. It is an uneven collection, but the effective selections are so very good that they justify the time that the reader will devote to gleaning the admirable from the not so admirable.

"The Incredible and Sad Tale of Innocent Eréndira and Her Heartless Grandmother" is the story of a child who accidentally knocks over a candle and burns down her grandmother's home. As retribution, she must sell her body to dozens of men each day for the rest of her life, or until she repays the damage done by the fire. The story seems to be a chapter lifted out of *One Hundred Years of Solitude*. In fact, the same thing does occur at one point in that novel, though the characters' names are different. There is a reference in "Innocent Eréndira" to the fact that she was traveling in the electoral campaign of Senator Onésimo Sánchez, and the story of the Senator appears in "Death Constant Beyond Love," written two years earlier. Mr. Herbert of "The Sea of Lost Time" (1961) is surely the same Mr. Herbert who shows up six years later in *One Hundred Years of Solitude*. All this is typical of what García Márquez has done in his work over the last twenty years. He has created a fictional world which is the subject matter of all his novels and stories, so that the same characters appear in different works, and the same strange physical and metaphysical phenomena occur in all these pieces of fiction.

Of course, this technique of creating a fictional reality that serves as the substance of more than one work is not unique to García Márquez. It was common in the work of the nineteenth century realistic novelists and, more recently, in the work of writers such as William Faulkner. It does pose a problem at times in García Márquez' fiction, however. Because of his unusual vision of reality, it is very obvious when he repeats himself. Tobías and Clotilde in "The Sea of Lost Time" spend their afternoons frolicking in bed, doing it "like earthworms, then like rabbits, and finally like turtles." This is amusing and gives a powerful impression of the personality of these characters, but it is so distinctive that the reader will surely remember that there are characters in *One Hundred Years of Solitude* who do exactly the same thing. In like manner, the characters' obsession with a smell of roses so palpable that Tobías could "pick it up in his hands and exhibit it" and Clotilde could brush it away like a cobweb is a phenomenon that occurs in several variations in the 1967 novel.

The problem of the repetitiveness of García Márquez' fiction has its source in the vastness of *One Hundred Years of Solitude*. It is an overwhelming work in which the author has perhaps exhausted the astounding view of reality that he created. Even though "Innocent Eréndira," "The Sea of Lost Time," and "Death Constant Beyond Love" tell stories that do not appear in the novel, the strange world of these stories is the same strange world of *One Hundred Years of Solitude*. It is a stark reality presented through the strong sensory perceptions of the characters. The dialogue is scant, as almost everything comes from the omniscient narrator who communicates the characters' vision of a metaphysical universe in which all things are possible. Thus, when Ulises stabs Eréndira's grandmother, her blood spurts out oily, shiny, and green, "just like mint honey," and covers him with "living matter that seemed to be flowing from his fingers" as he tries to wipe it away from his face. The dying Senator Sánchez fashions a butterfly from paper, which flutters about the room, is transformed into a lithograph, and then remains painted indelibly on the wall. The characters participate fully in this unusual reality, accepting it as normal. It is, in fact, a reflection of their hidden instincts and desires. Thus, the actions of these characters are just as marvelous and strange as their surroundings. The senator's newfound love, Laura Farina, her skin disturbed by a "glacial sweat," surrenders the key to her iron-padlocked chastity belt in exchange for a favor for her father, and the senator buries his face in her "woods-animal armpit," giving in to terror and weeping with rage at dying without her.

These are the techniques of literary realism—a wealth of exact detail, a predominance of description, and a thorough analysis of the motivation for the characters' behavior. García Márquez' fiction differs from the realistic novels of the nineteenth century, however, in that the reality of his novels and stories is characterized by remarkable magical qualities. For this reason, García Márquez is recognized as a leader of the Latin-American literary movement, Magical Realism (*realismo mágico*).

Therein lies the problem. The realistic novelist repeats himself constantly as he deals with the everyday, normal world familiar to his readers. No one notices because that world is ordinary and unsurprising. The "magical realist" cannot do the same thing; his world is too surprising and too unfamiliar. Of course, there is a justification for this repetition. If the world really is this way for these characters, it is entirely logical that their perceptions of this would be repetitive. Yet, because the readers surely do not see reality in these terms, the frequent duplication of unusual perceptions does not work very well.

In spite of this major limitation, these three stories are very effective. "Death Constant Beyond Love" is by far the finest of the entire collection. It is a precise, imaginative presentation of the death experience of a man who has spent his life in the self-imposed isolation of a political career.

There are nine stories written during the early period, 1947-1953. One of these, "The Woman Who Came at Six O'Clock" (1950), is different in tone and substance from all the other selections. It is a realistic dialogue between a bartender and a prostitute looking for an alibi to cover up a murder that she has just committed. García Márquez is not successful when he chooses this approach to the creation of fictional reality—his talent lies elsewhere. The other selections in this book reveal how innovative and imaginative he can be when he stays within the limits of the kind of fiction for which he has become famous.

The theme of death dominates the early stories. The first-person narrator of "The Third Resignation" (1947) is facing the moment when he will be "truly dead, or at least, inappreciably alive" after eighteen years in his coffin. The narrator of "Someone Has Been Disarranging These Roses" (1953) is a dead boy who stays in his chair in the corner while his childhood friend—the girl who was with him when he died—tends the roses on an altar in his room. Eva, of "Eva Is Inside Her Cat" (1948), is losing her beauty and craves an orange while thinking of the dead boy under the orange tree. She searches for her cat to inhabit its body and thus pass over into the strange, unknown world where all dimensions are eliminated. Finding everything turned to arsenic, she realizes that three thousand years have passed since she first decided to look for the cat. The twin whose brother has died in "The Other Side of Death" (1948) lives "between that noble surface of dreams and realities" and finds that the independence gained through the death of his twin is nullified by the decay of his own body. The old woman of "Bitterness for Three Sleepwalkers" (1949) loses her "natural faculty of being present" and wills the elimination of her vital functions, ending herself sense by sense.

Sense by sense: this is an important note to the fiction of García Márquez. His most notable achievement, evident in all his writing from 1949 to the present, is his use of forceful metaphoric language in which the metaphors are consistently sensorial. When one of his characters goes about carrying an "unexpected shadow in profile to her body" and giving off anguished shouts that have "a lot of remembered tree and deep river about them," the reader gains an impression of thorough knowledge of that character's interior state. At the same moment, the reader may know that these metaphors add up to a kind of nonsense. Often, it is indeed nonsense in the context of what one character calls "the other world, . . . the mistaken and absurd world of rational creatures." At other times, the metaphors are clear and delightful. In "Dialogue with the Mirror" (1949), the character who struggles with the opposing forces of the rational and the aesthetic smells breakfast cooking and senses that "a large dog had begun to wag its tail inside his soul." The man on "The Other Side of Death" feels death begin to flow through his bones "like a river of ashes."

Through this metaphorical language, García Márquez constructs an unusual universe dominated by perceptions which distort and remold reality according to a heritage of folklore, tradition, and myth passed down through generations to these characters. This process is clearest in *One Hundred Years of Solitude* and the stories of that period.

The earlier stories do not have the force of the writings of 1968-1972. Although some, such as "Bitterness for Three Sleepwalkers," are very good, they tend to be "set pieces" which seem to lack a context. It is as if they were wrested from some larger work which, given intact, would make them clear and firm.

Gilbert Smith

Sources for Further Study

Atlantic. CCXLII, August, 1978, p. 84.
Business Week. July 30, 1978, p. 13.
New Republic. CLXXIX, August 26, 1978, p. 44.
New York Review of Books. XXV, October 12, 1978, p. 61.
Time. CXII, July 10, 1978, p. 81.

INVENTING AMERICA
Jefferson's Declaration of Independence

Author: Garry Wills
Publisher: Doubleday & Company (Garden City, New York). 398 pp. $10.00
Type of work: History
Time: The 1770's
Locale: America on the eve of independence

A controversial analysis of the ideological influences upon Thomas Jefferson as he fashioned the Declaration of Independence within the context of the Enlightenment theories of the time

> *Principal personages:*
> THOMAS JEFFERSON, Virginia lawyer and author of the Declaration of Independence
> JOHN LOCKE, English Enlightenment *philosophe*
> FRANCIS HUTCHESON,
> THOMAS REID, and
> DAVID HUME, Scottish Enlightenment *philosophes*

Gary Wills has been a fairly active author over the past few years if one considers his *Nixon Agonistes*, random articles, and now this work on Thomas Jefferson and the Declaration of Independence. While Wills has earned something of a reputation for promoting novel viewpoints, this most recent work may be his most noteworthy endeavor.

One of the more significant assests of *Inventing America*—and there are several—lies in its invitation to see the Declaration of Independence within the context of its time. It would appear that Wills is particularly concerned that documents such as Jefferson's Declaration of Independence have become merely historical monuments to be revered but not necessarily appreciated for intent. As such, Wills attempts here to ferret out not only Jefferson's essential influences in writing the document, but also his creative purpose. While considerable controversy may be stirred by Wills's conclusions, his willingness to analyze the contents is admirable.

In many respects, the Declaration of Independence can best be viewed as a product of the Enlightenment. The document was shaped for a new and emerging society that vastly contradicted the major thrust of Western civilization by the 1700's. Prior to that time, much of the Western world had functioned along classic conservative lines which espoused the doctrine of "collective man." The underpinnings of the Western world had been the existence of a social hierarchy built by birthright, primogeniture, the dynastic principle, and the acceptance of one's fate as "God's Will." With this social hierarchy had come divine right absolute monarchies (particularly on the continent of Europe), state-supported (or at least favored) churches, an economic system which primarily served the interest of the state, and the nation-state itself. Under such a format, the individual in society was felt to have duties and obligations but not necessarily rights and privileges. The individual's talents, ambitions, and creativity were subservient to the loyalties one must show to crown, church, and nation.

The Enlightenment *philosophes* were essentially a reaction against such an order. Through scientific observation and the use of rational logic, they dissected society by the usage of no more an elaborate yardstick than nature. To Enlightenment thinkers, nature manifested the inherent perfection of the universe, and, as such, was the logical device whereby the value of any manmade structure could be measured. In short, the more "natural" a component of society proved to be, the greater evidence of its worth. For the *philosophes*, artificiality was not only the antithesis of perfection, but a virtual indictment, and nature dictated a substantial reexamination of society and its accepted systems. Such examination revealed to the *philosophes* a considerable deviation from nature and invited them to fashion a viable alternative.

That alternative turned out to be classic liberalism, although during the 1700's it was largely a theory built upon what the *philosophes* felt *ought* to be rather than what actually existed. Grounded in the notion that, on nature's terms at least, all men are created equal, classic liberalism reversed society's emphasis upon the good of the whole. In its place came the celebration of the individual as being endowed with tremendous capacities for self-development.

To the proponents of classic liberalism, each individual had the natural right to realize his potential. Furthermore, it was considered to be the highest responsibility of government to insure that this right was not infringed upon. Beyond this, however, nature guaranteed very little. The natural interaction of men and their environment would determine a "meritocracy," and those who failed to achieve would, in effect, have no one to blame but themselves.

Of course, the Enlightenment's promotion of the individual in keeping with nature's dictates was in no way an espousal of democracy. The *philosophes* saw in democracy an artificial, mass-oriented ideology which once again assured the public of influence which had not been earned. While democracy certainly was more humanitarian in its concern for the general public than classic conservativism, the *philosophes* felt that both ideologies suffered from a similar artificiality of guaranteed determinations.

In certain respects, one might say that Thomas Jefferson was the closest figure America had to the Enlightenment *philosophes* of Europe. His familiarity with Enlightenment concepts was evident in many areas, including his vision of a governmental form limited in its socioeconomic role. More particularly, Jefferson's Enlightenment ideals become evident in his primary justification for Americans seeking independence: the belief that Britain had violated the "natural rights" of Americans.

What distinguishes Jefferson from the purely liberal *philosophes* of the Enlightenment are his democratic impulses. He did not suffer from the same reservations concerning the masses of society that plagued the liberal intellects of France and England. It was Jefferson's perspective, perhaps aided by the potential possibilities of the American physical landscape, that saw the inherent weakness in classic liberalism. The liability can be summarized by the question of what is to be done with the losers. Even under an atmosphere in which classic liberalism prospers, there would remain a permanent segment of the society to whom nature would be less than kind.

Wills can be commended for his attention to those more democratic ideas of Jefferson which surfaced in his rough drafts of the original Declaration of Independence, but fell short in the chambers of practical politics. Wills is not particularly concerned here with the Declaration of Independence as a vehicle for justifying independence from Britain. Rather, the author's intention is to come to grips with what actually amounts to three documents: Jefferson's original undeleted version, the more practical and genuine Congressional form, and the "symbolic" document which lives today as an ideal of the American political culture.

Understandably, Wills points to Jefferson's original draft as the version most revealing of Jefferson's own creativity. That this Declaration of Independence is periodically at variance with the ideological thrust of John Locke and the classic liberal Enlightenment is not only unsurprising, but implicit evidence for its being edited by the tamer minds of the Continental Congress.

What *is* surprising is Wills's dismay at the Declaration of Independence in its present form: a mere statuesque symbol which Americans revere as a cherished component of our heritage rather than as a practical guide to political reality. That American citizens are not accustomed to analyzing the Declaration of Independence for its political intent may be regrettable, but it is hardly a revelation to anyone even remotely observant of American political culture. Studies have long indicated Americans to be among the lowest in Western democratic societies in terms of voter turnout and familiarity with political and governmental species; at best, they are often merely tolerant of politics as a necessary evil.

More valuable, however, is Wills's invitation to treat the Declaration of Independence as a concrete entity rather than as an unapproachable political Ten Commandments. To see the document put on public display for altar worship as was the case during the Red Scare of 1919-1921, is, in Wills's mind, detrimental to its greater worth as a signpost for American society. While a case can be made, as the author does, for the influence of Scottish *philosophes* upon Jefferson's thinking, the larger point may be missed. Wills seems intent upon dismantling the Declaration of Independence for analysis, and he becomes, in the process, something of a political mechanic anxious to discover what makes the system tick. His findings have led to the rationale for this book, but he may have hampered his larger goal by diffusing the honored veneer of the document itself.

Terry Alan Baney

Sources for Further Study

Best Sellers. XXXVIII, November, 1978, p. 259.
Commonweal. CV, October 27, 1978, p. 691.
New Republic. CLXXIX, August 26, 1978, p. 32.
Saturday Review. V, August, 1978, p. 42.
Time. CXII, July 31, 1978, p. 78.

JANUS: A SUMMING UP

Author: Arthur Koestler (1905-   )
Publisher: Random House (New York). 354 pp. $10.00; paperback $3.95
Type of work: Essays

A synthesizing condensation of the author's past three decades of writings on mentation, paranormal experience, biology, psychology, and creativity

In *Janus: A Summing Up*, Arthur Koestler successfully distills the past three decades of his writings on mind, paranormal experience, biology, psychology, and creativity. Because Koestler, now well into his seventies, is a Renaissance man—novelist, political journalist, philosopher, and in *Janus* an essayist bent on correlating a humanistic view of man with the empirical data of the life and physical sciences—*Janus* is able to contain coherently many diverse worlds. Moreover, Koestler incorporates these diverse materials within a General Systems Theory that encompasses all phenomena. This theory posits open systems of hierarchical levels of organization, rather like a branching tree which at each level allows a certain degree of autonomy, or wholeness, even while each level is constrained by being part of a greater whole. Koestler's metasystem thus provides the reader with a rare vision of the possible interconnectedness not only among the sciences, but also between the two cultures.

Given Koestler's productivity and range over the past thirty years (some twenty books and numerous essays), the task of *Janus* seems superhuman. A brief description of the major works synopsized here makes this clear: "The Yogi and the Commissar" (1944) focuses on free will and determinism; *Insight and Outlook* (1948) on hierarchical organizational principles that interrelate science, art, and social ethics; *Trail of the Dinosaur* (1955) on the possible extinction of humanity; *The Sleepwalkers* (1959) on the creative process of scientific geniuses such as Kepler and Brahe; *The Lotus and the Robot* (1961) on the paradox of self-transcendence; *The Act of Creation* (1964) on the positive freedom of creativity; *The Ghost in the Machine* (1967) and *Beyond Reductionism* (1969, Editor with J. R. Smythies of papers from The Alpbach Symposium) on the fallacies of biological and psychological reductionism; *The Case of the Midwife Toad* (1971) on the possibilities of Lamarckian biology; *The Roots of Coincidence* (1972) and *The Heel of Achilles* (1974) on the correspondence of paranormal experience and quantum physics.

Yet Koestler makes this mixture cohere, first, because he, like such comparable interdisciplinary writers as C. P. Snow or Robert Ardrey, has a sure grasp on science, and second, because all his diverse writings can be seen as variations upon a single theme—that of free will *versus* determinism. One of *Janus'* main contributions is that it makes explicit how Koestler's holistic systems theory resolves this central problem of freedom.

Here is the way the system works. According to Koestler, our empirical experience with the laws of nature suggests that all phenomena, be they psychological, social, biological, linguistic, electrical, or even inorganic, can be seen as tiered systems, or "holarchies." These holarchies are composed of interrelating systems whose levels of organizations, or "holons," increase in complexity: atom, molecule, organelle, cell, tissue, organs, and so on. Moreover, each level has its own governing principles: the atom operates differently from the molecule, the molecule differently from the organelle. Thus each level, or holon, is partially free because it obeys its own laws, while at the same time, it is subordinate to and determined by the larger system of which it is a part. Like Janus, the double-headed god, the holons have dual natures; they look both outward and inward. Although the laws of the higher level cannot be reduced to, nor derived from, the lower levels, nevertheless the phenomena of the lower level and their principles are implied in the higher level. Thus the freedom of each holon inheres in the new values and relationships not present in the lower level. The destiny of the holon, however, depends on the laws of the superior level, laws which the holon cannot predict and which to it must appear inexplicable. The holon, man, experiences his greatest freedom in the subjective experience of free choice which, even as it is free, is likewise limited by the greater wholes—biological, social, symbolic—to which man belongs.

Likewise, Koestler's concept of the dual nature of all living organisms can be seen as a partial solution to his concern with freedom. At every level, a living organism exhibits two contrary tendencies: the tendency towards self-assertion accounts for the holon's conservatism and individualism; on the other hand, the tendency towards self-transcendence, or integration, accounts for the holon's urge to be part of something greater than itself. Surprisingly enough, it is man's self-transcendent tendency which, according to Koestler, not only accounts for his creativity, but also for his destructiveness. It is man's need to devote himself to something greater than himself—an ideal, a faith, a demagogue—that results in the bloodshed and carnage distinguishing human history. It seems strange that Koestler lays war at the feet of the patriotic or conscripted foot soldier instead of at the head of Atilla or Hitler. Yet his theory would seem to be upheld by Stanley Milgram's well-known experiments on obedience and authority.

Koestler's views on man's inhumanity to man are provocative, yet unfortunately *Janus* offers only a feeble solution. The basic reason for man's predicament, argues Koestler, is that man is a biological mistake. That is, his new brain, the neocortex or reasonable "thinking cap," is merely overlaid or superimposed upon an older brain. This older brain, composed of reptilian and mammalian infrastructures, governs our passions and instincts. But because the vertical neural pathways between these two brains are inadequate, reason is often unable to control passions, and thus the organism works against itself. For this problem, as old at least as Plato, Koestler proffers a kind of *deus ex chemia*: he says science must discover a drug that will enlarge the brain's pathways and thus give more control to man's new brain.

Koestler offers no better solutions when he misapplies physical laws to biological or psychological data. For example, he uses the Law of Complementarity, which asserts that all elementary particles have dual natures of corpuscles and waves, to explain the holon's self-assertive (corpuscular) tendency and its self-transcendent (wave) tendency. Unfortunately, such explanation confuses more than it clarifies. In like manner, Koestler's transference of Werner Heisenberg's Principle of Indeterminancy to paranormal phenomena seems untenable. This principle, we recall, asserts that if a physicist accurately determines the velocity of a particle (which is simultaneously a corpuscle and a wave), he will be unable to fix its location, and vice versa. Koestler holds that there is a fundamental analogy between the inexplicable way paranormal phenomena operate, and between the behavior of quantum particles; neither can be comprehended by the usual laws of space, time, or causality. Five years ago, interest in QM as a basis for psi was so widespread that Koestler himself instigated and convened an important international conference of physicists and psychologists interested in psychical experience. Today, however, more and more physicists are quick to disclaim any association with investigations into paranormal realms.

More enduring, surely, are Koestler's insights on biology and psychology. Here his refutations of reductionism, as well as his application of the General Systems Theory to the life sciences, prove genuinely illuminating. Koestler is a lively controversialist. He argues against the neo-Darwinian (Darwin, amended by the geneticists) biologists' view that evolution, and thus man, is "nothing but" random mutations. He cites Waddington's well-known analogy that this is like hoping that by throwing bricks together in heaps, we should eventually be able to choose ourselves the most desirable house. While Koestler admits that the principle of natural selection works "like a weed killer" to eliminate unfavorable mutants (and most mutations are such), he asserts that it does not explain the emergence of new plant species. A favorable mutation such as the lens of an eye, for example, requires numerous other organic systems such as the retina, ciliary muscles, and so on, in order to function. The chances of there being simultaneous mutations in all these necessary ancillary systems is beyond an astronomical chance. Koestler confides that it is a well-known fact among biologists that neo-Darwinism is no longer a tenable theory. In its place, Koestler of course proposes his own holistic hierarchic system that allows for a kind of purposiveness, or inner direction (freedom), in evolution. According to the eminent biologist, W. H. Thorpe, although Koestler's views are controversial, recent developments in scientific knowledge tend to confirm them.

Just as the body of Koestler's insights on biology are valid, so are his views on psychology. Again, he convincingly attacks the reductionists—here the Behaviorists—who hold that learning is "nothing but" the differential reinforcement of random responses (that is, the learned behavior of boxed pigeons or rats who happen upon the right food lever). Moreover, he points up the absurdity of behaviorists consciously denying that there is such a thing as consciousness. Instead, Koestler asserts, psychologists need to study what distinguishes human beings from pigeons, not just how we are alike. Koestler suggests that new laws, new values obtain at every level of hierarchical organization; perhaps life, consciousness, language are such new laws.

Perhaps, too, creativity is such a new law, or freedom. Set within his critique on behaviorism and his definition of consciousness is Koestler's most positive statement on human freedom—his analysis of creativity. First proposed in *Insight and Outlook* (1948) and fleshed out in *The Act of Creation* (1964), this provocative and sometimes perplexing theory of the creative act posits another Janus-headed holon. Its cornerstone in the general systems theory is bisociation, or double vision, wherein we view two self-consistent but incompatible levels of organization simultaneously. Creativeness, then, arises, from the comparison of two hitherto unrelated ideas, or value systems. Humor, by its surprising juxtaposition of two unlike systems, elicits a physiological response—"Ha!" Scientific creation overlaps two unlike systems and thereby creates a new concept, eliciting an "Aha!" And finally, artistic creation systhesizes two overlapping patterns and thereupon evokes an "Ah!" Furthermore, creativity in both science and art is analogous in that each is engendered by a regression from the more rational areas back into the more primitive, nonverbal levels of ideation. This regression, or undoing, is then followed by a leap forward, but in a new direction. In fact, Koestler asserts that this creative undoing-redoing pattern runs as a *leitmotif* through biological evolution (as paedomorphosis, or juvenilization, which allows a species to retrace its steps by dropping off an adult stage), through the revolutionary turning-points in science and art, to the archetypal monomyths of death-and-resurrection, withdrawal-and-return, that structure all mythologies.

Final assessment of such a sweeping, all-inclusive vision as *Janus* presents is hazardous. Science is more fickle than art. If physicists currently deplore Koestler's mysticism, they applauded it a few years ago; if biologists are abandoning neo-Darwinism, they are doing it quietly. We will have to wait and see if, as Koestler asserts, evolution is a game of fixed rules and flexible strategies. Indeed, Koestler's ultimate gift, as presented in *Janus*, may not be his theory of holarchies, his analogies among diverse systems, but rather his evidencing of the creative tendency itself—his own curiosity, his openness to varied ideas, his wonder and awe at the mystery, beauty, and order of the universe. Koestler has said, "A true science of life must let infinity in and never lose sight of it." In *Janus: A Summing Up*, he shares this glimpse with the reader; it is a rare gift and we are grateful for it.

Shirley F. Staton

Sources for Further Study

America. CXXXVIII, July 3, 1978, p. 451.
Economist. CCLXVI, March 4, 1978, p. 107.
Library Journal. CIII, April 15, 1978, p. 878.
Nation. CCXXVI, May 6, 1978, p. 547.
New Republic. CLXXVIII, May 13, 1978, p. 34.
New York Times Book Review. April 2, 1978, p. 9.

JEFFERSON AND THE PRESIDENCY
Leadership in the Young Republic

Author: Robert M. Johnstone, Jr.
Publisher: Cornell University Press (Ithaca, New York). 332 pp. $15.00
Type of work: History and political science
Time: 1801-1809
Locale: The United States

A political analysis of the Jefferson presidency with emphasis upon the leadership role and performance of Jefferson within the confines of legal restraints and the political culture

        Principal personages:
        THOMAS JEFFERSON, third President of the United States
        JAMES MADISON, fourth President of the United States
        JOHN MARSHALL, Chief Justice of the United States Supreme Court
        ALBERT GALLATIN, Secretary of the Treasury

Robert M. Johnstone notes in his acknowledgments to this fine text an indebtedness to the late Clinton Rossiter for his varied conceptual assistance on the topic of the presidency. Clearly, Johnstone could have no finer mentor on the executive branch than Rossiter, who is widely regarded to be among a mere handful of premier authorities on the subject. Yet it is also curious to note that Johnstone implies that Rossiter may have had some reservations about the conclusions and perspectives that are put forth in *Jefferson and the Presidency*; and, although Johnstone does not elaborate on the particulars of Rossiter's remarks, one can speculate as to their nature.

One of the more controversial features of this work is the use of leadership analysis models fashioned originally by Richard Neustadt in his classic, *Presidential Power* (1964). Neustadt, a considerable authority on the presidency, offered a framework for ascertaining the relative level of success or failure of presidents in terms of their ability to govern within the context of altering political situations. The Neustadt model, however, was clearly designed to study the performance of presidential leadership during more contemporary times. In particular, the emphasis was upon the twentieth century figures traditionally looked upon as vanguard personalities in the rise of what Arthur Schlesinger, Jr., has termed "the Imperial Presidency." To suggest that such a model might also be applied to the presidents of the nineteenth century may not have been in keeping with Neustadt's intent. Yet this is, in fact, the thrust of Robert Johnstone's study of Thomas Jefferson.

Johnstone himself acknowledges that his approach may be subject to some immediate speculation, but he nevertheless feels that the application can be a valid method for analyzing policy decision-making as it relates to the use of executive authority. Beyond this, the author builds a strong case for focusing a greater degree of attention upon the role of individuals in such leadership situations—a focus which Johnstone suggests has been largely absent until only recently. The argument put forth in this text is that, because of a conceptual perspective which centers upon the context of events or the flow of society, historians have traditionally felt less inclined to view the individual personality as a critical element in governance. In fact, Johnstone goes so far as to imply that such an approach among American historians may be due to a cultural bias which honors, however unconsciously, the mass-oriented notions of democracy at the expense of dominant personalities.

The figure of Thomas Jefferson and his presidency was by no means a random historical selection on the author's part. Johnstone is blunt in his view that Jefferson was a primary element in the creation of presidential leadership more traditionally associated with the expansive presidency of Theodore Roosevelt. He portrays Jefferson as the presidential pioneer of the chief executive as "power broker," willing to cultivate and promote influence beyond the confines of precedent and constitutional legitimacy.

Johnstone divides his work into three segments which survey the nature of executive leadership, its context in relation to party, the press, and the other branches of the Federal government, and, finally, the limits which can occasionally curtail such executive performance. With Jefferson as the executive in question, Johnstone pursues his analysis from the basis of Neustadt's own central measurement theme: how is an executive to become an authority in fact as well as in name? That such a dilemma may very well have plagued leaders throughout antiquity offers Johnstone a key rationale for the validity of this study. Although the use of a contemporary model in the analysis of a noncontemporary leader may raise criticisms, the perplexities of effective leadership transcend any time barriers. As such, while the cosmetics of Jefferson's presidency may offer little resemblance to those of modern chief executives, the inherent nature of the leadership role has altered only superficially. The use of the Neustadt "bargaining" model for role analysis therefore becomes a mere device for gauging the effectiveness of that leadership.

To some degree, one might note that the use of such role analysis models suggests a debt to social psychology as much as history or political science *per se*. The model in question deals in the realms of situation variables and the perceived attitudes, assumptions, and expectations of the involved actors in any given environment. In keeping with such concepts, Johnstone approaches the nature of Jefferson's presidential leadership from the point of view of "role-set"; that is, Jefferson's ability to exert a meaningful leadership and a decisive influence upon policies in keeping with the shifting variables. It is the author's contention that the key ingredient in Jefferson's creative leadership role was his uncanny ability to place himself in the vanguard of party, public, and official opinions and expectations.

While Johnstone clearly feels that the use of such yardsticks as measurement tools in the analysis of presidential leadership has merit, he is also aware of the liabilities. An overly scientific or structural approach to the leadership style of any president may run the risk of dehumanizing the individual in question, resulting in an emotionless, formal portrait. The use of such a model may provide genuine insight into the manner in which leadership is exerted, but it may be immune to the equally revealing factor of motivation. Were man a purely rational animal, the availability of character profiles might offer the necessary input to answer the question, "Why did he do it?" And, despite the presence of generalized theories of behavior, there remains a paucity of models for studying motivation in terms of individual leadership.

Such problems would appear to at least subconsciously prey upon the author as he presents his analysis of Jefferson. And while Johnstone feels confident that his use of Neustadt's model allows for consideration of the uniqueness of each president and his environment, the absence of a solid technique for ascertaining motivation keeps Johnstone's book shy of being a breakthrough. In place of such a device, Johnstone suggests that such personality traits as desire and the capacity of leadership will have to suffice as admittedly nebulous variables.

As history, Johnstone's work here is not intended to be especially enlightening so far as factual content is concerned. The factual particulars regarding such covered topics as the Yazoo land claims dispute and the Embargo of 1808-1809 remain familiar to students of the Jeffersonian period. In addition, one could also safely add that it does not appear to be the author's intention to praise unduly or diffuse the figure of Jefferson as president. Rather, Johnstone prefers to offer Thomas Jefferson as a case study in the analysis of executive leadership beyond the limitations of legal grants or restrictions of power. Johnstone sets Jefferson in the position of attempting to come to grips with the problem of providing effective leadership that can bridge the constitutional barriers between the three branches of the federal government. That such a performance by a president, particularly one who took office in 1801, should be a standard by which leadership talents are measured may be a matter of some debate. Yet Jefferson's ability to conduct himself and the course of national affairs by meeting this challenge suggests to Johnstone that Jefferson was not only a viable leader, but a standard-builder by which future executives would be measured.

The critical factor of individual performance in a leadership role is underlined by Johnstone's attention on the Embargo crisis which closed Jefferson's presidency on a decidedly sour note. The issue is offered here not only as an illustration of the limits of executive rule which even a Jefferson could not consistently manipulate, but also as an indication that subsequent executives faced with inherited problems may or may not offer similar leadership capabilities. While James Madison is not a central character in this study, the specter of his offering an entirely new set of variables looms over the Embargo issue.

Although the nature of Robert Johnstone's approach to *Jefferson and the*

Presidency may stir debate, it is a fascinating look at the role-performance of one of the United States's most dynamic chief executives. It should also be noted that scholars would do well to emulate the amazing readability of Johnstone's style. Clearly, the author has perfected a writing talent which ought to insure that this work be absorbed by students and scholars from a broad spectrum. Anyone interested in the presidential years of Thomas Jefferson, as well as the nature of executive leadership, should find *Jefferson and the Presidency* stimulating.

Terry Alan Baney

Sources for Further Study

Choice. XV, October, 1978, p. 80.
Library Journal. CIII, April 1, 1978, p. 747.

JOURNEY TO THE SKY

Author: Jamake Highwater
Publisher: Thomas Y. Crowell (New York). Illustrated. 242 pp. $9.95
Type of work: Novel
Time: The mid-1800's
Locale: Central America, the United States, England

A novelization of the true adventures of John Lloyd Stephens and Frederick Catherwood as they search for the lost Mayan cities in the jungles of Central America

Principal characters:
> JOHN LLOYD STEPHENS, a lawyer and explorer who rediscovers the Mayan ruins
> FREDERICK CATHERWOOD, an artist and fellow explorer who rediscovers the Mayan ruins
> AUGUSTIN, the valet and overseer of the explorers' expeditions into Central America
> THE MULESKINNER, an insolent workman who handles the mules on the expeditions
> MARTIN VAN BUREN, President of the United States
> FRANCISCO MORAZAN, President of the Central American Federation
> RAFAEL CARRERA, Indian conservative leader who opposes Morazan's right to control of Central America

Jamake Highwater has enriched the reading public in the past with his penetrating looks into the cultural makeup of the Indian American. His last work, *Anpao: An American Indian Odyssey*, was honored with the 1978 Newbery Honor Award. Highwater, being of Blackfoot and Cherokee heritage, has energetically taken on the task of putting to the page the rich traditions of the First Americans. His previous works have explored the topics of Indian painting, dance, and music—all elements of the ceremonial experience that form the sacred for the various tribal nations. A storyteller in the best sense of the term, Highwater weaves tales that are as economical and colorful as Indian blankets. As he discards any excess material, especially any words that are unable to complete the desired pattern, the author escorts the reader between towering cliffs on an anguished trail that leads to wisdom. This is evident in his work, *Anpao*, which is a collection of Indian folklore tied together by the author's insertion of Anpao as the central character who searches for his place in the universe. The individual Indian and his relationship to tribe and fertile Earth are themes dealt with in *Anpao* and the rest of Highwater's canon. A mythical quality runs through his writings, rustling the trees, riding on the wind, and carrying the weary Indian back to his roots, where he can be one with Mother Earth; and the reader follows inquisitively and faithfully.

Jamake Highwater has in his latest entry, *Journey to the Sky*, brought together linked elements that are sure to lure the reader. The idea of high adventure, discovering a lost civilization, and the heroic efforts of the central characters, all pull the reader into the story until the journey is completed and glory has been justly awarded. *Journey to the Sky* is a novelized version not only of the actual adventures of John Lloyd Stephens and Frederick Catherwood as they penetrate the jungles of Central America on a diplomatic mission for the United States, but also of their search for the rumored lost cities of an ancient civilization. What they stumble upon is the world of the Mayas, a civilization which once flourished within the area of what is now known as Guatemala, Honduras, Chiapas, and Yucatan. The Mayas had reached their zenith between A.D. 250 and 900, after having commenced around 600 B.C. Eventually they were conquered by the Spanish, though their way of life had long since begun to deteriorate. Their great cities had been left deserted; this episode is still a matter of speculation. It could have been due to failing crops or an outbreak of disease. The jungle reclaimed the cleared land and overtook the structures until they were almost unrecognizable. At the height of their civilization, the Mayans surpassed all the peoples of the Americas in their knowledge of astronomy and mathematics as well as in the complexity of their calendar. They were able to make accurate observations of the heavenly bodies, independently come up with the concept of zero, and devise a writing system that was partly phonetic. When the Spanish arrived in the sixteenth century, they were befuddled by the half-hidden cities, deserted and crumbling, yet still possessing a magnificence. Even with the chains of the jungle stretched across the ruins, the elegance pushed them toward the sky and the viewer gazed at them in awe.

John Lloyd Stephens is considered the author of the finest travel record in American literature. He was sent by President Martin Van Buren on a diplomatic mission to the newly formed and unstable United Provinces of Central America. Between the years 1839 and 1842, he and his close friend and fellow adventurer, Frederick Catherwood, explored, tracked down government officials, and rediscovered the Mayan ruins of Central America. Stephens kept a journal—a vibrant narrative—of the entire experience. The publication of this journal, *Incidents of Travel in Central America, Chiapas, and Yucatan*, startled the reading public back in the United States; the bizarre and incongruous nature of what the explorers found sparked interest in Central America. Both Stephens and Catherwood were young and came from relatively wealthy families. Stephens was an attorney in New York when he received his assignment from the President; Catherwood was an English artist and architect.

At the time of the assignment, Central America was in the midst of bloody turmoil; it was unclear who had legitimate control of the United Provinces of Central America. A guerrilla war was taking place and skirmishes were common, making it highly dangerous for the two adventurers; they had to be careful not to antagonize either of the warring factions. It was nevertheless Stephens' duty to locate the rightful head of state and report back to Washington on the situation as he found it. Francisco Morazan, a liberal who wished to institute reforms, had been elected President of the Central American Federation and was recognized by North America, Great Britain, and France as the rightful authority. But Morazan's reforms aggravated the local Catholic clergy, which eventually sent ripples back to King Ferdinand of Spain and the Pope. Both refused to recognize Morazan as President, thus leading to the rise of Rafael Carrera, an Indian conservative. Carrera and his guerrillas marched against the Federation, and a full-scale civil war was under way by the time Stephens and Catherwood set foot inside the area. Five provinces had been set up after the separation from Mexico in 1823, and the fight for their control had commenced. There was the reform-minded Morazan on one side, and conservative, Catholic-backed Carrera on the other; in addition, there were a number of would-be generals ransacking the countryside for their own profit.

Even though they were in the area on government business, Stephens and Catherwood wished to search out the ruins they had read about in an old report written by Colonel Juan Galindo. But it is Stephens' own report of the ruins that is of note, for it was lively and historically significant. The first excursion, which took ten months, put the two men in contact with untrustworthy military officials and confusing political winds; thus, Stephens was led to conclude that the area would not soon see stability. His descriptions of the Mayan ruins form the bulk of his narrative; of particular note are his portrait of Copan, in the forests of northern Honduras, and his feelings for the people who must have constructed such a place:

> No remnant of this race hangs around the ruins, with traditions handed down from father to son and from generation to generation. It lay before us like a shattered ark in the midst of the ocean, her masts gone, her name effaced, her crew perished, and none to tell whence she came, to whom she belonged, how long on her voyage, or what caused her destruction—her lost people to be traced only by some fancied resemblance in the construction of the vessel, and, perhaps, never to be known at all.

Jamake Highwater's own style of writing is as straightforward, crisp, and weeded of unnecessary debris as is Stephens' narrative. Highwater has picked up Stephens' banner and carries it proudly so as to give the modern reader a feeling for the actuality of the adventure and its significance to the peoples of the Americas. The story moves forward unencumbered by distracting interjections. The words chosen facilitate the continuance of the journey. The jungle is presented as torturous, with insufferable humidity and insects that eat away at the flesh and spirit of the uninitiated white man. The magnificence of the Mayan world—or, at least, what can be imagined—seems to make the journey more than worthwhile. Though stymied by the political upheaval, impeded by fear, warfare, and local mistrust, the vision of this lost civilization keeps the explorers going. The reader senses the frustration, the plodding nature of discovery, the false trails, the surly and incompetent help, and the deteriorating health of both Stephens and Catherwood.

In researching for this novel, Highwater took three years to delve into the world of the Maya, journeying himself to Honduras, Guatemala, and Yucatan to retrace the steps of Stephens and Catherwood by plane, jeep, mule, and foot. He did his best to make the journey his own. This dedication on the author's part makes the novel seem all the more authentic, a truly bountiful helping of harrowing adventure.

The explorers showed great resoluteness on their journey. Stephens was a veteran of other expeditions into areas such as Greece and Crete, and Catherwood had much the same traveling background, having visited Egypt, Palestine, and Arabia for the purpose of making architectural drawings. The close bonds between the two is admirably portrayed by Highwater. Their respect for each other, and how their talents complemented each other, is vividly drawn. Stephens the writer and Catherwood the artist illuminate to the fullest extent possible the grandeur of the ruins they agonizingly locate and record. The reader grows fond of their valet, Augustin, a Mexican who looks after them. Their muleskinner, though, grates on the adventurers as well as the reader. He is rude and insolent, constantly threatening to disrupt the plans, and is as much of a pest as the mosquitoes. The friction that arises between the characters, and what the environment does to each of their temperaments, is brought bristling to the page by the author's acute and pointed writing style.

For presenting high adventure, *Journey to the Sky* is very much comparable to the tales of Robert Louis Stevenson and Rudyard Kipling. The narrative-journal kept by Stephens also reminds the reader of the detailed observations made by Sir Richard Burton on his treks to Africa. Highwater more than keeps pace with each in his commitment not only to fine, precise prose, but also to paying homage to the culture under study. The Mayans still remain somewhat of a mystery, which adds to their attraction, but the peoples of the Americas can look proudly to the ruins as symbols of the Mayans' cultural sophistication and take satisfaction that so great a series of monuments do exist.

The two expeditions Stephens and Catherwood undertake lead to the rediscovery of several ancient cities. Catherwood, suffering from a high fever, sketches at a furious pace the city of Uxmal; but he soon collapses and can continue no longer. It is decided to take a ship back to New York to recuperate. They leave the area for the first time in June, 1840, and do not return until October, 1841. Stephens' two-volume journal is a large success after it is published in 1841, though scholars are less enthusiastic and lag behind for another fifty years before concurring with Stephens' zest for the Mayan ruins. On the second expedition a young doctor by the name of Samuel Cabot accompanies them. They wish to finish the work they had begun fifteen months earlier at Uxmal. But illness strikes again, and all three have to be carried away on litters after their work is completed. They still take it upon themselves to journey to Kabah and Labna, the ruins of Chichen Itza, and the eastern extremity of Yucatan so they can view the island ruins of Isla Mujeres. On June 4, 1842, they set off for New York weary and homesick.

The friendship of Stephens and Catherwood continued, but at a distance. Highwater fills in the reader on the activities that consume the two after the Mayan expeditions. Stephens became involved with the Panama Railroad Company—becoming its President—and lured Catherwood, who was back in England, into the venture. After arriving in Panama, Catherwood became ill with malaria. Stephens was also hampered by poor health and a riding accident and was forced to return to New York. While he was away Catherwood heard of the discovery of gold in California and decided to try his luck and join the gold rush. Upon receiving the news back in New York of gold being found in California, Stephens believed that the railroad must be completed as fast as possible, and so he forced himself, though still weak, to journey back to Panama. Catherwood urged his friend to join him in California, but Stephens never did. On his way back to England, Catherwood met with his friend in Panama for the last time. Catherwood is to make another offer to Stephens concerning California gold, but the message never reached Stephens; he is found in a coma under a ceiba tree. The Indians believe that he is dead and name the tree the "Stephens Tree." A legend starts that the great explorer has died under the Mayan Tree of Life. Suffering from terminal hepatitis, John Lloyd Stephens died at the age of forty-seven on October 13, 1852. Two years later Frederick Catherwood sailed out of Liverpool for New York on his way back to California, still sensing the loss of his partner. In September, 1854, on board the ship *Arctic*, Catherwood met his own end when the *Arctic* collided with a French ship in a heavy fog and sank.

Highwater has brought these two adventurers to life as men of courage—figures who uncovered history. The Americas are in their debt, and Jamake Highwater has admirably paid back a portion of that debt with chiseled prose, the inclusion of illustrations, and a bibliography—all of which make up *Journey to the Sky*.

Jeffry Michael Jensen

Sources for Further Study

Library Journal. CIII, December 1, 1978, p. 2445.

JOYCE'S VOICES

Author: Hugh Kenner (1923-   )
Publisher: University of California Press (Berkeley). 120 pp. $8.95
Type of work: Literary criticism

A brief but perceptive examination of the various styles used by James Joyce in his fiction, especially Ulysses

To set the context for discussing this slim but fascinating book, we need to know about the subject of its all-too-brief discussion, the author who offers that discussion, and the series in which it appears, for what we have in *Joyce's Voices* is a special coming together of author, subject, and format to create a special kind of critical work.

We might deal with the subject first, for James Joyce is clearly the premier novelist of the modern age in English literature. He is known chiefly for four works, each one of which broke major new ground in terms of its treatment of subject and style. His *Dubliners*, a collection of short stories, chronicles in a series of sharply drawn vignettes the lives of a variety of residents of Ireland's capital city. His *Portrait of the Artist as a Young Man*, a brief novel, recounts the early years of Stephen Dedalus, Irishman and aspiring artist, as he seeks to break free of personal and cultural childhood restrictions and find his own literary voice. Joyce's next and most famous work, *Ulysses*, describes at great length one day in the life of Dublin and of three of its citizens—Leopold Bloom, his wife Molly, and Stephen Dedalus. Finally, *Finnegans Wake* records the unconscious activities of a single mind during a night's sleep. This last work is an enormously difficult one, and is probably one of the least read of all works by a major modern author. *Ulysses*, on the other hand, though also difficult in its way, has been found endlessly readable and fascinating by several generations of readers and critics who have subjected its pages to the most painstaking and careful sort of analysis. Much of this work has been done in the light of the novel's supposed parallels to Homer's *Odyssey*, or in terms of the book's efforts to record in minute detail the events of a single day in Dublin. It is this work of Joyce that is Kenner's special concern in *Joyce's Voices*; in the brief compass of one hundred pages, he has set out to reverse the major trends in literary criticism of the novel.

Hugh Kenner is one of America's most influential critics of the modern age in literature. A number of his earlier works, including his two studies of Ezra Pound, *The Poetry of Ezra Pound* and *The Pound Era*, are classics of modern criticism and cultural history. What makes Kenner's work so appealing is his breadth of reading and his ear for nuance, the wide range of literary and cultural material he can hear echoed in any given passage and bring to bear on its explication. He is also noted for the readability of his style and the associative quality of his thought. All these traits are fully on display in *Joyce's Voices*, with the result that it is a highly enjoyable as well as truly informative work of literary criticism.

The book appears in the "Quantum Books" series of brief critical studies from the University of California Press. Deliberately limited to one hundred pages or so, the books in this series are intended to treat a significant subject in a brief but important way. Intended to be read in an evening, these books still strive to be rich in detail and insight. What *Joyce's Voices* brings together is Kenner the scholar, Joyce the stylist, and the Quantum format to produce a truly delightful and brief but extremely helpful essay on Joyce's stylistic variety, especially as it is exhibited in *Ulysses*. The experienced Joycean scholar may find little here that is really new; he may also lament the absence of the usual elaborate scholarly apparatus. The literate general reader of Joyce, however, will find here a sprightly, challenging, rich, and insightful introduction to the deeper study of Joyce's work which will go a long way toward making Joyce's writing more approachable and all the more profoundly moving.

Kenner's central point is that too much energy has been expended in working out all the Homeric parallels to *Ulysses*. We need, instead, to be more aware of the variety of styles Joyce employs to create his fictional worlds, the ways those styles interact to create the fictional world, and the relationships those styles bear to the characters who use them to reveal their attitudes and personalities.

Kenner finds the truly significant Homeric parallel in *Ulysses* to be with Homer's dividing of the narration of his poem between himself and his Muse. *Ulysses* also contains a double process of narration, a duality of normative style, instead of the single authoritative narrative voice we may be more accustomed to from our reading of other fiction. In Joyce's *Ulysses*, in a fashion anticipated by other earlier writings by Joyce, the first narrator is sensitive to the special idioms of each character and thus reflects the unique world view, the unique perspective of each of the figures who populate the landscape of Joyce's Dublin. The second narrative presence, however, is aware of the realities of language as surface and style, and thus can play with the very medium of the novel's expression.

Kenner finds many of the special peculiarities of *Ulysses*, its most problematic passages, illustrative of this second narrative voice in its distinctively Irish concern for pose, for role, and for play of language, as opposed to the use of words to convey literalistic concepts of meaning or objective presentation. Some of the most helpful sections of this brief study are those in which Kenner renders the more difficult sections of *Ulysses* intelligible in terms of the special attitudes and devices of this second narrative presence.

Another helpful aspect of Kenner's discussion is his placing of the special narrative technique of *Ulysses*, and its effect upon the language which makes it up, in the context of the history of English prose style. The author finds the kinds of expectations we have for a true depiction of reality in fiction to be of relatively recent origin in the history of English writing. He notes that Jonathan Swift in *Gulliver's Travels* satirized this objective attitude toward fictional realities by making Gulliver see the entire world in objective terms, with predictably riotous results. Joyce, argues Kenner, is well aware that words do not create objective realities, but have their own logic and shape. In *Ulysses*, he builds a verbal world which calls attention to its surface, to its very artificiality, so as to recover a sense of the mythic and the ritualistic in fiction and to put us in touch with that very reality which so-called "objective" prose style cannot capture.

A review of a brief book should be brief as well; suffice it to say that the brevity of *Joyce's Voices* belies its importance. What Kenner has given us in this book is an easily accessible introduction to the complexities of *Ulysses* which should go a long way toward making the book's riches available to the nonscholarly reader. Intended as a companion to its much, much longer subject, this book will overcome the barriers which often stand between a master-work and its potential readers; it will make the task of appropriating *Ulysses* into our own world a richer, easier, and more delightful one. Kenner performs the true act of criticism; he does not explain away the literary work, but instead makes more available to us its unique experience in all its splendid complexity.

John N. Wall, Jr.

Sources for Further Study

Choice. XV, November, 1978, p. 1217.
National Review. XXXI, February 16, 1979, p. 244.
Yale Review. LXVIII, Winter, 1979, p. 266.

JUST REPRESENTATIONS
A James Gould Cozzens Reader

Author: James Gould Cozzens (1903-   )
Edited, with an Introduction, by Matthew J. Bruccoli
Publisher: Southern Illinois University Press (Carbondale and Edwardville) and Harcourt Brace Jovanovich (New York and London). 568 pp. $14.95
Type of work: Collected writings

A collection of six reviews and critical essays which focus on various aspects of Cozzens' work, an introductory essay by editor Bruccoli, and selections from Cozzens' writing

On the occasion of James Gould Cozzens' seventy-fifth birthday, Matthew J. Bruccoli has edited "an introduction for new readers of his [Cozzens'] works and an omnibus for the initiated." Samplings from the novelist's work, chosen by the editor and approved by Cozzens, include *Ask Me Tomorrow* in its entirety; excerpts from six other postapprenticeship novels; three short stories; six previously uncollected essays; and "Some Putative Facts of Hard Record," from his 1923 diary. The selections are arranged for reading in conjunction with the essays and reviews contributed by George Garrett, Jerome Weidman, Noel Perrin, Frederick Bracher, Brendan Gill, and Richard M. Ludwig. Particularly appropriate is the epigraph, a quotation from Samuel Johnson used by Cozzens in *Morning Noon and Night*: "Nothing can please many, and please long, but just representations of general nature."

Editor Bruccoli's Introduction is a biographical sketch and a comprehensive résumé of Cozzens' literary career, which officially began in March, 1920, with the publication of "A Democratic School" by the *Atlantic Monthly*. Described by Bruccoli as an "uneven" student, Cozzens decided early to become a professional writer. While he was at Harvard, he wrote his first novel, *Confusion*, published in 1924. This event caused considerable excitement in Boston, and the young student-author was persuaded to make several public appearances—all time-consuming an unsatisfactory from Cozzens' viewpoint. Finding himself in difficulty at Harvard, he took a leave of absence and never returned to complete his course work.

With his formal education at an end, Cozzens, who never at a loss for inspiration and material, continued to write. Part of his income was derived from other more ordinary jobs, however, including teaching, tutoring, editing, and library work. More and more he became fascinated with the idea of writing about the professional people in American society. Three years after he left Harvard, Cozzens married Bernice Baumgarten, who was his literary agent and to whom *Just Representations* is dedicated.

Bruccoli, in his concise review of Cozzens' work, pays tribute to the writer's dedication to his craft and to his uncompromising pursuit of excellence in his work. Since the Harvard days, Cozzens has never sought publicity, has never embraced social or political causes, and has been too absorbed in his profession to become involved with other activities which do not interest him. "His refusal to make concessions to inattentive readers" has been offered as one reason for Cozzens' failure to attract the readership his work deserves. In commenting on this idea, Bruccoli praises the clarity and dignity of Cozzens' style and defends his judicious use of uncommon words, his concise sentence structure, and his meaningful literary allusions, open or concealed. Bruccoli, like Cozzens himself, objects to categorizing the novelist as a conservative, an aristocrat, and a classicist. Rather, Cozzens insists that "he tries only to render life and people accurately as he sees them." Bruccoli adds that Cozzens respects intelligence, firmness, and self-discipline.

Excerpts from the 1923 diary and additional notes included in a letter from the author to Bruccoli are part of the front matter. Diary entries provide an insight into the mind of a fledgling genius frustrated at being at once student and author. His inner conflict is apparent.

Ask Me Tomorrow, subtitled *The Pleasant Comedy of Young Fortunatus*, published in 1940 and reprinted *in toto*, reflects Cozzens' own experiences as a tutor in 1926-1927. His student was a young American boy and the job afforded the tutor an opportunity to travel in Europe. As Bruccoli explains, Francis, the sensitive tutor and hero, is also becoming educated even as he tutors Walter in academic subjects. Fate plays a big part in the development of the plot, but Francis' own vanities must be recognized and tempered. The petulant, self-centered young man portrayed at the beginning matures in the course of events until he can accept a change in fortune with grace and be sincerely sympathetic with Mrs. Cunningham and her problems.

The variety of material in the Cozzens canon is discussed in "Whatever Wishful Thinking You May Wish: The Example of James Gould Cozzens," by George Garrett, teacher and author of *The Death of the Fox*. One reason college teachers do not use Cozzens' major novels, Garrett believes, is that college students are incapable of dealing with the form and content, and teachers find it difficult to bridge the gap between Cozzens and his potential youthful audience. Another reason is that "most professors hate the professionals." Cozzens, unequaled in his ability to portray doctors, lawyers, military men, and the clergy, has consistently declined to let politics influence his writing, whereas "for a very long time and dominantly so since World War II, in politics the Academy has been a sort of sacred grove, strongly dedicated to the Left."

Cozzens' so-called "professional" novels include six mature works: *The Last Adam* (1933); *Men and Brethren* (1936); *The Just and the Unjust* (1942); *Guard of Honor* (1948); *By Love Possessed* (1957); and *Morning Noon and Night* (1968). Most of the central characters in these books are mature men who believe in their chosen disciplines. Only John O'Hara, according to Garrett, is comparable to Cozzens in his treatment of this type. The professionals have earned a place in American literature, thinks Garrett, because these are people who have had a profound influence on American life in the twentieth century.

Essayist Garrett concludes with a discussion of luck in Cozzens' work. Convinced that luck is often the determining factor in success or failure, Cozzens expresses his conviction over and over in plot and characterizations. In praising Cozzens' technique, Garrett says, "He offers a superior example of the integrity of the craft, of the daring refinement of language, of the creation of fully realized characters who matter, of structures and patterns of experience which seem, in the major novels, to shadow the complex patterns of Fortune and Providence in our lives."

Three excerpts from *The Last Adam* illustrate the views of George Garrett. Dr. Bull, indifferent to public opinion, may be an incompetent doctor, but he is a vibrant man and necessary to the community. Henry Harris, thwarted in his ambition to attend Yale, compensates by making money. He has power. One excerpt includes the superb scene in which Dr. Bull confronts the members of the board. A woman reporter persists in writing up her story, but Henry Harris has only to make a call to the editor of the Sansbury *Times* to quash it. Both Dr. Bull and Henry Harris are necessary to the community.

Jerome Weidman, in "The Opening Up of Windows," comments on *Children and Others*, a collection of short stories published in 1964. It is notable, Weidman thinks, that stories written over such a long period (the first in 1930) and covering such a wide range of subjects should vary so little in excellence. Their one common denominator, he thinks, is the Cozzens intelligence. Weidman praises the superb sentence structure and preciseness of words. The hero characteristically found in the stories is "nearly always an acutely intelligent man born into a middle-class eastern family of tradition and a comfortable amount of worldly goods." Such a hero chooses one of the "suitable" professions—medicine, the law, the clergy—and he performs his military duty (as an officer). In analyzing a Cozzens scene in which an intelligent black man handles with wisdom and empathy a delicate situation involving race, Weidman concludes that "an artist [Cozzens] has opened up for us a secret window in a human heart."

Three short stories are used with Weidman's essay. The first is "The Way To Go Home," in which Meade Pons, head of a prestigious automobile agency in Havana, finds he must settle for a safe, mundane domesticity because he cannot go back to a more exciting life-style. In "Every Day's a Holiday," Mr. Jamison, not a college graduate but rich, fails to see himself reflected in his daughter and feels no real responsibility for her, although he excoriates Emily's irresponsibility. Finally there is "One Hundred Ladies," whose protagonist, Owen Fulton, is a Civil War veteran who tries unsuccessfully to recapture the romance of his war years by attending a Confederate reunion.

Like Meade Pons, Owen Fulton finds that he has taken a one-way road and cannot reverse his route.

Noel Perrin's "The Good Dukes" explores the essayist's idea that the dominant theme in Cozzens' novels is that of "order imposed on a meaningless world." In arriving at this conclusion, Perrin compares the dukes in Shakespeare to the ducal characters who appear in at least six of the Cozzens novels. These ordering characters, discussed at length, include Mrs. Banning, Henry Harris, and May Tupping in *The Last Adam*; Colonel Ross and General Beal in *Guard of Honor*; Ernest Cudlipp and Dr. Lamb in *Men and Brethren*; Abner Coates in *The Just and the Unjust*; Alfred Revere, Aunt Maud, Colonel Minton, and Arthur Winner in *By Love Possessed*; and Henry Worthington in *Morning Noon and Night*. Perrin perceives Arthur Winner as the most complete of these figures.

Because they possess power, ducal characters are not always "nice" people, says Perrin. They sometimes hurt other people, not because they want to but because they must in order to achieve their goals. For instance, Henry Harris, not wicked but lacking in human sympathy, enjoys manipulating people. In the later novels the ducal characters are intelligent and see their roles as ordering persons who must keep the world functioning, and extricating people in difficulty. Ernest Cudlipp in *Men and Brethren* exemplifies Cozzens' mature ducal characters.

Frederick Bracher's essay on style and technique is thorough and perceptive. Predictably he appreciates the long, complicated, but clear sentences and the rich vocabulary commanded by Cozzens. Words are not used because they are uncommon, but uncommon words are used because they enrich and express thoughts precisely. Bracher comments on Cozzens' penchant for using parenthetic elements and on his skill in working into his own text allusions and quotations from other writers, albeit this technique is sometimes overdone. Cozzens' own temperament is reflected, perhaps subconsciously, by certain recurring words. Bracher cites such words as *mortifying, harassed, crestfallen, qualms, chagrined, wounded feelings*; "Cozzens's diction reflects his pyrrhonist's temperament, his apoetic intelligence, and his troubled aloofness."

The novelist gives priority to the dramatic element in his novels rather than to character development. Fully formed at the outset, Cozzens' characters are at once involved in a crucial situation. Time covered by the action is usually brief and the locale particularized. Cozzens makes much of coincidence and dramatic irony. By harmonizing scene, weather, and event, he artfully creates whatever mood the subject dictates. Although Cozzens denies a conscious use of symbolism, it is there nonetheless. Examples of it abound.

Introductory to a study of *Guard of Honor* is Cozzens' own review of Oliver La Farge's *The Eagle in the Sky* (1949). In the review Cozzens displays his understanding of military matters and his appreciation for dedicated military men. *Guard of Honor*, which won for its author the Pulitzer Prize in 1949, is considered the best novel of World War II. In Oliver La Farge, Cozzens sees many of the same characteristics seen in Cozzens' characters in *Guard of Honor*.

"Summa cum Laude" by Brendan Gill is a review of *By Love Possessed* (1957). Gill's emphasis is on the inventive genius of Cozzens. The reviewer notes that Cozzens does not rely on autobiographical experiences but invents his characters, so the result is not a self-image but "images appropriate to the subject being treated." A Cozzens hero, conditioned to act well in society, feels morally bound to act when he unexpectedly encounters evil, even though his action may be futile. *By Love Possessed* has just such a hero in Arthur Winner, who in two days' time is confronted with repeated situations which challenge his whole code of conduct; "truth, honor, probity" prove to be totally irrelevant. "He [Winner] will get up, he will seem to survive the blows, but life will never be the same for him."

"The Profession of Literature" from *Morning Noon and Night* affords Cozzens an opportunity to express his own philosophy about writing professionally. Written in the first person, it doubtless reflects personal experience. At fourteen or fifteen, the hero decides to become a professor because that is the profession his background and training seem to dictate. He decides to become a professor who writes because his observation tells him that writing professors command special prestige and adulation. With wry humor Cozzens uses this character to explore the difficulties and discouragements encountered by such would-be writers who drift into the profession. His comments on the motivation of writers, the commercial aspects of publishing, and the luck involved in the whole process are revealing. A young writer who aspires only to create "just representations of general nature" becomes disillusioned. ("A butyric whiff of riper phoninesses to come taints ever so faintly the rare atmosphere."

Richard M. Ludwig, author of the final essay, "A Reading of the Cozzens Manuscripts," interprets the complex nature of Cozzens and his methods of composition as revealed in the manuscripts, books, and papers now housed in the Princeton University Library. Ludwig notes Cozzens' many revisions, his care in selecting titles, his obvious effort to eliminate firsthand observations, his striving for exactness. The essayist finds special interest in the development of *By Love Possessed* and includes four pages of manuscript plates to reinforce points made in the essay.

Attractive in appearance and meticulously edited, *Just Representations* will surely prove to be the omnibus that teachers, students, and Cozzens devotees have wanted and needed for a long time.

Mary Reynolds Peacock

Sources for Further Study

Booklist. LXXV, September, 1, 1978, p. 26.

Choice. XV, January, 1979, p. 1515.

Library Journal. CIII, September 15, 1978, p. 1766.

National Review. XXX, December 8, 1978, p. 1552.

New York Times Book Review. August 6, 1978, p. 10.

Virginia Quarterly Review. LV, Winter, 1979, p. 18.

KARL MARX
An Intimate Biography

Author: Saul K. Padover (1905-   )
Publisher: McGraw-Hill Book Company (New York). 667 pp. $18.95
Type of work: Biography
Time: 1818-1883
Locale: Western Europe

A comprehensive biography dealing with the intellectual development, political activities, and published writings of Karl Marx, but giving special emphasis to Marx as a human being

> *Principal personages:*
> KARL MARX, author of *The Communist Manifesto* and *Das Kapital*
> FRIEDRICH ENGELS, Marx's lifelong friend and collaborator
> JENNY MARX (*née* VON WESTPHALEN), Marx's wife
> HELEN DEMUTH, loyal servant, trusted adviser, and mother of Marx's illegitimate son
> MICHAEL BAKUNIN, Marx's anarchist rival for leadership of the First International

In an age when, as *Newsweek* recently admonished us, we are "more interested in personalities than issues," one approaches an "intimate biography" of Karl Marx with trepidation. The fears are, fortunately, unjustified, because Saul K. Padover is not an ordinary journalistic gossip monger. He is a knowledgeable, sophisticated scholar well prepared to do justice to the issues that are so important to understanding the issue-oriented man he is examining.

Padover devoted twelve years to the study of Marx, but the current biography is not the only fruit of that labor. Padover's name also appears on the seven volumes entitled *The Karl Marx Library* which appeared with impressive regularity from 1971 to 1977. These volumes contained, for the most part, Padover's original translations, often of material never before translated into English.

Padover neither hates nor worships Marx; his biography is therefore free of that particular type of distortion. However, Padover's freedom from the intense emotions that have led many a commentator to deviate from objectivity does not mean he is without a point of view. While Padover is neither a Marxologist nor an anti-Marxologist, he is a Jeffersonian democrat. Padover has written a biography of Jefferson and edited collections of Jefferson's work, and he is more at home with Jefferson's eclectic pragmatism than he is with Marx's systematic theory-building. As a result, this fine biography whets the appetite, but does not fully satisfy it. The reader unfamiliar with Marx will inevitably feel compelled to look elsewhere for a deeper understanding of Marx's thought.

Yet the standard exegeses of Marx's thought are further illuminated by this intriguing examination of the interaction between his thought and his experience. McGraw-Hill has done Padover a disservice by its marketing strategy, which leaves the impression that the book focuses exclusively on Marx's personal life. Although the early chapters reinforce that misleading impression, Marx's intellectual development, political activities, and published writings are all dealt with in this large and thorough volume. Padover's own characterization of the work in the Introduction is more accurate than that of his publisher: he writes that he has attempted "a comprehensive biography, with special emphasis on Marx as human being."

One of the advantages of Padover's work is that he has had access to scattered and often unknown materials that have been unearthed and collected by a number of researchers over the last few decades; as a result he is able to fill in some of the gaps in our knowledge of Marx's early years. He also provides a detailed genealogy of Marx's ancestors.

Marx turns out to have been the descendant of a remarkable collection of rabbis on both his father's and his mother's side of the family. His father, however, was a secularist, who had to overcome both his family's displeasure and the anti-Semitic prejudices of the broader community in order to become the leading lawyer in Trier, the town where Marx was born. His father's classical education was supplemented by a knowledge of the great writers and thinkers of the modern age, such as John Locke, Immanuel Kant, Gottfried Wilhelm Liebniz, and Isaac Newton. We know from the remarkable letters they exchanged while young Karl was a University student that theirs was a relationship of mutual devotion and respect. Karl's remarkable and impressive erudition, commented upon in extreme terms even by chance acquaintances, had its roots in a childhood admiration for his learned father.

However, it was a neighbor, Baron von Westphalen, who introduced Karl to great literature. They would go for long hikes together during which the Baron would talk of such figures as Goethe, Saint-Simon, and Cervantes. The Baron truly became a second father to Marx when Karl married his daughter Jenny, even though she was four years his senior. Their marriage was an extraordinary one, and although they went through extreme hardships together, their relationship remained intense and loving until her death finally separated them after thirty-eight years. Many others have detailed the bitter, vituperative quarrels that Marx engaged in with enemies, rivals, and even former friends, but Padover shows us as well the caring, loving man whose philosophical sympathy for the downtrodden can be recognized as more than an abstract belief; it was heartfelt emotion as well. Marx was as tender and caring with his children as he was with his wife. For the children, he was a companion, a friend, a playmate, and a delightful storyteller.

The more one knows about Marx, the harder it becomes to attribute his political activism to his childhood personality or his social circumstances or even the circumstances of his mature family life. Despite our modern tendency to find the sources of ideas or the explanation for their development in these nonintellectual realms, the wealth of biographical detail about Marx drives us back to admitting that in his case his actions and beliefs were intimately related to a process of intellectual development. It is impossible not to know that Marx was influenced by the Young Hegelians while a University student, because we all seem to have been told in college that Marx stood Hegel on his head. How many of us, however, have been told that Marx wished to be a poet and playwright when he started his university career? How many of us are aware of the plays and poems he wrote? How many of us realize that he studied jurisprudence only to satisfy his father? Most remarkable of all, Padover reports that the undercover police agents monitoring political troublemakers at the Gymnasium and the two Universities Marx attended, never mentioned him in their reports because he was so uninvolved in the political activism of his fellow students.

Not only were Marx's early inclinations not those of a political activist, but his early intellectual orientations were also not what we would today characterize as those of a Marxist. When Marx received his doctorate at the age of twenty-three, he seemed most interested in a position as a Professor of Philosophy. Moses Hess, a Young Hegelian in Cologne, claimed, after a relatively brief acquaintance with Marx, that Marx was the greatest living German philosopher. Although we now think of Hegelianism as the conservative philosophy that Marx abandoned, the Prussian government viewed the Young Hegelians of the time as a subversive force. When Marx's friend Bruno Bauer lost his position at the University of Bonn through the personal intervention of the Prussian King, Marx lost whatever hope he still harbored of being able to follow an academic career.

As a result Marx became a journalist, from which he earned money but not a living. In late 1841, the Prussian Cabinet issued a new, more sweeping censorship decree, to which Marx replied in a lengthy article "Remarks on the Latest Prussian Censorship Instruction." If this article is taken as a measure of Marx's thinking at the time, he had not yet abandoned liberal bourgeois ideology. His argument was couched in decidedly non-Marxist terms, and is basically a libertarian argument. The tone of the essay is in marked contrast to his diatribes against censorship in the *Neue Rheinische Zeitung* in 1848, by which time he was a Communist, a revolutionist, and what we would today call a Marxist.

In 1842, however, when Marx became the editor of the old *Rheinische Zeitung*, he was not a Communist, but a humanist who knew little about Communism or economics. Indeed, on his first day as editor he rejected in print both the theoretical soundness and practical potential of Communist ideas. It was not until his own thinking had changed, and he in turn had changed the content of Communist thought, that he embraced the European Communist movement.

The first step in that transformation was for the "Young Hegelian" to free himself of some aspects of the Hegelian system. Marx found Hegel appealing because his philosophical system linked German idealism with reality. On the other hand, Hegel was a supporter of the Prussian monarchical system that Marx rejected. Marx began to write his "Critique of Hegel's Philosophy of Law" in the summer of 1843 while still on his honeymoon. Although they had waited for seven years to marry, Marx, who compulsively overworked throughout his life, could not refrain from intellectual concentration and work at the very start of his marriage to the remarkably patient and understanding Jenny. In the "Critique of Hegel's Philosophy of Law," Marx rejects Hegel's identification of the monarchy with the Universal. He also rejects the idea that the Universal is the cause of the real, of the institutions of society. Instead, he for the first time identifies the proletariat as the universal class, asserts that institutions and ideas are the creations of human effort, and assigns to the proletariat the historic role of liberating mankind and revolutionizing the world. "The *head* of this emancipation is philosophy, its *heart* is the proletariat." Nevertheless, in a September, 1843, letter, Marx was still to describe Communism as ". . . separate from the humanist principle." He had not yet finished his transitional odyssey.

By October, 1843, the second step in his transformation had begun, with his move to Paris, the center of European revolutionary ferment. In Paris, Marx was to meet many famous revolutionaries and intellectuals. More importantly, he was to meet workers, real proletarians rather than theorists, who had in fact already created workers' organizations such as the Communist League and the League of the Just. Padover vividly points out the importance of the Paris experience. "In Paris, class divisions were palpable, sharp and uncompromising. Marx did not have to imagine or invent the class struggle; he only had to look around him."

Marx had moved to Paris to join with Arnold Ruge in publishing the *Deutsch-Französische Jahrbücher*. That ill-fated venture led to the third and final step in his transformation from skeptic to Communist. The first and last issue of the publication came out in February, 1844. It contained two articles by Friedrich Engels, whom Marx had met only briefly in November, 1842, in the office of the *Rheinische Zeitung*. Engels' "Outline of a Critique of Political Economy" deeply impressed Marx, reinforcing his increasing concern with economics. He began an intensive study of the classic English economists, and by the spring of 1844, was attempting a long essay on economics, which he never finished.

On August 28, 1844, Engels arrived in Paris for a stopover on his way from England to Germany. Marx and Engels spent ten enthusiastic days together, discovering their wide range of agreement on philosophic and social questions. During that stay they began their first collaboration together, an attack on Bruno Bauer and the Young Hegelians who followed him. Engels wrote the first four chapters of *The Holy Family*, while Marx wrote the final four chapters and the postscript.

From this point on Marx was part of the preexisting European communist movement, and a determined agitator for his own more theoretically sound version of communist ideology. What that meant is most succinctly expressed by what happened to the motto of the Communist League at its second congress in London, as a result of the determined prodding of Marx and Engels, which produced a number of other important changes as well. The old motto had been "All Men Are Brethren." The new motto adopted was "Proletarians of All Countries, Unite!"

Padover's comprehensive and detailed biography permits us to answer many questions about the interaction of Marx's life experiences and the development of his thought. Some readers may be tempted to criticize Padover for not doing more of the interpretative work for us. Yet a narrower interpretive focus usually implies a greater selectivity in the presentation of data. That would be a great loss in a work dealing with as fascinating and complex a man as Marx. For example, even Padover's endless detailing of the physical ailments suffered by Marx can be of unexpected importance in evaluating other interpretations in the literature. There have been attempts to develop elaborate psychological theories to explain Marx's inability to finish the four projected volumes of *Das Kapital*. While it must be admitted that emotional stress seems clearly associated with many of Marx's physical ailments, Padover demonstrates that the afflictions long preceded the *Das Kapital* project.

There are other areas as well in which Padover is useful precisely because he chooses to be a historian rather than a psychologist, political theorist, or polemicist. Of course, even as historian and biographer, Padover could not totally eschew interpretation. One or two examples may strike the reader as potentially controversial or, worse yet, flatly wrong. Nevertheless, Padover is generally sound, always thorough, and thoroughly readable. *Karl Marx: An Intimate Biography* is definitely to be recommended as an excellent introduction for the neophyte and a useful reference for the scholar who is an academic specialist on Marx.

Barry Faye

Sources for Further Study

Booklist. LXXV, October 15, 1978, p. 338.
Chronicle of Higher Education. XVIII, October 30, 1978, p. R9.
Library Journal. CIII, October 15, 1978, p. 2105.
Nation. CCXVII, December 23, 1978, p. 703.
New Republic. CLXXX, January 6, 1979, p. 28.
Time. CXIII, January 8, 1979, p. 77.

KOLYMA
The Arctic Death Camps

Author: Robert Conquest (1917-   )
Publisher: The Viking Press (New York). 254 pp. $10.95
Type of work: History
Time: 1927-1956, with concentration on the period 1935-1953
Locale: The far northeastern area of Siberia

A pioneer study in which Conquest discusses in detail the purposes, conditions, and results of the Soviet labor camps in Kolyma during the regime of Joseph Stalin

> *Principal personages:*
> JOSEPH STALIN, leader of the Communist Party of the U.S.S.R., Prime Minister and Dictator, 1929-1953
> GENRIKH YAGODA, head of the Soviet Secret Police, the NKVD, 1934-1936
> NIKOLAI I. YEZHOV, successor to Yagoda as head of the NKVD, 1936-1938
> E. P. (REINGOLD) BERZIN, head of Dalstroy and the camps in Kolyma, 1932-1937
> K. A. PAVLOV, head of Dalstroy and the camps in Kolyma, 1937-1940
> I. F. NIKISHOV, head of Dalstroy and the camps in Kolyma, 1940-1946
> MAJOR-GENERAL P. P. DEREVENKO, head of Dalstroy and the camps in Kolyma, 1946-1953
> MAJOR (LATER COLONEL) GARANIN, virtual head of the camps in Kolyma, 1938-1939

Robert Conquest, a British poet and political writer who has written such works as *Power and Policy in the USSR, Russia After Khrushchev,* and *The Great Terror,* has once more made a significant contribution to twentieth century Soviet Russian history by his latest book, *Kolyma,* which is an account of the prison life for the inmates of the Arctic Death Camps situated in northeastern Siberia during the regime of Stalin. Drawing upon contemporary eyewitness accounts of seventeen individuals, sixteen of whom were former prisoners and one of whom was a free individual who worked there, Conquest sets out to depict the atrocities committed upon Russians and ethnic minorities by Stalin and his regime.

The author did extensive research in order to write this book. The subject matter of this work is such that he could not, of course, use any materials in the Soviet State Archives and had to rely upon two major sources of information: eyewitness accounts and memoirs and indirect evidence. A good example of the latter is the fact that he diligently checked the various volumes of Lloyd's Register of Shipping for the tonnage and place and date of origin of the ships which were owned and operated by Dalstroy (The Far Northern Construction Trust), as these vessels were used exclusively to transport prisoners to Kolyma. His research clearly demonstrates that over three million people were transported there from 1937 until 1953. Of these, at least three million died during the same period. Using his first type of source, the eyewitness and contemporary accounts of his seventeen major sources, Conquest very cleverly and succinctly weaves these stories into a coherent unified account of what went on in these Soviet labor camps established by Stalin in the 1930's. What unfolds is a story of such horror, such barbarism, that for many of us today it is quite literally incomprehensible.

The story of Kolyma's inhabitants begins back in European Russia where they were arrested—usually at midnight—by agents of the Russian Secret Police, the NKVD. From various places in Russia, these hapless individuals were then transferred in overcrowded, dark, stinking cattle trucks or trains to the transit camps of Vladivostok, Nakhodka, and Vanino. These prisoners had already been beaten and tortured by the time they arrived in the transit camps, but in these camps conditions were much worse. The lack of adequate food supplies, incredibly crowded living areas and totally inadequate medical treatment allowed disease and starvation to run unchecked and many thousands of prisoners died before they were taken to Kolyma.

But for those who survived the long train journey and the transit camps, many more horrible experiences awaited. From the transit camps, the prisoners were taken aboard the ships of the NKVD, called the Dalstroy Line. This fleet of ships was actually a slave fleet, and the occupants of their holds underwent a "Middle Passage" from Vladivostok to Nagayevo, the port of Kolyma, as gruesome as any in the history of slavery. Ironically, the colors of this fleet were a broad white band with a blue stripe which symbolized the idea of hope. The typical hold of these ships consisted of three decks, each of which contained two-level bunks. Here the prisoners were confined and cramped in very small spaces, where the heat, the humidity, the stench were overpowering. In addition, the hardened criminals in the group terrorized, murdered, and raped those prisoners who were regarded as "politicals" by the authorities. In a sense, this voyage was the introduction of Kolyma to its future inhabitants. Fortunately, these voyages often only lasted one week.

At long last, the prisoners arrived at the port city of Kolyma, Nagayevo, located on the barren shores of the Sea of Okhotsk. This city was the gateway to a world of subarctic climate where in winter the temperature can reach −70 C., a world totally isolated from the rest of Russia, and a world of slave labor camps and gold mines.

The establishment of gold mining in 1927 was the *raison d'être* for the creation of the approximately 120 slave labor camps and mines during the following three decades. In 1931 Dalstroy, otherwise known as The Far Northern Construction Trust (a NKVD agency), was established with supervisory powers over all compulsory labor projects in northeastern Siberia. For a brief interlude, 1932-1937, when Dalstroy was governed by E. P. (Reingold)

Berzin, Kolyma's inhabitants experienced a "golden age" because Berzin was primarily interested in the mining and production of gold. It was during this period that the prisoners sent to Kolyma were at least provided with adequate food, clothing, and shelter. But Berzin was attacked for leniency towards the prisoners and was removed in 1937 (he was later shot for alleged espionage for Japan); he was replaced as the head of Dalstroy by K. A. Pavlov and I. F. Nikishov. The actual running of the camps and the prisoners was given to the infamous Major (later Colonel) Garanin, who was a special agent of the new chief of the NKVD, Nikolai I. Yezhov. The year 1938 began a new era called "the Garaninshchina" in Kolyma, in which the Stalin regime instituted a program whose policy had two goals: the production of gold according to the Five Year Plans enunciated by Stalin, and the extermination of the prisoners. The major legacy of this period, the concept that the lives of the prisoners were forfeited because they had been sent to Kolyma, remained enforced even after the fall and execution of Yezhov and Garanin in 1939 and was maintained until at least 1953.

The Kolyma System which evolved during the years 1937-1953 saw prisoners reduced to living in squalid, overcrowded, disease-ridden, unheated barracks; to eating rations of only eight hundred grams of bread a day if they were fortunate enough to maintain their quotas of gold production; to having their lives totally dominated by four things: work, food, tobacco, and the cold; to being given utterly inferior and shoddy clothing which gave little or no protection against Kolyma's subarctic climate. The work day was one of twelve, later extended after the outbreak of World War II to sixteen, hours in which the prisoners worked from 5 A.M. until 8 P.M. Of those prisoners who had not completed their work quota for the day, two additional hours of labor were expected. The prisoners were also given extraordinarily high quotas of gold to produce, yet accurate measurement of each worker's production was impossible to determine. The physical environment was so harsh that most prisoners fell into a vicious cycle. Individuals who could not keep up their work quotas were first reduced to five hundred, then three hundred grams of bread a day, which resulted in death by starvation. These conditions led to the emergence of two special groups of workers: the Katorzhniki, who were always chained while they worked and who perished to a man because they were denied blankets and mattresses at night, and the Dokhodyaga or "goners" who, before they died, had been reduced to an utter state of animal savagery and idiocy caused by lack of food and clothing. As Conquest clearly demonstrates, the Kolyma System remained unchanged, since the accounts of eyewitnesses about conditions in the camps and mines are basically the same, regardless of whether they were written in the late 1930's, the mid-1940's or the early 1950's.

One of the most interesting aspects of Conquest's book is his careful delineation of the social structure of Kolyma. In this penal empire there arose an elite of nine individuals and their families who were called the Devyatka ("niners") who were responsible for the administration of the Kolyma region. These individuals were given special privileges and, in their relationship with the prisoner population, they enjoyed many of the prerogatives which the Czarist aristocracy had over the serfs. Within the prison population itself, however, another complex social order was created. Here the leading group were the professional criminals—the "urkas"—who were encouraged by the prison authorities to intimidate and murder the "politicals" who were those prisoners sent to Kolyma for "counter-revolutionary" activity. Thus the urkas carried out their program of bitter warfare to the politicals with complete immunity and with the direct connivance of the leaders of Dalstroy, even though most of the political prisoners were innocent of their alleged crimes. The urkas stopped at nothing in their animus towards the politicals. They stole food and clothing, raped women politicals, and murdered male politicals if they resisted. In return, the prison authorities gave the urkas the best camp jobs and positions among the servile population of Kolyma.

A special feature of the social system of Kolyma was the role of women, who comprised no more than five or six percent of the total population. Conquest notes that there is a disproportionately large number of female eyewitness accounts, which suggests that as women did not have to work in the mines, they had a higher survival rate than their male contemporaries. However, here too existed the division between urka female prisoners and political female prisoners, where the former tyrannized over and scorned the latter. One resource for survival open to all women not available to men was, of course, their sex. In many cases, women survived by prostituting themselves to camp administrators and guards. If any children were born of this promiscuity, they were almost at once removed from the care of their mothers, who never saw them again.

In his summary, the author discusses some very impressive statistics which prove the central thesis of his book. He demonstrates how Kolyma from 1938 to 1940 went from having twenty-five gold mines with approximately 150,000 prisoners, to sixty-six mines with approximately 400,000 prisoners. In addition, from 1932 until 1954, Kolyma received at least 3,000,000 people, of whom at most only 500,000 survived. He makes a salient comparison between the Hitlerian concentration camps and those of Stalin and points out that Hitler's only lasted a decade and had no defenders in the West while Stalin's lasted over two decades and had many ideological supporters in Europe and America. Conquest is especially severe on those Westerners who deliberately, according to him, turned a blind eye towards the Stalin slave labor camp system, such as former Vice-President Henry A. Wallace and Professor Owen Lattimore, who visited Kolyma in the summer of 1944 and wrote glowing accounts of what they saw, and of the present Soviet regime. Indeed, to Conquest, the present Soviet government remains both the heir and the accomplice of the Kolyma System until such time that it publicly denounces the atrocities committed there during the Stalinist era.

Robert Conquest has a superb writing style and has accomplished a brilliant *tour de force* in integrating his source materials into a readable and intelligible narrative. His two appendices on the ships of the Dalstroy Line and the camps and mines of Kolyma are admirable in their inclusiveness. For scholarly readers, there is a criticism of the book in its incomplete footnoting system. However, this is a minor fault offset by the precise and almost photographic prose which depicts so vividly the barbarism and inhumanity of the Kolyma labor camps.

Michael G. R. Kelley

Sources for Further Study

Booklist. LXXIV, July 1, 1978, p. 1648.

Christian Century. XCV, September 13, 1978, p. 836.

Christian Science Monitor. LXX, October 13, 1978, p. 19.

Kirkus Reviews. XLVI, February 15, 1978, p. 212.

New York Times Book Review. June 18, 1978, p. 1.

Times Literary Supplement. May 12, 1978, p. 520.

THE LAST CONVERTIBLE

Author: Anton Myrer (1922-   )
Publisher: G. P. Putnam's Sons (New York). 506 pp. $10.95
Type of work: Novel
Time: 1970's, with major flashbacks to the 1940's
Locale: Massachusetts

*Starting as an explanation of how a 1938 Packard convertible, sequentially inher-
ited over the years by members of a clan of Harvard friends, came to rest finally in the
narrator's possession, this story becomes a sensitive and violent history of a representative segment of American life in the 1940's*

Principal characters:
GEORGE VIRDON, the narrator, a scholarship student at Harvard, a
World War II veteran, and now a publisher's reader
NANCY, his shrewish wife
RON, his daughter's lover, to whom he explains the generation of
the 1940's
CHRISTABEL FARRIS, his true, never-to-be-realized love
RUSS CURRIER, her lover
JEAN-JEAN DES BARRES, the original, aristocratic owner of the con-
vertible, "The Empress"
RON DALRYMPLE, one of George's lifelong friends
TERRY GILLIGAN, another of George's friends from Harvard

Anton Myrer is a courageous and gifted novelist. He never avoids the largest subjects, and he treats them with deep respect and skillful craft. Certainly
anyone interested in depictions of the 1940's in American life should go to his
fiction. That era was a vital and large event in American history. Typically set
mainly in that period, Myrer's latest novel, *The Last Convertible*, is commen-
surately enormous in its scope, ambitious in its intent, and remarkable in the
fullness of its achievement. It is obviously a major effort by a writer who cares
deeply about his country, his countrymen, where they are going, and why.

Myrer has written seven lengthy novels, each built and told with care and
attention to exact details of character, setting, and mood. He has written about
a restless array of subjects. In *The Tiger Waits*, for instance, he explored
international and national politics, along with the dramatic sociological
changes of America in the 1960's; and earlier, in the powerful yet unappre-
ciated *The Big War*, he wrote a moving novel about World War II. *The Big
War* has some of the most harrowing yet precisely written and effective descriptions of men in combat of any of the war novels of that era. Neither
Norman Mailer nor James Jones equals Myrer's masterful depictions of the
commingled hatred for and fascination with the "aliveness" of war. Those
sections in *The Last Convertible* describing combat also have a strong visceral
impact. In each of his subsequent novels as well, Myrer has continued to
explore the relationships between men and women in love, struggle, and turmoil.

Now, nearly forty years later, the World War II period still haunts Myrer, and in *The Last Convertible* he uses the period as the setting to help his generation come to grips with its children's attitudes towards the war in Vietnam. Myrer is adept at suggesting the delicate and deadly mixture which the decade of the 1940's was for him, with its acute sense of beginnings, its seemingly boundless future, and its imminent possibility of sudden death. This fusion produced a period of clearly defined, firmly grasped joys—pleasures made all the deeper for their defiance of death. Myrer survived the trauma of his war and came out of those years with values clarified and a desire to write about some of the things he deeply cared about.

In *The Last Convertible*, the author attempts to explain those hard-won joys. The Vietnam War years—the tumultuous, tradition-shattering 1960's— seem to have eroded, attacked or confused those very values Myrer's generation fought so tenaciously to protect. Today's world makes the old values, attitudes, music, and general style all seem "square." Typically, Myrer confronts this hurtful premise. He asks questions, analyzes, attempts resolutions, offers answers—he refuses, in short, to give up. Many of his generation have withdrawn into reactionary sullenness and despair as their children lose themselves in life-styles which seem radical and incomprehensible to their parents. Myrer loves his country and its people, old and young, too much to give up on them. They are alive, and therefore they have the potential for synthesis, change and the achievement of unity and human understanding.

The story of *The Last Convertible* opens in the early 1970's in a typical American home. The youngest daughter of the novel's narrator, George Virdon, reads aloud over breakfast a newspaper article announcing the production of the last convertibles in the United States. Although this news impresses George, it does not impress his wife, who is more worried about the live-in relationship their oldest daughter has with a young Vietnam War veteran named Ron. The parents are divided over the issue of their daughter's relationship: Nancy feels George is easygoing, unstructured, and remiss in his fatherly duties, while George feels that his child's trial marriage is something he and Nancy should have done years ago. Thus, Myrer quickly establishes the tenor of the 1960's by depicting the philosophical and sociological problems confronting his characters.

George, retiring to his automotive-hobby workshop with his daughter's lover in tow, finds himself offering an explanation—or more honestly, a justification—to the young man for the values his own generation holds. He begins with an explanation of how he has come to own "The Empress," a classic 1938 Packard convertible super-eight. His deep affection for the old car has caused his children to accuse him of "slobbering down memory lane." George's explanation includes how the car has been owned successively by five of his Harvard classmates. The story of the car becomes the story of the people who owned it and, through a flashback technique, the story of the entire generation of the 1940's.

In the substance and manner of gray-haired George Virdon's description of his remembered world and his time to the young man, there are significant revelations of Anton Myrer's deepest concerns. It is his ability as a novelist thus to combine seriousness of philosophical intent with narrative compulsion which makes him an important writer for Americans in our age. Confronted as we are with a swiftly changing world, we long for some guidance. Myrer suggests ways of finding this. Through humility, hard work, patience, and faith, his characters reach worthy goals, and they cherish beliefs which sustain them through disastrous events. To meet the challenge of inevitable change, man must draw on his strength derived from those constants which give value and a solid base to life: love, marriage, children, work, school, learning, friendship, loyalty, adherence to a code, and a sense of style befitting one's time. One must have resilience as well, and faith in one's self.

In the course of George's detailed reminiscence to Ron, he tells the story of his own courtship of Nancy and the falseness of the code reflected by it: rather than following his passion for the beautiful, gentle Christabel, he decides to defend and maintain a personal error of judgment so that no one else will be hurt. He tries to make Ron, the representative of a more impatient generation, understand how he can take sustenance, and even pride, in having loyally and faithfully upheld a forgivable mistake. Myrer shows the older generation as outer-directed to a fault and the younger generation as inner-directed to a fault. Through his story, the author moves the two generations closer together in human understanding.

For Myrer the world is an excitingly real place which, when it refuses to be embraced, must at least be faced. And, he suggests, it is up to us to make it work at its best. Myrer's strong characters illustrate that living requires as much giving as we can provide—and as much heartfelt taking as we are capable of. Life is complex, heartbreaking, awesome—and Myrer embraces it wholeheartedly. The author writes passionately as well about women; not since Walter D. Edmonds has there been an American writer who so deeply loves and enjoys the company of and the creation of interesting women. Women in all their variety fascinate, delight, and dismay him. He also is concerned about the diversities and the polarization of emotions in men. He knows how men react under stress, and is intrigued by their strengths and weaknesses, their friendships, and their loyalties.

Myrer writes about the necessity for friendship in a difficult world. He sees the main rallying point, the great leveler of differences to be human tolerance and affection, and he has his characters learn the need for loyalty. Early in their careers, the students at Harvard learn a double meaning for the musical phrase, "I'll get by—as long as I have you." That idea stated in many ways becomes a coda for George Virdon's time. He and his friends survive, or get by, because they have one another.

As the novel closes, each of these topics, these values Myrer espouses, has been changed by time, by circumstance, by history. Contemporary attitudes towards each of them have been altered. The novel suggests that this alteration is all—that the topics themselves still are of value, though redefined, re-emphasized.

The real strength of *The Last Convertible* lies in Myrer's uncompromising love of life. For his characters, such phenomena as major wars, miserable marriages, failures of ambitions, shatterings of traditions, all exist as part of the great adventure of being alive. For Myrer, a ride in a green Packard, top down, with the music of Tommy Dorsey wafting from the ornate dashboard, and a beautiful girl talking brightly in the seat nearby, and with a shining dream in one's heart, makes it all worthwhile. It will be different, he knows, for other generations, but their different dreams will nonetheless be beautiful. For Myrer, the manufacture of this country's last convertible marks the end of an aspect of style, not the end of style itself.

Thomas N. Walters

Sources for Further Study

Best Sellers. XXXVIII, May, 1978, p. 38.
New York Times Book Review. March 10, 1978, p. 14.
Newsweek. XCI, May 1, 1978, p. 83.
Time. CXI, June 19, 1978, p. 84.

THE LEFT-HANDED WOMAN

Author: Peter Handke (1942-   )
Translated from the German by Ralph Manheim
Publisher: Farrar, Strauss and Giroux (New York). 88 pp. $7.95
Type of work: Novel
Time: The present
Locale: Germany

A study of loneliness and alienation in an absurd world and of the inadequacy of language as a means of communication

> Principal characters:
> MARIANNE, called "the woman"
> STEFAN, called "the child"
> BRUNO, Marianne's husband
> THE PUBLISHER
> FRANZISKA, Marianne's friend
> THE ACTOR
> THE SALES GIRL

Peter Handke exploded onto the literary world in 1966 by means of his three plays, the first of which was aptly called *Offending the Audience*, and by making headlines, both here and in Germany, because of an outburst of criticism of the members of *Gruppe 47*. This association of German authors and critics was meeting at Princeton, and almost two hundred of Germany's most famous intellectuals were present to be lambasted by the twenty-four-year-old beatnik who idolized the Beatles—his first performed play was dedicated to John Lennon—and dressed and groomed accordingly.

The Left-Handed Woman is the seventh volume by this "angry young man" to be translated and published in the United States. Like most of Peter Handke's works, this one also deals with man's alienation and loneliness in an absurd world. Thirty-year-old Marianne, wife of a successful executive of a porcelain manufacturing company and mother of an eight-year-old son, is suddenly cast into loneliness. The novel starts with Marianne and her husband, Bruno, celebrating his return from an extended business trip to Finland. He tells her that in the isolation in the cold and dark North where he could not understand a single word of what people said, he had come to realize how strongly he and Marianne belonged to each other. They go through all the motions of a reunion of a married couple. The next morning Marianne awakens Bruno and informs him, while laughing at her own choice of words, "I suddenly had an illumination"—another word she had to laugh at—"that you were going away, that you were leaving me. Yes, that's it. Go away, Bruno. Leave me." He leaves her and she rebuffs every one of his future attempts at returning to his family and house.

Is Marianne correct in assuming that Bruno will leave her some day in the future? And is her instinct right, making her fend for herself before that day comes? The answer to these questions can never be definitely ascertained in the novel; but a similar experience in the life of Marianne's employer, the publisher, indicates that such an "illumination" is a private experience which has no relation to reality. The publisher is in a taxi once on a very dark evening with his girl friend, whom he loves very much. For a fleeting moment he sees a man on the sidewalk, and it flashes through his mind that the girl friend, in seeing that man, must realize what an old wreck is now embracing her and that she must be filled with revulsion. He immediately shies away from the embrace and breaks off all their relations, although it is doubtful that she ever even saw the man on the sidewalk.

The publisher's knowledge that his thoughts, his "illumination," have no basis in reality, does not change anything because in the novel the inner world and the outer world seem to have lost contact with each other. This feeling of dislocation between man's emotions and the reality around him is strengthened even further by a statement made by Marianne's friend, Franziska, who feels "that human thought is in pretty good shape but that life is elsewhere." Also Marianne's father contributes to this feeling when he states that at some time in the past he began "to live in the wrong direction."

Nowhere in the novel can the realm of inner emotions be brought into a natural relationship with outer reality. People live past one another without making contact. Where there is physical nearness there is emotional separation, and in a case where for a moment it appears that physical and emotional contact might occur between two characters, they are literally separated by an electric shock. This is when Marianne and The Actor first meet in the department store. There is an apparent reciprocal emotional attraction but when they stretch out their hands in greeting, they recoil from an electric shock caused by static electricity. Later on, when The Actor catches up with Marianne in a café and comes to her house, he talks about emotions. He tells her how he loves her, longs for her, and desires her, but these words spoken out into the real world leave Marianne unmoved and as empty as the late night bus which passes by with its strap handles swaying.

The inability to communicate by means of language and the boundaries of expression placed upon us by the available linguistic structure are matters of concern to Peter Handke and are at the center of his work, *The Inner World of the Outer World of the Inner World*. These and other concerns with language also play a role in the novel at hand. There is very little communication in the dialogues in the novel. They consist of lifeless clichés, but they also appear odd because the responses are almost always off the mark from what the reader would anticipate. What is spoken has become part of the outer world and cannot penetrate into the inner world of the conversation partner. Not only can language not convey emotions from one person to another, but it also may even be detrimental to emotions: as soon as they are verbalized, they become reality which cannot reach back into the realm of emotions. This is exemplified in the incident between The Actor and Marianne. When they first meet without talking, there seems to be mutual understanding and attraction; but when he verbalizes his feelings for her, this understanding and compassion are replaced by apathy. Similarly, Bruno's declaration of his feelings for his wife after his return from Finland immediately precedes Marianne's "illumination" and her request that he leave her.

Perhaps it is also fear of secularizing the essence of the characters which prevents the Narrator from using their names. With this in mind, Marianne's statement, "The more you have to say about me, the freer I will be of you," begins to make sense. The more her husband and friends bring into words that which had united her with them before, the less influence they exert over her.

After asking Bruno to leave, Marianne grows more and more quiet and avoids expressing any feelings. Therefore, she can say in her final statement, which, like the one quoted earlier, is made to herself in front of the mirror: "You haven't given yourself away. And no one will ever humiliate you again." This sounds like a victory statement after the impromptu party at her place. She has become immunized against the world around her, has accepted the inevitable fate, and has receded into a capsule of silence and loneliness.

Such a statement about the demise of language is interesting from an author whose early dramas were nothing but words. The author refused to call them plays, but rather "speaking pieces," *Sprechstücke*, and all traditional elements of the theater were eliminated from them. There was no play-acting, no staging, no theatrical illusionism at all, only a bare stage with actors as speakers—Handke does not want them to be called actors at all—addressing the audience. This apparent emphasis on the word changes in later plays as, for example, *Kaspar*, in which the hero of that name cannot speak. He is taught words for the objects around him by impersonal voices. However, at the end of the play, Kaspar concludes that the language taught him is useless, as it cannot express what he wants to say. The development from Handke's early speaking pieces through *Kaspar* culminates in his play, *My Foot My Tutor*, in which not one word is spoken. Like *Kaspar*, this play is concerned with presenting an aspect of the learning process, an aspect of the way in which an individual becomes aware of the forces around him, or within him, and takes steps to deal with these forces.

Both with respect to the debate about the efficacy of language and with respect to the analysis of a learning situation, one in which an individual is faced with previously unmet problems, *The Left-Handed Woman* is related to the plays mentioned. Some of the elements used to illustrate the demise of language in the novel have already been mentioned. However, to support the thesis that language in this novel is not merely a tool used to deal with a theme but is itself part of the central theme, it is necessary to return to them again.

Structurally the novel is not unlike the two plays mentioned. This novel of eighty-eight pages is broken into thirty-nine independent chapters which all show the woman, Marianne, in different situations. No attempt is made at tying the chapters together with a reference in one leading over to the other. The opposite is the case: each chapter is a self-contained unit. As the plays have blackouts between the skits or situations, so the novel has a very obvious, unusually large, spacing between each chapter. This spacing is always the same, whether the time span is long or short or whether there is a change of location or not. To make the division between chapters appear even stronger, the first word in each chapter is in heavy italics.

The lack of continuity and cohesion is seen also in other structural elements. Mention has already been made of the distortion created by having partners in a dialogue miss their cues, so to speak, thereby creating a halting effect since one statement does not logically follow the other. Increasing this duality and lack of continuity is the Narrator's way of identifying the speakers as in a drama. Thus an already staccato dialogue falls even more apart when every statement, no matter how short, is preceded by "The woman:," "The child:," and so on.

Looking in on situations without hearing any words spoken, as is the case with the play, *My Foot My Tutor*, is another device used in the novel. We see Marianne observe through the window a meeting of the women's association with which Franziska repeatedly tries to involve Marianne. We see her observe her son, Stefan, and his friend on the playground via a video transmission without sound. We see her in a shopping center notice a shopkeeper treating a foreign worker differently from the way he treats a local shopper, and many other similar situations. Soon it becomes clear that the novel as a whole is like the play, *My Foot My Tutor*. The reader is looking in on Marianne adjusting to loneliness, and he also gets a picture without sound, since he never hears Marianne put into words any of her feelings and thoughts. She—contrary to the other characters, especially Bruno—knows the limitation of language and accepts the consequences. As the character who was interviewed on the television program mentioned in the novel, and who was asked to tell about his loneliness and just sat there without opening his mouth, so Marianne at the end of the novel silently faces the world from her rocking chair on the terrace.

Because of the author's inability to deal with the characters as complete human beings, and because of his disregard for the spiritual side of man, the novel is cold and humorless. Fortunately, it consists of only eighty-eight pages of large print with plenty of spacing; otherwise, many readers might never complete it.

Sofus E. Simonsen

Sources for Further Study

Library Journal. CIII, June 15, 1978, p. 83.

New York Times Book Review. June 18, 1978, p. 10.

Newsweek. XCII, July 3, 1978, p. 83.

Time. CXI, June 19, 1978, p. 80.

LEON TROTSKY

Author: Irving Howe (1920-   )
Publisher: The Viking Press (New York). 214 pp. $10.00
Type of work: Biography
Time: 1877-1940
Locale: Russia

A condensed study of Trotsky's life and thought offering an introduction to his political and intellectual contributions to twentieth century history

> *Principal personages:*
> LEON TROTSKY, Russian Socialist leader and early Bolshevik leader who fell from power in the late 1920's
> VLADIMIR ILYICH LENIN, Russian revolutionary and theorist who led the Bolsheviks during the October Revolution of 1917
> JOSEF VISSARIONOVICH STALIN, leader and head of the Russian government from 1924 until 1953 who helped Russia become a totalitarian state

In this short but informative "political essay with a narrative foundation" about Marxist critic, polemicist, philosopher, and firebrand Leon Trotsky, Irving Howe offers readers who know little about Trotsky a comprehensive yet concise overview of the revolutionary leader's many contributions to Bolshevism, his disillusionment with Stalinism, and his years in exile. Though *Leon Trotsky* is, in Howe's words, "a small book on a large subject," it manages to include the major currents in the intellectual growth of its subject. The book is intended as an introduction to Trotsky's life and thought and as a critique of his political and intellectual role in twentieth century history.

As Howe sees him, Trotsky, though his life was a succession of painful episodes and his "message" to fellow socialists eventually fell upon deaf ears, remains a "figure of heroic magnitude" whose writings about the coming terrors of Russian totalitarianism were uncannily accurate. To Howe, Trotsky the social critic and polemicist is inseparable from Trotsky the man: his life was given over to the furtherance of the aims of the October Revolution.

Trotsky's life as a free-thinking revolutionary began early, even though his early circumstances hardly dictated that he would rise up against hereditary privilege and the suppression of the proletariat. Born into a prosperous family of Jewish landowners living close to the Black Sea, Trotsky (né Lev Davidovitch Bronstein) had a relatively easy life as a youth. However, he had an astonishing social conscience for the place and time in which he lived; Trotsky recalled, for example, that he was "shaken" by his father's brutal dealings with his peasants. Later, in a private school in Odessa, young Trotsky joined a demonstration against an instructor who harassed a boy because of his German origins. (Trotsky considered this episode, which ended with his expulsion from school, as his first true political "test.")

Trotsky, no longer a political virgin, increasingly gave himself over to radical causes, which Howe mentions in passing but fails to elaborate on. Among other things, we are told that the budding revolutionary was said to have exclaimed at one point, ". . . a curse upon all Marxists, and upon those who want to bring dryness and hardness into all the relations of life!" Howe implies that Trotsky's life became not a struggle against Marxism—for he embraced it with fervor at age eighteen—but a fight against all forces, whether outside or inside the Marxist movement, that would make life "hard" and "dry" for the masses of working people.

Trotsky's decision to enter the ranks of committed socialists was to make his life hellishly painful. For, not long after having joined socialist groups, Trotsky was arrested by the Czar's police and kept for months in solitary confinement, only thereafter to be sent to Siberia. Siberian exile, however, turned to his advantage, since he was given ample opportunity to study the literary classics as well as the newer writers—Zola, Ibsen, and Gogol. It was this Siberian period that helped Trotsky become so well acquainted with literature that he became a literary critic, a vocation that he turned to when politics soured his spirit.

In the years preceding the Revolution of 1917, Trotsky wrestled with what he termed "the organizational question"—the question of how best to create a worker/peasant alliance that would overthrow the Czar. In 1902, he met Lenin and other leading Russian radicals-in-exile living in London. Increasingly, he was referred to as a "leader" of the socialist movement. However, Trotsky found it quite difficult to jump to either the Mensheviks' side (the side of the group which was more moderate in its political aims than were the members of Lenin's group) or that of the Bolsheviks.

What plagued Trotsky in those prerevolutionary years and all the years to follow the formation of a one-party state was the implicit threat of totalitarianism in the Leninist/Bolshevik outlook. Lenin, calling for "severe discipline, strict centralism, hierarchic structure, and . . . a corps of 'professional revolutionists,'" seemed to be paving the way for a state as unresponsive to the workers as was the Czar's government. What Trotsky feared (and his worst fears would, of course, be realized) was that a clique of revolutionaries would dictate to the Russian masses—those who theoretically were to control their own destinies—what they could or could not do with their lives. Moreover, such a ruling clique would, he felt, go against the Marxist ideal of a classless society, since one group of people would place themselves at the top. In so believing, Trotsky prophetically forecast that "process of degeneration" which was to overtake the Bolshevik party in the 1920's.

Trotsky, at age twenty-six, provoked the Czar by becoming the chairman of the Soviet of Workers' Delegates in 1905. Since this Soviet badly frightened the Czar, Trotsky again found himself in Siberia, this time supposedly for "life." In exile, he wrote *1905*, his first major work. Unfortunately, Trotsky displayed a myopic vision of the world in *1905*, failing to understand the attachment workers in industrialized nations had to parliamentary forms of government, the lack of interest many Third World people would have in Communist doctrine, and, finally, the elitist nature of many so-called "people's revolutions." In addition, he failed to foresee the Stalinist type of authoritarian state (though he had vague fears of the Bolshevik Revolution going sour); he simply could not imagine former revolutionaries creating such a monstrous government. But, aside from these failings, Trotsky did accurately forecast the Russian October Revolution.

Howe, jumping from the events of 1905 to those of 1917, portrays the mature Trotsky as a seasoned thinker and man of action ready for a fight. At this point in the book, the Revolution is already an accomplished fact (apparently Howe felt that any discussion of it would be redundant, since many fine histories dealing with the uprising exist) and the ranks of the revolutionaries are badly split along ideological lines. The question is who will guide the new Russia now that the Czar has been toppled.

Howe does offer some discussion (though not much) of the power struggle among the liberal Kadets of the Provisional Government who "failed to understand that the revolution spreading across Russia was an elemental social upheaval, not to be wrenched to an abrupt halt at some point of convenience. . . ," the Social Revolutionists ("sincere, romantic, confused, divided"), the Mensheviks (who felt that backward Russia was not "ripe for socialism"), the Rightists who would restore the Czar-based government the Bolsheviks destroyed, and the Bolsheviks themselves, the party of Lenin.

Trotsky, having gone abroad to Western Europe and America for a time, came back to a divided Russia in 1917. The Provisional Government of Alexander Kerensky was unstable, since it had opted to have Russia stay in the Great War. After a brief term in jail, Trotsky and Lenin helped create a resurgent Bolshevik party which, in turn, masterminded the October Revolution.

Assuming the role of "Cruel Advocate" of Bolshevism, Trotsky thundered at the Mensheviks, "You are miserable bankrupts, your role is played out: go where you belong—to the dustbin of history." Howe observes that Trotsky's choice of words oozes with irony. For, though he had no inkling of it at the time, Trotsky would one day find himself in history's "dustbin."

After Lenin took power, Trotsky believed that, at long last, the Marxist dream of a socialist state had been fully realized. Such a rosy view was soon destroyed, however, as Bolshevism turned from the people's party into a totalitarian state. As Howe finds: "On the day the revolution succeeded it set loose energies of counter-revolution—from within its own flawed premises, from the selflessness of those who fought and died for it."

No ivory-tower theoretician or technocrat, Trotsky served the Bolsheviks first as Foreign Minister and then, more importantly, as Minister of War during the Red *versus* White Civil War. It was his leadership that gave the Bolsheviks the wherewithal to defeat the Whites. Once again, however, Howe says little about such large matters as the Civil War and its aftermath, opting instead to focus upon Trotsky's intellectual life.

After the war, Trotsky, though generally well regarded, was never made a part of the Bolshevik inner circle. Rather than battle against those who would push him aside, he made the mistake of absenting himself from the political fracas then going on. The inner circle, receiving no real opposition to their schemes, gradually steered the state from a people's democracy to a totalitarian regime though Trotsky was rather slow to realize what they were doing. In fact, Trotsky even reluctantly agreed to Lenin's idea that laborers be forced to do the state's bidding in order that Russia rebuild her agricultural and industrial base. This idea soon became policy, and helped usher in the totalitarian state.

Moreover, Trotsky did an "about-face" (albeit a temporary one) in his *Terrorism and Communism* (1920), by arrogantly supporting raw power as the means by which the masses must be governed in order that socialism might win the day. To Howe, this book marks one of the lowest points in Trotsky's career, for it marks his betrayal of his own best instincts: "If there is a single text that supports those who believe Leninism and Stalinism to be closely linked or to form a line of continuous descent, it is *Terrorism and Communism.*"

The tragedy of Russia after the Revolution's high hopes had been quashed was partly Trotsky's responsibility. When Soviet workers staged a rebellion, claiming that the Government did not care about their needs, the Bolsheviks, led by Trotsky, fired upon them at Kronstadt in one of the darkest events of the early Revolutionary period.

In Howe's estimation, although dissenting opinions were to be heard within Bolshevik ranks during the 1920's, those in power sensed their failure as true revolutionaries, and their isolation from the Russian people. Lenin, by alternately repressing political rights and easing economic policy, allowed the state to fall into what Howe calls the "Thermidor" of Stalinism.

As a counter-revolution, Stalinism, developing in strength throughout the 1920's, really came into its own in the 1930's; the "Old Bolsheviks" were purged in large numbers and a monstrous bureaucracy held life and death power over the Russians. With his personal fortunes waning during this troubled period, Trotsky used his brilliant mind to write hard-hitting critical essays about the terror of this new regime; politically, however, his life was becoming forfeit, as his foes pushed him further and further from the seat of power.

Sensing he was partly to blame (how much so we are not told, for Howe fails to go into detail) for the souring of the Revolution, Trotsky turned to reading great literature for solace; it was during this period (the late 1920's) that he wrote some of his best literary essays. By 1929, Trotsky, stripped of power, was first exiled to Asiatic Russia, then permanently exiled from Russia by Josef Stalin, his archenemy. Little was left for him to do but write and occasionally address his scattered followers in the countries where he lived (Turkey, France, and Norway). Driven from place to place, he finally settled in Mexico, only to be slain by a secret agent of Stalin. The fact that Stalin went out of his way to get rid of Trotsky demonstrates how fearful the former was of the latter; Stalin realized that Trotsky's pen was more to be feared than his sword, and took no chances.

It can safely be said that *Leon Trotsky*, though well written, is not a scholar's work. Howe does not in any way misrepresent his book. It is a solid, brief introduction to a multifaceted personality, a man who was a theorist, war hero, philosopher, literary critic, statesman, and politician. It is not, however, a portrait of the whole man, for we hear almost nothing about him as husband, son, and friend. *Leon Trotsky* is a "small book on a big subject" which serves to whet the reader's imagination by providing him with glimpses of Trotsky the theorist within the context of his age.

John D. Raymer

Sources for Further Study

Booklist. LXXIV, July 15, 1978, p. 1708.
Harper's Magazine. CCLVII, October, 1978, p. 96.
Library Journal. CIII, August, 1978, p. 1501.
Nation. CCXXVII, September 23, 1978, p. 38.
New York Times Review of Books. XXV, September 28, 1978, p. 277.
Times Literary Supplement. August 4, 1978, p. 878.

LERMONTOV
Tragedy in the Caucasus

Author: Laurence Kelly (1933-   )
Publisher: George Braziller (New York). Illustrated. 259 pp. $12.50
Type of work: Biography
Time: 1814-1841
Locale: Russia

A study of the life and work of the Russian Romantic poet Mikhail Lermontov, focusing on his period in the Caucasus

Mikhail Lermontov, perhaps Russia's greatest poet after Pushkin, was an enormously talented and thoroughly unpleasant person whose life was cut short in an unnecessary duel, which bordered on suicide. He had cast himself in the role of the morose and black humored Byronic hero at odds with society and had succeeded in getting himself exiled to the Caucasus, where he died at the age of twenty-six.

In this well-researched work, the first major biography of Lermontov in English, Laurence Kelly covers the whole of the poet's life, incorporating considerable background on the political and intellectual life of the time. His descriptions range from the court at St. Petersburg to the frontier life of the Caucasus, which appealed especially to that fiercely independent side of Lermontov that expressed itself in political opposition to the Czar and the autocratic regime. In addition to poetic genius, Lermontov was a gifted artist, and one of the more interesting features of this work is a collection of his drawings and sketches of scenes of villages, landscapes, battles, and native types, as well as other contemporary drawings that give a picture of the world that was so important in shaping Lermontov's poetic work.

In his Preface, Kelly recounts the conception of this book on his own journey to the Caucasus and Georgia in 1971, retracing Lermontov's steps. He has a strong feeling for this area, and some of the better parts of his book are those dealing with this little-known part of the world. This firsthand experience, along with exhaustive research, gives the work an important place in Lermontov scholarship. Among other finds, most important is the exhaustive account of the final duel, complete with eyewitness accounts, and a never before published report of Lermontov's last words—an insult to his opponent that almost surely was responsible for the fatal outcome.

To be sure, this exhaustive research is at times exhausting to the reader, as Kelly shows a fascination with detailed accounts of the most minor matters, such as details of military life and weaponry—which, though they picture the life Lermontov knew, deflect attention from the poet himself. The book runs the danger of focusing more on the man of action than the poet, and thus reversing the actual values for which Lermontov is remembered. This is all the more the case, since the poetry itself is so difficult to translate, and the versions presented in an appendix in most cases fall short of the music and power of the originals, a fact which Kelly himself recognizes and regrets.

Even without really significant literary criticism, however, the book is valuable, and certainly the drama of Lermontov's life should make him of interest to many who have no specific interest in Russian literature. The poet lived during a time of turmoil in Russia, as first Czar Alexander I and then Nicholas I attempted to clamp a lid on political expression in the years immediately following the invasion of Russia by Napoleon, years which throughout Europe were marked by an attempt to turn back the hands of the clock, to undo the liberalizing tendencies of the French Revolution. The Congress of Vienna, which ended in 1815, had attempted to restore toppled monarchies along with the privileges of the aristocracy, and throughout Europe the young generation of poets became spokesmen for nationalism and liberalism. They united political sentiment with the literary movement of Romanticism that had come to prominence in the "Storm and Stress" writers of Germany in the 1770's, and in England with Wordsworth, Shelley, Keats, and, above all, Byron. Byron's European reputation was enormous, and his *persona*, that of the moody outsider, satiric, mocking, feeding on his own emotions, became a model for a younger generation. Byron died in Greece in 1824, helping the cause of Greek liberty against the Turks. His work was already known in Russia and had cast a spell over Pushkin. The government, alarmed by the revolutionary sentiments of many of Byron's works, which often celebrated outlaws and brigands while attacking conventional society, attempted to impose censorship. In Russia Byron became a political figure, since literature in general was a forum for the expression of political thought; Romanticism in Europe became equated with political liberalism.

It was into this world that Mikhail Lermontov was born. His young mother died of consumption in 1817, and his father, a member of the minor gentry, turned to a life of dissipation. Mikhail's upbringing was therefore taken over by his grandmother, a woman of great determination. During his youth she took him three times to the Caucasus, and thus began the lifelong connection of Lermontov with what Kelly calls "the wild east." He describes traveling conditions and circumstances in the Caucasus in considerable detail. Doubtless these early exposures to the grandeur of the landscape and the primitive life of the mountains had a profound impression upon the youngster, and Kelly evokes many of the impressions that must have struck the growing poet-to-be.

A second major influence on Lermontov during his youth was the Decembrist uprising in 1825, the year Nicholas I came to the throne. The uprising, an attempt to bring modern Western liberal political ideas to Russia, failed, and the leaders were executed or exiled to Siberia. Among these leaders were friends of the family, and the young Lermontov could hardly avoid awareness of the events, which reverberated among the liberal thinkers for years as Czar Nicholas sought to prevent any repetition of the movement.

In 1828, Lermontov was enrolled in the "Noble Pension," a school for the aristocracy. It was during this period that he wrote his first verses, and Kelly stresses the role played in these earliest works by the lasting impressions of the Caucasus, mingled with Romantic sentiments of solitude, tragedy, sublime nature, and love of the primitive life. Also during this period, Lermontov began to draw the sketches illustrating his poetry. These tendencies continued through his years at Moscow University, beginning in 1830. After only two years, Lermontov dropped out and entered a military school in St. Petersburg, an atmosphere hardly conducive to the development of his artistic talent, if only by its sheer lack of privacy. Nevertheless, the loss of a former sweetheart whom he had left in Moscow produced an emotional reaction expressed in two plays, *Masquerade* and *The Two Brothers*, the first of which Kelly quotes at length. The entrance of Lermontov into the social and literary scene of the early 1830's in St. Petersburg shows further the development of some of the leading themes of his life and work: social and political criticism, conflict with the censors, personal disillusionment, and depression. These years were dominated in literature by Alexander Pushkin, whose *Evgeny Onegin* and *Queen of Spades* appeared between 1833 and 1836, and the still immature work of Lermontov went relatively unrecognized. It was the death of Pushkin in a duel in 1837 which brought Lermontov to prominence: in a single day he composed "The Death of a Poet," and later added a passionate postscript which was circulated privately, but which came to public attention and outraged the censors. As a result of these hastily written, overwrought lines, Lermontov was transferred into virtual exile—in the Caucasus.

The next years of Lermontov's life Kelly titles "The Grand Tour." His exile was to a region that he loved; he remained an officer, and his family had friends in all the frontier towns. Kelly details his life there, again describing the region in considerable detail and evoking the scenes that must have struck the poet, quoting as well from Lermontov's works to register his own impressions. His first months were spent at Pyatigorsk, where he took the mineral waters at the spa, having developed rheumatism on his journey east. He fell into social as well as literary circles there and met many of the exiled Decembrists who were serving their time in the Caucasus rather than Siberia. Lermontov sketched, wrote, visited, and traveled, stopping for some weeks in Tiflis and again adding to his store of impressions and experiences. Kelly interweaves Lermontov's poetry, notebook and diary excerpts, other contemporary accounts, and his own observations to create another vignette of an aspect of Lermontov's work. It is in these vignettes, rather than a thoroughgoing analytic approach, that the book has its greatest strength.

Following his brief return to the Caucasus, which was a crucial event in Lermontov's life, a pardon by the Czar brought him back to St. Petersburg, where his literary career blossomed. He joined the circle of the noted historian Karamsin and the editor Andrei Krayevsky, through whose influence much of his work escaped the censors. It was this period that produced the two works on which Lermontov's fame rests, the novel *A Hero of Our Time* and the poem "The Demon." *A Hero of Our Time* is actually not a novel, but a group of five short stories, each touching upon the character of the central figure, Grigory Pechorin, a young officer in the Caucasus. The stories rest heavily on Lermontov's own experiences, and thus the Caucasus becomes not merely the scene of his own childhood, exile, and death, but a key element in his literary work. This novel, which contains so much of Lermontov's own character and thought, is also, as its title indicates, a portrait of the post-Decembrist generation. It was even read by the Czar, who found it disgusting. Nevertheless, this novel, with "The Demon," established Lermontov's reputation. A number of significant works appeared in succession.

The poet's character, however, was not suited to the demands of St. Petersburg society and the guarded atmosphere of the royal court. He was prone to indiscretions, and at last ended in jail for dueling. The punishment once again was exile to the Caucasus, which was now embroiled in a war between the fiercely independent highland tribes and the occupying Russians. Again, the narrative blends Lermontov's poetry with his own accounts of his experiences and with a thoroughly researched depiction of the life of the area and the events and relationships which Lermontov encountered. This section is particularly well developed with all the background information to give one a good picture of the soldiers' life in the war—details of the procedure of running the gauntlet, of Russian and tribal tactics, of major personalities. At times, Lermontov seems to get lost in the welter of secondary information.

The second exile was broken by a two-month leave in 1841, and Lermontov returned once again to the capital. His literary career was assured; poems had continued to appear in his absence through the influence of Krayevsky, and a second edition of *A Hero of Our Time* was published. Lermontov hoped to remain, but his efforts to secure permission for a permanent return failed, and he returned to the Caucasus for the last time. His indiscretion brought about a chain of events which led to his death in a duel, which is recounted at length, including important previously unpublished information.

The literary evaluation of Lermontov as a poet is difficult for the English-speaking reader. By the leading writers of his day, he was regarded as second only to Pushkin, and that estimate is still held by many. That his life was tragically enmeshed in the political struggles of the time is clear; the role played by his own arrogant and intemperate character in his misfortunes is equally evident. Laurence Kelly provides a vivid picture of the poet and his times; the works themselves are woven into the narrative. While specialists may seek a more analytic treatment of the literary aspects of Lermontov's life, for the general reader this biography provides a glimpse of a fascinating era and of one of its leading figures.

Steven C. Schaber

Sources for Further Study

New Statesman. XCIV, November 25, 1977, p. 731.
New York Times Book Review. March 5, 1978, p. 10.
New Yorker. LIV, March 20, 1978, p. 152.
Times Literary Supplement. December 2, 1977, p. 1402.

THE LETTERS OF SIDNEY AND BEATRICE WEBB

Authors: Sidney Webb (1859-1947) and Beatrice Potter Webb (1858-1943)
Edited by Norman MacKenzie
Publisher: Columbia University Press (New York). 3 vols. 1,340 pp. $125.00
Type of work: Letters
Time: 1873-1944
Locale: England, the United States, Russia

> *An annotated collection of letters exchanging views on social and economic condi-*
> *tions between two social reformers and a world full of their acquaintances*

Readers only casually acquainted with societal forces in England's late Victorian period will nevertheless probably be aware of the influence of Sidney
and Beatrice Webb on the contemporary political scene. Beatrice Potter Webb
was the most notable woman of her time, and her husband, politician Sidney
Webb, was of only slightly less fame. Though the couple were active during
World War I, their letters to each other and to their associates carry few references to that conflict. They do, however, bridge the period between the fading
of the Liberals as a power in the British Empire and the rise of the Labor Party
as His Majesty's Loyal Opposition.

Norman MacKenzie, a sociologist at the University of Sussex and prominent in the London School of Economics and Political Sciences, has sifted
through several thousand letters the Webbs wrote to each other and to their
correspondents. He includes complete letters rather than merely excerpts of
important letters, and the entries are numbered, dated, and introduced by paragraphs explaining their significance to readers and future historians. When
Beatrice planned, late in life, to write an autobiography, she planned a three-
part division: Apprenticeship (1873-1892), Partnership (1892-1922), and Pilgrimage (1912-   ). MacKenzie follows her divisions. In addition, he assures prospective readers that, however uninteresting the letters are by Sidney
(a pleasant fellow even though a boring letter writer), those by Beatrice (often
charmingly written) offer an excellent intellectual survey of the era that
spanned the period between the publication of Darwin's *On the Origin of
Species* and the dropping of the bomb on Hiroshima.

Three threads give a sort of unity to this collection. One is Beatrice's personal story, smothered by trends, reports, and statistics; the second follows the
development of socialism in nineteenth century Great Britain; and the third
covers the careers of the Webbs, to whose tireless work and research many of
Britain's political and social reforms owe a considerable debt.

The first volume of 452 pages covers the first nineteen years of the Webbs'
letter-writing, while the other two books contain their production during over
half a century. Each book also includes a brief "Survey Chronology of the
Period Covered" and a List of recipients of the letters in it. Volume I also
provides a "List of the Potter Children." The first forty letters were written by
Beatrice, next-to-the-youngest of the Potter's nine daughters. (A younger

brother died at the age of four.) Letter No. 1, which Beatrice called "a nice little letter," is an uncorrected copy of the work of a four-year-old girl. Other early letters by her to parents, sisters, family servants, and so forth, asking for local news and reports on pets, are omitted. One significant letter gives details of her visit to some of her mother's poor relations in Lancaster, and conditions in the collectives where they lived. Another letter, written though never sent, confesses her own antidemocratic and anticollectivist biases with which she began this early survey of industrial conditions.

Beatrice was born into a wealthy industrial family, while Sidney came from an impoverished family—his father was an innkeeper, his mother a milliner. His ambitious parents nevertheless sent their two sons to France and Germany to learn languages, after graduation from a middle-class school in England; Sidney then took up legal studies. Beatrice describes Sidney as "Under average height" and "homely and plain." In later years, the couple was labeled "Beauty and the Beast," though photographs and paintings used as frontispieces in the books prove this is an exaggeration. Her letters concede that he was "unusually tolerant and with an extraordinary stock of abilities." In the literary and debating clubs he later joined, he revealed a clear and legal mind. It was in one of these clubs that he first met Bernard Shaw, and their friendship persisted.

Sidney's first letter in this collection, dated February 28, 1881, reported his defeat in a club election, though his opponent characterized him as "the ablest man in England." Another letter suggests the group be renamed "Fabian Society" instead of "Free Life Fellowship." The name was derived from the Roman general, Quintus Fabius Maximus (275-203 B.C.), who believed that victories could be won by delaying tactics while permeating the opposition. Members of the Fabians believed trade unions and objectionable labor movements could be destroyed by patience and by the books and pamphlets the members wrote against them. As MacKenzie reports, after Beatrice and others joined the Fabians in 1909, several groups disbanded or became part of a unified Labor Party, while the Fabian Society became a sort of Research and Publicity Agency.

Beatrice had originally come to London to assist Charles Booth in a survey of London, an effort which ended with the publication of the seventeen-volume *Life and Labor of the People of London* (1889-1903). Sidney, meanwhile, was involved in a fight to improve the British Poor Laws. At the beginning of the nineteenth century, to suppress vagrancy and begging, British towns passed a variety of laws that in 1834 were combined in a national law making each center of population responsible for its own social conditions. The law was a failure. The poor, the sick, and the insane were all lodged in the same shabby quarters. For nearly a century, reformers had been trying to stir up public interest to improve conditions; now the Fabians joined the endeavor, trying to improve education for poor children by making pamphlets and books available. Sidney Webb was largely responsible for the establishment of the London School of Economics and Political Science as an additional instrument.

Sidney was elected to the London Council, and his letters to various groups show his involvement in myriad problems. Other letters are about the private lives of fellow Fabians; H. G. Wells's illegitimate child is mentioned, as is Bertrand Russell's threat of divorcing his wife. Beatrice writes that she wants to celebrate their tenth wedding anniversary by a trip to Italy to work on the *History of Liquor in England.* Meanwhile, friends were begging for speeches and articles from Sidney, and Beatrice was appointed to a commission whose purpose was the end of segregation of the destitute under near-penal conditions. Beatrice's critical judgment was always in demand by author friends, who sent her their latest publications. She angered H. G. Wells by writing that she quit his badly written *Tono Bungay* to turn to the prophetic *War in the Air;* and amid it all, her husband was trying to persuade her to combine with him in the issuance of a new magazine, *The New Statesman,* to cover world conditions such as unrest in Ireland and the violence connected with the Women's Suffrage movement. At this point in the Webbs' hectic lives, Volume II begins.

Though the editor entitles one chapter "The Earthquake, July 1914-1916," its first letter shows that the Fabians were so concerned with their local situation that the outbreak of the World War came as a complete surprise. Even the letters dating from the vacation trip around the world between June, 1911, and May, 1912, MacKenzie comments, "show a curious detachment for a couple of social investigators." Beatrice could not make up her mind which side to favor; like many friends, she could not accept the thought of a conflict between two great capitalistic powers. She became melancholic, fearing she was suffering from the cancer that had killed three of her sisters. For several years, she had no incentive to tackle any important task. Though Sidney was called on to serve on a commission to determine postwar policy, Beatrice felt no urge to make suggestions and was barely tempted to co-edit his book, *Methods of Social Study,* as soon as he could gracefully retire from Parliament. One friend suggested a small cottage and estate to which he might retire to rest, so he bought it, and the couple used their leisure moments to improve and replant what they called Passfield Cottage.

From Passfield, the Webbs announced the conclusion of Volume I of *English Poor Laws,* gave a premature retirement party for Sidney, and received honorary degrees from the University of Munich.

From what they had read, the Webbs had an unrealistic idea of conditions in Russia; they happily accepted an invitation from the editor of *Pravda* to join fifty other Fabians "all over 50" in a visit to see Communism in action. From the first came disillusion. As their letters report, the trains were crowded, dirty and off schedule; the lack of a diner on the train forced all passengers to forage for food at every stop during their fourteen-hour trip.

Back in England, Beatrice collapsed with a kidney condition, but, following two operations and several months in a nursing home, she was able to return to slow writing. The default of German reparations, however, so reduced their income that they were glad to accept Shaw's generous check from his theater royalty to cover medical expenses and the cost of publication of her *Soviet Communism*. Sidney was asked to become Colonial Secretary and was elevated to the Upper House as Lord Passfield. Beatrice was slowly recovering and was now able to conclude her *Wages of Men and Women: Should They Be Equal?*

The three hundred letters of Volume III are filled with references to how the passing years have spread illness and death among the Webbs' circle. Wells's wife had died of cancer, as had Lady Courtney. Their old friend Graham Wallas was dead, as well as Lord Richard Haldane and "A. E." (George William Russell), the Irish poet. The deaths of several German Socialist friends are also mentioned. When these late letters are not about the deaths of friends, they are filled with reports of ill health and longing for vacations on the Mediterranean. Sidney complains on his eightieth birthday, "I am aging and feel 150." Except for her concern for the future of her semi-invalid husband, writes Beatrice, "I would gladly sleep and rise no more."

But it was Sidney who first gave way to the strain of his official duties in the Colonial Office. He suffered a stroke in 1938; his speech became blurred and he could no longer write. Beatrice took on the presidency of the Fabian Society and, despite her physical weariness and worries, substituted on other duties. She managed to survive till she completed her *Truth About Soviet Russia* (1943), then died. Sidney survived her by four years. Two months later, by popular desire, both were buried side by side, in Westminster Abbey, the only couple ever so honored.

Willis Knapp Jones

Sources for Further Study

Economist. CCLXVII, May 13, 1978, p. 133.
Guardian Weekly. CXVIII, May 21, 1978, p. 20.
New York Times Book Review. July 30, 1978, p. 7.
Observer. May 21, 1978, p. 16.
Times Literary Supplement. May 19, 1978, p. 551.

THE LETTERS OF VIRGINIA WOOLF
Volume III: 1923-1928

Author: Virginia Woolf (1882-1941)
Edited, with an Introduction and notes, by Nigel Nicolson and Joanne Trautmann
Publisher: Harcourt Brace Jovanovich (New York). 600 pp. $14.95
Type of work: Letters

The third volume of a projected six-volume collection containing 1,977 letters written in the period during which Woolf wrote her most famous novels, Mrs. Dalloway *and* To the Lighthouse

"It's odd how being ill . . . splits one up into several different people," wrote Virginia Woolf to Vita Sackville-West during one of an extraordinary number of minor illnesses: her critical brain, she said, could read and conceptualize, but it felt separated from the person who could write books; and her body was yet another person, going its own way.

Actually, Woolf might have been describing not an illness, but her state of creative health. Like so many makers, she lived in and moved amphibiously among several levels and layers of the world at once: the social, the domestic, the critical and journalistic, and the small, intensely private area where she wrote her novels and short stories. These lives were clearly interdependent; she needed an enormous social sphere in order to free the tiny space where she did her serious work. And yet, paradoxically, she firmly and fiercely kept these regions separated from each other. For her different lives there were different literary modes: her private, and relatively honest, feelings about herself, her friends, and her work went into her diary; there, for example, she was willing to admit jealousy of her husband's literary advances. For her public, social existence, however, she adopted the public mask of her letters, where she is by turns bright, witty, charming, demanding, affectionate, malicious, gossipy, and airy. They were the next best things to conversations. One assumes that she rarely reread or recopied them: "I can only write letters if I don't read them," she insisted. "Once think and I destroy."

That meant, however, that her letters rarely deal with her fiction or serious criticism or delve into the more intense areas of her emotional life. It can be startling, in fact, to call to mind that the letters of this volume, covering the six-year period from 1923 to 1928, coincided with what is generally conceded to be Woolf's major phase. Prior to this time she was, as she notes with some satisfaction in her diary, beginning to acquire something of a reputation, but it scarcely stretched very far beyond the range of Bloomsbury. But now came *Mrs. Dalloway* (1925), *To the Lighthouse* (1927), and *Orlando* (1928); as a bid for a place in the world of criticism beyond that provided by the horde of fugitive pieces that had poured from her pen, there was *The Common Reader* (1925); and she read the lectures that were later revised into *A Room of One's Own* (1929). Yet of all this creative activity and more, there is only the barest passing mention in the letters. Woolf may have been aware of what many writers know—that to speak of one's serious creative efforts is to inhibit that creation. The one exception, and it is only partial, was *Orlando*, written, as Nigel Nicolson points out, as "her most elaborate love-letter" to Vita Sackville-West.

For some years, Vita Sackville-West was one of the most important people in Woolf's life. Beautiful, charming, patrician, herself a writer and published by the Hogarth Press, she became for a time quite indispensable to Woolf. The salutations tell the story in outline. Married to Harold Nicolson, she was addressed at first simply as "Dear Mrs. Nicolson," which shortly became "My dear Vita," in itself innocent enough. Until the end of 1925, there was nothing to distinguish the letters to Vita from any others; they were no longer and no different in tone. In fact, longer and more affectionate letters during this period went to the French painter Jacques Raverat, educated in England, married to a friend of Virginia, and slowly dying abroad. It was to Raverat that she complained of the extensive homosexuality in her circle: "Have you any views on loving one's own sex? All the young men are so inclined." And the ladies, she notes, "are given to their sex too. My aristocrat [Vita] . . . is violently Sapphic." She then describes Vita's elopment with Violet Trefusis, also married, both women intending to spend the rest of their lives together but persuaded to return by their husbands. Obviously fantasizing, she tells Raverat "a secret, I want to incite my lady to elope with me next. Then I'll . . . tell you all about it." According to Nigel Nicolson, the two women did bed down together, for the first of about a dozen times, in December, 1925. Shortly thereafter, Vita was addressed as "Dearest Creature," and then as "Dearest Honey." Vita might speak directly to her diary and confess eventually to her husband; Woolf was more discreet. Speaking of the world at large, she writes, "Oh and Vita won't be here next week to adulterate it—you know what I mean Its a word I can't find at the moment." Two years later, there is a teasing but clear enough reference: "Should you say, if I rang you up to ask, that you were fond of me? If I saw you would you kiss me? If I were in bed would you. . . ." There seems to be general agreement that, whatever affection Woolf felt, there was little that could be termed intense physical passion; and, most certainly, her close and very necessary relationship with Leonard was untouched. But when Vita left England for some months to join her husband, who had taken a diplomatic post in Persia, the letters that followed her were long, detailed, and affectionate. Clearly Woolf meant it when she wrote: "I have missed you. I do miss you. I shall miss you."

At best, or worst, Woolf's "affair" with Vita could scarcely be all-consuming. There was a bustling round of people, parties, lectures, concerts, art exhibits, plays; there were house guests to be entertained, and as house guests she and Leonard were entertained; there was the kaleidoscopic movement of John Maynard Keynes, Roger Fry, E. M. Forster, Clive Bell, her

sister Vanessa Bell, Duncan Grant, Lytton Strachey, T. S. Eliot, Lady Otto-
line Morrell, the Sidney Webbs, and the host of titled and untitled folk that
moved among the members of the upper-middle-class intelligentsia. There was
the Hogarth Press to run and to see become something of a nuisance because of
its success; there were several extended trips abroad, in the course of which
the Woolfs adopted the traditionally sentimental tone of the Englishman rav-
ished by the life of the Mediterranean south—it was no doubt a symbolic necessity that, in Palermo, they see D. H. Lawrence and Norman Douglas sitting
side by side on a bench. Above all, there were the careers and often seedy love
affairs of their friends to hear about, to gossip about, to throw up their hands
about. All this was poured into the letters that were like grappling hooks linked
to her friends: "I am writing great heaps of rubbish," she told one correspondent; "do not blame me; for unless I *do* write something, [you] will let the
end of her line drop, and me go, for ever."

While constantly downed by headaches, flu, and innumerable unclassified
ailments, she and Leonard were able to put aside, for the moment, the fear of
mental breakdown that had dogged her earlier. A cold need no longer be
treated as the harbinger of disaster. So delightful did she now find London that
at long last the Woolfs gave up Hogarth House in Richmond and leased a
house in Bloomsbury, which not only became their own home but also that of
the press. Woolf was exultant: "London is incredibly beautiful—not with the
soft suburban beauty of Richmond: I find Bloomsbury fierce and scornful and
stony hearted, but as I say, so adorably lovely that I look out of my window all
day long."

London, of course, also provided Woolf with much more material for her
often malicious, sometimes inaccurate, but always amusing comments. "That
strange figure Eliot dined here last night," she wrote to Roger Fry. "I feel that
he has taken the veil, or whatever monks do." She was certain that whatever
was wrong with Eliot resulted from his unfortunate American training; to
Lytton Strachey she described "his highly American way, which is tedious
and long-winded to a degree." She no doubt felt that Eliot was fair game,
because, agonizing, diffident, and fearful, he resisted her efforts to provide a
fund for him that would enable him to leave his bank job and devote more of
his efforts to his poetry. The fund winds, like a comic-opera *leitmotif*, through
the letters until the last of many last words was finally written in 1927. Another strange figure was Desmond MacCarthy, whose friends were forever
conspiring, without success, to have him write the book they were certain he
had in him. "Of course we will bully the old wretch," Woolf wrote to his
wife. "Perpetual letters? Telegrams? Telephone? What do you advise? He
must be coerced." For him, too, a fund was raised and presented, and Woolf's
ultimate judgment of him is scarcely pleasant.

Max Halperen

Sources for Further Study

Atlantic. CCXLI, June, 1978, p. 101.

Booklist. LXXIV, June 15, 1978, p. 1593.

Christian Century. XCV, May 3, 1978, p. 48.

History Today. XXVIII, March, 1978, p. 205.

New York Review of Books. XXV, April 20, 1978, p. 16.

New York Times Book Review. May 14, 1978, p. 11.

LIFE IN THE FOREST

Author: Denise Levertov (1923-   )
Publisher: New Directions (New York). 135 pp. $3.95
Type of work: Poetry

A collection of sixty-eight fine lyrics, both in the confessional mode and chronological narrative sequence

The literary reputation of Denise Levertov has long been established, but with *Life in the Forest*, her most recent publication, she once again affirms her place and assures her permanence in the mainstream of *belles lettres*. Further, this volume of verse marks the poet's deliberate attempt to move beyond the freely confessional mode still currently in vogue and considered her forte. Striving to weave a narrative thread through poetic depictions of persons and places, scenes and landscapes, however, she still succeeds in imbuing them all with her personal voice and poetic presence.

Appropriately, the first of five sections comprising the collection is called a "Homage to Pavese," and as Levertov's notes corroborate, the poetry of Cesare Pavese more or less ratified the role she was obscurely taking in her own endeavors:

> Pavese's beautiful poems are about various persons other than himself . . . and in his accompanying essays he speaks of his concept of suggesting a narrative through direct recounting of events as such. . . . Those poems of my own which have, I feel, some humble affinity—however oblique—with what Pavese achieved in *Lavore Stanca*, tend to rather long lines and a discursive structure.

Significantly, then, "Human Being," the poem initiating the "Homage" group, establishes the seemingly dispassionate and disparate observations of a *persona* who metaphorically meditates upon man's timeless journey:

> . . .walking
> in doubt from childhood on; walking
> a ledge of slippery stone in the world's woods
> deep-layered with wet leaves—rich or sad: on one
> side of the path, ecstasy, on the other
> dull grief.

Thus, philosophizing upon life, death, love, loneliness, joy, and sorrow, Levertov runs the gamut of universal emotions and aspirations. Skillfully, she links the poems in this and within each subsequent sequence by reinstating words, images, ideas, and metaphors with varying tones, themes, or shades of meaning. In "Chekhov on the West Heath," for example, she suggests that the past is always with us—blending memory and desire, bringing us back to the place of our birth which "gives and gives, as we return" in need. In this long, discursive narrative she traces the ever-present influence of both author and heath of her childhood upon her later life and work. Conversely, in "A Woman Meets an Old Lover" the poet proposes—with interlocking phrase and ironic pun—a woman's apparent ability to obliterate the past and particularly a love that caused her pain:

> He who seemed always to
> take and not give, who took me
> so long to forget
> remembered everything I had so long forgotten.

Likewise, "A Woman Alone," a companion piece to the preceding poem, foregoes both the pleasure and pain of the past in a forgetfulness that alleviates self-pity, remorse, and moments of mourning for dear, departed lovers. Since "no one can walk the world any more," the woman acquires the ability to remain alone and the endurance to face a "euphoric solitude" devoid of guilt and deceit.

Following a series of poetic observations of fellow "travelers" through time—"A Young Man Traveling," "Fellow Passengers," and "A Mystery in Mexico," the first section concludes with a poetic sequence far more personal in phrase and more prophetic of the tone and themes extant in Section Two. Somewhat transitionally, then, the final phase of the "Pavese" collection pays fitting homage to the nostalgic impact of time past upon time present; while, concurrently, it prefigures the opening poems of the "Continuum" sequence in their elegiac longing for the lost garden of childhood and their pervasive guilt and grief for an aging mother's suffering and death.

In "The 90th Year," for example, the poet assumes the first-person approach of the confessional mode, as she juxtaposes the pleasurable memories of childhood past with the timeless process whereby a beloved mother grows weary of life and waits for the eternal peace of death. In this regard, the sequence assumes a narrative chronology all its own, as subsequent poems unfold the effects of age and infirmity—the mother's debilitating dependency and impending death. Symbolically refurbishing a familiar image, the poet suggests the mother's diminishing life through the demeaning encroachment of weather and weeds upon her otherwise idyllic garden. Thus, the crackling seedpods and broken blossoms prefigure the human "husk/a shell/from which the soul of life still struggles to be freed."

In "A Daughter (I)" and "A Daughter (II)," however, the *persona* focuses less upon the indignities of the dying and more intently upon the anguish of the bereaved on the eve and in the aftermath of a mother's death. With careful scrutiny to domestic detail, she perceives the mundane needs to which she must minister—the "milk to be boiled . . . hair to be brushed," and bandages to bind firm the "old bones" broken in a fall. And, in the manner of Emily Dickinson, she anticipates the meaningless words and myriad decisions to be determined for funeral, burial, and final disposition of effects. With both compression and concentration, Levertov strikes a compelling emotive response, as she simulates the agony of love lying inarticulate, locked like "a cube of Pain" in the daughter's throat. Further, she effectively assimilates the woman's doubt and dilemma—wondering if she should have remained those many years before, yet wishing even now to flee from the sight of her mother's silent suffering. More than ever, of course, she laments the precipitate passing of time:

> . . .one minute
> of communion, here in limbo.
> All the years of it,
> talk, laughter, letters. Yet something
> went unsaid. And there's no place
> to put whatever it was, now,
> no more chance.

In "Death Psalm. . ." the poet creates a somewhat ecclestiastical and incantatory mood:

> She remembered her griefs.
> She remembered the happiness.
> She watered the garden. . .
> She watched the passing of seasons and years.
> She did not die.

With hypnotic rhythm and anaphoric, alliterative refrain, she attempts to lure a "laggard death" who tauntingly steals insignificant "patches of flesh," yet shuffles past the waiting woman lying tubed, taped, incontinent in the hospital bed.

It is at last the legacy of the mother's love which helps alleviate the daughter's loss and her bereavement; and, ironically in "Earliest Spring," she expiates guilt and grief in the childhood rediscovery of spring—with its first significant signs of renewal and rebirth. Symbolically, then, in this and similar lyrics in the "Continuum" section, the poet suggests the perennial process of time and nature; and, imagistically, she employs the world of nature to reflect the inner weather of the soul. The majority of these poems, such as "Emblem I" and "Emblem II," manifest the close-knit kinship between form and content, image and idea, and suggest the source of creative energy and inspiration in the ideal emblems of nature's world. Further, they evince a remarkable spontaneity and simplicity which is enhanced by the natural cadence of Levertov's verse. As she explains, however, considerable care precipitates the casual effect of her achievement:

I believe every space and comma is a living part of the poem and has its function. . . . I believe content determines form, and yet that content is discovered only in form . . . form as means should never obtrude, whether from intention or carelessness, between the reader and the essential force of the poem. . . .

Consequently, the music of Levertov's verse does not obtrude upon or obscure her meaning. Yet by shifting caesuras, alternating heavy with a series of light, lyrical beats, she re-creates the music of the human voice in a variety of rhythmical speech patterns. Thus, piling participial phrases upon assonance and alliteration, the inspired "spirit" of "Emblem I" seemingly soars from the "cave of the winds" to the "wood of tasks," sweeping "poems and people" headlong "over open heath," heaving "a sigh that holds/a single note," and heading "far and far to the horizon's bent firtree." Conversely, the "quivering cocoon" of "Emblem II" in faltering, close-clipped cadence wrestles to release "its creased/compacted wings" from an enveloping shroud, and awaits fulfillment in poetic song.

Frequently, the lyrics in *Life in the Forest* explore the transience of time and the seasonal metamorphosis of nature's rhythms; but always they evince the pure, unbridled joy of discovering the mysterious in the mundane, or the fresh and fanciful phrase in the most familiar natural phenomenon. In "Scornful Reprieve," for instance, sound enhances sense with an ensemble of explosive *p*'s, as sky "plucks at knots of cloud, unfurling pellets/of leaden rain/singly, savagely/dropping to pock the pale/dust of the earth." Whimsically in "Alongside," Levertov celebrates the miracle of life with close and local scrutiny of the catbird and his colorful morning antics. Onomatopoeically, she re-creates the "catbird credenzas," as oblivious of his observer—and with "puffed throat/pumping"—he sings his "golden pizzicato" to a waiting world, soon to be "noon, hot, and silent." And in "Continuum," the poem concluding the section of similar name, the poet juxtaposes the timelessness of nature's forces with the time-worn temporal world—affirming the midnight song of the beetle and its brood of "minute stars" above the "crouching cities" and "cracked flagstone" of man's creation.

In "Modulations for a Solo Voice," the third and central section of the volume, Levertov returns again to the memories of time past and the realities of time present in a series of poems reverberating the theme of love. However, most of the "modulations," couched in the first-person confessional mode, seem to have evolved from actual experience and seemingly effect a narrative sequence through interlocking thought, phrase, and theme. As the poet's prefatory note explains, "These poems were written in the winter and spring of 1974-75, and might be subtitled, 'from the cheerful distance of 1978, Historia de un Amor.'" Chronologically, the series opens with an awakening of love, as the *persona*, wishing to "learn the lover by heart," regrets "there was only time/for the opening measures—a minor key." Sequentially, then, succeeding lyrics rise to a crescendo in their lament for the lover's absence and long for his return.

With remarkable versatility, Levertov manipulates images and metaphors softly modulating a similar theme—a woman's loneliness and alienation in the absence of her friend, lover, and source of inspiration. Some lyrics, such as

"Silk," enhance a series of sensory details with erotic overtones, as the *persona*, half awake, dreams her lover into existence—caressing his "silky hair, cornsilk, his voice of one substance with his words, with his warm flesh." And in "Silk II," she sustains the metaphor to embrace the "silk" of her lover's voice, "wrapping" herself in its warmth to diminish the distance between the two. However, in "The Phonecall," a barrage of alliterative images and adjectives re-create the bleak and barren landscape of her despairing soul: "Big bluejay black,/white sky in back; brittle/twisting bare random/branches." "Epilogue," the final poem and fitting epilogue for the medley of modulations, manages to transcend earlier expressions of anguish and alienation. Thus, with ironic contrasts between the illusion of love and the reality of life, the *persona* seemingly mitigates the pain and bitterness of her despair with understanding and acceptance:

> I thought I was linked invisibly to another's life
> But I found myself more alone with him than without him. . .
> I thought I was wounded to the core
> But I was only bruised.

In the fourth section, myriad moods are sustained in the clean, crisp clarity of detail and diction and the deceptively casual and colloquial style that have become the hallmark of Levertov's finest lyrics. The central portion of this group, in fact, invokes imagery of nature to embrace the physical and spiritual attributes of art, and to evince a poetic manifesto of artistic attitude and intent. In "Artist to Intellectual (Poet to Explainer)," therefore, Levertov links a series of whimsical rhetorical questions designed to discourage the frantic search for myth or prophetic vision in her verse. Rather, she contends, her creative imagination probes seed and shadow, channeling no chaos—consuming and creating "wildfires that none/shall measure." Further, she asserts, both poet and poem must not measure, but *be*—pausing not merely to touch, but "to taste eternity". . . burrowing into the heart of life and undulating in "exquisite rain":

> . . . returning, if so I desire, without
> reaching that goal the measurers
> think we must head for. Where is
> my head? Am I not
> worm all over? My own
> orient.

Significantly, too, the love lyrics concluding the "Waterfall" collection abound with the lush imagery of earlier sequences now fused with a kaleidoscope of color into a rich, new dimension. The verses abound with colorful contrasts, therefore, manifesting the poet's obvious love of language and her incomparable ability to color mundane observations with poetic music and metaphor:

What you give me is
the extraordinary sun
splashing its light
          into astonished trees. . .
     the flash of golden daylight
in the body's
midnight.

          . . .

Cloudy luminous rose-mallow sundown,
          suffusing the whole. . .
     one drop of crimson lake to a brimming
chalice
and we the lees of it. . .
          we are motes
of gold brushed from the fur
of mothwings, night is
breathing,
close to us,
dark, soft.

The fifth and final section of *Life in the Forest* bears the title of the text itself. And, as befitting its dedication to Jon, "brother in dream - Sometime lover - Friend - Imaginer," it traces the "metamorphic Journal" of a friendship, love, and prolonged separation. Interweaving recurrent images of river, forest, and sea, Levertov brings the collection to its culmination in a final affirmation of love and acceptance of life. Having poetically traversed through sickness, suffering, sorrow, and despair, she emerges from the dark night of the soul, it seems, and concludes in a final celebration of spring, love, art, and artistic inspiration. In "Metamorphic Journal," a three-part poem charting the vicissitudes of love ("December," "February," and "April"), the winter wanderer seemingly withdraws into the "grey-barked sapling" of her dryad soul—a soul slaking its "tree-thirst" in the river of life and love. Symbolically, as the chrysalis evolves into its final and mystifying April form, artist-lover, art and inspired imagination emerge as one:

When you love me well
     it is when imagination has flicked
          its fire-tongue over you. . .

You have
those moments of absolute sureness. . .
          those instants
when the Creative Spirit, sisterly,
takes a Wanderer's cold and burning hand
in hers
and they enter the dance.

Suggesting a similar yet singular timelessness, the poem "Magic" concludes the collection with its continuous one note:

> The brass or bronze cup, stroked at the rim,
> round and around, begins
> to hum,
>   the hum slowly
> buzzes more loudly. . .
> becomes
>   the. . .
>   one note,
> continuous,
>   gong
> of the universe. . .

With neither beginning nor end, the hum of the bell jar suggests the timeless
cycles of life itself—"heard/only those times we take the cup and stroke/the
rim," and only seeming to cease "when we cease/to listen." Similarly, in their
own preoccupations with the alternating rhythms of life, death, rebirth, and the
eternal aspects of love—for family, friend, and "sometime lover"—the lyrics
of *Life in the Forest* sound their own eternal song. As a woman at ease in the
world of nature and the world at large, Denise Levertov writes eloquently of
life, death, marriage, and motherhood. Sensitive yet avoiding the sentimental,
she touches upon and comes to terms with fears, frustrations, and the most
persistent problems that beset mankind. And, while professing to be neither
prophet nor mythmaker, nonetheless she strikes a universal chord in the timelessness of her themes and the transcendent wholeness and harmony of her
poetic achievements. Like the magical hum of the bell jar, however, the music
of her lyrics awaits those readers who "stroke the rim," and it shall only seem
to cease when we might cease to listen.

Phyllis De Leo

Sources for Further Study

Booklist. LXXV, October 1, 1978, p. 271.
Kirkus Reviews. XLVI, November 15, 1978, p. 1300.
Library Journal. CIII, September 15, 1978, p. 1752.

THE LIFE OF THE MIND
One / Thinking
Two / Willing

Author: Hannah Arendt (1906-1975)
Publisher: Harcourt Brace Jovanovich (New York). Volume One, 258 pp. $12.50;
  Volume Two, 277 pp. $12.50
Type of work: Philosophical essay

An account of the activity of thinking and the activity of willing, based upon the author's concept of the life of contemplation and containing an overview of perspectives on these activities from the pre-Socratics through Nietzsche and Heidegger

This work contains what in briefer form were Arendt's Gifford Lectures given at the University of Aberdeen in 1973 and 1974. Mary McCarthy has done a major job of editing. There is an interesting postscript by her on her role as editorial collaborator. She had previously worked on several of Arendt's texts, notably *On Violence* and *On Civil Disobedience*. The work was a kind of translating as well as editing, involving finding the proper English conceptual equivalents for terms initially given their meaning in a different language. While Hannah Arendt was alive, the process of "englishing" her Germanicized English idiolect was a collaboration that could be conducted by conversation and correspondence. After her death, it became a process of reconstruction. One can only admire Mary McCarthy's devotion and skill.

Past Gifford Lectures have given rise to James's *The Varieties of Religious Experience*, Whitehead's *Process and Reality*, Dewey's *The Quest for Certainty*, Marcel's *The Mystery of Being*, and Gilson's *The Spirit of Medieval Philosophy* (a work that Arendt greatly valued). Those familiar primarily with Arendt's social and political writings—totalitarianism, the Eichmann trial, on violence, and others—ought to be forewarned that these are works which, in the traditions of other Gifford Lectures, are generally concerned with questions of a metaphysical nature. They are in a way a continuation of her work *The Human Condition*, concerned with the related concepts of work, labor, and action. Her subjects here are the human faculties of "thinking" and "willing."

In *Thinking*, Arendt takes the position that all reality is appearance. This central tenet of idealism receives negligible epistemological argument. Indeed, to understand Arendt, one must realize that her primary categories are "activity" (the Greek term is *energeia*), the doing or making of something, and "passion," the result of activity. Thus, it is the activity of appearing that is intended—displaying and being-displayed-to. Whether appearances are states of some entities or entities in themselves is never made clear.

Human beings are part of this world of appearings and self-display, but unlike other living species, which fit themselves into a world of appearances by the act of self-display, men also present themselves in deed and word. The difference between self-display and self-presentation is that the latter involves a choice and presupposes an awareness of self (as thinking ego). Early on, the claim is made—as a kind of central paradox of human existence—that what distinguishes mental activities from other activities is a withdrawal from the world as it appears, but a withdrawal that is neither a leave-taking nor a transcendence of the world of appearance.

Much of Arendt's discussion of the activity of thinking derives from a distinction which, for her, has its origin in Kant (with a disclaimer that it may not be what Kant exactly had in mind). This is the difference between intellect *(Verstand)* and reason *(Vernunft)*. In her hands, intellect is concerned with cognitive processes whose proper scope is appearance, whose product is knowledge of science, and whose major concern is truth. Reason, on the other hand, is concerned with meaning: ". . . the faculty of thought . . . does not ask what something is or whether it exists at all—its existence is always taken for granted—*but what it means for it to be.*"

This is a major distortion of Kant. First, because Arendt does not explain that in Kant, intellect, like reason, has objects which are not derived from appearance (Kant calls these "a priori concepts"). Second, Kant's "ideas of reason" are not "meanings" in the sense which Arendt gives to that term. Meaning—the term is never explicitly defined—is used by her to discuss questions concerned with the value or worth of activities. It is her contention that we engage in thinking for its own sake and not in service to some other end. Arendt attributes to Kant the view that questions concerning these ideas of reason are "unanswerable." While this is true for Kant, there is an important ambiguity in the notion of what is unanswerable. For Kant the ideas of reason concern the permanence of self, whether the universe has a beginning, whether there is a causal agency different from natural law, whether God exists. And these are unanswerable in the sense that they are not provable or knowable. But in Arendt's hand "unanswerability" means (at least sometimes) not involving any relation to truth.

The thesis that thinking involves a withdrawal from the realm of appearance is connected for Arendt with the "invisibility" of the thinking ego and its objects. *"Every mental act rests on the mind's faculty of having present to itself what is absent from the senses."* Thinking is the creation of objects by *de*-sensing sensations, by *re*-presenting images; in short, it is the creation of a class of mental entities. Arendt has no special name for the products of thinking, as she conceives it. She does not, probably deliberately, employ the terms "concepts" or "ideas"—although she occasionally uses the term introduced by Brentano: "intentional objects." The claim that these objects are "invisible" is buttressed by an extended attempt to contrast the understanding of language with the apprehension of appearances. An example of what makes this a contrast is her belief that we understand language serially, whereas we grasp appearances immediately. The fundamental point is that language, although the vehicle and expression of thought, is not a "picture" of what it signifies. We distort the understanding of language when we impose upon it the metaphor of vision. The result is an all-encompassing notion of truth as adequation of understanding to thing, thereby distorting the function of language as a vehicle for communicating meanings.

Another theme associated with withdrawal is the contention that thinking involves a cessation of one's ordinary concourse with the world and with other persons and a consciousness of self. Indeed, it is less a consciousness of self than a dialogue between a person and himself. She quotes with approval Valery's interpretation of (rejoinder to) Descartes: "Sometimes I think and sometimes I am." This theme is purportedly related to the conjecture cited in the introduction and arising from her observations of Eichmann's behavior—that evil can arise from *thoughtlessness*, from the absence of intrapersonal dialogue, from a kind of mechanical adherence to prevailing mores. No real development of this theme is found in this work, however.

The more relevant motivation is Arendt's concern with the *Vita Contemplativa* (see her *The Human Condition*) as an ideal for human activity in ancient and medieval thought and its decline in modern thought. Thinking is an activity, in this view, conducted for its own sake (like flute-playing), not for the sake of something else (like flute-making). Philosophizing, in its original etymological sense, is perhaps a better rubric for the activity as here conceived. In the section "What Makes Us Think?," Arendt relates this activity to a pre-Platonic state of wonderment, to Stoical concerns with moral self-discipline, the state of acceptance and indifference which is the compensation for the frustrations of politics and life in general, to the Platonic notion of knowledge of being as *theoria*, and to what she takes to be the essence of the Socratic teaching, the conducting of a dialogue with oneself.

Arendt more than once alleges that there is an "immediate datum of consciousness" that is the evidence for a "mental faculty" which has been given the name of "the will." This datum has a problematic status in the history of philosophy, since it was, unlike thinking, not recognized before the first century of the Christian era, (Aristotle's *pro-airesis*, better translated as choice, is not in her view the same as will), and there is from the seventeenth century onward a strong tradition in philosophy, both among rationalists and empiricists, to deny what Arendt regards as authentic experience of the will. The central experience is that we know that we could have left undone what we in fact did.

Here, too, as in her discussion of thought, the categories of activity and passion are central to her exposition. She appropriates Kant's view that the will is "a power of spontaneously beginning a series of successive things or states."

This spontaneous beginning must be understood as a rejection of the Aristotelian principle that everything must be preceded by a state of potentiality. As an activity, the will is related to future matters; its "objects" are not objects but "projects." Will is a power to begin something new. Understanding of this experience of the will requires a view of time that the Greeks, who conceived of it in terms of the cyclical processes by which they measured it, did not possess, and thus they did not have a due appreciation for the different onto-logical import of future-tensed statements from past or present-tensed state-ments. The properties of the objects of the intellect are expressed in a kind of omnipresent tense—"a present which lasts." They are conceived to exist even when not presently entertained by consciousness. The "projects" of the will, on the other hand, are not absent in this sense when not entertained. They are things which "have never existed at all." Sometimes Arendt takes a more qualified view of the ontological status of "projects," which does not neces-sarily deny that they exist but emphasizes that the future is "a region where no such certainties exist." The character is contingent or random in a way that the objects of intellect are not.

This latter difference between contingency and determination, rather than that between objects and projects, seems uppermost in her discussion of the tension between the two mental activities and also of her explanation of why philosophers seem unable to come to terms with certain phenomena of the mind, resulting in the denial that experience of the will is authentic. In particu-lar, she believes that the soul demands of the mind "what will be was to be." This view, embodied in Hegel, however it misrepresents the nature of the life of the mind, is based upon an inherent inclination of the mental faculties. The contingency of projects as well as the determination of objects arises from the activities of willing and thinking. Every volition, although a mental activity, relates to the world of appearances in which its projects are to be realized; in flagrant contrast to thinking, no willing is ever done for its own sake or finds its fulfillment in the act itself. Every volition not only concerns particulars but looks forward to its own end when willing something will have changed into doing it.

A detailed comment is not possible here. The waters in which Hannah Arendt fishes are, sad to say, troubled. This is true of her attempt to distin-guish meaning from truth and of her identification of truth with the knowledge thereof, or with the ways of discovering or asserting truth. It may also be noted that she gives no clear reasons for distinguishing between the real status of objects of thinking and projects of willing. Perhaps these confusions arise from the fact that activity and passion is too narrow a foundation for the explanation of the mind's activity.

One comment should be made—a *caveat emptor* for the general reader. Arendt's interpretation of what some of the major figures intended is suspect, ranging from idiosyncratic to controversial but unsupported by the kind of argument that would make it plausible. One important case pointed out here concerns Kant, but there are others. A corresponding comment can be made about whom she chooses to discuss and whom she chooses to ignore. This is notable in *Willing*, where she jumps from Kant (with some discussion of Hegel) to Nietzsche and Heidegger, leaving out important idealists such as Fichte and Schopenhauer. More important, there is no discussion of the seventeenth century controversies, which involved Descartes, Hobbes, Spinoza, Leibniz and others, and no treatment of the empiricists.

These comments are made because it leaves the reviewer perplexed as to what she regards as valid *testimony* as to the existence and nature of thinking and willing. And this is especially important in view of the fact that Arendt does not employ methods of phenomenological analysis standard in that school of thought but relies heavily upon the existence of historical and cultural traditions which testify to the "authenticity" of experiences of thinking and willing. Her own disclaimers that she is not—and does not wish to be considered—a historian of philosophical ideas cannot exempt her from the responsibility of careful and reasonable complete interpretation.

Robert S. Metzger

Sources for Further Study

Commonweal. CV, September 1, 1978, p. 566.

Guardian Weekly. CXIX, September 17, 1978, p. 22.

Harper's Magazine. CCLVII, August, 1978, p. 84.

New York Review of Books. XXV, October 26, 1978, p. 16.

Observer. July 30, 1978, p. 26.

LOST TRIBES AND PROMISED LANDS
The Origins of American Racism

Author: Ronald Sanders
Publisher: Little, Brown and Company (Boston). 443 pp. $15.00
Type of work: History
Time: The fourteenth century to the mid-seventeenth century
Locale: The New World, Spain, Portugal, England, France, and Holland

> *A history of the exploration and colonization of the New World with emphasis on the origin and development of racism in the treatment of Jews in Spain and Portugal and of Indians and blacks in the New World*

> *Principal personages:*
> PRINCE HENRY THE NAVIGATOR, who undertook exploration of the coast of Africa to the Orient
> CHRISTOPHER COLUMBUS, discoverer of the New World for Spain
> HERNANDO CORTES, Spanish conqueror of the Aztec Empire
> BARTOLOMÉ DE LAS CASAS, Spanish defender of the Indians of the New World
> CAPTAIN JOHN SMITH, English explorer, colonizer, adventurer, and author
> MANASSEH BEN ISRAEL, Dutch Rabbi and messianic author of *Hope of Israel*

Lost Tribes and Promised Lands by Ronald Sanders is an exciting, thought-provoking, perplexing, and often infuriating book. This volume is the author's contribution to the growing body of writings on the origins of American racism. Sanders traces those origins to the period from the late fourteenth century to the mid-seventeenth century and concentrates his attention on the major colonizing powers—Spain, Portugal, England, France, and Holland.

Most of the book is the recounting of a familiar story: Portuguese exploration of Africa, the search for Prester John, the establishment of the African slave trade by the Portuguese, the efforts of Columbus, the Spanish conquest of the Indians of Central and South America, the work of las Casas, the beginnings of French colonization, English colonial undertakings, the legend of Captain John Smith and Pocahontas, the story of Squanto, and many other events of the colonization of the New World. All of these tales are told with great skill and enthusiasm by the author, but in hopping from one scenario to the next, Sanders conveys a looseness of organization throughout his book. What is unique about the Sanders treatment is a unifying theme with which Sanders attempts to weave together and explain the many episodes of his book.

Sanders believes that American racism had its origin in Spanish intolerance during the Age of Exploration, and he focuses throughout the book on the Jew. He attempts to show that in a sense, the Age of Exploration, the colonization of the New World, and the origin of American racism were all footnotes to the history of the Jew in the period. However, the author is unable to sustain this fascinating thesis throughout the work, and he frequently loses sight of it, sometimes for very lengthy portions of the book. While the author's thesis, although historically debatable, can be supported somewhat in examining Spain and Portugal, it can hardly be sustained when applied to English and French colonization efforts in the New World. Nonetheless, *Lost Tribes and Promised Lands* is a well-written and interesting account whose thesis merits serious consideration.

Sanders' argument portrays Spain in the Middle Ages as "the most tolerant land in Christendom." From the late fourteenth century onward, Spain became "fanatically intolerant" and "the history of the Iberian peoples was to be dominated by this development in the Old World and then in the New." This fanaticism generated the racism which the book attempts to explain. In A.D. 711, Islamic armies conquered much of the Iberian Peninsula, leaving Christians in control of the northwest, where they gathered strength over the next three centuries for a reconquest of Spain; that reconquest was partially successful by the mid-thirteenth century, but a part of Spain remained in Moorish control for more than a century longer.

Down to the late fourteenth century, Spain was characterized by an accommodation and synthesis among Islamic, Jewish, and Christian cultures living in the Peninsula in a harmony which produced the highest level of intellectual and cultural activities. In such an atmosphere of toleration, Jews found a haven in the Peninsula during the medieval period, and the gradual domination from the eleventh through the thirteenth centuries of the Christians over the complex, heterogeneous society brought little change in the toleration of Jews. However, as a consequence of growing intolerance, racism, and prejudice directed against Jews throughout Christendom, Spanish Christians during the course of the fourteenth century were infected with the disease of anti-Semitism.

On June 4, 1391, an outbreak of anti-Jewish rioting in Seville marked the beginning of a series of pogroms all over Spain. In Cordova, Toledo, Madrid, Majorca, Cuenca, Burgos, and other cities, Jews were killed, synagogues were looted or turned into Christian churches, Jewish communities were destroyed, and Jews were given the options of death, conversion, or flight. Such anti-Semitism accompanied the last phase of the *Reconquista* which culminated in the expulsion of the Moors and the Jews from Spain and the triumph of militant Christendom throughout the Iberian Peninsula.

As the final phase of the Christian conquest of Granada swept through Spain, it developed a fanaticism and a messianism that, fusing together religion and nationalistic reconquest, proved irresistible. The earliest victims of this fanaticism were the Jews, who became the objects of racism because Spanish Christians believed that they possessed tainted religious views; this belief, in the spirit of heated fanaticism, was then transformed into a conception of the Jews (and later other peoples) as a tainted people. Thus, religious difference became the source of racism as the Spaniards sought *"limpieza de san-*

gre" or "purity of blood." This racism was supported by both the Catholic Church and the Spanish monarchy.

The marriage of Ferdinand of Aragon and Isabella of Castile united the major kingdoms of Spain, reinforced the fanatical nationalism of the *Reconquista*, and strengthened the role of the Spanish Catholic Church in its advocacy of orthodoxy and *limpieza de sangre*. Working with the Spanish monarchy, the Church zealously maintained orthodoxy by means of the Inquisition. As a consequence of these agencies working together, the fifteenth century Spanish Jewish community was destroyed, and Jews were either expelled from Spain or forced to convert (sometimes with no alternative except death). Some converted Jews (*conversos* or New Christians) fully adopted Christianity, others adopted Christianity outwardly but remained secret practitioners of Judaism, and others abandoned Judaism temporarily until its practice could be resumed.

The Inquisition was employed mercilessly and brutally against *conversos* who were caught practicing Judaism. Moreover, in order to guarantee the purity of office holders, the test of *limpieza de sangre* was employed to require that Christians seeking promotion and office must prove that they had no taint of Jewish blood. *Conversos* became a marginal people, excluded from important Spanish positions and offices. Nevertheless, even from their marginal positions, *conversos* were able to exert, according to Sanders, an enormous influence on Spanish exploration and colonization of the New World. In fact, if we are to believe the author, that exploration and colonization was a Jewish and New Christian product sustained by *converso* messianism.

The story of that messianism began in 1375 with the production of the Catalan Atlas by Abraham Cresques, a Jewish cartographer (one problem of the book is a lack of adequate illustrations of the Catalan Atlas, which is discussed at length). Among other things, the Catalan Atlas cartographically depicted apocalyptic scenes from the Old and the New Testaments. Primary allusion to apocalypticism, however, was within the Jewish tradition, for "it is clearly a Jewish Messiah that Cresques has given us here." Sanders introduces at this point the messianic idea of an apocalypse redeeming Jews and recovering the Ten Lost Tribes of Israel. The messianic hope that the Catalan Atlas manifested eventually came to characterize Protestant, Catholic, and Jewish interest in exploration in the succeeding centuries. For Sanders, Abraham Cresques was the prophet of the messianic tradition of exploration and discovery. His tradition was advanced by Jewish-dominated schools of cartography and by a son of Cresques, Jafuda Cresques, who was forced to become a New Christian after the 1391 Seville pogrom, and who carried on the cartological heritage of his father. Changing his name after conversion to Jaime Ribes, he became after 1415 the chartmaker of Prince Henry the Navigator and was known as Master Jacome.

From this point, Sanders draws Portugal into his story. Portuguese exploration led to control of the Guinea slave trade, which placed Portugal in control of large numbers of black slaves. Arab literature had clearly depicted blacks as peculiarly suited to slavery as a consequence of their physical characteristics. At the outset of the Age of Exploration the Portuguese adopted the Arab view of blacks, who came to be seen as a mere commodity or a cargo to be shipped by the Portuguese wherever needed. It was easy for the inhabitants of the Iberian Peninsula to describe black slavery as an extension of the Christian *Reconquista* of the Moors. "The captives were being brought out from pagan darkness into the light of Christianity." In the same way that a racial taint had been attached to Jews, the idea of racial inferiority was similarly affixed to blacks in order to justify their enslavement. Having developed the theme of racism and its relationship to slavery, the author moves to a discussion of Spanish exploration and colonization of the New World.

According to Sanders, Spanish exploration and colonization of the New World was largely a product of New Christian or *converso* messianism. Basing his arguments on the studies of Salvador de Madariaga, Sanders emphasizes the New Christian background of Columbus and his supporters. New Christian messianism (the historical heritage of the Jewish messianism of Abraham Cresques) such as Columbus manifested leads Sanders to speculate: "How much this enterprise of discovery owes to New Christian initiative we can only guess; but it may well be that America began its history as a promised land of Spanish heresy." Masking his speculation behind expressions of tentativeness, such as "How much . . . we can only guess" and "it may well be," Sanders places the weight of his research and argumentation clearly in behalf of the speculation. The view of the book is that Spanish discovery, exploration, and colonization of the New World owed very much to New Christian initiative and that, in fact, "America began its history as a promised land of Spanish heresy."

The theme of the "promised land" of New Christian hopes was, after the discovery of Indians, also expanded to regard America as the home of the Ten Lost Tribes of Israel. This view developed in the course of the sixteenth and seventeenth centuries alongside the myth of the bestiality of the Negro, which was used to support the idea of the appropriateness of blacks for servitude. While blacks were undergoing dehumanization, the American Indians, badly treated by such conquistadors as Hernando Cortes and Francisco Pizarro, were being defended by such *conversos* or New Christian supporters as Peter Martyr, Vasco Nunez de Balboa, Bernardo de Sahagun, Diego Duran, and especially Bartolemé de las Casas.

Las Casas, probably a New Christian, wrote his *History of the Indies* in a "Hebraic" religious tone and in the tradition of the *Jewish Antiquities* of Josephus. Recognizing the historic oppression of the Jews, he undertook a defense of the Indians against similar Spanish oppression and sought the destruction of the cruel *encomienda* system under which Indians had been enslaved in the New World. As an alternative to the *encomienda*, las Casas in 1516 proposed the importation of Negro slaves. Ironically, therefore, black slavery was recommended by a humanitarian in order to prevent Indian slavery. In 1518, Charles V of Spain agreed to an *asiento de negros* permitting the purchase and importation to America of blacks. In the words of Sanders, "The coin thus minted was to remain currency for generations, one side of it consisting of a passionate relationship, alternating between love and hate, with the Indian, the other of indifference or contempt toward the Negro."

After 1518 las Casas continued his career as protector of the Indians, thoroughly criticized Spain in his *Brief Relation of the Destruction of the Indies* (written in 1540 and published in 1552), and significantly contributed to the "Black Legend" of Spanish cruelty to the Indians. For Sanders, las Casas, Peter Martyr, Sahagun and other supporters of the Indians represented sixteenth century Spanish humanism in contrast with the conquistador tradition which was a continuation of *Reconquista* and which sought conquest, plunder, and exploitation. According to Sanders, the Dominican order, of which las Casas was a member, represented Erasmian Humanism in the New World. The chief representatives in the New World of a militant Counter-Reformation heritage were the Franciscans and later the Jesuits. The Franciscans and the Jesuits sought the destruction of the Indian religion much more thoroughly than did the Dominicans. The humanistic messianism of las Casas and Diego Duran had been transformed into the far more militant messianism of the Franciscan zealots who desperately sought the salvation of the Indians. With Franciscan zeal, the New Christian messianism which had provided the stimulus for New World settlement and humane Christianization of the Indians reached its zenith.

Sanders next turns his attention to French, English, and Dutch efforts at exploration and colonization of the New World. In moving away from Spain toward the other colonizing powers, the thesis that Sanders built so speculatively and interestingly ceases to have any validity. Much of the remainder of the book is an elaboration of the ideas and insights of other scholars.

The French view of the Indian was mixed, and the relationship between Indians and French colonists in the New World was characterized at times by cooperation and at times by hostility. The French view, which vacillated between idealizing the Indian and considering him no better than a beast, was shared by the English. But the full force of bigotry was directed more against blacks than Indians. This bigotry is described by Sanders in an analysis of English literature focusing particularly on Shakespeare.

In his description of English colonization efforts, Sanders develops a dichotomy similar to that of his treatment of Spain. In the same way that he divides Spanish sentiment into advocates of *Reconquista*, Christian fanatics, conquistadors, and racists on the one hand, and humane, moderate New Christian sympathizers with the oppressed on the other, he also breaks English sentiment into two groups. Here the dichotomy is not so dramatic as in Spain. On one side, Sanders presents humanist nonracist sympathizers with the Indian, such as Sir Walter Raleigh, John White, Thomas Hariot, Roger Williams, and (at times) Shakespeare. On the other side are those who finally prevailed in America—practical, exploitative, land-hungry racists such as Captain John Smith, Christopher Marlowe, Reverend Samuel Purchas, and the Puritans. The views of the latter group led to the exploitation of the Indians, the massacre of the Pequot Indians, and black slavery in America.

The English slave trade really began in the West Indies colonies and spread to the North American continent. On the mainland of British North America, there was from the outset a conflict over the status of blacks. Some whites opposed black slavery by advocating personal liberty, while others favored black slavery for economic reasons. The materialistic view prevailed, and by the 1660's blacks were rapidly being imported into North America from the West Indies and elsewhere. Racism had been firmly established in the English colonies of the New World by the mid-seventeenth century.

After his description of English colonization in the New World, Sanders turns in a brief final chapter to Dutch colonization. Here the author's interest focuses on twenty-three Jewish refugees from Portuguese Recife who came to New Amsterdam in 1654 requesting to be allowed to settle. The cosmopolitan toleration and humanitarianism that characterized seventeenth century Holland extended to the New World and the Jews were allowed to stay. When the English seized New Amsterdam a decade later, the Jews were allowed to remain in the English colony of New York because they were regarded by the Dutch and the English as a religious minority rather than a race. At long last Jews had found a refuge in the New World, but the Indians were not so fortunate, and became lost tribes in their own land, while blacks endured subsequent centuries of slavery.

Saul Lerner

Sources for Further Study

Book World. August 27, 1978, p. E6.
Commentary. LXVI, August, 1978, p. 78.

A LOVER'S DISCOURSE: FRAGMENTS

Author: Roland Barthes (1915-   )
Translated from the French by Richard Howard
Publisher: Hill and Wang (New York). 234 pp. $10.00
Type of work: Novel

A nontraditional novel which reproduces the language of love, incorporating references to scores of other texts, conversations with friends, and personal experience

Is this the same Roland Barthes who proselytized a dry, cold-blooded style in *Writing Degree Zero*? Is this the remote guru of semiology and structuralist rhetoric who announced the demise of the autonomous ego? This latest book by the Frenchman picking up the intellectual torch long carried by Sartre represents an unabashed shift towards a patently sensuous subject (in the sense of topic *and* psychology) and style.

Barthes couches his new orientation in a method honed in *The Pleasure of the Text* (1975) and *Roland Barthes* (1977): an alphabetical organization of fragments, introduced here by a prefatory guide, the first section of which explains the necessity for the book. The next outlines its format, presenting three subheadings: figures, order, and references. Each of the eighty fragments has as its subject a figure (whose first letter relegates its position in the whole) ranging from "to be engulfed" (*s'abîmer*) to "will-to-possess" (*vouloir-saisir*). Central and longest among the figures (including Adorable, Waiting, To Write, Gradiva, Scene, and Suicide) stands I-Love-You. Barthes claims not to use "figure" rhetorically—although many figures seem to be rhetorical tropes as well as dramatic stances—but in a "gymnastic" or a "choreographic" sense. He compares the lover to an athlete, an orator, or a statue; the "figure," an economical affective articulation, he maintains, is the "lover at work."

Every fragment contains a "figure," briefly defined, preceded by a title not always identical with it (the title of "To Hide" is "Dark Glasses"), and followed by a text composed of from two to ten numbered paragraphs which bespeak a point (the sentimentality of love is today discredited and is the obscene in love); clarify a word as used in the context of this discourse ("Objects" are objects touched by the beloved); or identify a lover's experience (when the love affair is over, the lover continues to be anguished by a telephone that does not ring, like an amputee pained by his missing leg).

The "order" of this book is not, Barthes counsels, dialectical, but circular. The fragments refuse to form a syntagmatic chain, refuse to become a "story." If miscellany rules their arrangement by the arbitrary choice of nomination and alphabetizing, it also prescribes their content, which treats literature, psychoanalysis, music, personal experiences, and history. Their tone varies from anecdotal to aphoristic to argumentative to contemplative.

Third, Barthes categorizes his "references." That paragon of the Romantic novel, Goethe's eighteenth century *The Sorrows of Young Werther*, is most frequently cited. The modern philosopher clearly identifies with the lacrymose hero. Further sources include Plato, Zen, Freud, and Lacan, Christian mystics, Nietzsche, and Schubert. Barthes' more casual reading occasions the references to (among others) Proust, Flaubert, Gide, Mann, Balzac, and Racine. More personally, demure initials correspond to conversations with friends. With a bow to Renaissance printing, Barthes patterned a wide left margin, enabling the source to be cited directly alongside the borrowing. Footnotes often elaborate with quotations; and a Tabula Gratulatoria concludes the book. Barthes does not mention works of others in order to substantiate his own writing. His sources lose this vestment of authority, reborn as elements of the lover's discourse. Last but not least, the author's life infiltrates this telling which is not a story.

The final prefatory statement announces, "So it is a lover who speaks and who says," emphasizing the discourse, not the lover. Barthes' shift in orientation does not imply one in fundamental interest. His three recent books's concern with pleasure, self, and love notwithstanding, Barthes' "lover" utters such phrases as "I rub my language against the other. It is as if I had words instead of fingers, or fingers at the tip of my words. My language trembles with desire." For this lover, "orgasm . . . speaks and it says: *I-love-you.*" He can "fall in love with *a sentence*" and feels compelled (after Lacan) to identify "I-love-you" as a "holophrase." He thrills to phonic, syntactic, and narrative voluptousness. Not the average lover this.

It would be unfair and unproductive to reproach Barthes for simulating a lover quite like himself, one who instinctively raises a shield of abstraction. The reader is forewarned of the prominence accorded language at the expense of love in the passage defining "figure." The word "discourse" is rendered "dis-cursus," stressing its etymology—as Barthes is wont to do throughout the fragments. Deriving from the same root as "to run," "discourse" refers, very simply, to a "running" commentary or argument, in this case deployed internally by the lover to himself.

"Amorous discourse" (a more literal translation than "Lover's discourse") thus concentrates on the linguistic nature of the amorous sentiment. The text is a discourse on a brand of discourse (that of the lover) rather than on love itself. Eros resides not in the experience but in the language of love. Indeed, language satisfies the lover's erotic desire. The text exudes a profound sensuality. Its power emanates from its very aspiration to be physical. In the text, discourse is a "skin," an "envelope," a "glove," a "cocoon"; it can "suffocate" the beloved, it is "massive," "smooth," "soft." The lover's thoughts are tactile. For him, "the word is a tenuous chemical substance." Such considerations rarely troubled young Werther.

So much for the method and the subject. What does this specific amorous discourse actually say? Here we find Barthes the suicidal romantic. The predominant message tells of painful isolation. In the book's opening paragraph we read: "The necessity for this book is to be found in the following consideration: that the lover's discourse is today *of an extreme solitude.*" This solitary discourse, while spoken by many, remains "ignored, disparaged, or derided" by surrounding languages. Its utterance provides no pharmaceutical effect for the lover nor for itself: the lover continues to despair nostalgically for the unity offered by maternal and androgynous love.

Public opinion having discredited sentimental love, the sentimental lover remains "alone and exposed." A curious fraying of the discourse ("all the same, he could have. . . ," "He knows very well. . . .") and its intricate fragmentation duplicate the erosion of unity and confidence experienced by a subject in love. All the discrepancies between the lover's hopes and reality, the permanent distance posited between the babbling lover and the silent (and, we gather, unsentimental) object of this devotion correlate formally to the blank space that permeates the text.

There are two paradoxes fundamental to Barthes' philosophy at work here: one pertains to his radical opposition to so-called bourgeois myths, the second to the function of language in society. Barthes has so successfully shattered the stereotypes, braved the taboos, and demystified the myths of public opinion, that he—by dint of his militant intellect—was bound to attack the new conformity. Hence his "lover": an uncertain, infatuated hero of a most unfashionable (but undoubtedly seminal) novel. Sexuality having lost its cachet, sentimentality inherited the mantle of the taboo, so becoming the target for demystification. The second paradox relates directly to the "extreme solitude" of the discourse. Quite simply, language isolates. As much as one tries to use language as a means of constructing a common bond, language continues to alienate and to foster self-engrossment.

Reading (his) writing, Barthes teaches, must be multidimensional. The deft arranging and layering of his writing cannot but astound the reader. Throughout the fragments, however, the image of a scene glimpsed through a keyhole remains implicit. The figure entitled "Image" defines an image as "that from which I am excluded." The lover is excluded from the image "as if from the primal scene, which may exist only insofar as it is framed within the contour of the keyhole." A prime example of Barthes' fascination with images is his assertion that to fall in love is to become enamored of an image, framed in a situation, seen by surprise. Werther's first sight of Charlotte framed by the doorway serves as the archetypal reference. It is, therefore, all the more surprising that the English translation, excellent in other respects, eliminates the enchantingly seductive and highly pertinent picture used as a cover to the French edition.

This picture is emblematic in many ways. Most obviously, it too is a fragment: the central square of a much larger canvas, it portrays the linked arms of two people, the thumb of one's hand resting lightly on the edge of the other's sleeve. In *The Pleasure of the Text*, Barthes specifies the juncture of skin and garment as the body's most erotic part. Moreover, he chose this fragment of the larger work—a painting of Tobias and the Angel—with the same coyly provocative intent with which he selected his references, each, itself, a textual fragment: it is an enticement to observe a larger, more complex vista and to compute its relationship to the whole. The painting fragmented by Barthes corresponds to the story in the *Apocryphal Book of Tobit* of the Angel Raphael instructing Tobias to eviscerate a fish. The intricate ties this story, its source, and its depiction in the scene of the painting have to the text are too numerous to investigate here. Suffice it to say that like a scene viewed by the lover through a keyhole, the framed scene is both alluring and baffling. The selected fragment and the painting in its entirety function as a guide to the reading of the text.

In addition to its application to the references of the author's systematic learning, the keyhole imagery subsumes the personal level of the text as well. At the same time that he experiences the lure of knowledge and possession *through* the keyhole, the viewer is essentially solitary, excluded and literally *barred* from the scene he witnesses. Like the books of the Apocrypha alluded to by the cover picture, which stand outside the Bible, like the picture and the reader forever just outside the text, the lover can never absolutely possess or know the object of his affections. Canonicity will remain problematical and totality out of reach.

Union in love escapes the lover just as the guarantee of a unified meaning escapes the text. The lover and the text follow in the errant footsteps of Tobias. However, the ingenious musicality of the textual resonances and reverberations, the eloquently interwoven registers of discourse, and the restlessness of the lover saying all this to himself echo Barthes' own dogged quest for (structuralist) universals. Where the essays in *Image-Music-Text* (1977) seemed to juxtapose and distinguish these modes of human creativity, *A Lover's Discourse* effectively and fluently—albeit by means of a dictionary—reconciles the three.

The book is by no means what might, in contemporary parlance, be called "a good read," but it is a fascinating and elegant discourse. Barthes' Gallic intelligence combines rigor of thought and vast erudition with an ability to woo and captivate his reader. Having already sold more than sixty thousand copies in the original French edition and having received accolades from friend and foe, *A Lover's Discourse* promises to be Barthes' most popular work.

Linda Klieger Stillman

Sources for Further Study

Book World. October 29, 1978, p. E6.

Booklist. LXXV, September 1, 1978, p. 15.

Kirkus Reviews. XLVI, June 15, 1978, p. 669.

Library Journal. CIII, August, 1978, p. 1510.

New Leader. LXI, October 23, 1978, p. 14.

Publisher's Weekly. CCXIV, July 10, 1978, p. 123.

LUCKY EYES AND A HIGH HEART
The Biography of Maud Gonne

Author: Nancy Cardozo
Publisher: Bobbs-Merrill (New York). 468 pp. $15.00
Type of work: Biography
Time: 1866-1953
Locale: Ireland

The first detailed critical biography of Maud Gonne, Irish patriot and the inspiration of William Butler Yeats's great love poems; also a chronicle of Gonne's work in forming the Irish Republic, her struggle for women's rights and human rights throughout the Western world, and her relationship with Yeats

Principal personages:
MAUD GONNE, Irish patriot and crusader for human rights
WILLIAM BUTLER YEATS, Irish poet; her lover

The myth of modernity has relegated some genuine heroes to unjustified obscurity. In certain instances, a crucial figure of the past is remembered, if at all, for the wrong reasons with isolated or obscure or flamboyant details obscuring the greatness of the totality of the person. Such a fate has overtaken one of the noble figures of the early twentieth century: Maud Gonne, patriot, rebel, fighter for freedom, and the beloved of William Butler Yeats. Yet unfortunately she is remembered for the poems about her, not for her accomplishments in her own right; and they were many. In fact, it may not be far from the truth to maintain that Maud Gonne mothered an entire nation, the Republic of Ireland.

Maud Gonne MacBride was in every way a remarkable woman. She was much more than a fascinating footnote to the biography of Yeats, although in another sense their names, even as their lives, must remain inextricably intertwined.

Nancy Cardozo's new biography *Lucky Eyes and a High Heart* takes its title from a love poem by Yeats:

> She could have called over the rim of the world
> Whatever woman's lover had hit her fancy,
> And yet had been great-bodied and great limbed,
> Fashioned to be the mother of strong children;
> And she'd had lucky eyes and a high heart,
> And wisdom that caught fire like the dried flax,
> At need, and made her beautiful and fierce,
> Sudden and laughing.

This biography does more, however, than simply detail the famous relationship from Gonne's viewpoint rather than Yeats's; it sets the record straight. Maud Gonne would have been a great woman even if she had never met Yeats. A vigorous book written with insight and passion, it corrects the misinterpretations of forgetful historians. Throughout its more than 450 pages, it re-creates an era too little known to Americans, despite the large number of people in this country of Irish descent. Cardozo is an impeccable researcher, and her book is filled with enough facts to satisfy even the most erudite Yeats scholar. But the facts—the names, the dates, the places, the obscure facets of Irish history or British parliamentary maneuvering—never obscure Cardozo's central purpose: to make Maud Gonne live again.

Born in England in December, 1866, the daughter of a captain in the British Army, Gonne liked to say that she was two months old before she first breathed the air of freedom when her father was transferred to Ireland. Her love of Ireland and hatred of English oppression of the Irish never left her, even when the aims of the Easter Rising of 1916 came to fruition with the birth of the Republic of Ireland several decades later. In fact, one of the most interesting of the small details that crowd the pages of this book is Cardozo's story of Gonne's attitude toward Richard Ellmann, the great biographer of Yeats and Joyce. Ellmann visited Gonne in 1946, several years before her death in 1953. She wrote of him that "He appeared to be pro-British though he said nothing to make me think this and therefore may be inclined to underestimate Ireland's influence on Willie's [Yeats's] thought and work." Thus, even when the victories had been won and Ireland was free under the tricolor flag of the Republic, Gonne continued the battle for Ireland.

Cardozo is careful to indicate, however, that while Gonne's interests were centered upon Ireland and the struggle (violent if necessary) to achieve Irish freedom from what she conceived to be the yoke of English tyranny, her sympathies were essentially universal. Her humanitarianism manifested itself in struggles for women's suffrage in both England and America; in attempts to win freedom for political prisoners of whatever ilk; and, toward the end of her life, in her ability to equate the devastation of Hiroshima and Nagasaki with the annihilation of the Jews in the Nazi gas chambers. Maud Gonne, in other words, was a woman of passion, of great pity, and of great capacity for love. Her passion, however, became a passion put to use largely on behalf of Ireland.

Everywhere Cardozo's personal affection for her subject shines through the pages; it appears that the more the author got to know Maud Gonne the more the evanescent, vibrant personality of the great Irish patriot came alive for her. It is the reader's good fortune that Cardozo is able to communicate that multiple personality.

Gonne was a spectacular beauty, nearly six feet tall, with long red-gold hair. Yeats described her thus:

> I had never thought to see in a living woman so great a beauty. It belonged to famous pictures, to poetry, to some legendary past. A complexion like apple blossoms and yet face and body had the beauty of lineaments which Blake calls the highest beauty . . . and a stature so great that she seemed of a divine race.

Yeats, or at least so the myth goes, fell in love with her at first sight and seemingly, despite his later very happy marriage to Georgie Hyde-Lees, never really fell out of love with her, at least in a spiritual sense. One of the curious facts that Cardozo reveals is that Georgie and Maud developed a firm friendship, as if both women were certain of themselves and of their relationship with the great Irish poet, and nothing that the other could do or say would alter that relationship.

Lucky Eyes and a High Heart traces Gonne's life chronologically, through her early years in Ireland and France; her close relationship with her father; her meeting with Yeats and their love; their investigations of the occult; Maud's involvement with the French political activist Lucien Millevoye; her becoming his mistress and bearing his daughter Iseult; her conversion to radical politics; and her marriage to John MacBride, with its tragic results. It is all here in this remarkable book, and through it all looms the figure of William Butler Yeats. However, what results from this biography is not simply another retelling of that classic love story, now so familiar that it has become a modern myth. Rather, what emerges from these pages is the story of a great individual, not simply an aspect, however important, of the life of Yeats.

Cardozo carefully demolishes a myth that has grown up about the two lovers which pictures the wan poet sighing in the reeds and the iron woman at the barricades. According to this myth, carefully nurtured by all of Yeats's biographers including Ellmann, the relationship between the two was never consummated; the two shared "spiritual eroticism" but never physical union. Citing hitherto unpublished letters, reminiscences, and journals, Cardozo clears up this misconception; the fact of physical intimacy, while not critical, perhaps, makes both lovers seem much more human and real, not simply attenuated wraiths.

As the daughter of a British army captain, throughout her early years Gonne was almost totally unaware of the suffering of the Irish peasantry under the blind English administration. Her awakening to the problems of Ireland came when she was nineteen. She had gone down to the country for a formal ball, and, she says, ". . . while I was there I heard that families were being evicted for failure to pay rent by the man whose guest I was. They were clinging to their bits of furniture. They wandered about looking for a place to spend the night. I could not bear it."

Her transformation from debutante and belle of Dublin Castle to Irish hero was instantaneous and complete; it lasted for the rest of her eighty-seven years. Yeats was appalled by her passion, but Gonne sought out Irish radicals and became one of them. They were "radical," of course, only in the sense that they no longer believed that England would grant Ireland Home Rule through the parliamentary process. Britain's obstinacy and blindness about the "Irish problem" forced Gonne, John O'Leary, Padraic Pearse, and many others to prepare for revolution. When it arrived at Easter time, 1916, Maud was in France, frantic at being unable to get to Ireland and join her comrades in the abortive Rising. Maud's estranged husband, Major John MacBride, was executed by the British along with other leaders, thereby blindly helping to make the Rising a success by creating martyrs. "A terrible beauty is born," Yeats later wrote in "Easter 1916." It was a terrible beauty at least partially brought about by Maud Gonne MacBride, as well as by Pearse and the others.

No facet of Gonne's life has escaped Cardozo's attention. We hear of her trips to America to raise funds for the Irish poor; we learn of her conversion to Catholicism, not simply because she believed in the tenets of the Church, but because she also felt that she could be closer to the great masses of the Irish people if she shared their religious convictions. We are not surprised to discover that her love for her children was extraordinary. Some of her passion for humanitarian ideals was passed to her son Sean MacBride as well. A former member of the Irish Republican Army in the Irish civil war days of the early 1920's, Sean MacBride was once a cabinet minister in the Republic and later founded Amnesty International, whose work on behalf of political prisoners of whatever persuasion was honored in 1974 when MacBride was awarded the Nobel Peace Prize.

Amnesty also was another of Maud Gonne MacBride's great passions. Herself once imprisoned by the British for political activities, she immediately began a hunger strike. She was released from Kilmainham jail twenty days later by the shame-faced British. She was so weak that she had to be carried out on a stretcher, but she was the most cheerful hunger striker the prison doctor had ever seen, always smiling.

Maud seems to have been always angry, but she also seems always to have smiled. Her personality was so strong and so charming that it radiates through the pages of this book, unhampered by time or distance. She was in almost every way a great woman, a true patriot, a genuine human hero. In fact, the part she once played on the stage, that of *Cathleen ni Houlihan*, a part written for her by Yeats memorializing the mythic Great Mother of Ireland, could well be her epitaph. Cardozo's text catches that spirit well, as do the book's excellent illustrations and many photographs.

Yeats wrote in words that are still chanted by audiences in Ireland:

> They shall be remembered for ever;
> They shall be alive for ever;
> They shall be speaking for ever.
> The people shall hear them for ever.

Nancy Cardozo's fine biography makes it certain that Maud Gonne will be remembered forever as well.

Willis E. McNelly

Sources for Further Study

Booklist. LXXV, November 1, 1978, p. 452.

Kirkus Reviews. XLVI, October 1, 1978, p. 1100.

Library Journal. CIII, October 15, 1978, p. 2103.

Newsweek. XCII, November 6, 1978, p. 94.

Publisher's Weekly. CCXIV, October 2, 1978, p. 12.

THE MAN WHO SHOOK HANDS

Author: Diane Wakoski (1937-   )
Publisher: Doubleday & Company (Garden City, New York). 118 pp. $6.95
Type of work: Poetry

A collection of poems by and about a woman coping with middle age, loneliness, and a poor self-image

This book of poems is actuated by the motif of the man who shook hands, a private reference to a terrifying experience, but an experience so trivial and innocuous that it takes the poet many lines, many false starts, before she is able even to narrate its details, much less explain her terror. In fact, she never directly does. The final success of the book is that the poet voices this *leit-motif* through such a kaleidoscope of situations, events, and images that the fright ultimately becomes serious rather than trivial, destructive rather than innocuous.

The *persona* of the poems, the poet herself, gains stature as she narrates and explicates her confrontations with this overwhelming and oft-repeated experience of rejection and the resulting intense loneliness. Each poem becomes a facet reflecting a new way of experiencing the central thematic crux—the vast loneliness of a single, middle-aged woman, and the painful rejections she experiences when she tries to form attachments.

The encounters Wakoski narrates in her poems are primarily those with men, and they are unabashedly sexual, tenderly sensual. Late in the order of the collection, she writes of an encounter with a woman from whom she expects candor and friendship, and voices her anguished sense of betrayal and rejection when the woman is revealed as having been dishonest with her. The final poems deal with the poet's relationship to her mother. The character of the mother, a cold and bitter woman, is revealed almost as if by chance in poems expressing the poet's rejection of the mother. The poet sees her likeness to her mother, and sees herself doomed to becoming inevitably more and more like her as she too becomes bitter and outwardly cold as a result of rejection. At each painful though infrequent encounter with the mother, the daughter becomes progressively more aware of their irrevocable bond of kinship and similarity.

Throughout the collection, the poet earnestly and singlemindedly seeks the love and companionship of a man. Wistfully, romantically, she weaves poems of longing for her ideal man—she refers to him as the King of Spain—and dolefully, nostalgically, sometimes angrily, she recounts her experiences with men whom she had hoped would fulfill the role and mend the huge void in her life. The nadir of her search and hopes was reached in the terrible title experience:

> The man who shook hands with me, after making love,
> the last rung in some ladder to failure
> I've been descending.

The book begins with an essay seeking to explain or justify the poems that follow, since their relentless theme of loneliness and rejection could slip quickly into banality, soap opera, and self-pity. The poet is rightly concerned, for at times all three elements are present, although fortunately other positive strengths outweigh these flaws.

Wakoski has a fine sense of poetic diction, and her poems demonstrate a consistent linguistic appropriateness. The precision and care in choice of words give her work a professional smoothness and a richness of connotation which greatly enhances the semantic denotation. This talent for choosing the right word extends to and includes a fine instinct for the poetic line. It is a pleasure to enjoy the rhythms and sounds of language as Wakoski organizes them. She exhibits a sure instinct for the appropriate rhythm and length of line, together with a melodic patterning of sounds of speech which lift the subject matter out of the mundane and trivial ephemera of middle-age frustration and elevate it, at moments, to a high seriousness. The language of speech as transmuted by the poet into poetry is at once authentic and appropriate to the poem. Her words are the words of current, everyday, common speech, and her syntax is in everyday use.

The Man Who Shook Hands is divided into five sections, each of which deals with what might be loosely called a step in the progress of the poet's experience, reaction, and comprehension. Experience, however, for this poet is primarily emotion, with the event perceived as the genesis of the emotional experience. She explains this perception in the course of her opening essay and through the use of Wallace Stevens' poem, "Peter Quince at the Clavier," in which he insists that feeling is the reality, and beauty is immortalized in its fleshly embodiment rather than in transient mental images. So the poet asserts the primacy, the truth, of her emotional states, and the reality of her urge for fulfillment. She develops this idea further in "The blue swan, an essay on music in poetry," in which she asserts that history does not consist of the artifacts of the past, nor are tangible things its important reality; what is real and important are the dynamics of human interaction and people's emotional response to one another.

The first section of the book contains a long, tortuous essay to friends, self, and critics which attempts to explain the rationale for the title, as well as the poet's aesthetic stance. The essay is manifest evidence that prose is a totally inadequate and unsuitable medium for Wakoski to use for expression of her ideas and emotions. She then moves into poems expressing her bewilderment, frustration, despair, hope, and finally the consolation which poetry affords her. The bewilderment is touching as she expresses her sustained expectation of reciprocated love and understanding, and its unseemly failure to appear. She writes movingly of her tentative offers of herself, or more frustrating to her, her suppressed desires to offer herself which are rebuffed, ignored, or simply unrecognized. She can engage the sympathy of the reader deftly when she writes of her shyness, her sense of inadequacy, her imperfections, simultaneously with expressions of her longing to be loved as she loves. She finds refuge and articulation finally in her poems, and that is why these poems are mostly love songs to various men.

The imagery and metaphors of the poems are vivid, fresh, and compelling, and serve well to elicit sympathy for the poet's message by their precise fitness. The image of the poet as Cassiopeia immobilized in the sky and watching helplessly from afar as her beloved man moves away from her is striking and exact. The further image of the word as twin sister to the emotion—but quite separate from it—is a further extension of the Cassiopeia imagery, conveying the idea that neither the act nor the word is identical to the emotion. The richness of imagery is a delight in this volume of verse. Many of the images are poetic in the traditional sense: the moon, ocean, birds, sun, flowers, and many other images from nature are invoked repeatedly. But other images, such as the black mustache, the brass keyring, and running, are private images with a private set of associations which the poet shares and uses to induce the reader to enter her private world. That she is usually quite successful in both engaging the reader and in conveying her meaning lucidly through such imagery is testament to her skill.

The section entitled "Life is like a game of cards" represents an attempt to move from personal experience to philosophical consideration of the nature of human existence. But the interest these poems arouse does not result from abstractions or philosophical concepts. The poems return persistently to the immediacy of the present, or to the precision of an unforgettable memory. Wakoski is concerned with her special situation. She is forced to write about the fears that haunt her—fears about her self, her needs, her situation, and her dissatisfaction with her maturing body. While Wakoski probably strikes a responsive chord in the best of these poems, the anguish of self-pity, when it is sustained through so many poems, becomes a bit tiresome.

One poem, "Looking for the bald eagles in Wisconsin," occupies a section entirely by itself, and attempts to make an assertion of poetic license in the broadest sense of freedom to use whatever vehicles or images seem appropriate to the poet, even if they seem strange or ridiculous to anyone else. The poem is also an in-joke between poets, as the author explains in a note at the conclusion. The poem, which makes a good case for the use of unlikely imagery, loses some of its impact when it is reduced to a private communication among a few poets, and is found to be only secondarily a message to be shared with and appreciated by the general reader.

Despite these shortcomings, the poet writes convincingly of herself, her desires, her observations of life, and the details of her daily existence with an acuteness and vividness which transform the words into the vision of a woman facing life with great dignity, patience, and perseverance. She is also a poet creating her poems as surrogate satisfactions for the longings with which she contends. She speaks with a manifest honesty and seriousness. Her lines reveal herself, her world, and her range of interests with candor and vividness, and they ask from the reader a sympathy, understanding, and acceptance which one is inclined to grant on the merit of the poems. The volume is intensely personal, but to some extent it transcends the person and becomes the representation of a sustaining theme. It is this occasional transcendence which finally raises the poetry out of the self-pity and the pathetic, desperate hope-against-hopelessness ambience to make the volume a message about life and loneliness and an unending search for happiness, even in the face of apparently overwhelming odds against success.

Betty Gawthrop

Sources for Further Study

Choice. XV, October, 1978, p. 1056.
Southwest Review. LXIII, Summer, 1978, p. 303.

A MANUAL FOR MANUEL

Author: Julio Cortázar (1914-   )
Translated from the Spanish by Gregory Rabassa
Publisher: Pantheon Books (New York). 391 pp. $10.95
Type of work: Novel
Time: The recent past
Locale: Paris

The story of the revolutionary activities of a group of Latin American exiles in Paris

> Principal characters:
> ANDRÉS, a young Argentine
> MARCOS, another young Argentine
> THE ONE I TOLD YOU, omnipresent character, surrogate for the writer
> LUDMILLA, a young Polish woman
> FRANCINE, a young French woman
> MANUEL, a baby boy
> LONSTEIN, a Freudian character

Julio Cortázar is no newcomer to the English-speaking world, although his most famous story is normally associated with the Italian film director Michelangelo Antonioni who put *Blow Up* to film. Seven of Julio Cortázar's books, including *A Manual for Manuel*, have so far been translated into English. *Hopscotch*, one of Cortázar's longer novels, has received, perhaps, the greatest acclaim.

A Manual for Manuel is Cortázar's latest long and meaningful novel that has seen the light in translation. When the original *Libro de Manuel* was published in March, 1973, it was immediately hailed as the most "political" of the writings of this remarkable Latin American writer. Such an opinion is reflected in the flap of the jacket of the English edition, starting with the words "In his first political novel. . . ." This statement is both inaccurate and misleading. Political, though not partisan, are two previous novels: *The Winners* and *Hopscotch*. Indeed, all the works of Cortázar since the publication of *Las armas secretas* (*The Secret Weapons*) in 1959 fall into the political realm. This collection of stories that includes the original of "Blow Up" ("Las babas del Diablo"), and what now is considered as his best short story, "El perseguidor" ("The Pursuer"), is a narration of political consequence in the same perspective in which *A Manual for Manuel* is also political.

The wary reader will by now have guessed that the connotations of the very familiar word political as used in this essay differ somewhat, perhaps considerably, from the normally accepted usage and that an explanation is necessary. Cortázar shares with other well-known members of the group that has come to be known as the "boom" a nonpartisan political commitment, the bases and meaning of which can be best expressed in the writer's own words:

In Latin America (and in the rest of the world), politically committed intellectuals can be divided into two categories: those who understand political theory and know or think they know why they are engaged, and those who do not understand political theory but, nevertheless, are equally committed. Anyone who has read my books realizes that I belong to the second of these categories. . . .

Julio Cortázar shares with Gabriel García Márquez, Mario Vargas Llosa, Carlos Fuentes, and even Octavio Paz—though to a lesser extent—the conviction that artistic creation develops within a context that includes the historical circumstance and its political options, all of which ineluctably influence the work of the writer, whether he wishes or not, and will be reflected in it. They do not share the attitude of the Marxist critic, for whom only the writers who belong to the "oppressed" class or who have broken with the bourgeoisie and joined the "oppressed" can be considered as revolutionary. Their attitude can be compared, rather, to that of the American New Left in the late 1950's and 1960's. It is an irrational, rather than a logically systematic approach, based on vital motivation instead of on the acceptance of ideological discipline. It rejects organizational discipline while uncompromisingly adhering to the belief that the only acceptable basis for social behavior is the total absence of any exploitation of human beings.

In this search, Cortázar, an Argentine writer exiled in France, rejects the traditional view of the "Latin American liberal," of the bourgeois or petit bourgeois liberal transplanted to Europe where, far from the daily constraints of the oppressive society he has left behind, he can devote himself to "universal" ideas redolent of religious and metaphysical connotations. Quite the contrary, as the writer himself has explained, if he left Argentina in 1951 to take up residence in France permanently, it was in order to acquire a wider perspective and to rediscover bit by bit the true roots of Latin American life without losing sight of a global view of history and of mankind. The Algerian war, the conflicts in eastern Europe, the Cuban revolution, the Vietnam war, the events of 1968 both in France and in the United States were the crucial crises that contributed to develop the conscience of these intellectuals on a twofold perspective: on the one hand, the need for a rational praxis while, on the other, adopting an irrational motivation towards artistic creativity as well as in the individual's understanding of his situation in society.

Intuition, participation in a magic mode in the rhythms of men and events decide my route without seeking or giving explanations. . . . Unreasoningly, without prior analysis, I was suddenly living, full of wonder, the feeling that my ideological road coincided with my Latin American return.

The return of which Cortázar spoke was not merely a reference to the visit he paid to Cuba or to the Chile of Salvador Allende. It was also a recognition of the fact that since taking up residence in Paris, his books had had greater acceptance in Argentina and in the rest of Latin America and that this was a result of the more complex experience and the wider perspective gained from living in a world that ultimately surpassed the stricter individuality to which his original experience was limited.

Part of this wider perspective came about with a reexamination of the accepted notions of alienation. As a result of the industrial expansion of the 1940's and 1950's, it had become political dogma among traditional social thinkers in the 1960's to speak of the passivity of a working class that had abandoned its adversary role, having been tranquilized by a new prosperity that made the material benefits of the consumer society indifferently available to all classes. Coupled to the ideological bankruptcy of the Soviet system, this brought a serious reexamination of dialectical materialism. It was argued that the working class was no longer restive. An alternative view was proposed by the New Left thinkers, Wright Mills, Herbert Marcuse, Theodor Adorno, in whose view there was still a large mass of alienated humans, notably ethnic minorities confined to economic or racial ghettos. These marginal populations, they insisted, still existed even in the industrialized nations, but above all, in those nations that came to be known as the Third World. Marxist dialectic was no longer applicable; in its place, new-leftism relied, fundamentally, on violent confrontation not as part of a dialectically ordered process but, asystematically, as an expression of total intolerance towards every manifestation of bourgeois culture. History is seen, therefore, as a process of sudden revolt with attendant, indiscriminate destruction and without a constructive sequel. Instead of a long, conditioning process advocated by orthodox Marxism, we are left with an irrational, subjectivist series of succeeding and unforeseeable events.

Cortázar's latest book assumes this basic belief in the liberating potential of instinctive behavior, where the pleasure principle assumes a significant role. In the behavior of the Latin American revolutionaries of *A Manual for Manuel*, we recognize the by now familiar, seemingly incomprehensible deportment of the anarchists, Trotskyites, Maoists, hippies or yippies of the 1960's with their destructive purges of anything that, under the guise of order, constrains individual aspiration and the will to self-expression. The satisfaction of the pleasure principle is as evident in Cortázar's characters as it was among the youth of America in that fateful decade. There is a parallel in the lives of the Latin American revolutionaries of *A Manual for Manuel* between eroticism and freedom, as there was in the "make love not war" slogan of the Vietnam War protests. In their search for the satisfaction of the libido, the characters in Cortázar's book become aware that their yearning for personal fulfillment is twofold and dependent on the double assumption of an individual and a social role. They are conscious of social degradation at the hands of capitalism and of Fascist ideologies, as they are also conscious of the fact that their intimate lives are constantly and inescapably influenced by those external factors.

The Manuel to whom the title of the book refers is a baby boy for whom a scrapbook is being assembled. This scrapbook or *A Manual for Manuel* (the original title is the less alliterative and more meaningful *Book of Manuel*) is the unplanned collection of newspaper cuttings contributed by all members of the revolutionary group, somewhat euphemistically translated as The Screwery. Their ultimate objective is the kidnaping of The Vip, a high ranking Latin American diplomat. The Screwery's cover is the implausible gift of a turquoise penguin and a couple of royal armadillos for the Vincennes zoo. The narrative line becomes immaterial, though it gives the semblance of a plot in the novel, which consists of nonlinear development. Its primary theme is the parallel between a nonconformist, surrealist aesthetic and the affirmation of the individual against the unstoppable tide of political oppression and increasingly degrading persecution and torture. The action centers on four male characters, three of whom, Andrés, Marcos, and Lonstein, are identified by name, while the fourth—referred to as The One I Told You—fulfills the role of an omnipresent and omniscient manipulator. Against the concrete militancy of the three named actors, the impersonal fourth centralizes their efforts and appears to lead them toward greater political efficacy. But his reiterated call for an ethical stand is belied repeatedly by sadistic undercurrents in the frequently equivocal eroticism of the others. For example, the reiterative praise of masturbation in the lengthy discourse of Lonstein, and the anal intercourse forced by Andrés on Francine. We must, perhaps, see in such sexual encounters one more effort on the part of the writer to liberate Latin American eroticism from its age-old pruriency.

This is the only effective, albeit vicarious, liberation in *A Manual for Manuel*. For the rest, the view is pessimistic—as befits the subject—softened only by a benevolent ending. Worst of all the book ends with twelve pages of small print, in parallel columns, extracted from a press conference of the Forum on Human Rights relating cases of torture in Latin America, and statements of various American G.I.'s bearing witness to similar events in Vietnam. *A Manual for Manuel*, taken as a whole, is a very unsettling book which leaves the reader both puzzled and enlightened.

Alan A. Gonzalez

Sources for Further Study

Booklist. LXXV, November 1, 1978, p. 458.

Library Journal. CIII, November 1, 1978, p. 2261.

New Republic. CCXXIX, October 21, 1978, p. 41.

New York Review of Books. XXV, October 12, 1978, p. 61.

Time. CXII, November 6, 1978, p. 115.

MARGARET FULLER
From Transcendentalism to Revolution

Author: Paula Blanchard
Publisher: Delacorte Press/Seymour Lawrence (New York). 370 pp. $11.95
Type of work: Biography
Time: 1810-1850
Locale: Massachusetts, New York, and Western Europe

A biography of a noted American writer, conversationalist, and feminist

> Principal personages:
> MARGARET FULLER
> TIMOTHY FULLER, JR., her father
> MARCHESE GIOVANNI ANGELO OSSOLI, her husband
> RALPH WALDO EMERSON, transcendentalist poet and essayist

Although excellent studies of Margaret Fuller have been published during the past thirty-five years, her name is still likely to call up the image of a slightly absurd, egocentric bluestocking who once announced, "I accept the Universe." Paula Blanchard's fine biography ought to do much to restore balance to this distorted portrait of one of the most extraordinary women of nineteenth century America. Blanchard does not ignore the quirks of personality and style that made Fuller vulnerable to the scorn of men such as James Russell Lowell, Edgar Allan Poe, and Nathaniel Hawthorne. Yet she enables her readers to put these flaws into proper perspective as Fuller's own friends did, and to concentrate instead on her achievements.

In a society that expected women to be passive, dependent, and self-effacing, Margaret Fuller was strong-minded, ambitious, dramatic, and aggressive enough to make a place for herself in the transcendentalist intellectual circles of Boston and Concord; to give both moral and financial support to her family after her father's death; to explore New York jails and insane asylums as a reporter for Horace Greeley's *New York Tribune*; and to commit herself to the republican cause in the Roman revolution of 1848-1849. Her most dramatic defiance of convention was her romance with the Marchese Giovanni Angelo Ossoli, who became her lover, her husband, and the father of her son in a sequence never fully documented.

None of these things came easily. Margaret Fuller's life as Blanchard presents it has elements of a Greek tragedy. Her successes seem always to have been accompanied by physical and emotional pain.

Both her achievements and her suffering, Blanchard suggests, can be traced to the strong influence of her father, Timothy Fuller. The son of a Massachusetts clergyman and something of a radical in his student days at Harvard, he was a stern patriarch in his relationship with his submissive wife and their eight children. Blanchard describes him as a reserved man, "forever trying to crack his way out of his own shell." He demonstrated his devotion to his precocious firstborn by teaching her to read at the age of three and setting her soon afterward to translating gory passages from Homer and Virgil that gave her nightmares. She quickly learned that intellectual prowess was the way to win his approval, only recognizing years later the price she paid for neglecting her physical and emotional needs. At nine she squinted from near-sightedness, conversed like a pedantic adult, and lived almost totally isolated from other children.

Had she been a boy she might have gone on to Harvard and become a distinguished professor or clergyman, her pedantry and her lack of charm no great hindrance. But, as her father realized when she approached adolescence, Latin and Greek were useless assets for a woman in the 1820's, and he set about to transform her into a marriageable young lady. She was sent to dancing classes and finishing school in an effort to polish the curt, forthright, often satirical manner that made her seem rude at times. For the plain, stout, red-faced girl accustomed to winning praise for her intelligence, this change in emphasis apparently created conflicts of tensions that brought about much of her later unhappiness. All of her adult life was in some respect a struggle to reconcile the conflicting demands of her "masculine" side—her intellect—and her "feminine" nature—that part of her that longed for love.

Yet she had gifts that enabled her to move beyond these conflicts and slowly create for herself a place in society. She was a brilliant conversationalist, and she had an empathy with others than enabled her to form close friendships with both men and women all through her life. Her family's efforts to provide her with womanly accomplishments did not prevent her from continuing to educate herself at an astonishing rate; one of her contemporaries compared her reading with that of the historian Gibbon.

Blanchard traces Margaret's development through her teens and early twenties as she and her friends, future transcendentalists and abolitionists such as James Freeman Clarke, William Henry Channing, Frederick Henry Hedge, Elizabeth Peabody, and Lydia Maria Child, read and discussed the works of German and English Romantics. These children of New England Puritanism were greatly attracted by the writers' emphasis on "the awesome responsibility of the individual for his own moral development" and their assertion "that the unfolding of human consciousness, or soul, must be to some degree divinely assisted from within." Margaret was moved most deeply by Goethe and hoped for years to be able to write his biography.

Examining the state of her soul filled only one part of her life at this time, however. As the oldest daughter in a growing family, she had substantial domestic responsibilities, especially after the Fullers moved from Cambridge to Groton in 1832. Blanchard devotes several pages to a description of the household duties that had to be shared by the servants and the women in a typical family of the time. Since the Fuller income, although adequate, provided wages for only one servant, Margaret was required to assume many of these responsibilities for her ailing mother. She managed to sandwich in her reading of Goethe, Schiller, and Thomas Jefferson between hours of tutoring six young children and attending to domestic chores.

This was also a period, Blanchard speculates, when she was searching for a direction for her life. She apparently concluded fairly early that she would not marry. Though she was accepted as an equal by her male friends in Cambridge, they did not look upon her as a future wife. As Blanchard puts it, ''The price of being one of the boys was being one of the boys.'' The choices open to an unmarried woman, as Margaret was painfully aware, were either teaching or remaining under the paternal roof. She was in fact exploring the possibility of teaching in Kentucky, where her friend James Freeman Clarke was minister of a church, when her father died suddenly in 1835.

Timothy Fuller's death was both a liberating force and an oppressive burden for his daughter. She had, in effect, to assume the role of *pater familias* for her dependent frail mother, her sister Ellen, and five schoolboy brothers, the youngest mildly retarded and difficult to handle. There was a small inheritance, but if the younger children were to have an education, Margaret would have to earn the money.

This need provided the impetus that moved her more and more into the world. In the winter of 1836 she began teaching in Bronson Alcott's experimental school where students learned through uninhibited discussion. In addition, she set up evening classes in German and Italian literature for women, whose access to serious formal education was almost nonexistent. It was here that she found her talents most fully used and appreciated. Alcott's school proved too free and experimental for most Boston parents, however, and she had to take a job in a school in Providence for the next year and a half.

Once the family financial situation was stabilized, she moved them to a new home near Boston where she was able to tutor a few private pupils, work on her translation of Goethe's *Conversations with Eckermann*, which was published in 1839, and renew her friendship with the men and the handful of women who formed the Transcendental Club, the most influential of whom was Ralph Waldo Emerson. Out of her participation in this group came her famous "Conversations." For four years she offered, for a fee, a series of discussions on such subjects as Education, Fine Arts, and Greek Mythology. These sessions were for the most part limited to women, for Margaret was convinced that they needed to "fully engage their minds in an atmosphere that was as free as possible from censure." She firmly believed that women were innately as intelligent as men and lacked only their education and self-confidence.

Her connections with the transcendentalists brought her another responsibility in 1839 when she agreed to edit the *Dial*, a new review designed to provide a forum for the literary, philosophical, and theological opinions of the group. For two years she struggled to keep the magazine going, often writing half of the material herself. Her *Dial* articles, Blanchard points out, varied widely in quality, but at least three of them were of major significance. Her essay on Goethe brought new appreciation of his work in the United States; her "Essay on Critics" made her one of the country's first serious literary critics; and "The Great Lawsuit" drew attention to the condition of women in her time. At thirty-three she was keenly aware of their limited opportunities and of their subjugation in most marriages, and she argued forcefully in her article for equal educational and vocational opportunities for them.

At this period in her life she seems to have felt an increasing need to move beyond the abstract concerns of the transcendentalists, and in the summer of 1843, she and a woman friend spent several weeks traveling in the frontier country around Chicago and Milwaukee. The plight of the Indians, especially the Indian women, seems to have aroused her strongest passions. Her account of the trip, *Summer on the Lakes*, records her indignation at the callous treatment of the native Americans by the white settlers.

Her movement from the contemplative to the active life, in Blanchard's view a natural outgrowth of "Transcendentalism, Unitarianism, and her father's Jeffersonian liberalism," took her in 1845 to New York to work for Horace Greeley. At his urging she enlarged "The Great Lawsuit" into a long feminist document, *Women in the Nineteenth Century*, and its publication coincided with her first articles on New York prisons and the plight of the women, mostly prostitutes, who were incarcerated in them. She soon had a national reputation as a radical thinker and suffered considerable criticism for her frankness from "good" society. Even Emerson viewed her new career with some coolness.

While Fuller's professional achievements brought her increasing recognition and satisfaction, her emotional life during her twenties and thirties was considerably less smooth. Her nature was essentially passionate and singularly incompatible with the resolutions of lofty detachment from ordinary human emotions that dot the pages of her journals. She found outlets for her unfulfilled need to love and be loved in intense friendships with both men and women, expressing her feelings in extravagantly sentimental phrases that more than once led men either to flight or to expectations of commitments she was unwilling to make. She fell in love at least twice with men who did not return her feelings and broke off relations by announcing their intention to wed someone else.

Still hurt by the second of these rejections, she set off for Europe in 1847, intending simply to travel and write of her experiences for Greeley. But when she reached Italy she found the opportunity to fulfill both her need for significant action and her need for love. She had written of herself a few years earlier: "Once I was almost all intellect; now I am almost all feeling. Nature vindicates her rights, and I feel all Italy glowing beneath the Saxon crust." She sensed an immediate kinship with the land and its people, and she sympathized with the republican spirit that was gathering force in Rome.

Shortly after her arrival she met Ossoli, a gentle, unintellectual man several years younger than she. Within a few months they became lovers. Blanchard notes that in character and personality he resembled her mother, whose love for her was probably the most stable, uncomplicated force in her life. The differences in their religion, nationality, and age made marriage nearly impossible; but Margaret, altogether abandoning the "Anglo-Saxon crust," apparently decided to be guided by her feelings. Her time of unalloyed happiness was very brief. She discovered that she was pregnant and wrote a friend, without describing the circumstances behind her statement, "I have known some happy hours, but they all lead to sorrow; and not only the cups of wine, but of milk, seem drugged with poison for me."

Her son was born in September, 1848, in a village not far from Rome, bringing both the greatest joy she had ever known and desperate anxiety during periods when he was ill and separated from her. He remained with a nurse while she and his father took part in the bloody siege of Rome that ended with the French occupation of the city in June, 1849. While Ossoli fought for the unification of his country, Margaret was in charge of a hospital for wounded soldiers, working herself to the point of collapse day after day. Once Rome had been occupied and Ossoli's cause lost, there was nothing to hold them there, and they spent the last year of their life together in a brief period of domestic tranquillity with their son in Florence, where Blanchard believes they may have been married. Economic necessity soon forced them to make new plans. They finally decided to return to the United States where Margaret hoped to support them with her writing.

The tragic end of their story is well known. Their ship struck a sand bar off Fire Island, and all three Ossolis drowned in sight of land. Yet in Blanchard's view their death may in some ways have been less tragic than the life that awaited them. Margaret's critics had received the news of her surprising marriage and motherhood with malicious glee, and even her friends were dubious about the wisdom of her return. She herself had foreseen problems of adjustment for her husband in an alien culture and faced realistically the difficulties that the difference in their ages might later present. In addition, the past three years had taken enormous psychic toll of the strength that had earlier enabled her to balance many responsibilities successfully.

Her short life, as Blanchard describes it, does not really seem incomplete. She had accomplished more than most people do in twice the time, and she had achieved a measure of personal happiness that she never expected to experience.

The success of this biography rests not only on the sensitive portrayal of the central figure, but also on the fully developed background against which she is set. Drawing on wide-ranging research, Blanchard vividly characterizes the society in which she lived and the people who most affected her. This wide canvas may cause problems for the nonspecialist reader—it is not easy to keep track of all the transcendentalists—but it cannot be regarded as a major flaw.

What differentiates this book from other studies of Margaret Fuller are its implicit ties with the women's movement of the 1970's. Her struggle to win acceptance in a male-dominated society is seen throughout the biography as the prototype of similar efforts today. Blanchard's last paragraph aptly states her perspective on her subject: "Ultimately she should be remembered for what she was rather than what she did. Her achievement cannot be measured except in terms of the handicaps under which she gained it. . . . Given the circumstances of her life, it took an uncommon variety of strength and courage to continue to accept the Universe, warts and all."

Elizabeth Johnston Lipscomb

Sources for Further Study

Atlantic. CCXLII, August, 1978, p. 84.
Booklist. LXXV, September 15, 1978, p. 146.
National Review. XXX, November 10, 1978, p. 1428.
New York Times Book Review. July 23, 1978, p. 12.
Wall Street Journal. CXCI, August 7, 1978, p. 10.

MAX PERKINS: EDITOR OF GENIUS

Author: A. Scott Berg
Publisher: E. P. Dutton (New York). 498 pp. $15.00
Type of work: Biography
Time: 1884-1947
Locale: New York, Connecticut, and Virginia

A biography of the Scribner's editor who became known for working with Fitzgerald, Hemingway, and Wolfe

> *Principal personages:*
> MAXWELL PERKINS
> LOUISE PERKINS, his wife
> ELIZABETH LEMMON, a close friend
> F. SCOTT FITZGERALD
> ERNEST HEMINGWAY
> THOMAS WOLFE

Maxwell Perkins, though not a household name, was certainly the most famous editor of our time, discovering and helping to shape the careers of such famous writers as F. Scott Fitzgerald, Ernest Hemingway, and Thomas Wolfe, as well as notables such as Ring Lardner, Edmund Wilson, John Marquand, and, his last find, James Jones. A. Scott Berg began his work on Perkins at Princeton as an honors thesis under the direction of Carlos Baker, and he has pursued every possible lead for eight years. Now, thirty years after Perkins' death, the editor stands revealed in a book of nearly five hundred pages and a series of helpful photographs.

The first point to be made is that Max Perkins would have been horrified by this biography. All of his life he chose to remain in the shadows; a shy and intensely private man, he always avoided publicity. He once said he wanted to be "a little dwarf on the shoulder of a great general advising him about what to do . . . , without anyone's noticing," and one recalls that he threatened to resign his job at Scribner's if Thomas Wolfe included him and his editorial colleagues in his fiction. Especially would he be shocked at the revelation of his drinking problem, his secret "love letters," and his daughter's struggle with mental illness.

If the biography had to be written, perhaps Berg is the man for the job. This is patently a young man's book, with the virtues and flaws the term implies. Berg unquestionably admires his subject, treating him with all possible kindness—even at the risk of turning Thomas Wolfe into something of a villain. Although he had Malcolm Cowley's *New Yorker* profile and Perkins' published letters, *Editor to Author*, to begin with, he has made excellent use of the Scribner's files, interviewed everyone who knew and worked with the editor, including his platonic love, Elizabeth Lemmon, who turned over her letters to him. (Apparently without irony she referred to them as her "Aspern papers.") The author has also had the cooperation of Perkins' five daughters.

Berg has aimed, obviously, at a popular biography. Instead of dwelling at length on Perkins' New England village background and education, or his early life as a journalist, he moves rapidly to his rise as a young editor at Scribner's. Much of the bulk of the book is devoted to Perkins' most famous writers; in fact, often more space is devoted to Fitzgerald, Hemingway, and Wolfe than to the editor himself. Although the publishers (and one notes that Scribner's did not publish this book) lay claim to presenting new facts, anyone who has read a biography of these three novelists will soon grow weary of the stale gossip about them. Here we are treated again to the story of Hemingway's fight with Max Eastman, Wolfe's troubles with his aging mistress, Aline Bernstein, and Fitzgerald's reaction when he discovered that Zelda had stolen his material in her novel *Save Me the Waltz*.

To be fair, however, Berg is capable of more than purveying the gossip one expects in a biography of a Hollywood queen. He does trace the gradual rise of Maxwell Perkins in the staid house of Scribner's. The workings of the publishing firm are clearly sketched, and a number of his colleagues are admirably drawn, most notably the poet-editor John Hall Wheelock. Well handled, too, is Perkins' friendship through the years with Van Wyck Brooks, who suffered a series of breakdowns while working with the patient and loyal editor.

Was Perkins an editor of genius? Clearly Berg thinks so, and there is no question that Perkins could recognize new talent when he encountered it. Certainly he was right to follow his hunch and argue for Fitzgerald's first novel—after the Scribner's board had twice rejected it. More important, he was able to see the genius in *O Lost*, the huge manuscript that became Wolfe's *Look Homeward, Angel*. And there are numerous other such examples: his judgment of Ring Lardner's stories and his encouragement of John Marquand. Moreover, he was often helpful in revising individual books, in selecting titles, and in organizing stories for anthologies—as in the case of Wolfe, Fitzgerald, Lardner, and Hemingway. This was a task which he thoroughly enjoyed, whereas he had to work against the grain on many books of nonfiction.

On the other hand, it needs to be stressed that, in spite of his intuitive powers, Perkins was often wrong. He had curious blind spots as a reader and editor. For example, he thought Faulkner's *Sanctuary* a "horrible book"; he believed that Hemingway's *Fifth Column* was a great play and that Caldwell's Maine stories were better than his Georgia tales. His background in literature was not especially strong; he majored in economics at Harvard and had worked first as a journalist. Consequently, he felt out of his depth with many great works of the past. More germane here, he was a slow reader, a very poor speller (as his letters indicate), and a slipshod proofreader. As a consequence, there were scores of serious errors in Fitzgerald's *This Side of Paradise*, and Thomas Wolfe was mortified at the numerous errors in *Of Time and the River*—many of them resulting from Wolfe's difficult handwriting and Perkins' refusal to allow him to correct the galleys. As Perkins grew older and his health deteriorated, he realized that his judgments were often dubious, and he came to be far less demanding in asking for revisions, as was the case with Alan Paton's *Cry, the Beloved Country.*

It should be noted, too, that Perkins was limited and conservative in his tastes—although not nearly as conservative as the men at Scribner's who set the company's policy in the 1920's. It is painful today to read how much of his time was spent arguing Hemingway into cutting out four-letter words—incidentally, words that Perkins could not bring himself even to say. It is hard to believe that a truly great editor would object to "bitch" or "dry loins" or caution a writer like Marjorie Kinnan Rawlings to cut back on the realistic dialogue in her fiction so that her novels could be recommended to young readers.

Yet, when all of this is said, one cannot deny that Perkins' instincts were generally correct. He did stand up for Fitzgerald and guide him through *Tender Is the Night* (though he might have been more helpful on the false start), and he was right in his suggestions about fleshing out Gatsby's character in the earlier novel. He was also right in suggesting the cuts in Wolfe's *Look Homeward, Angel.* Such instances could be multiplied. As Berg's quotes from numerous letters indicate, Perkins was also loyal and faithful to his writers, occasionally lending them money out of his own pocket. They respected his opinions, and a number of his women writers rather pathetically "worshipped" him—as his young biographer comes close to doing in this book.

Whether Perkins was an editor of genius is debatable; nevertheless, Berg makes his subject come totally alive. Perkins was obviously a complex and unhappy man—at times even a desperate man. Toward the end of his life he drank too much, though he was a tower of strength to Fitzgerald and Wolfe, among others. Berg makes much of the split in his nature; from the Evartses he inherited a Yankee sense of duty and morality, from the Perkinses a sensual streak. As a result, there was in him a lifelong struggle of "Cavalier versus Roundhead." As he aged, Perkins suppressed the "wild" side of his nature, no doubt enjoying vicariously the messy affairs and exciting lives of the writers he worked with.

Perkins' marriage was an unhappy one, and he retreated more and more into his editorial duties. His wife was a frustrated actress and playwright and, later a convert to Catholicism. Perkins was not sympathetic to her ambitions. It is understandable, but nonetheless ironic, that he was more supportive with his writers, even Zelda Fitzgerald, than with his wife Louise—though he did help get her published at Scribner's. Apparently he never thought of divorcing Louise—though Berg reveals his "affair" with Elizabeth Lemmon, a Virginia woman of startling beauty. Perkins rarely visited her, and though he apparently loved her—or said he did—their relationship seems to have remained a platonic one. Wolfe makes it clear in his fictional portrait of Foxhall Edwards in *You Can't Go Home Again* that Perkins did not like women, and the editor did have a reputation as a misogynist—in spite of working well with such women authors as Marcia Davenport and Taylor Caldwell.

As he grew older, Perkins became more and more eccentric. He liked to wear a hat in his office, doodled drawings of Napoleon, ate the same food for days on end. He was as superstitious as Hemingway and also believed in phrenology. As his marriage failed, his work became everything to him, with the exception of his daughters. He had never shown very much interest in the theater or music or art, nor did he apparently ever hold any firm religious beliefs. He did not like travel or vacations and complained because Scribner's did not keep the office open on weekends.

Berg observes that Maxwell Perkins became a father-figure to many of his authors, most notoriously to Thomas Wolfe. (He never suggests that this might pose very real dangers to the editor-author relationship.) No doubt Perkins was disappointed in not fathering a son, and perhaps without realizing it he began to look on Fitzgerald and Wolfe as surrogate sons. Fitzgerald even refers to him in a letter as "a parent." Although this did not have serious results with most of his writers, it proved disastrous with Thomas Wolfe, who was perhaps the least secure of the writers. Although Perkins did not generally socialize with his writers, he worked long hours with Wolfe on the interminable manuscript which became *Of Time and the River*. Wolfe visited in the home and became almost a member of the family. In the end, Louise Perkins became jealous of the time her husband spent with the novelist. Later, when Wolfe broke with Perkins and Scribner's, the rupture had much in it of a son repudiating his father in order to discover and assert his own identity.

On the other hand, there was none of this in Perkins' relationship with the women writers he edited. In spite of his well-known antipathy for the sex—which he and his biographer made light of—he got along well with such novelists as Marcia Davenport and Marjorie Kinnan Rawlings. Perkins was always attractive to women—and, as the numerous photographs show, he was a handsome man, until overwork and poor health aged him prematurely. Since women knew of his unhappy marriage, there were a number of offers of sympathy and comfort. According to Berg, he was always careful to keep his distance; if he ever went beyond the love letters he wrote over many years to Elizabeth Lemmon, it is not mentioned.

One side of Perkins needs further exploration: why did he not write himself? A number of his authors asked him this question, but Berg does not answer it satisfactorily. After all, he did write for the *Harvard Advocate* when he was a student, and his first real job was in journalism. Perkins always said that he did not write because he was an editor. But there seems to be some evidence that, like many editors, he was a frustrated writer who could never realize his secret ambition. This might account, in part, for the fact that he was an obviously unhappy man; some compelling urge in him had been thwarted.

Whether or not this is true, Perkins was capable of coming up with creative ideas, even whole plots, for his writers. For example, he gave Rawlings the general idea—and some of the episodes—for her most famous novel, *The Yearling*, as well as whole outlines for stories and novels to other writers. If he were a frustrated writer, might not this explain his well-known proclivity for reworking the manuscripts of others—while all the while disclaiming any ambitions as a writer? His forcing Wolfe to follow *Look Homeward, Angel* with a long novel that he himself helped shape—he even provided the novelist with the theme, as well as the overall structure—is a case in point. (For some reason, Berg does not mention Wolfe's short novel "K-19" or the other novellas that Perkins eventually fitted into *Of Time and the River*.)

One further flaw is that Berg does not question his published sources enough. For example, he quotes Erskine Caldwell's *Call It Experience*, retelling the story of Caldwell's burning three suitcases of rejected manuscripts at the end of his apprenticeship in Maine. As Malcolm Cowley and others have made clear, Caldwell's so-called autobiography is often pure fiction. Perhaps the author did burn some of his early work, but there have been two recent articles on a "lost" collection of poems and an unpublished novella entitled "The Bogus Ones." (Incidentally if one can trust Caldwell's version of the story, one of the main reasons he left Scribner's after *Tobacco Road* was owing to Perkins' eccentric behavior. The only time the editor took him to lunch, he ordered for both of them: orange juice and peanut butter-and-jelly sandwiches.)

A. Scott Berg seems to be a dauntless researcher, traveling thousands of miles for over a hundred interviews, and sifting through thousands of letters. However, style is not his strong suit. He would have done well to follow Fitzgerald's advice to Wolfe to be more selective: he includes too much of everything. His style is breezy and colloquial ("Max was hung over throughout the interview," "everything went haywire for Wolfe"); and at times it clashes too obviously with the restrained style of Perkins' own letters. As one finishes the book, one can only wish that Perkins had been alive to edit it—but then, of course, he would have rejected the project out of hand.

Guy Owen

Sources for Further Study

Book World. July 23, 1978, p. F1.

Christian Century. XCV, October 4, 1978, p. 932.

New York Times. July 24, 1978, p. C17.

New Yorker. LIV, July 31, 1978, p. 74.

Saturday Review. V, August, 1978, p. 57.

Sewanee Review. LXXXVI, October, 1978, p. 572.

THE MELLONS
The Chronicle of America's Richest Family

Author: David E. Koskoff (1939-   )
Publisher: Thomas Y. Crowell (New York). 602 pp. $14.50
Type of work: Biography
Time: The nineteenth and twentieth centuries
Locale: The United States, especially Pittsburgh, Pennsylvania

A history of an enormously wealthy American family which highlights Andrew W.
Mellon as well as many lesser known of the family members

> *Principal personages:*
> THOMAS MELLON, the founder of the family fortune
> THOMAS ALEXANDER (T. A.),
> JAMES ROSS (J. R.),
> ANDREW WILLIAM (A. W.), and
> RICHARD BEATTY (R. B.), his sons

The name Rockefeller is equated by the general public with money, for the Rockefellers are a large and very wealthy family. The Mellon name, however, is not as widely recognized, though the Mellon family is just as large and far wealthier. The Rockefellers are known as philanthropists. The Mellons have also given enormous sums of money through their charitable foundations. They have founded and endowed the National Gallery of Art in Washington, D.C., and heavily support other arts and cultural events directly and more recently through public television.

The Mellon family far outshines the established Rockefellers and DuPonts in wealth, topping even the newer wealthy family names of Getty and Hunt. The Mellon fortune is diversified and complex. The Gulf Oil Corporation, for instance, is only the tenth largest industrial corporation in the world, yet its annual revenues are greater than those of any state in the union. The Mellon fortune controls the Gulf Oil Corporation. The Mellons are the principal stockholders of Alcoa, and the major stockholders in many of the other "Fortune 500" businesses.

David E. Koskoff, in *The Mellons: The Chronicle of America's Richest Family*, describes who the Mellons are and how they became so wealthy. This is not a genealogy; he does not list every family member with equal emphasis on each. Rather, it is a family history, highlighting certain of the family members and glossing over others.

Much of the personal detail in the book is grounded in family genealogical sources, for there were many family members who recorded such information for posterity. In the first section of the book, which highlights the founder of the fortune, Thomas Mellon, Koskoff relies heavily on *Thomas Mellon and His Times*, an autobiography which the founder had privately printed for his descendants in 1885. Koskoff quotes extensively from this work, allowing

Judge Mellon's own words to provide for the reader a fairly clear picture of his character and values.

Thomas Mellon was born in Northern Ireland in 1813 of Scotch-Irish parentage. His family immigrated to western Pennsylvania in search of better farmland when he was five years old. His father was a hard-working and thrifty farmer who assumed that his son would be also. Young Thomas, however, had other ideas. He had been allowed to attend school for brief intervals and read incessantly from Pope, Shakespeare, and the like. The turning point in his life came, however, with his reading of the autobiography of Benjamin Franklin. He found Franklin's values the same as his own and their early circumstances parallel. While Thomas's own father discouraged his son's ideas of leaving the farm to enter a profession, the Franklin autobiography inspired him to try. Thereafter, Thomas Mellon relied on no one else but himself for support or inspiration.

The words "self-made man" are often used to describe such persons, but such a phrase does not provide the entire picture. The real significance lies in the way in which these persons go about "making" it. Single-mindedness and the ruthless drive toward a particular goal seem to be characteristic of their actions. Some want to acquire power; some want to acquire fame; Thomas Mellon wanted to acquire money.

His thoughts about entering an honorable profession were overshadowed by his drive for money soon after he left the farm. From his observations of the townsfolk, he decided that to be genteel was very nice, but to be wealthy and genteel was much nicer. He decided on the profession of law because he could, through it, cultivate many of the "better" people and because it was the quickest way for someone with no capital to make money. This cold analysis of his goals and methods is reflected in a number of the quotations from his own writings which Koskoff has selected for inclusion and typifies his approach to all decisions, including that of choosing a proper wife.

Once Thomas had amassed a sizable amount of money, he quit the practice of law and, aside from a term on the bench which forever labeled him old Judge Mellon, turned to business pursuits so that his money could make more money.

Koskoff devotes many pages to descriptions of the Judge's relationship with his sons, again illustrated by long quotations in his own words. The boys were reared in a somewhat humorless but certainly conscientious manner, with particular emphasis on mental discipline and the development of keen business judgment. The great family fortune was amassed rather than its initial core squandered because this second generation learned to handle money wisely from the cradle onward.

The four boys were Thomas Alexander known as "T. A.," James Ross or "J. R.," Andrew William known as "A. W.," and Richard Beatty or "R. B." The family in both its private and its public dealings had the habit of using the

initials instead of the names of its members. Koskoff, quite naturally, uses them
also whenever he refers to one of these sons, although the device creates much
confusion for the reader in the earlier sections of the book, before the individual personalities have become distinct. Throughout the work, however, the
author has provided clearly drawn genealogical charts as each new generation
is accommodated. There are also several pages of photographs, grouped for
easier comprehension, but with somewhat inadequate captions. Each of these
four young men headed his own extensive branch of the family, and as each
family member thereafter is described, he or she is tagged with the appropriate
family branch.

The Mellons who populate the center section of Koskoff's book come in all
varieties. Some are very family-oriented, others more individualistic. Some
take their money seriously, some are frivolous. The closeness of the early
generations began to diminish in the 1930's with the deaths of the branch
founders, and as the assets have been divided among more and more family
members, so has the power.

Much attention is given to Andrew W. Mellon, or "A. W.," the most successful of the old Judge's sons. Andrew W., with his brother Richard B., did a
great deal to build the family fortune. As business partners they were involved
in supplying raw materials, notably money, to the budding industries of Pittsburgh. These early investments netted them many powerful friends as well as
large interests in many industries that were just entering a boom period.

It was A. W. who served as Secretary of the Treasury and who, according
to many of his foes, caused the Great Depression in the 1930's. He served as
ambassador to Great Britain, and used the opportunity to cement a relationship
between the family's Gulf Oil Corporation and the oil interests in British-
protected Kuwait. A quiet and austere man, A. W. was fairly conservative in
business, but knew how to take a calculated risk. One of those risks turned out
to be a marriage late in life that ended in an all-too-public divorce. His name is
now frequently seen by the public, however, through the National Gallery of
Art, which he founded, and the support given through his foundations to many
cultural endeavors.

Koskoff also highlights several other key family members including William Larrimer Mellon, who was the prime mover behind the Gulf Oil Corporation, and Richard King Mellon, sometimes called "The General" for his
penchant for dressing up in his reserve officers uniform. It was The General
who presided over the "Pittsburgh Renaissance" after World War II.

There are some less public-spirited and business-minded Mellons, and Koskoff does not neglect to mention them. Notable among these are Matthew
Mellon who was all too interested in the Nazi Party during the 1930's and
Billy Hitchcock, a descendant who thirty years later was a leading manufacturer and distributor of LSD for the hippie generation. On a more positive
note is Larry Mellon, very quiet and shy, with a facility for languages, whose

admiration for Albert Schweitzer led him to become a medical missionary at the age of thirty-seven.

Many of the middle generations did little more than enjoy their wealth and the power, prestige, and luxuries that it occasioned. Some of the younger Mellons that Koskoff encountered, however, seem to be reconsidering their current responsibilities and future roles.

Most of the family enterprises now run themselves with little direct attention from the family (as opposed to those of the DuPonts and Rockefellers by contrast). The family is most active with their banking interests, which reflect the more conservative elements of family business acumen. The old Pittsburgh saying "Nothing moves in Pittsburgh without the Mellons," while quite true in the days of Andrew W. and Richard B., is true today only insofar as it refers to the Mellon Bank, for the Bank is still important to finance in that city.

Koskoff, especially in his summary, becomes a little too fascinated with the fine points of corporate ownership in the family business to be exactly true to his stated purpose of family history. However, it is indicative of his thorough investigation of the family and family matters. He has obviously spent much time and effort tracking down family members as well as corporate statistics. His efforts are calendared in his bibliography and the resulting detail is recorded in the extensive index.

One wishes, however, that the writing had been more carefully edited for a smooth flow of thoughts. The vignettes of the lesser Mellons are not as clearly grouped or carefully introduced as they could have been, and the result is often a jumble of interesting characters without a clear pattern of their relationship to or significance for one another. The chronological approach in this case might have been supplanted by a more linear explication of the family branches.

The author wisely does not attempt to draw any all-encompassing conclusion at the close of the volume. After a thorough presentation of the family's current business status, he describes the individuals of the newest Mellon generation and leaves the reader to draw his own conclusions as to their futures.

Margaret S. Schoon

Sources for Further Study

Best Sellers. XXXVIII, July, 1978, p. 118.

Esquire. LXXXIX, June 6, 1978, p. 35.

Library Journal. CIII, July, 1978, p. 1397.

National Review. XXX, September 15, 1978, p. 1161.

THE METAMORPHOSIS OF GREECE SINCE WORLD WAR II

Author: William H. McNeill (1917-   )
Publisher: University of Chicago Press (Chicago). 264 pp. $12.95
Type of work: History
Time: 1946 to 1976
Locale: Greece

A history of Greece since World War II which emphasizes the role of villages in modernization and urbanization and stresses the tensions between heroism and materialism in modern Greek life

> *Principal personages:*
> ALEXANDER PAPAGOS, Greek Prime Minister, 1952-1955
> CONSTANTINE KARAMANLIS, Greek Prime Minister, 1955-1963 and 1974-present
> GEORGE PAPANDREOU, Greek Prime Minister, 1963-1965
> GEORGE PAPADOPOULOS, Greek Prime Minister, 1967-1973
> KING CONSTANTINE, Greek King, 1964-1968

William H. McNeill has written an exceedingly interesting account of post-World War II Greece in *The Metamorphosis of Greece Since World War II*. Based on his observations of Greece from 1946 to 1976, the book focuses on six rural villages in an attempt to discern the most significant characteristics of Greek life and the ways in which modern Greece has reflected these characteristics.

For McNeill, three key elements have influenced Greece throughout its history: "the centrality of exchange and the critical importance of the skills of the marketplace," heroism, and Orthodox universalism. Although mentioning Orthodox universalism and describing aspects of religion in Greece, McNeill neglects this factor to emphasize the historic tension in Greece between market behavior and heroic behavior. He argues that the "polarity and uneasy existence between market behavior and heroic behavior constituted . . . the major axis of traditional Greek life and continue to inform the national experience in our time." McNeill develops this tension in his analysis of Greek society prior to 1941.

McNeill explains market behavior as a heritage of the nature of the major Greek exports—olive oil and wine. Since these commodities did not deteriorate as rapidly as grain, for example, wine and oil merchants "could afford to wait indefinitely until the price was right." Greeks, then, had an enormous advantage in their commercial dealings and learned to enjoy that advantage to the fullest.

The nature of Greek exports arose from the geography of the land, which precluded large-scale grain production and mandated small-scale farming efforts. This assured Greece of a society that was not divided between rich landowners and serfs or peasants. The higher degree of equality which prevailed throughout Greek society in turn encouraged market behavior.

Greek market behavior kept trade flowing around the Mediterranean throughout Greek history. Under Alexander of Macedon, conquest of the Persian Empire placed Greeks in administrative positions throughout the Middle East. Even under the Roman Empire, Greek-speaking merchants, administrators, and military leaders guaranteed that Greek remained the official language of government, and became the official language of the Eastern Church just as it became a tradition of Byzantine civilization. This heritage was suddenly ended in 1453 when Turks assumed domination of the Eastern Empire and Greeks ceased to be the ruling class.

By the seventeenth century, however, Greeks had taken on the important role of serving as intermediaries in relationships between Christian governments and the Turkish Empire. In this capacity and as merchants, they were again able to attain a fairly significant level of involvement in the trade and politics of the Mediterranean; their role was augmented when trade was opened with Russia after 1774, and in the economic boom that followed, trade was pushed to Vienna, Marseilles, and other markets. A Greek diaspora manifesting market behavior had sustained these trade and political relationships for some two thousand years until it was eclipsed by the events of 1821.

The Greek War for Independence undermined Turkish confidence in Greek and in Christian-Turkish relations. The important role of the Greeks as intermediaries suddenly collapsed, and for over a hundred years after 1821 the critical work of Greeks in facilitating trade and politics existed only in history. After the Greek War for Independence, Greece sank into an economic and political lethargy. The Greeks produced only enough commodities for subsistence. Greek cities remained small and insignificant. Hunger and starvation frequently stalked the small mountain villages of Greece.

Hunger and privation led to the assertion of the heroic ideal in the form of violence. Mountain villagers swept from the hills to prey on the villages of the plains and on trade caravans. The result was that after 1830 Greece became a small, insignificant, violent kingdom; and few Greeks were content with the form their country took after the Greek War for Independence.

In the twentieth century, numerous political *coups* produced no basic change in the lives of everyday people or in the place of Greece in world events. Insignificance was translated into genuine suffering and privation during the period of Greek occupation from 1941 to 1944. As starvation befell mountain villages, the heroic tradition that traced itself back to Homer and expressed itself in the acts of Achilles was asserted against the Nazis and their allies. The vehicle for such heroism was a coalition of leftist political parties that recruited members from all over Greece and mounted a campaign of violence, sabotage, and harassment against the occupation forces. After the occupation the leftist coalition sought rule of Greece. This was resisted by Great Britain and the leftists discredited themselves by their violence against political enemies. Eventually, the leftist coalition decided to lay down their arms as a consequence of the agreement of Varkiza in February, 1945. The Greek army emerged after 1945 as a strongly anti-Communist and antileftist unit that contributed to the eventual dissolution of the leftist coalition.

The postwar Greek government had to cope with monumental devastation and destruction, political unrest, and hunger. The first order of business was economic recovery. England was in no position to sustain Greece and withdrew its support; but the United States, through the Truman Doctrine, provided aid to both Greece and Turkey, and in April of 1948, Marshall Plan assistance was also extended to Greece. Throughout the period, the Greek government had to cope with leftist guerrilla activity that lasted until 1949.

Such expedients as the introduction of new crops, rebuilding of stocks and herds, repairing of damaged buildings, and the construction of roads were undertaken. By the early 1950's these efforts were beginning to bear fruit. The communication network spread throughout Greece, reduced the isolation of small villages, and weakened the tradition of localism. New crops began to enhance prosperity. Life became progressively easier—particularly for women. A national electrical grid made a higher standard of living possible. By the 1950's, Greece's economic recovery was well on its way to spectacular success.

The United States had contributed significantly to this success, and American leaders were disappointed about lack of change in another area of Greek life: the Greek government remained far too subject to corruption, bribery, and graft. Also, in the context of the hostilities that pitted Western democracies against Communist states in the late 1940's and 1950's, Greece was required to maintain a strong army even though such a policy inhibited her ability to remain economically self-sustaining. The Greek standing army, dedicated to heroic behavior and fundamentally opposed in attitude to the prevailing market behavior of most Greeks, was to play an increasingly significant role in Greek politics after 1950.

In 1952 Field Marshal Alexander Papagos headed the Greek government. Under his leadership the foundations for economic improvement were laid which, under his successor (Papagos died in 1955), Constantine Karamanlis, expanded into a boom. Karamanlis remained Prime Minister until 1963, and was Greece's most effective political leader of the postwar period; under his leadership, living standards improved throughout Greece, private capital was channeled into new construction and factories, and migration within Greece and to other countries was encouraged. Greek mountain villages which had historically been centers of poverty and violence, enjoyed higher standards of living by the late 1950's and 1960's.

As Greek prosperity grew, the issue of Cyprus came to the forefront of attention. In the early 1950's Greece had infiltrated Greek Cypriot villages in an attempt to encourage Greek domination of the Island. The opposition of Turkey was evident, and finally a treaty was worked out in 1959 to permit the establishment of an independent government for the Island. Greece was not at all pleased with this arrangement, and under the "jingoistic" leadership of George Papandreou, the issue was manipulated in 1961 in an unsuccessful attempt to oust the Karamanlis government. Karamanlis remained in power until 1963 when he resigned over a disagreement with the Greek royal family.

The resignation of Karamanlis brought the election of George Papandreou, who governed until 1965. Greek population had been declining in the 1950's as jobs in German factories increased migration abroad. For the first time since World War II concern began to be expressed about the emptying of the countryside. The Papandreou government provided no solutions for the nation's major problems, and as a result of conflict with the royal family, Papandreou's government was replaced by that of Panagiotis Kanellopoulos. A deteriorating economic situation resulted in a *coup* by a group of Colonels on April 21, 1967. The leader that emerged as Prime Minister was George Papadopoulos.

Papadopoulos attempted to restore "the wholeness of Hellenism" to Greece by offering the heroic alternative to the marketplace tradition of Karamanlis. Nationalism and patriotism were stressed, but to no avail. The wealthy were taxed, and corruption contaminated the government, which was able to affect little change in the market behavior of citizens. In 1967, King Constantine attempted to overthrow the Colonels, but he failed and was forced into exile. In 1973, Papadopoulos declared the establishment of a Greek republic, but military authority was not relaxed. Papadopoulos was replaced in 1973 when his control over the military had weakened. The major problem with which the military failed to deal effectively, however, was Cyprus.

The Greek government launched a *coup* in Cyprus in mid-1974. Turkey refused to accept Greek domination of the island and invaded Cyprus, seizing the wealthiest and best part of the island. Because of Turkish military strength, Greece could do nothing to retrieve the island or improve the position of Greek Cypriots. Amid an atmosphere of disillusionment and failure, Constantine Karamanlis was called out of retirement to help. He restored democratic government as soon as possible, held popular elections in November, 1974, and returned his government to power. Under Karamanlis, political stability returned along with democratic government. It was anticipated that with the suppression of the heroic behavior of military dictatorship the market behavior would permit continued economic improvement of Greece. Market behavior characterized life in the villages of Greece as well as in Greece's major cities.

Between 1946 and 1976, McNeill studied at firsthand six Greek villages: Old Corinth, New Elftherohori, Kerasia, Kotta, Kardamili, and Lofiscos. Starting out amid the extreme hardship and poverty that was the legacy of the occupation, McNeill observed the pervasive idiosyncratic localism of each village; in his book, he discusses the commitment to rural values and the centrality of the family unit in Greek village life. Each village worked to resolve its own particular problems from 1946 to 1976, and each village, some more fully than others, was rewarded with considerable success by the end of the period.

The economic success of the villages has created enormous changes in the past thirty years. Modernization has brought the villages fully into the twentieth century as standards of living improve, electric power plants are built, and communications systems are steadily improved. Each village's history has, of course, been different; but the point McNeill does not stress heavily enough is how much *alike* all the villages are in their loyalty to the nuclear family, in their cooperation among families, in the effectiveness of their market values, and in their respect for traditional values. These factors make the villages more alike than different from one another, while McNeill tends to stress differences. Regarding some topics—such as the role of the nuclear family and traditional values—McNeill hinted at the outset that he would emphasize the Orthodox universalism which he suggested was one of the foundations of Greek heritage. However, his choice not to follow up this line of reasoning throughout the volume weakens his own central thesis.

Tradition and the role of the family have also been important aspects in the development of Greece's major cities, Athens and Salonika. Because Greek society is organized into nuclear family units, the transition of the family from village life to city life has been comparatively smooth. Newcomers can rely on nuclear families as a source of support and comfort; because of this, individual disorientation has been less of a problem than in most other countries which undergo urbanization.

However, as Athens and Salonika have grown, the countryside of Greece has become depopulated. This is happening because of greater opportunity and higher living standards possible in the cities. In other words, the attractive force is the market behavior that seeks improvement in one's situation and pervades Greek life. The alternative view of heroism characterizes the lower ranks of the army and seeks the virtue and beauty of the countryside. However, even the military attempt to retire in or around the cities, suggesting the lack of substance of the heroic ideal in the 1970's in comparison to the reality of market behavior.

Although market behavior characterizes the cities, rural traditions have also penetrated the urban environment. Rural interest in land has induced city dwellers to purchase homes as soon as possible. The rhythm of work of the village pervades cities. Patronage systems that characterize city life are also a legacy of the haggling of village life.

However, some traditional village ways are also, in McNeill's view, declining in the cities, as witnessed in modifications of marriage arrangements relating to dowries, in weakening support of the elderly and the establishment of homes for the aged, and in widespread use of birth control methods. It is precisely in this area of changing traditional values that McNeill fails to test his thesis of the importance of Orthodox universalism as an ingredient of

Greek life. Thus, when he discusses Orthodox, market and heroic behavior, it is his description of the former that is most deficient throughout the book. Readers are left with uncertainty as to the significance of Orthodoxy in the family structure and in the formation of traditional values. Traditional values could well be partly a legacy of the Orthodox universalism that McNeill leaves unexplored.

The lack of a careful analysis of the nature of the nuclear family and traditional values is particularly troublesome as McNeill describes the highly successful Greek experience over the past thirty years. In his view of the future, he stresses two areas of potential instability in Greece. These are uncertainty about the future of the nuclear family, and the dangers of Greek militarism. While the latter has been fully explored throughout the volume, the former requires elaboration. Nevertheless, McNeill's very interesting account merits serious consideration as a well-written and thoughtful reflection not only on Greek life, but on the processes of modernization and urbanization in the twentieth century.

Saul Lerner

Sources for Further Study

Library Journal. CIII, August, 1978, p. 1507.

MILTON AND THE ENGLISH REVOLUTION

Author: Christopher Hill (1912-   )
Publisher: The Viking Press (New York). 541 pp. $20.00
Type of work: Biography
Time: 1608-1674
Locale: England

A critical biography of John Milton that investigates the poetry and prose of England's renowned Protestant radical and his influence on the course of political and religious events in seventeenth century England

> *Principal personages:*
> JOHN MILTON, a poet, prosemaster, scholar, religious and political activist
> OLIVER CROMWELL, Lord Protector of England
> WILLIAM LAUD, Archbishop of Canterbury
> CHARLES I, King of England, 1625-1649
> CHARLES II, King of England, 1660-1685
> ANDREW MARVELL, a poet and Milton's amanuensis
> GENERAL GEORGE MONCK, Duke of Albermarle
> ELIZABETH MINSHULL, Milton's third wife
> JOHN DRYDEN, a poet and playwright

John Milton is one of England's most misunderstood poets and thinkers. Those who have read his great epic poem *Paradise Lost* or reviewed any of his religious and political tracts know from personal experience that his ideas are not easily accessible. Indeed, in the words of Milton's critics and admirers alike, he is difficult, ambiguous and often seemingly contradictory. For the past forty years, the poet's literary stock has fluctuated dramatically. Eminent scholars and poets have challenged Milton's rather awesome reputation, and they have done so on the grounds that much of his verse is undeserving of high praise. Others argue that his ideas are outdated, his thinking muddled, and his Renaissance views obsolete even for the seventeenth century. In addition, there are those who disapprove of Milton the man and view him as a harsh, inflexible, self-righteous Protestant radical who was absolutely rigid in his religious beliefs and never gave his adversaries the benefit of a single doubt.

Christopher Hill's study of Milton is an attempt to view this great English figure with sympathy and understanding—to exorcise, if you will, the "Puritan" image which, for many of his modern readers, still clings to the poet. The approach Hill employs is historical; not only does it study numerous aspects of Milton's life in depth, but it seriously challenges much of what Milton would have us know about himself. According to Hill, the self-portrait that Milton prepared for posterity is not at all accurate. Indeed, Milton's own portrait is almost as damaging as those prepared by his severest critics. Hill attempts to correct this view and show Milton not as the rigid, brooding intellect whose enormous learning alienated him from many of his contemporaries, but as a great patriot and poet who devoted his energies to liberating his countrymen from religious and political tyranny.

In composing a balanced account of his subject, Hill reviews the major events in Milton's life and closely analyzes the better known controversies surrounding him, both public and private. Hill is equally interested in the origin of Milton's ideas on a number of subjects—including church, state, government, kingship, and divine rights. He also examines the poet's thinking on education, censorship, literature, marriage, and divorce. But central to this study is the author's focus on Milton's support of a cultural revolution aimed at destroying the magical power of kingship.

John Milton was born into a rather prosperous Puritan household in 1608. He entered Christ's College, Cambridge, in 1625, the same year that Charles I succeeded his father to the throne. After taking his M.A. degree, Milton returned to his home to complete his education, rejecting a career in the Anglican Church because of its episcopal organization. A few years later he made the Grand Tour (1638-1639), returning to England in time to witness Charles' difficulty with Parliament and the Scottish bishops. By 1642, the King was at war with Parliament; within six years, the Royalist forces were defeated, the King was under arrest, and Cromwell's Parliamentarians were in control of England. A few months later, however, the Revolution recommenced, with the King and Scotland at war with England. Cromwell was called upon to command the New Model Army and at the Battle of Preston defeated the King's coalition. For his part in a war against England, Charles I was tried for treason and beheaded in 1649. In 1653 Cromwell was made chief executive officer of the land, Lord Protector of the Commonwealth of England, Scotland, and Ireland.

In many respects, Milton was prepared for these events: he had a deepseated distrust of clerical authority, and he was equally suspicious of the monarchy. When Cromwell appeared on the scene, Milton was convinced that England would have the opportunity to free herself from the ancient dogmas of kingship and achieve a new social and religious system for her people. In addition, Cromwell was a Puritan with religious views similar to those of Milton. This meant that the Anglican bishops would be divested of their enormous ecclesiastical powers. To Milton, it was unthinkable that one Christian should have authority over another. It is not surprising, then, that Milton became the official spokesman for the Revolution and the Commonwealth. In 1649 he published two tracts in support of the new "Free" State of England, *Tenure of Kings and Magistrates* and *Eikonoklastes*. These papers not only supported Parliament's new form of government, but they also defended the regicide as being necessary before England's first Republic could be founded.

Despite the many favors bestowed upon him during Cromwell's rule (his appointment as Secretary for Foreign Tongues to Council of State being the most prestigious), Milton was never timid about criticizing the Revolution or the Commonwealth it brought into existence. When Parliament enacted a bill of censorship during the First Civil War, Milton attacked it in *Areopagitica*, one of the most eloquent defenses of a free press in the English language. After the Protectorate was established to "protect the Revolution's achievements," Milton clearly perceived that this was a dangerous step toward reestablishing the monarchy, in form and substance, essentially giving to Cromwell the power which Parliament had denied Charles I.

But the remarkable thing about Milton—and Hill's study carefully considers this factor—was his loyalty to the ideas which formed the Revolution and outlined new religious and social arrangements for England. Upon the collapse of the Commonwealth and the subsequent restoration of the monarchy, it might have been expected that Milton would recant his former views or take them with him to the scaffold. Many of his associates were beheaded during the bloody purge which occupied Charles II and his ministers during the early months of the Restoration. Milton was, of course, arrested. After all, he was the author of the definitive argument in defense of regicide, and he had served and supported the government which had officially abolished the monarchy. He was not harmed, however, nor was he long detained, although his assets were impounded and he was deprived of all revenues and public offices. Yet he refused to make peace with the King who spared his life or publicly renounce the principles of the Revolution or the achievements of the Commonwealth. It is not likely that he would have exhibited the same degree of compassion for his captors had the circumstances been reversed.

Milton's greatest period of political and social influence occurred during his first five years of service to Cromwell (his failing eyesight and eventual blindness diminished his contributions later in the regime). He was known throughout Europe—for better or for worse—as the defender of the English Revolution. The Restoration brought an end to Milton's public life, but it allowed for more concentrated activity in his private one, especially in the sphere of poetry. Ironically, whatever opinions we have about Milton are largely formed from reading his verse and not from scrutinizing his public service to the Cromwellian government. His remaining years in seclusion were almost exclusively devoted to his monumental epic poems—*Paradise Lost*, *Paradise Regained*, and *Samson Agonistes*. Milton was, ostensibly, writing poetry, but he was also engaged in the great social and religious debates which illuminated and gave purpose to the Commonwealth. What Milton was forced to leave in public life he rediscovered in his epic poems. The struggle for freedom, the justification of God's ways to man, the formation of reasonable governments, became the subjects of Milton's literary efforts. And while a prisoner of the forces he had struggled to destroy, Milton continued to believe in and serve the ideas responsible for his captivity. If Charles II thought Milton's age, blindness, or reduced circumstances made him less of a threat to monarchical ideas, he was mistaken. The Age of Kings was all but over; the power of Parliament was on the rise.

Hill's study of Milton makes it very clear that the poet's ideas are still current today; indeed, Hill describes his subject as a great libertarian who understood the meaning of individual freedom more profoundly than any of his contemporaries. And his great epic poems continue to define this concept in language still pertinent. In addition, Milton's criticism of social and ecclesiastical institutions anticipates the views of a number of modern humanists. For Milton, the most important "institution" was the individual, and he urged his countrymen to draw from within themselves the spiritual energy needed to make life on earth dignified and worthy of God's trust. Finally, in Hill's assessment, Milton was a great literary artist who embodied all the best of that which preceded him and prepared the way for those who followed. Milton's mastery of the epic form, still regarded among literary critics as the greatest of all, places him in the company of Homer, Vergil, Dante, and Spenser.

Still, the reader without specialized interest or training in seventeenth century English political and religious affairs will have some difficulty with much of Hill's very admirable study. This is not to say that the author does not advance a sound argument in defense of Milton's reputation; nor does he fail in preparing a benevolent portrait of England's famous radical Protestant. Indeed, the scholarship in *Milton and the English Revolution* is impressive. Equally convincing is Hill's solid study of the major poems and prose pieces. Those students who seek a moderate and sympathetic portrayal of John Milton—poet and political activist—will not be disappointed. But there will be some readers who will wonder why Milton's poetic reputation is in need of critical defense, or why his political views require such elaborate justification. Still others may very well question whether it is necessary first to see Milton as a warm and loving figure before the wisdom and utility of his ideas can be fully appreciated.

Don W. Sieker

Sources for Further Study

Books West. I, March, 1978, p. 37.
History: Reviews of New Books. VI, August, 1978, p. 175.
Modern Age. XXII, Summer, 1978, p. 325.
Sewanee Review. LXXXVI, July, 1978, p. 414.

MIRABELL: BOOKS OF NUMBER

Author: James Merrill (1926-   )
Publisher: Atheneum Publishers (New York). 182 pp. $10.95
Type of work: Poetry

A verse drama about the nature, history, and destiny of matter and spirit

Continuing the Ouija board format adopted in ''The Book of Ephraim'' in James Merrill's *Divine Comedies*, *Mirabell* presents itself as a record of the poet (JM) and David Jackson's (DJ) contact with W. H. Auden (WHA) and Maria Mitsotaki (MM or MAMAN)—their close friends among the dead—and with 741 (Mirabell), a nonhuman spirit who spends much of the book revealing that the ''God of Biology'' is moving the world toward ''Paradise'' through a coded reincarnation of souls in the ''Research Lab'' of evolution.

The significance of number is a major concern in the book. Mirabell's number (741) itself relates to the 14 spirits of which he is one and to the 14 syllable lines he speaks in on the Ouija board. The book has 10 sections, though ''10'' is seldom formalized as such: they begin with 0 and end with 9, and each section has 9 subparts. The Angel Michael speaks the last line of the book in 10 syllables. The point seems to be that only the messenger of light can express a pure 1.0; everything else is always a fraction off, as in the case of Akhnaton and Nefertiti, who had built a diamond pyramid conduit to the sun's energy, which, though it occasioned an impressive advance in human ability, had a fractional flaw which caused the first atomic explosion in human history.

The ''Research Lab'' itself predicates 9 ascending stages, of which a given soul may achieve one; the book itself progresses through 9 sections in its approach to the source of light. Also, not only is Mirabell one of 14 messenger spirits, but he relates that there were 14 energy zones on prehuman Earth which anchored it to the ''platforms'' his kind maintained above it.

Regarding souls formed between lives to ''soak up densities and be reborn'' (densities being various engineered combinations of the 4 elements), the maximum density in any age resides in 5 extraordinarily powerful souls. Human souls like JM and DJ's, moreover, have identity numbers composed, in Mirabell's idiom, of the number of their previous lives, the ratio of animal to human densities, talent rating, and finally of both the stage among the 9 at which the soul originally made contact with the spirit world and the stage at which it will ultimately arrive.

5 is a critical and often referred to number. The pentagram is mentioned as a hedge against chaos, and the 5th section of the book describes the 5 principal characters (JM the ''scribe''; DJ his intimate and ''the shaping hand of nature''; WHA and MM the dead; Mirabell the messenger) as a sort of atomic model which makes illumination possible. Indeed, selected souls, whose ''densities'' have been carefully formulated, are capable of ''V'' work which helps to insure the ''onward dance of things.''

As he uses number, Merrill uses color to structure the book. It begins with blue (the blue-eyed bats in the carpet), which generally stands for reason and was absent from the sun-worshiping kingdom of Akhnaton and Nefertiti; it ends with "the red eye of the sun," for "It is in red that power lives," and the poet has moved from accumulating the evidence to apprehending the source of this power.

The nature of perception and understanding is thus one of James Merrill's preoccupations. "WE ARE U YOU ARE WE EACH OTHERS DREAM," and "DREAM, FACT & EXPERIENCE ARE ONE," Mirabell says, implying that his messages are implicit in the poet's mind.

Some of the more exotic messages which Mirabell uncovers are the origin of Atlantis and the invention by its centaurlike inhabitants of Mirabell's kind, the latter of whom build and maintain sky platforms after the Earth's crust sinks. The program, moreover, for the last three thousand years of man's own history has included the gradual supplanting of religion by the "scribe" or poet—has, indeed, provided for a new "monotheism of language."

The source of language and the nature of poetry also concern Merrill. Mirabell says of himself and his colleagues, "WE SPEAK FROM WITHIN THE ATOM," and JM sees poetry as ". . . the formula made word." Among the book's more charming notions is that pastoral poetry results from the cloning of plant souls in humans; among its more petulant notions is that homosexual unions produce the best climate for poetry and music; and among its more rigorous notions is that poetry is essentially metaphor and that the poet is an instrument through which messengers such as Mirabell (the true Mercury) speak. As Auden goes on to say in rhymed couplets when JM complains that the words of this gigantic poem are not his, JM owes his work to powers which precede and supersede him, as well as to his poet ancestors, among whom Auden includes Thomas Hardy, Thomas Campion, John Milton and John Dryden. "FACT IS IS IS FABLE," Auden concludes, criticizing thus the sense of distinction on which egotism thrives, and foreshadowing the Angel Michael's pronouncement at the end that God is the "ACCUMULATED IN-TELLIGENCE" in the history of cell life.

There is a pervasive informality in the book signaled by the first half-line "Oh very well then" (reminiscent of the "Hang it all . . . ," which begins Pound's second *Canto*) and embodied by such matters as "the Age / . . . of the Wrong Wallpaper," the illness and death of DJ's parents in Greece, DJ's operation in Boston, and by allusions to private events involving Merrill and David Jackson and, among other acquaintances, their friends Maria and Auden and the latter's dead intimate Chester Kallman. This casualness gives a realistic texture to a mystical situation, and perhaps allows the poet to commit himself to that situation without seeming foolish or grandiose, though, as Mirabell remarks opaquely to JM, ". . . YR NONCHALANCE / IS THE SLEEP OF A VAST TRAVAIL. . . ."

One appreciates Merrill's sense of drama, his feel for dialogue, and his fastidious prosody. If there is a flaw in his literary skill and informal approach to ontological matters, it is that the first seems deliberately exhibitionist and the second a droll romp, as though the mysteries of being were subject less to awe than to gossip. If the adjustment of ancient and profound concerns to modern metaphors remains an intriguing enterprise here, the work's vision—wide though it be—seems taken for granted, its passions effeminate, and its sense of myth self-conscious and cute. Merrill's venture, in short, is more a museum of and a critique on its materials than a hypnotic transmission, in the manner of the great myths, epics, and dramas, of continually resonant images.

Mark McCloskey

Sources for Further Study

New York Review of Books. XXV, December 21, 1978, p. 34.
Publisher's Weekly. CCXIV, October 23, 1978, p. 53.

MOKSHA
Writings on Psychedelics and
the Visionary Experience (1931-1963)

Author: Aldous Huxley (1894-1963)
Edited by Michael Horowitz and Cynthia Palmer
Publisher: Stonehill Publishing Company (New York). 298 pp. $12.95
Type of work: Collected writings

A chronologically arranged sampling of writings on visionary and psychedelic experience from the last thirty years of Huxley's life, including personal correspondence, essays, addresses, and excerpts from his Utopian novels

On November 22, 1963, while his family gathered (except Laura Huxley, his wife) to watch television bring the assassination of John F. Kennedy to the stunned world, Aldous Huxley died peacefully and painlessly, slipping quietly into the "realm of Light" under the influence of LSD. What was there about this man who, two years before, had given a lecture at M.I.T. that caused traffic to jam all the way across the Charles River into Boston?

Huxley in his usual modest fashion blamed the tie-up on his having been around for so long: "If I live to be a hundred, I shall be like Stonehenge." In an uncharacteristic stroke of misanalysis, Huxley left the question unanswered. Perhaps it simply *seemed* that he had been around for a long time. The Eisenhower generation of college students had read his *Point Counter Point* in Contemporary Fiction classes, and Jocelyn Brooke, attending college in England in the 1920's, had called him "the wicked uncle" and recalled the excitement adolescents felt over his advanced ideas, his intellectual one-upsmanship, and his superb prose style. He seemed to have lived, as Einstein, longer than he did, because of his tremendously productive outpouring and the fact that he rode out his life to the end on a vast wave of enthusiasms and projects. All this was made even more amazing because of his almost total blindness since he was sixteen and his lengthy and losing battle toward the end of his life with cancer of the tongue.

"Moksha" is a Sanskrit word meaning "liberation from the body." The "moksha-medicine" of *Island* was a far different drug from the soma of *Brave New World*. Soma was dispensed by a benevolent and paternal government to provide pleasure and escape from a totalitarian regime whose citizens were victims of chemically induced apathy and euphoria, while Moksha provided visionary information about the Other Reality to be used for the welfare of the public. *Moksha* is a collection of addresses, essays, letters from the last years of Huxley's life, and portions from his novels, *Brave New World* and *Island*, and the long essay *The Doors of Perception*. Among the many contributions this sampler from the immense fabric of Huxley's thought offers is an insight into the breadth and depth of one man's intellectual accomplishments. *Moksha* can also be liberating for the reader in a time (as Huxley knew) that is extremely unsympathetic to visionary experiences (which is why so few are reported).

T. S. Eliot knew men could stand only so much reality. So where does one go for escape, if not to visionary worlds? The problem is that the search for ecstasy has destroyed many people who have used alcohol, which is often unsatisfactory and self-destructive; other drugs, such as heroin and cocaine, are of poor-quality transcendence and can have dangerous, if not fatal, effects. These, said Huxley, provide a pitiful substitute for the sacramental drugs which he foresaw as offering almost pure benefits, if used and prepared for properly.

This collection of writings is introduced by Dr. Alexander Shulgin and Dr. Albert Hofmann, the scientist who isolated psilocybin, the active ingredient in peyote; both men were pioneers of psychotropic substances. Aided by Huxley's second wife, Laura Archera Huxley, the editors proceed chronologically from Huxley's 1931 discovery of the German pharmacologist Lewin's survey of psychoactive drugs, *Phantasia*, and through his loving acquaintance with Dr. Humphrey Osmond, who was present in 1952 when Huxley first took mescaline and opened his own "doors of perception," a phrase he borrowed from William Blake's *Marriage of Heaven and Hell*. Huxley was the first person to inquire into and record the literary and humanistic uses of the psychodelic (Huxley spelled it with an *o*) drugs.

Whereas the collection provides only windows, only limited access for seeing into Huxley and his work, it does stimulate the imagination of the reader, tempting him to reexamine similar works dealing with the expansion of the senses; Huxley's own *Island* and *The Doors of Perception*; Grover Smith's monumental *Letters of Aldous Huxley*; *Centuries of Meditation* by Thomas Traherne; *Confessions of an English Opium Eater* by Thomas De Quincey; and even *The Tibetan Book of the Dead*.

Mescaline for Huxley was not the cause of, but the occasion for, entrance into a world where Love is the primary and fundamental cosmic fact, where gratitude is the primary emotion, and where subject and object are one. Such ideas raise questions that transform and transcend the misshapen universe that we have created for ourselves by means of "culture-conditioned prejudices." The visionary experience, Huxley's writings reveal, permits entry, whether spontaneous—induced by yoga, fasting, sensory deprivation, or sleep deprivation—or chemically induced by mushrooms, morning glory seeds, or drugs into the consciousness of "certain kinds of mental activity normally excluded as possessing no survival value." Therefore, as we become acculturated, we retain what we perceive as "useful," discard or repress what is not. We consequently are seen as living in more than one universe at a time: a liberating prospect, immense with spiritual and philosophic implications. The questions raised here about the power and abuse of language, both verbal and nonverbal, which Huxley felt education must emphasize, create pebble-in-the-pond ripples out into intellectual waters. If words do not exist for ideas which have no pragmatic usefulness, how does one conceive and communicate these realities? This is the challenge and quest of the poet.

Therefore, *Moksha* shakes us up, stimulates our questions, reminds us of what we have forgotten. It does not propose to show us Huxley, the flesh-and-blood man; instead we see him through the eyes of the "faithful" who clearly lionized him. Huxley revealed little of himself as a private man in his own writings. He was a tender husband, affectionate friend, staunch upholder of population control and conservation, bridge between science and ethics and religion and philosophy, courageous voyager into inner space, and prophet who urged cooperation and foresight among the world's thinkers and planners. He was worried about the use of chemical persuasion and the fading of spontaneity in technical society. In the future, control will be based, Huxley believed, not on terror, which is inefficient and wasteful, but on painless government-provided tranquilizers. He wished to warn us, not to dwell in the Other World as a hermit, believing, as Pascal, that "The worship of truth without charity is idolatry."

This collection lends a view, if not personally illuminating, of a man who was the still, calm center of a vast and lively network of literary and scientific influences, intellectual currents, spiraling interests regarding the future, self-created controversy, and great misunderstandings about the nature of his work. The letters reveal his enormous sincerity, caution, and ethical responsibility for his pioneering work and its applications. His addresses reveal a man of humor and mildness, whereas one reads his essays in the 1970's with the same excitement that young Brooke and his schoolboy friends experienced in the 1920's. Some will feel the irony of the gap between Huxley's views and the psychedelic abuses of the 1960's, some pessimism at Huxley's vision of goodness, love, and fundamental sanity, some his enthusiasm to be precisely that of the schoolboy: innocent, naïve, and uninitiated. One sees Huxley's ideas distorted, his fears justified, and his predictions rapidly coming true. What optimism one may have left untouched by cynicism perhaps can be rekindled by reading *Moksha* and expanding one's mind with views of other universes and messages brought back from these continents, which exist for visionaries as substrata of all existence, past, present, and future.

Agnes McDonald

Sources for Further Study

Booklist. LXXIV, June 1, 1978, p. 1530.
Library Journal. CIII, April 1, 1978, p. 764.

MOMO

Author: Émile Ajar (Paul Pavlovitch)
Translated from the French by Ralph Manheim
Publisher: Doubleday & Company (Garden City, New York). 182 pp. $6.95
Type of work: Novel
Time: 1970
Locale: Paris

A sentimental story of a castoff Arab boy and a retired prostitute which won the Prix Goncourt

Principal characters:
> MOMO, the son of a prostitute abandoned at the age of three
> MADAME ROSA, an aging former prostitute who cares for the children of prostitutes
> KADIR YOUSSEF, Momo's father
> MONSIEUR HAMIL, a retired Algerian carpet salesman
> MADAME LOLA, a transvestite

The story told in *Momo*, which has become familiar to American filmgoers from the movie *Madame Rosa*, is narrated in the first person by Momo (short for Mohammed). Momo has spent his life at Madame Rosa's boarding house which she maintains for the children of prostitutes who are still working in the profession. Madame Rosa is Jewish, sixty-eight, weighs 220 pounds, and has survived a long professional career and a stay in a German concentration camp. Momo is ten, the son of an Arab prostitute and possibly an Arab father—"There's always a mystery when a kid gets born because a woman who hustles for a living hasn't been able to stop it in time with hygiene"—and he is Madame Rosa's principal helper in taking care of the boarding children who sometimes number as many as ten. The children are Jewish, Arab, French, Vietnamese, Malian, Senegalese, and others; no distinction is made between the races.

Momo has been with Madame Rosa since he was three. Mothers of the other children come to visit them on Sundays and to take them to the country for holidays, but no one comes for Momo. He wants to know his mother but realizes that Madame Rosa is the only mother that he will ever know. He longs for an identity and for love. Madame Rosa relies on him, and when his father, Monsieur Kadir Youssef, does come to see him eleven years after leaving him with Madame Rosa, she is thrown into such a panic by the possibility of losing the child that she lies and insults the father, who dies of a heart seizure from the frustration of the scene. Momo remains with Madame Rosa, loving and caring for her until her death in her bizarre "country home." As the story ends, it seems that a truly happy life with a family is about to begin for Momo.

Following the great success of the novel in France, *Publisher's Weekly* succeeded in arranging an interview with the elusive author. Ajar talked of his first novel, *Gros-Câlin*, saying that it is "a book about loneliness, just as

Momo is about loneliness. It should be important for critics because it contains my other two books." In *Gros-Câlin*, the principal character dealt with his loneliness by sharing his home with a python. The third novel, *Pseudo*, is "a fanciful version of everything that happened to Ajar after the publication of *Momo*."

In *Momo*, the principal characters are either lonely or isolated. Momo is certainly of the first group. The oldest and longest tenured of the boarders, he longs for friends of his own age and for motherly love. Monsieur Hamil, a retired Algerian carpet salesman, is his closest friend and teacher, since Momo does not attend school. Momo believes that Monsieur Hamil, being Moslem, must know something of his parents, but Monsieur Hamil says that he knows nothing. Another friend is Madame Lola, a thirty-five-year-old Senegalese transvestite and former boxer who works the Bois de Boulogne and desperately wants to adopt a child.

Perhaps Ajar's greatest strength, at least as exemplified in *Momo*, is his talent as a portraitist and as a painter of the *milieu* in which the action of the novel takes place. The characters come to life, with their fears, doubts, loneliness, ambitions, joys, cruelties, and compassions. Madame Rosa is loving, jealous, forgiving—she is human. Madame Lola is kind, carnal, good-humored, and wretched. The carpet salesman, a procurer from Niger for whom Madame Rosa writes letters, is equally well drawn.

The *quartier* of Belleville and its inhabitants are created in an effective and believable manner. The seventh-floor walk-up apartment which is home to Madame Rosa and her charges is the logical place for her to be. The rent is less there since there is no elevator, and the difficulty of reaching it is further protection from the police and the dreaded Public Welfare which might take the children from her. Those who live in the apartment building are from varied origins: Madame Lola, the transvestite; a retired employee of the French Railways; the four Zaoum brothers who are movers; and others—all are aware of one another but do not intrude unnecessarily into one anothers' lives. The tenants of this building and of several nearby are mostly black, with large groups of Jews and Arabs on adjoining streets. These people perform the most menial tasks, among which are street sweepers and street walkers.

Ajar demonstrates a very compassionate, tolerant understanding of prostitutes, their problems, and the socioeconomic groups from which large numbers of them come. It is a profession like any other, and those who practice it go through a routine existence involving the daily grind known well to other types of workers. The fear of having their children taken from them because they are illegitimate is pervasive. In their prime, satisfaction comes from numbers of clients, money earned, and thoughts of a secure retirement in family surroundings. In retirement, particularly for Madame Rosa, pleasure is derived from remembering that she was once desirable.

Certainly Momo is an appealing, lovable child whose understanding of

Madame Rosa and of the other principal characters is extraordinary. His loyalty and his willingness to endure while trying to alleviate Madame Rosa's discomfort, anxiety, and despair are admirable. He has the childlike qualities of curiosity and fantasy that make him credible. A problem arises, however, when Ajar begins putting philosophical statements into the mouth of Momo, who, despite his very rude introduction to life, could hardly have these mature, often cynical observations to make on the human condition. These remarks, frequently inserted, stretch the reader's credulity, as seen in the following examples of ten-year-old Momo's musings: "Banania. . . . Take it from me, that little son of a bitch was a case, four years old and still happy." "I'm not going to write history all over again, but I can tell you that the black people have suffered an awful lot, and we should try and understand them when we can." "I've often noticed that people end up believing what they say. They can't live without it. I'm not saying that to sound like a philosopher, I really believe it." The visibility of Ajar in Momo's thoughts and words destroys a great deal of the pleasure that might come from this contemporary "tranche de vie."

Mary Paschal

Sources for Further Study

Library Journal. CIII, April 1, 1978, p. 773.
New Republic. CLXXVIII, April 22, 1978, p. 34.
New York Times Book Review. April 2, 1978, p. 15.
New Yorker. LIV, April 10, 1978, p. 143.
Saturday Review. V, March 4, 1978, p. 31.